AGING
Social Change

AGING

James G. March, Editor in Chief
Graduate School of Business
Stanford University
Stanford, California

Aging: Biology and Behavior, edited by James L. McGaugh and Sara B. Kiesler

Aging: Social Change, edited by Sara B. Kiesler, James N. Morgan, and Valerie Kincade Oppenheimer

Aging: Stability and Change in the Family, edited by Robert W. Fogel, Elaine Hatfield, Sara B. Kiesler, and Ethel Shanas

AGING
Social Change

Edited by

SARA B. KIESLER
Department of Social Science
Carnegie-Mellon University
Pittsburgh, Pennsylvania

JAMES N. MORGAN
Institute for Social Research
University of Michigan
Ann Arbor, Michigan

VALERIE KINCADE OPPENHEIMER
Department of Sociology
University of California, Los Angeles
Los Angeles, California

ACADEMIC PRESS
A Subsidiary of Harcourt Brace Jovanovich, Publishers
New York   London   Toronto   Sydney   San Francisco

NOTICE: The project that is the subject of this report was approved by the Governing Board of the National Research Council, whose members are drawn from the Councils of the National Academy of Sciences, the National Academy of Engineering, and the Institute of Medicine. The members of the Committee responsible for the report were chosen for their special competences and with regard for appropriate balance.

This report has been reviewed by a group other than the authors according to procedures approved by a Report Review Committee consisting of members of the National Academy of Sciences, the National Academy of Engineering, and the Institute of Medicine.

The National Research Council was established by the National Academy of Sciences in 1916 to associate the broad community of science and technology with the Academy's purposes of furthering knowledge and of advising the federal government. The Council operates in accordance with general policies determined by the Academy under the authority of its Congressional charter of 1863, which establishes the Academy as a private, nonprofit, self-governing membership corporation. The Council has become the principal operating agency of both the Academy of Sciences and the National Academy of Engineering in the conduct of their services to the government, the public, and the scientific and engineering communities. It is administered jointly by both Academies and the Institute of Medicine. The Academy of Engineering and the Institute of Medicine were established in 1964 and 1970, respectively, under the charter of the Academy of Sciences.

This project was supported by Grant No. NO1-AG-8-2111, awarded by the National Institute on Aging.

ACADEMIC PRESS, INC.
111 Fifth Avenue, New York, New York 10003

United Kingdom Edition published by
ACADEMIC PRESS, INC. (LONDON) LTD.
24/28 Oval Road, London NWI 7DX

Library of Congress Cataloging in Publication Data
Main entry under title:

Aging, social change.

Papers from a workshop entitled "The elderly
of the future," held May 3-5, 1979, in Annapolis,
Md., which was organized by the Committee on
Aging, National Research Council and sponsored
by the National Institute on Aging.
    Includes bibliographies and index.
    1. Aging--Social aspects--Congresses.
2. Aged--United States--Socioeconomic status
--Congresses. I. Kiesler, Sara B., Date.
II. Morgan, James N. III. Oppenheimer,
Valerie Kincade. IV. National Research Council
(U.S.). Committee on Aging. V. National
Institute on Aging.
HQ1061.A484   305.2'6   81-14959
ISBN 0-12-040002-2   AACR2
ISBN 0-12-040022-7 (pbk.)
PRINTED IN THE UNITED STATES OF AMERICA

81 82 83 84   9 8 7 6 5 4 3 2 1

COMMITTEE ON AGING

JAMES G. MARCH (Chair), Graduate School of Business, Stanford University

JAMES R. DUMPSON, Associate Director, New York Community Trust Foundation

ROBERT W. FOGEL, Department of Economics, Harvard University

ELAINE HATFIELD, Department of Sociology and Department of Psychology, University of Wisconsin–Madison

JACQUELYNE J. JACKSON, Duke University Medical Center

JAMES S. JACKSON, Institute for Social Research, University of Michigan

M. POWELL LAWTON, Philadelphia Geriatric Center

JAMES L. McGAUGH, Department of Psychobiology, University of California, Irvine

SIDNEY W. MINTZ, Department of Anthropology, Johns Hopkins University

JAMES N. MORGAN, Institute for Social Research, University of Michigan

VALERIE KINCADE OPPENHEIMER, Department of Sociology, University of California, Los Angeles

ROBERT R. SEARS, Department of Psychology, Stanford University

ETHEL SHANAS, Department of Sociology, University of Illinois at Chicago Circle

ROY L. WALFORD, Department of Pathology, School of Medicine, University of California, Los Angeles

SARA B. KIESLER, Study Director, Department of Social Science, Carnegie-Mellon University

ELAINE McGARRAUGH, Administrative Associate, Committee on Aging, National Research Council

Contents

6

Political Characteristics of Elderly Cohorts in the Twenty-First Century

NEAL E. CUTLER

7

The Welfare State and the Political Mobilization of the Elderly

RICHARD G. FOX

8

Life-Stage Effects on Attitude Change, Especially among the Elderly

DAVID O. SEARS

9

Aging and Opportunities for Elective Office

JOSEPH A. SCHLESINGER AND MILDRED SCHLESINGER

III

ORGANIZATIONS

10

The Aging of Work Organizations:
Impact on Organization and Employment Practice   243
SHELBY STEWMAN

11

Some Consequences of Organizational Demography:
Potential Impacts of an Aging Work Force on
Formal Organizations   291
JEFFREY PFEFFER

12

Reform Movements and Organizations:
The Case of Aging   331
W. RICHARD SCOTT

IV

SOCIAL AND EMOTIONAL RESOURCES

13

Dilemmas of Social Support: Parallels between Victimization and Aging   349

CHRISTINE DUNKEL-SCHETTER AND CAMILLE B. WORTMAN

14

Convoys of Social Support: A Life-Course Approach   383

ROBERT L. KAHN AND TONI C. ANTONUCCI

15

The Role of Expectancy in Adaptation to Aging   407

ROBERT R. SEARS

16

The Self-Concept and Old Age   431

JOEL COOPER AND GEORGE R. GOETHALS

List of Contributors

Numbers in parentheses indicate the pages on which the authors' contributions begin.

Toni C. Antonucci (383), Institute for Social Research and Department of Family Practice, University of Michigan, Ann Arbor, Michigan 48106

Robert N. Butler (1), National Institute on Aging, 9000 Rockville Pike, Bethesda, Maryland 20205

Sidney Cobb* (75), Division of Biology and Medicine, Brown University, Providence, Rhode Island 02912

Joel Cooper (431), Department of Psychology, Princeton University, Princeton, New Jersey 08540

Neal E. Cutler† (127), U.S. Senate, Special Committee on Aging, Dirksen G-233, Washington, D.C. 20036

James A. Davis (93), Department of Sociology, Harvard University, Cambridge, Massachusetts 02138

Christine Dunkel-Schetter** (349), Department of Psychology, Northwestern University, Evanston, Illinois 60201

* Present address: North Easton, Massachusetts 02356.
† Present address: Andrus Gerontology Center, University of Southern California, Los Angeles, California 90007
** Present address: Department of Psychology, University of California, Berkeley, Berkeley, California 94720.

RICHARD G. FOX (159), Department of Anthropology, Duke University, Durham, North Carolina 27706

JOHN FULTON (75), Division of Biology and Medicine, Brown University, Providence, Rhode Island 02912

GEORGE R. GOETHALS (431), Department of Psychology, Williams College, Williamstown, Massachusetts 01267

E. A. HAMMEL (11), Department of Anthropology, University of California, Berkeley, Berkeley, California 94720

GIORA HANOCH (543), Center for the Social Sciences, Columbia University, New York, New York 10027

MARJORIE HONIG* (543), Center for the Social Sciences, Columbia University, New York, New York 10027

ROBERT L. KAHN (383), Institute for Social Research and Department of Psychology, University of Michigan, Ann Arbor, Michigan 48106

JENNIE KEITH (453), Department of Anthropology and Sociology, Swarthmore College, Swarthmore, Pennsylvania 19081

SARA B. KIESLER† (41), National Academy of Sciences, National Research Council, Washington, D.C.

C. K. MCDANIEL (11), Department of Anthropology, University of California, Berkeley, Berkeley, California 94720

JAMES N. MORGAN (587), Institute for Social Research, University of Michigan, Ann Arbor, Michigan 48106

JEFFREY PFEFFER** (291), Graduate School of Business, Stanford University, Stanford, California 94305

JOSEPH A. SCHLESINGER (205), Department of Political Science, Michigan State University, East Lansing, Michigan 48824

MILDRED SCHLESINGER (205), Department of Political Science, Michigan State University, East Lansing, Michigan 48824

W. RICHARD SCOTT (331), Department of Sociology, Stanford University, Stanford, California 94305

DAVID O. SEARS (183), Department of Psychology, University of California, Los Angeles, Los Angeles, California 90024

ROBERT R. SEARS (407), Department of Psychology, Stanford University, Stanford, California 94305

BETH J. SOLDO (491), Center for Population Research, Georgetown University, Washington, D.C. 20057

* Present address: Department of Economics, Hunter College, New York, New York 10021.

† Present address: Department of Social Science, Carnegie-Mellon University, Pittsburgh, Pennsylvania 15213.

** Present address: Graduate School of Business Administration, Harvard University, Boston, Massachusetts 02163.

SHELBY STEWMAN (243), School of Urban and Public Affairs, Carnegie-Mellon University, Pittsburgh, Pennsylvania 15213

RAYMOND J. STRUYK (513), The Urban Institute, 2100 M Street, N.W., Washington, D.C. 20037

JUDITH TREAS (561), Department of Sociology, University of Southern California, Los Angeles, California 90007

K. W. WACHTER (11), Demography and Statistics, University of California, Berkeley, Berkeley, California 94720

CAMILLE B. WORTMAN (349), Research Center for Group Dynamics, Institute for Social Research, University of Michigan, Ann Arbor, Michigan 48106

Foreword

This book is one of three volumes examining some possible social and behavioral science research perspectives on aging. The others are: *Aging: Stability and Change in the Family*, edited by Robert W. Fogel, Elaine Hatfield, Sara B. Kiesler, and Ethel Shanas; and *Aging: Biology and Behavior*, edited by James L. McGaugh and Sara B. Kiesler. The papers were solicited by the Committee on Aging of the National Research Council in response to a request from the National Institute on Aging.

The reason for the request was uncomplicated. As the phenomena of aging became more salient to private lives, effective research on aging becomes more critical to public policy and personal understanding. Most analyses suggest that there will be more money for research on aging over the coming years and that shifts in research funding will be incentives for shifts in research attention. Past experience warns, however, that although financial resources are necessary for an outstanding research program, they are rarely sufficient. In order for a public agency to influence the direction of important research, it must entice the community of scholars not only with money but also with a sense of the challenges and opportunities that the field provides. It must influence the individual professional enthusiasms that collectively determine the allocation of significant research creativity. In such a spirit, the National

Institute on Aging asked the National Research Council's Committee on Aging to organize a series of workshops at which experienced gerontologists and other social and behavioral scientists might discuss research ideas of possible relevance to future work on aging.

Organizing and implementing the workshops and the resulting volumes have involved many members of the research community. The 14 members of the Committee on Aging, the 65 contributors to the volumes, the 63 other participants in the workshops, and the 80 colleagues who reviewed the papers submitted for the volumes all contributed their time and expertise. In many cases, this represented a considerable personal commitment. On behalf of the committee, I want to thank this large band of generous colleagues, and particularly the editorial group of Robert W. Fogel, Elaine Hatfield, Sara B. Kiesler, James L. McGaugh, James N. Morgan, Valerie Kincade Oppenheimer, and Ethel Shanas. With no personal gain and little glory, they did the job. At the usual risk of promoting ordinary behavior into heroics, I calculate the professional fees foregone as being on the order of $1,000,000 and happily record the amount as a grant from the research community to the Academy and the Institute.

For most of the scientists who participated in this effort, however, the activity has had little connection to eleemosynary instincts. What more could a reasonable person ask from life than that it provide a few opportunities to exchange ideas with people who have some? The willingness of important research scientists to write papers for these volumes attests to the intellectual stimulation they found in fundamental research questions about aging. On behalf of my research colleagues, therefore, I want to thank the National Institute on Aging and the National Academy of Sciences for their parts in creating some occasions for such pleasures.

In particular, we owe a debt to some Washington colleagues. The original request to the Academy came from Robert N. Butler, Director of the National Institute on Aging, to David A. Goslin, Executive Director of the National Research Council's Assembly of Behavioral and Social Sciences. Both of them, as well as Betty H. Pickett, former Associate Director of the extramural collaborative research program of NIA, Matilda White Riley, Associate Director of NIA for social and behavioral research, and Shirley P. Bagley, health scientist administrator at NIA, contributed considerably to the climate of support that sustained the effort.

In addition, there was a small, tolerant staff in Washington. Elaine McGarraugh of the Committee on Aging and Christine L. McShane of the Assembly of Behavioral and Social Sciences managed the many details of bringing the papers together for the books. They cajoled an unlikely crew of widely scattered contributors with patient humor and peristaltic persistence and edited the volumes for the Academy with the sweet and sour sense and firmness that distinguish good editors. The one indispensible person, however, was Sara B. Kiesler. Before she left to return to academe, she served as study director for the project. Without her exceptional professional breadth and imagination, as well as her high style of dealing with ideas and people, the committee would have been unable to function. She deserves primary credit for having brought it all together.

As usual, it is necessary to exonerate all of these people, as well as the United States government, the National Academy of Sciences, the Assembly of Behavioral and Social Sciences, the National Institute on Aging, and innumerable universities from responsibility for what the individual authors say. The sensible things they have written are doubtless attributable to their colleagues and to the Committee on Aging. But the foolish things are their own.

JAMES G. MARCH, CHAIR
Committee on Aging

Preface

Reaching old age is becoming a universal experience in American society. Yet the socioeconomic and political environment the aged face is constantly shifting, as is the influence of the elderly population on the society at large. In planning this volume, the major objective was to encourage scholars from a variety of social and behavioral sciences to bring their particular perspectives to bear on the question of social change and its implications for the elderly. A special emphasis was placed on those changes most likely to occur in the next 25 years and on the general characteristics of social processes that would have particular relevance for the remainder of this century and the start of the next.

The authors were asked to reflect on the lives of old people from the perspective of data and theory in their own disciplines. They were asked to pose researchable questions and testable hypotheses. Their ideas, it was hoped, would indicate what researchers are learning about old age as it has been and as it may be in the future.

The topics of this volume were chosen on the basis of some guesses about the future as well as judgments of interesting and important research. One focus is on public policy. Understanding how policies are formulated, implemented, or improved has obvious implications for the old, many of whom rely heavily on public services and income. Further, recent work on the role of demographic and social change in public policy raises many new questions about our assumptions concerning aging and programs for the elderly. A second emphasis of the volume is the organization of business, government, and social institutions. Modern life, whether for old or young, takes place within organizations; organizational continuity and change is an emerging area of research both of practical significance for those who will manage the old (or be managed by them) and of general theoretical importance. Finally, the volume stresses everyday life, that is, the personal resources and living conditions of the old. Social ties and attitudes about ourselves and others as well as the arrangement of retirement, jobs, households, medical care, and community services are what link public policies and organizational behavior to the well-being of individuals. New research on these links is revealing the real challenges of old age as we face the new century.

In all three areas, we have assumed that research priorities should be guided at least in part by foreseen problems, tempered both by awareness that we cannot predict all the problems and by the fact that some research topics are more intrinsically exciting and/or more feasible than others. We hope the research agenda implicit and explicit in this volume will excite new activity by scientists not traditionally considered to be gerontologists.

The idea of this volume originated in 1978 with the Committee on Aging of the Assembly of Behavioral and Social Sciences at the National Research Council. The committee, chaired by James G. March of Stanford University, worked on this project in cooperation with David A. Goslin, Executive Director of the Assembly, and the leading individuals from the sponsoring federal agency, Robert N. Butler, Betty Pickett, and Matilda Riley of the National Institute on Aging. A workshop entitled "The Elderly of the Future" was held May 3–5, 1979, in Annapolis, Maryland. It was planned by a group consisting of the editors of this volume, James March, and members of the Committee on Aging, James R. Dumpson, M. Powell Lawton, and Robert R. Sears. The discussers and reviewers (whose names appear in Appendix A and Appendix B, respectively) were an important source of ideas and provided feedback to the authors. Elaine McGarraugh was administrative associate to the committee and organizer-in-chief of the many reviews and revisions of the chapters. Christine McShane read and edited every chapter in this volume. The editors are very grateful to these many colleagues.

PART **I**

ANTICIPATING
THE FUTURE

chapter 2

The Kin of the Aged in A.D. 2000: The Chickens Come Home to Roost

E. A. HAMMEL
K. W. WACHTER
C. K. McDANIEL

In all human societies, the ties of consanguinity and affinity have formed the warp and weft of social groups. In the technologically simplest and demographically sparsest societies, kinship is often the only basis of internal organization. In the technologically most developed and demographically densest, kinship provides the basis for the formation of groups that have the greatest emotional significance for most persons. Kinship provides each person with a set of known individuals from which important groups are formed.

There are three components to the process of group formation. First, purely demographic events produce individuals of particular biological connections. Of course, social understandings constrain the demographic events. Second, the operative cultural system defines which individuals will be recognized as kin, how they will be classified, and what their rights and obligations are. Indeed, by extension, the cultural system may define some persons who are not consanguineal or affinal kin into these same groups; the boundary between kin and nonkin is not always sharp. Third, individual preferences and interactions will further refine the map of kinship and the roles of the participants. Our concern here is the force of the constraints imposed by demographic processes. Although demography does not determine what the kinship map will be, it furnishes the

11

AGING
Social Change

basic materials that are refined by cultural and individual forces. If cultural prescription and individual preference are to draw the map for particular persons, what does demography provide?

Our earlier research has shown that different demographic rates indeed have an influence on what a cultural system and individual preferences can achieve in group formation. The establishment of stem family households (parents with one married child) is loosely constrained by demography (Hammel and Wachter 1977, Wachter et al. 1978, Chapter 4). LeBras (1973) has discussed the coexistence of lineal kin in modern and eighteenth-century France. Hammel et al. (1979) have shown the effect of incest taboos on marriage possibilities in small populations. Goodman et al. (1974, 1975) and Goldman (1977, 1978) have addressed the estimation of vital rates from knowledge of kinship structure, as have McDaniel and Wachter (1979), Wachter (1980), and McDaniel and Hammel (1981). The research we present here is close to that of LeBras, but proceeds by way of Monte Carlo simulation, using current versions of the SOCSIM microsimulation programs (Hammel et al. 1976).

THE PROBLEM

Our interest is directed toward the existence of three-generational kinship groups under different regimes of demographic rates. The problem has two aspects:

1. What is the kinship universe of the aged (defined here as those over age 70)? How many of the aged have siblings, and how many siblings? How many of these have children and grandchildren, and how many?
2. What is the position of the middle generation in this three-generational structure? How many persons in the middle generation have minor dependent children? How many have aged, possibly dependent parents? How many have both kinds of dependents at the same time, and what is the weight of this simultaneous responsibility?

Measuring the kinship universe of the aged defines the set of persons from whom emotional support is most likely to come or at least from which it is culturally expected. Cummings and Schneider (1963), for example, have shown that the sibling sets of the elderly re-form even after years of dormancy to replace social linkages lost through the death of spouses. Material support for the elderly has been culturally expected

of their children, and the laws of some states may require filial contribution before public assistance can be given. Those of the aged who
have no kin are the most likely to become dependent on public assistance
for their material welfare and social well-being.

Measuring the responsibilities of the middle generation estimates the
degree to which persons in it may be placed in a difficult position,
psychologically or materially, by virtue of their simultaneous responsibilities. The conflict between filial and parental duties may be sharp. It
can be expected to increase as the number of minor children and of aged
parents increases for members of the middle generation—phenomena
dictated by the demographic rates.

Ancillary to these concerns are those of the familial environment of
socialization. Growing up in a large sibling set is different from growing
up in a small one. Growing up with living grandparents is different from
growing up without them.

Policy issues are importantly affected by variation in kin-based groups
in all these areas—the social environment of the aged, the burdens imposed on the economically productive segment of the population through
responsibility for the young and the aged, and the milieu in which the
young are socialized.

For the purposes of this chapter, we examine a simulated population
at three points in historical and projected time. We use a simulacrum
of the white population of the United States in 1950 under the then
current demographic rates, in 2000 under the low fertility projections of
the Bureau of the Census, and in 2000 under the high fertility projections
of the Census Bureau. At each of these points, we examine the kinship
universe of all persons in the population, by 5-year age groups, recording
living grandparents, parents, siblings, spouses, children, and grandchildren. Similarly, for the 5-year age groups of the adult population, ages
20–69, we examine the numbers of their dependents. Insofar as cultural
rules constrain demographic rates to certain ranges, we have used our
own intuitive understandings of the current social system in selecting
demographic regimes and in interpreting the meaning of kinship. We do
this not because we feel the current system must persist but because we
have more uncertainty about where it is going than about where it is or
has been. Our results, however, are easily reinterpretable if others wish
to change the assumptions.

Computation of the dependents is complex. First, any child under age
18 is counted as a dependent of its biological parents, if those are alive,
and the responsibility is shared between them. Thus, if only one parent
is alive, the total burden falls on that parent, but if both are alive, each

bears half the burden. Orphaned siblings under 18 are counted as a burden on their siblings over 18, and the burden is shared among the older siblings. Parents are counted as dependent if they are over age 70. If a parent over 70 has a spouse under 70, half the burden of the older parent is taken by the younger spouse, and the remaining half is shared between all the biological children of the older person. The responsibilities of two spouses are shared between them, and what we examine in the final analysis is the dependency burden of couples, not of individuals. The results presented here do not examine the responsibilities of widowed persons. These differ from those of couples only in bearing the full burden of minor children, but the number of widowed persons with minor dependents is quite small. The simulations did not include divorce (see methods, following), so that the dependencies of divorced persons are also unexplored.

METHODS

The critical information for analysis of networks of living kin and of dependency in three-generational sets consists of the joint age distributions of parents and children across three generations. We need to know the distribution of ages of children by ages of parents and at the same time the distribution of the ages of the grandparents. No reliable source on this subject was available to us. Data of the Bureau of the Census are generally household-based. A count of the children of parents is likely to lose the older children, because they have left home, and since stem and joint families (those with married siblings) are rare in this country, the ages of the grandparents are unlikely to be found in any household survey. Data on the distribution of ages of living children by age of parent may be found in some fertility surveys, but the critical information on ages of grandparents, linked to the ages of their children and grandchildren, is, again, unavailable. Age-specific distributions of the kin of noninstitutionalized aged will be biased toward exclusion of the aged without kin, since the latter are more likely to be institutionalized. One could assume statistical independence of the joint age distributions of parents and children in two adjacent generations and from these estimate the joint age distribution across three generations from census data. One could adapt the methods of Goodman et al. (1974, 1975), estimating the proportion of persons in some age class who simultaneously have ascendants of some degree over a critical age and descendants of some degree under another critical age. However, these methods seem risky because of the fuzzy boundaries between generations in the kinship sense and age sets in the demographic sense. Additionally, changing demographic rates over time make estimation of any distributions by such methods virtually impossible. A possible but still difficult alternative would be a Markov transition matrix analysis, but that would make estimates of variance problematic.

Simulation has disadvantages as a modeling technique. First, it is inelegant compared with analytic models, and its picayune detail may obscure underlying regularities. Second, by its very nature it forces attention to the particular rather than to the general. But this may be an advantage under some circumstances, in requiring one to think hard about the complex processes being modeled. Simulation has some advantages, too. First, it allows one to avoid the strong assumptions of some analytic modeling, substituting weaker ones on particulars. Second, it permits one to select those subprocesses that will be modeled closely against external evidence and to handle others in a more stylized fashion or ignore them. The investigator thus has something like experimental control over the variables. In these simulations, we have sought to match external evidence particularly in the parity-specific rates, in the distribution of family size, in age structure, and in the proportions of persons married, by age. In other words, we have sought to hew closely to those population characteristics that might affect fertility. We have been content to use stylized inputs or to ignore migration (except for global corrections), divorce, differentiation of remarriage rates, the age gap between spouses, and the possibility of heritable fecundity. Furthermore, we have changed the regimes of rates by 10-year periods, even though changes of rates in the populations of interest occurred more continuously.

We should also specify two caveats. First, it is not our intention to replicate history in every detail but only in those details thought reasonably important to the focus of interest. Second, it is not our intention to predict the future; we only wish to model some of its aspects if particular conditions prevail. These conditions include not only the stated rates but also the cultural understandings about institutions that permit us to translate biology into social facts. Briefly, it is our purpose to illustrate a range of outcomes for particular demographic rates and social assumptions.

Because persons who were aged in 1950 must have been born in the late 1800s, we need to recapture the structure of the population about that time and project it forward according to the demographic rates appropriate in each time period. We began our simulations with a population structured roughly like the United States white population in 1900 and projected it forward. Our method was as follows:

1. A population of 1000 single individuals was constructed with ages proportional to the $L(x)$ column in the life table for the United States native white population in 1900.
2. This population was simulated through the events of death, marriage, and birth using rates designed to preserve an age structure like that in (1). This simulation was repeated 25 times, producing 25 different populations, each with an age structure like that in (1) but differing through random variability and with the individuals in each population linked among themselves by ties of blood and marriage.
3. The population whose females aged 0–49 best fit the female age structure of the United States white population in 1900 was chosen from the set of 25. This is the "starting population" for the simulations to follow.
4. Mortality, fertility, and nuptiality rates were then established for decades centering on 1905, 1915, 1925, . . . , 1995. Details are given in the Appendix. All rates are aggregate rather than stratified ones and thus do not pertain to any specific subgroup of the population; they represent at best average expectations. Briefly, mortality rates for 1905 to 1945 are based on Coale and Zelnick (1963) and for 1955 and 1965 on Historical Statistics of the United States (1975). For 1975 through 1995, they are based on 1976 male and female white yearly survivorships in Table B-3 of "Projections of the Population of the United States, 1977 to 2050," Bureau of the Census, Current Population Reports, P-25, No. 704, July, 1977.

Fertility rates for 1905 through 1915 are based on parameters estimated by Sanderson (1978) for the model schedule in Coale (1971). From 1925, they are parity-specific. For 1925 to 1945, they are calculated to match average cumulative proportions of cohorts reaching each parity by given years in Table 114 of Grabill *et al.* (1958), a summary table paralleling the material in Heuser (1976). For 1955 and 1965, the rates are from the Bureau of the Census Subject Report, "Childspacing and Current Fertility," Tables 71–77. For 1975 through 1995, rates are based on the central birth rates of "Projections of the Population of the United States, 1977–2050," Table A-6, using projection (1) for high fertility and projection (3) for low fertility to the year 2000.

Nuptiality rates for 1905 and 1915 derive from Sanderson's (1978) parameter estimates for Coale and McNeil's (1972) model schedule of cumulative first marriage proportions. For 1925 to 1955, the first marriage rates are computed to match the cumulative proportions married by cohort in Grabill *et al.*, Table 116 (1958). The 1965 probabilities of marriage and remarriage from the National Center for Health Statistics, "Marriage Trends and Characteristics" (1971) serve for 1965 and to the year 2000. Divorce rates were left at zero, since the fertility rates were computed by assigning to marital fertility all births to ever-married women. We do not believe that the omission of divorce importantly affects the analytical results to be presented, since responsibility for children is allocated to the natural parents, and in our ethnographic view the ties of consanguinity often remain strong even through divorce. What we do omit is the additive effect to kinship networks of step- and half- relationships established by divorce and remarriage, and we may misjudge the responsibilities of married couples if the remarriage of divorced persons is nonrandom with respect to their dependency burdens. Although there is anecdotal evidence on the expansion of kindreds through serial monogamy, we have discovered no reliable way to quantify it and regard its overall effect as moot.

5. The starting population of 1900 was simulated 20 times through the year 2000. In all 20 simulations, the rates for the decades centered on 1905, . . . , 1975 were those derived from the historical data, as previously indicated and in the Appendix. For all these, the mortality and nuptiality rates of 1975 were also used for 1985 and 1995. For 10 of the 20 simulations, the fertility rates for 1985 and 1995 were set in accord with the low fertility projections just described and in the Appendix, whereas for the remaining 10 they were set in accord with the high fertility projections.

6. We examine the kinship information provided by these simulations at three points—1950, 2000 under the low fertility assumption, and 2000 under the high fertility assumption, providing a historical base point and a range of possibilities five decades afterward. We call these points "1950," "2000LO," and "2000HI" for convenience. We also examine a variety of purely demographic statistics derivable from the simulation outputs to check the consistency of the runs and their correspondence with observed historical phenomena.

RESULTS

Demographic Results

1. Table 2.1 displays the age and sex structure of the 1900 starting population. Table 2.2 shows the structure of the white population of the United States in that year for comparison.

TABLE 2.1
Structure of the Starting Population

Age	Males		Females	
	N	Proportion	N	Proportion
0	52	.102	58	.114
5	45	.089	58	.114
10	70	.138	56	.110
15	56	.110	48	.095
20	47	.093	45	.089
25	40	.079	36	.071
30	43	.085	44	.087
35	27	.053	35	.069
40	35	.069	34	.067
45	25	.049	25	.049
50	16	.032	21	.041
55	15	.030	16	.032
60	16	.032	12	.024
65	10	.020	10	.020
70	7	.014	7	.014
75	2	.004	2	.004
80	1	.002	1	.002
85 +	1	.002	0	.000
Total	508	1.003	508	1.002

2. Table 2.3 shows the crude birth, death, and growth rates of the simulated population for the decades centering on 1905, . . . , 1995 as well as the observed or presumed rates from the data sources 1905–1975. The rates achieved in the simulated population are divided into those for the high fertility runs and the low fertility runs. Although the fertility differences took effect only after 1970, there are differences between the two classes of runs before that because of the stochastic character of the simulations.

3. Table 2.4 shows the population of white females (in millions) computable from the two sets of simulation runs and from the observed historical data, allowing an adjustment for migration up to 1930 in each of the census decades since 1900.

4. Table 2.5 shows the proportions of women with at least one child in 1970 having one, two, three, or four or more children, by 5-year cohorts of women from 1920–1924 to 1940–1944, as computed from the high and low fertility simulation runs and as taken from the historical sources.

5. Table 2.6 shows the proportions of women in 5-year age groups

TABLE 2.2
Structure of the U.S. White Population in 1900[a]

Age	Males		Females	
	N	Proportion	N	Proportion
0	4320	.120	4160	.119
5	4040	.112	3910	.111
10	3700	.103	3580	.102
15	3440	.095	3350	.095
20	3220	.089	3160	.090
25	3120	.086	2980	.085
30	2810	.078	2630	.075
35	2500	.069	2310	.066
40	2250	.062	2100	.060
45	1760	.049	1690	.048
50	1440	.040	1450	.041
55	1150	.032	1240	.035
60	882	.024	962	.027
65	645	.018	673	.019
70	431	.012	478	.014
75	244	.007	257	.007
80	110	.003	121	.003
85+	42	.001	52	.001

[a] From A.J. Coale and M. Zelnick, *New Estimates of Fertility and Population in the United States*. Excerpts from Tables 16 and 17, pp. 181–182, in adapted form. Copyright © 1963 by Princeton University Press. Reprinted by permission of Princeton University Press. See the original tables for qualifications in the higher ages.

TABLE 2.3
Crude Rates[ab]

Year	Birth			Death			Female growth		
	LO	EXP	HI	LO	EXP	HI	LO	EXP	HI
1905	25.6	29.6	25.6	13.9	15.4	13.5	12.5	12.9	13.4
1915	23.1	28.1	23.1	13.0	13.5	13.4	10.8	13.5	10.3
1925	23.4	23.5	24.3	12.1	11.2	11.5	11.1	11.6	12.2
1935	17.8	18.2	18.1	11.2	10.4	11.1	6.4	7.1	7.3
1945	22.9	22.3	23.2	10.9	10.0	10.4	11.6	12.6	13.6
1955	21.9	23.6	22.4	10.2	9.3	10.1	11.4	16.5	12.6
1965	17.5	18.7	17.5	10.3	9.4	9.6	7.9	10.2	7.8
1975	12.7	—	13.1	9.2	—	9.1	3.5	—	4.6
1985	12.8	—	18.0	10.0	—	10.1	2.7	—	7.6
1995	7.1	—	16.0	12.0	—	10.4	−4.1	—	5.3

[a] All rates are per 1000. Expected growth rates are for the female population only, based on total female population adjusted for migration, from Coale and Zelnick (1963, p.182).
[b] LO indicates the rates observed for the simulations in which fertility in 1885 and 1995 was according to the low-fertility projections, HI those for the high fertility projections. EXP birth and death rates are those for all whites, averaged over decades of yearly crude rates, from Historical Statistics of the U.S. (1975, p.49, 59).

TABLE 2.4
Total Female Population (in Millions)[a]

Year	LO	EXP	HI
1900	38.9	38.9	38.9
1910	44.0	44.2	44.4
1920	49.1	50.6	49.3
1930	54.9	56.8	55.7
1940	58.6	61.0	59.9
1950	65.8	69.2	68.7
1960	73.8	81.6	78.0
1970	80.0	91.0	84.4
1980	82.9	—	88.4
1990	85.2	—	95.4
2000	81.8	—	100.7

[a] LO and HI are the average numbers of females in the 10 simulations with the low and the high fertility projections, respectively, before 1980, multiplied by the factor 38.85/508 million to make them comparable to the total U.S. white female population. The EXP for 1930 to 1960 are from Coale and Zelnick (1963), Tables 17 and 18; for 1970, from Historical Statistics of the U.S. (1975, p.14). Before 1930, the EXP figures make allowance for migration in the Coale and Zelnick figures by solving for those numbers which, when subject to the expected crude birth and death rates of Table 3, would produce the 56.8 million of 1930.

TABLE 2.5
Proportions in 1970 of Women at Parities 1, 2, 3, 4+ out of Those Having at Least One Child in 1970[a]

Cohort		Parity				Age
		1	2	3	4+	
1920–1924	HI	.107	.234	.209	.450	
	EXP	.159	.301	.233	.305	45–49
	LO	.091	.198	.230	.481	
1925–1929	HI	.136	.263	.222	.397	
	EXP	.129	.272	.243	.356	40–44
	LO	.121	.248	.237	.394	
1930–1934	HI	.126	.332	.303	.239	
	EXP	.105	.254	.260	.381	35–39
	LO	.158	.301	.237	.304	
1935–1939	HI	.201	.364	.262	.173	
	EXP	.126	.297	.275	.302	30–34
	LO	.217	.421	.216	.146	
1940–1944	HI	.363	.369	.209	.059	
	EXP	.253	.388	.221	.138	25–29
	LO	.337	.409	.174	.079	

[a] HI and LO as defined earlier. EXP taken from Bureau of the Census (1970), Table 88.

TABLE 2.6
Female Age Distributions[a]

Year	Age	LO	EXP	HI
1930	0	36.53	38.51	37.70
	20	29.48	31.99	29.45
	40	21.45	20.67	20.79
	60	12.51	8.85	11.96
	100			
1950	0	33.85	32.46	34.72
	20	29.47	31.15	29.64
	40	22.62	23.34	22.14
	60	14.04	13.03	13.45
	100			
1970	0	33.69	35.20	33.80
	20	27.48	25.57	27.94
	40	23.15	22.93	23.06
	60	15.60	16.31	15.12
	100			
1990	0	23.17	—	27.63
	20	31.36	—	29.73
	40	24.86	—	23.60
	60	20.56	—	19.01
	100			

[a] HI and LO as defined earlier. EXP taken from Coale and Zelnick (1963, p.182) for 1930 and 1950 and from Historical Statistics of the U.S. (1975, p.16). for 1970.

for the two simulation sets (Table 2.3) and the historical data as of 1930, 1950, 1970, and for the simulations alone, for 1990.

6. Table 2.7 gives the cumulative proportions of women married, by age group, for cohorts born 1890–1894, . . . , 1915–1919, for the two simulation sets, and for the historical data.

The crude birth rates in both simulation sets are lower than those in the historical data by about 4 or 5 per 1000 in the first two decades, quite close for the next three, and about 1 per 1000 low for the decades 1950–1970. The crude death rates achieved are about 1 or 2 per 1000 low in the first decade, close for the second, and then about 1 per 1000 high until 1970. In consequence, the crude growth rates are generally low throughout the span 1900–1970, with an error ranging from about .5 to almost 3 per 1000. The major effect of these errors can be seen in the comparisons of the total white female population (Table 2.4): In 1970 the simulated population in the low fertility set falls short of the observed population by 12% and in the high fertility set falls short by 7%. Some

TABLE 2.7
Cumulative Proportions of Women Married[ab]

	Cohorts								
	1890–1994			1895–1999			1900–1904		
Age	LO	EXP	HI	LO	EXP	HI	LO	EXP	HI
15–19	.076	.082	.091	.097	.086	.089	.085	.089	.112
20–24	.424	.464	.442	.397	.473	.407	.433	.490	.452
25–29	.677	.728	.696	.715	.749	.725	.747	.755	.753
30–34	.831	.845	.846	.849	.852	.852	.855	.844	.830
35–39	.883	.882	.891	.875	.880	.875	.893	.883	.853
40–44	.888	.893	.898	.875	.895	.881	.906	.892	.872
	1905–1909			1910–1914			1915–1919		
	LO	EXP	HI	LO	EXP	HI	LO	EXP	HI
15–19	.083	.093	.074	.064	.091	.070	.070	.081	.044
20–24	.463	.483	.453	.393	.467	.421	.441	.476	.409
25–29	.721	.742	.727	.709	.753	.739	.818	.810	.805
30–34	.839	.844	.830	.902	.870	.893	.940	.906	.918
35–39	.913	.894	.902	.943	.916	.935	.946	.931	.940
40–44	.931	.916	.922	.956	.931	.946	.955	—	.950

[a] EXP from Grabill et al. (1958), Table 116, pp. 324–325. *The Fertility of American Women.* New York: John Wiley & Sons.
[b] HI and LO as defined earlier.

of this shortfall reflects the absence of migration in the simulations, for which no correction was made after 1930.

Despite these differences in rates and aggregate population figures, the structural match between the simulated and historical populations is quite good. The size of the discrepancies in the female age pyramids (Table 2.6) diminishes from 1930 to 1970 and is small in any case, smallest in the later simulation years in the higher age groups, a critical point in examining the position of the aged in the year 2000. The proportions of women at the various parity steps (Table 2.5) match the historical data rather well, with the largest discrepancies in the earliest cohort and at the highest and lowest parities. The proportions of married women in the simulations (Table 2.7) fit very well with the estimates for cohorts of United States white females made by Kiser et al. (1958).

The structural characteristics of the simulated populations in 1950 and under the two fertility assumptions for 2000 are the most important because it is these structural characteristics that underlie the presence and absence of kin. The crude birth, death, and growth rates are in themselves of little importance except as they correlate with the structural characteristics. Thus, although the simulations could have been adjusted and rerun to match the historical data more closely in these areas of discrepancy, we thought it advisable to hold to the population obtained because of the good structural fit.

Kinship Results

In the figures presented on numbers of living kin, the solid lines pertain to the population in 1950, the lines with short dashes pertain to the population in the year 2000 under the high fertility assumption (2000HI), and the line with long dashes to the population in 2000 under the low fertility assumption. Each pair of line types (solid, short-dashed, long-dashed) represents the 95% confidence limits of our estimates.

WIVES AND HUSBANDS

The expected number of spouses per person across the age groups is given in Figure 2.1. Happily, as in any monogamous population, the

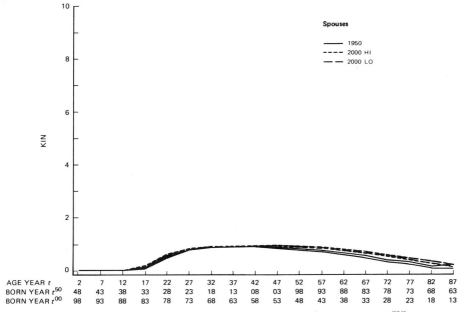

Figure 2.1. Expected number of spouses per person across the age groups. (Where $t =$ midpoint of 5-year age groups for any trace, 1950 or 2000, t^{50} indicates date of birth of persons aged t in 1950, and t^{00} indicates date of birth of persons aged t in 2000.)

expected number is never greater than one. It is zero in the age groups below 17, climbs as the proportion of persons married increases, then declines as mortality takes its toll. There are no differences between the 2000HI and 2000LO projections, both showing an improvement in mortality over 1950. This means that under the simulation assumptions, aged persons in 2000 can expect to have a living spouse more frequently than did persons their age in 1950. Generally, their expectations of companionship and mutual support will be marginally better.

PARENTS

Figure 2.2 shows the expected numbers of living parents across the age groups. Again, there are no differences between the runs for the year 2000 other than stochastic ones and a marked improvement over 1950 in survivorship of parents. Of course, in the upper age ranges, the number of living parents expected approaches zero.

SIBLINGS

Figure 2.3 shows the expected numbers of living siblings across the age groups. This plot is quite complex in its genesis. Examine first the

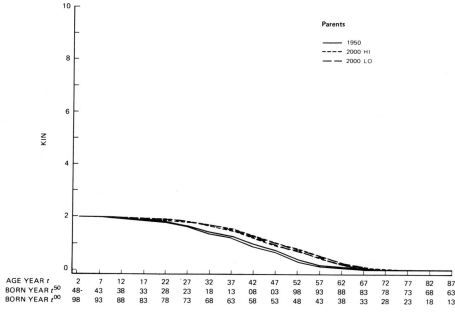

Figure 2.2. Expected number of living parents across the age groups. (Where t = midpoint of 5-year age groups for any trace, 1950 or 2000, t^{50} indicates date of birth of persons aged t in 1950, and t^{00} indicates date of birth of persons aged t in 2000.)

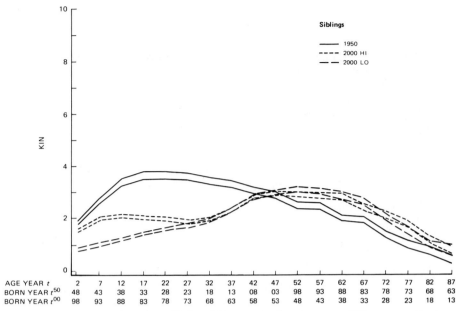

Figure 2.3. Expected number of living siblings across the age groups. (Where t = midpoint of 5-year age groups for any trace, 1950 or 2000, t^{50} indicates date of birth of persons aged t in 1950, and t^{00} indicates date of birth of persons aged t in 2000.)

trace of the plot for 1950 across the age groups. Note for purposes of interpretation that movement from left to right in the plot means not only an increase in age of the persons considered but also movement back in time to the dates of their birth and to the demographic conditions then in force. The expected number of siblings rises from a low for persons aged 2 to a higher point for those aged 12, after which the rate of increase slows, then ceases. Persons aged 2 are very likely to have siblings as yet unborn, while older persons are decreasingly likely to have siblings yet unborn. Thus, some of the increase we see is simply the filling out of sibling sets. The slope for 1950 is much steeper than that for 2000LO, however, indicating that fertility was higher in 1950. Indeed, what we see in the increase in siblings for persons aged 2 and 7 is the fertility rates of the decade 1940–1950, and the tapering off reflects the rates for the decade 1930–1940. Fertility rates in 1920–1930 were slightly higher and much higher in 1910–1920, but the larger number of siblings expected on those grounds for persons of middle age and older in 1950 is diminished by increasing mortality. Thus the expected number of living siblings declines.

The general form of the 2000HI and 2000LO curves is similar. Both exhibit an increase in expected number of siblings as persons increase in age, reflecting family building, but the peak is very much to the right, occurring for persons aged about 42 to 67. All of that difference from the 1950 trace cannot be attributed to family building. Persons aged 42 to 67 in 2000 were born between 1933 and 1958; the peak occurs for those aged 52, born in 1948. The height and "lateness" of this bulge in expected siblings can thus be attributed in part to the increase in fertility as the country emerged from the depression and to the high fertility after World War II. Another component of difference between the number of expected siblings for persons aged 40 and older in 1950 and in 2000 is the different mortality rates across the 50-year span. Persons over 40 in 1950 were born before 1910; those over 40 in 2000 were born before 1960; mortality rates were heavier throughout the lives of the first group (1950) than for the second (2000). At the extreme right of the graph are persons born well before 1900: The differences are underestimated because mortality rates before 1900 were yet heavier, but the starting population was created using 1900 mortality rates.

The two traces for 2000 show some differences. For persons aged 32 and over, they are only stochastic, reflecting the different sequences of random events under identical rates. For persons under 32, we see a slower rate of family formation, stemming from the lower fertility assumptions of the 2000LO simulation, the fertility rates having diverged in 1970. As we will see later, general conditions under the assumptions of 2000HI will converge on those of 1950, except for the improvement in mortality. In this graph, if the projections had run to 2050, we might expect the 2050HI trace to look much like the 1950 trace for persons aged about 22 and under but then to continue to the right with a much slower decline.

The general picture from this graph is that persons over age 70 in year 2000 can expect to have about one more living sibling on the average that did persons of the same age in 1950. Under the high fertility assumptions after 1970, by 2050 the aged might well have even more living siblings than those of the same age did in 1950.

CHILDREN

Figure 2.4 shows the expected numbers of children across the age groups. That number climbs from age 17 to 47 for the 1950 population, reflecting the accumulation of children through the end of the reproductive period. It then declines slowly under the pressure of mortality against the children of those who are over 47. The trace under the assumption of high fertility from 1970 to 2000 matches the 1950 curve closely until

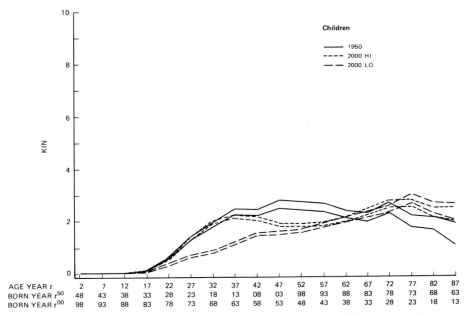

Figure 2.4. Expected number of children across the age groups. (Where t = midpoint of 5-year age groups for any trace, 1950 or 2000, t^{50} indicates date of birth of persons aged t in 1950, and t^{00} indicates date of birth of persons aged t in 2000.)

age 37, after which it drops off to rejoin the 2000LO trace, reflecting the lower fertility rates of the 1970s and 1960s; the number of expected children under the low fertility assumption climbs more slowly still. By 2000, under either fertility assumption, the expected number of children for persons aged 62 is about the same, and about the same as in 1950. Note that the expected numbers of children for both 2000HI and 2000LO continue to climb to a peak for persons aged 77. The increase to that point is attributable in large part to the fertility of the 1950s. If the simulations had run to the year 2050, the effects of the different fertility projections would have been visible further to the right in the graph. Under high fertility, the expected number of children would be greatest, enjoying both the increased fertility and improved mortality. This number would be greater than in 1950 and of course greater than that under the low fertility assumption. The number under the low fertility assumption might well be less than in 1950, despite the improved mortality.

Briefly, persons over 70 in 2000 can expect more children than could persons over 70 in 1950, and this difference could increase by 2050 if fertility again soared.

GRANDCHILDREN

As observed in Figure 2.5, the expected number of grandchildren naturally climbs with age, reflecting fertility in the senior generation, fertility and survival in the middle generation, and survival in the junior one. In 1958, this number peaked for persons aged 72, presumably reflecting the high fertility of this cohort, the children of whom were born around the first or second decade of the twentieth century, and perhaps the modest recovery of the fertility of their children after the depression. For the year 2000 traces, this number peaks for persons aged about 77, reflecting their own fertility in the 1950s. The trace for 2000LO is lower, reflecting the lower fertility levels of the middle generation in the mid-1980s, compared with those in the 2000HI projection. It is remarkable how close the 2000HI projection is to the 1950 trace, showing the effect of the recovery of fertility combined with improved mortality. Generally, persons aged about 70 and over in 2000 can expect to have four or five grandchildren, just about what persons of the same age had in 1950.

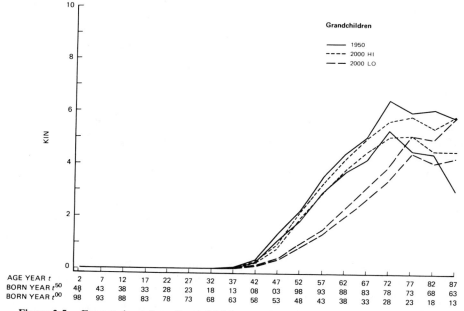

Figure 2.5. Expected number of grandchildren climbs with age. (Where t = midpoint of 5-year age groups for any trace, 1950 or 2000, t^{50} indicates date of birth of persons aged t in 1950, and t^{00} indicates date of birth of persons aged t in 2000.)

GRANDPARENTS

Figure 2.6 shows the expected number of grandparents. In 1950, it is about 3 for persons aged 2, and in 2000 about 3.5 because of the decline in mortality. Naturally, the number of grandparents declines, reaching zero for persons in their late thirties and early forties. What is important here is that children raised in the late years of this century will have a better chance of knowing their grandparents than their parents did. It is also important to note that some persons in their late thirties and early forties may be members of four-generational kinship sets, possibly with some responsibility to members of all four generations.

TOTAL PRIMARY KIN

Figure 2.7 shows the traces of the total primary kin across the age groups. Through age 47, the population in 1950 had more living primary kin. After that, mortality takes its toll among the kin of the older half of the population, primarily in the death of parents and siblings. In 2000,

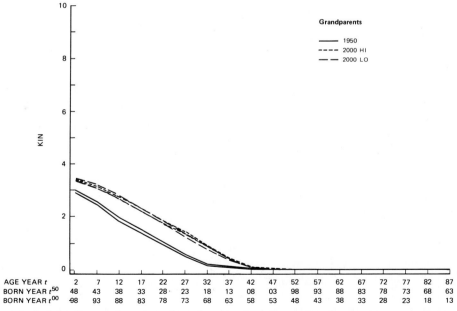

Figure 2.6. Expected number of grandparents. (Where t = midpoint of 5-year age groups for any trace, 1950 or 2000, t^{50} indicates date of birth of persons aged t in 1950, and t^{00} indicates date of birth of persons aged t in 2000.)

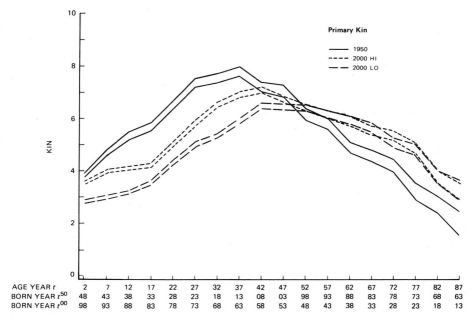

AGE YEAR t	2	7	12	17	22	27	32	37	42	47	52	57	62	67	72	77	82	87
BORN YEAR t^{50}	48	43	38	33	28	23	18	13	08	03	98	93	88	83	78	73	68	63
BORN YEAR t^{00}	98	93	88	83	78	73	68	63	58	53	48	43	38	33	28	23	18	13

Figure 2.7. Traces of the total primary kin across the age groups. (Where t = midpoint of 5-year age groups for any trace, 1950 or 2000, t^{50} indicates date of birth of persons aged t in 1950, and t^{00} indicates date of birth of persons aged t in 2000.)

the older segment of the population has more primary kin than the 1950 population, regardless of the fertility assumptions because of the improvements in mortality, and because that segment of the population was born into rather large sibling sets. Generally, the aged population in 2000 can expect to have larger kin networks than the aged in 1950 had. If the projections were extended to 2050, there would be a divergence between the 2000HI and 2000LO populations, the former having more living children and thus more living kin.

DISCUSSION

Overall, with respect to the potential sources of social and material support, the aged in 2000 will be in a better position than the aged in 1950. The aged of 1950, born in the late nineteenth century, came of large families so that they had relatively many siblings. They produced large families in the early twentieth century, so that they have many children. Some of their children in turn produced large families before the depression or after World War II. The aged of 2000, born in the early depression or before, came from reasonably large families. They married and raised families in the baby boom of the 1950s, so that they have many children, who will begin family formation in the late 1970s or early 1980s. Under the low fertility assumptions, the aged of 2000 will acquire fewer grandchildren than under the high fertility assumption, but they will nevertheless have some by virtue of their own large production of children. They will also benefit from the higher survival rates of siblings and of children compared with the aged population in 1950.

We can see from Figure 2.7, however, that as time advances beyond 2000, the position of the aged may deteriorate. The peaks of kinship for the aged in 2000 occur because of the timing of fertility cycles. Persons now aged 50 through 70 have all the kin they will have, except for grandchildren. If fertility drops, they will be denied the grandchildren, and their sources of support will diminish.

The situation for the younger age groups who might provide social and material support for the aged reflects these patterns of difference. We present here only the total dependency burden estimates for couples for the three populations, 1950, 2000HI, and 2000LO, across the age groups of the adult population. Computations of the dependency burden could be made in other ways, for example, by individuals, by considering widowed persons not remarried as residual couples, or by including divorce in the simulations, and so on. Nevertheless, since our purpose is to show general patterns under different demographic rates, and since couples are still the most frequently encountered familial core, we take advantage of this simplicity in the presentation. Each set of lines depicts the 95% confidence intervals of our estimates.

1950. Figure 2.8 shows the dependency burden on couples across the age ranges. The lower set of lines of the plot is the parental component, the upper set is the parental plus dependent child component. (The sibling component is minuscule and is omitted for clarity of presentation.) Notice that the total dependency burden rises from age 22 until 37 as children are born to couples. It then begins to drop as children pass age 18, despite the fact that responsibility for parents is increasing, not to drop off until age 47, when mortality diminishes the number of living parents. The peak dependency burden is about 2.5 persons, and the responsibility for aged parents is only about .12, or 5% of the total at that point. Parental responsibility peaks for persons aged 47 at about .3 out of a total responsibility of about 1.6, or about 20%.

2000HI. Figure 2.9 shows the dependency burden under the high fertility assumption for the years 1970–2000. The general picture is similar to that of 1950, although the peak burden is about .25 lower, and after

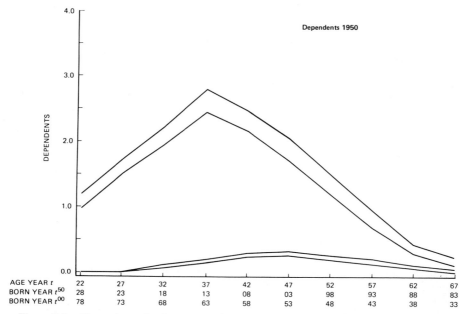

Figure 2.8. Dependency burden on couples across the age ranges. (Where t = midpoint of 5-year age groups for any trace, 1950 or 2000, t^{50} indicates date of birth of persons aged t in 1950, and t^{00} indicates date of birth of persons aged t in 2000.)

age 37 has a larger parental component. At age 37, the parental component is again about 5% of the total responsibility. At its peak (for age 52) it is about half the total responsibility. We can expect that if the simulations were continued for longer, the high fertility assumptions might accumulate a stronger effect, adding a dependent child component much like that of the 1950s to the higher parental component caused by more favorable mortality rates in the senior age groups.

2000LO. Figure 2.10 shows the dependency burden under the low fertility assumption for the year 2000. The parental component is the same as under the high fertility assumption. The dependent child component is lower under lower fertility, and thus the total burden is lower. The peak burden also occurs about 5 years later in the life of the middle-aged, reflecting age-specific differences between the fertility schedules for the high and low assumptions. The parental component here is about half the total, and at its own peak (for age 52), it is about two-thirds the total.

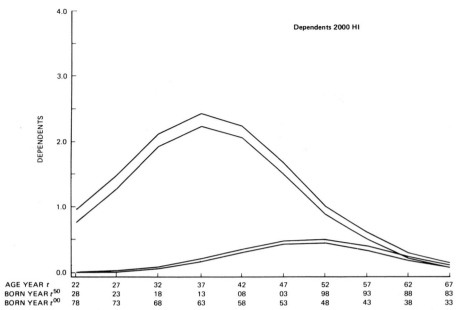

Figure 2.9. Dependency burden under the high fertility assumption for the years 1970–2000. (Where t = midpoint of 5-year age groups for any trace, 1950 or 2000, t^{50} indicates date of birth of persons aged t in 1950, and t^{00} indicates date of birth of persons aged t in 2000.)

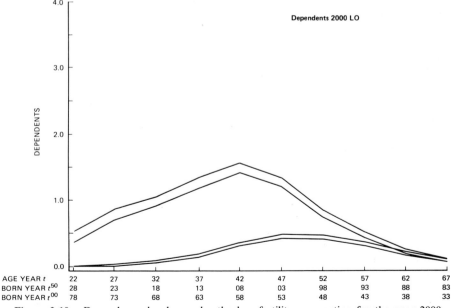

Figure 2.10. Dependency burden under the low fertility assumption for the year 2000. (Where t = midpoint of 5-year age groups for any trace, 1950 or 2000, t^{50} indicates date of birth of persons aged t in 1950, and t^{00} indicates date of birth of persons aged t in 2000.)

CONCLUSION

Overall, the middle-aged are in about the same position in 2000 under the high fertility assumption as they were in 1950, and their position could be worse by 2050 if that high level of fertility were to continue. Their position is much more favorable under the low fertility assumption in 2000, about one dependent less at peak. The proportion of available psychic and material resources provided by the middle generation to dependents goes much more to the elderly in 2000LO than in 2000HI or 1950; the claims of the elderly will meet with less competition from the young. At the same time, the elderly acquire a larger kinship base if fertility goes up.

We must again offer caveats to the presentation. Everything in the analysis depends on the accuracy of the rates employed and on the population structures generated. It was extremely difficult to find and correct the historical rate sets in order to provide rates that were internally consistent and whose interaction in demographic process produced population structures and other indices that matched observations in the real world. We declined to model some processes (e.g., divorce and remarriage, continuously changing rates, etc.) partly out of an unwillingness to take too many shots in the dark. Similarly, everything in the analysis depends on the continued viability of our assumptions about social relations, for example, the sharing of the dependency burden between spouses. We stress again that we are not predicting the future but only projecting the effect of certain assumptions. These initial assumptions could be altered, but real alternatives must be offered. We have seen no point in publishing the effects of all combinations of assumptions for the same reason that the availability of hand or machine computational techniques makes it unnecessary to publish tables of the results of all possible problems of arithmetic.

We believe that our methods have important virtues in the exploration of the effects of demographic conditions on social relations. Our results here confirm the general nature of projections by other scholars, for example, by Easterlin (1978). We are impressed by the replication, in the area of kinship relations, of the same mirroring of 1950 in 2000 that can be projected for employment, the structure of higher education, and other areas (Easterlin, 1978). We are intrigued to find the same intergenerational conflict of interest between the middle-aged and the elderly, contrasting the dependency burden and sources of kinship support, that one sees in macrocosm in the projected state of the Social Security system. The processes of fertility, marriage, and mortality that have the family as their arena also create the environment for their own enactment in future. In an inspiring passage in "The Sociological Imagination," C.

Wright Mills (1959, pp. 1–5) put forth the major task of social science as the understanding of how the lives of ordinary men and women are shaped by enormous forces beyond their control. Demography is such a force, and those who produce it visit it on their descendants.

APPENDIX

Mortality

For 1905 to 1945, we have taken q_x values from Coale and Zelnick (1963, pp. 184 and 185) for males and females. These q_x values are for decades centered on census years. We have converted them to the 1905, 1915 . . . series by the transformation $q_x(y) = 1 - \text{SQR}[(1 - q_x(y - 5)]*[1 - q_x(y + 5)]$, because in fact Coale's cohorts are subject to each of the rates of preceding and following life tables for half of the decade. These tables are sex-specific but not marital-status-specific. They have been converted to monthly rates. They are specifically for whites and are based on census figures corrected for enumeration errors.

For 1955 and 1965, the death rates are derived in the following way from *Vital Statistics of the U.S. 1971 Mortality* II, Part A. Table 5-4 on page 5.8 of that volume gives survivorships in 5-year age groups for white males and white females for 1949–1951,1959–1961, and 1970. After splitting the 15–20 group into 15–17 and 17–20, these are converted to 5-yearly probabilities of death by $1 - [\ell(x)/\ell(x-5)]$. These are then fed into a program that takes geometric averages of the rates to obtain rates for 1965 and 1955.

For 1975 on, we have taken Table B-3 in *Current Population Reports*, P-25, No. 704, which gives estimates of 1-year survival rates for white males and females. Multiplying successive survival rates together over each age span gives survival rates across that span (e.g., 0–1, 1–4, 5–9) and subtracting these from one gives the rates to be converted to monthly rates. The rates for 1976 are used for all years from 1975 on. Note that the table also gives "ultimate" male and female rates, undistinguished by sex. In various cases, these are lower than the 1976 survival rates, presumably because of the mixing of white and nonwhite populations, which is the reason for not taking them for 1990–1995.

Fertility

For 1905 and 1915, the rates are not parity-specific. They are based on the model marital fertility schedules of Coale (1971) with parameters chosen on the basis of Sanderson (1979, p. 341), and the technical memorandum cited there. The parameters ϕ, M, and m are chosen from Sanderson's values for 1900, 1910, and 1920 by linear interpolation to 1905 and 1915. Values for the natural fertility constants $n(a)$ and family limitation parameters $v(a)$ are taken from Coale and Trussell (1974). The form of the table is $r(a) = Mn(a) \exp[m \, v(a)]$ for yearly rates, and monthly rates are obtained by dividing by 12.

For 1925 through 1945, fertility rates are based on Table 114 in Grabill *et al.* (1958, pp. 320 and 321). For our purposes, this summary table is an adequate substitute for the detailed breakdowns on cumulative proportions achieving parity states by cohort in Heuser (1976). From the proportions in the table our rates have been computed with the Parifying Program WPARIFY by Ruth Deuel with homogeneous rather than heterogeneous fertility. This program iterates through rates successively approaching rates that give target, average, cumulative proportions from Grabill's Table 114 in each 5-year birth cohort reaching a parity state by a given exact date. Period fertility results from a reordering of the cohort fertility tables, picking out all rates pertaining to each given exact date. The rates are parity-specific and relate to native white women.

Rates from the parifying program have been adjusted in certain cases. We obtain rates for 17–20-year-olds by ignoring the outputs for 15–19 from the parifying program and multiplying the 20–24-year-old rates for each parity and period by .483460, the ratio we obtain by extrapolating linearly the (*a*) values in Coale's (1971) model schedule back beyond age 20.

For 1935 and 1945, we obtain the parity 5 for 20–24 (which the parifying program computed at zero, presumably because of insufficient cases at risk, not because of zero rates for cases at risk) by taking parity 4 for 20 to 24 and multiplying by the ratio of parity 5 for 25–29 to parity 4 for 25 to 29. For 1925, the Grabill-Kiser-Whelpton table gives no rates beyond age 35, these cohorts being too old. We have therefore taken round numbers for these rates following the general pattern of 1930 and 1935. For the rates at zero parity, we use in the parifying program person years at risk obtained from the cumulative proportions married in Table 116 of Grabill, Kiser, and Whelpton.

For 1955 and 1965, we have used the 1970 Census Subject Reports volume on *Childspacing and Current Fertility*, Tables 71 to 77: "Averaged annual probabilities of first child births to women who at the start of the calendar year were ever married and childless," etc. up to "Averaged annual probabilities of fifth and higher order births to women who at the start of the calendar year were ever married and already had four or more children." We use the sections for white women and convert to monthly rates by $1 - (1-r)^{1/12}$. We carry over the rates given for four or more children to our category of five or more children. For 1955, we have used the averaged annual probabilities for 1955 to 1959 and for 1965 the averaged annual probabilities for 1965–1969. These are somewhat off the central years. For 1965, we could average the 1960–1965 with the 1965–1969 rates, but we have not done so. The minimum birth interval in the SOCSIM program is set to 9.

For 1975, 1985, and 1995 we base our rates on the Central Birth Rates in Table A-6, page 78, of the *Census Current Population Reports* pages 25–704 for July 1977. For each age group, we calculate the ratio of each given year's rate to the 1965 rate, and then multiply all our parity-specific, marital–status-specific rates for that age group by this factor. Note that the central birth rates given in the table are general fertility, *not* marital fertility, so a procedure like ours appears essential.

The 1985(1) and 1995(1) rates are the high-fertility projections. The same rates with (3) are the low-fertility projections.

Nuptiality

For 1905 and 1915, we base our marriage rates on the model function of Coale and McNeil (1972) using parameters taken from Sanderson (1979), interpolated linearly between 1900 and 1910 and between 1910 and 1920. Note that the Coale and McNeil formula was developed for proportions ever married, but Sanderson has used it as if it were proportions currently married in estimating his parameters. The function gives a density value $g(a)$ for the distribution of time to first marriage by the relation

$$g(a) = C_1 \exp\{C_2 A(a) - \exp[C_3 A(a)]\}$$

where $A(a) = a - a_o - 6.06k$ and the Cs, k and a_o are parameters taken from Sanderson. The density values $g(a)$ are successively used to calculate rates per month, of first marriage, by

$$r = 1 - [1 - 5*g/(\text{survivors of marriage at start})]^{1/60}$$

This assumes that the density is constant over each 5-year period. We could refine these estimates by using 1-year values of $g(a)$, calculating the cumulative proportion married, and then the rates that would result in this cumulative proportion function, but we have used the cruder approximation, considering the crudeness of Sanderson's estimates in the first place. This results in missing the supposed proportion ever-married by about 2%. We adjust the 1905 and 1915 marriage rates for

15–19-year-olds to bring the proportions married by age 20 into line with those in Grabill, Kiser, and Whelpton, giving monthly rates of .002705 and .003101.

For all periods before 1965, the probabilities of marriage for widowed and divorced have been obtained by multiplying the probability for single people aged 20–25 by the ratio of probability of marriage for widowed or divorced of each age group to probability for single people aged 20 to 25 that obtains in the 1965 tables.

For 1925 to 1955, we have used first marriage rates calculated from the cumulative proportions of cohorts ever married by given exact years in Table 116 of Grabill, Kiser, and Whelpton by Ruth Deuel's WPARIFY program described under fertility rates. These pertain to native white cohorts.

For 1965, we have taken probabilities of marriage and remarriage from National Center for Health Statistics publication 21.21, *Marriage Trends and Characteristics* (1971), DHEW 72-1007, page 28. These are yearly probabilities of marriage, broken down between single women, widowed women, and divorced women, but aggregated into varying age groups. They have been disaggregated for the single rates in such a way as to match the proportions remaining unmarried by each end of period in the original table, but to decline progressively within the age categories lumped together.

Divorce

For the moment, we are leaving the divorce rates at zero, since our fertility rates are computed by assigning all births to ever-married women to marital fertility.

REFERENCES

Bureau of the Census (1970) *Childspacing and Current Fertility*. Subject reports. Washington, D.C.: U.S. Department of Commerce.

Bureau of the Census (1975) *Historical Statistics of the United States, Colonial Times to 1970*. Bicentennial edition, part 1. Washington, D.C.: U.S. Department of Commerce.

Bureau of the Census (1977) *Projections of the Population of the United States, 1977 to 2050*. Current Population Reports, Series P-25, No. 704. Washington, D.C.: U.S. Department of Commerce.

Coale, A. J. (1971) Age patterns of marriage. *Population Studies* 25:193–214.

Coale, A. J., and McNeil, D. (1972) The distribution by age of the frequency of first marriage in a female cohort. *Journal of the American Statistical Association* 67:743–749.

Coale, A. J., and Trussell, J. (1974) Model fertility schedules: Variations in the age structure of childbearing. *Population Index* 40:185–285.

Coale, A. J., and Zelnick, M. (1963) *New Estimates of Fertility and Population in the United States.* A Study of Annual White Births from 1855 to 1960 and of Completeness of Enumeration in the Censuses from 1880 to 1960. Princeton, N.J.: Princeton University Press.

Cummings, E., and Schneider, D. M. (1963) Sibling solidarity: A property of American kinship. *American Anthropologist* 63:498–507.

Easterlin, R. A. (1978) What will 1984 be like? Socioeconomic implications of recent twists in age structure. *Demography* 15:397–432.

Goldman, N. (1977) The Demography of Kin. Unpublished D.Sc. thesis, Harvard University.

Goldman, N. (1978) Estimating the intrinsic rate of increase of a population from the average number of older and younger sisters. *Demography* 15:499–508.

Goodman, L., Keyfitz, N., and Pullum, T. (1974) Family formation and the frequency of various kinship relationships. *Theoretical Population Biology* 5:1–27.

Goodman, L., Keyfitz, N., and Pullum, T. (1975) Addendum to "Family formation and the frequency of various kinship relationships." *Theoretical Population Biology* 8:376–381.

Grabill, W. G., Kiser, C. V., and Whelpton, P. K. (1958) *The Fertility of American Women.* New York: John Wiley and Sons.

Hammel, E. A., Hutchinson, D. W., Wachter, K. W., Lundy, R. T., and Deuel, R. Z. (1976) The SOCSIM Demographic–Sociological Microsimulation Program Operating Manual. University of California, Berkeley, Institute of International Studies Research Series, No. 27.

Hammel, E. A., McDaniel, C., and Wachter, K. W. (1979) Demographic consequences of incest tabus. *Science* 205: 972–977.

Hammel, E. A., and Wachter, K. W. (1977) Primonuptiality and ultimonuptiality: Their effects on stem–family–household frequencies. Pp. 113–134 in R. D. Lee, ed., *Population Patterns in the Past.* New York: Academic Press.

Heuser, R. (1976) *Fertility Tables for Birth Cohorts by Color, U.S. 1917–1973.* No. 76-1152. Washington, D.C.: U.S. Department of Health, Education, and Welfare.

LeBras, H. (1973) Parents, grandparents, bisaieux. *Population* 28:9–37. [Translated with revision in Wachter, Hammel, and Laslett (1978, pp. 163–188).]

McDaniel, C. K., and Hammel, E. A. (1981) Evaluation of Three Kin-Based Measures of *r*. Program in Population Research Working Paper No. 2. Institute of International Studies, University of California, Berkeley.

McDaniel, C., and Wachter, K. W. (1979) Estimating Demographic Parameters from Genealogical Structure: Simulation Assessment of the "Living Sisters" technique. Paper presented at the American Association of Physical Anthropologists, San Francisco, 1979.

Mills, C. W. (1959) *The Sociological Imagination.* New York: Oxford University Press.

National Center for Health Statistics (1971) *Marriage Trends and Characteristics.* No. 72-1007. Washington, D.C.: U.S. Department of Health, Education, and Welfare.

National Center for Health Statistics (1971) *Vital Statistics of the United States, Volume 2: Mortality.* Washington, D.C.: U.S. Department of Health, Education, and Welfare.

Sanderson, W. (1979) Quantitative aspects of marriage, fertility, and family limitation in nineteenth century America: Another application of the Coale specifications. *Demography* 16:339–358.

Wachter, K. W. (1980) The sisters' riddle and the importance of variance when guessing demographic rates from kin counts. *Demography* 17:103–114.

Wachter, K. W., Hammel, E. A., and Laslett, P. (1978) *Statistical Studies of Historical Social Structure.* New York: Academic Press.

chapter 3

The Aging Population, Social Trends, and Changes of Behavior and Belief

In this chapter, I consider how changing characteristics of our population and related exogenous conditions may alter attitudes and beliefs about older people. The chapter applies current social–psychological theory to attitude change about older people. The basic argument is that exogenous demographic, economic, and social conditions change behavior and that behavior changes attitudes. This idea may be used as a framework for research to understand future stereotypes of older people, changing attitudes about social issues involving the elderly, and new attitudes about aging.

GENERAL MODEL

The general theoretical model of attitude change adopted in this chapter is that various exogenous forces cause behavior to change, which in turn causes attitudes to change (see Figure 3.1). Exogenous forces include such conditions as changes in the demographic age structure, swings in the economic and political health of the nation, and various changes in social norms.

41

AGING*
Social Change

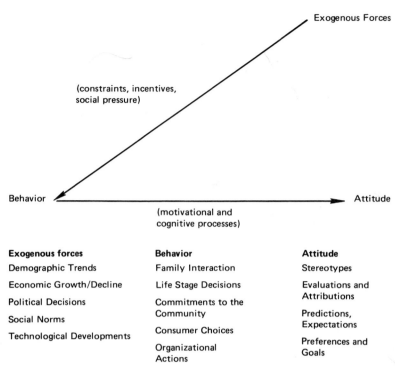

Figure 3.1. General model of attitude change.

In the first phase of the model, these external conditions and trends influence the immediate context in which individuals and their families act: The context affects their behavior. An example of the effect is the demographic trend toward improved life expectancy, which can increase the average person's number of older relatives. This increased number of relatives is part of the context of family interaction. Perhaps it means that people spend holidays with family members rather than traveling alone or with friends. Or perhaps they turn down jobs offered in faraway towns to stay near elderly parents. In this instance, the mortality rate is considered the exogenous force and the holiday activities or decision not to move are the behaviors influenced by it.

Exogenous forces influence behavior through constraints on decisions, perceived incentives, and social pressure. A family deciding whether to move West, for instance, may be constrained by having a grandmother's welfare to consider. Exogenous demographic conditions also attach incentives to the family's alternatives. For example, redistribution of the population toward the South and the West affects the family's judgments about job opportunities there. Finally, explicit and implicit social pressures on the family transmit social norms about behavior or imply sanctions for violating norms. The family may feel that staying with Grandma is the right thing to do, despite their personal preferences.

The three factors—constraints, incentives, and social pressures—are considered intervening variables in the model that link general external circumstances to individual decisions and actions. Although often they are much more complex than the previous examples indicate, for the purposes of this discussion only a simple effect is assumed: On average and for large groups of individuals, stronger incentives and pressures as well as more constraints (or fewer alternatives) will increase the probability and strength of exogenously caused behavior.

Researchers have uncovered many important areas of behavior that are influenced by exogenous forces. Increasing divorce and remarriage among older people, for example, has meant that many of them now acknowledge two or even three "immediate" families (see Furstenberg 1981), which means changes in family interaction patterns and access to more relatives across the age span. Important decisions about one's life are another set of behaviors influenced exogenously. Such decisions as to have or to delay having children or to retire earlier or later are in part a function of past living standards and future prospects in one's occupational class (e.g., Easterlin 1973, Morgan 1979, Oppenheimer 1981). Commitments to the community (such as volunteer work and voting), consumer choices (such as buying and selling a house), and organization or group action (such as committing funds to building a nursing home) are other categories of behavior that social psychologists have typically studied as internally caused by preexisting attitudes and socialization but that are also influenced exogenously.

In the second phase of the general model, behavioral changes caused by exogenous forces influence attitudes. Social psychologists have studied many kinds of attitudes in the last several decades. These include:

1. Stereotypes of people—that is, beliefs about the attributes of group members (e.g., Bruner and Tagiuri 1954, Hamilton 1979).
2. Evaluations of people and their behavior and attributions of causality for their behavior (e.g., Anderson 1967, Zajonc 1968, Jones and Nisbett 1971, Nisbett and Valins 1972).
3. Predictions and expectations, including "social schemata," chains of behavior that seem to go together (Nisbett and Ross 1980, Ross et al. 1977, Snyder and Swann 1978).
4. Preferences and goals (e.g., Zander 1968, Maloney and Schonfeld 1973).

The general model draws on two major theoretical views in social psychology to explain how behavior affects the kinds of attitudes just listed. First, there are motivational theories, which include dissonance, equity reactance, commitment, and self-awareness theories (Festinger 1957, Walster *et al.* 1973, Brehm 1966, C. Kiesler 1971, Duval and Wicklund 1972). These theories differ among themselves in some important ways, but not for purposes of the model discussed here. All of the motivational theories predict that an individual's own behavior arouses motives or drives that in turn change attitudes. Generally, the motives concern self-enhancement or protection of self, and the attitude change is in the direction of maintaining self-esteem. For instance, suppose a man commits himself to financial responsibility for an aged parent whose resources are otherwise limited; suppose also that the man's decision implies some lesser contribution to his children's education than he had originally intended. The man would be motivated to justify and explain his new position to himself. To satisfy this motive to justify his decision, the man could change his attitudes. He might increase his liking of the parent (improving his parent's deservingness) or come to feel more confident that people in general care for their elderly relatives (increasing the social desirability of his decision).

To summarize the simple role of motivation in the general model, exogenously caused behavior is assumed to arouse individual motives, usually to justify the behavior and protect self-esteem. Post hoc justification leads to attitudes that place the behavior in a good light from the actor's point of view.

The kinds of attitudes that change because of motivational processes include: stereotypes that enhance the desirability of one's in-groups (Campbell 1967); evaluations and attributions that "explain" behavior (e.g., Grune and Lepper 1974, cf. Bandura *et al.* 1977); expectations for the future or past history that are revised to reflect positively on the desirability and rationality of decisions (Aronson 1966); and changes in preferences and goals that make behavior consistent retrospectively (Jones and Berglas 1978). The model does not specify which kind of attitude will change in particular cases, however; this must be evaluated separately.

In contrast to the motivational view, cognitive theories of attitude change focus on the role of thinking, learning, and remembering in attitude change (e.g., Bem 1972, Harvey 1976, Harvey *et al.* 1978, Taylor and Crocker 1979, Cacioppo and Petty 1979, Petty *et al.* 1980). Here, too, there are some important differences among theories, but a general statement is possible. It is asserted that behavior influences an individual's information, and that the individual's inferences from information or from memories of information influence attitudes (e.g., Ross and Sicoly 1979, Snyder and Uranowitz 1978). For example, reading what newspapers say about nursing home fires provides information affecting one's inferences and attitudes about the dangers of nursing homes. Cognitive theoretical research aims at discovering what individuals will infer from such pieces of behavioral information.

According to the cognitive approach, it is the informative aspect of behavior that changes attitudes, and anyone's behavior can be informative. Either behavior in general or one's own behavior can change attitudes. Hence, the man who agrees to take care of his aged parent acquires information about himself from his behavior. His behavior speaks of a generous benefactor helping a person in need. However, he might reach the same conclusion about someone else who was to care for his aged parent or about all people who take care of their parents. The attitude that he is a generous person, then, is not necessarily a self-enhancing one; cognitive theories explain its acquisition quite well.

To summarize the simple roles of cognition in the general model, exogenously caused behavior produces information. Inferences are drawn from the behavioral information; they make sense of it. Inferences are used in developing and changing attitudes. Again, the general model does not specify which kinds of attitudes will change in specific cases, only that they will end up intelligibly related to the behavior.

The rest of this chapter is divided into four sections. The first section describes the application of the general model to the case of an aging population, especially its effects on behavior and attitudes about the elderly and aging. In the second section, it is proposed that the behaviors that are changed by the aging of the population will vary in the extent to which they involve motivational and cognitive processes of individuals. The third section describes the effect of individual motivational processes on attitudes about older people and aging. The fourth section describes the attitudinal effects of individual cognitive processes. These last sections show that motivational and cognitive theories predict different kinds of attitude change and complement each other.

APPLICATION TO THE AGING POPULATION

The general model proposed here can be applied to the case of an aging population (see Figure 3.2). An aging population may be defined informally as a change in the age distribution of the nation toward an increasingly older average age and a larger proportion of older persons in the total. In its final effect on attitudes, the aging population is theoretically interchangeable with any exogenous trend in society, as long as the behavioral effects are the same. (Behavior is the crucial factor

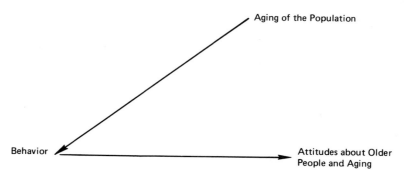

Aging and Proportion of Older People

Number and Proportion of Older People

Advances in Health, Education, Political Power, and Standard of Living of Older People

Change in Dependency Ratio

Small Family Size, Divorce, Migration and Other Demographic Correlates of Social Change

Behavior Characteristics

Contact with Older People

Change in Attributes of Older People

Decisions Affecting Older People (including intergenerational exchanges)

Making Plans for Old Age

Attitude Characteristics

Stereotypes of Older People and Attributions of Causality

Social Issues: Evaluations and Beliefs

Attitudes about Aging in One's Own Life

Figure 3.2. Application of the model.

intervening between exogenous conditions and attitude change.) However, demographic aging as we are experiencing it in this country has features that suggest a relatively strong indirect effect on attitudes about the elderly and aging.

One effect of the aging of the population is that a large number of people are more involved with older people. There is more personal contact or interaction with older people and more learning about social and personal issues related to aging, such as retirement and long-term health care. Advances in the health, education, political clout, and living standard of older people will also increase contact and knowledge of them, because older people will appear more frequently in the community, in business, and in politics.

Increased contact with older people and knowledge of them will affect attitudes about the kind of people they are (stereotypes) as well as attitudes about the social issues that affect them (see, e.g., Insko and Wilson 1977). These changes of attitude will occur even if more contact only elaborates current impressions of older people. Enriching perceptions of older people would help popularize new subcategories of older people (e.g., young-old versus old-old) and cause greater awareness of the heterogeneity of outlook and needs of older people.

The demographic aging of the population is likely to affect attitudes relevant to social issues even more strongly, however, because of the public and private decisions to be made about older people (Wack and Rodin 1978). Although advances in the well-being of older people is true generally, a minority of older people are poor, ill, or too frail to care for themselves. This minority is growing disproportionately faster than the overall group of persons over 65. Declines in mortality are increasing the numbers of people who are very old, the numbers who have no immediate family, and the numbers who have very few financial assets. As a result, public organizations responsible for older people and also relatives of poor, alone, sick, or frail older people will have to make difficult decisions about their care. More intergenerational decisions and transfers of resources will be necessary. The decisions may involve higher taxes targeted to social security and Medicare, more publicly supported housing and community facilities for older people, more government regulation of family responsibilities for elderly parents, more professionalization of services and specialized training for people serving older clients, and more pressure on employers not to discriminate against older people. If the numbers of older persons increase and they support these decisions and the decisions actually are implemented, the total effect on attitudes about social issues affecting older people could be considerable.

Another demographic characteristic of the aging population is its (noncausal) association with significant social change, such as smaller family size and higher divorce rates (e.g. Waring 1975). These changes are circumstantial but significant because of the likelihood that social change plus a larger population of older people will have a synergistic effect on behavior and attitudes. For example, because of the increase in the numbers of single people and childless people and the decrease in household size and the number of marriages, both old and young Americans may seek close relationships outside the immediate family to a greater degree than they did in earlier times. In addition, smaller and less permanent households may promote a less disciplined family life because of fewer domestic responsibilities and less isolation of family members from people outside the family. This extrafamilial interaction and loosening of family ties will take older people out of tight family circles. Some will seek equally close circles of age peers. But others will break tradition to participate in age-integrated recreational and work activities such as active sports, political campaigning, and attending college. This proximity and association of young and old could lead to more frequent cross-peer friendships and kin-like relations.

Old age is a unique "stigma" because most people expect to acquire it eventually. In addition to having effects on attitudes about older people, the demographically aging population will cause many people to think more about their own old age, to plan for it, and to change attitudes about their own aging. For example, the trend toward building communities exclusively for the elderly and toward designing condominium facilities that will be attractive to them provokes middle-aged couples to buy homes now for future use in retirement. These purchasing commitments could affect attitudes about the desirability of attaining the age of retirement.

In addition to changing attitudes about aging, exogenous social change will combine synergistically with the greater numbers of elderly to affect an individual's plans for old age. For instance, the highly publicized divorce rate has apparent ill effects on older women, many of whom are left in financial straits. Seeing this, younger women may be encouraged to seek employment or work more hours as a way of ensuring their own security in old age. The two factors—a salient divorce rate and seeing more older women who live alone—interact so that the total effect on women's employment would be greater than the sum of the two exogenous forces.

All of the previous arguments are to the effect that characteristics of the aging population are pervasive, and either alone or in combination will affect behavior and decisions involving older people and one's own aging, which in turn will affect attitudes about older people and aging.

Another reason the aging population is important is that it is salient, and the causes of behavior and decisions in the future will be attributed more frequently (and perhaps inaccurately) to the aging population or to the older age of people. For example, higher government expenditures for services to the sick and poor may be blamed on political pressures exerted by older people (Hudson 1978). On the individual level, people may attribute the decisions of older individuals or families who move, buy an apartment, support a candidate, or take up a hobby to their advanced age (see S. Kiesler 1975).

The "graying of the nation" as well as the aging of individuals will be a likely target of causal attribution for many political, economic, and family decisions because age is a highly visible and discernible aspect of people. Like gender and race, age is an attribute that people use in initially categorizing individuals and groups (see Taylor *et al.* 1978). This makes age (also gender, race, and other physical characteristics) a much-used key to organizing the social environment in thought, and as a result age easily comes to mind as a causal variable (Cantor and Mischel 1979).

Attributing the cause of behavior to people's age obviously is related to attitudes about older people and aging. In fact, attributions of cause are attitudes, and they are often significant ones (e.g. Nisbett and Borgida 1975). For instance, some people believe that age causes declines of intelligence and extreme social behavior (e.g., both talkativeness and withdrawal). These theories could lead to the exclusion of older people from informal social and work groups. Such exclusion would elicit behavioral confirmation of the attributions in older people (see Word *et al.* 1974, Zanna and Pack 1975, Snyder *et al.* 1978, Messe *et al.* 1979).

Our aging population, then, will affect attitudes about older people and aging for two general reasons. First, the aging population is a strong exogenous force. Characteristics of the aging population will increase contact with older people, change behavior toward them, and affect preparations that people make for their own aging, all tending to integrate older people into society. Second, it is argued that the aging population is a conceptually relevant exogenous force. The aging population will seem to change behavior independent of its actual effects. This perception will result from the salience of age as an attribute of people and is itself an attitude.

Because of the previous arguments, the application of the general model to aging (Figure 3.2) posits a significant connection between the demographic aging of the population and individuals' attitudes about older people and aging. It is this connection to which the remainder of this chapter is addressed.

General Behavioral Effects of the Aging Population

In this section, I consider the motivational and cognitive effects of exogenously changed behavior. In order to understand how increased contact with older people, decisions affecting the elderly, changes in attributes of older people, and planning for old age affect attitudes, we must first examine more closely the motivational and cognitive processes activated by behavior change.

The general idea that behavior influences attitude is an old one, but Festinger's dissonance theory (1957) was the first well-tested model of the effect in social psychology. Festinger asserted that behavior has motivational implications and affects attitudes through motivational processes. Attitude change is a response to personal drives or tension (motivation) aroused by behavior.

In dissonance theory and other motivational models, certain perceptions of behavior are important because of their influence on motivation. These perceptions of behavior include its being seen as freely chosen or internally motivated. They are perceptions that increase the personal relevance of behavior and its implications for self.

More recently, an approach to studying how behavior influences attitudes has used theories of information processing from cognitive psychology (e.g., Nisbett and his colleagues' work [Nisbett and Ross 1980], which draws on the experiments of Kahneman and Tversky [1973]).

Recent information processing and social cognitive theories do not address behavior, but they imply that attitudinally relevant aspects of behavior are those that activate attentional, encoding, retrieval, and other processes of thought and memory. These aspects of behavior include its salience and perceived connection with other behavior. These features of behavior make it informative in the sense that it can be meaningfully organized in memory.

The significance of the distinction between motivational and cognitive processes is that they differ functionally. Motivational processes are correlated with variables that are personally relevant and change attitudes that touch individuals' feelings about themselves. Cognitive processes are correlated with aspects of behavior that are informative and cognitively activating and that change attitudes more generally.

The lists of variables correlated with each set of processes is not the same among theorists, but there is general agreement on each side. Personally relevant and motivating behavior is correlated with the explicitness of one's behavior, with perceived choice, perceived low exogenous pressure, and experiencing of the consequences of the behavior. Informative and cognitively activating behavior is correlated with salience of behavior, its association with prior classification of behavior in memory, and its consistency or inconsistency with inferential processes.

Each grouping of characteristics of behavior implies a different effect on attitudes and has been used in various studies of attitude change. For example, taking an explicit public position on a social issue activates the motivational process of psychological commitment. Commitment causes resistance to persuasive attacks on the attitudes one has or develops to justify the public stance (C. Kiesler 1971, also McGuire 1964). Among characteristics important in cognition, salience focuses attention on gender or racial minorities in groups and promotes attributions of causality for a group's behavior to them (Taylor *et al.* 1979, Taylor and Fiske 1978).

In some few cases the motivational and cognitive processes activated by behavior lead to the same predictions for attitude change. For example, motivational theories predict that post hoc justifications of expenditures of effort cause egocentric attitudes, such as explaining away one's failures but taking credit for one's successes (Schlenker and Miller 1977). An example would be blaming one's difficulties in obtaining a promotion on a hidden negative attitude of senior employees and then believing the promotion they actually support is entirely due to one's own ability to persuade them. Cognitive theories also predict egocentrism. For instance, because of our having expected our own efforts in work to be successful (at least more frequently than we expect failure) and having organized our memories to confirm those biased expectations, we will remember good outcomes of our own performance better than we remember bad ones. This would make for egocentric attitudes (e.g., Miller and Ross 1975). Such overlapping predictions are of concern to theorists interested in identifying the underlying variables that cause attitude change (Bradley 1978).

In this chapter, we are concerned with the application of both motivational and cognitive processes to attitudes about older people and aging. The evidence so far suggests that the distinction between motivational and cognitive processes is useful for our purposes in the following sense: Examining personally relevant behavior and the variables that have been studied as aspects of such behavior (e.g., perceived choice) seems most likely to result in clear predictions of self-enhancement and post hoc justifications of behavior affecting older people as well as plans for one's old age. Informative behavior and the variables associated with it, on the other hand, seems most useful for clearly predicting attitude change that reduces ambiguity about older people and aging and helps maintain an organized concept of age. It would seem reasonable to expect, however, that both sets of processes might converge toward the same end product, that is, attitudes about older people and age that are somewhat self-promoting rather than "fair," and clear or consistent rather than "accurate."

Motivational Processes

When the general model is applied to the effects of an aging population on attitudes about older people and aging and motivational processes are viewed as intervening between behavior and attitude, the result is an emphasis on the motivating effects of a person's own behavior (Figure 3.3). Motivational theories assert that behavior that activates motives must be relevant to a person's view of himself or herself; this relevance is difficult to predict unless it is the person's own behavior that is examined (cf. Jones and Davis 1965).

Three areas of personal behavior would seem most relevant to the present discussion: personal contact with older people, decisions made affecting older people, and plans made for one's old age. In each of these areas of behavior, the potential relevance of behavior to self is relatively obvious.

A person's capacity for attention to or involvement with his or her own behavior must be limited nevertheless. Only so much of one's own behavior can be pursued with thought and reflection about its implications for self (Langer 1978, Langer and Newman 1979). Therefore, we look for conditions that make one's personal behavior psychologically motivating. These conditions are those that create the perceptions alluded to in the last section—that rivet the choice and responsibility for one's own behavior on oneself.

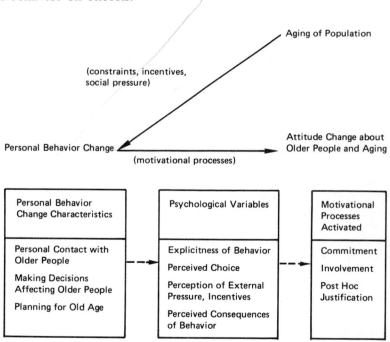

Figure 3.3. Application of the general model, motivational process aspects.

The first perception is that one's behavior is clear and explicit, as with a public statement or observed behavior. Because such behaviors involve others and are hard to revoke, they are both involving and committing (C. Kiesler 1971). An example of explicit behavior is declaring to one's family and employer the intention to retire. The announcement would increase one's psychological involvement in retirement and commitment to it.

A second perception is of high personal choice. When people perceive they have chosen their actions, they cannot easily deny them or avoid feeling responsibility for them. As a result, they rationalize the value of their choices. For example, voluntary retirement will cause persons to enhance the perceived attractiveness of retirement (cf. Kimmel *et al.* 1978) and of the people with whom they interact more frequently (e.g., Tyler and Sears 1977).

A third perception is of weak external (exogenous) pressure on one's behavior. Regardless of what is actually the case, the perception that one has control of one's behavior and acts for reasons of internal preference increases commitment and post hoc justification. For example, retiring despite insufficient retirement income or other external incentive to fully explain why one retires enhances one's impression of retiring because of personal preference. If one retires voluntarily and partly without sufficient external pressure or incentive, one is liable to become more intrinsically motivated to retire. This intrinsic motivation could include heightened perceptions of the value of leisure time or a desire to spend retirement time in nonmarket but useful work (see Lepper and Greene 1975, Folger *et al.* 1978). Of course, the opposite effect would occur if one postponed retiring without external pressure or incentive to do so (such as delaying retirement even though one must work for inadequate pay).

The motivational theories assert that greater pressure and stronger incentives reduce commitment and post hoc justification of behavior. The prediction for persons who retire voluntarily is that modest pensions and high foregone wages will lead to greater increases in intrinsic motivation and positive attitudes about retirement than will high pensions and modest foregone wages. For persons who delay retirement, modest foregone pensions and high wages would improve attitudes about work, but not so much as high foregone pensions and modest wages would. In sum, the greater the outside influence people perceive on their decisions, the less they will change their attitudes enhancing the value of their actions or preferences.

A final important perception is that one's behavior must seem to have consequences and implications for oneself. This condition is satisfied when personal behavior has an outcome that must be faced. For example, suppose a man retires and then experiences much more boredom than he had imagined. As a result he would have to explain his retirement to himself in view of the negative consequence. The prediction would be that he discovers retrospectively other good aspects of retirement or explanations of his decision to retire (I did it to satisfy my wife; I was in poor health).

Here it is implied that negative consequences of action and failure to achieve goals can lead to attitudes that nevertheless support previous poor choices. This suggests that preferences and goals will change in response to success (or ambiguous consequences) more readily than they will change in response to failure (see Zander 1968). For instance, decisions to delay retirement while building savings that turn out to be less than expected will reduce financial aspirations less than successful decisions to delay retirement and to save will increase financial aspirations. In our culture, which typically distorts the ideal and actual rationality of decisions, the result is overrationalizing decisions whose outcome is poor, that cause conflict, or that are otherwise unproductive (see Morgan 1979, for data on retirement decisions).

All of the predictions in the previous examples about retirement have a parallel in other kinds of attitude changes about older people and aging. Some of these are illustrated in Table 3.1. The predictions of Table 3.1 are speculative, but they have a basis in previous research on social change. The data of Mason et al. (1976), for example, shows that increased ideological support for dual careers and changes in sex roles followed the dramatic increases of women's employment. The work of Blake (1974) on expressions of ideal family size in polls suggests that ideals followed changes of actual family size. Natural experiments of S. Kiesler (1977) support the idea and show the effect of perceived choice. Larger-scale studies of attitudes have also shown the effect of fertility behavior on attitudes (Ryder 1979, Lee 1979). Finally, evidence from the negative income tax experiments indicates how foregone wages result in justifications such as increases in nonmarket work (Devaney 1979).

In sum, data on large-scale changes of behavior indicate that exogenous forces do cause attitude change through post hoc justification of behavior. The data encourage predictions that the aging population will bring about new attitudes about the elderly and aging that justify or rationalize demographically caused changes of behavior.

PERCEPTIONS OF CHOICE AND PERSONAL RESPONSIBILITY

One of the most difficult theoretical questions about motivation and attitude change concerns perceptions of choice and responsibility when

TABLE 3.1
Examples of Attitude Change in the Motivational Process Model

Exogenous forces associated with aging population	Behavior	Motivational process (individual)	Attitude change toward older people and aging
Examples of change in stereotypes			
Increased numbers of older people	More people in middle-age have responsibility for aged relatives	Perceived responsibility for (family) consequences	Believed importance of grandparents
Increased proportion of older people in population	Consumers buy products marketed for older persons	Perceived choice of "mature" products: clothes, household goods, etc.	Older people viewed as more innovative, flexible, and "mature"
Smaller family size	Older people seek close relationships among far relatives and outside family	Attribution to individuals (not to external pressure) for cross-age relationships	More variability accepted in older persons' friendships
Example of change in social issue beliefs			
Laws banning age discrimination	More people work with older employees	Post hoc justification of adjustments needed (e.g., postpones promotion of young workers)	Greater valuing of employee stability, discipline, and loyalty
Shift in nature of dependency ratio (more old dependents; fewer young dependents)	Shift in public expenditures (e.g., from schools and playgrounds to parks and tennis courts)	Increased involvement of adults in community services	Legitimization of public services for adults (e.g., camps and colleges)
Examples of change in attitudes about one's own aging			
Improved health and physical condition of older people	More people expect "second careers" (postretirement employment)	Perceived control over life events; choice of risks	"Retirement" redefined or replaced as stage of life
Increased numbers of older working couples; older women have more financial independence	Decisions to readjust or coordinate work and retirement; more older couples divorce	Subjective uncertainty over role choices	Attitudes adjust to new roles for independent older women

behavior changes as a result of exogenous forces. In general, when personal behavior responds to features of an aging population, the effect on attitudes will depend on how influential the features seem to be. The paradoxical prediction is that strong exogenous characteristics associated with our aging population (such as large increases in social security outlays) are more likely to change behavior (such as working more hours to increase after-tax income) but also more likely to be perceived as the responsible cause of the behavior change. Since lack of choice and responsibility for one's behavior reduces commitment to it and minimizes tendencies toward self-justification, any changes in attitude that took place would only reaffirm beliefs in external causes (e.g., "I'm working more only because my taxes are too high").

The opposite effects exogenous forces can have are illustrated in Figure 3.4. In the figure, the exogenous variable is inflation, the behavior is delayed retirement, and the attitude is justification of delayed retirement, that is, improved attitudes toward employment in old age. In the figure, inflation at moderate levels is assumed to be just barely strong

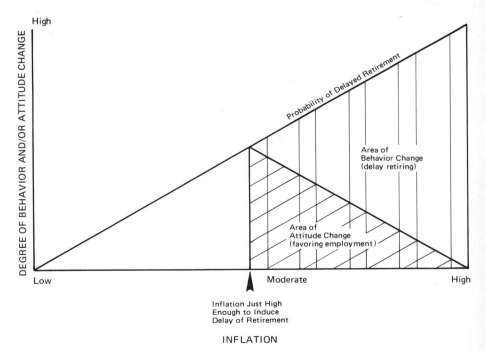

Figure 3.4. Example of inflation as an exogenous force causing behavior and attitude change in hypothetical group of older persons.

enough an incentive to cause a hypothetical group of people to change their behavior, that is, to delay retirement. At this point, attitude change justifying the decision is greatest. If inflation is any greater than that just needed to change the behavior, however, attitude change is reduced. The reason for the reduced attitude change is that the extra incentives to delay retiring only reduce perceived choice.

The perception of own choice and responsibility versus external pressures (or incentives) is obviously crucial. It would be useful to identify those exogenous forces whose influence is more or less associated with personal decisions in the minds of the public. Which social trends do we view as limiting individual choice and which as expanding it?

Most experimental research in social psychology that has used manipulated levels of choice has proceeded intuitively. Perceived choice or responsibility (which are not always identical) have been manipulated by informing subjects they had choice, by pointing out or allowing them to experience the consequences of decisions, by informing them their decisions are deviant or unlike others', by offering bogus alternatives or similar alternatives, and by inducing them to declare they have made their "own" decisions publicly. Observing the effects, researchers have concluded that choice and responsibility derives from feelings of personal control (Wortman 1976), subjective rather than objective uncertainty (Harvey 1976), discounting of external attributions of cause (Kelley 1967, 1973), and from having to face the negative outcomes of one's choices (Cooper and Worchel 1970).

This theoretical work suggests some hypotheses regarding personal choice or responsibility and exogenous forces:

1. Strong and independent exogenous forces reduce perceived choice and responsibility—because they reduce perceived control. They cannot be ignored as causes of behavior and threaten freedom of choice.
   Examples: Rising prices; clear political pressures from retired persons' lobbies; high demand for housing units built for older people.
2. Conflicting or rapidly changing exogenous forces reduce perceived choice and responsibility—because they reduce perceptions of control and increase objective uncertainty.
   Examples: Inflation (as a disincentive to retire) along with organizational pressures to retire early; social change in family stability and structure; unclear political crises.
3. Exogenous forces that people view as positive increase perceived choice and responsibility—because having positive alternatives causes higher perceived control and subjective uncertainty.

Examples: Improvements in services actually available to old people; economic recoveries; technological inventions.

4. Exogenous forces that attract various groups of people to deviate from norms or innovate increase perceived choice and responsibility—because innovation and variability denote personal independence and cause discounting of external attributions.
   Examples: Increased popularity of "preventive" medicine and exercise; increased frequency of unmarried couples living together.

5. Exogenous forces representing gradual and long-term social change increase perceived choice and responsibility—because they are subtle and encourage internal attributions but increase subjective uncertainty.
   Examples: Married women entering (or staying in) paid employment; the decline in large family size.

These hypotheses, while somewhat speculative, suggest the behavior changes that, in an aging population, will also place the onus of the behavior on those who change. Table 3.1, in illustrating the kinds of attitude change predicted by motivational processes, builds on the hypotheses to predict behavior.

Cognitive Processes

Anyone's behavior has the potential to influence the development of attitudes. But according to research on cognitive processes (mostly on memory and problem solving) only a limited portion of behavior will actually influence attitudes through its value as information.

One limit to the informativeness of behavior is lack of fit with prior organization of thought, especially firmly held expectations. For example, contact among age groups might have no effect whatsoever on what younger people think older people are like (and vice versa) because any actions of either side that might disconfirm expectations are simply ignored (see Rose 1980). Furthermore, each age group will forget the behavioral data but remember the conclusions they drew from it (Trope 1978).

Another limit to the informativeness of behavior is that only so much behavior can claim a person's attention. A number of cognitive processes correlated with the active use of information—notably clustering, categorization, and organization in encoding and recall—require attention and effort (see Hasher and Zacks 1979).

A third limit to the informativeness of behavior is imposed by active inferential processes that make use of some pieces of behavioral information more than others. For instance, observers sometimes (but not always) use concrete actions of one person rather than general observations of behavior to predict what people will do in the future (Tversky and Kahneman 1973, Quattrone and Jones 1980, Nisbett and Borgida 1975).

Because information's usefulness is limited, at least three psychological variables attached to behavioral information will determine the eventual effect of behavior on attitudes about older people and aging. The discussion of attitude change in this section is organized around these variables and is summarized in Figure 3.5.

The first variable is observers' current expectations of older persons and aging. These expectations will determine how new behavioral information is encoded and retrieved (e.g., see Anderson and Pichert 1978). An analysis of Rose (1980) suggests that new information is encoded or recalled so that it bolsters old stereotypes. The second variable is the salience of observed behavior affecting older people. Salience influences attention and evaluative inferences, which in turn will influence judgments and attributions of causality to older persons or to age (see Taylor and Fiske 1978). The third variable is stability and change of the per-

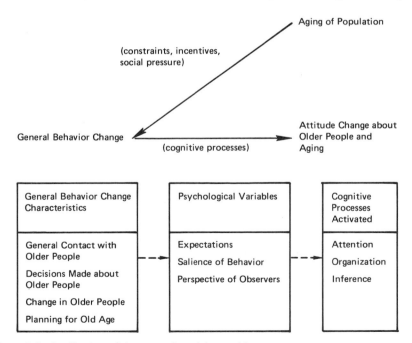

Figure 3.5. Application of the general model, cognitive process aspects.

spective of observers of older people, aging, and those involved in decisions affecting older persons. Changes of perspective affect attributions for social and personal change (see Jones and Nisbett 1971, Silka 1980) and hence attitudes about the interests and goals of older people and about the nature of aging.

EXPECTATIONS

In an earlier section, it was claimed that because apparent chronological age is an easily distinguishable and distinguishing characteristic of people, age is used to categorize them and their behavior. Older age is the central attribute used in comparing a person's resemblance with prototypical older people who define various stereotypes such as "grandma," "elder statesman," and "senior citizen" (Brewer 1979). These stereotypes, like other categories based on age (e.g., teenagers), create firmly held and rather global expectations of behavior. For example, one expects any grandmother to behave sweetly toward children. The stereotypes therefore influence the categorization of older people in many broad taxonomies: of personality, occupation, stage of life, interests, and so on. Table 3.2 illustrates the potential influence by listing some of the attributes associated with three possible stereotypes of older persons.

Notice that most of the attributes in Table 3.2 are simple, lack concreteness, and cannot be tested against reality; many of the attributes are negative in tone and carry connotations of extreme behavior. These characteristics are typically correlated with unelaborated person categories, that is, categories that are global, undetailed, and poorly connected to behavioral (operationalized) concepts (see Linville 1979).

The traditional stereotypes of older people (as depicted in Table 3.2) are extremely important expectations because of the general tendency of all people to sort new information about people using categories of group membership (Taylor et al. 1979) and to distort its meaning or recall so that what is remembered is consistent with existing expectations (e.g., Hamilton et al. 1980). Hearing that an older female acquaintance carries important job responsibilities might cause traditionalists to wonder how she manages to fulfill her grandmotherly and domestic roles. Seeing her male counterpart with his grandchildren will remind them of his interpersonal skills as an executive. Behavioral information about older people, then, usually will be organized around their membership in global age-defined categories and the simplistic stereotypes associated with those categories.

TABLE 3.2
Attributes Associated with Photographs of Elderly People[a]

Three "Grandmothers"		Three "elderly statesmen"	
Version 1	Version 2	Version 1	Version 2
Accepting	Accepting	Aggressive	Aggressive
Helpful	Helpful	Intelligent	Intelligent
Trustworthy	Trustworthy	Conservative	Conservative
Traditional	Traditional	Dignified	Dignified
Serene	Serene	Neat	Neat
Kindly	Kindly	Authoritarian	Authoritarian
Optimistic	Optimistic	Traditional	Intolerant
Calm	Calm		Competitive
Cheerful	Cheerful		Strong-willed
Neet	Neat		Active
Emotional	Dignified		Aware

Three "senior citizens"		Unsorted	
Version 1	Version 2	Version 1	Version 2
Lonely	Lonely	Traditional	Kindly
Old-fashioned	Old-fashioned	Conservative	
Traditional	Weak		
	Worried		

[a]The attributes listed were selected by a majority of subjects from a list of 44 traits, one-half positive and one-half negative, previously implicated in stereotypes of the elderly. Also, different subjects sorted 40 photographs into groups of, for example, grandmothers. Matching attributes with groups of photographs generated two versions of each stereotype. Adapted from Brewer (1979).

Because of the distortions described above, one could argue that exogenous trends producing behavior change (e.g., greater contact with older people; planning for old age) would serve only to reaffirm traditional attitudes and stereotypes. But there are two ways changes of behavior could change expectations significantly.

First, Cantor and Mischel (1979) and others have reported that many stereotypes and person categories have subcategories in the same way that object categories do (Rosch 1978). An example they use is "religious devotees" and "social activists" as subcategories of "committed persons." Attributes attached to subordinate categories are much richer in detail, patterned, behaviorally concrete, and situation-specific than the attributes of global categories. Also, attributes of subordinate categories overlap; they may be less polarizing of groups than more global categories.

Knowing people relatively well not only causes less categorization on the basis of only one or two central characteristics but promotes greater attention to configurations of attributes across time and place (see Cantor and Mischel 1979). Therefore, obtaining greater total amounts of information about older people and observing them in different settings (e.g., employed in nontraditional jobs) should cause the formation of more subcategories of older people: rich grandmothers versus ordinary grandmothers; mean elder statesmen versus wise elder statesmen; sick aged versus active and bright aged. While these elaborations of thinking would not banish categorization on the basis of old age, they could contribute to the impression of variability among groups of older people and heighten expectations that older people hold membership in other person categories. When appropriate, we might more readily think of an older John C. Smith as a competitive person in games, a sympathetic listener to his friends, and an incisive problem solver for the community as well as a man enjoying his retirement.

A second way new information could change expectations is through automatic processing of information about older people and aging.

Research on memory encoding processes (e.g., Kahneman 1973, Posner and Snyder 1975, Schneider and Shiffrin 1977) has shown that certain mental operations occur automatically, without effort, are unaffected by practice and motivation, and possibly not by learned expectancies and conceptual biases either. Among these automatic operations is the remembering of the frequency of events such as written words, visual images, opinions, and observed attributes of a person (see Hasher and Zacks 1979).

That frequencies elicit automatic "event-driven" memory processes rather than effortful "concept-driven" processes is significant for this discussion because of the implication that exogenously caused changes in the frequency of behavior will be encoded and recalled without bias even though the categories into which they fall are biased. For instance, we could perceive that more older people are joggers these days but continue to perceive the prototypical jogger as a young person.

Nevertheless, frequency information could change the perceived implications of being categorized as an older person or of aging itself. For instance, as we learn that retired people are taking paid jobs, retirement will imply taking a rest with less certainty, and the association of old age and illness will be weakened. This change of meaning need not depend on the truth of changes in behavior; frequencies of assertions affect meaning, too (Hasher et al. 1977). Hence, the more often we hear it asserted that half the residents of retirement communities are gainfully employed, the more true it will seem. And the more "retired" people

frequency of decisions

we think are employed, the more likely we are to believe that older people are active, energetic, and capable.

The mental association of old age and negative attributes (e.g., low productivity, ill health) is particularly significant in that intercorrelations of rare attributes are exaggerated (Hamilton and Gifford 1976). When older people's behavior seems more like that of middle age, however, the inappropriate over-association of old age and negative attributes should decline. We may see instead an overestimation of the correlation of high productivity and good physical condition with older age (e.g., overestimates of the productivity of older workers).

Since the frequency of decisions about issues involving old age will also increase in the future, perceptions of these decisions should also change. To the extent that the frequency of certain decisions is processed automatically, the perception will change as to how extreme or rare they are and thus how "normal." For example, if the frequency of decisions to retire before 65 were to increase, the definition of "early" retirement would shift downward.

The public definition of what is extreme and what is normal may be viewed as a shift in scales of judgment. Research on social judgment (Upshaw 1969, Eiser and Osman 1978) indicates that increasing the range of a behavioral distribution (or skewing the distribution) widens scales of evaluative judgment (or moves them up or down). As illustrated in Figure 3.6, what now constitutes excessively early or late retirement will seem less excessive (and abnormal) as the distribution of retirement age becomes more variable.

In summary, research on automatic processing of frequency information suggests that even if people continue to categorize each other on the basis of age, old age categories will overlap more with those of middle age, and behavior associated with advanced years will seem more attractive.

SALIENCE

Many opinions about older people can be described as social schemata. Social schemata are organized sequences of behavior attached to particular situations. For instance, in the retirement schema, old people take up oil painting and they walk in parks. Schemata are often miniature stories about parts of life such as the stereotypical story of retirement. Schemata are also implicit personality theories. For example, there is the idea that as people age they mellow (see Langer 1978). The encoding and recall of social schemata is an effortful process requiring attention, although less so with practice and experience.

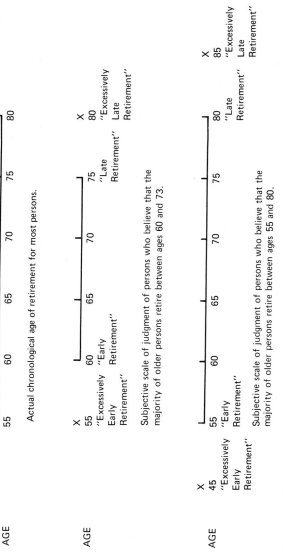

Figure 3.6. Effect of perceived frequency of retirement at various ages on perceptions of how extreme and excessive the age of retirement is.

Because salient human behavior is behavior that stands out and commands attention, it may be highly amenable to effortful processing and to detailed organization, including incorporation into social schemata. Behavior made salient by our aging population as well may be increasingly better organized in thought and remembered in terms of detailed social schemata. This implies that people will be more conscious of the role of older age in schemas of social behavior and public decisions ranging from jogging to investing money.

The latter effect would be of minor interest if not for the fact that focusing attention has the further effect of biasing one's evaluations and judgments. Salient people, attributes, and behavior are not only remembered, but inferred to be important. Salient people are perceived as causes of events. For instance, Taylor et al. (1979) showed that people overestimate the effects on a group of a minority in the group, that is, of the salient portion of the membership. Vinokur and Burnstein (1978) showed that people who give novel arguments in a group are salient and are more persuasive than those who offer old familiar arguments. McArthur and Post (1973) showed that merely sitting people beneath a lighted lamp heightens their perceived importance as influencing events. This research implies a shift in the presumed importance of older people as a result of exogenous forces making their behavior more salient.

A related argument, mentioned earlier, is that salient aspects of the aging population as a whole will seem causal. Characteristics of the aging population such as the gray lobby and divorce among older people will be held responsible for social change generally, and public choices affecting older people such as changes in taxes will be viewed as more politically and economically influential.

PERSPECTIVE

The implication of much of the research on cognitive processes is that new behavioral information will elaborate and exacerbate attitudes about the elderly and aging but will not change them drastically. Exogenous events, however, may change the perspective of those exposed to new behavioral information and in that way cause a fundamental revision of attitudes.

Changes of perspective, which occur when people become members of new groups or have to change their goals, influence attitudes through the interaction of perceiver changes with information changes. For instance, a person who moves from Group X (clerk) to Group Y (retired clerks) will be changing as a perceiver: reorganizing his or her mental categories of "our interests" and "their interests," for example. In forming attitudes, the change of perceiver's perspective is coupled with any new information received from acquaintances in the new group and actions as a member of the new group. The discovery that pensions are inadequate, which is learned as a result of retirement as a clerk, is evaluated with a new perspective for organizing that information. (At the least it has relevance to self-schemata.) One outcome may be the addition of attitudes, as when the retired clerk becomes an amateur expert and advocate for pension reform. More generally, exogenously caused changes of perspective by large groups should lead to reattributions of cause for social change and conflict including new attributes about the role of older persons in society.

The research on changes of perspective and their effects on attribution is based on the theoretical work of Kelley (1967), Jones and Nisbett (1971), and others. A general finding about perspectives is that observers tend to view behavior as internally caused by the personality and preferences of actors (Ross 1977). In contrast, actors view their own behavior as a reasonable response to the situation and to others. The reasons for this difference in the attribution of observers (them) and actors (us) is that actors have a unique perspective. Consider: (*a*) From our own visual perspective as actors, we can observe and attend to other people and situations better than we can observe and attend to our own behavior, so other people and situations readily come to mind as a cause of our behavior (e.g., Storms 1973). Furthermore, (*b*) we know that in the past we have responded differently to different people and situations (Ross and Scioly 1979). Finally, (*c*) although we can remember images of the behavior of others, we recall verbally encoded schemata of our own behavior (Lord 1980). As a result, our own behavior seems embedded in a whole configuration of personal plans and thoughts about the circumstances of behavior.

The self versus other difference of perspective causes a significant difference in attitudes about the self as compared with attitudes about others. One's own visions, one's own interests, and one's own groups seem reasonable and rational, that is, responsive to actual constraints, incentives, and pressures from outside forces. In contrast, others seem more responsive to their own internal preferences and agendas. In conflicts between only two people, each person attributes the cause of the problem to the other's motives or personality (Orvis *et al.* 1976), in part because of each person's necesssary difference of perspective and its effect on attributions. If groups are involved in conflicts of interest, the difference of perspective accounts for opposing views of the cause of the conflict; that is, for each, the aggressor is the other side.

An example of attributional conflict is illustrated in Figure 3.7. In the figure, an older employee attributes his decision to delay retirement to the situation: the attractiveness of his work and the money he earns. The employer's young colleague, however, attributes the decision to delay retirement to the personality of the older man (except when the older employee's financial situation clearly accounts for the delay of retirement).

Attributional conflict caused by differences of perspective varies with perceptions of exogenous conditions. Two variations of exogenous conditions are shown in Figure 3.7: technological change and retirement benefits, each of which increase internal attributions of the delay of retirement. According to attribution theory, in delaying retirement, despite high retirement benefits and the fact that his or her skills have

Conditions Under Which Retirement Is Postponed

	Foregone Retirement Benefits Relatively Good	Foregone Retirement Benefits Relatively Poor
Technological Obsolescence of Older Workers Is High	Old worker: "I work because I like working and it keeps me young." Young colleague: "He only keeps working because he has no outside interests." XXX	Old worker: "I can't afford to retire." Young colleague: "He works for the money but he doesn't deserve it." XX
Technological Obsolescence of Older Workers Is Low	Old worker: "I work because I enjoy it." Young colleague: "He keeps working because he has no outside interests." XX	Old worker: "I can't afford to retire." Young colleague: "He works for the money." X

Figure 3.7. Examples of an attributional conflict over the causes of delayed retirement. (X's denote degree to which external circumstances fail to explain why older workers remain on the job [delay retiring] and the degree of attributional conflict. Where XXX exists, two external forces are inconsistent with working and attributional conflict is greatest.)

become obsolete, the older worker attributes his or her behavior to the value of the work itself.

Figure 3.7 contains an implied hypothesis as to how changes of perspective in our aging population may alter attitudes. First, the figure shows how intergroup conflict between young and old could be reduced or heightened by changes in the perception of causal exogenous conditions. For example, interage conflict would decline if strong exogenous forces irrelevant to age, such as international conflict, took the "blame" for differences of interest between young and old but not for their interests in common. Even more change of attitudes would result from redistributing age group memberships. The old now prefer to see themselves as middle-aged (Bultena and Powers 1978). If only exogenous conditions were to increase the attractiveness of older age as an attribute (e.g., greater power of older persons in work organizations) and the lines separating age groups moved, perspectives on attributional conflict would move, too.

One way exogenous forces change perspectives is suggested in an analysis by Silka (1980). According to her analysis, individuals have difficulty observing changes in themselves, whether the change concerns their organization of information or their inferences from it. As a result, they attribute change in themselves to social change. An example is when people get used to stories of criminal attacks on old people and come to think that crime against old people has declined.

Other examples: A committee of citizens is to decide on a major urban sports facility for the elderly, but political differences cause the discussions to last several years. Because of their increasing familiarity with the arguments supporting the facility, the committee perceives a large increase in the numbers of athletic older persons. Here again, change in frequency of opinions heard changes perceivers, who in this case perceive a group to have changed. (Nevertheless, it is unclear whether the 75-year-old jogger will replace the 75-year-old porch sitter as a prototype of old age.)

Another example is a committee of citizens who learn that no local nursing home has facilities for active sports and are moved to recommend that such facilities be built. Having acted as though old people who get sick may get well again, the committee perceives that the clientele of nursing homes has changed drastically.

The previous examples suggest that exogenous changes associated with our aging population that change public group memberships and goals and change information about other people at approximately the same time will also alter beliefs about older people significantly. In the past, simultaneous changes of social groups and goals and of information about social groups were caused by economic growth in the 1920s, the depression of the 1930s, World War II, and the civil rights movement. These forces realigned economic and political groups (e.g., industrialists hired educated youth; government officials devised large public programs for the poor), and behavioral information about the groups changed as well (e.g., people learned how schooling benefited the young; they heard that the poor deserved relief). The interaction of these two phenomena produced new attitudes about the young, the poor, minorities, and women. Today, the aging population is a force with similar potential for changing attitudes about the aged.

CONCLUSION

According to the models used in this chapter, large demographic, economic, and social trends often bring about significant changes in individual behavior. The significance of change in behavior is its subsequent effect on attitudes. Our aging population will have far more importance than merely commanding public resources and increasing family responsibilities for aged relatives. It will create new ideologies of age, new expectations of work and workers, and new norms of kin interaction. Changes in our society change all of us as individuals.

ACKNOWLEDGMENTS

I am grateful to colleagues at Carnegie-Mellon University for their suggestions. I used Lee Sproull's models of socialization in devising the figures used in this chapter. I drew on conversations with Lynne Reder for the section on cognitive processes. Susan Fiske provided comments on a draft of this chapter.

REFERENCES

Anderson, N. H. (1967) Averaging model analysis of set size effect in impression formation. *Journal of Experimental Psychology* 75:158–165.

Anderson, R. C., and Pichert, J. W. (1978) Recall of previously unrecallable information following a shift in perspective. *Journal of Verbal Behavior* 17:1–12.

Aronson, E. (1966) The psychology of insufficient justification: An analysis of some conflicting data. Pp. 115–133 in S. Feldman, ed., *Cognitive Consistency*. New York: Academic Press.

Bandura, A., Adams, N. D., and Beyer, N. (1977) Cognitive processes mediating behavioral change. *Journal of Personality and Social Psychology* 35:125–139.

Bem, D. J. (1972) Self-perception theory. In L. Berkowitz *Advances in Experimental Social Psychology,* Vol. 6. New York: Academic Press.

Blake, J. (1974) Can we believe recent data in birth expectations in the United States? *Demography* 4:25–44.

Bradley, G. (1978) Self-serving biases in the attribution process: A reexamination of the fact or fiction question. *Journal of Personality and Social Psychology* 36:56–71.

Brehm, J. W. (1966) *A Theory of Psychological Reactants.* New York: Academic Press.

Brewer, M. B. (1979) A Cognitive Model of Stereotypes of the Elderly. Paper presented at the annual meeting of the American Psychological Association, New York.

Bruner, J. S., and Tagiuri, R. (1954) Person perception. In G. Lindzey, ed., *Handbook of Social Psychology,* Vol. 2. Reading, Mass.: Addison-Wesley.

Bultena, G. L., and Powers, E. A. (1978) Denial of aging: Age identification and reference group orientations. *Journal of Gerontology* 33:748–754.

Cacioppo, J. T., and Petty, R. E. (1979) The effects of message repetition and position on cognitive responses, recall and persuasion. *Journal of Personality and Social Psychology* 37:97–109.

Campbell, D. T. (1967) Stereotypes and the perception of group differences. *American Psychologist* 22:817–829.

Cantor, N., and Mischel, W. (1979) Prototypes in person perception. In L. Berkowitz, ed., *Advances in Experimental Social Psychology,* Vol. 12. New York: Academic Press.

Cooper, J., and Worchel, S. (1970) Role of undesired consequences in arousing cognitive dissonance. *Journal of Personality and Social Psychology* 16:99–206.

Devaney, B. L. (1979) An Analysis of the Impact of Negative Income Tax on the Time Allocation of Women. Paper presented at the meetings of the Population Association of America, Philadelphia.

Duval, S., and Wicklund, R. A. (1972) *A Theory of Self-Awareness.* New York: Academic Press.

Easterlin, R. A. (1973) Relative economic status and the American fertility swing. In E. B. Sheldon, ed., *Family Economic Behavior.* Philadelphia: J. B. Lippincott.

Eiser, J. R., and Osmon, B. E. (1978) Judgmental perspective and value connotations of response scale labels. *Journal of Personality and Social Psychology* 36:491–497.

Festinger, L. (1957) *A Theory of Cognitive Dissonance.* Stanford, Calif.: Stanford University Press.

Folger, R., Rosenfield, D., and Hays, R. P. (1978) Equity and intrinsic motivation: The role of choice. *Journal of Personality and Social Psychology* 36:557–564.

Furstenberg, F. F., Jr. (1981) Remarriage and intergenerational relationships. In R. W. Fogel, E. Hatfield, S. B. Kiesler, and E. Shanas, eds., *Aging: Stability and Change in the Family.* New York: Academic Press.

Grune, D., and Lepper, M. R. (1974) Effects of extrinsic rewards on children's subsequence intrinsic interest. *Child Development* 45:1141–1145.

Hamilton, D. L. (1979) A cognitive–attributional analysis of stereotyping. In L.Berkowitz, ed., *Advances in Experimental Social Psychology,* Vol. 12. New York: Academic Press.

Hamilton, D. L., and Gifford, R. K. (1976) Illusory correlation in interpersonal perception: A cognitive basis of stereotypic judgments. *Journal of Experimental Social Psychology* 12:392–407.

Hamilton, D. L., Katz, L. B., and Leirer, V. O. (1980) Organizational processes in impression formation. In R. Hastie, T. Ostrom, E. Ebbesen, R. Wyer, D. Hamilton, and D. Carlston, eds., *Person Memory: The Cognitive Basis of Social Perception.* Hillsdale, N.J.: Lawrence Erlbaum Associates.

Hasher, L., Goldstein, D., and Toppino, T. (1977) Frequency and the conference of referential validity. *Journal of Verbal Learning and Verbal Behavior* 16:107–112.

Hasher, L., and Zacks, R. T. (1979) Automatic and effortful processes in memory. *Journal of Experimental Psychology: General* 108:356–388.

Harvey, J. H. (1976) Attribution of freedom. Pp. 73–96 in J. H. Harvey, W. J. Ickes, and R. F. Kidd, eds., *New Directions in Attribution Research,* Vol. 1. Hillsdale, N.J.: Lawrence Erlbaum Associates.

Harvey, J. H., Ickes, W. J., and Kidd, R. F. (1978) *New Directions in Attribution Research,* Vol. 2. Hillsdale, N.J.: Lawrence Erlbaum Associates.

Hudson, R. B. (1978) The "graying" of the federal budget and its consequences for old-age policy. *The Gerontologist* 18:428–440.

Insko, C. A., and Wilson, M. (1977) Interpersonal attraction as a function of social interaction. *Journal of Personality and Social Psychology* 35:903–911.

Jones, E. E., and Berglas, S. (1978) Control of attributions about the self through self-handicapping strategies: The appeal of alcohol and the role of underachievement. *Personality and Social Psychology Bulletin* 4:200–206.

Jones, E. E., and Davis, K. E. (1965) From acts to disposition. In L. Berkowitz, ed., *Advances in Experimental Social Psychology,* Vol. 2. New York: Academic Press.

Jones, E. E., and Nisbett, R. E. (1971) *The Actor and the Observer: Divergent Perceptions of the Causes of Behavior.* Morristown, N.J.: General Learning Press.

Kahneman, D. (1973) *Attention and Effort.* Englewood Cliffs, N.J.: Prentice-Hall.

Kahneman, D., and Tversky, A. (1973) On the psychology of prediction. *Psychological Review* 80:237–251.

Kelley, H. H. (1967) Attribution theory in social psychology. In D. Levine, ed., *Nebraska Symposium on Motivation,* Vol. 1. Lincoln: University of Nebraska Press.

Kelley, H. H. (1973) The process of causal attribution. *American Psychologist* 28:107–128.

Kiesler, C. A. (1971) *The Psychology of Commitment: Experiments Linking Behavior to Belief.* New York: Academic Press.

Kiesler, S. B. (1975) Actuarial prejudice toward women and its implications. *Journal of Applied Social Psychology* 5:201–216.

Kiesler, S. B. (1977) Post hoc justification of family size. *Sociometry* 40:59–67.

Kimmel, D. C., Price, K. F., and Walker, J. W. (1978) Retirement choice and retirement satisfactions. *Journal of Gerontology* 33:575–585.

Langer, E. J. (1978) Rethinking the role of thought in social interaction. In J. H. Harvey, W. J. Ickes, and R. F. Kidd, eds., *New Directions in Attribution Research,* Vol. 2. Hillsdale, N.J.: Lawrence Erlbaum Associates.

Langer, E. J., and Newman, H. M. (1979) The role of mindlessness in a typical social psychological experiment. *Personality and Social Psychology Bulletin* 5:295–298.

Lee, R. D. (1979) Shooting at a Moving Target: The Relation of Period Fertility Rates to Changing Desired Completed Family Size. Paper presented at a meeting of the Population Association of America, Philadelphia. (Available from author, Population Studies Center, University of Michigan, Ann Arbor, Michigan 48109.)

Lepper, M. R., and Greene, D. (1975) Turning play into work: Effects of adult surveillance and extrinsic rewards on children's intrinsic motivation. *Journal of Personality and Social Psychology* 31:479–486.

Linville, P. W. (1979) Dimensional Complexity and Evaluative Extremity: A Cognitive Model Predicting Polarized Evaluations of Outgroup Members. Unpublished Ph.D. dissertation, University of North Carolina.

Lord, C. G. (1980) Schemas and images as memory aids: Two modes of processing social information. *Journal of Personality and Social Psychology* 38:257–269.

Maloney, J. C., and Schonfeld, E. P. (1973) Social change and attitude change. Pp. 191–215 in G. Zaltman, ed., *Processes and Phenomena of Social Change*. New York: John Wiley and Sons.

Mason, K. O., Czajka, J. L., and Arber, S. (1976) Change in U.S. women's sex–role attitudes, 1964–1974. *American Sociological Review* 41:573–596.

McArthur, L., and Post, D. (1973) Figural emphasis and person perception. *Journal of Experimental Social Psychology* 13:520–535.

McGuire, W. J. (1964) Inducing resistance to persuasion: Some contemporary approaches. Pp. 191–229 in L. Berkowitz, ed., *Advances in Experimental Social Psychology*, Vol. 1. New York: Academic Press.

Miller, D. T., and Ross, M. (1975) Self-serving biases in the attribution of causality: Fact or fiction? *Psychological Bulletin* 82:213–225.

Messe, L. A., Stollak, G. E., Larson, R. W., and Michaels, G. Y. (1979) Interpersonal consequences of person perception processes in two social contexts. *Journal of Personality and Social Psychology* 37:369–379.

Morgan, J. N. (1980) *Retirement in prospect and retrospect*. In A. Duncan and J. Morgan, eds., *Five Thousand American Families*. Ann Arbor, Mich.: Institute for Social Research.

Nisbett, R. E., and Borgida, E. (1975) Attribution and the psychology of prediction. *Journal of Personality and Social Psychology* 32:932–943.

Nisbett, R. E., and Ross, L. (1980) *Human Inference: Strategies and Shortcomings in Social Judgment*. Englewood Cliffs, N.J.: Prentice-Hall.

Nisbett, R. E., and Valins, S. (1972) Perceiving the causes of one's own behavior. Pp. 63–78 in E. E. Jones, D. E. Kanouse, H. H. Kelley, R. E. Nisbett, S. Valins, and B. Winer, eds., *Attribution: Perceiving the Causes of Behavior*. Morristown, N.J.: General Learning Press.

Oppenheimer, V. (1981) The changing nature of life-cycle squeezes: Implications for the socioeconomic position of the elderly. In R. W. Fogel, E. Hatfield, S. B. Kiesler, and E. Shanas, eds., *Aging: Stability and Change in the Family*. New York: Academic Press.

Orvis, B. R., Kelley, H. H., and Butler, D. (1976) Attributional conflict in young couples. Pp. 353–386 in J. H. Harvey, W. J. Ickes, and R. F. Kidd, eds., *New Directions in Attribution Research*, Vol. 1. Hillside, N.J.: Lawrence Erlbaum Associates.

Petty, P. E., Ostrom, T. M., and Brock, T. C., eds. (1980) *Cognitive Responses in Persuasion*. Hillsdale, N.J.: Lawrence Erlbaum Associates.

Posner, M. I., and Snyder, C. R. R. (1975) Attention and cognitive control. In R. L. Solso, ed., *Information Processing and Cognition: The Loyola Symposium*. Hillsdale, N.J.: Lawrence Erlbaum Associates.

Quattrone, G. A., and Jones, E. E. (1980) The perception of variability within ingroups and outgroups: Implications for the Law of Small Numbers. *Journal of Personality and Social Psychology* 38:141–152.

Rosch, E. (1978) Principles of categorization. In E. Rosch and B. B. Lloyd, eds., *Cognition and Categorization*. Hillsdale, N.J.: Lawrence Erlbaum Associates.

Rose, T. L. (1980) Cognitive and diadic processes in intergroup contact. In B. L. Hamilton, ed., *Cognitive Processes in Stereotyped and Intergroup Behavior*. Hillsdale, N.J.: Lawrence Erlbaum Associates.

Ross, L. (1977) The intuitive psychologist and his shortcomings: Distortions in the attribution process. In L. Berkowitz, ed., *Advances in Experimental Social Psychology*. New York: Academic Press.

Ross, L., Lepper, M. R., Strask, F., and Steinmetz, J. (1977) Social explanation and social expectation: Effects of real and hypothetical explanations of subjective likelihood. *Journal of Personality and Social Psychology* 35:817–829.

Ross, M., and Sicoly, F. (1979) Egocentric biases in availability and attribution. *Journal of Personality and Social Psychology* 37:322–336.

Ryder, N. B. (1979) Changes in Parity Orientation from 1970–1975. Paper presented at the meeting of the Population Association of America, Philadelphia. (Available from author, Office of Population Research, Princeton University, Princeton, New Jersey 08544.)

Schlenker, B. R., and Miller, R. S. (1977) Egocentrism in groups: Self-serving biases or logical information processing? *Journal of Personality and Social Psychology* 35(10):755–763.

Schneider, W., and Shiffrin, R. M. (1977) Controlled and automatic human information processing: I. Detection, search, and attention. *Psychological Review* 84:1–66.

Silka, L. (1980) A Theory of Change Misjudgment. Unpublished manuscript, University of Lowell, Lowell, Massachusetts.

Snyder, M., and Swann, W. B., Jr. (1978) Hypothesis-testing processes in social interaction. *Journal of Personality and Social Psychology* 36:1202–1212.

Snyder, M., Tanke, E. D., and Berscheid, E. (1978) Social perception and interpersonal behavior: On the self-fulfilling nature of social stereotypes. *Journal of Personality and Social Psychology* 35:656–666.

Snyder, M., and Uranowitz, S. W. (1978) Reconstructing the past: Some cognitive consequences of person perception. *Journal of Personality and Social Psychology* 36(9):941–951.

Storms, M. D. (1973) Videotape and the attribution process: Reversing actors' and observers' points of view. *Journal of Personality and Social Psychology* 27:319–328.

Taylor, S. E., and Crocker, J. (1979) In E. T. Higgens, P. Hermann, and M. P. Zanna, eds., *The Ontario Symposium on Personality and Social Psychology,* Vol. 1. Hillsdale, N.J.: Lawrence Erlbaum Associates.

Taylor, S. E., Crocker, J., Fiske, S. T., Sprinzen, M., and Winkler, J. D. (1979) The generalizability of salience effects. *Journal of Personality and Social Psychology* 37:357–378.

Taylor, S. E., and Fiske, S. T. (1978) Salience, attention, and attribution: Top of the head phenomenon. In L. Berkowitz, ed., *Advances in Experimental Social Psychology,* Vol. 2. New York: Academic Press.

Taylor, S. E., Fiske, S. T., Etcoff, N. L., and Ruderman, A. J. (1978) Categorical and contextual bases of person memory and stereotyping. *Journal of Personality and Social Psychology* 36:778–793.

Trope, Y. (1978) Inferences of personal characteristics on the basis of information retrieved from one's memory. *Journal of Personality and Social Psychology* 36:93–106.

Tversky, A., and Kahneman, D. (1973) Availability: A heuristic for judging frequency and probability. *Cognitive Psychology* 5:207–232.

Tyler, T. R., and Sears, D. O. (1977) Coming to like obnoxious people when we must live with them. *Journal of Personality and Social Psychology* 35:200–211.

Upshaw, H. S. (1969) The personal reference scale: An approach to social judgment. In L. Berkowitz, ed., *Advances in Experimental Social Psychology,* Vol. 4. New York: Academic Press.

Vinokur, A., and Burnstein, E. (1978) Novel argumentation and attitude change: The case of polarization following groups discussion. *European Journal of Social Psychology* 8:355–368.

Wack, J., and Rodin, J. (1978) Nursing homes for the aged: The human consequences of legislation-shaped environments. In M. Bush and A. Gordon, eds., People and Bureaucracies. *Journal of Social Issues* 34:6–21.

Walster, E., Berscheid, E., and Walster, G. W. (1973) New directions in equity research. *Journal of Personality and Social Psychology* 25:151–176.

Waring, J. M. (1975) Social replenishment and social change: The problem of disordered cohort flow. *American Behavioral Scientist* 19:237–256.

Word, C. O., Zanna, M. P., and Cooper, J. (1974) The nonverbal mediation of self-fulling prophecies in interracial interaction. *Journal of Personality and Social Psychology* 10:109–120.

Wortman, C. B. (1976) Causal attributions and personal control. Pp. 23–52 in J. H. Harvey, W. J. Ickes, and R. F. Kidd, eds., *New Directions in Attribution Research,* Vol. 1. Hillsdale, N.J.: Lawrence Erlbaum Associates.

Zajonc, R. B. (1968) Attitudinal effects of mere exposure. *Journal of Personality and Social Psychology* 9:1–27.

Zander, A. (1968) Group aspirations. Pp. 418–429 in D. Cartwright and A. Zander, eds., *Group Dynamics.* New York: Harper and Row.

Zanna, M., and Pack, S. (1975) On the self-fulfilling nature of apparent sex differences in behavior. *Journal of Personality and Social Psychology* 11:583–591.

chapter 4

An Epidemiologic Gaze into the Crystal Ball of the Elderly

SIDNEY COBB
JOHN FULTON

I keep six honest serving men:
(They taught me all I know)
Their names are What and Where and When
And How and Why and Who.
                    Rudyard Kipling

"In the High and Far-Off Times . . . O Best Beloved" there was no computer, only a crystal ball. Since we are not sure that one is better than the other, we have combined some crystal ball gazing with some computing to make four predictions. These predictions are followed by some presentation of their foundations and reliability, and we will conclude with some discussion of the implications for research and planning. Both our recurring references to Kipling's "The Elephant's Child" and Figure 4.7 are intended to keep the reader reminded that though prediction is a risky business, it can be used to stimulate curiosity and planning. The focus is on change in survivorship, mortality, and morbidity predicted from certain rather obvious social and behavioral trends. No mention is made of areas in which we see no reason to forecast change on a social basis.

AGING
Social Change

PREDICTIONS AS WE APPROACH THE YEAR 2020

A. There will be a greater increase in longevity than the mortality trend lines now predict. This may involve a decrease in morbidity among the elderly.
B. There will be an increase in the sex ratio (M/F) among older people. This will presumably lead to a reduction in the proportion of elderly women who are lonely and depressed.
C. There may be a relative increase in survivorship into old age among those who are well educated.
D. The pattern of disease in the population will change toward
    (1) less malignant disease
    (2) less chronic obstructive lung disease
    (3) less arteriosclerotic disease
    (4) more disease of bones and joints
    (5) more senile dementia
    (6) less suffering from hypertension because a larger proportion of hypertensives will be receiving therapy

Our four predictions are based on a number of observations and projections, to which we now turn.

PREDICTORS

Certain Behaviors Will Change

(1) The per capita consumption of cigarettes will continue to decrease along the lines suggested by Figure 4.1. The tar content of cigarette smoke will continue to decrease both as a result of changes in the tobacco used (see Figure 4.2) and as a result of the increasing use of filters. The decrease in cigarette consumption appears to have begun earlier and to be proceeding more rapidly among men than among women (see Figure 4.3). Among men there is a striking difference by educational level in time of the beginning of the decrease. For women, this difference is less striking. In this connection, it is encouraging to note that at Brown University only about 5% of the medical students and about 13% of the college students smoke (Marshall and Hollinshead 1979) compared with 38% of the general population of equivalent age across the country (Surgeon General 1979).

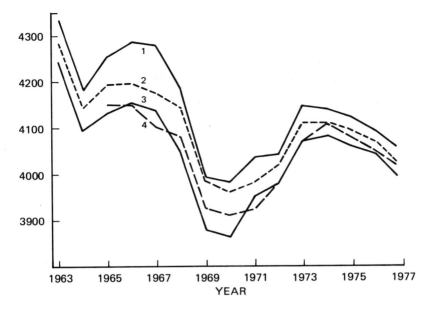

1. Based on Department of Agriculture total U.S. consumption series.
2. Based on Federal Trade Commission consumption series.
3. Based on Department of Agriculture domestic consumption series.
4. Based on Maxwell Reports' domestic consumption series.

Figure 4.1 Annual consumption of cigarettes per person aged 18 years and over, 1963–1977. (From Surgeon General 1979, Figure 2, p. A-23.)

(2) As continuing inflation erodes disposable income, the proportion of red meat in the American diet will probably decline, while the proportion of grain and fiber will probably grow. This trend will be amplified if the cost of red meat rises faster than the cost of grain and fiber. As the information about the dangers of red meat and the benefits of whole grains and fiber becomes more widely disseminated, it seems likely that the best educated will be the first to accept and act on the information, given that education is positively correlated with (*a*) the ability to accept and use new information, (*b*) self-discipline, and (*c*) future orientation, all of which seem logically related to the probability of changing one's health-damaging habits.

Similarly, the ever-growing American appetite for alcohol may be curbed by the erosion of disposable income. However, this is not so likely to be related to social class because the economic and educational effects are much more complex. In fact, during the 1970s, total alcohol

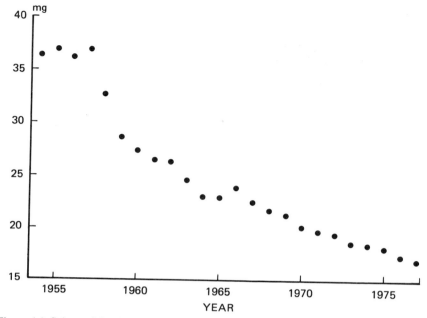

Figure 4.2 Sales weighted average "tar" per cigarette, 1954–1977. (From Surgeon General 1979, Figure 3. p. A-24.)

consumption per capita in Rhode Island appears to have leveled off after a very steady rise during the 1960s (Burns 1977).

(3) Although it is hard to document trends in interpersonal behavior, it seems likely that the frequency of socially supportive behavior is increasing. This is suggested by recent increases in communal living, the hospice movement (Stoddard 1978), and the use of the relaxation response (commonly in the form of transcendental meditation), and by a definite decrease in the use of skin color as a marker in interpersonal and intergroup activities. These changes are likely to be beneficial to health and longevity in a nontrivial way (Cobb 1976, Benson 1975, Harburg *et al.* 1978, Berkman and Syme 1979) (see Figure 4.4). They have at least the possibility of partially offsetting the continuing trends to divorce- and mobility-based disruption of the family, which are known to have negative health effects (Chen and Cobb 1960).

Figure 4.3 Percentage of people smoking cigarettes by year and group. All males from Gallup, 1979; National Clearinghouse of Smoking and Health, 1979. Rhode Island physicians from Burgess *et al.* 1978. All women from Gallup, 1979; National Clearinghouse of Smoking and Health, 1979. College educated women from National Clearinghouse of Smoking and Health, 1979). (*See facing page.*)

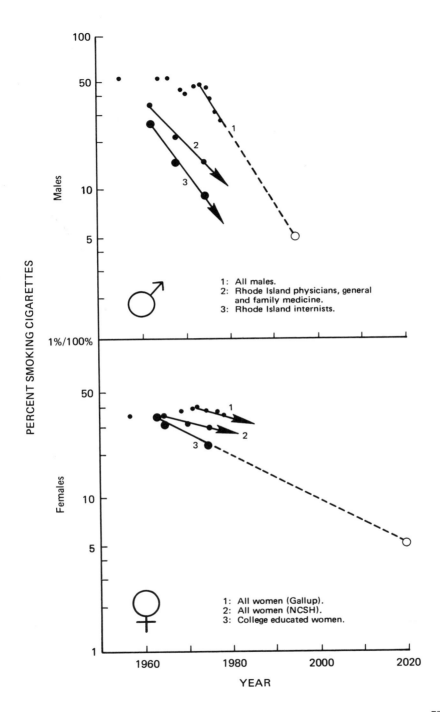

100

50

Males

10

5

1: All males.
2: Rhode Island physicians, general
   and family medicine.
3: Rhode Island internists.

PERCENT SMOKING CIGARETTES

1%/100%

50

Females

10

5

1: All women (Gallup).
2: All women (NCSH).
3: College educated women.

1

1960   1980   2000   2020

YEAR

Work Patterns Will Change

(1) The labor force participation of women will continue to increase (see Figure 4.5).

(2) The 30-year trend toward reduced labor force participation by the elderly (U.S. President 1978) will be blunted, if not reversed, by the recent proscription of mandatory retirement by an amendment to the Age Discrimination in Employment Act of 1967 in combination with continuing inflation.

(3) Patterns of exposure to the risks of travel will change. First, continuing reduction in gasoline supplies with increasing cost per gallon will reduce highway fatalities. This will affect the survivorship of men more than of women, because men have higher highway accident mortality rates than women, largely because of greater exposures (Baedenkopf *et al.* 1956). Second, because of increases in employment, independence, and discretionary income, the exposure of women to the risk of highway travel will increase relative to the exposure of men.

(4) Patterns of exposure to other environmental hazards are not changing in obvious, systematic ways that are apparent to the authors, so they are not useful in prediction.

(5) As the proportion of gross national product available for health gradually levels off, there will be increasing attention to prevention both in private practice and in public programs. Analyzing risk factors and changing health habits will be emphasized (Seward and Sorensen 1978). This trend toward prevention will support the changes in health habits through the already burgeoning health education movement.

CONNECTIONS

Since, like the Elephant's child, O Best Beloved, you may ask a "new fine question," we propose some answers about how we moved from predictors to predictions.

The prediction of an accelerating increase in longevity is more than the trend line prediction, and one that is undergirded by the emerging trends in health habits. Reducing exposures to cigarette smoke, improved diet, perhaps some leveling off of alcohol consumption, possibly continued improvement in interpersonal relations, and substantial reduction in high-speed automobile travel will all contribute to a general increase in longevity. It is to be hoped, but not ensured, that the increase in longevity will be associated with an increase in enjoyable, productive time, not just an increase in years of dependency and discomfort. Unfortunately,

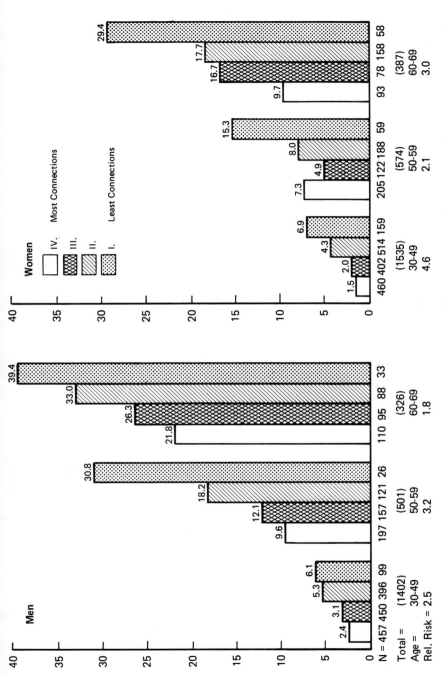

Figure 4.4 Age and sex-specific mortality rates from all causes per 100 for Social Network Index, Human Population Laboratory Study of Alameda County 1965–1974. (From L. F. Berkman and S. L. Syme, Social networks, host resistance and mortality: A nine-year follow-up study of Alameda County residents, *American Journal of Epidemiology* 109:190, 1979.)

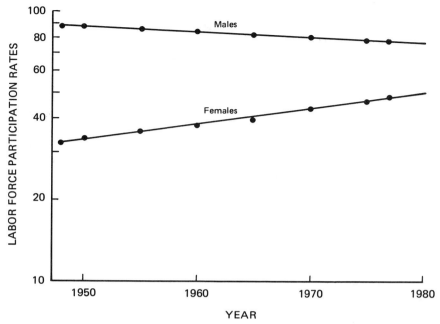

Figure 4.5 Civilian labor force participation rates by sex 1948–1977. (From U.S. President 1978, Table A-4.)

the trend is toward an increasing prevalence of chronic illness and disability as longevity increases (Gruenberg 1976). Perhaps the trend toward increasing social support will extend to the aged. Brown *et al.* (1975) have shown that social support prevents depression, which is the scourge of old age, and Lowenthal and Haven (1968) have shown this specifically for older people. However, the increasing tendency of the elderly to establish themselves in colonies may not be helpful in this regard. Bonds to younger people, especially family, are probably more important, for Berkman and Syme (1979) suggest that family and friends are more important to survivorship than are church and other group memberships.

There are several reasons for believing that the sex ratio will increase, that is, survivorship will increase more rapidly for men than for women. The first is the relative distribution and probable trends of smoking behavior. Our best estimates are presented in Figure 4.3. These suggest that the proportion of smokers might drop to 5% by 1995 among men and by 2020 among women. It should be noted that in predicting the drop to 5% smoking among women by 2020 we have used the trend line for college women. This was done in the belief that women as a group will soon start catching up with men. These projections are surely rather unstable, but in order to illustrate what they might imply, we have used them in the life table analysis described in the Technical Appendix. This analysis indicates that between 1970 and 2020 the expectation of life at age 65 for men would increase about 1.25 years, while the expectation of life at age 65 for women would increase less than .25 year. As a result, there would be a substantial increase in the sex ratio (M/F) in the older age groups as shown in Figure 4.6.

It might be argued that the rate of change of the sex ratio is exaggerated because women may eventually assume the same rate of decrease in smoking that we now see in men. However, this potential exaggeration will probably be offset by two other trends, the effects of which are less easily estimated. The first is the increasing participation of women in the labor force. Visual inspection of Figure 4.4 suggests that if current

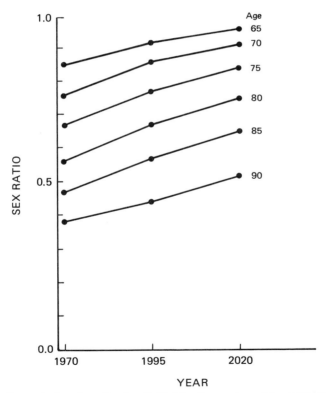

Figure 4.6 Sex ratio (number of males divided by the number of females) by year, given the decline in smoking posited in the text. (See Technical Appendix.)

trends persist, they might bring us to equal participation by the turn of the century. If we interpret the trends correctly, much of this increase will have to come from women entering blue-collar jobs. These women will be exposed to occupational hazards from which they were previously insulated. Some increases will surely also take place in the proportion of women in the executive suite. Since the type A behavior that contributes to coronary heart disease (Jenkins 1971) is probably more related to one's current environment than to one's genes or childhood environment, we may begin to see an excess of coronary heart disease in executive women in the same way that Hinkle *et al.* (1968) found an excess of coronary diseases among the minority of men who came into executive positions without a college education. This trend is already appearing among women in clerical and sales positions who are married to blue-collar workers (Haynes and Feinleib 1980). In general, women will have greater need to drive (to and from their jobs) and more disposable income to afford driving, and thus be more exposed to the hazard of death on the highway. This will begin to alter the long-time excess of males over females in highway deaths.

Since smoking cigarettes and eating diets high in beef and low in fiber are predicted to wane most rapidly among the well educated, it is reasonable to suppose that both arteriosclerotic disease, including coronary heart disease, and stroke, and cigarette-related cancer will develop a negative social class gradient, that is, will become least frequent in the highest social classes. Since these two diseases constitute a significant fraction of the causes of death, it seems likely that the survivorship advantage of the upper classes will reverse its downward trend and start increasing again. Although life table analysis using the available data on the difference in smoking habits between those with a college degree and those without revealed nothing but an insignificant advantage in survival for the well educated, the present generation of college students seem much less prone to smoke than their predecessors, which should increase the advantage. If a simple survey done on undergraduates at Brown University is reliable and representative of college students across the country, one would expect that in the proximate future, the population of recent college graduates would contain about one-third as many smokers as the rest of the population. If this is truly the case, and if diets are improved more rapidly by the well educated, then the predicted advantage in mortality will accrue. This is clearly the weakest of the four predictions, but it is important because trends started by high-status people tend to persist.

The pattern of disease and the requirements for medical care are surely going to change along with the changes in mortality. The postulated lower incidence of cigarette-related cancer will obviously affect morbidity and mortality at the same rate. Changing dietary and smoking habits should similarly affect both morbidity and mortality from atherosclerosis. On the other hand, if Hammond and Garfinkel (1969) are right that the bulk of the decrease in coronary heart disease morbidity after cessation of smoking takes place in the first or second year, then one must infer that most of the effect must be on mortality among those who already have established atherosclerosis. If the effect were primarily on the long, slow process of atherogenesis, the change would not be so prompt. This suggests that the number of people with extensive atherosclerosis may actually increase for a while because the mortality rate will fall faster than the morbidity rate. It is hard to envision the kinds of problems that this might create. In this connection, it is encouraging to note that the incidence may already be declining as fast as the mortality from stroke, (Garraway et al. 1979, Cooper et al. 1978).

The prediction that diseases of bones and joints will assume greater importance is simply based on the facts that osteoporosis, Paget's disease of bone, and osteoarthrosis all increase in frequency with advancing years. As people live longer, more people will require treatment for bone and joint disease. Similarly, more people will come under treatment for senile dementia (Gruenberg 1978) even if the proportion of the elderly with atherosclerotic brain disease should begin to decrease before 2020.

The prediction that the proportion of hypertensives receiving treatment will continue to increase is largely based on a trend line extrapolation, but if as we expect there is an increase in emphasis on prevention in the practice of medicine, the early detection and treatment of hypertension will be among the front-runners for emphasis on secondary prevention.

Unfortunately, there is no real reason to suppose that disability or institutionalization in the elderly will decrease. In fact, it has been shown that the proportion of the elderly in institutions increased from 1950 to 1970 despite the reduction in the proportion in state mental institutions (National Institute of Mental Health 1977).

CAVEATS

There is a great need for more ongoing, comparable morbidity data on the basis of which trends can be identified. The National Health Surveys, the Cooperative Health Statistics System, and the data from our large prepaid health insurance plans all provide useful data. Gillum

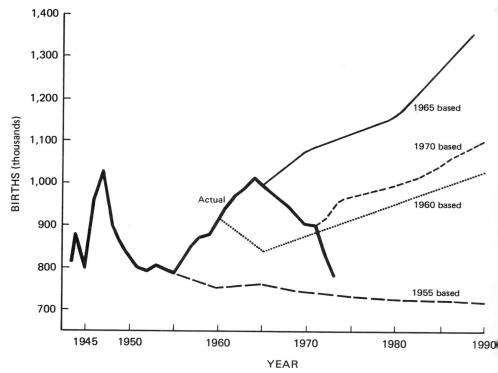

Figure 4.7 Comparisons between actual and projected live births, United Kingdom for 1955, 1960, 1965, and 1970. (From Alderson, 1977, p. 65. The original data were derived by Alderson from several Her Majesty's Stationery Office sources specified in his text.)

(1978) has proposed community surveillance for cardiovascular disease, and cancer registries are now commonplace. Nonetheless, though the methods are available, comparability and continuity are often inadequate, and too little information is being collected on two important conditions: senile dementia and alcoholism.

If life is to improve in quality rather than deteriorate as it lengthens, then research efforts must be directed at those disabling and/or painful diseases that increase in frequency through the oldest age groups. These would include, but not be limited to, senile dementia, depression, osteoporosis, osteoarthritis, and Paget's disease of bone. With respect to these diseases, basic reasearch is needed at all levels—molecular, cellular, organ, organismal, and population—for all of these diseases are still largely indeterminate with respect to etiology. Progress in understanding etiology will perhaps move us closer to prevention and/or treatment. In the meantime, considerable attention is warranted to the possible role of paramedical and nonmedical personnel in the prevention, management, and rehabilitation of these conditions. We must push past the enervating concept that these diseases are inevitable concomitants of aging and find ways to deal with them.

It is fun to make predictions, but just to remind ourselves, authors and readers alike, that most crystal balls are flawed, we include Figure 4.7 from a recent book by Alderson (1977). We hope that our optimistic predictions do not turn out to have been just wishful thinking.

TECHNICAL APPENDIX

Degree–sex–age-specific cohorts were subjected to mortality rates over the 50-year period, 1970–2020:

$$l_x^{s,d} = \text{degree–sex–age-specific cohort,}$$

where

d = whether or not members of the cohort have received college degrees
s = sex of members of the cohort
x = age of members of the cohort

The initial value for each cohort was derived from the l_x column of the U.S. life table, 1969–1971 (note a):

$$l_x^{s,d} = {}^{US}l_x^s \cdot S \cdot D,$$

where

S = sex-ratio at birth, 1.05 for males, 1.00 for females
D = proportion of the cohort who either have received college degrees, or who have not, depending on the value of d (note b).

Sex–age-specific mortality rates for smokers and nonsmokers were derived from the q column of the U.S. life table, 1969–1971 (note a), sex–age-specific ratios of the mortality of people who had ever smoked to the mortality of people who had never smoked (note c), and sex–age-specific proportions of the United States' population, 1970, who had ever smoked and never smoked (notes d,e):

$$^{US}_{n}q_x^s = ({}_n t_x^s \cdot {}_n r_x^s \cdot {}_n q_x^{s,NS}) + [(l - {}_n t_x^s) \cdot {}_n q_x^{s,NS}] ,$$

where

n = width of the age group (in this study, 5.0)

t = proportion who have ever smoked

r = mortality ratio, ever-smoked/never-smoked

$_nq_x^{s,NS}$ = sex–age specific mortality rate for nonsmokers (actually, of never-smokers, but used as a best estimate of the mortality rate for nonsmokers)

$_nq_x^{s,SM}$ = $_nr_x^s \cdot {}_nq_x^{s,NS}$ = sex–age-specific mortality rate for smokers.

Before applying a mortality rate, q, to a cohort, l, in a given time period, l was split into current smokers and current nonsmokers degree–sex–age-specific proportions of current smokers and nonsmokers (notes d,e). Deaths were calculated separately for smokers and nonsmokers, then summed and subtracted from l. Degree–sex–age-specific proportions of current smokers and nonsmokers were derived from estimates of the same for the United States, 1970 (notes d,e), and assumptions that the proportion of current smokers could be reduced to .05 for all males by 1995 and all females by 2020. Proportions for intervening dates were calculated using linear interpolation. Mortality rates were applied for 5-year periods.

Notes

(a) National Center for Health Statistics (1975) *United States Life Tables: 1969–1971.* Washington, D.C.: U.S. Government Printing Office.

(b) Bureau of the Census (1973) *Census of Population: 1970. Detailed Characteristics.* Final Report PC(1) - D1. United States Summary. Washington, D.C.: U.S. Government Printing Office.

(c) Hammand, E. C. (1966) Smoking in relation to the death rates of one million men and women. In W. Haenszel, ed. *Epidemiological Approaches to the Study of Cancer and Other Chronic Diseases.* Washington, D.C.: U.S. Government Printing Office.

(d) National Center for Health Statistics (1970) *Changes in Cigarette Smoking Habits between 1955 and 1966.* Vital and Health Statistics. Series 10, No. 59. Rockville, Md.: U.S. Department of Health, Education, and Welfare.

(e) U.S. Department of Health, Education, and Welfare Public Health Service (1976) *Adult Use of Tobacco, 1975.* Washington, D.C.: U.S. Department of Health, Education, and Welfare.

REFERENCES

Alderson, M. (1977) *An Introduction to Epidemiology.* Littleton, Mass. PSG Publishing Co.

Baedenkopf, W. G., Polan, A. K., Boek, W. E., Korns, R. F., and James, G. (1956) An epidemiological approach to traffic accidents. *Public Health Reports* 71:15–24.

Benson, H. (1975) *The Relaxation Response*. New York: William Morrow.

Berkman, L. F., and Syme, S. L. (1979) Social networks, host resistance, and mortality: A nine-year follow-up study of Alameda County residents. *American Journal of Epidemiology* 109:186–204.

Brown, G. W., Bhrolchain, M. N., and Harris, T. (1975) Social class and psychiatric disturbance among women in an urban population. *Sociology* 9:225–254.

Burgess, A. M., Jr., Casey, D. B., and Tierney, J. T. (1978) Cigarette smoking by Rhode Island physicians 1963–1973: Comparison with lawyers and other adult males. *American Journal of Public Health* 68:63–65.

Burns, T. F. (1977) *Apparent Consumption of Alcoholic Beverages in Rhode Island 1934–1976*. Dept. of Anthropology, Brown University mimeo.

Chen, E., and Cobb, S. (1960) Family structure in relation to health and disease. *Journal of Chronic Diseases* 12:544–567.

Cobb, S. (1976) Social support as a moderator of life stress. *Psychosomatic Medicine* 38:300–314.

Cooper, R., Stamler, J., Dyer, A., and Garside, D. (1978) The decline in mortality from coronary heart disease, U.S.A., 1968–1975. *Journal of Chronic Diseases* 31:709–720.

Gallup Poll (1979) American Institute of Public Opinion. Cited by Surgeon General.

Garraway, W. M., Whisnant, J. P., Furlan, A. J., Phillips, L. H., II, Kurland, L. T., and O'Fallon, W. M. (1979) The declining incidence of stroke. *New England Journal of Medicine* 300:449–452.

Gillum, R. F. (1978) Community surveillance for cardiovascular disease: Methods, problems, applications: A review. *Journal of Chronic Diseases* 31:87–94.

Gruenberg, E. M. (1976) The Failure of Success. The Rema Lapouse Lecture, American Public Health Association Annual Meeting October 19, 1976.

Gruenberg, E. M. (1978) Epidemiology of senile dementia. In B. S. Schoenberg, ed., *Advances in Neurology*, Vol. 19. New York: Rover Press.

Hammond, E. C., and Garfinkle, L. (1969) Coronary heart disease, stroke and aortic aneurism. *Archives of Environmental Health* 19:167–182.

Harburg, E., Gleibermann, L., Roeper, P., Schork, M. A., and Schull, W. J. (1978) Skin color, ethnicity and blood pressure I: Detroit Blacks *American Journal of Public Health* 68:1177–1183.

Haynes, S. G., and Feinleib, M. (1980) Women, work and coronary heart disease: Prospective findings from the Framingham Study. *American Journal of Public Health* 70:133–141.

Hinkle, L. E., Whitney, L. H., Lehman, E. W., Dunn, J., Benjamin, B., King, R., Plakun, A., and Flehinger, B. (1968) Occupation, education, and coronary heart disease. *Science* 161:238–246.

Jenkins, C. D. (1971) Psychologic and social precursors of coronary disease. *New England Journal of Medicine* 285:244–255 and 307–317.

Lowenthal, M. F., and Haven, C. (1968) Interaction and adaptation: Intimacy as a critical variable. *American Sociological Review* 33:20–30.

Marshall, R. M., and Hollinshead, W. H. (1979) Personal communication.

National Institute of Mental Health (1977) Psychiatric Services and the Changing Institutional Scene 1950–1985. Publication No. (ADM) 77-433. Washington, D.C.: U.S. Department of Health, Education, and Welfare.

National Clearinghouse of Smoking and Health (1979) Data from adult use of tobacco, 1970, 1975. In *Smoking and Health*. (PHS) 79-50066. Washington, D.C.: U.S. Department of Health, Education, and Welfare.

President, U.S. (1978) *Employment and Training Report of the President*. Washington, D.C.: U.S. Government Printing Office.

Seward, E., and Sorensen, A. (1978) The current emphasis on preventive medicine. *Science* 200:889–894.

Stoddard, S. (1978) *The Hospice Movement*. New York: Vantage.

Surgeon General (1979) *Smoking and Health*. (PHS) 79-50066. Washington, D.C.: U.S. Department of Health, Education, and Welfare.

PART II

GOVERNMENT AND POLICY

chapter 5

Conservative Weather in a Liberalizing Climate: Change in Selected NORC General Social Survey Items, 1972–1978[1]

JAMES A. DAVIS

This chapter traces the changes in 12 especially volatile items in the National Opinion Research Center (NORC) General Social Survey 1972–1978 (11 national priority questions and reports of changes in one's finances) and an abortion item that showed an unexpected plateau pattern. Despite sociological predictions of a trend toward liberalism stemming from demographic changes (the Stouffer hypothesis), the set, as a whole, showed a conservative direction consistent with the claims of recent pop sociology. The paradox is resolved by a multivariate causal model that shows both patterns of change to be operating. The metaphor of a slow, long-term trend toward liberalism in the opinion climate plus a sharp, short-term shift toward conservativism in the opinion weather is introduced to interpret the results. The striking absence of interactions in the data casts doubt on the hypothesis that the young or the better educated tend to lead other groups as opinions shift.

In the months of February and March 1972 through 1978, the National Opinion Research Center, with heroic inhibition of its urge to improve

[1] Preliminary versions of these materials were reported at the 1978 meetings of the American Sociological Association, San Francisco, California, September 5, 1978, and the National Research Council Workshop on Stability and Change in the Family, Annapolis, Maryland, March 24, 1979. This research was supported by National Science Foundation Grant Number SOC77-03279.

question wordings, asked identical questions of national samples of adult Americans in its General Social Survey (GSS). (For an explanation of the survey, see the Appendix.) This rigidity was, oddly enough, in the service of studying change. Because the questions are repeated, one may use the cumulative file ($N = 10,652$) to track trends for some 200 items, over 6 years, within a variety of social groups, using repeated samples from the same statistical universe.

The dates span President Nixon's trip to Peking (February 1972) to the middle of Jimmy Carter's initial term in office. Though 6 years may be too short to catch the movements of deep currents, enough froth has swirled around on the surface to justify some attempt at summary. In particular, these were the years of Watergate (the break-in was June 17, 1972, and President Nixon was pardoned on September 8, 1974), the end of the Vietnam adventure (South Vietnam surrendered on April 30, 1975), and the first years since 1958 when the real-money–GNP-per capita declined (1974, 1975).

A year ago, I ventured a review of the changes from 1972–1977 (Davis, 1978a). Operating in the wholesale mode, I drew these conclusions:

Of 160 items that appeared with identical wordings in four or more General Social Surveys, 1972–1977:

1. About one-fourth are clearly nonconstant. Of these, almost two-thirds show a significant trend or direction, and almost one-half (44%) can be described neatly by fitting a straight line.
2. About one-fourth may be changing, but sampling variations can not be ruled out as an alternative explanation.
3. About one-half are either constant or changing so little that repeated surveys of size 1500 cannot detect the fluctuations.

These figures may be of some use as a benchmark for assessing the rate of change in contemporary American. Assuming the GSS is a reasonable sample of the variables sociologists think to be important—and it should be since it was designed by panels of sociologists for that purpose—the 25–25–50 figures suggest: The rate of change in most sociological variables is a bit less than the talk-show authors and pop sociologists would imply, but a good deal larger than the frozen-in-amber formulations in sociology tests.

A year later I am in no mood to redo hundreds of calculations in last year's report. My impression (and that of the GSS staff in Chicago) is this: With the exception of the attitudes toward abortion discussed below, 1978 was "more of the same."

Instead, I wish to move from wholesale to retail, from counts of items to particular topics. I have chosen 13 questions, 12 of them (11 national priority ratings and 1 measure of financial changes) because of their high rate of change during 1972–1977 and one (attitude toward abortion on demand) because of an unexpected shift in 1978.

While the main criterion was action, the questions discussed here also shed some light on an apparent paradox. It is commonly believed that we are in a period of reaction to social and political attitudes. In the *New York Times*, for example, Peter Ross Range writes, "In 1972, the country was on the cusp of what has now been recognized as the conservative turn of the 1970s [1979, p. 74]." Quite possibly, as we shall see. At the same time, however, sociological research (e.g., Stouffer 1955, Davis 1975b, Taylor *et al.* 1978) suggests a long-term movement toward liberalism. Since study after study shows better-educated and younger Americans to be more liberal, and since older Americans are inexorably replaced by better-educated, more-recently-born cohorts, there is every reason to expect a long-term trend toward liberalism.

The assertions are not logically contradictory. Technically, they specify a model in which the cohort effect and the aging-period effect have opposite signs. Nevertheless, it may be useful to sort out the two possible effects and estimate their sizes.

Thus, the aims of this chapter: to track 13 relatively volatile items in the GSS 1972–1978 and to sort their changes into two portions—that produced by the changing of the generational guard and that produced by the tides and eddies of the period 1972–1978.

THE TRENDS

Table 5.1 gives the wording and marginal results for an 11-part item on national priorities (asked annually beginning in 1973) and a question on financial progress.

The national priorities question allows us to track the popularity of liberal programs such as "solving the problems of the big cities" or "improving the conditions of blacks" along with such conservative favorites as "halting the rising [sic] crime rate" and "the military, armaments, and defense." Since all 11 imply cash outlays (the question refers to "many problems . . . none of which can be solved easily or inexpensively"), we can watch the complete data set, looking for a simultaneous downturn that might signal the highly publicized "taxpayers' revolt."

To boil things down a bit, I will summarize the trichotomous answers by an index, the proportion "too little" minus the proportion "too

TABLE 5.1
Marginal Trends for Selected GSS Items[a]

Item	Year						
	1972	1973	1974	1975	1976	1977	1978
"We are faced with many problems in this country, none of which can be solved easily or inexpensively. I'm going to name some of these problems, and for each one I'd like you to tell me whether you think we're spending too much money on it, too little money, or about the right amount."							
Space exploration program (NATSPAC)[b]							
Too little		.074	.077	.076	.094	.102	.117
About right		.343	.310	.340	.304	.407	.416
Too much		.583	.612	.583	.602	.490	.466
Little–much		−.509	−.535	−.507	−.508	−.388	−.349
Improving and protecting the environment (NATENVIR)[b]							

About right	.315	.567(?)	.520(?)	.552(?)	.431(?)	.497(?)
(Too little)	—	.335	.380	.371	.425	.398
Too much	.075	.078	.100	.097	.119	.105
Little–much	+.535	+.509	+.420	+.435	+.338	+.329
Improving and protecting the nation's health (NATHEAL)[b]						
Too little	.611	.640	.627	.603	.565	.557
About right	.342	.313	.321	.346	.366	.368
Too much	.047	.047	.052	.051	.069	.074
Little–much	+.564	+.593	+.575	+.552	+.496	+.483
Solving the problems of the big cities (NATCITY)[b]						
Too little	.483	.495	.457	.415	.391	.369
About right	.393	.393	.419	.385	.405	.432
Too much	.124	.112	.124	.200	.203	.199
Little–much	+.359	+.383	+.333	+.215	+.188	+.170
Halting the rising crime rate (NATCRIME)[b]						
Too little	.645	.670	.652	.658	.658	.645
About right	.308	.281	.291	.263	.278	.292
Too much	.047	.049	.057	.079	.064	.063
Little–much	+.598	+.551	+.595	+.579	+.594	+.582
Dealing with drug addiction (NATDRUG)[b]						
Too little	.658	.606	.547	.587	.556	.550
About right	.281	.328	.365	.337	.354	.361
Too much	.060	.065	.088	.075	.090	.089
Little–much	+.598	+.546	+.459	+.512	+.470	+.461

(Continued)

97

TABLE 5.1 (Continued)

Item	Year						
	1972	1973	1974	1975	1976	1977	1978
Improving the nation's education system (NATEDUC)[b]							
Too little	—	.491	.506	.486	.495	.469	.516
About right	—	.418	.407	.396	.405	.428	.368
Too much	—	.090	.087	.118	.110	.103	.116
Little–much	—	+.401	+.419	+.368	+.377	+.366	+.400
Improving the conditions of blacks (NATRACE)[b]							
Too little	—	.326	.308	.262	.266	.244	.229
About right	—	.457	.482	.493	.473	.505	.507
Too much	—	.217	.210	.245	.261	.252	.264
Little–much	—	+.109	+.098	+.017	+.005	-.008	-.035
The military armaments and defense (NATARMS)[b]							
Too little	—	.111	.170	.168	.246	.241	.281
About right	—	.508	.520	.523	.491	.535	.508
Too much	—	.380	.311	.309	.263	.224	.211
Little–much	—	-.269	-.141	-.141	-.017	+.017	+.070
Foreign aid (NATAID)[b]							
Too little	—	.042	.029	.051	.026	.031	.034
About right	—	.253	.207	.204	.204	.298	.284
Too much	—	.706	.764	.744	.771	.671	.682
Little–much	—	-.664	-.735	-.693	-.745	-.640	-.648

welfare (NATFARE)

Too little	—	.199	.221	.235	.125	.118	.113
About right	—	.285	.355	.332	.260	.274	.291
Too much	—	.516	.425	.433	.614	.608	.596
Little–much	—	−.317	−.204	−.198	−.489	−.490	−.448

"During the last few years, has your financial situation been getting better, getting worse, or has it stayed the same?"
(FINALTER)[b]

Better	.433	.424	.391	.355	.359	.383	.410
Same	.387	.411	.390	.364	.413	.395	.402
Worse	.180	.164	.219	.281	.228	.222	.188
Better–worse	+.253	+.260	+.172	+.074	+.131	+.161	+.222

[a] Each proportion is based on between 1350 and 1500 cases. Youngest respondents in later years are excluded as explained in Table 5.4
[b] Standard GSS mnemonic for this item.

much." A value of 1.00 would mean that everyone that everyone answered "too little," a value of .000 would indicate equal proportions saying "too little" and "too much," and a score of − 1.00 would mean unanimity for "too much." Scores in Table 5.1 range from + .598 (for crime and drugs in 1973) to − .735 (foreign aid in 1974).

The financial item, "During the last few years, has your financial situation been getting better, getting worse, or has it stayed the same?" is a standard Michigan Survey Research Center (SRC) question. Using a similar trichotomous index (better minus worse), it shows a range from + .260 in 1973 to + .074 in 1975. Despite the economic vicissitudes of the period. "betters" outnumbered "worses" each year.

While the 12 questions in Table 5.1 were chosen for closer scrutiny because they were among the most volatile measures 1972–1977 (Davis 1978a), the abortion questions in Table 5.2 were chosen because of an unexpected shift from 1977 to 1978.

Respondents were asked whether abortions should be legal under six conditions: mother's health endangered, pregnancy because of rape, strong chance of a serious defect in the baby, low family income, mother is single and doesn't wish to marry, mother is married and doesn't want any more. Marginal frequencies for the first three differ substantially from those for the second group. For the former sometimes called "hard reasons," endorsement is high (79% for each item in any year), while for the latter, "soft reasons," "yes" answers are concentrated in the 40–50% range. Thus, throughout the period—"right-to-life" forces to the contrary notwithstanding—there was virtually unanimous support for abortion when motivated by hard reasons, and throughout the period— "pro-choice" forces to the contrary notwithstanding—American adults split down the middle on soft reasons.

The pattern of change for the abortion items is shown in the bottom panel of Table 5.2. Between 1972 and 1973, all six items showed statistically significant increases in favorability—possibility because of the January 22, 1973, Supreme Court decision favorable to abortions (though an analogous Supreme Court decision on capital punishment the year before did not produce a change in the GSS death penalty item). From 1974 to 1977, all six items remained virtually constant, but the next year there was a downturn in favorability. In 1978, the six items showed an average drop of − .042 in endorsement, the three soft items averaging − .070, the three hard items a trivial − .013.

Since the three hard reasons did not show the unanticipated turn in 1978 and since the three soft reasons appear to behave in much the same way, I will use just one of six for further analysis—"married and doesn't want any more children."

I now turn to Figure 5.1 to examine the direction and patterns of change. In Figure 5.1, the proportions and trichotomous indices are rescaled to equal zero in their first reading and sorted into three groups, Figures 5.1(a), (b), and (c).

Figure 5.1(a) plots seven items with unambiguous trends up or down:

1. Spending priority for defense[2] showed a steady increase from 1973 to 1978. In 1973, it had a negative score of $-.269$, while by 1978 it was a slightly positive $+.070$.
2. Spending priority for space increased considerably in 1977 and 1978 after a virtually constant value from 1973 through 1976.
3. Spending priorities for blacks, solving drug addiction, environment, and cities showed parallel downward trends.

Figure 5.1(b) shows three priorities that remained constant[3] throughout the period—foreign aid, education, and crime. Constancy is not so colorful as change, but these results are of some technical interest since they argue against year-to-year changes in sampling, interviewing, question order, and the like as explanations for changes in the other items. The ability of GSS to come up with constancy in many items adds to its credibility when it does appear to spot changes.

Three items, shown in Figure 5.1(c), showed irregular changes—statistically significant departures from homogeniety that cannot be comfortably fit by straight lines.

1. Financial progress shows a U-shaped pattern that makes sense in the light of the economic trends of the period. Reports of progress dropped in 1974, bottomed out in 1975 (even then "getting better" outnumbered "getting worse" by 36% to 28%), and have been improving since. By 1978, the absolute index, $+.222$, had almost recovered its 1972 level of $+.253$.
2. Welfare priority shows a reversed U, which is presumably related

---

[2] A series of very similar, but not identical, Gallup and Harris items on defense spending for 1960, 1969, 1971, 1973, 1974, 1976, 1977, and 1978 suggests that the long-term trend is more complicated. The series shows a sharp drop in military spending priority between 1960 and 1969 (the Vietnam period) followed by a steady rise since. In 1977, "too little–too much" for the Gallup–Harris series was back to its 1960 level ($+.04$ for 1977, $+.03$ for 1960) and in 1978, the index ($+.16$) was more favorable than at any time since the beginning of the Kennedy administration (see *Public Opinion,* 1979, p. 25).

[3] Strictly speaking: 1972–1977 analysis did not reject the null hypothesis that the years could be samples from a common pooled value for both responses (too little, too much) for crime and education, and "too little" for foreign aid. "Too much" did show significant variation for foreign aid, but there was no apparent trend. Since 1978 results looked essentially similar; no significance test was made for them.

TABLE 5.2
Marginal Trends in Abortion Attitudes (Proportion "Yes")[a]

Item	Year							
	1972	1973	1974	1975	1976	1977	1978
"Please tell me whether or not *you* think it should be possible for a pregnant woman to obtain a *legal* abortion if:							
(a) the woman's health is seriously endangered by the pregnancy?	.869	.923	.924	.907	.908	.905	.906
(b) she became pregnant as a result of rape?	.791	.835	.865	.837	.837	.838	.832
(c) there is a strong chance of serious defect in the baby?	.786	.845	.851	.832	.839	.855	.820
(d) the family has a very low income and cannot afford any more children?	.488	.534	.548	.532	.531	.534	.474

(e) she is not married and does not want to marry the man?	.435	.491	.500	.482	.503	.498	.411
(f) she is married and does not want any more children?	.397	.477	.466	.457	.462	.465	.403
Year-to-year changes							
Health endangered		+.054	+.001	−.017	+.001	−.003	+.001
Result of rape		+.044	+.030	−.028	.000	+.001	−.006
Serious defect		+.059	+.006	−.019	+.007	+.016	−.035
Low income		+.046	+.014	−.016	−.001	+.003	−.060
Not married		+.056	+.009	−.018	+.021	−.005	−.087
Doesn't want any more		+.080	−.011	−.009	+.005	+.003	−.062
Mean =		+.056	+.010	−.018	+.007	+.002	−.042

[a] Ns are based on all cases and range from 1414 to 1539.

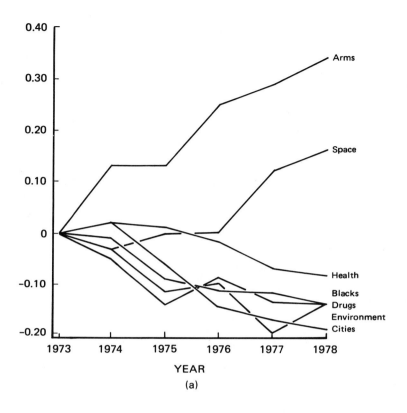

(a)

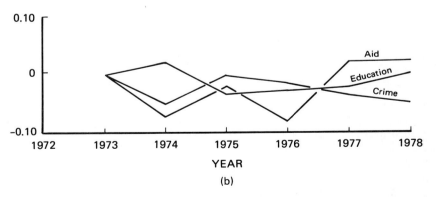

(b)

Figure 5.1. (a) Stems showing definite trends in favorability, more–less (1973 set to .000); (b) items showing no clear-cut changes; (c) items showing curvilinear changes. (For finances, score-better–worse; for abortion, score-proportion "yes.")

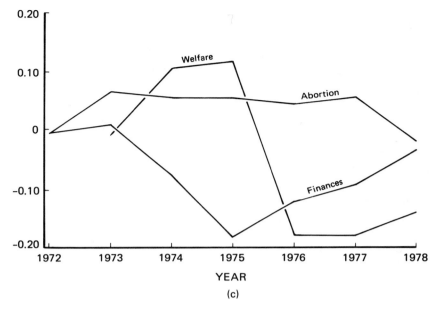

Figure 5.1 (continued)

to economic trends. Welfare priority dipped to a fairly constant value in 1976 through 1978, a value that was well below the 1973 level, One feels, but cannot document, that the American public regretted its temporary softheartedness toward the poor and unfortunate.

3. Abortion, as explained above, shows a reversed U or perhaps better, a "mesa" pattern, up in 1972 and then down again in 1978.

Does all of this amount to a conservative tide? It depends on what one means by conservative and what one means by tide. In terms of the political vocabulary of university people, it looks that way. Increased backing for arms and space, decreased priorities for health, blacks, drugs, environment, cities, and a stalemate on abortion are not likely to generate much applause from the left—new, old, or middle-aged. But conservatism is a notoriously slippery word, and it may not mean the same thing to a national cross-section of people. Table 5.3 treats respondents' self-reports of liberalism–conservatism.

The top panel in Table 5.3 perhaps suggests a conservative trend in self-descriptions. Indeed, one can fit the data nicely with a linear trend of $-.0058$ per year for liberal and $+.0105$ for conservative. Unfortu-

TABLE 5.3
Attitudes and self-reported Liberalism and Conservatism

(a) Trends in self-report					
Category	1974	1975	1976	1977	1978
Extremely liberal, liberal, slightly liberal	.305	.301	.288	.289	.282
Moderate, middle of the road	.400	.400	.399	.388	.383
Extremely conservative, conservative, slightly conservative	.295	.298	.313	.323	.335
Total	1.000	.999	1.000	1.000	1.000
N	1410	1397	1401	1453	1435

(b) Self-report and attitude (1972–1977 pooled)

Item	+ Category	Proportion plus among:			Trend in Figure 5.1
		Liberals	Conservatives	Difference	
Big cities (NATCITY)	Too little	.628	.438	+ .190	Down
Environment (NATENVIR)	Too little	.678	.492	+ .186	Down
Blacks (NATRACE)	Too little	.404	.224	+ .180	Down
Health (NATHEAL)	Too little	.706	.557	+ .149	Down
Abortion (ABNOMORE)	Yes	.560	.422	+ .138	"Mesa"
Welfare (NATFARE)	Too little	.265	.125	+ .140	Inverted U-shape
Education (NATEDUC)	Too little	.591	.458	+ .133	No change
Military (NATARMS)	Too little, about right	.161	.272	− .111	Up
Foreign aid (NATAID)	Too little	.058	.032	+ .026	No change
Crime (NATCRIME)	Too little about right	.942	.924	+ .018	Constant
Space (NATSPAC)	Too little, about right	.103	.104	− .001	Up
Drugs (NATDRUG)	Too little	.594	.594	.000	Down

nately, the differences are so far from statistical significance (p = .868 for liberal, .556 for conservative) we suffer no compulsion to treat the lines seriously.

Nevertheless, indirect support for a conservative trends appears in the bottom panel of Table 5.3. There we see eight of the priority items are associated with self-description and, among them, the four liberal priorities (cities, environment, blacks, and health) moved down and the one conservative priority, military, moved up.

But Figure 5.2 puts these changes in still another perspective. Despite definitive conservative trends, the rank order of national priority scores in 1978 was much the same as in 1973 (Spearman rank correlation = +.900). Despite the many changes, only two pairs reverse their positions. Military matters no longer take second place to helping blacks, and space now outranks welfare. Save for fighting crime and drug addiction, and liberal goals of environment, cities, health, and environment remained top in priority through the early 1970s.

In sum, if I had to choose a word to summarize the net shifts in Figure 5.1, it would hardly be "liberal," and its converse, "conservative," would not be unjustified; but before one begins to drown in the images of riptides of reaction or compelling currents of conservativism, one should also bear in mind (*a*) three ideological items (education, welfare, and abortion) did not show any directional shift in 1972 through 1978; (*b*) self-identification as liberal or conservative did not show any statistically significant change; (*c*) analyses not reported here suggest that civil liberties items for blacks (as opposed to spending for blacks) were definitely not moving down and were perhaps moving up (see Taylor *et al.* 1978); and (*d*) the essentially liberal rank order of the items remained much the same from 1973 to 1978.

AN UNDERCURRENT OF LIBERALISM?

Qualifications and complexities aside, the 1972 to 1978 trends in marginals don't appear to give much support to the Stouffer demographic hypothesis (Stouffer 1955)—that morticians and school teachers would give us a progressively more progressive climate of opinion.

The hypotheses go like this:

1. Newer generations (more recent birth cohorts) tend to be better educated.
2. Better-educated people tend to be more liberal, regardless of age.
3. Newer generations tend to be more liberal, regardless of education.

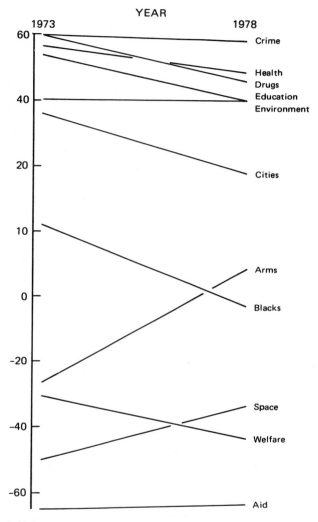

Figure 5.2. Initial and final scores (better–much) for national priority items.

4. Consequently, as newer, better-educated generations replace older generations, the liberal proportion of the population will rise.

The hypothesis was shown to account for about half the increase in liberalism on civil liberties from 1954 to the early 1970s, the remaining half being a shift toward liberalism within all cohort and education categories (Davis 1975b).

To test these ideas for the items in Tables 5.1 and 5.2, I divided the cases into three cohorts, those born in 1918 or before, those born from 1919 to 1938, and those born from 1939 to 1954, arbitrarily splitting the years to give roughly equal groups for the 1972–1978 pooled data. As shown in Table 5.4, the older cohort was in its middle fifties or older during the study period, the middle cohort was "in its forties" and the young cohort was in its twenties and thirties. (For simplicity, respondents born after 1954 were excluded even when they began to turn up in the later years.) Inevitably, cohort composition of the samples changed year-to-year, as shown in Table 5.4. The young cohort comprised .327 of the total in 1972 and .425 in 1978; the older cohort dropped from .321 to .248.

Hypothesis (1), naturally, was well-supported: the proportions with 13 or more years of school running .197, .292, and .422 as one moves from older to middle to young, the proportions with zero to 11 years of schooling running .582, .350, and .189.

As a consequence of cohort change and the cohort–education correlation, the GSS samples improved their levels of education during the

TABLE 5.4
Definition of Cohort Groups

Category	Group			
	Young (born 1939–1954)	Middle (born 1919–1938)	Older (born 1918 or before)	
Age in				
1972	18–33	34–53	54+	
1973	19–34	35–54	55+	
1974	20–35	36–55	56+	
1975	21–36	37–56	57+	
1976	22–37	38–57	58+	
1977	23–38	39–58	59+	
1978	24–39	40–59	60+	
Proportion of cases in [a]				
1972	.327	.352	.321	1.00
1973	.343	.358	.299	1.00
1974	.363	.341	.296	1.00
1975	.372	.338	.290	1.00
1976	.383	.307	.310	1.00
1977	.372	.374	.255	1.00
1978	.425	.327	.248	1.00

[a] Younger cohorts excluded.

TABLE 5.5
Educational Composition of Samples over Time[a]

Year	Years of school completed			Difference 13 + versus 0–11
	0–11	12	13 +	
1972	.398	.319	.283	− .115
1973	.362	.329	.309	− .053
1974	.344	.330	.325	− .019
1975	.358	.334	.308	− .050
1976	.362	.331	.308	− .054
1977	.376	.321	.303	− .073
1978	.323	.339	.338	+ .015

[a] See Table 5.4 for explanation of excluded cases.

6-year period as shown in Table 5.5 In 1972, respondents with zero to 11 years of schooling outnumbered those with 13 or more by more than 10 points (.398 versus .283); in 1978, the categories were just about equal (.323 versus .338). The 1980 GSS will no doubt show the United States to be across an important social watershed— having become a nation in which more adults (age 18 and over) have some college education than have no high shcool diploma.

So far, we have seen that surveys over as short a period as 6 years show definite demographic changes of the sort required by the Stouffer hypothesis.

What about hypotheses 2 and 3? To test them, I:

1. Cross-tabulated education (0–11 versus 12 versus 13 +) by cohort (young versus middle versus older) by opinion by year.
2. Analyzed the results using "d-systems" (Davis 1975a), choosing the following base categories: for cohort, middle; for education, 12 years. That is, for cohort, the setup asked whether young respondents are more liberal (or whatever) than middles and middles more liberal than older—within each year and educational group; for education, it asked whether 13 + s are more liberal than 12s and 12s more liberal than 0–11s—within cohorts and years.

Table 5.6 gives the detailed results. The table may be read as follows:

Consider, for example, cohort and cities (row 4 of part (a) of Table 5.6). The figures + .073*, .036, and .952 mean: (a As weighted average across education categories and years, respondents in the young cohort are + .073 higher than middles on "too little"; (b) the estimated two-sigma confidence interval for that difference is .036; (c) since .073 is larger than .036, the difference is significant, as indicated by the asterisk;

and (d) when we fit a model assuming no interactions for the (d) of +.073, the chance probability for such discrepancies as did turn up is .952, much higher than .05—that is, the interactions are not significant.

The comparisons are defined so that four pluses indicate a consistent association with "youth" or better education. For example, the four pluses for environment and youth indicate that youngs are more likely than middles to say "too little" and less likely to say "too much"; middles are more likely than olders to say "too little" and less likely to say "too much. In other words, younger cohorts are consistently more favorable to environment as a national priority.

To summarize the many details in Table 5.6, I will call an association "present" when (a) at least two differences are significant and (b) the significant differences all have the same sign. Using these criteria, we can sort the outcomes in Table 5.6 into the nine cells of Figure 5.3. Figure 5.3 says

1. Five items are related to both education and cohort. Younger and better-educated respondents give higher priority to the environment, space, and race, lesser priority to arms, and report more favorable financial changes.
2. Two items are related to cohort but not to education. Younger respondents give higher priority to cities and education.
3. One item is related to education but not to cohort. Better-educated respondents are more favorable to abortions.

		Less Favorable	Neither	More Favorable
ASSOCIATION WITH EDUCATION, BETTER EDUCATED ARE . . .	More Favorable		Abortion (curve)	Environment (down) Finances (curve) Race (down) Space (up)
	Neither		Health (down) Crime (no change) Drugs (down) Aid (no change)	Cities (down) Education (no change)
	Less Favorable	Arms (up)		Welfare (curve)

Figure 5.3. Summary of results in Table 5.6.

TABLE 5.6
Cohort, Education, and Opinion Items, 1972–1978[a]

Item	Comparison	Too little			Too much–sign reversed			Average difference –number significant
		Difference	2 Sigma	Interval	Difference	2 Sigma	Interval	
(a) Cohort and opinion, net of education and year								
Space	Young–middle	− .005	.020	.834	− .026	.036	.940	− .001/1
	Middle–older	+ .028*	.018	.294	− .035	.038	.894	
Environment	Young–middle	+ .142*	.036	.908	+ .049*	.018	.907	+ .85/4
	Middle–older	+ .108*	.040	.939	+ .040	.026	.984	
Health	Young–middle	+ .029	.038	.896	− .005	.016	.898	+ .010/0
	Middle–older	− .003	.038	.914	+ .017	.016	.965	
Cities	Young–middle	+ .073*	.036	.952	+ .041*	.024	.962	+ .051/3
	Middle–older	+ .065*	.040	.990	+ .026	.030	.970	
Crime	Young–middle	− .020	.036	.916	+ .009	.016	.948	.000/0
	Middle–older	+ .008	.038	.863	+ .005	.018	.996	
Drugs	Young–middle	+ .017	.036	.944	+ .003	.020	.989	+ .014/0
	Middle–older	+ .029	.040	.978	+ .008	.011	.995	
Education	Young–middle	+ .070*	.036	.068	+ .055*	.020	.243	+ .076/4
	Middle–older	+ .118*	.040	.701	+ .060*	.028	.973	
Race	Young–middle	+ .054*	.034	.999	+ .053*	.032	.521	+ .045/3
	Middle–older	+ .068*	.034	.904	+ .005	.036	.996	
Arms	Young–middle	− .057*	.028	.952	− .066*	.032	.212	− .032/2
	Middle–older	− .001	.032	.991	− .004	.032	.920	
Aid	Young–middle	+ .017*	.012	.958	+ .040*	.032	.982	.014/2
	Middle–older	+ .005	.012	.978	− .006	.036	.954	
Welfare	Young–middle	+ .058*	.026	.282	+ .071*	.036	.974	+ .030/2
	Middle–older	+ .017	.026	.599	− .024	.040	.998	
Finances		Better			Worse (sign reversed)			
	Young–middle	+ .068*	.034	.920	+ .017	.028	.974	+ .043/2
	Middle–older	+ .103	.034	.847	− .015	.030	.429	
Abortion		Yes						
	Young–middle	+ .028	.034	.992	—	—	—	+ .026/0
	Middle–older	+ .025	.036	.751	—	—	—	

[a] See text for detailed explanation
* Significant at the .05 level (estimated sampling variances doubled to compensate for clustering).

TABLE 5.6 (Continued)

Item	Comparison	Too little			Too much–sign reversed			Average difference –number significant
		Difference	2 Sigma	Interval	Difference	2 Sigma	Interval	
		(b) Education and opinion, net of cohort year						
Space	13 + versus 12	+ .073*	.024	.930	+ .148*	.038	.974	+ .092/4
	12 versus 0–11	+ .028*	.018	.948	+ .119*	.038	.985	
Environment	13 + versus 12	+ .072*	.036	.997	+ .010	.018	.897	+ .034/2
	12 versus 0–11	+ .057*	.038	.956	− .003	.022	.981	
Health	13 + versus 12	+ .017	.038	.896	− .005	.016	.924	+ .006/0
	12 versus 0–11	− .003	.038	.902	+ .017	.016	.965	
Cities	13 + versus 12	+ .064*	.038	.995	− .014	.028	.993	+ .017/2
	12 versus 0–11	+ .034	.038	.944	− .015	.026	.829	
Crime	13 + versus 12	− .064*	.036	.916	− .009	.016	.998	+ .001/3
	12 versus 0–11	+ .053*	.036	.758	+ .025*	.018	.918	
Drugs	13 + versus 12	− .059*	.038	.453	− .010	.020	.999	− .017/1
	12 versus 0–11	− .011	.038	.993	+ .013	.020	1.000	
Education	13 + versus 12	+ .063*	.038	.318	+ .007	.020	.963	+ .016/1
	12 versus 0–11	− .007	.038	.542	.000	.022	.848	
Race	13 + versus 12	+ .051*	.034	.612	+ .052*	.032	.882	+ .015/2
	12 versus 0–11	− .033	.034	.919	− .011	.034	.891	
Arms	13 + versus 12	− .024	.028	.997	− .166*	.034	.587	− .065/2
	12 versus 0–11	− .027	.032	.984	− .042*	.032	.356	
Aid	13 + versus 12	+ .010	.012	.970	+ .063*	.034	.442	− .006/3
	12 versus 0–11	− .024*	.012	.998	− .071*	.034	.943	
Welfare	13 + versus 12	− .002	.024	.675	.030	.038	.942	− .049/2
	12 versus 0–11	− .085*	.028	.238	− .139*	.038	.868	
Finances		Better			Worse (sign reversed)			
	13 + versus 12	+ .067*	.034	.734	− .011	.028	.783	+ .058/3
	12 versus 0–11	+ .116	.034	.739	+ .062*	.030	.813	
Abortion		Yes						
	13 + versus 12	+ .160*	.036	.883	—	—	—	+ .134/2
	12 versus 0–11	+ .111*	.036	.975	—	—	—	

4. One item shows a mixed pattern. Younger respondents and the less-well-educated gave higher priority to welfare.
5. Four items—health, drugs, aid, and crime—show no consistent association with either demographic variable.

According to the Stouffer hypothesis then, we should have seen steady *increases* in:

- Priority for environment, which went down—Figure 5.1(a)
- Priority for spending on blacks, which went down—Figure 5.1(a)
- Priority for cities, which went down—Figure 5.1(a)
- Priority for education, which showed no trend—Figure 5.1(b)
- Favorability toward abortion, which showed no net trend—Figure 5.1(c)
- Perceived financial progress, which, if anything, went down—Figure 5.1(c)
- Priority for space, which did go up—Figure 5.1(a)
- A decreased priority for arms, which went up—Figure 5.1(a)

Thus, at first glance, seven of eight items seem flatly to refute the Stouffer hypothesis. But, of mathematical necessity, if cohort and/or education are consistently correlated with a dependent variable, and if cohort composition is changing, then the population must be moving in a progressive direction.

The paradox is quickly resolved by viewing the data as a causal system whose variables are year, birth cohort, education, and liberalism. Figure 5.4 is their flow graph.

The five propositions of the system are represented by these five parameters:

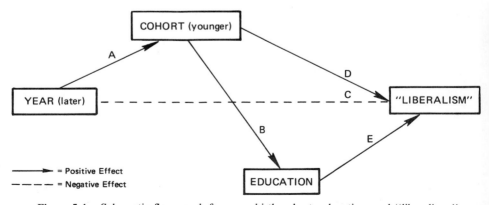

Figure 5.4. Schematic flow graph for year, birth cohort, education, and "liberalism."

A = The later the year the *greater* the proportion from younger cohorts.

B = Within each year, the younger the cohort the *higher* the educational attainment.

C = Within cohort and education combinations, the later the year the *less* proportion liberal.

D = Within year and education combinations, the younger the cohort, the *greater* the liberalism.

E = Within year and cohort combinations, the greater the education, the *greater* the liberalism.

For simplicity, I set the coefficient for year and education to zero, assuming (as can be documented from other studies) within cohort groups the year-to-year changes in educational level among adults are trivially small.

Ignoring the specific statistics temporarily, we can focus on the association between year and liberalism, that is, change in attitude (a 10-point positive association between year and liberalism is the same thing as a 10-point increase in liberalism from $year_1$ to $year_2$). Applying flow graph principles:

$$\text{Change in liberalism} = -C + (A * D) + (A * B * E).$$

In English, the change in liberalism is the sum of:

$-C$ = a negative shift within each cohort and education group

$+(A*D)$ = increased liberalism because later samples tend to have more respondents from younger cohorts and younger cohorts tend to be more liberal, regardless of their educations

$+(A*B*E)$ = increased liberalism because later samples tend to have more respondents from younger cohorts, younger cohorts tend to be better educated regardless of the year, and better-educated respondents tend to be more liberal regardless of year and cohort.

The actual data flow graphs are more complicated since (*a*) cohort and education are trichotomies and (*b*) except for abortion, the dependent variable is an index (too little minus too much, or better minus worse). In the first situation, one presents two of the three categories in the graph, dropping the other (called the "base") to avoid redundancy (see Davis 1975a, for details). In the second, one creates an index by running a positive coefficient of $+1.000$ from too little (better) and a negative coefficient of -1.000 from too much (worse), each running into a compositive variables, little minus much (better minus worse).

Figure 5.5 shows the actual graph with data for change in priority to the environment, 1973 to 1978. In English:

Between 1973 and 1978,

$A1$ = the proportion in the young cohort increases $+.082$;
$A2$ = the proportion in the older cohort decreased $-.051$.

Within each year . . . compared with respondents in the middle cohort: . . . the proportion with 13 or more years of education is . . .

$B1$ = $+.130$ higher in the young cohort;
$B2$ = $-.161$ lower in the young cohort;
. . . the proportion with zero to 11 years of education is . . .
$B3$ = $-.095$ lower in the older cohort.
$B4$ = $+.232$ higher in the older cohort.

Within education and cohort combinations, compared with 1973 respondents, 1978 respondents were:

$C1$ = $-.138$ lower on too little;
$C2$ = $+.034$ higher on too much.

Within year and education combinations, compared with respondents in the middle cohort:

. . . respondents in the young cohort were . . .
$D1$ = $+.142$ higher on too little;
$D2$ = $-.049$ lower on too much.
. . . respondents in the older cohort were . . .
$D3$ = $-.108$ lower on too little;
$D4$ = $+.040$ higher on too much.

Equation (1) now expands like this:

(C) = Direct effect of year
 = $(C1*1) + (C2*-1) = (C1 - C2)$
 = $(-.138) - (+.034) = -.172$
$(A*D)$ = Indirect effect via cohort replacement
 = $(A1*D1*+1) + (A1*D2*-1) + (A2*D3*+1) + (A2*D4*-1)$
 = $[(A1)*(D1 - D2)] + [(A2)*(D3 - D4)]$
 = $(+.082) * [(+.142) - (-.049)] + (-.051) * [(-.108) - (+.040)]$
 = $(+.0157) + (+.0075) = +.0232$
$(A*B*E)$ = Indirect effect via cohort effect on educational composition
 = $(A1*B1*E1*+1) + (A1*B1*E2*-1) + (A1*B2*E3*+1)$
 $+(A1*B2*E4*-1) + (A2*B3*E1*+1) + (A2*B3*E2*-1)$
 $+(A2*B4*E3*+1) + (A2*B4*E4*-1)$

$$= (A1*B1 + A2*B3) * (E1 - E2) + (A1*B2 + A2*B4) *$$
$$(E3 - E4)$$
$$= (+.0155) * (+.082) + (-.0250) * (-.060)$$
$$= +.0028$$

So the total change in the environmental priority index from 1973 to 1978 equals:

1. Stoufferian
   via cohort replacement   +.0232
   via educational composition   +.0028
                                                                    ─────────
                                                                    +.0260
2. Residual, within category change   −.1720
                                                                    ─────────
                                                   Total   −.1460

There is no paradox. Stouffer was right—in that the index was shifted up +.026 by changes in demographic composition; and the pop sociologists are right—in that an additional −.172 drop in environmentalism remains. Of course, the amateurs are more right in that −.172 is a lot bigger than +.02 6.

Table 5.7 shows similar results for the complete set of opinion items. (I left out finances because I think the relationships there represent an aging effect, not a cohort effect.)

As expected, the Stoufferian process has produced definite liberal trends in those items for which Figure 5.3 suggested an association with cohort and/or education. However, just as in the case of environment, the effects are all very small (but reliable, since the constituent coefficients are all highly significant) and generally swamped by the residual changes.

The results lead me to shift metaphors in midstream, as it were. The notion of a conservative tide implies (*a*) everything is going in the same direction (*b*) if we were to wait, things would reverse. Neither is justified by the GSS data. Although small in magnitude, the Stoufferian trend toward liberalism is clearly present in the GSS surveys, even in as short a period as 6 years; furthermore, we have no evidence that the conservative within category (residual) effect will stop or reverse.

Perhaps we can do better by leaving the water and taking to the air. Instead of tides and waves, I think we should invoke the well-known distinction between climate and weather— that is, the difference between long-term changes in climate (ice ages and the like) and the short-run storms and air masses that produce the day's weather.

The GSS results suggest this: The long-term liberal ("warming"?) trend in attitudes and opinions continued through the early 1970s, but

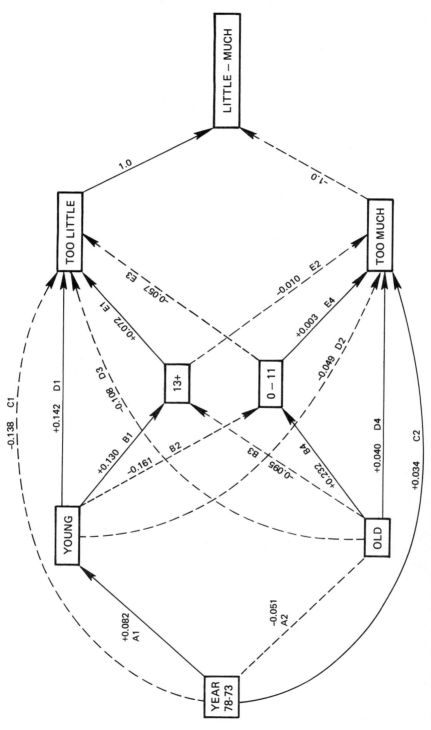

Figure 5.5. Flow graph for change in "Environment," 1973–1978.

TABLE 5.7
Flow Graph Results for Twelve Opinion Items

| Item | Cohort | Change 1973 to 1978[a] due to: | | | |
		Cohort and education	Total indirect	Direct	Total
Environment	+ .0232	+ .0028	+ .0260	− .172	− .146
Education	+ .0193	+ .0010	+ .0203	− .009	+ .011
Cities	+ .0140	+ .0024	+ .0164	− .206	− .190
Arms	− .0103	− .0047	− .0150	+ .345	+ .330
Race[b]	+ .0125	+ .0005	+ .0130	− .159	− .146
Health	+ .0094	+ .0001	+ .0095	− .091	− .082
Abortion[a]	+ .0036	+ .0053	+ .0089	− .016	− .007
Space	+ .0007	+ .0071	+ .0078	+ .137	+ .145
Welfare	+ .0102	− .0050	+ .0052	− .165	− .160
Aid	+ .0046	− .0012	+ .0034	+ .012	+ .015
Drugs	+ .0035	− .0011	+ .0024	− .139	− .137
Crime	− .0002	+ .0008	+ .0006	− .014	− .013

[a] Abortion data are for 1972 to 1978.
[b] Item was asked of whites only, but cohort and education coefficients are based on all races.

politicians and practical opinion analysts were wise to wear policy over-coats and mittens since the attitude and opinion weather was dominated by a large-scale conservative "cold front."

TRACKING THE CONSERVATIVE COLD FRONT

So far, we have looked at overall change without considering subgroup differentials. My sociological imagination tells me we may have been missing some very interesting differences. In particular, it is widely believed new ideas (a) start in the most educated groups and then trickle down to the hoi polloi and (b) start among the flexible young people and then percolate up to their relatively rigid elders. The same data analyzed in Tables 5.6, and 5.7 , and Figure 5.3 enable us to examine these hypotheses.

Actually, the answer appears in Table 5.6 in the columns headed "Interaction." If some group, for example respondents with 13 or more years of education, were first on the block—that is, they changed their opinions before those in other groups—their distance from other groups would vary with time. We might expect the difference between their opinions and others to go up when they begin to change and then to go down when the backwoods persons caught up with their trendy beliefs.

Technically, such a pattern implies lots of interactions in the data (Davis 1978b), that is, difficulty in fitting the data using the same percentage differences in each year.

The figures in the "Interaction" columns in Table 5.6 are probabilities for the 100 chi square tests for interaction. To make the tests, the computer program compared the raw data with the proportions implied by a no-interaction model. If the discrepancy were strong, the probabilities would be small, while, conversely, if the data were devoid of interactions, the discrepancies will be small and the chi square probabilities will be large.

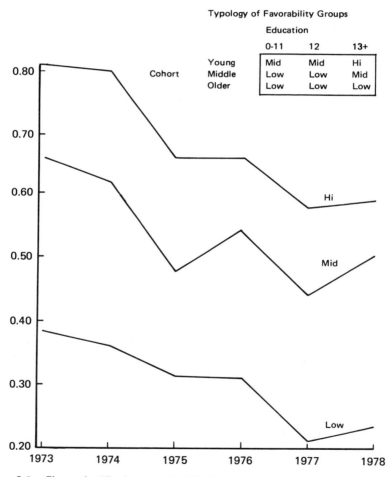

Figure 5.6. Change in "Environment" within favorability groups.

The data in Table 5.6 show a remarkable absence of sociological imagination. None of the 100 chi square tests is significant at the .05 level, the median probability is .920, and 74% of the probabilities are .85 or higher. Granted, it required a large interaction to be statistically significant, and the blanket hypothesis of no interaction at all might conceal some effects (with four variables, for example, it might be that the BCD interaction was nonzero but it got lost because ACD, ABD, and ABCD interactions were so small the hypothesis of no interactions at all came off well); nevertheless, the sample size is nontrivial (8000 or

Figure 5.7. Change in "Finances" within favorability groups.

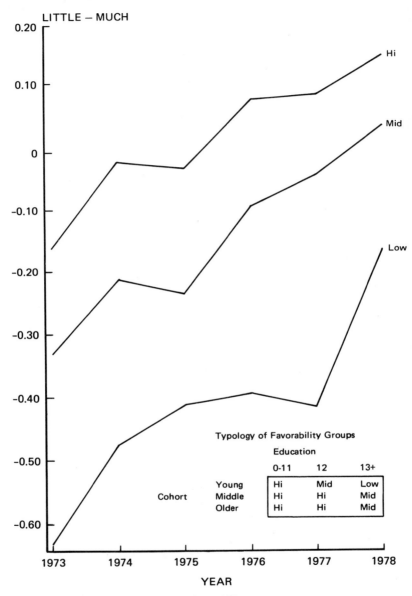

Figure 5.8. Change in "Arms" within favorability groups.

122

more cases per variable) and therefore substantial interactions should show their faces through low probabilities in the chi square tests.

Direct inspection of the data confirms the impression given by the chi square tests. Figures 5.6–5.10 illustrate.

The figures show the trends within subgroups for five arbitrarily selected items. The point is simple and clear. The lines move together, in parallel, the no-interaction property meaning that subgroups maintain a constant distance from each other while each is changing. While all five illustrate this point, two are especially interesting. Figure 5.7 shows— despite claims that recent economic trends have pressed especially hard on the younger cohorts and the middle class—the young, better-educated respondents are consistently the most favorable on financial changes and the older, less well-educated are the least. The "low" group shows the only negative values of the better-minus-worse index for the period 1972 to 1978—but all three subgroups move together, dipping down in 1974 and 1975 and moving upward again in 1976, 1977, and 1978. The economic

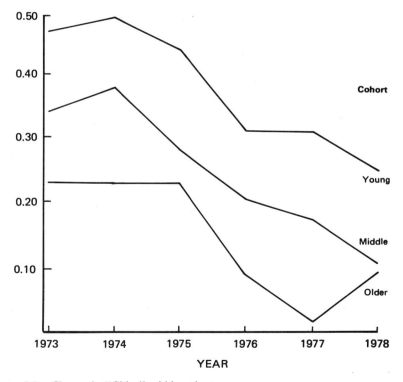

Figure 5.9. Change in "Cities" within cohorts.

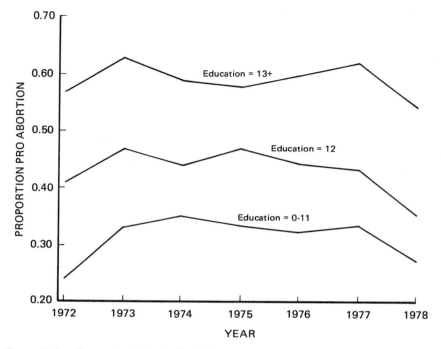

Figure 5.10. Change in "Abortion" within educational groups.

weather of the 1970s seemed to hit all these subgroups at the same time. Figure 5.10 is also of special interest since one might argue in the other cases that the "bellwether" shifts might have occurred before 1972. For abortion, however, the 1978 change was not the continuation of a previous pattern; nevertheless, the three education groups moved together, maintaining virtually constant distances apart.

In sum, the weather of conservativism not only obscured the long-run climatic changes in liberalism, but the sharp change in temperature seems to have hit the various age-education combinations at exactly the same time and with exactly the same strength, producing a remarkably interaction-free set of data that gives no support to the hypotheses about subgroup differences in opinion leadership,

CONCLUSION

During the relatively brief period 1972 to 1978, the GSS managed to show not only striking change (in selected items), but a lopsided combination of two change models operating simultaneously. There is definite evidence for a long-term climatic trend toward liberalism, predicted by Samuel Stouffer in 1954; but these changes are overshadowed by a conservative shift in the weather that appears to have hit both bellwether groups such as the young and the better educated and backwater categories such as the old and poorly educated at about the same time and with the same impact.

APPENDIX

The General Social Survey

The NORC General Social Survey (GSS) is an annual personal interview sampling of the United States adult population funded by the National Science Foundation. Surveys have been completed in 1972, 1973, 1974, 1975, 1976, 1977, and 1978 and additional studies will take place in 1980 and 1982.

SAMPLING

The universe is the total noninstitutionalized English-speaking population of the continental United States, 18 years of age or older, carried out in the late winter (most interviews are carried out in March). In 1972 to 1974, the design was of the modified probability type with quota elements introduced at the final stage. In 1977, 1978, 1980, and 1982, the design is full probability, with predesignated respondents. In 1975 and 1976, random halves of the sample were executed each way. (Although the anticipated significant differences in variances turned up in the experiment, no differences of importance to the vast majority of research users were detected [Stephenson, forthcoming].) Both designs have an average cluster size of five respondents.

Sample sizes average 1520, with a total of 10,652 cases from 1972 to 1978.

CONTENT

The items cover a deliberately wide variety of content: detailed background characteristics with special emphasis on current and parental socioeconomic status; abortion, sex, and sex roles; racial attitudes (mostly limited to whites prior to 1978); morale and satisfaction measures; a vocabulary test; crime and violence; the Stouffer measures of tolerance on nonconformists, etc. Roughly half the items are permanent and appear each year. The others are assigned to one of three rotation schemes arranged so zero-order correlations for any two variables in the plan can be obtained at least every two surveys. Items have been dropped because of extreme marginal distributions and one or two items have been added each year. The 1972 study has fewer variables than the later ones because it had a smaller budget.

Many items are exact replications of questions from one or more prior national surveys, so the time span of analysis can be cast back before 1972, sometimes as far as the 1940s.

DISTRIBUTION

GSS was designed to be placed in the public domain on completion of coding and data processing (usually on July 1 of the same year) to give research workers in a variety of institutions access to recent, high-quality data and to promote standardization in sociological research. Codebooks and data sets are not copyrighted and users are free to copy and/or distribute the materials. Major vendors for the data are the Roper Public Opinion Research Center, Yale University, the Inter-University Consortium for Social and Political Research, University of Michigan; and CONDUIT. In the fall of 1978, the National Opinion Research Center created a cumulative tape and code book of all 10,652 cases, which is sold by the Roper Center for approximately $55.

REFERENCES

Davis, J. A. (1975a) Analyzing contingency tables with linear flow graphs: D systems. Pp. 111–145 in D. Heise, ed., *Sociological Methodology 1976*. San Francisco, Cal.: Jossey-Bass.

Davis, J. A. (1975b) Communism, conformity, cohorts and categories: American tolerance in 1954 and 1972–1973. *American Journal of Sociology* 81(November): 491–513.

Davis, J. A. (1978a) Trends in NORC General Social Survey Items 1972–1977. National Opinion Research Center. GSS Technical Report No. 9.

Davis, J. A. (1978b) Studying categorical data over time. *Social Science Research* 7(June):151–179.

Public Opinion (1979) Vol. 2, No. 2, March/May, 1979.

Range, P. R. (1979) Will He Be the First? *New York Times Magazine*. March 11, 1979.

Stephenson, C. B. (forthcoming) Probability sampling with quotas: An experiment. *Public Opinion Quarterly*.

Stouffer, S. A. (1955) *Communism, Conformity, and Civil Liberties*. Garden City, N.Y.: Doubleday.

Taylor, D. G., Sheatsley, P. B., and Greeley, A. M. (1978) Attitudes toward racial integration. *Scientific American* 238(June):42–49.

chapter **6**

Political Characteristics
of Elderly Cohorts in
the Twenty-First Century[1]

NEAL E. CUTLER

The purpose of this chapter is to identify and discuss political characteristics of elderly cohorts in the early decades of the next century. The task is not to predict which party will be victorious in the presidential election of 2024, but rather to identify factors in a number of different research areas that either directly or indirectly are likely to influence the politics of future cohorts of the elderly.

In general, many of these factors are themselves nonpolitical. Consequently, much of this chapter considers various consequences of secular trends and the recent demographic metabolism of the United States. While some of these factors have been previously identified as being relevant to the politics of aging, some have not, and it is the intent of this chapter to bring a variety of such factors together in a coherent discussion.

The concept of *cohort* is particularly useful and important for a discussion of the political and politically relevant characteristics of the future elderly. While the elderly of tomorrow share with historically prior groups of elderly their chronological location in the life-cycle, the key differences, of course, are found in their historical or generational lo-

[1] The research program of which this paper is a part is supported by National Institute on Aging Grant Number AG00133-02.

AGING
Social Change

cation. That is, all birth cohorts undergo the processes of birth, development, and death. What is important for political analysis is the consideration of the historical and demographic context in which particular birth cohorts experience aging. In short, underlying all sociopolitical cohort analysis is the perhaps too obvious premise that both individual and societal aging is or can be dramatically different in different historical and demographic contexts. The perspective of what we have elsewhere called "political gerontology" is a consideration of aging and political factors in this historical–demographic context (Cutler 1977a).

While it is true that many of the politically relevant characteristics of the future elderly are rooted in the demographic attributes of successive birth cohorts, it is also true that more general societal trends, which are not directly a product of demographic dynamics, are also important. In particular, two such secular trends will be discussed: the increasing educational level of the American population over the past 60 years and the decline in partisanship over the past 20 years. Whether these two trends have been directly accelerated by population trends is outside the scope of this chapter. What is clear, however, is that the various demographic and nondemographic trends, political and nonpolitical factors overlap and interact so as to produce, if not unique, at least different cohort profiles of politically relevant experiences and characteristics. As one way of outlining the topics that are being considered here, a schematic portrayal (Figure 6.1) is presented.

The discussion first considers the consequences of the demographic metabolism of the United States. Since detailed demographic analysis of the older population is available elsewhere, our discussion is a brief overview of the major contours of data describing the growth in the absolute and relative size of the older population, trends in dependency ratios, etc. In considering the genesis of potential frustrations held by the elderly of the first decades of the twenty-first century—frustrations that are likely to take on substantial political significance—we also consider the Easterlin model of economic and fertility cycles. Although fairly well-known in the fields of demography and economics, the relevance of Easterlin's work to social gerontology is only beginning to be appreciated.

The chapter next considers two general nondemographic trends. First, since education has long been found to be a correlate of a range of social and political behaviors, cohort patterns of improvement in educational levels describe cohort patterns of potential political resources. Second, the one manifestly political trends considered here is that of the decline in partisanship within the American electorate. As future cohorts of the elderly are less partisan than prior older cohorts, the political system

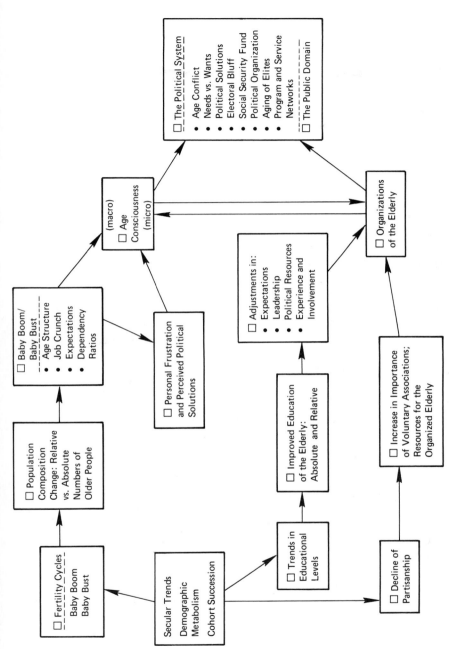

Figure 6.1. Cohort succession, age consciousness, and politics: a heuristic model.

may expect the elderly to organize outside the traditional party structure. Indeed, one of the key intervening concepts in all of the trends outlined in Figure 6.1—demographic metabolism, educational levels, and decline in partisanship—and the political system is that of age consciousness. As the political system (macro analysis) and aging members of specific birth cohorts (micro level) become increasingly age conscious, age will become an increasingly salient dimension of political organization and behavior.

Figure 6.1 is meant to be heuristic, rather than empirically descriptive, and is in no way meant to suggest either a "systems model" of the politics of age, or a complete causal sequence of events. Several aspects of the politics of age are not considered here. Attitudes toward specific clusters of public policies are not included—not because they are unimportant, but because the generational nature of such trends (as contrasted with aging and period explanations) has not been well established. In general, furthermore, the schematic presented in Figure 6.1 represents aggregate or macro analysis. Not included in this discussion, for example, are such individual-level processes as the effects of low fertility on family structure, sibling patterns, and birth order—variables that could be of potential political significance. As we enter the final approximately 230 months of the twentieth century, the time seems appropriate to identify and assess these key factors and trends that research suggests are likely to have substantial impact on the political characteristics of the elderly in the twenty-first century.

DEMOGRAPHIC METABOLISM AND CHANGES IN THE AGE COMPOSITION OF THE POPULATION

As recently as 10 years ago it seemed that only gerontological and demographic specialists were substantially familiar with the dramatic changes that the age structure of the American population is undergoing. The political fallout of the demographic processes was only beginning to be felt. When the decade of the 1960s came to an end, the Administration on Aging and Medicare, both called for by legislation enacted in 1965, were in their infancy. Public discussions of the financial integrity of the social security trust fund were relatively infrequent.

The decade of the 1970s, by contrast, exhibited substantial age consciousness on the part of the American society and government. A national network of local "Area Agencies on Aging" was begun in 1973. The National Institute on Aging was established to give greater visibility and independence to the basic research efforts in aging supported by the federal government. The Congress passed a number of major aging-related pieces of legislation, including pension reform laws, age discrimination laws, and the national abolition of age-based mandatory retirement. Both houses of Congress established permanent committees on aging.

Demographic facts that were somewhat esoteric in the 1960s became known and understood by the mass media and the public in the 1970s. In general, it is now widely recognized that the baby boom of the 1940s and 1950s will represent something of a senior boom in the early decades of the twenty-first century. While such terms as *dependency ratio* and *cohort* may not punctuate cocktail party conversation, the ideas behind these concepts have circulated beyond the halls of academic departments and government planning bureaus.

The demographic portrait of the aging population need not be repainted in great detail here. As a rough sketch, though, we know that in 1870 (when data on the age distribution of the national population began to be reported) the 65 and older age group represented a little over 1% of the population. This had increased to 4% by 1900, and to almost 7% by 1940; the 1970 census reported that 10% of the national population was age 65 or over. This uninterrupted increase in the relative size of the older population is estimated to continue, as it is expected that the proportion of the population represented by the 65 and over age group will be 11% at the turn of the century, 13% by 2020 and in excess of 15% by the middle of the twenty-first century (see Table 6.1).

The same data expressed in absolute numbers of older persons are

TABLE 6.1
Basic U.S. Census Data for Three Age Groups, 1930–2050[a]

	1930	1940	1950	1960	1970	2000	2020	2050
Young (under 18)[b]	47.61	45.31	47.08	64.20	69.64	56.90	50.31	43.79
Work force (18–64)[b]	68.53	77.34	91.95	98.56	113.50	157.15	157.60	134.89
Old (65 +)[b]	6.63	9.02	12.29	16.56	20.07	31.82	45.10	52.31
Total[b]	122.77	131.67	151.32	179.32	203.21	245.87	253.01	230.99
Young (under 18)[c]	38.8	34.4	31.1	35.8	34.3	23.1	19.9	19.0
Work Force (18–64)[c]	55.8	58.7	60.8	55.0	55.9	63.9	62.3	58.4
Old (65 +)[c]	5.4	6.9	8.1	9.2	9.9	12.9	17.8	22.6

[a] Sources: 1930–1940: Bureau of the Census (1943, Table 8, p.26). 1950–1970: Bureau of the Census (1973, Table 37, p.32). 2000–2050: Bureau of the Census (1977, Table 12, p.71).
[b] Numbers given in millions.
[c] Numbers given in percentages.

no less dramatic. In 1940, there were 9 million persons in the 65 and over category. By the 1970 census, this figure had more than doubled to over 20 million. By 2020, it is estimated that another doubling will have taken place, as the 65 and over group will include over 40 million persons.

Not too long ago, most average citizens would have attributed the growing size of the older population to improvements in mortality. Indeed, in introducing the subject of the demographic antecedents of political gerontology to public and student groups over the past several years, I have followed the presentation of the demographic trends with a question concerning the audience's opinion as to whether the causes were to be found primarily in fertility, in mortality, or in migration—the three basic elements of the demographic metabolism. Inevitably, the response has been framed in terms of mortality.

When told the correct answer is found in the dynamics of fertility and not of mortality, many of these groups have quickly pointed out the well-publicized improvements in life expectancy in the United States (Deming and Cutler 1981). After all, if average life expectancy in 1900 was 47.3 years and 70.9 years in 1970, doesn't this "prove" that people are living longer? In fact, of course, those numbers reflect changes in life expectancy at birth, and the improvements are improvements in infant mortality. Improvements in the life expectancy of older persons, while notable, are not so dramatic; life expectancy at age 65 was 11.9 years in 1900 and 15.2 years in 1970.

Thus, the basic facts concerning this country's demographic change have become public knowledge. Evidence of the public nature of these facts and the age consciousness stimulated by them are the various government laws and institutions born in the 1970s, noted earlier. The mass media devote increasing attention to the issue, in both its statistical and its personal side. Indeed, the cover story of *Newsweek,* February 28, 1977, focused on changes in the age composition of the American population; the title of the cover story was "The Graying of America." And in words, pictures, and charts, *Newsweek* told its readership that the "graying of America" was a baby boom (i.e., cohort phenomenon).

The baby boom increase in the absolute and relative numbers of older people in the American population represents one side of the demographic coin. The other side of the coin is represented by the baby bust fertility decline of the 1960s and 1970s. By the beginning of the 1970s, demographers recognized that as a consequence of a number of factors (e.g., availability of birth control, changing value systems concerning family size, increasing female entrance to education and labor force pools), the baby boom years were over and fertility rates had dropped.

Estimates of the age composition of the future population are based on empirical estimates of the survival of already-born cohorts into old age, plus projected estimates of future births (i.e., those persons who would be the younger working population at the time when the baby boom babies are in old age). Among the more plausible assumptions underlying estimates made in the early 1970s was that fertility would decline to the "replacement" fertility rate of 2.10 births per female. On this basis, dependency ratios could be calculated, demonstrating the statistical relationship of one component of the population to another. The old age dependency ratio—the ratio of the 65 and over "dependent group" to the 18–64 "working group"—could be calculated and projected for future years. Using Series E population estimates of the Census Bureau available in the early 1970s, old age dependency ratios reinforced the view that the older population was dramatically increasing within the American population.

In the years during which the baby boom cohorts are in their adolescence and working years, the old age dependency ratios remain fairly stable: .167 in 1960 and .177 in 1970 and 2000. As the baby boom moves into old age in the first decades of the next century, the baby bust cohorts of the low fertility 1960s and 1970s become the working population, and dependency ratios rise accordingly: .213 in 2020 and .257 in 2050.

Yet even these might be underestimates of the relative sizes of the "working" and "dependent" population groups. If the current trend toward earlier retirement continues (but see below for a reconsideration of this assumption), then age 65 becomes an unrealistic basis for the computation of old age dependency ratios. In the 1970s, labor force trends indicated that many workers would rather retire earlier than later, even if this means lowered social security benefits. The average age of new social security retirees thus moved closer to 62 than 65.

Consequently, if we recompute just the 1970 old age dependency ratio, but change the definition form 65+/18–64 to 60+/18–59, we begin to see the potentially dramatic effects of aggregate retirement decisions and practices on the labor force composition. The computational "adjustment" changes the 1970 old age dependency ratio from .177 to .273; this new 1970 dependency ratio is higher than that projected for the year 2050 (.257) using the more traditional 65+/18–64 formula. Consequently, to the degree that political programs, demands, and "backlash" are connected to the relative sizes of the older and the working populations, these simple computations suggest the increasing political salience of the age composition of the population.

The old age dependency ratio is affected by yet another factor, that of increasingly declining fertility. While demographers in the early 1970s noted that fertility had declined to the replacement rate, by the mid-1970s fertility had declined even more. In the same month that *Newsweek* made "The Graying of America" its cover story, the Census Bureau publicly reported that in 1976 American fertility had reached a historical low, being 1.8 births per woman. Consequently, the denominator of the old age dependency ratio in the twenty-first century may be represented by an even smaller population than earlier anticipated.

As is the case with other statistical social indicators, a dependency ratio does not cause social or political situations, but merely reflects underlying demographic patterns, which in turn may reveal the dynamics of social pressure and change. The absolute value of a dependency ratio is, by itself, of little meaning; rather, it provides us with one kind of statistical indicator of recent historical (and possible future) changes. It is, as one analyst recently stated, a "quantitative clue" to underlying social dynamics.

Beyond this, a questioning of the component elements of a statistical social indicator forces us to examine the underlying assumptions concerning the process that the social indicator represents. It is of both factual and heuristic value, therefore, to raise the following three kinds of questions about the old age dependency ratio: First, is it appropriate to focus on an old age dependency ratio, since a very large group of society's dependent population (i.e., children) is not included in the old age dependency ratio? Second, to what extent do quite recent trends in retirement patterns suggest that the numerator (i.e., the older persons) will be getting smaller rather than larger—that is, later retirement rather than early retirement? Third, what role does the possibility of dramatic biomedical developments in life extension technology play in the overall estimate of longevity and the future mix of older and younger persons in American society?

On the first question, it may be argued that any dependency ratio that does not include that component of society's overall obligation including that to children presents a distorted picture of actual dependency. Furthermore, the argument may continue, the aging or graying of American society implies a relatively smaller younger population, and hence the growth in the older population does not itself necessarily mean an increase in overall dependency, but just a shifting of societal emphases and resources. Another version of this argument suggests that the terms *young* and *old* should not be used at all, but simply *workers* and *nonworkers* or a similar ageless distinction.

The use of the old age dependency ratio does not imply, of course, that all older persons are nonworking dependents and that all younger persons (18–64 years old) are in fact employed. Rather, for purposes of comparison using readily available census data, the age groups are used in full recognition that some distortion is present. The more important issue, however, is the use of an old age dependency ratio compared with a total dependency ratio in which both pre-adults and senior citizens are combined; the formula might then be: (under 18 + over 65)/18–64. If one assumes that the financial costs of the younger and older societal dependents are equal and thus directly interchangeable, then it would be important to note the decline in the number of children as the number of old people increases.

Such costs are not directly interchangeable, however, for several reasons. First, except for education, most of the costs of youthful dependency are borne by the family and not by public budgets. While much family care is also provided to old people, major public expenditures (e.g., social security, medicare) directed toward the older population are unequalled in the case of young children. Second, public expenditures for younger persons (mainly education) are typically local and state expenditures for school construction and maintenance and for teacher salaries and pensions. Decline in enrollments will not completely eliminate these expenses. Even if actual dollar savings can be identified, there is no mechanism whereby these local and state government dollars will be automatically transferred to the federal budget, where most of the governmental supports for older persons are located (Storey and Hendricks 1979).

Third, and perhaps most critical, it would be difficult to argue that the dollar cost to public budgets of a younger dependent is equal to the dollar cost of an older dependent. In recent testimony before a joint hearing of the Select Committee on Population and the Select Committee on Aging of the House of Representatives, demographer Donald Cowgill estimated that "support of older people from the public coffers is about three times that going in the direction of support of a child [Cowgill 1978, p. 31]."

Concerning trends in retirement patterns, there is evidence that work and retirement factors and trends might serve to mitigate the incidence of actual overall societal dependency even when the size of the older population is growing. In 1978, the trend of the 1970s toward early retirement appeared to decline. That is, while early retirement continues, the rate has slowed down. In considering this recent trend as a signal for the future, several factors should be briefly noted:

- Federal legislation has prohibited mandatory retirement at age 65 in most occupations in private-sector employment.
- As inflation reduces the value of fixed-income pensions, more and

more older workers want to continue to work rather than retire on
their pension benefits.

- The labor force mix of, roughly stated, blue-collar and white-collar
jobs is changing toward the latter, and it is the blue-collar workers
who have typically indicated a stronger preference for early retirement.
- Future cohorts of older workers have better health and education
levels than prior cohorts of older workers.
- At least three recent government changes in social security rules
are conducive to labor force participation by the elderly and thus
serve to reduce actual dependency.

—The amount of money a social security retiree may earn without
reduction in benefits is being raised.

—The overall exemption of this earnings limitation now held by
workers at age 72 will drop to age 70 in 1982.

—The 1% increase in social security benefits per year for each year
worked beyond age 65 has been raised to 3% per year.

To the degree that these factors and trends continue in the 1980s and
1990s, the computation and interpretation of the old age dependency
ratio will have to be adjusted accordingly.

It was noted earlier that the recent and future growth of the older
population is due primarily to fertility factors rather than to changes in
mortality. Nonetheless, in the past few years there has been a rather
notable decline in old age mortality, which raises the issue of the possible
impact of major breakthroughs in biomedical life extension technologies
on the mixture or ratio of young and old in American society.

Medical and biological experts disagree over the realistic likelihood,
and even the possibility, of major extensions in the life-span within the
next 50 years. For present purposes, however, the question is whether
and to what degree such changes would affect the age composition of
the society. If such a breakthrough did occur, then the numbers of older
persons presented in Table 6.1 would be underestimates of the magnitude
of the graying of American society. Thus, the political consequences of
an aging society, discussed in the later sections of this chapter, are likely
to be even more dramatic if such life extension developments take place
in the next few years and thereby increase the number and proportion
of older persons in the first decades of the twenty-first century.

Despite differences in such predictions among biomedical experts, the
likely impact of this kind of development on the the demography of the
United States is less uncertain. Jacob Siegel, senior demographic statistician for the Bureau of the Census, recently reemphasized that the
increasingly older composition of the population is due primarily to the

postwar baby boom. As to the question of possible biomedical developments that could decrease mortality and thus increase the number and proportion of older persons, Siegel stated: "The research to date also indicates that any reasonable projection of mortality doesn't essentially affect the percentage of the elderly, and that the percent is primarily determined by recent trends in the birth rate and by changes in the number of births long past; that is, 65 years ago [1978, p. 7]."

This overall assessment about the relative percentage of older persons should be tempered, however, with recognition of the increasing numbers of "older old" persons in the population, a phenomenon that was not accurately forecast 10 years ago. As social scientists and policy planners increasingly recognize, defining old age simply as the traditional 65 and older age group is becoming less and less useful. Recent evidence suggests that the 80 and older segment of the population has grown dramatically beyond the estimates of demographers in the past 10 years. Since it is this population of "old-old" that represents the more dependent group, undifferentiated description of the older population (as 65 and older) generally hides the actual proportionate growth of these potentially more dependent older persons.

In recent testimony before the Senate Special Committee on Aging, Harold Sheppard (1978) noted the discrepancy between estimates of the 80 and older group in the year 2000 made in 1970, and the same estimates made in 1977. Decreases in mortality within this older old age group indicate that "by the year 2000, even if there is no further progress in the death rates, we can expect 1,725,000 more Americans 80 and older than we had expected for that year as recently as 1971 [p. 56]."

This discussion of the criticisms and utility of the old age dependency ratio, in light of recent evidence of changing work, retirement, and older old age mortality experience, suggests that our social definitions of old age may evolve chronologically upward over the next 20 years. The social and financial costs of dependency may well accelerate in the next two decades. What this discussion reemphasizes, however, is that stereotypes and images of aging are changing. The social and political concerns of "old age" may well continue to begin at age 60 or 65, since this has been the age threshold that the baby boom cohort has come to recognize as the traditional beginning of old age. Nonetheless, demographers may need to develop a new set of dependency ratios in which the growing proportion of people in their 70s and 80s are accurately portrayed, since this population group more realistically represents the traditional image, and costs, of "old age."

Despite these problems with age-related social indicators, the rough outlines of the future demographic profile of age groups are fairly well known. All of the persons who will be counted among the older population in the early decades of the twenty-first century are already born. Consequently, virtually all of the indicators that are available suggest that the baby boom cohorts of the 1940s and 1950s will age in the context of programs and benefits that will not only cost more but will also have to be financed by the smaller baby bust cohorts of the 1960s and 1970s. It is not surprising, therefore, to find even contemporary critics of domestic federal spending talking in terms of the "graying of the national budget." And, given the demographic dynamics already described, it is not a radical conjecture to say that older cohorts in the twenty-first century will be even more involved in a society characterized by an age consciousness and the politics of age than is currently the situation.

DEMOGRAPHIC METABOLISM AND
THE EASTERLIN MODEL

While the preceding section has discussed something of the futurology of aging and the aged, the primary concern of this chapter is a consideration of the sources and nature of politically relevant characteristics of cohorts of elderly in the first decades of the twenty-first century. One way of considering the cohort *gestalt* of the baby boom–senior boom cohort is by reference to the work of economic demographer Richard Easterlin. Easterlin's work focuses on the cyclical nature of causal interrelationships among age structure of the population, employment rates and opportunities, fertility, and, in keeping with the cyclical orientation of his model, the age structure of the population.

While Easterlin's work has been described as "exciting," "innovative," "a great contribution," and a "tour de force," it has also been described as "ludicrous," "time-bound,' "sexist," "amateurish," and "dubious" (Collins 1979). Obviously, Easterlin's research goes far beyond the narrow concerns of this chapter. Despite his more general theoretical concerns and despite its controversial nature, the Easterlin model is especially relevant to a consideration of the characteristics of the elderly cohorts of the twenty-first century, since much of his work focuses on the context and aggregate experiences of the baby boom cohorts of the 1940s and 1950s.

Of additional gerontological interest, Easterlin's predictions suggest that the accepted wisdom concerning continued decline in fertility may well be overturned in the 1980s and 1990s. If fertility does indeed rise in the last decades of the twentieth century, then estimates concerning the proportion of older persons in the population and similar age-relevant demographic factors will be subject to change. While Easterlin has been doing research on long-term economic–demographic cycles for several years, renewed interest in the work has followed from the delivery (and subsequent publication) of his 1978 presidential address to the Population Association of America: "What Will 1984 Be Like? Socioeconomic Implications of Recent Twists in Age Structure." The publication of the address in *Demography* (Easterlin 1978) and discussion of it in *Psychology Today* (Collins 1979) provide the basis of our reference to it here.

Easterlin argues that a small birth cohort creates a scarcity of younger workers for the labor force; hence members of that smaller cohort will have an easier economic time throughout their life-cycle. There will be more jobs than workers, so jobs will come easier, and the scarcity of younger workers will drive the price of wages up for these cohort members.

Central to the Easterlin model is the impact of this optimistic economic outlook on the fertility behavior of this smaller birth cohort. The entire process of family formation accelerates; marriage rates increase, families have children earlier in their life-cycle, and total fertility increases. Of course, fertility rates can increase to such an extent that a baby boom is caused. Thus, the low fertility or baby bust cohorts of the 1920s and 1930s produced the baby boom of the 1940s and 1950s—aided and extended by war, postwar economic prosperity, etc.

If a relative scarcity of younger workers (i.e., a smaller birth cohort) provides economic well-being and stimulates family formation, the non-scarcity of younger workers found in a large baby boom cohort produces the opposite, according to Easterlin. "In large cohorts, there is a glut of young people in the labor market, the competition for jobs increases, and there is a subjective feeling that times are tough in relation to the aspirations young people formed as children at home [Collins 1979, p. 35]." The subjective feelings that times are tough can have an impact on a fairly broad range of behaviors on the part of the cohort members. Among the affected behaviors that Easterlin empirically considers are divorce, suicide, political alienation, and even the decline in the precollegiate SAT scores.

In terms of the Easterlin model, the most important impact of the perceived tough times on the part of members of the larger birth cohort is on their own family formation and fertility behavior. With jobs more difficult to find, wages lower, and outlooks gloomier, marriages are delayed and fertility declines. The cyclical nature of the Easterlin model can thus be seen across the 1920–1970 period. The smaller cohorts, born in the 1920s and 1930s, produced the baby boom of the 1940s and 1950s.

The later more "crowded" cohorts, with their less optimistic economic outlook, experienced an aggregate decline in fertility (as well as decline in marriage and increase in divorce), and in so doing, produced the baby bust years of the 1960s and 1970s.

The Easterlin research is particularly relevant to this discussion in that it provides a statement concerning the general relationship between the size of a birth cohort and its aggregate psychology. The diminished outlooks, the frustrations that may be manifest in increasing rates of suicide, divorce, and political alienation, all contribute to and are component parts of the aggregate social–psychological aging of the baby boom birth cohorts who will be the senior boom cohorts of the next century. As Easterlin notes directly, "this analysis also shows that a cohort carries its fortunes, good or bad, depending on its size, throughout its life cycle [Easterlin 1978, p. 404]." Its political values as well are so carried.

A final implication of the Easterlin model is relevant to the politics of old age in the early decades of the next century—one that could alter our expectations of the aggregate relationship of young to old, of working to dependent populations. The cyclical analysis of baby bust to baby boom to baby bust over the period 1920–1970 is, roughly speaking, supported by a combination of empirical trend data and a creative matching of the model to the data. Thus, the next prediction of the model is that the current baby bust years of the 1960s and 1970s will lead to increased fertility as the smaller baby bust cohorts begin to benefit from the scarcity of younger workers that characterizes, and fuels, their generation's favorable position.

Most discussion of demographic futures suggests that the current low levels of fertility will continue into the foreseeable future. Such factors as the openness of the occupational structure to women, birth control technology and availability, and evolving value orientations directed at fulfillment outside the traditional family-and-children model—to say nothing of inflation and the desirability of two-income families—all suggest that family formation should continue to be delayed with a concomitant continuation of lowered fertility. Easterlin's cyclical model, to the contrary, predicts an upturn in fertility. And it is here that Easterlin's model had been criticized. For example, it may be true, as Easterlin argues, that the women's movement may have been more the effect of increased female labor force participation than the cause of such participation (Easterlin 1978). Whatever the causal structure of this set of factors, however, societal values and norms may have become fundamentally altered such that when the current baby bust cohorts arrive at the childbearing years, they may not return to the family-versus-career patterns that characterized their grandparents in the baby bust year of the 1920s and 1930s.

If the Easterlin predictions do come to pass, then demographers will have to alter somewhat estimates of the proportion of elderly in the population, as the proportion of babies and younger persons will increase. Trends in dependency ratios, similarly, will have to be recalculated and reassessed. Easterlin does not predict a new baby boom, but only an increase in fertility. And he has identified demographic studies other than his own that yield fertility and labor force predictions consistent with his predictions (if for different theoretical reasons). Consequently, the Easterlin model has yet additional relevance to the research, estimates, and speculations of interest to gerontologists.

COHORT DIFFERENCES IN EDUCATIONAL ATTAINMENT

When the social scientist interested in cohort phenomena moves beyond demographic considerations of population size, structure, and composition, the ground becomes theoretically treacherous. As scholars from a number of disciplines have noted and discussed, the disentanglement of cohort, aging, and historical period effects is difficult (Cutler 1977b, Glenn 1977, Hyman 1972, Riley 1973, Schaie 1977). One characteristic of great importance to an understanding of the potential political orientations and behavior of the elderly—educational attainment—fortunately does not have this ambiguity: recent increases in cohort-specific rates of educational attainment clearly reflect cohort rather than individual aging factors.

Education is important in considering the political behavior of any group, including the aged. Among the strongest and most repeatedly documented generalizations found in the social sciences is the proposition that education is related to social and political involvement (Lipset 1960, Milbrath and Goel 1977, Verba and Nie 1972). The joining of voluntary associations, for example, is strongly related to formal level of educational attainment.[2] While voting is the most common of political behaviors, involvement above and beyond voting is highly correlated with educational level (see Miller and Levitin 1976, Nie et al.). And, as is well known, educational attainment is often a precondition to higher

---

[2] The relationship between socioeconomic status, of which educational level is a critical indicator, and membership in voluntary associations, has been found to be one of the most well-documented relationships in social scientific studies. (For example, see Erbe 1964, Freeman et al. 1957, Hodge and Treiman 1968, Smith and Freedman 1972.)

levels of occupational and income status that, in turn, provide other resources for political interest, involvement, and influence.

As is widely recognized, the average educational level of the American population has been steadily rising over the past 50 years. Given the well-documented relationship between educational attainment and sociopolitical involvement, it is especially important to recognize that this improvement in educational levels has been a clear cohort phenomenon. That is, the rising educational trend is "caused" by the addition to the population of incoming cohorts that are better educated than the cohorts who preceded them. Conversely, the cohorts dying out of the population during this period are substantially less educated than the cohorts entering the system.

These general patterns are illustrated in Table 6.2, which presents the educational distribution for selected age groups over the period 1952–1976; for this illustration, education has been dichotomized as "no education through incomplete high school" versus "complete high school (or equivalence) or higher." Each of the time points coincides with a national presidential election.

The data for the 65 and older group reveal a steady if slow progression toward higher educational levels. The educational levels of the total population have improved at a somewhat faster rate. The source of aggregate change in cohort terms may be seen through an examination of the trend in educational levels for the youngest age group (i.e., the entering "political" cohort for each election year). At mid-century, only

TABLE 6.2
Educational Composition of Selected Age Groups[ab]

Age group	1952		1956		1960		1964		1968		1972		1976	
	Low	High	Low	High	Low	High	Low	High	Low	High	Low	High	Low	High
21–24	45	55	33	67	39	61	30	70	19	81	14	86	1	99
25–34	47	53	34	66	36	64	29	71	21	79	22	78	3	97
35–44	58	42	48	52	36	64	34	66	34	66	26	74	8	92
45–54	67	33	59	42	47	53	50	50	39	61	40	60	13	87
55–64	76	24	65	35	68	32	62	38	55	45	55	45	29	71
65 and older	81	19	78	22	71	29	67	33	71	29	70	30	48	52
Total	62	38	51	49	48	52	45	55	41	59	38	62	18	82

[a] Each year was taken from the University of Michigan Center for Political Studies presidential election national survey. The data were provided by Inter-University Consortium for Political and Social Research through the USC Political and Social Data Laboratory.

[b] Low education is defined as no education through incomplete high school. High Education is complete high school (or equivalence) and higher.

slightly more than half the youngest cohort had a "high" education. A quarter of a century later, the trend had virtually reached its limit, as almost 100% of the entering cohort had at least a high school education.

Given the cohort-specific nature of the educational trends, we can return to the question of the political resources of the future elderly by estimating the educational level of older people in the first decades of the twenty-first century. The 21–24 age group in the 1976 sample will all be at least 65 years old by the year 2020, demonstrating that the future elderly will be much better educated than even the older group of a few years ago. While less than one-fifth of the 65 and older age group in 1952 had a "high" level of educational attainment, by 2020 almost all of the 65 and older group will have that level of education— a rather substantial reversal. While not all educated people will be actively involved in politics, the educational resources for involvement and activity will certainly be greater for tomorrow's older population than it has been in the past.

While these data suggest that the future elderly will have markedly improved educational levels compared with those of previous elderly cohorts, a recent analysis by Palmore (1976) indicates that the future elderly will also be better off in terms of the relative status of the old as compared with younger age groups. Palmore argues that not only is the educational status of the old improving, but also the disparity between young and old is diminishing. This was not always the case, however. In an earlier analysis of the period 1940–1969, Palmore and Whittington (1971) found that although the educational status of the elderly was improving in absolute terms, such gains did not keep pace with the gains being made by the 14–64 age category; thus, the relative status of the older group declined.

In projecting relative educational status gains for the period 1970–1994, however, Palmore found that the elderly do in fact gain both in absolute and relative terms. Although Palmore does not present his data as such, his findings are the logical outgrowth of the dynamics of cohort succession. As the patterns in Table 6.2 suggest, in the 1950s through the 1970s the most dramatic educational improvements are for the entering cohorts. Between now and the end of this century, however, the entering cohorts will not improve at the same high rate as in the preceding 25 years. Thus, the accumulation of educational gain for the older cohorts will represent net gains in the relative status of the elderly. In political terms, this is significant in that to the degree that educational levels do indeed represent political resources, the twenty-first century will not exhibit the educational disparity between young and old that has characterized most of the twentieth century.

POLITICAL ORIENTATIONS OF
FUTURE ELDERLY COHORTS:
THE EROSION OF PARTISANSHIP

Throughout almost three decades of systematic empirical research concerning the political behavior of the American population, the dominant mechanism by which members of the public have found to orient their various policy attitudes and vote decision has been that of partisanship, a social–psychological identification with one of the two major political parties. Although issues, candidates, and campaign–media strategies in specific elections have at times lowered the importance of partisanship, in general party symbols have been the single most important mode by which members of the political system organize their political orientations (Campbell *et al.* 1960).

Evidence is accumulating, however, that strongly suggests that partisanship is declining, and that the decline reflects pervasive generational cohort change in the American political system. This is particularly germane to the present discussion, for if future cohorts of elderly do not organize their political tendencies in partisan terms, other forms of political orientation, both psychological and organizational, are likely to emerge. Furthermore, although any kind of prediction about future politics is hazardous, the evidence of the cohort-based demographic changes previously summarized suggests that age factors may well become a major set of orientations on the domestic American political scene in the twenty-first century.

Partisanship is one of the few areas of political behavior research that has been empirically studied with sufficient frequency and regularity, and with consistent operational definitions over time, to warrant the drawing of empirically guided conclusions about trends. Furthermore, within the study of partisanship, there has ben a significant, recurring interest in the question of age, aging, and cohort succession. Indeed, as will be noted shortly, age and cohort studies of partisanship have included cross-sectional, time-sequential, panel, and even cross-national research designs.

One of the earlier statements in this area was based on an age analysis of cross-sectional data collected in the 1950s. The authors of the now classic *The American Voter* suggested that the politics of the New Deal had produced a generational effect on new voters of that period, such that in the 1950s, when those voters were in the middle of their life-cycle, they were more Democratic in orientation than would be expected given the Republican climate of the 1950s (Campbell *et al.* 1960). This conclusion, however, might be thought of as "cohort specific," and the generality of cohort versus aging effects remained to be established using more appropriate longitudinal data bases.

One early (and unfortunately widely cited) study of this kind argued that the processes of aging produce a conversion to political conservatism. The study focused on an analysis of the relationship between age and identification with the Republican party as found in a sequence of cross-sectional Gallup polls taken at 4-year intervals from 1946 through 1958. While the analysis concluded that the data demonstrated a linear change in the conservative direction as a function of aging, I have demonstrated that such a conclusion was not supportable when the data were reanalyzed using the appropriate techniques of cohort analysis (Crittenden 1962, Cutler 1969, reprinted in Kirkpatrick 1974).

A later study (Glenn and Hefner 1972) focused on the same set of analytic issues but used a much more expansive data base (surveys taken at 4-year intervals from 1945 to 1959), a formal cohort analysis methodology, appropriate controls for sex and education, and statistical corrections for the underrepresentation of lower-class respondents found in the early Gallup polls. The authors concluded that "this study should rather conclusively lay to rest the once prevalent belief that the aging process has been an important influence for Republicanism in the United States [pp. 31–47]."

While these studies demonstrate that cohort effects are stronger than aging effects in understanding the *direction* of partisanship, of greater relevance to the present discussion is the question of trends in the decline of partisanship in general—that is, a decline in the public's identification with either party. A first complication in this question is the fact that, descriptively, in cross-sectional tabulations, older age groups are more strongly partisan than younger age groups, and this descriptive generalization holds for the past three decades.

An innovative analysis based on a survey of the British electorate in the mid-1960s discovered that it is not aging per se but a variable confounded with aging that appears to be responsible for the descriptive relationship between age and strength of partisanship. Butler and Stokes (1969) hypothesized that the key variable in explaining strength of partisanship is the length of time that a person maintains that partisanship: The longer it is held, the stronger the attachment becomes. The analytic problem, of course, is that for people who do not change their partisan attachments, age and duration of partisanship progress together.

In their British study, consequently, Butler and Stokes (1969) divided the sample into those who had changed their party affiliation in the past 10 years and those who had not, and then examined the relationship between age and partisan strength for each group. They found, as hypothesized, that age was not ubiquitously related to strength of partisanship. Within the group of changers, all age groups were equally weak in their partisanship.

A similar conclusion, pertaining to the lack of age patterns in strength of partisanship, was derived from a trend study of American elections (Cutler 1976). In a study of the 1964, 1968, and 1972 national elections, I examined age distributions in five measures of partisan flexibility (partisanship versus presidential vote, presidential vote versus congressional vote, presidential vote in current versus previous election, straight versus split ticket voting at state and local level, and preelection presidential preference versus actual vote). While there were interesting variations among age groups and across the three elections, "In general it should be concluded that older voters are not characterized by less partisan flexibility than the rest of the electorate [p. 34]."

Thus far the evidence supports two conclusions: The first, descriptively, is that variations in chronological age are associated with variations in partisanship; the second, analytically, is that there is no evidence for interpreting such patterns in aging or developmental terms. That is, it does not appear that the middle or later years of the life-cycle bring about inevitable changes either in the direction or strength of partisanship.

Given the proposition that aging does not appear to account for substantial differences in partisanship, what, then, of the other major interpretation of chronological age differences, that of cohort or generational effects? This question is especially germane to the present discussion as we attempt to describe the likely orientation to political issues of future cohorts of the elderly. Three elaborate studies, each using different data bases, provide evidence supportive of the cohort interpretation of declining partisanship in the United States. The first two are time-sequential cohort studies based on multiple cross-sectional data sets; the third is a nationally representative panel study.

In the earlier cited analysis of national Gallup polls spanning the period 1945–1969, Glenn and Hefner (1972) noted increasing independence (i.e., lack of identification with either major party) in the 1965–1969 period. The analytic question posed above—whether age group differences reflect changes caused by the aging process—was answered in the negative: "Apparently, the different cohorts were not responding to different stimuli arising from different stages of the aging process." And while they suggest that their data are not definitive, it is concluded that "the older cohorts, as aggregates, always had stronger party identification than the younger cohorts, probably because their early political socialization occurred when the two major parties were more salient in American life [p. 43, 44]."

A much more definitive conclusion in the same direction is provided by Abramson's (1976) cohort analysis of the sequence of National Election Studies conducted by Michigan's Center for Political Studies (CPS) over the period 1952–1974, and encompassing all 11 of the presidential and mid-term congressional elections of that period.[3] Abramson analyzed partisanship in several ways, contrasting partisans versus independents, and within those who did identify with one of the two parties, strong partisans versus weak partisans. All of the analysis pointed to substantially lower levels of partisanship among the more recent cohorts. The cohort analytic logic and design of the analysis led Abramson to the following conclusion: "The low level of partisan identification among young Americans appears to result from fundamental differences between the formative socialization of persons who entered the electorate during the postwar years and that of their elders. . . . the overall decline in party identification results largely from generational change [p. 469]."

In 1965 Jennings and Niemi conducted an interview study with a nationally representative sample of high school seniors; separate interviews were held with the parents of the student respondents. Eight years later, the dual sample was reinterviewed with a 67% and 72% completion rate for the student and parent samples, providing an unbiased representative panel subset of the original sample. Among the variables studied was partisanship, and given the maturational emphasis of the study, aging effects were a major focus of the analysis (Jennings and Niemi 1975).

Based on previous theory and research, the authors expected partisanship to increase in the student sample over the 8-year period, as youthful independence and lack of involvement in partisan electoral decisions would respond to the presidential and congressional elections to which they were exposed. The parent or adult sample would then act as a kind of social–biological control, as their partisanship would also have been exposed to the events of the 8-year period. In short, this

---

[3] The standard measure of party identification developed by Michigan's Center for Political Studies, used in their National Election Studies since the early 1950s, and employed in hundreds of other studies as well, is based on a pair of questions: (1) Do you consider yourself to be a Republican, a Democrat, an Independent, or what? (2) If the respondent said Republican or Democrat, the second question was: Would you say that you are a strong (D or R) or weak (D or R). Independents were also "pushed" a bit further in terms of their potential partisanship; if "independent," the second question was: Would you say that you lean more toward the Democrats or toward the Republicans. Consequently, a 7-point scale is available: Strong Democrat, Weak Democrat, Independent-Lean Democrat, Independent, Independent-Lean Republican, Weak Republican, and Strong Republican. In much research, the "independent leaners" are simply combined with the "pure independents."

national panel study would be able to directly test the life-cycle hypothesis that people become more partisan as they mature.

In fact, while in the aggregate the parents' partisanship remained stable over the 8-year period, the students became less, not more, partisan:

> The change in the partisan distribution of the filial generation between 1965 and 1973 is startling. The proportion of Independents, already high in 1965, rose another 12 percent, to include almost half the sample. At the same time, the proportion of strong identifiers was cut nearly in half. Such an increase in the proportion of Independents at a time in the life cycle when we would ordinarily have expected the beginning of a long term decline, provides a compelling argument for a generation effect [p. 1325].

At this point in the development of research on trends in American partisanship, there appears to be substantial evidence that the well-documented relationship of chronological age to partisanship is a generational cohort phenomenon. Although the contemporary elderly in general have high levels of partisanship, this reflects their own generationally based socialization experiences, not the influence of the aging process. And, while it is not usually appropriate to suggest trend extrapolations from cross-sectional age data, the burden of the research evidence suggests that this prohibition is lessened for the case of partisanship. With this in mind, then, what is the prognosis for the partisanship of the older population in the early decades of the twenty-first century?

Table 6.3 presents age distributions of partisanship based on the 1976 National Election Survey. Using the standard measures, we computed two indicators of partisanship: (1) partisan identifiers versus independents, and (2) within each of the two major American parties, strong versus weak identifiers. Although partisans substantially outnumber independents, the youngest age group in 1976 has twice as many independents as the 65 and older age group.

When those respondents in the "partisan" column are arrayed in terms of the strength of their attachment to either of the two major parties, we see that weak attachment, in 1976, outdistances strong attachment in all age groups. The pattern is especially notable among the younger age cohorts. It is also interesting to note that the age pattern in strong versus weak attachments is generalizable across both Republican and Democratic parties, although strong identification is more infrequent among Democrats than among Republicans.

Finally, we should note (as was done in connection with the educational data presented in Table 6.2) that the youngest age group in the 1976 data will all be in the 65 and older category by the year 2020. To the degree that such an extrapolation does indeed point to the future

TABLE 6.3

Age Distribution of Partisanship, Independents, and Strength of Partisanship, 1976[a]

	All respondents			Democratic identifiers			Republican identifiers		
	Indepen- dents	Parti- sans		Strong	Weak		Strong	Weak	
21–24	32	68	(388)	18	82	(195)	29	71	(68)
25–34	31	69	(686)	20	80	(351)	28	72	(123)
35–44	28	72	(419)	23	77	(207)	37	63	(96)
45–54	20	80	(398)	33	67	(217)	43	57	(102)
55–64	18	82	(404)	38	62	(224)	40	60	(110)
65 and older	16	84	(508)	41	59	(267)	47	53	(159)
Total	25	75	(2802)	29	71	(1459)	38	62	(656)

[a] From University of Michigan, Center for Political Studies, 1976 National Election Survey. Data were provided by the Inter-University Consortium for Political and Social Research through the USC Political and Social Data Laboratory. (Age group N's given in parentheses.)

nature of partisanship among the older cohorts of the next century, it is apparent that the political party attachment will not be the major mechanism by which the older population will be oriented toward politics. At the very least, it must be concluded that the older cohorts of tomorrow will be rather different from the older cohorts of the present time.

In sum, although social scientists have not analytically solved the "cohort analysis problem" (i.e., the ambiguity of cohort, age, and period effects in the interpretation of a specific set of observed age differences) in the case of political partisanship the results are relatively clear. All of the analyses reviewed here suggest that partisanship is declining in the United States, and that this decline can be traced to a generational cohort mechanism. More specifically, data from a variety of studies cumulatively suggest that the young cohorts entering the American political system since the mid-1960s are substantially less partisan than the cohorts who preceded them. Since several analyses suggest that this has been a cohort rather than an aging phenomenon, the most appropriate conclusion, and prediction, is that as these younger cohorts age, they will remain less partisan in their political orientations than historically prior cohorts.

Despite the general agreement of the various studies, it is important to note that the cohort-based conclusion does not unequivocally state that a new partisan upsurge cannot take place in future years. A realignment of the political parties could take place so that the less partisan younger persons of today could become more partisan middle-aged persons in the first decades of the next century. Cohort analysis does not suggest that social and political attitudes are absolutely fixed in adolescence and young adulthood.

What the cohort-oriented studies of partisanship do suggest, however, is that when these younger cohorts reach middle age and old age, they will have experienced youthful political socialization environments substantially different from their parents. While their parents may have been raised in the partisan-charged years of the Depression, these younger members of the political system will have had their early political exposure in the weak (if not anti-) partisan era of the 1960s and 1970s. Consequently, any rebirth of partisanship that does take place in the next 20 years or so will do so within the context of a relatively weak level of partisanship within the younger population. This set of factors, then, provides the context in which it may be reasonably argued that forms of political orientation (such as age) other than the traditional party structures may well emerge in the early decades of the next century.

THE ORGANIZED ELDERLY AND AGE CONSCIOUSNESS

The preceding discussion has noted that as a consequence of the historical alteration of high and low fertility periods, the first decades of the twenty-first century will be characterized by a relatively large old age population and, simultaneously, by a relatively small younger working population. While these population estimates do not inevitably predict age conflict, certainly the stage is set for political controversy in which the needs and demands of different age groups will play a significant role.

It has also been suggested that senior citizens in these early years of the next century should be understood not simply as an age category but as a generational cohort. In this context, we should recognize that elderly cohorts of the early twenty-first century will be the survivors of the politically involved and experienced baby boom cohorts of the 1940s and 1950s. This group has witnessed and been involved in such sociopolitical experiences as the civil rights movement, the Vietnam war, the women's movement, Watergate, other minority rights and liberation movement, and similar public political events.

In the aggregate, furthermore, tomorrow's elderly cohorts will be better educated than the elderly of today, and indeed, will have higher levels of formal education than the elderly of any period in the country's history. At the same time, research demonstrates that current tendencies in the political behavior of the American electorate are linked to the dynamics of the generational cohort process. In particular we find a decreasing reliance on traditional political party allegiances as the primary mechanism by which the public organizes its political orientations and chooses its leaders.

Thus, the elderly cohorts of the not-too-distant future will be markedly different from past elderly cohorts in terms of demography, socioeconomic status, and partisanship. Yet there is another cohort-related factor of potentially greater relevance to the politics of age in the twenty-first century than those already considered: age consciousness.

As noted at the beginning of this chapter, it is only within the past decade that the United States has begun to take societal cognizance of the changing age structure of the population and its potential impact on economics, social organization, and politics. As a result, contemporary older persons were already in their older years when society began to develop programs and institutions for the elderly. By contrast, tomorrow's elderly are already being socialized to the potential politics of age. To put this another way, one of the most dramatic contrasts between the elderly of today and the generational cohorts who will constitute the elderly of tomorrow is the portion of their life-span in which they and the society in which they live have been age conscious.

In a most important essay on this subject, sociologist Matilda White Riley outlined the nature of age consciousness at both the individual and societal levels of analysis (Riley 1971). Perhaps the best way to conceive of age consciousness, she suggests, is by analogy to class consciousness: Every individual may be objectively described in terms of his social class (e.g., in terms of income, occupation, education, etc.). At the same time, however, an individual may not be conscious of that social class location or attribute. Furthermore, even if the individual is generally aware of some kind of social class "belongingness," the individual may not act socially or politically on the basis of that subjectively held class consciousness; that is, it may simply not be important to that individual.

What is said about the individual and social class can also be said about society as a whole. That is, every society can be said to have some kind of class structure, but all societies are not equally conscious of that structure. And, as with individuals, even if a society recognizes the class structure, it may not behave in a class-conscious fashion; that is, class may not be a major source or basis of socioeconomic and political organization and conflict. In sum, while all individuals and societies have social class attributes, it is only under some historical situations that these attributes become a basis for individual identification and action and social organization and possible conflict.

It is in this context, Riley reasons, that class consciousness and age consciousness are analogous. Every individual has an age. Yet it is not always the case that individuals identify themselves in terms of their age. And, furthermore, even when such identification is present, it is not always the case that such identification is the basis for individual or collective action. The societal analogy is also relevant. All societies have an age structure, but it is only under certain conditions that age structure stimulates societal age consciousness, and similarly, only under certain historical conditions in which societal age consciousness becomes translated in sociopolitical organization and conflict.

As the United States has moved into the final quarter of the present century, we have begun to witness the increasing evolution of societal age consciousness. As noted earlier, the number and scale of governmental programs, laws, and institutions of direct relevance to the elderly have multipled substantially. There can be little question but that the demographic dynamics of alternating baby boom and baby bust are in large part responsible for this increasing societal age consciousness. Simultaneously, the political consciousness and aggregate experiences of the baby boom cohorts of the 1940s and 1950s have interacted with the demographic dynamics to stimulate and enhance age consciousness for both the individual members of the cohorts and the larger society that is beginning to respond to them.

To say that the interaction of demography and politics produces a politically relevant age consciousness is not to argue, however, that the inevitable outcome is intense conflict between old and young. Foner (1974) argues that just as the age stratification of society can produce tensions, there are two distinct mechanisms that serve to reduce age-related conflict. First, in age-heterogeneous groups, such as church and work organizations, the goals and interests of the group itself may override the members' age differences on political matters. Second, the inevitability of aging implies that, since during their lifetime all persons experience youth, adulthood, and old age, each group thereby has the experiential base for empathizing with the other. In these ways, Foner concludes, although the dynamics of age stratification produce a strong potential for age-based political conflict, "at the same time there are age-related mechanisms for reducing sharp age struggles [p. 194].

Consideration of the conflict-reducing potential of age-heterogeneous groups and voluntary associations suggests that the role of age-homogeneous organizations should also be examined. Indeed, in the evolving politics of age, there is evidence that social and political organization not only reflects age consciousness, but is a significant part of the dynamic process that encourages its development.

Pratt's research on the "gray lobby" in the United States (Pratt 1974, 1976) notes that historically previous organizations of the elderly did not have lasting political impact for two major reasons. Such organizations were either organized around a single issue, and then dissipated when the issue was absorbed by the major political parties and institutions, or were organized around a single personality, and then dissipated when that individual left the scene.

By contrast, modern associations of the elderly have different organizational bases. The larger associations are neither single-issue groups nor are they dependent on the organizational energies of a single charismatic older leader. The two largest associations, the National Council of Senior Citizens (NCSC) and the American Association of Retired Persons (AARP), for example, have national membership constituencies that number in the millions, and are organizationally linked to other, non-age organizations. Such linkages, in turn, can provide several valuable (and politically relevant) resources, including middle-level leadership and bureaucratic structure, access to political institutions, and financial resources in addition to those provided by the older membership.

The political involvement of the NCSC and the AARP is substantial. Each maintains extensive offices involved in the analysis and drafting of legislation, predominantly at the federal level but also in selected state capitals. Political mobilization and information dissemination is accomplished through national networks of local organizations, chapters, and affiliates. Both national organizations are involved in substantial mass direct mail operations.

The "circulation of elites" is also apparent between national government and these organizations. For example, Nelson Cruikshank, longtime president of the NCSC, had previously been the head of the AFL-CIO's Department of Social Security and was later the President's White House counselor on aging. John Martin, U.S. Commissioner of Aging in the Nixon Administration, is currently a senior analyst at the AARP national headquarters. Bernard Nash, executive director of AARP for 5 years in the early 1970s, was previously assistant to the Commissioner on Aging during the Johnson Administration.

Despite the mixture of social and political concerns that are of interest to NCSC and AARP, the monthly newsletters of both organizations are predominantly political in content. The front pages of both monthly newsletters are virtually devoted to legislative and executive decisions, proposed, pending, or completed, at the national level. News of state policies and laws are also reported, although not with the same frequency or intensity as are national political happenings. Although the thousands of older persons who join these organizations each week may be primarily interested in the specific programs and services provided, an important consequence of their membership is the continuous stream of information that is received describing the role of politics in the issues of importance to the lives of older persons. Although systematic research in this area is just beginning, there is some indication that the involvement by older persons in even nonpolitical groups, clubs, and associations tends to increase their political involvement and perception of old age issues in political terms (Trela 1971, Cutler and Mimms 1977).

This latter point brings us back to the issue that began this section of the discussion: age consciousness. While we know of no empirical research concerning the long-term effects of the information materials continuously disseminated by national associations to their millions of older members, the likely effect is to promote age consciousness, that is, to promote the subjective feeling among older persons that they are part of an age-based collectivity, that the problems and frustrations that they face are experienced also by thousands or even millions of other older persons, and that some part of the solutions, remedies, and resources may be found in collective social and political activity. While the causes of emerging age consciousness are still to be identified, recent research has begun to explore the contours and implications of age consciousness among older persons in the United States.

Most of the published studies of age consciousness, or what we have called "subjective age identification," have focused on small or unique samples (Peters 1971, Cutler 1981a). Our own research in this area, however, explores the antecedents and correlates of age identification as measured in recent representative samples of the national population of the United States. When chronologically older persons are divided into those who subjectively identify themselves as old and those who do not possess any predominant age identification, a variety of socio-economic attitudinal differences can be seen. For example, of those aged 60 and over in a 1972 national sample, the subjectively old were found to be more liberal on traditional "New Deal" kinds of scope-of-federal-government issues, more conservative on contemporary issues of social importance (e.g., abortion, marijuana, women's liberation), and more pessimistic with respect to their own and the society's future economic well-being (Cutler 1981b).

At this stage in the research on age consciousness, it cannot be said for certain if the attitudinal patterns uncovered are relatively enduring or simply reflect period effects. What the political attitude research does reveal, however, is that age consciousness does appear to represent an important nonchronological dimension of aging that is of substantial potential relevance in understanding the political manifestations of an aging society. As additional nationally representative studies incorporate measures of age consciousness, we can begin to document and untangle the cohort, aging, and period effects that affect the correlates of age identification.

One challenge to the importance of the concept of age consciousness in contemporary society suggests that it is nothing more than a subjective psychological surrogate for various "disadvantaged" statuses (e.g., poverty, widowhood, retirement). Indeed, in some earlier research, an identification by old persons as old was itself conceptualized as a measure of maladjustment on the grounds that a well-adjusted older person would not identify himself as old (Phillips 1957).

More recent research, and research that is methodologically more sophisticated, however, has documented the proposition that age identification per se is empirically distinct from such potential correlates as low self-esteem, negative evaluations of old age, etc. (Brubaker and Powers 1976, Ward 1977). An analysis of the 1972 national sample mentioned earlier employed multiple regression techniques to examine the combined impact of chronological age, widowhood, retirement, sex, income, education, and subjective social class identification on age identification to test the hypothesis that age identification was nothing more than a surrogate for "disadvantaged status." Among respondents aged 50 and over, the analysis revealed that all of the predictors combined yield a Multiple R of only .295, or 8.6 % of the explained variance (Cutler 1975). While this research does not indicate what the precise antecedents of individual age consciousness are, it is clear that it is something more than the sum of indicators of the negative aspects of old age.

Although it remains for future research efforts to trace trends and casual patterns in age consciousness, one historical distinction is already evident: As suggested earlier, perhaps the most significant difference between contemporary elderly and future elderly cohorts is the proportion of their lives during which they will have lived in an age-conscious society. In sum, there is ample reason to believe that future cohorts of the elderly will be substantially more age-conscious than contemporary older persons, and that the society of the first decades of the twenty-first century will be substantially concerned with politics of age.

REFERENCES

Abramson, P. R. (1976) Generational change and the decline of party identification in America: 1951–1974. *American Political Science Review* 70:469.

Brubaker, T. H., and Powers, E. A. (1976) The stereotype of "old"—a review and alternative approach. *Journal of Gerontology* 31:441–447.

Bureau of the Census (1943) *U.S. Census of Population: 1940.* Volume II, Characteristics of the Population. Washington, D.C.: U.S. Department of Commerce.

Bureau of the Census (1973) *Statistical Abstract of the United States: 1972.* Washington, D.C.: U.S. Department of Commerce.

Bureau of the Census (1977) *Projections of the Population of the United States: 1977–2050.* Current Population Reports, Series P-25, No. 704. Washington, D.C.: U.S. Department of Commerce.

Butler, D., and Stokes, D. E. (1969) *Political Change in Britain.* New York: St. Martin's Press.

Campbell, A., Converse, P. E., Miller, W. E., and Stokes, D. E. (1960) *The American Voter.* New York: John Wiley and Sons.

Collins, G. (1979) The good news about 1984. *Psychology Today* (January):34–48.

Cowgill, D. (1978) Testimony given in Consequences of Changing U.S. Population: Demographics of Aging. Joint Hearing before the Select Committee on Population and the Select Committee on Aging, U.S. House of Representatives, 95th Congress, Second Session, Volume I, May 24, 1978.

Crittenden, J. A. (1962) Aging and party affiliation. *Public Opinion Quarterly* 26:648–657.

Cutler, N. E. (1969) Generation, maturation, and party affiliation: A cohort analysis. *Public Opinion Quarterly* 33:583–588.

Cutler, N. E. (1975) Socioeconomic Predictors of Subjective Age. Paper presented at the annual meeting of the Gerontological Society.

Cutler, N. E. (1976) Resources for senior advocacy: Political behavior and partisan flexibility. In P. A. Kerschner, ed., *Advocacy and Age: Issues, Experiences, Strategies.* Los Angeles: University of Southern California Press.

Cutler, N. E. (1977a) Demographic, social–psychological, and political factors in the politics of aging: A foundation for research in "political gerontology." *American Political Science Review* 71:1011–1025.

Culter, N. E. (1977b) *The Application of Cohort Analysis to Cross-Sectional Data in Gerontological Research.* Los Angeles, Andrus Gerontology Center, University of Southern California.

Cutler, N. E. (1981a) Subjective age identification. Pp. 731–787 in D. M. Mangen and W. A. Peterson, eds., *Research Instruments in Social Gerontology.* Kansas City: University of Missouri Press.

Cutler, N. E. (1981b) Age and political behavior. Pp. 374–406 in D. S. Woodruff and J. E. Birren, eds., *Aging: Scientific Perspectives and Social Issues,* 2nd ed. New York: Van Nostrand Reinhold.

Cutler, N. E., and Mimms, G.E. (1977) Political Resources for the Elderly: The Impact of Membership in Nonpolitical Voluntary Associations upon Political Activity. Paper presented at the annual meetings of the American Political Science Association.

Deming, M. B., and Cutler, N. E. (1981) Demography of the aged: Pp. 31–69 in D. W. Woodruff and J. E. Birren, eds., *Aging: Scientific Perspectives and Social Issues,* 2nd ed. New York: Van Nostrand Reinhold.

Easterlin, R. A. (1978) What will 1984 be like? Socioeconomic implications of recent twists in the age structure. *Demography* 15:397–432.

Erbe, W. (1964) Social involvement in political activity. *American Sociological Review* 29:198–215.

Foner, A. (1974) Age stratification and age conflict in political life. *American Sociological Review* 39:194.

Freeman, H., Novak, E., and Reeder, L. G. (1957) Correlates of membership in voluntary associations. *American Sociological Review* 22:528–533.

Glenn, N. D. (1977) *Cohort Analysis*. Beverly Hills, Calif.: Sage Publications.

Glenn, N. D., and Hefner, T. (1972) Further evidence on aging and party identification. *Public Opinion Quarterly* 36:31–47.

Hodge, R. W., and Treiman, D. J. (1968) Social participation and social status. *American Sociological Review* 33:722–740.

Hyman, H. H. (1972) *Secondary Analysis of Sample Surveys: Principles, Procedures, and Potentialities*. New York: John Wiley and Sons.

Jennings, M. K., and Niemi, R. G. (1975) Continuity and change in political orientations: A longitudinal study of two generations. *American Political Science Review* 69:1325.

Kirkpatrick, S. A., ed. (1974) *Quantitative Analysis of Political Data*. Columbus, Oh.: Charles E. Merrill.

Lipset, S. M. (1960) *Political Man*. New York: Doubleday.

Milbrath, L. W., and Goel, M. L. (1977) *Political Participation*. Chicago: Rand McNally.

Miller, W. E., and Levitin, T. E. (1976) *Leadership and Change: The New Politics and the American Electorate*. Cambridge, Mass.: Winthrop.

Nie, N. H., Verba, S., and Petrocik, J. R. (1976) *The Changing American Voter*. Cambridge, Mass.: Harvard University Press.

Palmore, E. (1976) The future status of the aged. *Gerontologist* 16:297–302.

Palmore, E., and Whittington, F. (1971) Trends in the relative status of the aged. *Social Forces* 50:84–91.

Peters, G. R. (1971) Self-conceptions of the aged, age identification, and aging. *Gerontologist* 11:69–73.

Phillips, B. S. (1957) A role theory approach to adjustment in old age. *American Sociological Review* 22:212–217.

Pratt, H. J. (1974) Old age associations in national politics. *Annals of the American Academy of Political and Social Science* 415:106–119.

Pratt, H. J. (1976) *The Gray Lobby*. Chicago: University of Chicago Press.

Riley, M. W. (1971) Social gerontology and the age stratification of society. *Gerontologist* 11:79–87.

Riley, M. W. (1973) Aging and cohort succession: Interpretations and misinterpretations. *Public Opinion Quarterly* 37:35–49.

Schaie, K. W. (1977) Quasi-experimental research design in the psychology of aging. In J. E. Birren and K. W. Schaie, eds., *Handbook of the Psychology of Aging*. New York: Van Nostrand Reinhold.

Sheppard, H. L. (1978) Testimony given in Retirement, Work, and Lifelong Learning. Hearing before the U.S. Senate Special Committee on Aging, 95th Congress, Second Session, Part 1, July 17, 1978.

Siegel, J. S. (1978) Testimony in Consequences of Changing U.S. Population: Demographics of Aging. Joint Hearing before the Select Committee on Population and the Select Committee on Aging, U.S. House of Representatives, 95th Congress, Second Session, Volume 1, May 24, 1978.

Smith, C., and Freedman, A. (1972) *Voluntary Associations: Perspectives on the Literature*. Cambridge, Mass.: Harvard University Press.

Storey, J. R., and Hendricks, G. (1979) *Retirement Income Issues in an Aging Society*. Washington, D.C.: The Urban Institute.

Trela, J. E. (1971) Some political consequences of senior center and other old age group memberships. *Gerontologist* 11:18–123.

Verba, S., and Nie, N. H. (1972) *Participation in America*. New York: Harper and Row.

Ward, R. A. (1977) The impact of subjective age and stigma on older persons. *Journal of Gerontology* 32:277–232.

chapter 7

The Welfare State and the
Political Mobilization of the Elderly

RICHARD G. FOX

Whether the aged population of the United States (and other Western societies) will emerge as an actual political constituency demanding and requiring national recognition and rewards is essential for determining the future of the elderly. This chapter argues that since the end of World War II and especially since the efflorescence of the welfare state in the last 20 years, there has been a weakening of political identification and movements based on the objective class structure. Concomitantly, there has been a rise and rapid growth of politicized groups based on ascriptive, or presumably ascriptive, characteristics such as ethnicity and sex. The conditions of the larger society as well as the increase in the aged population seem propitious for a similar mobilization of the elderly. Certain contemporary developments among the aged, particularly the label of *agism* used as a potent political symbol, perhaps presage the construction of political identities based on age.

I should make clear that this tentative judgment of the possibilities of age-based mobilization does not depend primarily on the aging literature, which is filled with programmatic opinions rather than actual studies along these lines. Rather, my support comes from a portrayal of the nature of American welfare state society and the emergence of an ascriptive politics in conjunction with that type of society. This ascriptive

159

AGING
Social Change

politics, in the form of ethnic nationalist movements in Wales and Canada studied by my students and me (Fox *et al.* 1978, 1981) was equally unpresaged in the social science literature yet is undeniably real in the identities of individuals and in political consequences. The argument is therefore cast in the most general terms and should be considered as a prolegomenon to the much larger job of research that must be undertaken to resolve this question. The specific form and strategy of this research, at least from an anthropological perspective, is suggested at the conclusion.

I begin by placing the discussion within an evolutionary conception of human society derived from the cultural anthropologist Julian Steward. The application of the evolutionary approach to the contemporary United States then leads to specifying the character of welfare state society and to indicating the sorts of political groupings to which such states are or may become prone. These states appear susceptible to the mobilization of the aged as one form of political expression and organization. Yet a consideration of the literature on the politics of the aged, which I undertake next, discerns a consensus against projecting future political identity among the elderly. Instead, this literature generally favors viewing aging associations as continuing their present-day lobbying efforts in the absence of a substantial and active political constituency based on such identity. I then consider the counterexample of ethnic nationalist movements, whose development of symbols and organization based on ascriptive identity presents a model of what may transpire among the aged. My concluding remarks suggest how certain newly developed symbols and organizations among the aged apparently presage political evolution similar to that undergone by ethnic nationalist movements and how such matters might be researched using an anthropological approach to the study of complex societies.

AN EVOLUTIONARY VIEWPOINT

Anthropological study of complex societies is a natural outgrowth of the discipline's concern with cross-cultural variation—that is, with explanation of the range of human society. A necessary adjunct of this enterprise is a cultural evolutionary approach, which sets cross-cultural variation within a causal framework of increasing institutional complexity and specialization. The most lucid formulation of cultural evolution as it entails the differentiation of social institutions and therefore the changing character of social cohesion and conflict was made by Julian Steward a quarter of a century ago. Steward proposed through his concept of "levels of socio-cultural integration" that cultural evolution involves not only quantitative increase in complexity but also qualitative reformation of society through the appearance of new institutions of social control. These "emergent forms" create novel relationships linking the parts of the society. Steward (1955) wrote

> In the growth continuum of any culture, there is a succession of organizational types which are not only increasingly complex but which represent new emergent forms . . . simple forms, such as those represented by the family or band, do not wholly disappear when a more complex stage of development is reached, nor do they merely survive fossil-like. . . . They gradually become modified as specialized, dependent parts of new kinds of total configurations [p. 51; see also Steward 1950, p. 110].

Steward applied his concept of levels of sociocultural integration to several evolutionary types: the nuclear family, the folk society, and the state. My major concern is with the state level, which Steward (1955) characterized in this manner

> What may be called roughly a state level of integration is marked by the appearance of new patterns that bring several multifamily aggregates, or folk societies, into functional dependence upon one another within a still larger system [There follows a list of the productive, distributional, religious, military, and other dependencies within a state.] . . . . The system of controls arising from economic, military, and religious needs creates a political hierarchy and a social system of classes and statuses. Qualitatively new institutions appear on the state or national level: government structure and control over those aspects of life which are of state concern; social stratification; and national cultural achievements [p. 55].

Steward saw his concept of integration levels as an analytic tool for delineating the emergent forms of social integration over the course of evolution and for marking the changing organization and relationships of social segments like community in the wake of such emergent forms. Anthropologists following Steward's lead have put forward more rigorous typologies of cultural evolution at nonstate or prestate levels of integration (see Fried 1967, Service 1962, Sahlins 1972). Yet little has been done by anthropologists to qualify the portrayal of the state level of sociocultural integration presented by Steward, except that the modern nation–state is distinguished from earlier, ancient, or primitive states (as, for example, the "segmentary state" type; see Southall 1956).

Failing to entertain and explore the notion of continued cultural evolution after the emergence of nation–states begs the question of whether new emergent forms have appeared (or, more correctly, are useful to distinguish for analytic purpose). It assumes by default that the organization and relationships characteristic of the nation–state over the last centuries, including the nature of political opposition and organization, sufficiently specify state organization in late twentieth-century states. It therefore precludes, by definition and inattention, the emergence of new political identities, such as ascriptive ones, in response to novel forms of sociocultural integration. In the following section, I consider the evidence for recognizing a new level of sociocultural integration—the welfare state—that elicits political mobilization based on ethnicity, sex, and (potentially) age instead of class. It is important, however, to locate this new state level within Steward's general framework for two reasons: (1) in order to recognize that although ascriptive identities such as sex, age, and ethnicity exist at previous levels of sociocultural integration and may have been the basis for organizations, they are fundamentally transformed in character and function when they appear within the welfare state integration level (as, Steward argues in the quote above, is true of institutions such as the family); and (2) in order to avoid interpreting the novel developments at one level of sociocultural integration through analyses or models that are appropriate to another level. This basically antievolutionary approach is exemplified by attempts to explain ethnic nationalism in Western societies as a recrudescence of primordial loyalties not fully eradicted by the nation–state or as an ascriptive veneer coating class conflict under conditions of internal colonialism (see Hechter 1975). Both treat this phenomenon as an aberration of the politics of the nation–state rather than as a novel mobilization in response to a very different level of state integration. Similarly, attempts to measure the possibilities of political mobilization of the elderly in terms of class or interest-group formulas appropriate to the nation–state pass over the novelty of welfare state organization to which the aged must adapt.

THE WELFARE STATE LEVEL OF
SOCIOCULTURAL INTEGRATION

The economic power, the communication and transportation capability, the political control enjoyed and exercised by contemporary Western states gives them a puissance over and penetration into the private and public existence of individual citizens unlike that of previous state forms. Social scientists over the last 20 years have increasingly recognized the emergent characteristics of this new, welfare state as it appears in advanced industrial societies after World War II and have documented its use of state subsidies, grants, pensions, and other rewards to regulate conflict, co-opt dissidence, and promote cohesion in society.[1] Janowitz (1978 p. 20, 124), for example, writes that social stratification in such states is not simply an outcome of occupation and class, but is also a result of the "claims and expectations generated by the welfare state." Gouldner (1968, 1970) has shown how even the ascendancy of the functionalist paradigm in sociology may be dictated by the allocations for research provided by the welfare state; and he has also argued that much sociological research funded by such states, by impugning the efficiency and fairness of community and local-level welfare institutions, legitimates the welfare state's supersedure of such intermediate institutions in favor of its increasingly unmediated intrusion into social life (compare Reiter 1972 for France).

If, in fact, the welfare state is an emergent form of sociocultural integration—one that appears fully developed in societies with advanced industrial capacities and highly elaborate divisions of labor (compare Janowitz 1978), then we should expect that not only would the links between such states and their populations be different from previous state levels of integration, but also that, by extension, the forms of political mobilization characterizing these states would not conform to the class-based politics associated with the nation–state from the nineteenth through the early twentieth centuries. This expectation would be even stronger if we accept Fallers's argument about the class-based politics of the nineteenth-century nation–state. Fallers (1973) suggests that although this class-based politics is sometimes portrayed as a natural consequence, or simple reflection, of objective class divisions and conflicts, it is an ideological construction or political charter, linked to particular forms of the state:

> There seems to be, at any rate in societies of Western tradition, a certain affinity between the idea of the nation–state and that of the class/stratum sort of inequality. . . . The stratigraphic image, then, appears in the context of struggles between those whose power renders them more-than-equal citizens and those whose lack of it renders them less. Through the activities of ideologists who interpret social experience, it passes into cultural and subcultural tradition, where it appears as sociology and ethnosociology [p. 28].

---

[1] Janowitz (1976, pp. 2–3) defines the welfare state in terms of three attributes: (1) government allocates at least 8–10% of the gross national product to welfare, including health, education, community development, and poor relief expenditures; (2) the political principle exists that government, through grants and institutions, can and should intervene to correct or augment the well-being of its citizens apart from what the marketplace and the occupational reward system will allow; (3) decisions as to how to allocate such government grants and the missions of government welfare institutions reflect "political demands and consent and not authoritarian decisions."

The ideological constructions based on class and the political mobilization to which they give rise do not continue their salience in welfare states. Many scholars have documented the welfare state's increasing coopting of dissidence into a "managerial" competition for government benefits and away from a revolutionary disavowal of the system or away from radical demands for its reconstruction (compare Field and Highley 1972). The diminution of the latter represents the declining salience of class-based political ideology, activity, and organization. This development has been referred to as the "politics of consensus" (Lane 1965; p. 877), "depoliticization" (Torgerson 1962, p. 160), "the waning of opposition" (Kirchheimer 1957, p. 150), or in the best known statement, the "end of ideology" (Bell 1962, Lipset 1977). Abramson (1975) writes of the decline in class-based partisan voting in postwar America due to prosperity, equalization of economic rewards, reduction in lifestyle differences, and the conservative strategies of trade unions. Wilensky notes, "'with advancing industrialism and urbanism traditional indices of class, present income and occupational category no longer serve to distinguish life styles and mass political attitudes and behaviors' [quoted in Janowitz 1978, p. 131, see also Janowitz 1978, p. 98, 130]."

Rarely did these commentators suggest that new forms of mass political identity, action, and organization might come to replace the increasingly jejune class-based forms when the welfare state proved unable or perhaps unwilling to solve all social problems or failed to reward certain segments of the population adequately. Instead, they often argued as if the termination of class-based ideologies and organizations of political opposition was an "end to (all political) ideology" and betokened the weakening of political consciousness and participation in general.

Recently, however, there has been a growing recognition of the welfare state's susceptibility to the organization of mass political opposition, or wide political strata, on the basis of appeals to ascriptive characteristics (see Fox, et al., 1981). Janowitz (1978) presents this insight most forcefully

> With the advent of advanced industrialism, age paradoxically becomes more and more a societal-wide dimension of self-identification and collective attachment. . . . Likewise, under advanced industrialism the ascriptive characteristics of race and sex emerge as profound sociopolitical issues, in good measure because they produce inequality in social stratification and economic rewards [p. 132; for a similar position on ethnic politics, see Bell 1975].

The susceptibility of welfare states to political appeals based on ascription and to attempts at organizing wide strata on the basis of such ascriptive political identities rests on: (a) the legitimacy and therefore recognition welfare states are willing to give to these ascriptive or "cultural" appeals (compare Eidheim 1968 on the Samish [Lappish] movement). Often the very economic base of an ethnic political movement depends on subsidies provided by the welfare state (as Cimino 1977 reports for the Acadians in Canada), or the demands for special considerations in hiring, education, and other matters find their purchase in the legal nooks and crannies of welfare state legislation (as Aull 1978 discovered for Welsh-language schools); (b) such ascriptive political groups work directly through appeals or confrontations with the welfare state bureaucracy, rather than through electoral contest (the Welsh, Scottish, and Acadian movements have gained much more from such lobbying than they have through the normal electoral channels). Given the highly bureaucratic nature of the welfare state and its managerial orientation to political control, this direct confrontation through lobbying efforts is more effective in gaining concessions and is also probably more acceptable to welfare state leaders.

Recognizing the welfare state as an emergent evolutionary form, therefore, has led to the expectation of a waning of class-based political mobilization and its replacement by new political strata based on ascriptive "diacritica," one of which might be an aged identity. I now turn to a review of the literature on the politics of the elderly to see to what extent this possibility has been entertained and researched.

THE POLITICS OF AGING

The literature on the politics of aging in the United States confirms the increasingly important role of the welfare state in the policy and direction of age-based voluntary organizations (see Pratt 1974, 1976; also Binstock 1976 for an overview of this literature), but it is divided as to whether this portends the development of "senior power" or "gray power" as a foundation for mass political action.

The intrusion into age-related matters by the American welfare state begins with the social security legislation of the 1930s and achieves an even higher level of government involvement with medicaid and the other legislation for the aged in the late 1960s and early 1970s. The White House Conference on Aging in 1971 provided a public venue for many age-based organizations and symbolized the heightened role of government in this sphere (Pratt 1976, p. 138). This increased governmental intrusion, direction, and definition (of the problem of the aged) occurs coterminously with a growing number of aged persons and yet with the continuance of insufficient income, inadequate medical benefits, and other detractors from the "good life" in this population (Binstock 1972, p. 266). All of these factors have underwritten a greater politicization of age-based voluntary organizations, which, furthermore, is increasingly directed at the welfare state administration rather than at legislators in the Congress.

Although these developments are generally agreed upon in the literature, their consequences for age-based organizations like the American Association of Retired Persons (AARP), the National Council of Senior Citizens (NCSC), and the more recent Gray Panthers, their members and, ultimately, the politics of "senior power" is in debate. In a 1962 article, Rose (1968) foresaw the emergence of the aged as a cohesive political force, whereas in 1965 Streib wrote of the aged as only a "statistical aggregate," having "little feeling of solidarity, consciousness of kind, or group spirit [Streib 1968, p. 36]." Closer to the present, Pratt suggests that "there can be no reasonable expectation that the elderly will become [an] autonomous, independent force in elective politics [1976, p. 215]." He believes that the leaders of age-based voluntary organizations will try to gain concessions from the welfare state on the basis of "alleged support from a cohesive and militant constituency [1976, p. 216]," but that the state will respond sceptically and may call their bluff. A similar view is held by Binstock; he foresees no major growth in the political strength of the aged (1976, p. 397), believes that if the bluff of the age-based associations is called, they will not be able to muster a sufficiently cohesive constituency and therefore will go down to defeat (1974, p. 210), and suggests that future improvements in the condition of the aged will require political cohesion with other, non-aged, underprivileged segments of the American population (1972, p. 279).

The weight of current opinion is against the formation of an effective and cohesive political identity and organization for the aged. Clearly, such a development is circumscribed by many difficulties, among them the constant turnover in the potential constituency through death and disabling disease, the lack of strategic placement of the aged in the production economy, the pejorative estimate of aging in the wider society, the dissavowal of an elderly identification among the aged, and the continued salience of previous and long-standing occupational, educational, religious, and political party identification for the aged.

Yet some of these same disabilities existed and continue to exist among the ethnic and sex-based (women's) categories that have recently mounted political movements based on appeals to cohesive group identity and that have developed influential associations representing this identity to government. The problem with the literature on the politics of aging is that it approaches the question of senior power as if categorization of the present situation were a sufficient prognostication of future processes. That age-based voluntary associations have not mobilized a constituency of the aged at present does not mean that they cannot do so in the future and, more important, does not mean that the processes of such mobilization have not been set in motion. This same overly synchronic perspective led commentators in the 1950s to claim that the formation of mass age-based voluntary organizations was impossible, yet such a development occurred in the 1960s (see Pratt 1976, p. 39). It disallows the purposeful activities of ascriptive elites in the creation of a women's political movement and identity that did not exist in its present form 20 years ago (see Freeman 1973) and, as I shall show, of modern Welsh and Acadian political identities that did not exist in their present guise before 1960. Furthermore, it does not take sufficient account of the changing composition and numbers of the aged and the future stresses to be placed on the political process as a growing number of aged people attempt to increase or maintain their perquisites from a decreasing labor force (see Neugarten 1974). Most of all, there seems to be retention of the idea that political movements must take class forms for successful mobilization (as in Binstock's notion, cited above, that the aged must make common cause with other underprivileged segments of the population); the welfare state as an emergent evolutionary form is thereby ignored, and the consequences for political activity of this evolution go unnoted.

I suggest as an alternative that the politics of aging be viewed in the context of a general contemporary emergence of ascriptively based political mobilization and groups in welfare states; more specifically, I believe that an investigation of the age-based organizations will show them to be undergoing, at the level of leadership and mass membership, transformation in symbols and identity through political interaction with the welfare state. These possibilities are unresearched in the current literature on aging I have available to me. As a possible template for their future development, I offer in the following section a brief discursion into the mobilization of ethnic political identities in Wales and Acadia.

ETHNIC NATIONALIST MOVEMENTS

Previous research on ethnic nationalism in Wales and among francophones (Acadians) in New Brunswick has confirmed two premises about the upsurge in Western industrial nations of political mobilization based on ascription.

The research indicates that these movements are not outcomes of reasserted primordial identities or atavisms of "tribalism," as some modernization theories hold. Rather, their growth and florescence are recent reactions to the welfare state's increasing power over and intrusion on regional or community organizations and identities. Some case materials follow to illustrate this point.

Although Wales was incorporated into the English political and administrative system in the middle of the sixteenth century, attempts to mobilize Welshmen for political purposes on the basis of ethnicity did not occur until the nineteenth century. The early organizational basis of Welsh identity depended on the spread of nonconformist sects of Christianity among the population in the eighteenth and nineteenth centuries and the inculcation of Welshness and preservation of Welsh language accomplished by the nonconformist preachers in their chapels (see Verdery 1976). At first, the nonconformist leaders acted mainly as brokers between their parishioners and the local Welsh gentry, who were thoroughly anglicized, but they soon moved to memorializing the central government for improvements in local education and preservation of Welsh culture. The democratic electoral reforms introduced in Britain after 1868 brought the nonconformist leaders into a more public political arena, but they operated mainly as a pressure group from within the Liberal Party, which depended heavily on Welsh support. Their objectives remained predominantly "cultural," that is, disestablishment of the Anglican church, education, and temperance. As the British state in the nineteenth century became increasingly the guarantor for general social welfare and education, so the Welsh leaders through political pressure prosecuted their local interests with it—and won major concessions.

At the end of the nineteenth century, this developing Welsh ethnic politics was dislodged by the growth of a strong class-based political movement centered in the industrial areas of southern Wales and institutionalized in the Labour Party. The Welsh nonconformist elite was generally unsympathetic and even hostile to the working-class movement, and it grew increasingly so as a British working-class identity and organization, personified in the union lodge, came to replace Welsh ethnicity and the nonconformist chapel as the central symbol and institution of community life. Thus, when Lloyd George and other members of the Welsh nonconformist elite attempted to form a nationalist party in the late 1880s, they were unable to amalgamate leaders from industrial South Wales, and the party (Cymru Fydd) was short lived.

Little more is heard of Welsh nationalism until after World War II. Even though the Welsh Nationalist Party (Plaid Cymru) was formed in 1925, it remained a small, basically "cultural," and, in the opinion of

many English, eminently laughable—but most certainly, generally unsuccessful—political organization until the middle of the 1960s. The
party's recent electoral victories depend on the growth of the British
welfare state and the concomitant burgeoning of many Welsh ethnic
organizations demanding recognition and reward from the state. Some
of these Welsh organizations are created by the welfare state within its
own bureaucracy; the Welsh Office and the Welsh National Water Development Agency have developed some autonomy from central government, if for no other reason than to justify greater allocation of powers
to themselves within the national bureaucracy. Other Welsh organizations are community-level responses to state intrusiveness: The Welsh
Schools Movement attempts to establish publicly funded Welsh-language
schools. Still others are Welsh splinter groups from British organizations,
like the Farmers' Union of Wales, the Wales Trades Union Council, and
the Community Councils Association of Wales. They contend that they
can better represent Welsh interests if they organize on a "national"
basis than if they only worked within the British parent organization.

These Welsh organizations share a common origin as reactions to or
as the results of welfare state intrusion. They direct their demands at
the welfare state bureaucracy and attempt to manipulate the state's own
resources and institutional involvement at the local level against the state
and in the interests of their (Welsh) advancement and autonomy. The
politics of ethnicity, or regionalism, carried forward by Welsh nationalists
at present is like the ethnic culturalism pursued by the nineteenth-century
nonconformist leaders. What has changed is the arena in which these
appeals to ethnicity and demands for perquisites take place: from brokerage between nonconformist elite and local anglicized gentry to a more
public and politicized brokerage between nationalist elite and the welfare
state. And this change of venue is a result of the evolution of nation–state
to welfare state. The continued success of such organizations depends
on appeals to Welsh identity and an ever-widening mobilization of Welsh
population on ethnic lines. At this moment, the greatest impediment to
the formation of a wide political stratum based on ethnic appeals is the
continued salience of class-based political identity in industrial South
Wales, which disrupted the growth of the nationalist movement at the
end of the nineteenth century.

A similar, but less developed ethnic nationalism characterizes the
Acadians, who represent a large majority of the population in the northern
and northeastern counties of New Brunswick. The Acadians are the
descendants of the French Catholics whom the British expelled from
Nova Scotia in 1755 but who returned to less fertile areas of the Canadian
Maritimes in 1763.

The advent of an organized Acadian ethnicity occurred in response to various acts of the New Brunswick provincial legislature in the late nineteenth century. The Common Schools Act of 1871 and the Municipalities Act of 1877 legitimated the parish structure of the Catholic church throughout Acadia as the provisioner of basic education and public welfare. These acts by a pre-welfare state essentially bequeathed autonomy to Acadian regions and made control of the provincial Catholic church tantamount to control over the Acadian population. At about the same time, an Acadian elite consisting mainly of priests and lawyers began to emerge from Collège St. Joseph, founded in 1864 by Quebec missionaries. This elite (as I shall detail) constructed an Acadian ethnic identity and organizations that were primarily directed at political power within the Catholic church in the early twentieth century. In the 1920s and 1930s, this elite pursued ethnic goals through the formation of local credit unions and a mutual aid society that developed into a major insurance company.

The Catholic church remained the primary institution controlling Acadian social welfare, education, and community life in general until well after World War II. The nascent Canadian welfare state, however, began to assume a greater role in the 1940s, when the provincial legislature passed various acts to centralize and strengthen primary education and to fund it adequately. (Education is in Acadia, as in Wales and perhaps most societies, the earliest point of entry for the welfare state— as befits the major institution for maintaining social control, enforcing social conformity, and reproducing the system of stratification). In the 1950s, the increasing cost of education and other social welfare taxed the Catholic church beyond its capabilities, and a church-related Acadian educational association began demanding greater provincial funding for schools. Thus was launched the interaction of Acadian associations with provincial government.

In the 1960s, the New Brunswick administration began a major intervention into provincial education and social welfare. It enacted a provincial property tax for education, formed a French-language university, and (with federal aid) inaugurated a major economic development scheme for the Acadian northeastern counties. These actions fully displaced the Catholic church as a local organization providing social welfare and necessarily forced the Acadian elite, who had once found employment and status within or attached to the church's control over community life, to turn to provincial government for perquisites or redress of inequalities. About this time, the Canadian federal government instituted a policy of funding Official Language Minority Associations, which began subsidizing an Acadian association in 1969. From the necessity of confronting provincial government and on the basis of the federal subsidy, a militant and public Acadian association, the Société des Acadiens du Nouveau-Brunswick (SANB), was formed in 1973. (This developed from an older association representing the Acadians throughout the Maritimes.) The SANB has continued to prosecute its demands with the provincial government for greater recognition of the French language, more government jobs for French speakers, and fuller efforts to improve the condition of the francophone poor in the rural areas. Like the Welsh, then, this elite has moved ethnic politics away from the competition for control of the Catholic church and into a more public and politicized arena—the confrontation with government.

This research on ethnic nationalist movements also confirmed the strategic importance of ethnic elites in the creation or attempts at creation of a mobilized population. Such movements do not spring up "naturally" from sudden mass perception of inequality or identity. Rather, the manipulation of symbols and the inauguration of organizations by elites promotes ethnic group identity and novel political protest. As I have previously shown, these elites and their organizations often preexist the fully intrusive welfare state and are then mainly involved in political brokerage at the community level (as with the nonconformist elite) or within specific regional institutions (as with the Acadian struggle within the Catholic church). State intrusion forces such elites to cast themselves into competition for access and rewards from the state bureaucracy, otherwise the welfare state erodes their functions and thereby undermines their previous roles as brokers at the community or regional level. (If the state is successful and offers sufficient inducements, the ethnic elite may, of course, be coopted or choose to "pass.") The welfare state, however, imposes its own requirements for legitimacy on these elites and their organizations: Rewards are given largely to the extent that elites can imbue their ethnic constituency with a common set of ascriptively based symbols and goals that supersede the differences in occupation, education, and other functional differences within it and that decree consistent ethnic political response. A major focus in the Welsh and Acadian research has therefore been on the transformed activities and evolving policies of the ethnic nationalist elites and their organizations. As they have moved from their original local level and private sector objectives to an increasingly public and politicized relationship with welfare state administration, so they have manipulated new or revitalized symbols of identity and political action to develop a large, self-conscious ethnic constituency with which to legitimize their demands.

Among the Welsh, there has been a movement away from the religious symbols of common identity that characterized the nineteenth-century movement and toward the secular (and therefore more readily accepted by the welfare state) symbols of Welsh culture, and especially Welsh language, in the twentieth century. Language has been the major avenue by which Welsh leaders have won concessions from the state, but it became somewhat of a liability as the only or major symbol of identity when attempts were made to mobilize the population of South Wales, most of whom have minimal acquaintance with the language and many of whom grew up with a strong British trade union orientation. It is striking, therefore, that as the Welsh efforts turned south, their symbolic statements increasingly broadcast notions of "internal colonialism (symbols of Welsh economic deprivation in relationship to England) and calls for redress of the presumed imbalance in regional development (although the language continues to be a unifying force among the elite). The evolution of symbols has therefore been from appeals to the unity of the Welsh in their opposition to the established church to their unity as possessors of a common culture to, at present, their shared deprivation as a result of English exploitation.

Acadian developments show similar symbolic changes. The original evocation of ethnic identity by elites accompanied elite efforts to wrest control over the provincial Catholic church hierarchy away from the Irish. This identity, propounded at the end of the nineteenth century, rested heavily on a common religion and on a common history of Acadian martyrdom during the 1755 Expulsion at the hands of the British (with whom the Irish were identified). As the ethnic battleground moved from the Catholic church to the New Brunswick government, there was a corresponding shift in the symbolic definition of Acadian identity. This change was only accomplished after the older generation of ethnic leaders had been supplanted by a more militant younger one, whose members often came from lower class backgrounds. (A similar generational change has occurred in the Welsh movement over the last decade, although with much less intraelite conflict.) The new identity being promulgated rests on a secular base shorn of the specific history of the Acadians. Its major symbol is the need of francophones in New Brunswick to preserve their language and culture against anglophone domination and the necessity of equality of opportunity for all French speakers in the province. The altered definition of identity allows the Acadian leadership to solicit the allegiance of the predominantly francophone population of Madawaska County in New Brunswick, which formerly resisted inclusion in the Acadian ethnic movement because it did not recognize this historical pedigree. The secularism of the symbols is more acceptable to the welfare state, as in Wales, and permits legitimate public confrontations with government over education, employment in the bureaucracy, provision of bilingual services, and other matters defined by the welfare state as within the orbit of government. That this identity appears more salient than any based on appeals to class is apparent in the utter failure of Le Parti Acadien, a breakaway radical wing of the ethnic movement that promulgated class symbols, which failed to generate any support in the early 1970s.

POLITICAL MOBILIZATION OF THE ELDERLY

The ethnic nationalist data indicate how elites attempt to mobilize wide political strata on the basis of the construction of ascriptive symbols and how these attempts are elicited and often inadvertently aided by the bureaucratic intrusion of the welfare state. Is it too flamboyant a speculation to suggest that the same process may lead to the mobilization of the elderly? The increasing involvement of age-based associations in direct political lobbying and the appearance of the Gray Panthers are harbingers of such developments; if nothing else, they attest to the existence of aged elites. (Whether they are actually elderly or not is a subsidiary, although interesting, question.) These elites depend for their legitimacy and rewards on the continuance and enhancement of their brokerage roles between the welfare state and the supposed constituency of the elderly they represent. For much of the past and even today in Wales and Acadia, the elite's representation of the extent and cohesion of their constituency has been in advance of the reality. "In advance" is an important phrase because it indicates that each successful act of brokerage by the elite enhances the reality of the ascriptive population they represent. Successes in Acadia and Wales have always whetted, rather than dulled, the appetite of the ethnic elite for further government concessions as we might expect on the model of interest group politics. In fact, the Welsh now call for such major reorganizations of British government and reallocations of social wealth that it would be fair to call them revolutionary, just as were nineteenth-century working-class demands. The only limit set on demands is the price exacted by the elites for their agreement to "pass," and given the upcoming conflict over the social security system and the moral and fiscal quandary brought on by a decreasing number of young workers supporting an expanding number of old retirees, I can foresee demands so great as to appear revolutionary, or a reaction so strong as to represent an economic and moral reordering of basic social institutions.

It may be that ethnic nationalisms will not serve as appropriate models for the mobilization of the elderly. The argument would run that one is ethnic for a lifetime, whereas one is old for a much shorter time; ethnic leaders and followers are not by the very definition of their ascription likely to suffer from poor health and failing faculties; ethnic brethren do not have a preexisting vita of occupation, political preference, and life-style to condition them, whereas the aged do. But there are counter-arguments: Ethnicity is no more "for life" than is an aged identity. Both come into play only from the time that and only for as long as the identity is recognized. Ethnic leaders therefore often have previous "lives" to surmount, as, for example, in Wales, among those who must learn the Welsh language that was not spoken in their childhood homes. Fur-thermore, although the elderly population suffers greater physical in-firmities, it also possesses certain advantages in relation to mobilization: a constantly replenishing supply of adult potential converts; a populace with much experience in dealing with public institutions; time for political participation unlimited by occupational and child-rearing duties; removal from direct reprisals by employers; and a set of diacritica (the physical attributes of age) that is apparent and therefore cannot easily be situa-tionally set aside (as, for example, can an ethnic language by a bilingual).

   I think it ill-advised to pursue these speculations about the future in the absence of research with which to evaluate them. Furthermore, to be overly concerned with the characteristics of the elderly that may preclude or enhance their mobilization is to fall into the same trap as treating the "diacritica" defining an ethnic population as once-given and unchanging. New symbols and new circumstances bring new or regen-erated or redefined ethnicities. Such persuasive symbols and the orga-nizations with which they are linked by a process of mutual reinforcement are essential, as Trela recognizes when he notes their absence among the aged: "Their age is not a salient point of political reference for most older people; there is no system of beliefs and values that shapes the political life of the aged, and except in rudimentary form, the aged have no effective political organization [1976, p. 145]."

   I should like, therefore, to present in the remainder of this chapter some recent symbolic formulations concerning the elderly that I believe are precursory to, and omens of, the attempted mobilization of an elderly movement. Social scientists have often served as intentional or uninten-tional ideologues for political movements; witness the use of the internal colonial "theory" among the Welsh and the analogy drawn between American blacks and French Canadians, the so-called white nigger model, by francophone Canadian intellectuals. It will therefore come as no surprise that these symbols are (at least in the citations I give of them) articulated by professional students of the elderly.

Writing in *The New Republic* of 2 December, 1978, David Hackett Fischer documents a symbolic charter for an elderly political movement by noting a conceptual reorientation toward the elderly taking place in the field of gerontology. This changing formulation of the nature of aging and the study of the aged, although evidently presented as an objective viewpoint by scholars studying the aged, could just as easily function as the symbolic foundation for the mobilization of the aged. This changing scholarly conception of aging could serve such a function because it removes many of the most pejorative images attached to oldness. Fischer (1978) writes:

> Only a few years ago [the "grey movement"] was mainly concerned with old age. Today, it is mostly about aging.
> . . . The idea of old age as a life-stage is yielding to a more dynamic conception of aging as a life-process . . . to a conception of aging as a great continuum.
> . . . The shift from a static idea of old age to a dynamic model of aging is of great importance. . . . If aging is a great continuum, without discrete physiological breaks, then the conventional life-stages which we use to organize our thoughts and institutions begin to appear as social artifacts which are arbitrarily imposed upon the life-cycle. And if the legitimacy of life-stages is called into question, then so also are the age-stereotypes and the systems of age stratification which rest upon them [p. 33].

Without in any way contesting the intellectual worthiness of approaching aging as a continuum, I must also suggest that Fischer's statement could serve as a manifesto for an aging movement. His use of the term *grey movement* throughout without complete definition also assumes a corporate grouping, although, curiously, or perhaps tellingly, the gray movement at times seems to refer to the aged themselves and at other times to the scholars who study the aged. This assertion of such a movement's existence in the mass media in advance of its substantial reality, and in the absence of explicit definition, has the character of a self-fulfilling prophecy. It is also the most obvious technique consciously or unconsciously used by an elite to further its own brokerage role. This could be as true for leaders of a potential age-based political movement as it evidently is for gerontologists asserting their intellectual brokerage (and thus their necessity) with universities and government. But such origin myths have effects on the populations the elite presumably represents, and they work to bring them into a reality that before has only been presupposed.

Fischer then speaks of a change in goals pursued by the aging, from desiring guarantees of economic security in old age to wanting autonomy from "bureaucratic aging," that is, from government paternalism that restricts the choices of when to work, where to live, and how to exist for the aged. How easily this statement could be used as political rhetoric.

Fischer goes further: He provides through review of the ostensibly objective observations of scholars as to what the aging want (need?) the rationale for a new incorporation of the elderly into associations based on a common, and possibly politicized, aged identity and writes of the core symbol being used, or that could be used, to implement this incorporation. He notes the work of family historians like Laslett impugning the notion, once held by gerontologists, that the problems of the elderly arise from the breakdown of the extended family. He credits Shanas with discovering that the aged do not lose contact with their relatives and do not suffer unduly from loneliness and isolation and quotes Comfort to the effect that what the elderly need are friends, not relatives. Fischer then sets out the new direction followed by gerontologists, a direction that would appear to bring their scientific objectivity even closer into service as ideology for an elderly political movement

> Gone (or going) from gerontology today is a nostalgia for ordered, holistic, communal structures [linking the generations together] which never existed in the past. . . . Today the primary purpose is to encourage the formation of pluralistic networks of association which might respond to variations of individual taste. Associations are being spawned in great profusion by the age movement today. They range from cultural and political and economic organizations of high sophistication to basement centers where "senior citizens" in rocking chairs listen to Lawrence Welk and make macaroni jewelry. . . . A new sort of social comity is in the making . . . a complex modern *Gesellschaft,* an open and pluralistic social system where adults of every age are recognized as autonomous individuals who have a right to *choose* their associative relations . . .
>
> In the age movement, all those things are increasingly being done not *to* older Americans but *by* them [1978, p. 34].

Fischer sums up the new thrust of the gray movement as a change from distaste for "gerontophobia," fear of aging and the elderly, to militance against "agism," institutionalized prejudice on the basis of age. This symbolic transformation is, I believe, an important precursor of an elderly political movement, even though Fischer evidently does not perceive it in this light; he alternates ambiguously between seeing agism as a core symbol of his gray movement and treating it as a direct response to objective social conditions. Undoubtedly, agism is both, but I wish to emphasize its symbolic valence in terms of the combinations it provides for mobilization of the aged.

The symbol of gerontophobia explained or expressed the distaste for aging and the aged as a psychological phenomenon, perhaps rooted in the presumed natural antipathy of humans to their failing capabilities in old age and their fear of approaching death. Bunzel (1972, p. 116) defined it as "a mass neurosis with the seat in the individual." The symbol of agism by contrast, blames society and social institutions for this miso-gerontism. It establishes a corporate responsibility and a recognition of kindred exploitation shared or suffered by all the old. It provides an external locus, in society itself, for the pejorative self-concept held by the elderly and explains it away as a false image perpetrated by society on both young and old in order to perpetuate institutionalized agism. The symbol of agism also deemphasizes the differences between the "young-old" and the "old-old" in favor of their common persecution. (This deemphasis is also effected by the ideology of "aging as a contin-uum.") Taken to its logical extreme, deemphasis permits the Gray Pan-thers to enlist the "young-young" in dubious battle with the evils of society. Not least important, the symbol of agism also serves as a di-rective to political action against an unfair system. It therefore helps answer the question of how the aged can be mobilized against a younger generation, that is, in a collective sense, composed of their children. But if these children suffer from the social malaise of agism, is it not simply a continuation of their now elderly parents' duty to disabuse them of such discriminatory notions? Probably more important, the very term *agism* as well as its symbolic meaning permits a gray movement to link its objectives with other, now-legitimized political dissent—against rac-ism and sexism—to prove its bona fides as more than an octogenarian crackpottery.

The development of the symbol agism over the last decade shows this passage from explaining age discrimination as psychological malaise to blaming society for it. Butler's 1969 definition has a heavy psychological flavor: "Age-ism reflects a *deep-seated uneasiness* on the part of the young and middle-aged—a *personal revulsion* to and distaste for growing old [p. 243; emphasis added]." By 1975, Butler speaks of agism as a product of social institutions and the prejudice against the aged they create (Butler 1975, p. 11–16). Writing in 1979, Comfort equates agism and society most forcefully. In an article entitled "Good-by to Ageism," Comfort defines the very process of aging as a social conspiracy visited on the aged by a demeaning society: "Basically, aging is not a biological or physical transformation. It is a political transformation that is laid upon you after a set number of years, and the ways of dealing with it are political and attitudinal [1979, p. 10]." Comfort, who sees the plight of the aged as analogous to that of blacks and women, urges the aged to become "bloody minded" and defiant of society's distaste for them. He suggests a cure for agism that directs action at society: "The things we individually can do to improve our own aging, and that of others, lie overwhelmingly in the sociogenic sector. . . . The most important of these is the militant exposure of society's stupid callousness to those who reach a given year [1979, p. 9]."

I do not aim to demean Dr. Fischer and the other gerontologists noted by showing them as ideologists for an aging movement; they are probably aware of these other functions their thoughts may serve. What I do hope to show is the recent formulation of potent symbols on which an active and mass political movement of the elderly might be based. I would expect such symbols to be articulated first by the aging associations and their elites through the newsletters, magazines, annual reports, and other communications that serve as vehicles for the transference of symbols to their constituents. The evidence that I have had time to assemble is slight, which may be more an artifact of the lack of research on the symbolic content of these documents than a true reflection.

In the Gray Panther *Network* for March/April 1979, Maggie Kuhn notes that "racism, sexism, and ageism are closely related in this society. All are directed toward people who are powerless and seen as inferior [1979, p. 12]." Elsewhere in that issue, several correspondents assert similar symbolic formulations: "We live in a real word with real, and mostly bad people in control"; "Gray Panthers believe our system should put people before profits"; "the reason that we have the problems we do—ageism, sexism, racism, housing shortage, no quality health care, escalation of arms, race, etc.—is simply because this system is a system based on the profit motive [Gray Panther *Network* 1979, p. 8]." Besides the clear assertion of society's guilt for the plight of the elderly and others, there is also a very interesting assimilation of a class argument to an aging organization, similar to what has happened among Welsh nationalists, that is, all aged are one in their exploitation by society.

Even more telling is the evocation of these new symbols in a letter in the *Network* from Edward E. Marcus:

> The notion that later maturity is distinguished by all kinds of intolerable woe is both blind to truth and unfeeling. Worse, it is a sign of prejudice against age, of age discrimination, of ageism.
>
> Death comes to all. But most seniors are not dying. Rather, they are being killed or, at best, deprived of the opportunity to live fully, richly, enjoyable [sic], by social attitudes which are malicious and demeaning.
>
> Many seniors share these negative attitudes themselves and hate themselves because they are now old. . . . But, by denying age in ourselves and in others, we deny life itself . . . [1979, p. 5].

The Gray Panther *Network* undoubtedly does not provide a random sample of the symbols being communicated to the elderly by age-based associations. But before relegating the paradigm pursued by this other Kuhn to the bone pile she has so often disdained, we should note its espousal in less radical aging associations. No one would accuse the AARP, publishers of *Modern Maturity,* of radical politics and policies, yet in the February–March, 1979 issue of this magazine, Alex Comfort writes of the social malaise of agism in terms similar to what I have taken from the *Network* (see earlier quotes). Does confluence of ideology indicate increasing confluence of action between AARP and the Gray Panthers? Perhaps not, yet in February 1979 Gray Panthers and members of the NCSC joined in Washington, D.C., to protest against proposed decreases in social security benefits.

Again, we come to the limits of the research that has been done to date. I therefore move on to some conclusions about how the potential mobilization of the elderly might be studied, based on the model provided by the investigation of ethnic nationalism.

CONCLUSION

The major argument of this chapter has been the futility of trying to resolve whether the elderly will be mobilized with the data at hand and without adopting a cultural evolutionary viewpoint encompassing the society in which the aged are set. The data that would be illuminating are first, the determination of the equivalent of an ethnic elite among the aged and second, the determination of this elite's symbolic and behavioral efforts at the local level to engender political identities. Recognition of this scholarly and nonscholarly elite would come from analysis of the symbols of identity for the aged that they construct and the propagation of these symbols among the elderly they presume to represent. It would also emerge from studying the interactions, "the web of group relations [Wolf 1956]," linking age-based associations at the national level with their affiliates at the local level as lines of organization along which elite efforts run and by which they are, in turn, directed. The variety in age-based associations provides a positive opportunity for this research. The AARP, NCSC, and the Gray Panthers, for example, developed from different organizational backgrounds, adopted dissimilar missions, promulgated divergent philosophies, and solicited distinctive memberships. A content analysis of the various communications of these age-based associations and their elites (including any seconded gerontologists) would establish whether, given their varied backgrounds, the symbols espoused have remained dissimilar or have evolved toward greater consistency around a common image of the aged or a common battle against agism and the enactments of the welfare state. A similar proposition could be investigated by studying the actual organization of these various age-based associations at the local level and their relations with the national leadership. Do they continue to differ in the way they organize the elderly at the community level and the way they define their mission there? Or has there been a growing conformity among them as they all have increasingly been drawn into confrontation with the welfare state and have adopted a brokerage role between their elderly constituents and government, a brokerage that requires or rewards the political mobilization of the elderly? Up to this point, research on the elderly seems to have ignored the construction of symbols and appears to have been confined to the lobbying efforts of age-based associations at the national level. An analysis of local-level organization and the communication of symbols that might underwrite political action at this level would be salutary. In such research, anthropology could have an important role, not only because of the change in venue from national to local level but also because of a shift in emphasis from overt activities to the symbolic constructions underlying them, that is, the creation of "culture."

I have attempted to demonstrate what an anthropological and cultural evolutionary approach, which for me are the same, has shown about ethnic nationalisms and what it might show, or at least where it might lead us to look, about the political mobilization of the aged. Using modernization theories and other fundamentally nonevolutionary perspectives brought many social scientists a few years ago the chagrin of exaggeratedly reporting the death of ethnicity, even when it was about to become most alive. Prescience of this sort is hardly rewarding to the scholar or rewarded by the state, but beyond these considerations, our own future elderly identities may shame us for any present-day myopia we permit to curtail our investigation of the possible mobilization of the elderly.

REFERENCES

Abramson, P. R. (1975) *Generational Change in American Politics*. Lexington, Mass.: Lexington Books, D.C. Heath.

Aull, C. (1978) Ethnic Nationalism in Wales: An Analysis of the Factors Governing the Politicalization of Ethnic Identity. Ph.D. dissertation, Department of Anthropology, Duke University.

Bell, D. (1962) *The End of Ideology: On the Exhaustion of Political Ideas in the Fifties.* New York: The Free Press.

Bell, D. (1975) Ethnicity and social change. In N. Glazer and D. Moynehan, eds., *Ethnicity, Theory and Experience.* Cambridge, Mass.: Harvard University Press.

Binstock, R. H. (1972) Interest-group liberalism and the politics of aging. *The Gerontologist* 12:265–281.

Binstock, R. H. (1974) Aging and the future of American politics. In F. R. Eisele, ed., Political Consequences of Aging. *The Annals of the American Academy of Political and Social Science* 415:197–212.

Binstock, R. H. (1976) Political systems and aging. In R. H. Binstock and E. Shanas, eds., *Handbook of Aging and the Social Sciences.* New York: Van Nostrand Reinhold.

Bunzel, J. H. (1972) Note on the history of a concept-gerontophobia. *The Gerontologist* 12(2):116.

Butler, R. N. (1969) Age-ism, another form of bigotry. *The Gerontologist* 9(4):243–246.

Butler, R. N. (1975) *Why Survive? Being Old in America.* New York: Harper and Row.

Cimino, L. (1977) Ethnic Nationalism Among the Acadians of New Brunswick: An Analysis of Ethnic Political Development. Ph.D. dissertation, Department of Anthropology, Duke University.

Comfort, A. (1979) Good-by to ageism. *Modern Maturity* 20(1):8–11.

Eidheim, H. (1968) The Lappish movement: An innovative political process. Pp. 205–216 in M. J. Swartz, ed., *Local-Level Politics.* Chicago: Aldine-Atherton.

Fallers, L. (1973) *Inequality: Social Stratification Reconsidered.* Chicago: University of Chicago Press.

Field, G. L., and Highley, J. (1972) *Elites in Developed Societies: Theoretical Reflections on an Initial Stage in Norway.* Sage Professional Papers in Political Science 3. Beverly Hills, Calif. and London: Sage Publications.

Fischer, D. H. (1978) Book review. *The New Republic* 2 December 1978:31–36.

Fox, R. G., Aull, C., and Cimino, L. (1978) Ethnic Nationalism and Political Mobilization in Industrial Societies. Pp. 113–133 in L. Ross, ed., *Interethnic Communication.* Proceedings of the Southern Anthropological Association no. 12. Athens, Ga.: University of Georgia Press.

Fox, R. G., Aull, C., and Cimino, L. (1981) Ethnic nationalism and the welfare state. Pp. 198–245 in C. Keyes, ed., *Ethnic Change.* Seattle: University of Washington Press.

Freeman, J. (1973) Origin of the women's liberation movement. *American Journal of Sociology* 78:793–802.

Fried, M. H. (1967) *The Evolution of Political Society: An Essay in Political Anthropology.* New York: Random House.

Gouldner, A. (1968) Sociologist as partisan: Sociology and the welfare state. *The American Sociologist* 3:103–116.

Gouldner, A. (1970) *The Coming Crisis of Western Sociology.* New York: Basic Books.

Hechter, M. (1975) *Internal Colonialism: The Celtic Fringe in British National Development 1536–1966.* Berkeley: University of California Press.

Janowitz, M. (1978) *The Last Half-Century: Societal Change and Politics in America.* Chicago: University of Chicago Press.

Kirchheimer, O. (1957) The waning of opposition in parliamentary regimes. *Social Research* 24:127–156.

Kuhn, M. (1979) *Gray Panther Network,* March–April, 1979.

Lane, R. E. (1965) The politics of consensus in an age of affluence. *American Political Science Review* 59:874–895.

Lipset, S. M. (1977) The end of ideology and the ideology of the intellectuals. Pp. 15–42 in J. Ben-David and T. N. Clark, eds., *Culture and Its Creators*. Chicago: University of Chicago Press.

Marcus, E. E. (1979) Approaches to ageing: Ever onward and upward. *Gray Panther Network*, March–April 1979.

Neugarten, B. (1974) Age groups in American society and the rise of the young-old. In F. R. Eisele, ed., Political Consequences of Aging. *The Annals of the American Academy of Political and Social Science* 415:187–199.

Pratt, H. J. (1974) Old age associations in national politics. In F. R. Eisele, ed., The Political Consequences of Aging. *The Annals of the American Academy of Political and Social Science* 415:106–119.

Pratt, H. J. (1976) *The Gray Lobby*. Chicago: University of Chicago Press.

Reiter, R. R. (1972) Modernization in the south of France: The village and beyond. *Anthropological Quarterly* 45:35–53.

Rose, A. M. (1968) The Subculture of the Aging: A Topic for Sociological Research. Pp. 29–34 in B. L. Neugarten, ed., *Middle Age and Aging*. Chicago: University of Chicago Press.

Sahlins, M. (1972) *Stone Age Economics*. Chicago: Aldine-Atherton.

Service, E. R. (1962) *Primitive Social Organization; an Evolutionary Perspective*. New York: Random House.

Southall, A. (1956) *Alur Society*. Cambridge: W. Heffer.

Steward, J. H. (1950) *Area Research: Theory and Practice*. Social Science Research Council Bulletin 63. New York.

Steward, J. H. (1955) *Theory of Culture Change*. Urbana: University of Illinois Press.

Streib, G. (1968) Are the aged a minority group. Pp. 35–46 in B. L. Neugarten, ed., *Middle Age and Aging*. Chicago: University of Chicago Press.

Torgerson, U. (1962) The trend towards political consensus: The case of Norway. *Acta Sociologica* 6:159–172.

Trela, J. E. (1976) Status inconsistency and political action in old age. Pp. 126–147 in J. F. Gubrium, ed., *Times, Roles, and Self in Old Age*. New York: Human Sciences Press.

Verdery, K. (1976) Ethnicity and local systems: The religious organization of Welshness. Pp. 191–227 in C. A. Smith, ed., *Regional Analysis Volume II Social Systems*. New York: Academic Press.

Wolf, E. R. (1956) Aspects of group relations in a complex society: Mexico. *American Anthropologist* 58:1065–1078.

chapter **8**

Life-Stage Effects on Attitude Change, Especially among the Elderly

DAVID O. SEARS

The relative malleability of people's attitudes at different stages of their lives has been the subject of many scholarly debates over the years. Psychologists have not played much of a part in these debates, however; they have been dominated by sociologists and political scientists. Even the current vogue of "life-span developmental psychology" has given little attention to problems of attitude changes. This chapter is one distinctly sociopsychological effort to delineate some of what is already known about this problem and to spell out some outstanding research questions, especially those implicating the elderly. It takes off from a much longer manuscript in preparation (Sears 1982), part of which has appeared elsewhere (Sears 1975).

FOUR HYPOTHESES

Many hypotheses have been posed about how individuals' attitudes vary with their age or life stage. Oversimplifying only a little, these hypotheses can be grouped into four basic ideas: (1) The *lifelong openness* notion suggests that attitudes have an approximately uniform po-

183

tential for change at all ages; it essentially asserts that age is irrelevant for attitude change. (2) The *life-cycle* view suggests that people are particularly susceptible to certain attitudinal positions at certain life stages; it essentially posits interactions between age and attitudinal position. Familiar examples would be the alleged radicalism of youth and conservatism of the aged (hence the old French saying, "He who is not a radical at 20 has no heart; he who is one at 40 has no head"). (3) A third view could be termed the *impressionable years* viewpoint, which suggests that people are unusually vulnerable in late adolescence and early adulthood to changes of any attitudes, given strong enough pressure to change. In other stages of life, people are resistant to change, and of course, even in the vulnerable stage, they do not change in the absence of substantial pressure to change. Hence, this view asserts interactions of age and pressure to change, with attitudinal position irrelevant. A special and particularly interesting instance of the impressionable years hypothesis is the *generational* effect; this occurs when those in the appropriate life stage (late adolescence and early adulthood) are subjected to a common massive pressure to change on some particular issues (e.g., when the nation is engaged in an unpopular war). It presumably yields interactions of birth cohort and attitudinal positions.[1] (4) The final viewpoint is *persistence*, which suggests that the residues of early (preadult) socialization are relatively immune from attitude change in later years. This asserts a simple main effect of age with attitude change (or perhaps attitude formation) occurring primarily in the preadult years.

No matter which viewpoint one prefers, all of us would concede that attitudes vary a good deal in their intrinsic resistance to change. People can be highly committed to or ego-involved in some attitudes, but not at all in others. Following a substantial amount of earlier research (e.g., Sherif and Cantril 1947, Converse 1970), we have suggested that individual attitudes can be thought of as falling somewhere on a dimension of affective strength running from "enduring predispositions" to "non-attitudes." The life-cycle distinctions just made are largely moot for attitudes at the "non-attitude" or low ego-involvement end of this dimension, since they are plainly extremely malleable. They become interesting only for attitudes that are relatively more resistant to change. My suggestion is that such attitudes can be identified in public opinion data using three criteria: short-term stability, consistency over variations in item wording, and influence over attitudes toward new objects linked

---

[1] Actually, generational theorists usually argue that generational effects are limited still further to specific demographic subgroups, for example, the intelligentsia or some regional or religious subgroup (see Mannheim 1952).

to them. Some simple contemporary examples are political party iden-tification, racial prejudice, and evaluations of Richard Nixon. So the following discussion will be largely confined to attitudes identifiable as of at least moderate ego-involvement (i.e., as passing some minimum thresholds of stability, consistency, and power).[2]

It should also be noted that these attitudes generally have the most societal importance. They tend to focus on the issues that get the most attention from the media and in ordinary conversation. They tend to reflect the most recurrent and controversial issues. And they provide the predispositions that help people organize the ongoing flow of information input on many different political and social issues. So an understanding of attitude change on these particular issues has some special priority.

There is no perfect methodology for testing aging effects on attitudes. The seemingly obvious candidate, a longitudinal study, is obviously very expensive and almost never done on the scale required for testing among these viewpoints. But even a longitudinal study is basically flawed meth-odologically, since it can normally track only one birth cohort. Hence it confounds period with life-stage effects and cannot assess cohort ef-fects. Hence, my strategy has been to consider a wide variety of other kinds of data as well, including cross-sectional surveys, short-term panels, cohort analyses, and correlational analyses of the impact of such life events as social and geographical mobility, status discrepancy, mass communications, and needs arising from one's social and economic life situation. Each, when considered alone, has shortcomings that prevent unequivocal interpretation. But because each can illuminate some sep-arate part of the larger beast, they are a good bit more telling when considered together.

A SIMPLE MODEL

Any single viewpoint would transparently be an oversimplification, not only for a population but no doubt normally for any single individual as well, considering the plethora of attitudes anyone has. Nevertheless,

---

[2] Describing this dimension as "affective strength" should be contrasted with the con-cept of "centrality" (Converse 1975, Rokeach, 1968), which, to my mind, bears too many additional implications (e.g., of interdependence in some structural sense). One can be strongly affectively committed to a particular position without its centering a highly dif-ferentiated cognitive structure. Similarly, there is some overlap with conceptualizations emerging from the much more cognitive standpoint of those studying "schemas" and "schematic thinking" (e.g., Markus 1977, Taylor and Crocker, 1980). The differences remain to be hammered out.

a simple view can have heuristic value. So let us hazard a description of the life course of some modal, "typical" political predisposition.

For most purposes, political socialization begins in late childhood and early adolescence, and many crucial attitudes are first acquired at that point. How strong and persistent they are at that stage is open to more debate. A weighted average notion (e.g., Anderson 1971) would predict rapid early increases in strength, since attitude strength at any given stage would be a function of prior exposure. But thereafter strength ought to be rather stable; after a certain point, further exposure should have relatively little impact. The conventional wisdom is that attitudes are usually still quite malleable into early adulthood (Jennings and Niemi 1974, Vaillancourt 1973).[3] And through the remainder of the life-cycle, there appear to be reliable, though rather small, continuing increases in strength (Converse 1976).

This original acquisition depends a good bit on the simplicity, salience, recurrence, and constancy of the attitude object, if the literature on parental transmission is a useful guide (Niemi 1974, Tedin 1974). Hence, a much-discussed, simple, and chronic political object, such as "Democrats" or "Richard Nixon," ought to evoke earlier and more durable attitudes than an occasional, changing, or complex one, such as government energy policy.

Finally, resocialization ought still to be possible in late adolescence or early adulthood, given either powerful pressures to change or weak earlier socialization. Newcomb's (Newcomb et al. 1967) Bennington study described impressive social pressures on late adolescents and considerable (though hardly universal) resocialization of attitudes toward the most salient political objects of the day. Persistence of those attitude changes depended on the maintenance of strong social reinforcement. The Watts riot resocialized many young blacks previously indifferent to violent forms of protest, presumably because it presented some rather new attitude objects (Sears and McConahay 1973). But even with late adolescents, resocialization is difficult with firmly entrenched attitudes, as witness Stuart Cook's (1970) difficulties in changing whites' racial prejudices despite using the best sociopsychological techniques—protracted equal-status cooperative activities.

---

[3] Our view is a little different. Many more children express attitudes than really have them. But it is possible to screen out those with "nonattitudes." The residual group, those with "genuine" attitudes, plainly increases in size through adolescence. But the intrinsic strength of their attitudes may not increase markedly (at least according to one study; Sears and Smith, 1975). Hence an "all or nothing" model of attitude acquisition may be most appropriate, with the frequency of real attitudes approaching asymptote in early adulthood and strength increasing rather little. But this may complicate the picture more than is warranted for the purpose of this chapter.

By this view, then, affective "mass" is built up over time, making attitude change progressively more difficult with age.[4] Attitudes become stronger with time, just as any learned preference does with long practice and reinforcement. This is consistent with some combination of the persistence and impressionable years hypotheses previously cited.

RESEARCH ON ATTITUDE CHANGE ACROSS THE LIFE-SPAN

If this simple description of the life-span is correct, two general findings should recur in the public opinion literature. One is that, in the absence of systematic pressure to change, attitudes ought to be more unstable over time among youthful cohorts than among older ones, everything else being equal. The other is that systematic pressures to change ought to produce little systematic attitude change among older people, and substantial change among younger ones (say, up to age 25) only if the pressure is powerful.

This view is supported by research in a number of different areas. Much of it has been done for other purposes but can usefully be brought to bear on this problem. The argument made elsewhere (Sears 1975, 1982) can be reviewed only briefly here, to give some sense of the approach taken.

For the first proposition, greater attitude instability among youthful cohorts, longitudinal studies are most appropriate. The best of these is the Jennings and Niemi (1978) panel, composed of a national sample born in 1948 and of their parents, interviewed in both 1965 and 1973. Over a wide variety of political and nonpolitical dispositions, it is clear that the younger cohort changed substantially more than did the older one. Similarly, Gahart and Sears (1979) found racial prejudice correlated .61 from 1972 to 1976 (using the Michigan election studies panel) among those aged 21–28 (in 1976), and .75 among those aged 45–60.[5]

For the second proposition, that older cohorts change their attitudes less than do younger ones in response to systematic pressure to change, a number of research literatures fortunately provide relevant evidence. (1) Cohort analyses have assessed stage-specific pressures to adopt specific attitudinal positions; (2) self-interest should induce pressure to adopt

---

[4] Converse (1962) used the term *informational mass,* but it may be that information per se is incidental to this process; affective strength may or may not be based on substantial amounts of information.

[5] It should be noted that these estimates are probably biased upward to some extent, since sample attrition was likely to screen out disproportionate numbers of persons with low political involvement and thus unstable attitudes.

specific self-serving policy attitudes and can itself vary considerably independent of life stage; (3) mass communications represent another simple category of pressure to change; (4) geographical and (5) social class mobility can expose the adult to new social norms and to strong conformity pressures; and (6) status discrepancies can arise in adulthood and create tensions that are thought to promote certain kinds of attitude change. This is surely not an exhaustive list, but is perhaps a reasonable start.

Cohort analyses have been done of many different attitudes with the intention of testing life-cycle effects (i.e., age-specific proclivities for certain attitudinal positions). These have almost invariably found generational rather than life-cycle effects. People do not become more racially prejudiced, Republican, or conservative as they age, nor do they align their votes more with their social class (Abramson 1975, Gahart and Sears, 1979, Glenn, 1974). Being young does not promote being a political independent (Glenn, 1972). In all these cases, generational effects hold instead; being of recent vintage has bred less racial prejudice, less partisanship in general and Republicanism in particular, less conservatism, and less class voting. Hence the attitudes with which each cohort has entered adulthood have largely persisted (at least when aggregated across the cohort) rather than being deflected into some age-specific changes.[6]

Another potential systematic source of pressure to change is self-interest. People's selfish interests change over time (e.g., their taxes go up, their children enter and then leave school, etc.), and this could conceivably induce self-serving changes in political attitudes. On the other hand, standing predispositions dating from earlier socialization may override these later-life changes in self-interest, leaving the person's political attitudes more or less unaffected by them. To test this, we have conducted an extensive series of studies pitting private self-interest against long-standing predispositions (such as party identification, racial prejudice, or liberalism–conservatism) as determinants of policy attitudes and voting preferences. These studies test whether adult interests deflect one's attitudes away from the course set by earlier attitude acquisition, thereby testing the "openness" model. The studies have assessed the effects of several kinds of personal racial threats (such as busing, neighborhood desegregation, crime, or economic competition on the racial

---

[6] Of course, cohort analyses cannot conclusively rule out life-cycle effects because cohort, age, and period effects can never be perfectly unconfounded. But for age to have an effect undetected in cohort analyses, it would have to be perfectly offset by opposite period effects (e.g., the times becoming less conservative at exactly the same rate that aging cohorts were becoming more conservative). It is possible but seems like a long shot.

political attitudes of whites [Kinder and Sears, 1981]), of economic self-interest (such as falling personal financial fortunes, unemployment, inadequate medical insurance, or property tax burdens), of crime victimization, of energy crises, or the vulnerability of close relatives or friends to war. This research is best summarized by Sears *et al.* (1980). (See also Sears *et al.* 1979, Kinder and Kiewiet 1979.)

Self-interest turns out to have remarkably little effect on policy attitudes. For example, self-interest in the busing issue (as indexed by having children in public school in districts with busing, or in which it is likely) is essentially uncorrelated with whites' opposition to it, and personal employment problems have little relationship to attitudes toward government job policies. Of all these issues, the only real exceptions were strong and significant self-interest effects on a property tax reform measure (Proposition 13) in the 1978 California election (Sears 1978) and on opposition to busing in Los Angeles in the period just before a desegregation plan was announced (Allen and Sears 1978). However, even in both these cases, standing predispositions accounted for large shares of the variance, and in the case of busing, much more than did self-interest. So these studies are generally consistent with the notion that adults' policy preferences are difficult to alter through changes in their self-interests. That is, the openness point of view is inconsistent with this evidence.

The minimal effects model of mass communication effects, so popular 20 years ago (Klapper 1960), argued that the media rarely produced major changes in established attitudes. This view has come under considerable attack in recent years from communications specialists. The growth of massive exposure to television has been accompanied by equally widespread assumptions about its persuasive impact. Extensive and reliable reviews have been produced by Comstock *et al.* (1978) and Kraus and Davis (1976). But these revisionists turn out not to argue that television generally changes attitudes very much; instead, they find and emphasize the discernible media impacts they uncover on other dependent variables, especially information diffusion and "agenda-setting." Another fallback position is the "uses and gratifications" approach, which asserts that motives for exposure determine impact; hence attitude change should not be expected in all cases because people may be using the media to satisfy other needs, such as entertainment. In any case, it is hard to see any major shift in the nature of evidence on the media's persuasive impact on adults' attitudinal commitments. It still seems minimal, at least on the most important of their attitudes, even in today's much more refined and sophisticated research.

Either geographical or status mobility can expose people to systematically different norms from those dominating their original environments and therefore to systematic pressure to change attitudes. The most systematic quantitative analysis (Brown 1979) of the effects of geographical mobility finds considerably more adaptation to the destination's partisan norms among young than old migrants. As would be expected from the "impressionable years" formulations, there is virtually no adaptation among those older (over 35) migrants who have spent less than 11 years in their destination environment. The one contrary result is some significant adaptation among older migrants with longer residence in the new locale. However, the small size of this group does not allow for appropriate controls on self-selection, and the findings would certainly be more persuasive if replicated.

Status mobility affords another opportunity to test for attitude changes in later life, particularly in societies with strong class-based norms regarding social and political issues. There are, generally speaking, two hypotheses specifying how social mobility might produce change in social and political attitudes. Mobility might produce psychological tensions that become displaced, altering such attitudes as those toward minorities. Or mobility might induce resocialization to the prevailing norms of the class of destination. There is an extensive literature on this problem, which can only be alluded to here. Many apparent mobility effects are almost certainly due to selective recruitment (i.e., to the persistence of class-inappropriate early socialization [Thompson, 1971]). Status tensions do not seem to induce systematic attitude change. Some preadult anticipatory resocialization also occurs. Yet mobile young adults do seem to adapt somewhat (though not completely) to the political norms of their destination social class (e.g., Abramson 1972). The extent to which such mobility effects continue to occur through the rest of the life-span is unclear, but the best current guess is that the lion's share of mobility-instigated resocialization is accomplished in late adolescence and early adulthood. This age effect is accentuated by the greater frequency of mobility at this life stage.

Finally, adult status discrepancies (i.e., inconsistencies among different indices of social class) have often been hypothesized to induce tensions that result in attitude changes in the direction of ultraconservatism, racial prejudice, or egalitarian radicalism (Lenski 1954). An extensive empirical literature has succeeded mainly in establishing that such inconsistencies rarely yield anything other than simple main effects of the constituent status dimensions. For example, rich Catholics' partisan preferences tend to fall halfway between those of the rich in general and those of Catholics in general. The only two exceptions seem to represent clear instances of the persistence model: Jews and blacks of high achieved status are "too liberal." This seems plainly traceable to the persistence of strong ethnic socialization rather than to any adult radicalization due to the shock of status tensions (Knoke 1972).

So, at least at some very crude level, important political and social attitudes appear largely to resist sytematic change in adulthood, whether the pressures derive from stage-specific needs, self-interest, mass communications, geographical and status mobility, or status discrepancy. Late adolescence and early adulthood is a period of life at which attitudes are more responsive to such pressures. Normally, though, such pressures are probably either weak or offsetting, so extensive resocialization is probably more the exception than the rule in this stage. The data are, of course, in most cases not completely adequate, there are exceptions, there is a good bit of "error variance" (however unexplained variance is to be interpreted in this context), and this characterization could never be anything but crude. Nevertheless, it seeems to me to be at least a helpful overall heuristic to argue that some combination of the "persistence" and "impressionable years" notions best describe the life course of political and social attitudes most important to ordinary people and most consequential for society.

DETERMINANTS OF LIFE-STAGE EFFECTS

Scarcely any research exists on why this age-related slowdown occurs in the potential for attitude change, however. And the several major alternatives differ consequentially.

Affective Mass

The cumulative total of affectively toned information to which a person has been exposed in his or her lifetime tends generally to increase with age, at least on issues with regular, recurrent, high levels of controversy and communication. Certainly partisanship meets this standard because of regular elections and their associated campaigns. So do racial issues, perhaps excepting the period of relative invisibility between Reconstruction and the civil rights movement (Johnson et al. 1971). By simple information integration theories, such cumulating past exposure ought, by itself, and even if completely passive, to create an increasing inert affective mass, making change increasingly difficult. This explanation would predict some substantial differences across issues, depending on total information flow, which have not yet been examined.

Active Practice

Attitudes get stronger with practice. This has been shown in a number of contexts, including those involving role playing, cognitive dissonance, or immunization (McGuire 1969). The assumption in *The American Voter* (Campbell *et al.* 1960), perpetuated but never tested in Converse's later writings (1976), was that party identification becomes stronger with age because the citizens have histories of more votes and arguments for their party's candidates as they get older. This explanation, too, would predict some substantial differences across issue areas, dependent on level of active participation rather than mere passive exposure—perhaps a difficult, but not impossible, distinction to make.

Information Flow

Age groups may differ in the amount and novelty of information they are normally exposed to. For example, young people attend college more than older people do and hence are exposed to more new ideas. On the other hand, older people tend to watch television more than younger people do. In any case, it is hard to see how this variable could explain age differences in attitude change in any simple way, since the main effects of either experience are not dramatic (Feldman and Newcomb 1971, Comstock *et al.* 1978).

Information Processing Skills

There may also be age-related changes in cognitive processing abilities that affect the potential for attitude change. This is a complex research area, and a brief glance at it cannot represent it very accurately. But it may be helpful to note that the dimensions investigated in this line of aging research might in turn affect the potential for attitude change. For example, some contend that intellectual abilities associated with experience (e.g., general information, similarities, associational fluency) may increase with age. Inhibitory problem-solving skills may also increase. At the same time, older people may be more susceptible to interference effects and declines in short-term memory and in the capacity for perception of relationships that involve reorganization of material (e.g., Craik 1977, Horn 1970).

On the face of it, all these effects of aging on processing abilities would seem to facilitate the preservation of old ideas and inhibit the free acceptance of new ones. However, it should be noted that the direction and magnitude of such age effects are still open to controversy. And no one knows how important such skills are in determining attitude change. Indeed, in experimental research, learning has turned out not to be nearly so important as originally expected (McGuire 1969). So this is quite a speculative category of explanation.

Social Support

Both experimental and survey research testify eloquently to the great contribution social support makes to resistance to attitude change (e.g., Berelson *et al.* 1954, Hovland *et al.* 1953, Newcomb *et al.* 1967). Indeed it is safe to say than an attitude strongly supported by an individual's immediate primary groups is next to impossible to change.

Moreover, the stability of primary groups and their attitudinal sup-portiveness vary considerably and systematically across the life-span. The frequency of disruptive changes in primary groups of several kinds is highest in late adolescence and early adulthood. Geographical mobility, entering and/or changing specific work environments, status mobility, higher education, entering marriage or other intimate relationships, and military service are all most common in this early life stage (Carlsson and Karlsson 1970). And there is some evidence (though it is much less extensive) that primary groups are increasingly attitudinally homoge- neous with age (e.g., Berelson *et al.* 1954). Certainly attitude similarity is a powerful determinant of interpersonal attraction (Byrne 1971), so it is plausible that over time, people are increasingly able to assemble supportive family, work, and friendship groups. Nevertheless, there surely is enough natural variation in the attitudinal supportiveness of primary groups, and life events disrupt it enough, to permit some as-sessment of their role in age-related declines in attitude change.

Identity Diffusion

Finally, some psychodynamic influences may vary across age. The simplest is perhaps Erikson's (1968) notion of identity diffusion: Young people are still seeking their own identity with respect to their values and attitudes just as much as in other areas of life. Identity may then crystallize around attitudes and protect them from change.

LIFE STAGE AND ATTITUDE CHANGE:
SOME OPEN QUESTIONS

It should be apparent that much remains to be clarified. Before moving on to the specific problem of how the elderly fit into all this, let me highlight some of what seem to me the more interesting general research issues.

One is the intrinsic strength or weakness of pre-adult attitude acquisition. Much of this analysis assumes that such attitudes are inherently quite resistant to change after early adulthood. But that is far from clear; indeed, some prominent researchers dissent quite vigorously (e.g., Jennings and Niemi 1978). They argue not only that important attitudes have the potential for substantial change well into adulthood, but also that much change does in fact occur even under ordinary circumstances, in the absence of massive pressure to change. I feel confident that short-term panel studies (e.g., spanning 2 or 3 years), if carried out on a sufficiently broad age range, could help illuminate this question considerably.

A second is the general issue of resocialization in late adolescence or early adulthood. To what extent does resocialization occur under ordinary circumstances? What about extraordinary circumstances, such as revolutions, national defeats in war, or times of sweeping social change? And what preconditions are required for successful resocialization? Some have been outlined in past analyses (e.g., Newcomb *et al.* 1967, Sears and McConahay 1973) but with suggestive rather than definitive data. A related problem concerns the impact of varying intellectual, political, or social *zeitgeist* or, more generally, "period effects" of any kind. Our argument, like Mannheim's (1952), would look for persisting effects in subsets of birth cohorts youthful at the time of the events. For example, certain elections may leave marked effects on particular generations, as may assassinations, wars, charismatic leaders, depressions, depressed public moods, and so on. Many opportunities for such studies exist in other countries, where the political systems undergo great changes, wars and revolutions occur, etc. The buildup of large-scale, long-term data archives should facilitate such studies, though, of course, they can never definitively rule out alternative interpretations. And they still would be missing the more fine-grained interpersonal and psychological detail that social psychologists would prefer.

A third general issue concerns the connectedness between personal life and one's political and social attitudes. To what extent and under what conditions does the former influence the latter? A rich tradition of connecting personal and public life exists at the case study level, Lane's

(1962) essays being perhaps among the most provocative examples. More quantitiative studies often find much less connection (e.g., Campbell *et al.* 1960, Kinder and Sears, 1981). Life-cycle theorists such as Erik Erikson and Daniel Levinson are filled with speculations about how changes in life stage affect one's political thinking. This could potentially be a particularly interesting problem for the elderly, since their lives change so dramatically in so many ways (health, social relationships, work, finances, etc.; see Cutler 1977). But all stages of life involve major changes. Research exploring the connections between personal life and attitudes toward public life has generally not paid much attention to life-cycle considerations.

Finally, all of this discussion presupposes a concentration on strong commitments rather than on "non-attitudes." There are still numerous open life-cycle questions regarding this distinction. Among them are the association between affective strength and informational mass; to what extent does this change with age? What about "schematic thinking"; does this increase with age, and does it contribute to added resistance to change? Such research would help clarify the relationship between affective and cognitive components of important attitudes and how it changes with age and experience.

THE ELDERLY

Now how does all this apply to the elderly? The most simple-minded version of the burden of the anlysis to this point is that major social and political attitudes become increasingly resistant to change with age. Why they do is unclear. And certain conditions may exist that would allow for more openness, such as changes in social support, information flow, practice, or delayed changes in intellectual functioning, or some combination. But if they do exist, they must be statistically abnormal, making persistence the most common outcome. In any case, the implication would certainly seem to be that the major social and political attitudes of the elderly are very hard to change. In the rest of this chapter, let me offer a couple of possible exceptions to this view and raise some questions about processes that may make old age again something of an "impressionable" period, even though a far cry, perhaps, from the openness of youth.

Attitude Change in Old Age

One scrap of evidence comes from Brown's (1981) study of migration. People who changed counties (or congressional districts) after the age of 35 and who had lived in the new locale for at least 11 years, were substantially more likely to share the dominant party identification of this new environment than would be expected by chance. While self-selection (or even chance, given the relatively low n for this group) could account for part of the finding, it seems to hold up across enough controls to be believed. And it would suggest some adaptation among people well beyond the "impressionable period" (though, of course, by no means elderly, on the average).

Clearer evidence of change in later life comes from the Gahart and Sears (1979) study of whites' racial prejudices in the early 1970s. As shown in Table 8.1, the stability coefficients (test–retest Pearson r's) across the 1972–1976 period increase predictably from age 21 to age 60. But then it drops enormously, from .752 for those 45–60 to .552 for the 61+ contingent.

And this drop seems not to be a matter of chance. While one finding cannot establish a phenomenon any more than one swallow makes a spring, there are some special reasons for taking this one seriously. The number of cases involved is large, it is one of the few panel surveys carefully done across the full adult life-span, the dependent measure is based on fairly reliable scales and well-established items, and it focuses on attitudes that clearly fit our definition of high commitment. Moreover, it is an exceedingly robust finding within this data set; it holds impressively even when age cohorts are broken into much narrower slices.[7] And it holds across a number of controls, as we shall see.

Finally, it seems partly to reflect a meaningful shift. There has been a general long-term decrease in whites' racial prejudice since the early 1950s, which continued in this period. But the amount of liberalizing change in this panel study was inversely related to age, as shown also in Table 8.1. That is, if the early 1970s still was part of a liberalizing period, old people were somewhat more responsive to the period effect. In absolute terms, this change was small in all cohorts, but there is some evidence that some part of the lowered stability is meaningfully directional.[8]

---

[7] When the age range is broken down into 14 4-year cohorts, the steady increase in stability to asymptote at age 30, lasting to age 60, is quite striking (.49, .66, .71, .72, .70, .73, .76, .75, .73, and .77), as is the steady decrease thereafter (.65, .62, .52, .50) despite the small N's for these narrower cohorts (median $N = 75$). This inverted-U-shaped relationship seems to us quite robust.

[8] This is not just a regression effect, of course, since the birth cohorts were not selected on the attitude dimension. Nor is it a ceiling effect, since no cohort was especially extreme on these items.

TABLE 8.1
Stability of Racial Prejudice in Whites from 1972 to 1976, by Age and Education[a]

Age (1976)	Stability coefficients[b]			Mean change	Mean change[c]	
	Any college	No college	All respondents	Mean change	t	p
21–28	.66 (81)	.51 (58)	.61 (139)	+ .74	1.57	n.s.
29–44	.77 (151)	.59 (185)	.71 (336)	− .16	.58	n.s.
45–60	.86 (116)	.63 (191)	.75 (307)	−1.03	3.85	<.001
61+	.67 (55)	.50 (206)	.55 (262)	−1.58	4.62	<.001
All respondents	.78 (403)	.59 (640)	.70 (1043)	− .65	4.06	<.001

[a] From Gahart and Sears 1979. Data from Center for Political Studies 1972–1976 election studies panel.
[b] Entries are test–retest Pearson correlations. Number of cases in parentheses.
[c] Entry is mean increase in racial prejudice from 1972 to 1976, on a 10-item, 40-point scale.

EXPLANATIONS

To explain this apparent sudden "openness" among the elderly, the same potential explanations can be addressed as were raised earlier. An obvious one is lowered cognitive capacity. The fact that the elderly shifted most in the dirction "appropriate" for the period effect (more tolerance), rather shifting around in some random manner, argues against that. The high level of consistency of the constituent attitude scales also argues against incapacity. If old people were losing their capacity to process political information, the reliability of the 10-item prejudice scales ought also to diminish with age. But as shown in Table 8.2, that is not the case: Their alphas are in the same ballpark as those for younger people.

Another version of the lower-capacity argument is that older people are less educated and therefore less politically involved, which would show up in a variety of ways (less informed, less consistent, less participatory, etc.). Glenn (1969) and Verba and Nie (1972), for example, find they can largely erase the apparent lowered "opinionation" and political participation among the elderly by using appropriate education controls. It is certainly true that the old are less educated; in the Center for Political Studies panel (Gahart and Sears 1979), the proportion with some college drops dramatically, from 58 percent in the youngest cohort through 45% and 38% in the middle, to only 21% among the elderly. And it is also true that less educated people have substantially less stable attitudes, as shown in Table 8.1 ($r = .78$ for the college-educated, while $r = .59$ for the rest). But the drop in stability among the elderly is substantial among both education groups; it is really unaffected by the ed-

TABLE 8.2
Cronbach Alpha Coefficients for Racial Prejudice Scale, by Age and Education[a][b]

Age (1976)	Any college		No college		All respondents	
	1972	1976	1972	1976	1972	1976
21–28	.75	.72	.64	.78	.71	.77
29–44	.79	.81	.73	.71	.75	.78
45–60	.83	.82	.70	.75	.77	.79
61 +	.63	.75	.72	.67	.68	.70
All respondents	.79	.79	.73	.72	.78	.77

[a] From Gahart and Sears 1979.

[b] Entries are Cronbach alphas for the 10-item, 40-point racial prejudice scale for each of two administrations.

ucation control. So the alleged lack of political capacity seems unlikely to explain this reemergence of openness.[9]

The elderly constitute the age cohort most exposed to television, especially to television news, so perhaps they are most influenced by it. Comstock *et al.* (1978, p.113) report that the ratings for television news are twice as high in the 50 + group as in the 18–49 set. I have earlier expressed my skepticism about the persuasive powers of television, and normally with very strong attitudes like racial prejudices we would expect very strong reinforcement effects rather than markedly changed attitudes. Still, it is true that most studies assess only very short exposures to the media, and here we are concerned with cumulative impact over 4 years. In any case, we have no evidence on this point. So it is possible that the substantially greater exposure to period-specific information in the news may promote some surprising period effects among the elderly.

The elderly are particularly vulnerable to loss of social support for their attitudes as well as for everything else. They may lose their work companions through retirement, their family companions through death and children's mobility, their friends through death and migration, and so on. Again, we have no direct way of determining whether these support changes explain this increase in attitude change. We would need better migration data, of the sort Brown (1981) used, or social network data, of the sort Eulau (1978) advocates. However, we do know about retirement; 8% of those (originally) aged 41–56 retired during the 4 years of the study, while 55% of those 57 and over did. But the drop in stability with age was actually greater (from .75 to .52) among those who did not retire than among those who did (.57 to .56). Similarly, changes in marital or employment status did not explain attitude instability: The drop occurred both among those with a constant social environment and those for whom it changed.

A Mini-Agenda for Research on Aging

So it turns out that we have no very good explanation for this particular drop in attitude stability, which may reflect a more general phenomenon of surprising openness among the old. Or it may not. At least it serves as the occasion for raising some more general issues about the potential

[9] Of course, survival in such a 4-year panel sample favors the robust and healthy, probably particularly so for the elderly, leaving an artificially capable group of old people.

for attitude change in old people. Let us assume that, in fact, affective mass builds up with time, making change more difficult, and that whatever changes in cognitive capacity occur serve on the average to reinforce this closed-mindedness. Why, then, might old people ever have a new thought? Again, to reiterate, research ought to be done on both media impact and social networks among old people. But two other areas might prove profitable as well.

Another feature of a long life is great change in attitude objects. An issue like race may have been a more or less permanent fixture in American politics, but its specific manifestations have changed quite radically. Consider the enormous changes in the attitude object blacks pose for whites. In the eighteenth century, blacks were thought of as jungle savages, then as slaves, positioned socially somewhere between domestic farm animals and hired hands. Before the turn of this century, my grandmother learned to call them "colored"; Booker T. Washington was prominent. In the late 1960s, we described them as "new urban blacks" in the time of Eldrige Cleaver, Stokely Carmichael, and the Black Panthers (Sears and McConahay 1973). In 1789, the issue was what fraction of a human being a black slave represented. In 1954, the issue was formal quotas and other barriers excluding blacks from normal participation in daily life. In 1979, the issue was formal quotas and other barriers forcibly including blacks in normal participation in daily life.[10]

What happens when attitude objects change? The drift of current research suggests that attitudes may be more specific to the original attitude object than once thought.[11] This seems to me the burden of the current attitude–behavior literature; attitudes are associated only with behaviors very specifically similar to them (Schuman and Johnson 1976). In our research on attitudes toward public leadership (Sears 1981), the same implication holds: Attitudes toward individual leaders bear little relationship to attitudes toward political leaders as a class. "Congress" is a different attitude object from "Congressman X" summed across 435 instances, and attitudes tend to be rather specific to their respective

[10] The point was once made for me in quite a different context. I vividly remember my grandfather, at the age of 95, telling me in the 1970s about his triumphs while a teenager in Missouri in the 1890s, cutting river-bottom timber and painstakingly hauling it with a horse and wagon up onto the river bluff—but pausing, distracted momentarily by the sight of a bright red Boeing-727 jet climbing through the sky out the window behind me. His mind was bouncing back and forth for a moment across a span of 80 years, between a very slow horse with a very tippy wagon and a sleek jetliner. All attitude objects are surely not constant across the life-span, regardless of how stable their associated attitudes are.

[11] Put another way, if an attitude is thought of as an affective response conditioned to the original attitude object, this suggests the generalization gradient tends to be rather steep.

objects. The argument made by Lipset and Schneider (1978) about affirmative action is based on the same assumption: Whites resist it because it represents a new attitude object that evokes other attitudes than did Selma and Martin Luther King. It violates attitudes of Protestant individualism that were never evoked, one way or the other, by the civil rights struggles of the 1950s and 1960s.

The research issue here focuses on the process by which people arrive at attitudes toward new objects on the basis of predispositions learned in response to old objects. The cognitive consistency theories were designed to account for this and do a good job up to a point. But they are mute on the cognitive processes by which old people do (or do not) address new problems with old predispositions. If they do not vary much, if old predispositions do not transfer very flexibly to new objects, age could promote change.

A last issue concerns self-interest. Clearly the marked changes in life situations that occur to old people—reduced income, limited mobility, the need for medical care, and so on—produce a new set of self-interests (Cutler 1977). When might that generate attitude change? Not often, we argue (Sears *et al.* 1980). But perhaps sometimes. Perhaps when the issue is very tangible, immediate, and concrete, as with property tax limitations (Sears 1978), or perhaps with social security. Or perhaps people generalize from the experience of losing one's vitality, earning power, and so on to greater tolerance for victims of prejudice and injustice. The broader issue here concerns the conditions under which private life situations become politicized and precipitate changes in political attitudes. Little is known about that.

CONCLUSION

I have tried to present a simple model of the change in important attitudes through the life-span. This by itself raises a number of fundamental issues for social psychologists. Not the least of these is the striking stability of major attitudes. A humbling case concerns college-educated people aged 45–60, certainly a capable and well-informed group. Tables 8.1 and 8.2 show their stability in racial prejudice (.86) to be almost identical to the reliability of the scale (.83). This means almost no change in 4 years except for measurement error. The presumed determinants of this resistance to change vary in interesting and sometimes correlated ways across the life-cycle and need to be unscrambled. Examination of the oldest life stage may reveal some surprises, including perhaps more openness to modern ideas than usually expected. It is my belief that such research can address basic problems of attitudes and cognitive process in a fruitful way and often one more meaningful than is possible with brief, more controlled experimentation. Certainly when one considers an attitude's trek across the life-span, one is forced to come to grips with a real landscape.

ACKNOWLEDGMENTS

Thanks are owed to Martin T. Gahart for research collaboration and to Thad Brown, M. Kent Jennings, and Sara Kiesler for their helpful comments.

REFERENCES

Abramson, P. (1972) Intergenerational social mobility and partisan choice. *American Political Science Review* 66(December):1291–1294.

Abramson, P. (1975) *Generational Change in American Politics*. Lexington, Mass.: D. C. Heath.

Allen, H. M., Jr., and Sears, D. O. (1978) White Opposition to Busing in Los Angeles: Is Self-interest Rejuvenated? Paper presented at the annual meeting of the American Psychological Association, Toronto.

Anderson, N. H. (1971) Integration theory and attitude change. *Psychological Review* 78:171–206.

Berelson, B. R., Lazarsfeld, P. F., and McPhee, W. N. (1954) *Voting: A Study of Opinion Formation in a Presidential Election*. Chicago: University of Chicago Press.

Brown, T. A. (1981) On contextual change and partisan attributes. *British Journal of Political Science* (in press).

Byrne, D. (1971) *The Attraction Paradigm*. New York: Academic Press.

Campbell, A., Converse, P. E., Miller, W. E., and Stokes, D. E. (1960) *The American Voter*. New York: John Wiley and Sons.

Carlsson, G., and Karlsson, K. (1970) Age, cohorts, and the generation of generations. *American Sociological Review* 35:710–718.

Comstock, G., Chaffee, S. H., Kutzman, N., McCombs, M., and Roberts, D. (1978) *Television and Human Behavior*. New York: Columbia University Press.

Converse, P.E. (1962) Information flow and the stability of partisan attitudes. *Public Opinion Quarterly* 26:578–599.

Converse, P. E. (1970) Attitudes and non-attitudes: Continuation of a dialogue. Pp. 168–189 in E. R. Tufte, ed., *The Quantitative Analysis of Social Problems*. Reading, Mass.: Addision-Wesley.

Converse, P. E. (1975) Public opinion and voting behavior. Pp. 75–170 in F. I. Greenstein and N. W. Polsby, eds., *Handbook of Political Science*, Vol. 4. Reading, Mass.: Addison-Wesley.

Converse, P. E. (1976) *The Dynamics of Party Support: Cohort-Analyzing Party Identification*. Beverly Hills, Calif.: Sage Publications.

Cook, S. W. (1970) Motives in a conceptual analysis of attitude-related behavior. Pp. 179–231 in W. J. Arnold and D. Levine, Eds., *Nebraska Symposium on Motivation, 1969*. Lincoln, Neb.: University of Nebraska Press.

Craik, F. I. M. (1977) Age differences in human memory. In J. E. Birren and K. W. Schaie, eds., *Handbook of the Psychology of Aging*. New York: Van Nostrand Reinhold.

Cutler, N. E. (1977) Demographic, social-psychological, and political factors in the politics of aging: A foundation for research in "political gerontology." *American Political Science Review* 71:1011–1026.

Erikson, E. H. (1968) *Identity: Youth and Crisis*. New York: Norton.

Eulau, H. (1978) The Columbia Studies of Personal Influence in Voting and Public Affairs. Unpublished manuscript. Stanford University.

Feldman, K. A., and Newcomb, T. M. (1971) *The Impact of College on Students: Vol. I. An Analysis of Four Decades of Research*. San Francisco: Jossey-Bass.

Gahart, M. T., and Sears, D. O. (1979) Attitude Stability Through the Life Cycle: An Initial Investigation of Racial Prejudice as a Function of Environmental Consistency. Paper presented at the annual meeting of the Western Psychological Association, San Diego.

Glenn, N. D. (1969) Aging, disengagement, and opinionation. *Public Opinion Quarterly* 33(Spring):17–33.

Glenn, N. D. (1972) Sources of the shift to political independence: Some evidence from a cohort analysis. *Social Science Quarterly* 53(December): 494–519.

Glenn, N. D. (1974) Aging and conservatism. *Annals of the American Academy of Political and Social Science* 33:176–186.

Horn, J. L. (1970) Organization of data on life-span development of human abilities. Pp. 423–466 in L. R. Goulet and P. B. Baltes, eds., *Life-Span Developmental Psychology: Research and Theory*. New York: Academic Press.

Hovland, C. I., Janis, I. L., and Kelley, H. H. (1953) *Communication and Persuasion*. New Haven, Conn.: Yale University Press.

Jennings, M. K., and Niemi, R. G. (1974) *The Political Character of Adolescence*. Princeton, N.J.: Princeton University Press.

Jennings, M. K., and Niemi, R. G. (1978) The persistence of political orientations: An overtime analysis of two generations. *British Journal of Political Science* 8:333–363.

Johnson, P. B., Sears, D. O., and McConahay, J. B. (1971) Black invisibility, the press, and the Los Angeles riot. *American Journal of Sociology* 74(4):698–721.

Kinder, D. R., and Kiewiet, D. R. (1979) Economic grievances and political behavior: The role of collective discontents and symbolic judgments in congressional voting. *American Journal of Political Science* 23:495–527.

Kinder, D. R., and Sears, D. O. (1981) Prejudice and Politics: Symbolic racism versus racial threats to the good life. *Journal of Personality and Social Psychology* 40:414–431.

Klapper, J. T. (1960) *The Effects of Mass Communication*. New York: The Free Press.

Knoke, D. (1972) Community and consistency: The ethnic factor in status inconsistency. *Social Forces* 51(September):23–33.

Kraus, S., and Davis, D. (1976) *The Effects of Mass Communication on Political Behavior*. University Park, Penn.: Pennsylvania State University Press.

Lane, R. E. (1962) *Political Ideology: Why the American Common Man Believes What He Does*. New York: The Free Press.

Lenski, G. E. (1954) Status crystallization: A non-vertical dimension of social status. *American Sociological Review* 19:405–413.

Lipset, S. M., and Schneider, W. (1978) The Bakke case: How would it be decided at the bar of public opinion? *Public Opinion* 1:38–44.

Mannheim, K. (1952) The problem of generations. In P. Kecskemeti, ed., *Essays on the Sociology of Knowledge*. London: Routledge and Kegan Paul.

Markus, H. (1977) Self-schemata and processing information about the self. *Journal of Personality and Social Psychology* 35:63–78.

McGuire, W. J. (1969) The nature of attitudes and attitude change. Pp. 136–314 in G. Lindzey and E. Aronson, eds., *The Handbook of Social Psychology, Vol. 3,* 2nd edition. Reading, Mass.: Addison-Wesley.

Newcomb, T. M., Koenig, K. E., Flacks, R., and Warwick, D. P. (1967) *Persistence and Change: Bennington College and Its Students after 25 Years.* New York: John Wiley and Sons.

Niemi, R. G. (1974) *How Family Members Perceive Each Other.* New Haven, Conn.: Yale University Press.

Rokeach, M. (1968) *Beliefs, Attitudes and Values: A Theory of Organization and Change.* San Francisco: Jossey-Bass.

Schuman, H., and Johnson, M. P. (1976) Attitudes and behavior. *Annual Review of Sociology* 2:161–207.

Sears, D. O. (1975) Political Socialization. Pp. 96–136 in F. I. Greenstein and N. W. Polsby, eds., *Handbook of Political Science: Vol. 2, Micropolitical Theory.* Reading, Mass.: Addison-Wesley.

Sears, D. O. (1978) The Jarvis Amendment: Self-interest or Symbolic Politics? Unpublished manuscript. University of California, Los Angeles.

Sears, D. O. (1981) The Person-Positivity Bias. Unpublished manuscript. University of California, Los Angeles.

Sears, D. O. (1982) *Political Attitudes Through the Life Cycle.* San Francisco: W. H. Freeman (in preparation).

Sears, D. O., Hensler, C. P., and Speer, L. K. (1979) Whites' opposition to "busing:" Self-interest or symbolic politics. *American Political Science Review* 73:369–384.

Sears, D. O., Lau, R. R., Tyler, T. R., and Allen, H. M., Jr. (1980) Self-interest versus symbolic politics in policy attitudes and 1976 presidential voting. *American Political Science Review* 74:670–684.

Sears, D. O., and McConahay, J. B. (1973) *The Politics of Violence: The New Urban Blacks and the Watts Riot.* Boston, Mass.: Houghton-Mifflin.

Sears, D. O., and Smith, T. (1975) How Strong are Preadults' Political Attitudes? Paper presented to the annual meeting of the Western Psychological Association, Sacramento.

Sherif, M., and Cantril, H. (1947) *The Psychology of Ego-Involvements.* New York: John Wiley and Sons.

Taylor, S. E., and Crocker, J. (1980) Schematic bases of social information processing. In E. T. Higgins, P. Hermann, and M. P. Zanna, eds., *The Ontario Symposium on Personality and Social Psychology, Vol. 1.* Hillsdale, N.J.: Lawrence Erlbaum Associates.

Tedin, K. L. (1974) The influence of parents on the political attitudes of adolescents. *American Political Science Review* 68(4):1579–1592.

Thompson, K. H. (1971) Upward social mobility and political orientation: A re-evaluation of the evidence. *American Sociological Review* 36(April):223–234.

Vaillancourt, P. M. (1973) Stability of children's survey responses. *Public Opinion Quarterly* 37:373–387.

Verba, S., and Nie, N. H. (1972) *Participation in America: Political Democracy and Social Equality.* New York: Harper and Row.

chapter 9

Aging and Opportunities
for Elective Office

JOSEPH A. SCHLESINGER
MILDRED SCHLESINGER

The aging of America has significant implications for the American structure of political opportunities that have yet to be explored. Between 1900 and 1975, the older population of the United States, those over 55 years of age, increased dramatically. Another dramatic increase in this age group is expected during the first decades of the next century, as the cohorts of the post World War II baby boom age become over 55 years (Siegel 1978, p. 3). One observer has termed this phenomenon an "impending population upheaval . . . comparable to the immigration tide in the late nineteenth and early twentieth centuries and the immigration of blacks to the North after World War II . . . [Samuelson 1978, p. 1712]," events of considerable import for political opportunities in the United States.

Of even more consequence for the opportunity structure than their numbers are the qualities of aging Americans. It is indeed true that along with the increase in the number of older Americans has come a change in the "social meaning of growing old" (Eisele 1974). Demographers and gerontologists have identified a group of "young-old," those ranging in age from 55 to 75, whom they expect increasingly to possess relative good health, relative affluence, and a relatively high level of education. Largely free of family responsibilities, this group will also possess, to

AGING
Social Change

the extent that the trend toward early retirement continues, a considerable amount of leisure time (Neugarten 1974).[1] These are characteristics that we associate with political elites, and indeed that is the way Bernice Neugarten depicts the young old of the 1990s. Reminding us that they will include those who actively participated in the major political and cultural movements of the 1960s and 1970s, she concludes: "These experiences and these attitudes combined with their higher educational and occupational levels, will probably lead the future young-old to exert a potent influence upon government. Compared to the young-old of the 1970s the young-old of the 1990s are likely to wield their influence through direct political action . . . [Neugarten 1974, p. 197]."

Given the characteristics of the future young-old that we have singled out, one form of direct political action may well be the search for elective office. At first glance, elective office appears as an excellent outlet for the energies of the politically aware, healthy, leisured, and educated young-old. The only age requirements are, after all, minimum requirements. Apart from these, entry into an elective political career can come at any age and without special prior training.[2] Elective politics, it is true, is a risky venture. There is no sure guarantee of election, and, once elected, there is no guarantee of tenure in office. For the vast majority of elective offices in the United States, the rate of turnover is high. Of course, the obverse of this situation is the great number of political opportunities available. Certainly, there is no guarantee of a steady and adequate income. Yet perhaps no group is in a better position to take such risks than the young-old we have described.[3]

Our task, then, is to consider to what extent the American structure of political opportunities will be able to accomodate a potentially unprecedented number of aging political aspirants. This question is by no means farfetched. Elsewhere in this volume, Neal Cutler convincingly argues that the future elderly will be far more age-conscious than those of the present. Yet already age-consciousness appears to have been added to consciousness of class, race, and sex. Consciousness in the latter instances inevitably provoked the question: How open is elective office to blue-collar workers, to blacks, and to women? Certainly we

---

[1] There is now a real question as to the economic feasibility of early retirement, even before the proportion of older Americans shifts perceptibly after the turn of the next century (see, for example, Sheppard and Rix 1977; Neugarten and Hagestad 1976, p. 39). This would not, however, necessarily affect the trend toward second careers.

[2] ". . . the political role in modern democracies . . . has a peculiarly flexible or volitional character that frees it from many of the direct and obvious constraints of age . . . [Foner 1972, p. 120]."

[3] Put differently, they are subject to fewer role conflicts than other age groups (Foner 1972, p. 129).

should now expect to hear the question: How receptive is the elective system to older aspirants in a society that has already moved to ban age discrimination as well as sex and racial discrimination in employment and has acted to end mandatory retirement?

Unfortunately, the literature that can help us with our task is slight. Politicians and political journalists, it is true, frequently worry in public about the timetables of political careers; this may well account for the ready availability of age data on both successful and defeated candidates for elective office. Yet political scientists have made little extensive use of such data to analyze age as an important independent variable affecting political careers.[4] Most often they have used age along with a host of other characteristics, such as social and economic status, occupation, and education to describe the politician's background. Such descriptions have led political scientists to comment on the comparatively advanced age of individuals in high positions of leadership (Hudson and Binstock 1976, pp. 377–378; Binstock 1974, p. 211). The question of the longevity of political careers is not irrelevant to our concerns. Freed from a fixed retirement age, how many and what types of officeholders can and do carry on long-term careers with only the impending threat of electoral defeat to contend with? Or is the trend toward early retirement and second careers also discernible among politicians? Our first concern, however, is with the relatively neglected question of the age of access to elective office. To what extent will the American structure of political opportunities allow the future young-old to launch political careers? How high will they realistically be able to set their political aspirations?

To answer these questions, we need first to map out the timetables of elective political careers that have emerged in the United States. For the numerous elective offices, from city councillor to president, timetables do exist. Amidst the apparent chaos, there is indeed an office-holding hierarchy. Without the prescript of law, individuals ascend from one office to another. Moreover, without legal prescripts, they often do so in an orderly time progression. This is not to say that age patterns for office have hardened within the American political system. Taking into account minimal legal age requirements, we can easily demonstrate that a variety of elective offices have been acquired at a variety of ages— which is by no means irrelevant to our concern for the political opportunities open to the young-old. Equally relevant, however, is the recognition that for all its openness, political opportunity in the United States has form. The form is due in part to the frequent disposition of particular offices to particular age groups.

[4] For the recognition by other social scientists of the importance of personal timetables, see Clausen 1972, pp. 462, 511–512; Neugarten 1974, pp. 44, 49–50.

Having identified the age patterns for elective offices and considered their pervasiveness, we need to try to explain their existence. The explanations we offer are four: institutional, organizational, motivational, and demographic. In offering these explanations, we have tried to be as sensitive as our data have allowed to the analytical distinctions that concern social scientists examining the effects of aging on social and political processes: the effect of biological aging or the life-cycle, the effect of cohorts, the effect of historical time periods (Hudson and Binstock 1976, p. 369, Bengston and Cutler 1976, Cutler, in this volume, Riley *et al.* 1972, pp. 11, 14, 16, 29, 45, 61, 69, 75, 527, 608, 610, 612). Nevertheless, our explanations can be summarized essentially in the following statements: (1) The institutional explanation suggests that the relative size and importance of individual political institutions and the relationships between institutions affect the age patterns for elective office. (2) The organizational explanation focuses on the effect of organized efforts for recruitment, notably those of political parties, on the ages of officeholders. (3) The motivational explanation considers the relation between ambition for office and age as a critical factor in the determination of the timetables of elective political careers. (4) The demographic explanation looks to the composition of the population from which candidates are drawn and to the effect of the size, longevity, and sex composition of particular age groups on the age distribution of elective officeholders. Alterations in institutions, in party organization, in human motivation, especially ambition, and in population groups will all vitally affect the political opportunities of the future young-old.

AGE PATTERNS AND ELECTIVE OFFICE IN THE UNITED STATES

The ages at which elective offices are achieved in the United States are not random. Definite age patterns have emerged, at least for the more conspicuous elective positions. The evidence suggests that age patterns developed gradually during the nineteenth century as the practices of American democracy were being established. After the turn of the twentieth century, for approximately the next five decades, a relatively stable political system nurtured relatively stable and well-defined age patterns for elective office. Following the political changes of the 1960s have come changes in the age patterns of the 1970s. The facts that age patterns developed in a political system whose age requirements for office have been minimal and that these patterns have been subject to change are of considerable significance for the political opportunities of the young-old.

During the first decades of the Republic, the opportune ages for the achievement of elective office were by no means clear. While the modal age distributions for the achievement of conspicuous state and federal offices were distinct, the distribution of ages for each office lacked focus and was widely dispersed (see Figure 9.1). Thus, from 1800–1809 the largest group of United States representatives were first elected in their late thirties, the largest group of senators in their late forties, the largest group of newly elected governors in their early fifties. At the same time, for each office the modal age group was not conspicuously dominant. By the mid-nineteenth century the age distribution for each office had become more focused; moreover, the age distributions for the three offices had come to look very much the same: At either end of the age scale, fewer individuals achieved office than those in the middle; for all three offices the modal age groups were in their forties. By the early twentieth century, the focus of age distributions was much sharper: U.S. representatives were winning their first elections predominantly in their early forties, and senators and governors in their late forties.

As for the length of careers in office, the situation was again a changing one. Throughout the nineteenth century, the overall length of service in each of the three offices was relatively brief. No office emerged as a potential career office until after the turn of the twentieth century, when the average senate term approached 8 years (Ripley 1969, p. 43). In the first years of the Republic, despite the official 6-year term, the average length of service in the Senate was a mere 2.5 years, well below that of service in the House, which was averaging 5.66 years, or 2.83 official terms. During the nineteenth century, senate service rose slowly to an average of 4 years in the 1830s. Only in the 1870s did it begin to rise again, but the average length of service did not exceed the official 6-year term until 1900. Meanwhile, service in the House took a somewhat reverse course, though it, too, noticeably increased after 1900. After the high of 5.66 years in 1811, the average length of service in the House dropped to a low of 3.38 years in the 32nd Congress of 1853. It then rose slowly until 1901, when it reached 6.22 years (Polsby 1968, p. 146). Gubernatorial service followed a course similar to that of service in the House. Initially, the average length of service was 4.9 years, although official terms varied from 1 to 4 years, with 1-year terms dominating (Kallenbach 1966, p. 187). By 1850–1859, average gubernatorial service had dropped to 2.94 years, after which it rose to 3.39 years in the decade 1900–1909 (Schlesinger 1970). It would appear, then, that real possibilities

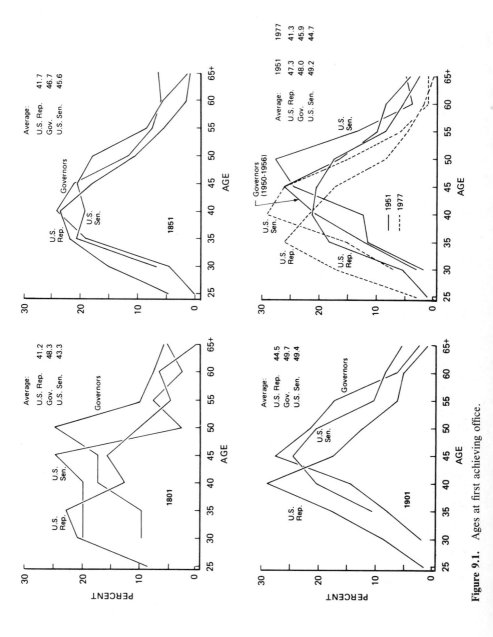

Figure 9.1. Ages at first achieving office.

for extended elective careers had not yet emerged by the end of the nineteenth century.[5]

Age Patterns in the Period of Stability, 1910–1960

After the turn of the twentieth century and for the next five decades, age patterns for higher elective office were quite clear, and the federal legislature emerged as something of a haven for careerists restricted by no formal retirement age. For this period, we can indeed establish a hierarchy of offices according to the ages at which each office was most likely to be achieved. The higher the office, the more focused or narrow the dispersion of ages at which first election typically came. At the top of the hierarchy was the president, elected most frequently between the ages of 50 and 55 (see Figure 9.2), a more focused distribution than that of the nineteenth century, when presidential ages were distributed throughout the fifties. Senators also were now winning their first election mainly in their early fifties. Governors were still taking office for the first time in their late forties, while U.S. representatives ranged more widely in age at first election, from the late thirties to the early forties.

This age-step pattern was not fortuitous since most higher elective officials arrived at their positions via offices beneath them. Thus, 7 of the 10 presidents elected during the period had been either governors or senators. Of the senators elected for the first time during this period, 48% had been either governors or U.S. representatives; only 8.22% had had no prior public office experience. Almost 40% of the governors came from statewide elective or state legislative office; only 8.11% had had no prior office experience (Schlesinger 1966, pp. 91–92). Of the representatives serving in 1951, a majority had been either public attorneys or state legislators; only 18.2% had had no prior office experience (*Biographical Directory of the American Congress, 1774–1971*). Moreover, most higher elective officials had begun their careers in public office well before they achieved election to higher office. Of the major party candidates who ran for the offices of governor and senator between 1900 and 1958 (senators from 1914), three-fourths had started their public office careers by the time they were 40; of this group about half had started in their thirties (Schlesinger 1966, p. 177). When we also consider the predominance of a single profession, the law, among higher elective

---

[5] From what little evidence we have, it may be that the nineteenth century saw an even sharper rise in turnover in state legislatures. In Connecticut, the percentage of legislators reelected from the previous year was 54.0 in 1800, 22.6 in 1830, 12.7 in 1860, 9.3 in 1880, and a mere 5.2 in 1889 (Luce 1924, p. 356).

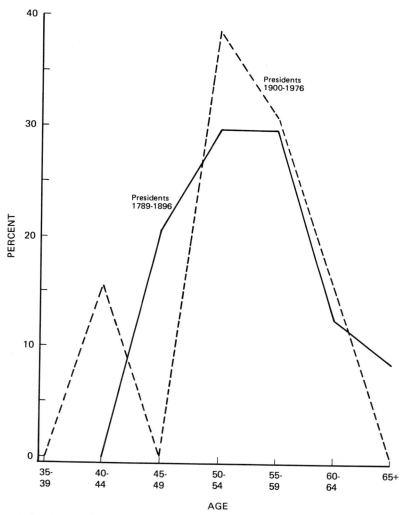

Figure 9.2. Ages at first achieving presidency.

officials, we realize how careerist elective politics had become (Schlesinger 1966, p. 178, 1957a, Eulau and Sprague 1964).

Other political scientists have chosen to comment on the relatively advanced age of American political leadership (Hudson and Binstock 1976, pp. 377–378). We wish to emphasize the dominance of the middle-aged and the middle-aged who first served both an office and a professional apprenticeship. This is not to say that American politics had come to bar the nonlawyer over 50 and without prior office experience from higher elective office. Such a person was, however, taking the less common route. Of the major party candidates for governor and senator, only 6% were 50 or older when they entered politics; of these only 21% were lawyers. Yet of this small group of older candidates, less than half (43%) were able to capture their nominations without prior public office experience (Schlesinger 1966, pp. 178–182). Thus, while higher elective office as a second career was a distinct possibility during the period of stability, it was hardly the norm.

If elective politics at higher levels was not an optimal second career choice, could it nevertheless provide for extensive careers continuing past customary retirement ages? Executive elective office offered few such opportunities. Apart from the obvious limited tenure of presidents, gubernatorial service was also brief. After the turn of the twentieth century, gubernatorial service rose slowly to an average of 4.6 years in 1950–1959, not quite returning to the average length of service for the early 1800s. Federal legislative office, on the other hand, emerged during the twentieth century as a careerist's office. By 1939, the average length of senatorial service was 8.5 years. It remained relatively stable until 1965, when it reached 10 years; in 1967, the average length of service rose to 10.5 years. In the House, the average length of service increased even more. By 1931, it averaged 8.96 years; by 1951, 9.46 years; in 1961, the average length of service for U.S. representatives peaked at 11.3 years. In both houses, the averages masked careers of much greater length that extended well beyond the age of 65.

Thus far we have considered only the opportunities for higher elective office because the data were more manageable. But the obvious question remains: Once the American political system had stabilized, how did various age groups fare in lesser offices? Data for the lower houses of five selected state legislatures (Vermont, Connecticut, South Dakota, Pennsylvania, and Michigan) for the years 1950–1959 indicate that age distributions for first elections were generally more dispersed or less focused. The age curves were flatter than that of the U.S. House of Representatives of the same period (see Figure 9.3). The exception was the state of Vermont, whose legislature, in contrast to the House, heavily favored older legislators. In Vermont, the number of legislators increased in each advancing age bracket until the age bracket over 50 accounted for 64% of the state's new legislators. In contrast, only 22% of the new House members were in this age group.

At the same time, the length of service in the Vermont legislature was very brief, though it lengthened during the period of stability. For the years 1951–1960, the average number of new legislators each term was 57.3%, down from the high of 84.3% in 1931–1940. Service in the other state legislatures was also brief, although it varied. Like Vermont, how-

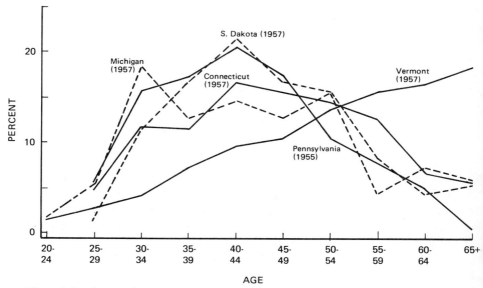

Figure 9.3.   Ages at first attaining legislative office.

ever, all four legislatures registered a decline in the turnover of personnel. In 1951–1960, the average number of new legislators every 2 years in Connecticut was 49%, down from 56.2% in 1931–1940; the number in South Dakota was 42.1%, down from 59.3%; the number in Pennsylvania was 30.4%, down from 51%; the number in Michigan was 26.3%, down from 46.5%. The movement in these legislatures toward longer service was part of a national trend. The composite turnover figure for the lower houses of all state legislatures in 1951–1960 was 44% every 2 years, down from 58.7% in 1931–1940 (Shin and Jackson 1979). Nevertheless, state legislative careers were not yet emulating those in the federal congress. State legislatures were more hospitable to the late starters in elective politics, but hospitality was bought at the price of less extensive legislative careers.[6]

The differences as well as the similarities that we have just noted in state legislative age and tenure patterns indicate that it is important to consider not only national patterns but also regional and state trends. For regions and states have varied considerably in their treatment of various age groups for elective office. In the period of stability, New England, the Border states, the South, and the West had distinctive age patterns for higher office. The age pattern of New England and the

---

[6] While we do not have the data for the local elective offices of city councillor and county commissioner, we would speculate that the age and tenure patterns would be similar to those of state legislatures.

Border states set the national norm of age progression for the offices of U.S. representative, governor, and senator that we have discussed. The age patterns of the Midwest and the Middle Atlantic states were similar but not so neat. The age distributions were flatter in the Midwest; the differences in the ages of governors and senators were also much smaller than elsewhere. In the Middle Atlantic states, the ages at first election to the governorship concentrated more strongly in the late forties, while senators winning their first election were somewhat older than elsewhere. U.S. representatives also first entered Congress somewhat later, typically in their late forties.

The age pattern of the South and West was distinctive because senators typically won their first election at an earlier age than governors. In both regions, U.S. representatives were also conspicuously younger than elsewhere. The age pattern of the two regions was clearly related to the regional treatment of the office of senator as a career office. In the South, at least, strong assurance of long tenure in office undoubtedly had its impact on the selection process, producing younger senatorial candidates than elsewhere. The same observation was true for southern representatives, who also entered Congress earlier than elsewhere and then went on to serve longer terms (Schlesinger 1966, pp. 187–192).

Further differences in age patterns were distinguishable among the individual states. To get some idea of the states' treatment of older aspirants for higher office, we classified the states according to the ages at which the major party candidates for governor and senator had begun their careers in public office. When we ranked the states according to the percentage of candidates who began their careers at 40 or older, the range was considerable, from a high of 55% in Oklahoma, to a low of O in Mississippi (see Table 9.1). This ranking helps dissect the southern age pattern. Of the four states in which 10% or less of the candidates began their public office careers at 40 or older, three were in the South; only one southern state was among those states in which more than 20% of the candidates started their careers late; Virginia (23%). In contrast, in 8 southern states, 50% or more of the candidates started their careers before age 30. States hospitable to late starters were less concentrated regionally, though more than one New England and Middle Atlantic state were represented. In only one state, Oklahoma, did a majority of the candidates make a late start. On the other hand, the southern states aside, most states did not severely penalize late starters. In more than half the states, 20% or more of the major party candidates had begun their careers at 40 or older.

The age and tenure patterns that we have been describing emerged and stabilized in the decades between 1910 and 1960. Since that time, alterations have begun to occur that are of considerable importance for

TABLE 9.1

Ranking of States According to Percentage of Major Leaders Who First Entered Public Office at Age 40 or Older (Major Party Candidates for Governor and Senator, 1900–1958)[a]

		Percentage			Percentage			Percentage			Percentage
1.	Oklahoma	55	13.	Indiana	31	25.	North Dakota	22	37.	Iowa	17
2.	Delaware	48	14.	New York	29	26.	Maryland	21	38.	Kentucky	16
3.	Connecticut	41	15.	Arizona	28	27.	West Virginia	21	39.	North Carolina	15
4.	Pennsylvania	39	16.	Illinois	26	28.	Texas	20	40.	Nevada	14
5.	Idaho	36	17.	Colorado	26	29.	Georgia	20	41.	Washington	14
6.	Kansas	36	18.	Wisconsin	25	30.	Tennessee	20	42.	New Hampshire	14
7.	New Jersey	36	19.	Montana	25	31.	Rhode Island	19	43.	Ohio	13
8.	Vermont	34	20.	Missouri	24	32.	Utah	19	44.	South Carolina	11
9.	Oregon	33	21.	Virginia	23	33.	New Mexico	19	45.	Alabama	10
10.	Maine	32	22.	California	22	34.	Louisiana	18	46.	Minnesota	9
11.	Michigan	32	23.	Nebraska	22	35.	Florida	18	47.	Arkansas	8
12.	Wyoming	31	24.	South Dakota	22	36.	Massachusetts	17	48.	Mississippi	0

[a] Adapted from Schlesinger 1966, p. 190.

the opportunities of the young-old in elective politics. For all three major offices in American elective politics the trend now is in favor of younger officeholders. This has been especially true of the Congress. The optimal age for election to the House is now in the late thirties, for the Senate in the early forties (see Figure 9.1). This trend has not been accompanied by a marked change in the number of individuals entering Congress without prior office experience. The marked change has been in the increased number of senators and representatives with state legislative experience. This trend represents a return to the nineteenth-century practice (Table 9.2). It also heralds a potential change in the age patterns of state legislatures that may well work to the disadvantage of the late starter in politics. Also noteworthy is the decline in the number of senators who came from the governorship, from 28.6% in the 1950s to 15% in the 1970s, a shift that accompanies the change in the age rankings of the two offices. As in the nineteenth century, senators are now typically

TABLE 9.2
Selected Prior Public Office Experience[a]

	Congress served (year elected)				
	7th (1800)	32nd (1850)	57th (1900)	82nd (1950)	95th (1976)
	U.S. Representatives				
No prior office	14.7	14.6	15.6	18.2	21.1
State legislature	74.1	59.4	40.5	33.3	43.9
	U.S. Senators				
No prior office	2.4	4.1	4.3	7.1	11.0
State legislature	78.1	74.0	55.4	38.1	45.0
U.S. Representative	34.2	39.7	38.0	28.6	32.0
Governor	4.9	16.4	19.6	27.6	15.0

	Governors (elected governors only)				
	1800–1809	1850–1859	1900–1909	1950–1959	1970–1975[b]
No prior office	7.0	1.6	9.4	5.3	14.0
State legislature	75.4	69.8	57.0	43.6	40.0[b]
U.S. Representative	38.6	23.8	16.8	9.8	14.0[b]
U.S. Senator	15.8	5.6	0.7	4.5	—

[a] Based on data in *Biographical Directory of the American Congress 1774–1971* and 95th Congressional data from Barone, Ujufusa, and Matthews (1978).

[b] 1970–1975 data are from Sabato (1978) and the percentages differ in that they are of penultimate office rather than experience. This understates the amount of state legislative experience in the latter group of governors. In the period 1900–1949, only 17.8% of governors had the legislature as a penultimate office.

winning their first elections at a similar or somewhat earlier age than governors. At the same time, there is evidence that the ages of new governors are also declining. While the average age of governors in 1951 was 48, the average age in 1977 was 45.9 years (Sabato 1978, p. 32). Recent trends in the ages of higher elective officeholders, then, would not appear to be favoring the young-old.

No more do recent trends appear to be favoring the continuation of elective office careers beyond the common retirement age of 65. The number of voluntary retirements in the House has increased: In 1966, there were 12, in 1978, there were 30. Between 1966 and 1974, 25.4% of the House retired; of these members, more than half retired before the age of 65. A disproportionate number of retirees were late starters: Over 40% had not entered the House until after 50, while fewer than 25% of the entire House had entered at this late age (Frantzich 1978). At the same time, between 1940 and 1970, the percentage of senior representatives, those with 10 or more terms, who died in office declined from 34.8% to 23.5%, while those who retired because of electoral defeat increased from 15.2% to 39.6% (Bullock 1972). Similarly, the unprecedented turnover in senate personnel in the elections of 1976 and 1978 marked the end of a number of long senatorial careers.[7]

It should be noted, however, that the trend toward longer tenure in the state legislatures has continued. In 1971–1976, the national average for the number of new legislators dropped again, to 37.3%. The average also dropped again in all five of the legislatures we considered earlier. The largest decline came in Vermont, where the average number of new legislators per term dropped to 37.3%. But the number also fell in Connecticut to 40.2%, in South Dakota to 38.5%, in Michigan to 24.6%, and in Pennsylvania to 23.4%. It remains to be determined whether the state legislatures are in fact beginning to support extended legislative careers. To the extent that they do so and to the extent that they become more important training grounds for higher office as well, they may reduce political opportunities for the young-old.

AGE PATTERNS FOR ELECTIVE OFFICE AND POLITICAL INSTITUTIONS

How can we account for the age and tenure patterns we have just described? What factors must we monitor to detect changes in age pat-

---

[7] Treas (1977), in applying a life-table analysis to senate careers between 1945 and 1970, concludes that increasing seniority does not make senators less liable to electoral defeat.

terns for elective office? Certainly institutional arrangements and institutional developments are a principal factor. The size of institutions, their relative importance, and the relationships of offices within and between institutions have helped determine the timetables of American elective officials.

The size of an institution accounts for the number of opportunities that those meeting minimum age requirements—the only age requirements for elective office in the United States—must share. Size is defined not only by the number of official positions within a given institution but also by the length of term of office and the rate of turnover in office, both of which contribute to the actual number of people that an institution encompasses. The larger the number of official positions, the shorter their term of office; the more rapid the turnover of officeholders, the larger will be the number of political opportunities. The larger the number of political opportunities, the greater the likelihood that a wide variety of age groups can aspire to the offices of a particular institution, or at least that careerists will not dominate. Obversely, the smaller the number of offices, the longer the term of office; the lower the rate of turnover, the more likely that the officeholders' ages will be focused.

Ages will also be more or less focused, depending on the relative importance of the institution. If the institution is relatively unimportant, if its influence is small, and if the power and the perquisites that go with its offices are few, then the offices are likely to attract a mixed lot of candidates, including candidates of mixed age groups. On the other hand, the more important the institution and the more desirable its offices, the more likely they will attract candidates with substantial resources—financial, organizational, or simply physical. Such candidates are most likely to come from the middle-age spectrum and will surpass the younger in money and following and the older in energy.

While some offices are more important than others, they have relationships with lesser offices that are likely to affect the age patterns of both. Offices are often perceived as having a special or manifest relationship that facilitates movement between them. The more important office appears to require prior office experience of a particular type, the lesser office looms as a training ground because both offices perform similar or complementary functions. This relationship can be reinforced by the need to please the same or part of the same constituency. If an office is perceived as a training ground, it will tend to attract younger, career-oriented candidates. If an office is seen as requiring prior office experience, the age at which it can be achieved will tend to rise. At the same time, the chances of the older, inexperienced candidate seeking such office as a second career will be reduced.

We can demonstrate the relation between institutional arrangements and age patterns with a brief overview of the American experience. The period of unfocused age distributions coincided with the period of unsettled institutional arrangements that characterized much of the nineteenth century. During the early years of the Republic, the size and status of state and federal offices were indeterminate. Washington had not yet become the nation's political mecca. Few federal elective officials chose to remain there the entire year: Most senators and represenatatives did not bring their families to live in the capital (Young 1966). Moreover, after service in the federal Congress, it was by no means unusual for senators to return to the House or the governorship, and for senators and representatives to return to the state legislatures where most had begun their political careers. Senators, of course, were chosen by the state legislatures until 1914, and during these early years were often viewed as the legislatures' delegates rather than as independent officials (Riker 1955). Governors, too, had a close attachment to the state legislatures. Although most came to be popularly elected, in the early years they were nominated by legislative caucus. Like senators and representatives, they had, more often than not, risen from legislative ranks. Like senators and representatives, they did not rule out a return to the legislature after gubernatorial service.

The relative status of offices was kept uncertain well into the nineteenth century because of the political ethic that triumphed under Andrew Jackson, which equated democracy with the widespread distribution of elected offices enforced by their frequent rotation. Thus, congressional seats were frequently viewed as offices to be rotated among the various counties comprising a legislative district (Kernell 1976). In such an ethos, no well-ordered committee system or methodical progression to the leadership developed in Congress to encourage long service; brief service could bring positions of power, as Henry Clay demonstrated by winning the speakership in the House during his first term (Polsby 1968). Similarly, expectations, if not always the law, limited gubernatorial service to two terms. And the official terms were brief, predominantly 1-year terms in 1820, and predominantly 2-year terms in 1860. Not until 1900 were gubernatorial terms about equally divided between 2- and 4-year terms.

While institutional practices were contributing to high turnover, thereby blurring the relative importance of offices, the institutions themselves were expanding in size with something of the same effect. The steady entry of new states along with the growth in population had its greatest impact on the House, which grew from 142 members in 1800 to 391 members in 1900. At the same time, the states' elective executive offices were expanding to include not only the governorship but such positions as secretary of state, state treasurer, and state attorney general. One result was to dilute the importance of the governorship.

The pool of political opportunities was also kept large and the status of offices blurred by diffuse electoral timing. State elections were held at any time during the year. Not until 1872 did Congress require that federal elections all fall on the same day. Even then exceptions were provided for; not until 1960 did Maine hold its congressional elections at the same time as other states. As a consequence, potential office-seekers were not limited in the choice of offices they could seek, nor were they or incumbent officeholders forced to make decisions about which offices were more important or desirable. Thus, throughout the nineteenth century, the growth of American political institutions and the relatively free flow of office movement contributed to the relatively broad distribution of ages to elective office that we traced.

After the turn of the twentieth century, important institutional changes took place that worked to limit the size of institutions and clarify their status. In the wake of these changes, came the more focused distribution of ages for higher elective office. The direct election of senators enacted for the elections of 1914 resulted from the increasing power of the Senate and contributed to the Senate's establishment as the major elective position beneath the presidency (Rothman 1966, Ripley 1969). Direct election broke the senators' close ties with the state legislatures, thereby forcing them to rely for power, not primarily on the position of "state political boss" but on position within the internal hierarchy of the Senate, a position that by the end of the nineteenth century had come to depend on seniority (Ripley 1969). Evidence of the appreciation in value of senate office in the twentieth century was the increase in the number of senators whose political careers ended in senate service. In 1851, less than half (47.9%) ended their careers with senate service; in 1951 81% did so. After the turn of the century, there was a precipitous decline in the number of senators willing to accept federal cabinet posts (Huntington 1965). Movement from the Senate to the governorship also ended. On the other hand, the identity of senatorial and gubernatorial constituencies brought about by the direct election of senators is part of a picture that includes an increase in the number of governors going on to the Senate. The number rose from 16.4% in 1851 and 19.6% in 1901 to 27.6% in 1951. Thus, the governorship established itself as a transitional office during the first decades of the twentieth century.

Since the 1950s, however, the transitional status of the governorship has lessened somewhat, as the number of opportunities for the governorship has decreased. Since the 1950s, an increasing number of states have adopted the 4-year term for governor. By 1968, only 12 states did not have the 4-year term (Kallenbach 1966). By 1976, this number had been reduced to 4. Such changes in gubernatorial tenure coincide with the decline we noted in the number of senators first serving in the governorship and the decline in senatorial ages.

On the other hand, the position of the House established in the first decades of the twentieth century as both a career office and a manifest office, or obvious stepping-stone to the Senate, has only been slightly modified by recent institutional changes (Price 1971). By 1910, the number of House seats stabilized at the present 435. Shortly thereafter, the slow decline in turnover that came at the end of the nineteenth century was given impetus by important internal reforms, notably those weakening the power of the Speaker, which strengthened the importance of seniority and orderly advancement[8] (Polsby 1968). Careerism in the House was also encouraged by the adoption of uniform electoral timing for federal and state offices, which force the representative to seek other offices always at the risk of losing his House seat. As a result, the number of representatives whose public careers ended with House service increased from 39.7% in 1851 to 76.8% in 1951. The number of senators who had served as representatives declined from 39.7% in 1851 to 28.6% in 1951. Nevertheless, the House remained the single most important manifest office for the Senate and its importance has increased somewhat in the 1970s. One possible explanation is the reapportionment of legislative districts that followed the Supreme Court's decisions of the 1960s and which has brought congressional constituencies more into line with those of the state as a whole.

Reapportionment, however, has had the most significant consequences for the size and status of the states' legislatures. An immediate effect was the reduction in the size of the legislatures: a net decline of 238 legislative seats as well as the continued decline in the rate of turnover that we noted earlier. Concurrently, there has been the resurgence of the importance of state legislative experience in the careers of higher elective officials, which we also noted. Reapportionment, then, by bringing the constituency of the state legislature closer to the constituencies of higher elective offices may well have set in motion the changes in age patterns for state legislative office on which we speculated earlier.

AGE PATTERNS FOR ELECTIVE OFFICE AND POLITICAL PARTIES

Another institution that helps explain age patterns for elective office is the political party, the extraconstitutional organization whose primary

---

[8] To the extent that recent reforms reduce the importance of seniority, the length of House careers may decline (Ornstein and Rohde 1978).

function is to recruit and advance candidates for office. A tightly knit organization, one that controls access to many different offices, will, we expect, reward those who have served the organization and promote experienced individuals to higher offices at advanced ages. But American parties, for the most part, have not been such organizations. They have generally not been capable of keeping under their control the whole range of offices that a long-range promotional system requires. Among other things, state laws have made it difficult for parties to take complete charge of their own nominations. The effect of such limitations has been often to place the burden for office-seeking less on the organization as a whole and more on the individual candidate. To the extent that the quest for office depends mostly on the individual candidate, we expect the advantage to lie with the most vigorous, the individual capable of amassing the resources that the organization might otherwise provide. Under such circumstances, the advantage appears to lie with the younger, experienced candidate. At the same time, the premium placed on individual initiative in the candidate-oriented arrangement appears to leave the older political neophyte more options than the tightly knit political organization.

Parties, however, do not operate as independent organizations. Much of their behavior is determined not by internal needs but by their relations with other parties or by party competition. We would expect highly competitive conditions to deprive parties of secure control over nominations for office and to expand the routes for advancement, thereby blurring promotional patterns, including age patterns. But American parties have never fit the perfect two-party competitive mold. The chances at winning office have seldom been evenly distributed between the two parties. The closer one party has come to dominating elections for a range of offices, the closer it has come to developing age promotion patterns.

The American two-party system has gone through several stages of development since the early contests between Federalists and anti-Federalists (Key 1955). The period in the mid-nineteenth century when Whigs and Democrats vied for office was the most evenly competitive (McCormick 1966). Each party was capable of winning a variety of offices in most areas of the country. It was also the period during which ages for elective office were the least focused. The post-Civil War era ushered in strong sectional ties to either the Republican or the Democratic party. But competition remained sufficiently strong so that neither party was assured control of the presidency or the Congress. The partisan realignments that followed the election of 1896, on the other hand, intensified the parties' regional bases and created large areas so solidly committed to either the Republican or the Democratic party that the minority party atrophied and in some cases ceased to field candidates at all (Key 1956, Burnham 1970). It was within this party system, which prevailed for the first six decades of the twentieth century, that focused age distributions for elective office emerge.[9]

One result of the unevenness of competition in the post-1896 party system was to remove the risks of interparty competition from public office careers in much of the political terrain. Most local offices, state legislatures, and congressional districts were predictably either Republican or Democratic. The domination of constituencies by a single party was furthered by the adoption of the direct primary between 1903 and 1920 (Key 1956). This method of nomination channeled most serious candidates through the dominant party. The major contest, if there was one at all, took place in the primary election. The primary especially facilitated the task of reelection for the incumbent representative or senator, a natural favorite with the party because of the advantages accrued through seniority. Even in states where major statewide offices such as the governorship were competitive, in states such as New York, Massachusetts, Ohio, or Illinois, each party had its strongholds from which a candidate might more easily capture a primary nomination and go on to contest the office. In either competitive or noncompetitive situations, the direct primary gave the advantage to the manifest office-holder whose visibility provided the most important assistance the primary electorate received in voting. Thus in some one-party states, officeholders were able to establish within the framework of the primary an office promotional arrangement. In Vermont, Republican speakers of the legislature moved to the office of lieutenant governor and then on to the governorship (Schlesinger 1957b). Whether by conscious design or not, age progression easily fell into line with this movement from office to office.

At the same time, the primary also influenced party organization by making it more difficult for a single organization to control nominations for many different offices, even within one-party areas. Within one-party areas, it was therefore possible for different types of party organizations to emerge. At one extreme were the loose candidate-oriented factions of the one-party South (Key 1949). As we have seen, southern politics indeed favored the young careerist and was least hospitable to the older neophyte. At the other extreme was the urban "machine" of the East and Midwest. In charge of both nominations and elections, such orga-

[9] The realignments of 1928 through 1936 did alter the party system by transforming what were once Republican strongholds into Democratic strongholds. Note, for example, the shifts in partisan support in cities such as Chicago, Pittsburgh, and Detroit or the alteration in Rhode Island. The basic tendency for one party to dominate remained.

nizations demonstrated a preference for candidates with long and loyal service. In his study comparing the Democratic candidates for Congress in the core city of Chicago with those in the outer areas and the suburbs, Snowiss (1966) found that the city candidates were significantly older and had more office experience. Similar evidence emerged from a study of four state legislatures. Where the state allowed the party most control over the nominating system, as in the closed primary in Pennsylvania or the convention system in Connecticut, legislators were older and experienced. Where the state allowed the party the least control, as in the nonpartisan primary in Minnesota or the blanket primary in Washington, candidates were older neophytes (Tobin 1975).

Since 1960, the American two-party system has undergone significant changes that have resulted in a far more evenly competitive system. Today, there are relatively few constituencies, including those in the South, that can be said to belong safely to either party. While the ability of incumbents to win reelection appears, if anything, to be increasing (Mayhew 1974), in elections without incumbents, either party can win in most of the country. Increasingly, voters have demonstrated their willingness not only to shift their votes from party to party from election to election, but also to divide their votes between the parties for different offices in the same election. Such voting behavior has encouraged the candidate-orientation of American parties already advantaged, among other things, by the direct primary. Candidates unable to win on the basis of the party label alone have had to rely more and more on their own resources. Among such resources, youthful vigor has not been the least important, especially at a time when the electorate has been expanded to include the 18-year-old voter and campaign techniques have been expanded to include television, a medium placing the highest priority on appearance. It is within a more competitive, candidate-oriented party system that we have charted the declining ages of senators, representatives, and governors.

The question arises, however, whether the age patterns we have distinguished differ not only over time and by region but also from party to party. The evidence would indicate that in the period of stability Democratic candidates for the major elective offices and the state legislature were consistently younger than Republican candidates (Walker 1960, Fishel 1973, Matthews 1960, Seligman et al. 1974, Tobin 1975). The difference may well be attributable to the Democratic party's involvement with candidate-oriented politics in the one-party South and with candidate-oriented politics in competitive areas elsewhere. Whatever the reason, the shift toward a more evenly competitive party system throughout the nation has brought a decline in the age of Republican officeholders, bringing them closer in terms of age to their Democratic counterparts. In the Congress elected in 1956, 68% of the Democrats had won their first election to the House before they were 45 compared with 53% of the Republicans. In the House elected in 1976, 68% of the representatives of both parties had won their first election before the age of 45. A similar decline took place in the Senate, although the decline was considerably greater for both parties. In 1956, 31.6% of the Democrats had won their first election to the Senate before they were 45, compared with only 18.7% of the Republicans. In 1976, 54.4% of the Democrats and 44.7% of the Republicans had won their first election to the Senate before the age of 45. Since Democratic membership in Congress has increased between 1956 and 1976, the decline in the ages of senators and representatives is due to both the persistence of the Democratic party in choosing younger candidates and the shift in the Republican party to match the Democratic image (see Table 9.3). A similar trend has been noted among governors. Sabato has noted that the newer Republican governors in the South are even younger than the Democrats. If, then, the older candidate might once have looked to the Republican party, it would appear that he or she now has little reason to choose between the two parties on the basis of their treatment of older political aspirants.

AGE PATTERNS FOR ELECTIVE OFFICE AND MOTIVATION: AMBITION FOR OFFICE

Institutions provide the opportunities for office; parties are the conduits through which office is reached. But motivation, primarily ambition, supplies the force for office-seeking. Do we have any reason to suppose that ambition for office is related to the life-cycle? If ambition for office is in part a response to an individual's perception of opportunities, then age patterns for office should both guide us to and be influenced by the distribution of political ambition among age groups. Is, for example, the diffuse age distribution for a particular office in part the result of ambition diffusely distributed among a variety of age groups? If the age patterns for a particular office are well defined, is it in part because certain age groups see that office as their preserve? To the extent that age patterns delimit the prospects for individual offices, we should expect age patterns to arouse or dampen ambition in such a way as to reinforce themselves.

For most of the period we have been examining, we have no direct tests of the relation of ambition to age patterns. Studies have been done,

TABLE 9.3
Changing Ages at Achieving Congressional Office (Republican and Democratic Differences)

Ages at first election	House percentage								Senate percentage							
	Republicans		Democrats						Republicans		Democrats					
	1956	1976		1956	1976				1956	1976		1956	1976			
55+	11.8	6.3		8.7	6.5				27.1	7.9		23.6	8.1			
45–54	35.0	25.6		24.7	25.4				54.2	47.4		45.1	37.1			
35–44	39.2	50.0		48.8	46.9				18.7	44.7		27.4	43.5			
Under 35	14.0	18.0		17.8	21.2				0.0	0.0		3.9	11.3			
Total	100.0	99.9		100.0	100.0				100.0	100.0		100.0	100.0			
N	202	143		234	292				48	38		51	62			
Mean age	44.2	41.6		42.1	41.0				51.3	46.3		47.8	43.7			

however, of the ages and ambitions of selected state legislators and city councillors during the late 1950s and early 1960s, a period during which the American structure of political opportunities was still relatively stable. The striking finding of these studies was the decline in the percentage of officeholders expressing ambitions for higher office with each advancing age group (see Table 9.4) (Wahlke *et al.* 1969, Hain 1974, Prewitt and Nowlin 1969, Prewitt 1970, Dutton 1975). A sizable majority of the younger legislators (those under 46) in New Jersey, California, Tennessee, and Ohio expressed ambitions for higher office (Hain 1974). This was also true for the majority of city councillors in the San Francisco Bay area under the age of 36 (Prewitt 1970). In contrast, among legislators who had reached the age of 56, only one-third expressed progressive ambitions; only 10% of the city councillors in this age group did so. Hain also demonstrated in his follow-up of careers of the legislators a strong positive relationship between those who expressed ambition for higher office and those who subsequently took action to achieve it. At the same time, it is important to note that each office attracted ambitious individuals in different proportions. In each age group a larger proportion of state legislators expressed ambitions for higher office than did city councillors. These studies indicate that there is a strong tendency for age patterns to reinforce themselves by focusing the ambitions of political aspirants. Nevertheless, ambitions do not uniformly decline with age. The office itself draws those with progressive ambitions to a greater or lesser degree.

TABLE 9.4
Age and Political Ambitions of Legislators and City Councillors[a]

Ages	State legislators expressing ambitions for high office		City councillors expressing ambitions for higher office	
	Percentage	(N)	Percentage	(N)
30 and less	81	16	100	4
31–35	78	46	53	17
36–40	75	75	43	42
41–45	77	73	41	64
46–50	62	77	23	73
51–55	60	55	13	61
56–60	37	43	10	40
61–65	31	39	10	59
66 +	12	42		
Total	59	466	26	360

[a] Adapted from Hain 1974. Quoted by permission of the University of Utah, copyright holder.

There is some reason to believe that age patterns for elective office have directed the ambitions of American officeseekers and that ambition, in turn, has affected age patterns for elective office. This may become even more demonstrable if a new, more venturesome young-old seek to enter elective politics. In a study of United States representatives who sought higher office, Rohde (1979) found that they tended to be candidates who had won their seats initially by defeating incumbents in a primary or general election. He argued that either because of some personal quality or because of the experience, the ambitious representatives were greater risk takers. It may well be that the emergent young-old, operating from a position of relative affluence and relative freedom from family responsibility, will contain a larger proportion of political risk takers, ambitious for higher office, despite their late entry into politics. (On risk taking and age, see also Riley *et al.* 1972, p. 427). Such older candidates may well find their ambitions fueled by recent institutional and partisan changes that have disrupted earlier established age patterns. Immediately, these changes have worked to the advantage of the younger candidate. But they could well work to the advantage of any candidate bringing exceptional personal resources to the electoral contest.

AGE PATTERNS FOR ELECTIVE OFFICE:
THE DEMOGRAPHIC EFFECT

Finally, we should consider the composition of the population from which candidates are drawn for its effect on age patterns. Have elective elites responded directly to changes in the age composition of the general population or the electorate? This would not appear to be the case. The increase in life expectancy over the history of the United States has not yet increased the chances of the older citizen for elective office. If anything, those chances appear to have been greatest when life expectancy and the median age of the population was lowest, at the beginning of the nineteenth century. If demographic factors affect age patterns for elective office, it is most likely due to short-run variations in birth rates as well as to generational differences in morbidity, education, income, and political experience.

Variations in the size of birth cohorts may influence the relative chances of their members. The era of the Great Depression saw a decline in the birth rate. Someone born in 1935 was 35 in 1970 and a central figure in the age group capturing in unprecedented numbers positions in the House, the Senate, and the state capitals. Indeed, expanding opportunities in all fields would appear to have reduced the competition for positions of prominence faced by this relatively small birth cohort (Neugarten and Hagestad 1976, p. 45). To the extent that the size of the depression birth cohort has contributed to changes in the age patterns of higher elective officials in the 1970s, the chances for elective office careers of the much larger cohort born after World War II may be considerably fewer, as they come of age politically during the 1980s.

The ability of any age group, however, to attain elective office ultimately depends on its financial, educational, physical, and political resources. Everything we know about people who run for office indicates that they are on the whole better educated, more affluent, more energetic, and more politically efficacious. At least in the past, these qualities have not been strongly associated with the older segments of the population. If, however, the older segments in the future contain a sizable core of relatively healthy, active, educated, financially secure, and politically alert individuals, we may well see some notable increase in the proportion of older citizens seeking elective office.

POLITICAL OPPORTUNITIES FOR THE YOUNG-OLD: WOMEN IN POLITICS

How successful will the future young-old be in their search for elective office? One aspect of America's demographic profile has special relevance for a discussion of political opportunities for the future young-old: the increasing predominance of women among older Americans. A striking characteristic of aging America is the advantage that women hold over men in life expectancy, an advantage that women are expected to retain. At the beginning of the century, women were only slightly advantaged (2.9 years). Between 1900 and 1974, however, whereas male life expectancy at birth increased 20 years, female life expectancy increased 25 years. As a result, in 1974, life expectancy for the American male was 68.2 years, for the American female 75.9 years. The disparity has become most glaring in the age group 65 years and older. In the 1930s, the numbers of men and women in this age group were about equal. By the 1970s, there were only 69 men to every 100 women 65 or older. By the year 2000, this ratio is expected to fall to 65 men per 100 women, despite the trend toward the convergence of male and female life-styles (Siegel 1978, pp. 12,28,42). The societal implications of this phenomenon have already become apparent, including, among others, the high proportion of widows in this age group. A trend of related interest is the increasing number of women aged 55–64, accounted for largely by the widowed and divorced, who are returning to the work force at the very time men in this age group are retiring in greater numbers (Siegel 1978, pp. 45,47,50).

Our concern is with the effect that the discrepancy in life expectancy between the sexes and its societal implications may have on the American structure of political opportunities. One expert demographer has called the discrepancy serious enough to require that "the social goal of greater equality" for men be achieved through a program of "affirmative action" (Siegel 1977, p. 23). However worthy this social goal, we are interested in whether the advantage of women in life expectancy and their need for social and economic independence in later years may in any way alter the disparity between elective officeholding of men and women.[10]

Solicitude over the token number of women in political office has come to equal, if not exceed, that over the position of minorities in American politics. An increasing number of studies are documenting the minor role of women while seeking among the successful women officeholders clues to the success and failure of women politicians (Bullock and Heys 1972, Diamond 1977, Dubeck 1976, Gehlen 1977, Githens 1977, King 1977, Kirkpatrick 1974, Lee 1976, Mezey 1978, Prestage 1977, Werner 1966, 1968). Invariably, these studies single out the age patterns of women in elective office: their relatively late arrival after family responsibilities have diminished. Women have made their greatest mark in state legislatures, where opportunities are most numerous.[11] They have been most successful in the legislatures in which older men have most easily initiated office careers: the outsize legislatures of the less populous New England states—Vermont, New Hampshire, Maine, and Connecticut.[12] These are the so-called citizen legislatures whose sessions are

---

[10] Any discussion of women's advantaged position with respect to life expectancy should be qualified by their disadvantaged position with respect to chronic, disabling diseases (Siegel 1978, p. 28).

[11] Even here women do not play a major role. In 1974, women made up only 9.1% of the lower houses in state legislatures and only 5% of the upper house (Diamond 1977, p. 25). The improvement in their position has been steady but slow. Between 1920 (ratification of the nineteenth amendment) and 1925, the number of women in state legislatures rose from 31 to 146; during World War II, the number reached a high of 228; during the Korean War, a high of 296 (Werner 1968, pp. 42–43). The largest increases have come during the 1970s. The number rose from 334 in 1971–1972 to 610 in 1975–1976 (Diamond 1977, p. 180).

[12] Connecticut was the only one of these state legislatures to reduce its size in response to the Court's apportionment decisions. But women have continued to be able to get elected (Diamond 1977, p. 18).

brief, remuneration is low, and turnover is unusually high. The recruitment process, therefore, is relatively nonselective, and women and retired men have provided a pool of talent for offices for which competition is minimal and in which younger men are willing to serve only briefly and to use for political or nonpolitical advancement. Studies of both male and female officeholders have singled out age as the most important deterrent to ambition for higher office (Prewitt and Nowlin 1969, Hain 1974, Githens 1977, p. 205, Diamond 1970, pp. 111–112, Kirkpatrick 1974, pp. 184–185, 214). Little wonder, then, that students of women in politics, without exception, decry their late start.

Our interest, however, lies in whether a woman's advantaged position with respect to life expectancy can alter both her career perspectives and the judgment of voters, causing them to distinguish between the older male and female candidate seeking higher office. At least for the time being, the successful female officeholder provides a good example of what the young-old can aspire to in politics. Politics has been for most women legislators a second career. To enter upon that career, they have not needed to follow the path of the typical successful man, a career in the law and an early staking out of elective office. Theirs has been an entirely different pattern, consisting of homemaking and volunteer work of either the partisan or nonpartisan variety. Far more than their male counterparts, female legislators have first been the envelope stuffers of American political parties.[13] For the most part, the female officeholder's work experience outside the home has been discontinuous. Where she has had experience, however, it has been primarily in education and business rather than in the law (Kirkpatrick 1974, p. 61, Werner 1966, p. 46, King 1977, p. 288). Although students of women in politics bemoan women's late start, female officeholders can find age an advantage. Age deflects the antagonism of younger women tied to household responsibilities; it also defuses the "sex" issue, allowing women to stand before men as authority figures, as matriarch or teacher, rather than as mate (Kirkpatrick 1974, pp. 101–102, 114, Diamond 1970, p. 110). If, in addition, the female officeholder can infer a life-span longer than her male counterpart, her late start may not necessarily disadvantage her for a full political career, which includes several offices of increasing status.

On the other hand, the picture of women as the late starters in American politics should be qualified. When we examine the careers of women who advanced beyond the state legislature, a pattern not at all

---

[13] Female legislators had prior local office experience in somewhat uniform proportions, though they were more likely to have been on a school board than on a city council (Diamond 1977, p. 42).

dissimilar to that of "careerist" male officeholders emerges. The highest office held by women in any number has been that of U.S. representative, although the number is small enough to limit the value of any generalizations. Between 1917 and 1970, 67 women sat in the U.S. House of Representatives. Of these, almost half (48%) were women who acceded to the seats of their late husbands. As would be expected, congressional widows at the time of their first election were older, on the average, than their male colleagues. Regularly elected congresswomen, however, were somewhat younger.[14] They were also more likely to be lawyers than women state legislators or congressional widows.[15] Even more than their male colleagues were they likely to have held elective office prior to their election to Congress.[16]

It would also appear that women have been participating, albeit in a small way, in the shifting age patterns that we have found for the Congress as a whole. When we combine congressional widows with the regularly elected women who sat in the House between 1917 and 1970 and compare the pool with the "aged" House of 1950, the age patterns of both sexes are similar (see Table 9.5[A]). When we compare the regularly elected women of 1976 with their male colleagues, the age patterns are also similar (see Table 9.5[B]). As with congressmen, the percentage of women who first won election to the House under the age of 40 has risen sharply.[17] Moreover, the percentage is more than twice that of the entire House elected in 1950.

Nevertheless, both before and after 1970, women deviated most strikingly from their male colleagues in the percentage who were able to win election to the Congress for the first time at 55 or older. Given the small pool of women with which we must deal, it is with extreme caution that we speculate whether, among the young-old, women may be able to aspire to greater success, that is, advancement in politics. In any event, the state of women in politics is in flux. Changes in life-style (i.e., in

[14] The mean age at first election of the widows who sat in the House between 1917 and 1970 was 52; the mean age of regularly elected women was 46.8, while the mean age of all freshmen elected in 1968 was 47.6 (Bullock and Heys 1972, p. 421).

[15] The breakdown of their previous experience is education 37%, law 20%, and business 11% (Bullock and Heys 1972, p. 418).

[16] During the 80th through 90th Congresses, 69% of regularly elected women compared with 59% of all freshmen in the House had held prior elective office (Bullock and Heys 1972, pp. 419–420).

[17] In contrast to women's slow but steady progress in state legislatures, the number of women in the House has been small and fluctuating. After reaching a high of 19 in the 1961 Congress, it has fluctuated from 10 in 1969, to 14 in 1973, 18 in 1977, and 16 in 1979 (Werner 1968, p. 42, Gehlen 1977, p. 1306, Kirkpatrick 1974, p. 21, *Congressional Quarterly* 1978, p. 3, Barone, Ujifusa, and Matthews 1978).

TABLE 9.5
Age at First Election to U.S. House of Representatives (A) and Age at First Election to U.S. House of Representatives of Those Elected in 1976 (B)

All members 1950[a]		Women 1917–1970[b][c]	
Ages	Percentages	Ages	Percentages
A			
25–34	6.7	30–35	3.0
35–39	10.1	36–40	15.8
40–44	21.2	41–45	19.0
45–49	20.3	46–50	23.8
50–54	17.2	51–55	17.4
55–59	18.5	56–60	11.7
60 plus	7.0	60 plus	9.5
55 plus	15.5	56 plus	21.2
Under 40	16.8	40 and under	18.8

All members		Women[d][e]
Ages	Percentages	Percentages
B		
25–29	3.0	0.0
30–39	17.1	14.2
35–39	26.2	21.4
40–44	21.8	28.5
45–49	17.1	7.1
50–54	8.3	7.1
55–59	4.6	7.1
60 plus	1.9	14.2

[a] From *Biographical Directory of American Congress.*
[b] $N = 63$, including 29 congressional widows.
[c] Based on Gehlin 1977, p. 307.
[d] $N = 14$.
[e] From Barone *et al.* 1978.

family size), in the assignment of family responsibilities, in the accession of women to the profession of law, and in the attitudes of women toward political participation are bound to affect the age patterns of women in politics (Kirkpatrick 1974, pp. 246–250). Along with the changing demands of electoral politics, they are bound to advantage younger women. The question arises, however, and it is worth some future observation, as to whether the older woman, given her advantage of life expectancy and the established female political career pattern, may be better able to survive in American electoral politics than her male counterpart.

POLITICAL OPPORTUNITIES FOR THE YOUNG-OLD:
THE GENERAL PICTURE

Our exploration of age patterns in American elective politics would indicate that, despite its relative openness, American politics has not been especially cordial to the older political neophyte. The American political community has at no time eagerly sought out or openly welcomed the successful businessman approaching retirement and ready at last to transfer his managerial skills to government. This is not to say that he has been barred from American politics—but his has not been the easiest route. While American governors, senators, and presidents have not come from the youngest ranks the law allows, nor have they all been lawyers with extensive public office careers, neither have they been predominantly graybearded corporate executives or generals untainted by prior elective office experience. Moreover recent trends have brought the most conspicuous American officeholders closer to the ranks of the experienced, youthful middle-aged than to the ranks of the inexperienced young-old. And these trends may well be reaching down to the lesser offices, the state legislatures, the county commissions, and the city councils, which have traditionally been more hospitable to older political neophytes. To the extent that reapportionment has brought the constituencies of the state legislature, the county commission, and the city council into line with the constituencies of higher elective offices, to the extent that their powers and perquisites, including financial remuneration, have increased, these bodies have become increasingly attractive to the younger candidate, seeking either a training ground for higher office or, alternatively, an extensive career in a single office. Such a juvenescence of elective officialdom, should it persist into the future, could contain the germ of a representational crisis if it were accompanied by the development of an increasingly age-conscious, politically active elderly cohort.

On the other hand, institutional, partisan, and demographic changes could also work to the political advantage of the future young-old. Factors that tend to enhance political opportunities in general (e.g., increased competition for office, candidate-oriented political organization, the weakening of congressional seniority) could work to the advantage of a variety of age groups. So could any future changes designed to equalize political resources such as the extension of the public financing of elections to include elections for Congress, state, and local government. If in one time period institutional and partisan changes have worked to the advantage of younger birth cohorts, they may well work to the advantage of these same cohorts as they age, accompanied by unprecedented physical, educational, and financial resources. Much will depend on the extent to which institutional and partisan changes arouse and fire the ambitions of older political aspirants.

Of particular interest should be the opportunities for the young-old in town, city, and county governments. Our analysis has focused on the opportunities for the more conspicuous offices because of the ready availability of the data and existing studies. But the great bulk of electoral opportunities exist at the local level, and they may well be especially attractive to the young-old. For one thing they require less geographic mobility. But more important, many of the issues likely to interest this age group—housing, medical care, police protection, public transportation, and recreation—have increasingly become issues that local political institutions can directly affect. Future research, then, might best emphasize the political opportunities for the young-old in local government, while continuing to monitor their opportunities for higher elective office.

REFERENCES

Barone, M., Ujifusa, G., and Matthews, D. (1978) *The Almanac of American Politics 1978.* New York: E. P. Dutton.

Bengston, V. L., and Cutler, N. E. (1976) Generations and intergenerational relations: Perspectives on age groups and social change. Pp. 130–159 in R. H. Binstock and E. Shanas, eds., *Handbook of Aging and the Social Sciences.* New York: Van Nostrand Reinhold.

Binstock, H. (1974) Aging and the future of American politics. *The Annals of the American Academy of Political and Social Science* 415:199–212.

Biographical Directory of the American Congress 1774–1971 (1971) Washington, D.C.: U.S. Government Printing Office.

Bullock, C. S. III (1972) House careerists: Changing patterns of longevity and attrition. *American Political Science Review* 66:1295–1305.

Bullock, C. S. III, and Heys, P. L. F. (1972) Recruitment of women for Congress: A research note. *The Western Political Quarterly* 25:416–423.

Burnham, W. D. (1970) *Critical Elections and the Mainsprings of American Politics.* New York: W. W. Norton.

Clausen, J. A. (1972) The life course of individuals. Pp. 457–514 in M. W. Riley, M. Johnson, and A. Foner, eds., *Aging and Society* 3. New York: Russell Sage Foundation.

Congressional Quarterly (1978) *Weekly Report,* 36(no. 45): 3252.

Cutler, N. E. (1977) Demographic, social-psychological, and political factors in the politics of aging: A foundation for research in "political gerontology." *American Political Science Review* 71:1011–1025.

Diamond, I. (1977) *Sex Roles in the State House.* New Haven: Yale University Press.

Dubeck, P. (1976) Women and access to political office: A comparison of female and male state legislators. *Sociological Quarterly* 17:42–52.

Dutton, W. H. (1975) The political ambitions of local legislators: A comparative perspective. *Polity* 7:504–519.

Eisele, F. R. (1974) Preface. *Annals of the American Academy of Political and Social Science* 415.

Eulau, H. and Sprague, J. D. (1964) *Lawyers in Politics: A Study in Professional Convergence*. Indianapolis, Ind.: Bobbs, Merrill.

Fishel, J. (1971) Ambition and the political vocation: Congressional challengers in American politics. *The Journal of Politics* 33:25–56.

Fishel, J. (1973) *Party and Opposition: Congressional Challengers in American Politics*. New York: David McKay.

Foner, A. (1972) The polity. Pp. 115–159 in M. W. Riley, M. Johnson, and A. Foner, eds., *Aging and Society*. New York: Russell Sage Foundation.

Frantzich, S. E. (1978) Opting out: Retirement from the House of Representatives 1966–1974. *American Politics Quarterly* 6:251–274.

Gehlen, F. (1977) Women members of Congress: A distinctive role. Pp. 304–319 in M. Githens and J. Prestage, eds., *A Portrait of Marginality*. New York: David McKay.

Githens, M. (1977) Spectators, agitators, or lawmakers: Women in state legislatures. Pp. 196–209 in M. Githens and J. Prestage, eds., *A Portrait of Marginality*. New York: David McKay.

Hain, P. L. (1974) Age, ambitions, and political careers: The middle-age crisis. *The Western Political Quarterly* 27:265–274.

Hudson, R. B. and Binstock, R. H. (1976) Political systems and aging. Pp. 369–400 in R. H. Binstock and E. Shanas, (eds.), *Handbook of Aging and the Social Sciences*. New York: Van Nostrand Reinhold.

Huntington, S. P. (1965) Congressional responses to the twentieth century. Pp. 5–31 in D. B. Truman, (ed.), *The Congress and America's Future*. Englewood Cliffs, N.J.: Prentice-Hall.

Kallenbach, J. E. (1966) *The American Chief Executive*. New York: Harper and Row.

Key, V. O., Jr. (1949) *Southern Politics*. New York: Alfred Knopf.

Key, V. O., Jr. (1955) A theory of critical elections. *Journal of Politics* 17:3–18.

Key, V. O., Jr. (1956) *American State Politics*. New York: Alfred Knopf.

Kernell, S. (1976) Ambition and Politics: An Exploratory Study of Political Careers of Nineteenth Century Congressmen. Paper delivered at 1976 meeting of the American Political Science Association.

King, E. G. (1977) Women in Iowa legislative politics. Pp. 284–303 in M. Githens and J. Prestage, (eds.), *Portrait of Marginality*. New York: David McKay.

Kirkpatrick, J. (1974) *Political Woman*. New York: Basic Books.

Lee, M. M. (1976) Why so few women hold public office: Democracy and sexual roles. *Political Science Quarterly* 91:297–314.

Luce, R. (1924) *Legislative Assemblies*. Boston: Houghton Mifflin Company.

Matthews, D. R. (1960) *U.S. Senators and Their World*. New York: Vintage Books.

Mayhew, D. R. (1974) Congressional elections: The case of the vanishing marginals. *Polity* 6:298–302.

McCann, J. C. (1972) Differential mortality and the formation of political elites: The case of the House of Representatives. *American Sociological Review* 37:689–700.

McCormick, R. P. (1966) *The Second American Party System*. Chapel Hill, N.C.: University of North Carolina Press.

Mezey, S. G. (1978) Does sex make a difference? A case study of women in politics. *The Western Political Quarterly* 31:492–501.

Neugarten, B. L. (1974) Age groups in American society and the rise of the young-old. *Annals of the American Academy of Political and Social Science* 415:187–198.

Neugarten, B. L. and Hagestad, G. O. (1976) Age and the life course. Pp. 35–55 in R. Binstock and E. Shanas, eds., *Handbook of Aging and the Social Sciences.* New York: Van Nostrand Reinhold.

Ornstein, N. J. and Rohde, D. W. (1978) Political parties and Congressional reform. Pp. 280–294 in J. Fishel, ed., *Parties and Elections in an Anti-Party Age.* Bloomington, Ind.: Indiana University Press.

Polsby, N. W. (1968) The institutionalization of the U.S. House of Representatives. *American Political Science Review* 62:144–168.

Prestage, J. L. (1977) Black women state legislators: A profile. Pp. 401–418 in M. Githens and J. Prestage, (eds.), *A Portrait of Marginality.* New York: David McKay.

Prewitt, K. (1970) *The Recruitment of Political Leaders: A Study of Citizen-Politicians.* Indianapolis, Ind.: Bobbs-Merrill.

Prewitt, K. and Nowlin, W. (1969) Political ambitions and the behavior of incumbent politicians. *The Western Political Quarterly* 22:298–308.

Price, H. D. (1971) The congressional career—then and now. Pp. 14–27 in N. Polsby, (ed.), *Congressional Behavior.* New York: Random House.

Riker, W. H. (1955) The Senate and American Federalism. *American Political Science Review* 59:452–469.

Riley, M. W., Johnson, M., and Foner, A. (1972) *Aging and Society, Volume Three: A Sociology of Age Stratification.* New York: Russell Sage Foundation.

Ripley, R. B. (1969) *Power in the Senate.* New York: St. Martin's Press.

Rohde, D. W. (1979) Risk-bearing and progressive ambition: The case of members of the U.S. House of Representatives. *American Journal of Political Science* 23:1–26.

Rothman, D. J. (1966) *Politics and Power, the United States Senate 1869–1901.* Cambridge: Harvard University Press.

Sabato, L. (1978) *Goodby to Good-Time Charlie: The American Governor Transformed 1950–1975.* Lexington, Mass.: Lexington Books.

Samuelson, R. J. (1978) Aging America—who will shoulder the growing burden? *National Journal* 10:1712–1717.

Schlesinger, J. A. (1957a) Lawyers and American politics, a clarified view. *Midwest Journal of Political Science* 1:26–39.

Schlesinger, J. A. (1957b) *How They Became Governor.* East Lansing, Mich.: Governmental Research Bureau.

Schlesinger, J. A. (1966) *Ambition and Politics: Political Careers in the United States.* Chicago: Rand McNally.

Schlesinger, J. A. (1970) The Governor's place in American politics. *Public Administration Review* 30:2–9.

Seligman, L. G., King, M. R., Kim, C. L., and Smith, R. E. (1974) *Patterns of Recruitment: A State Chooses Its Lawmakers.* Chicago: Rand McNally.

Sheppard, H. L. and Rix, S. E. (1977) *Graying of Working America.* New York: The Free Press.

Shin, K. S., and Jackson, J. S. III (1979) Membership turnover in U.S. state legislatures: 1931–1976. *Legislative Studies Quarterly* 4:95–104.

Siegel, J. S. (1977) Recent and Prospective Demographic Trends for the Elderly Population and Some Implications for Health Care. Paper prepared for the Second Conference on the Epidemiology of Aging, March 28–29, 1977.

Siegel, J. S. (1978) *Demographic Aspects of Aging and the Older Population in the United*

States. Bureau of the Census, Current Population Reports, Special Studies Series P-23, No. 59. Washington, D.C.: U.S. Department of Commerce.

Snowiss, L. M. (1966) Congressional recruitment and representation. *American Political Science Review* 60:627–639.

Tobin, R. J. (1975) The influence of nominating systems on the political experiences of state legislators. *Western Political Quarterly* 18:553–566.

Treas, J. (1977) A life table for postwar Senate careers: A research note. *Social Forces* 56:202–207.

Wahlke, J. C., Eulau, H., Buchanan, W., and Ferguson, L. C. (1962) *The Legislative System*. New York: John Wiley and Sons.

Walker, D. B. (1960) The age factor in the 1958 Congressional elections. *Midwest Journal of Political Science* 4:1–26.

Werner, E. (1966) Women in Congress: 1917–1964. *Western Political Quarterly* 19:16–30.

Werner, E. (1968) Women in state legislatures. *Western Political quarterly* 21:40–50.

Young, J. S. (1966) *The Washington Community, 1800–1828*. New York: Columbia University Press.

BIBLIOGRAPHY

Barber, J. D. (1965) *The Lawmakers: Recruitment and Adaptation to Legislative Life.* New Haven, Conn.: Yale University Press.

Campbell, A. (1971) Politics through the life cycle. *Gerontologist* 2(Summer):112–117.

Lehman, H. C. (1963) *Age and Achievement*. Princeton, N.J.: Princeton University Press.

Verba, S., and Nie, N. H. (1972) *Participation in America: Political Democracy and Social Equality*. New York: Harper and Row.

PART III
ORGANIZATIONS

chapter 10

The Aging of Work Organizations: Impact on Organization and Employment Practice[1]

SHELBY STEWMAN

For some purposes, the national labor force has been treated as an idealized national competitive market system. For other purposes, the national labor force has been divided into, at a minimum, dual markets, and, in some cases at the other extreme, into organizationally administered (hence internal) labor markets (Doeringer and Piore 1971). To understand the processes of aging in work organizations, it is important to continue to impose the idea of separate, multiple labor markets operating within each organization. In this chapter, the work organization will be treated as such a collection of internal labor markets. Thus, to grasp the relationship between individual aging and the organization's age distribution over time, I would argue we should first analytically break apart the organization into its multiple internal labor markets (ILMs). We can then investigate the aging process within each ILM. Having separately examined each ILM, we can then put them together to form the organizational labor force. The overall image is obtained thus by first viewing aging in a fragmented organization, with each separate labor force having its own "market" system.

[1] The writing of this chapter was in part supported by National Science Foundation Grant Number SOC 77-16240.

AGING
Social Change

A second pair of conceptual lenses that I wish to impose is the treatment of jobs and job vacancies as theoretical equivalents to workers and careers. Thus, I might wish to consider the aging of jobs and job vacancies as well as the aging of workers and careers. One reason for doing so is that stochastic models of careers have not been very good in career forecasting thus far (Stewman 1976a, 1976b). Moreover, an apparent reason for this failure lies in the one-sidedness of the models—treating individuals and labor supply at length but ignoring the causal mechanisms operating from the demand side of the process via job vacancies. In brief, one major problem has been that the distribution of careers has not been postulated as a joint function of supply and demand or of workers and jobs. In this chapter, I will emphasize the role of vacancies as primary determinants in explaining the aging processes in organizational ILMs.

Several properties of vacancy processes are important for our purposes. First, vacancies may be a key factor in causing persons to move and in determining the timing of such moves. The phrase, "when the opportunity presents itself," expresses this point. Initial generation of such opportunities within internal labor markets is caused by two types of events: a new job's being created or an individual's leaving a job, thus opening a vacancy. Once these initial openings occur, if someone inside the organization takes the job, he or she then opens another vacancy and so on, creating a chain reaction of individual moves. This chain reaction concludes either when the vacant job is abolished or when a person outside the ILM is recruited to fill the job (see White 1970, Stewman 1975).

Within an ILM, jobs are often organized into hierarchies of administrative responsibility, job complexity, etc. Moreover, these hierarchical tiers are also designed as incentive mechanisms for individual careers. The higher steps serve as rewards for individuals as they continue working, and the sequence of steps taken coincides with an individual's breadth of experience, level of performance, and, of course, associated aging. Thus, we might generally expect the hierarchical grades of jobs to vary greatly by age of the staff, with the "older and wiser" individuals at the top and the younger novices at the bottom. This would most likely be the case if an individual remained in an organization throughout his or her life or if an individual stayed in one career-line. On the other hand, if mid-career change became a normal occurrence for persons aged 40–70 or older, then our expectations regarding aging and hierarchical jobs would indeed need to be modified. In this chapter, I will attempt to shed insight into the relationship between aging and organizational internal labor markets. The vehicle for doing so will be a vacancy model of organizational labor. I will simulate worker redistributions over a 20-year period (or longer, in some cases). The simulation is intended to illustrate possible effects of individual aging and managerial strategies of hiring and promotion in particular.

The chapter is organized as follows: a brief description of the opportunity model in section 1, presentation of the parameter estimates or guesstimates and the simulation design in section 2, followed by a discussion of the findings or results in section 3. Five topics will guide the discussion on results: (1) promotion rates per grade, (2) age distribution within a grade, (3) grade distribution within an age group, (4) seniority distribution within a grade and (5) the joint age–seniority distribution by grade. Aging implications for younger workers may be seen using the promotion rates. Organizational "age lumps" and "age echo booms," as in national populations, are brought to light by examining the age distributions by grade and for the overall ILM.

A different perspective is gained if we look across grades and examine the manner in which age is distributed. By comparing the grade distribution for a particular age group, we may address the issue of aging and an individual's grade level. Seniority distributions denote experience mix per grade and have possible implications for productivity. And, labor costs are also related to seniority distributions within grade, and especially to staff concentrations at the highest-paid seniority levels. Perhaps of most interest is the overall view gained by examining the joint age–seniority organizational staff profile. Very different profiles will be shown to result from alternative managerial practices and age-dependent worker exit decisions.

THE OPPORTUNITY MODEL

As a point of departure, I will oversimplify and suggest that two basic types of processes depict ILM staff flows. In the more simple one, some attribute (or set of attributes), such as age or, more realistically, seniority, determines internal promotions. The craft trades are a case in point. The usual demographic aging type of model would portray such an attribute-driven process, using age, and hence I will not deal with that type of staff flow. The second type of process is one in which jobs are established at specific levels in the job hierarchy, denoting the need for such tasks to be performed, and individuals move into these jobs as they become vacant, not by the individual's aging or reaching a certain level of seniority. An administrative or managerial labor market is an example. In these cases, individual careers are an outcome of fluctuations in labor demand or job vacancies over time. Hence, rather than take fixed age- or seniority-specific promotion rates, as are used in demographic aging models of a national population, I will assume that age and seniority promotion rates and the resulting age and seniority profiles are unstable and must be derived from an underlying opportunity process. In reality, of course, both supply and demand interact and the opportunity process to which I refer incorporates both of these facets.[2]

Two types of decision makers are considered in the opportunity model presented in this chapter: managers selecting who will be promoted, hired, or terminated and workers deciding to stay or leave. For tractability and illustrative purposes, I will make rather extreme assumptions regarding the promotion, hiring, and exit decisions. I will assume that managerial selection is based on seniority in present grade and that managerial hiring and a worker's exit behavior are based on age. Clearly, multiple attributes of individuals are considered by managers, but assumptions regarding the form of the attribute distribution and cohort effects over a future 20-year period preclude their inclusion. The promotion selection assumption is simply that seniority effects are conditional on: the number of opportunities available, managerial preference by seniority given a vacancy, and the sufficiency of labor at the desired seniority levels. Given the preference structure, it is the matching of vacancies and labor supply over time that determines individual rates of movement and subsequent age-seniority distributions.

Age is assumed to be ignored by managers making promotion decisions. This is not to imply that age is unimportant for job performance. Recent legislation, the Age Discrimination Act of 1967 and the Age Discrimination in Employment Act Amendments of 1978, and recent judicial decisions, Griggs versus Duke Power Co., a 1971 U.S. Supreme Court decision, and Hodgson versus Greyhound Lines, Inc., a 1974 decision by the U.S. Court of Appeals, Seventh Circuit, strongly support the idea that job performance, not an individual's age, should be the heart of the matter in employment discrimination, whether it be hiring, promotion, or termination. That these civil rights issues arise at all points

---

[2] By the use of comparative statics and an insightful reformulation of stable population theory, Keyfitz (1973) provides an excellent analysis of individual careers where the timing of promotion is conditional on an available vacancy. See Stewman and Konda (1981a) for an elaboration. The results from Keyfitz's demand model and career results from a variation of the model to be presented here are compared in Stewman and Konda (1981a), and considerable consistency between the two is found. The present analysis, though distinct, may therefore be related to both of these works.

to the importance of age in employment practice. However, it also high-lights an area of great uncertainty—what is the relationship of age and the aging process to job performance? This is an important area for future research. Perhaps more important, if we widen the focus a bit more and place aging and work in the context of individual development throughout life, then a much more important issue arises—what brings wisdom and discernment to one's own life? And how does work fit into this larger developmental framework? It is reasonable to think that aging and the accumulation of experiences are important in changing how an individual attends to certain types of events and cognitively organizes them—events within the work environment as well as those that extend beyond work and thereby cast the work environment itself and today's events into a wider purview. Faunce (1972) has theorized that work success (promotions, raises, recognition) means different things to dif-ferent people, depending on how much self-investment is given to work relative to other areas and how important such success is in the eyes of those outside the immediate work circle, such as family, close friends, and other persons important to that individual. Sofer (1970) has shown that mid-career managers have explicit age-related promotion expecta-tions and that promotion by age 40 is viewed as crucial for further "advancement." Sheehy (1976) points to the early thirties, for men, as a time to concentrate on climbing career ladders and becoming recognized in the career-line, and to the forties as a time for expanding into other areas. For women, on the other hand, she points out that in today's age 30–40 cohort, many women are just beginning their first serious career, and the second half of life is more career-oriented than the first. Ob-viously, this would vary by age entry point. Women initiating careers in their twenties should more closely follow the pattern pushing for career recognition in the thirties. It seems reasonable to postulate that self-investment in work, perspective on the meaning of work, and an indi-vidual's organization of work and attention to different facets of that work may all change with age or with the life cycle, thereby potentially affecting job performance. What these changes are and how they link with attributes other than age and seniority is largely unexplored, nor will I touch on this area directly in this chapter. Instead, lacking such information, I suggest that the implications of aging for work are poten-tially strong enough to warrant a diverse age mixture in our work or-ganization. Moreover, I will vary managerial hiring practice and exit behavior by age to illustrate potential organizational profile impacts. For instance, hiring decisions will be varied to capture the impacts of a policy restricting entry to individuals in their twenties versus a policy having uniform hiring across all age bands, including the sixties.

The exit decision by the worker is assumed to be a function of age. Just as seniority effects were assumed conditional on the available opportunities, age is assumed to operate conditional on being overlooked for promotion. Advancement opportunities seem less important at the ends of the work life age distribution, where job adjustment and retirement decisions dominate. Hence, no distinct opportunity impact will normally operate at these points in the model. Alternatively, for the intermediate years of age, the assumption of exit decisions as contingent on promotion decisions seems to fit with an individual's anticipating promotion or not accepting an outside offer until it is compared with internal offers. Scope of reasonable parameter estimates for exit behavior and a desire to keep the model simple in design resulted in ignoring grade level seniority as an attribute affecting exits, once its effect on promotion was taken into account.

The final aspect of the model to be discussed is the chain reaction of promotion opportunities across grades after a vacancy enters the ILM. This process was briefly described in the introduction. Here, I merely note that if a vacancy is filled by a person in another grade within the ILM, another vacancy is generated for yet someone else to fill, and so on until a person is recruited from outside. Thus, instability in vacancy entrances at any higher grade in the job hierarchy will directly affect all lower grades and affect the promotion chances of the individual in those grades. The modeling of this type of opportunity process has its roots in White's (1970) vacancy chain model and Bartholomew's (1963, 1973) renewal model. In the model here, a chain reaction occurs, although the complete vacancy chain concept, as described by White (1970), is no longer necessary since all horizontal vacancy moves within a grade (person transfers) are ignored. In brief, the chain effect is achieved without the chain itself. In this respect, perhaps the model more closely follows the renewal modeling of Bartholomew (1973). Again, however, an essential feature of Bartholomew's model is discarded. The constant grade size and age and seniority distributions per grade necessary for renewal theory no longer hold. The model is less pure from the standpoint of mathematical theory but more realistic from an opportunity labor theory point of view. The most recent vintage of the model is given in Stewman (1978) and Konda and Stewman (1980).[3] Here age is incorporated, but the model remains essentially the same. The terms are defined below and the equations follow.

[3] A dynamic multivariate choice model conditional on opportunities has also been developed by Stewman and Konda (1981b).

Terms

$n_i(a,t)$	The number of persons of age a in grade i at time t
$n_i(s,t)$	The number of persons having seniority s within grade i at time t
$n_i(a_s,t)$	The number of persons of age a having seniority s within grade i at time t
$n_i(t)$	The number of persons in grade i at time t
$n_{i,i+1}(a,t)$	The number of persons of age a in grade i at time t who are promoted to grade $i + 1$ by time $t + 1$
$n_{i,i+1}(s,t)$	The number of persons having seniority s within grade i at time t who are promoted to grade $i + 1$ by time $t+1$
$n_{i,i+1}(t)$	The number of persons in grade i at time t who are promoted to grade $i+1$ by time $t+1$
$n_{io}(a,t)$	The number of persons of age a in grade i at time t who leave the ILM by time $t+1$
$n_{io}(t)$	The number of persons in grade i at time t who leave the ILM by time $t+1$
$\alpha_i(a_s,t)$	The proportion of persons of age a having seniority s within grade i at time t of all persons of age a in grade i at time t
$r_i(a,t)$	The number of recruits from outside the ILM who enter grade i at age a in the time interval $(t, t+1)$
$r_i(t)$	The total number of recruits from outside who enter the ILM at grade i in $(t, t+1)$
$v_i(t)$	The number of vacancies in grade i at time $(t, t+1)$ subject to managerial decisions
$j_i(t)$	The number of new jobs created in grade i in the time interval $(t, t+1)$
$J(t)$	The organizational ILM growth in number of additional jobs
ρ_i	The probability a new job is allocated to grade i
$\lambda_{i+1,o}$	The probability that an individual outside the ILM will be selected to fill a vacant job in grade $i+1$
$\lambda_{i+1,i}(s)$	The probability that an individual having seniority s within grade i will be selected for promotion to grade $i+1$, given a vacant job there

$\delta_i(a)$ The probability that a recruit of age a will be selected from outside the ILM to fill a vacancy in grade i

$p_{io}^*(a)$ The probability that an individual having age a will leave the ILM given that he or she was not promoted

$p_{io}(a,t)$ The unconditional probability that an individual having age a in grade i at time t will leave the ILM before time $t+1$

$p_{i,i+1}(s,t)$ The probability that an individual having seniority s within grade i at time t will be promoted to grade $i+1$ before time $t+1$

The equations showing the two basic staff flow parameters and the number of hires are given below. I have assumed promotion to the immediately higher grade only and that recruitment from outside the ILM occurs only at grade 1, the lowest grade. A brief statement regarding each equation will be made, as well as any additional assumptions other than those discussed above.

Promotion

Assume a k grade ILM with k being the highest grade. Then, an individual m having seniority s within grade i at the time t has the following promotion probability

$$\Pr\left[\begin{array}{c|ccc} m \text{ is in} & m \text{ is in} & m \text{ has} & \text{there is a} \\ \text{grade } i+1 & \text{grade } i & \text{seniority } s & \text{vacancy available} \\ \text{at time } t+1 & \text{at time } t, & \text{within grade } i, & \text{in grade } i+1 \end{array}\right],$$

$$\bar{p}_{i,i+1}(s,t) = \frac{\bar{v}_{i+1}(t)\,\hat{\lambda}_{i+1,i}(s)}{\bar{n}_i(s,t)}, \tag{1}$$

$$\hat{\lambda}_{i+1,i}(s) = \frac{\Sigma_t\, n_{i,i+1}(s,t)}{\Sigma_t\, n_{i,i+1}(t)}, \tag{2}$$

$$\bar{v}_{i+1}(t) = \sum_{l=i+1}^{k} \bar{n}_{lo}(t) + \bar{j}_l(t), \tag{3}$$

$$\bar{n}_{lo}(t) = \sum_a \bar{n}_l(a,t)\bar{p}_{lo}(a,t), \tag{4}$$

$$\bar{j}_l(t) = J(t)\hat{\rho}_l, \tag{5}$$

$$\hat{\rho}_l = \frac{\Sigma_t\, n_i(t)}{\Sigma_t\, \Sigma_i\, n_i(t)}. \tag{6}$$

Equation (1) postulates that the promotion probability of an individual having seniority s within grade i is dependent on the number of available vacancies in grade $i+1$, $\bar{v}_{i+1}(t)$, the managerial preference probability for an individual with seniority s, $\hat{\lambda}_{i+1,i}(s)$, and the number of persons at grade i who have this attribute, $\bar{n}_i(s,t)$. The product $\bar{v}_{i+1}(t) \hat{\lambda}_{i+1,i}(s)$ is the expected number of opportunities that will be filled by persons of seniority s. The managerial preference function, Eq. (2), is estimated from the total number of upward movers from grade i to $i+1$, $n_{i,i+1}(t)$; it is the percentage from this group who have seniority s, $n_{i,i+1}(s,t)$. The total number of expected vacancies available in the destination grade, $\bar{v}_{i+1}(t)$, in Eq. (3), is the sum across all higher grades of the two modes of vacancy entrance to an ILM—a person exiting $\bar{n}_{lo}(t)$, and a new job creation, $\bar{j}_l(t)$. The summation across grades depicts the chain reaction of opportunities beginning in each of the higher grades, $l = i + 1$ to k. The number of persons leaving grade l, $\bar{n}_{lo}(t)$ in Eq. (4) is the sum of all persons having age a who leave. The equation for the probability of exiting at age a will be given below. The number of new jobs at grade l, $\bar{j}_l(t)$ in Eq. (5) is simply the total number of new jobs $J(t)$ multiplied by the allocation probability of new jobs to that grade, $\bar{p}_l$. Eq. (6) represents this allocation as the same proportion as has held in the estimation period, a conservative assumption at best.

Two final remarks need to be made regarding the place of age in the promotion equation. First, I have assumed no age effect for managerial selection; therefore, once the number of vacancies that will be filled by persons of seniority s is decided, the selection will be random within that seniority level, meaning a consequent age effect proportional to the age distribution in that seniority level. Second, when there is an insufficient supply of labor at seniority s to fill the specified number of vacancies, $\bar{v}_{i+1}(t) \hat{\lambda}_{i+1,i}(s)$, then the $\hat{\lambda}$s are assumed to maintain their relative magnitude and the remaining $\hat{\lambda}$s are renormalized to fill the vacancies remaining empty. That is:

$$\hat{\lambda}'_{i+1,i}(s) = \frac{\hat{\lambda}_{i+1,i}(s)}{1 - \hat{\lambda}_{i+1,i}(s^*)}$$

where s^* denotes the seniority level with insufficient supply.

Exits

An individual m with age a is assumed to have the following exit probability:

$$\text{Pr}\begin{bmatrix} m \text{ exits} \\ \text{between} \\ \text{time } (t,t+1) \end{bmatrix}\begin{array}{ccc} m \text{ is in} & m \text{ has} & m \text{ was not} \\ \text{grade } i \text{ at} & \text{age } a, & \text{selected for} \\ \text{time } t, & & \text{promotion} \end{array}$$

$$\hat{p}_{io}^*(a) = \frac{\Sigma_t n_{io}(a,t)}{\Sigma_t \left[n_i(a,t) - n_{i,i+1}(a,t)\right]} \tag{7}$$

The effect of making exit behavior conditional on not being promoted is to raise the exit rate when promotions decrease from the mean promotion rate during the estimation period and to decrease the exit rate when promotions increase. This may be shown parametrically as follows:

$$\bar{p}_{io}(a,t) = \hat{p}_{io}^*(a) \left\{ \sum_s \bar{\alpha}_i(a_s,t)[1 - \bar{p}_{i,i+1}(s,t)] \right\} \tag{8}$$

where

$$\bar{\alpha}_i(a_s,t) = \frac{\bar{n}_i(a_s,t)}{\Sigma_s \bar{n}_i(a_s,t)} = \frac{\bar{n}_i(a_{s,t})}{\bar{n}_i(a,t)} . \tag{9}$$

Equation (8) shows the time dependency of exit rates for the initial population of age a in the time interval $(t,t+1)$. This instability can arise from two sources: an unstable age distribution within seniority levels, $\bar{\alpha}_i(a_s,t)$, and the time dependent promotion probabilities at a seniority level, $\bar{p}_{i,i+1}(s,t)$, which was postulated in Eq. (1).

Stayers

An individual who is neither promoted nor leaves is then advanced in both age and seniority.

Recruits

Recruitment is also vacancy dependent. The managerial choice is dual: the mix of internal staff to external recruits and the age of recruits.[4] In this paper, only the latter choice is considered since recruitment is at the lowest grade.[5] Hence,

[4] It should be noted here that judicial decisions have ruled that unless age-based hiring discrimination can be shown to be related to job performance, it is illegal.

[5] To incorporate the internal–external choice at each grade Eq. (10) would simply be $\bar{r}_i(a,t) = \delta_i(a) \lambda_{io} \bar{v}_i(t)$ (10′) and Eq. (3), the vacancy equation determining $\bar{v}_i(t)$, would become

$$\bar{v}_i(t) = \bar{n}_{io}(t) + \bar{j}_i(t) + \sum_{l=i+1}^{k} \left\{ \prod_{\tau=l+1}^{l} (1 - \lambda_{\tau o})[\bar{n}_{lo}(t) + \bar{j}_l(t)] \right\}. \tag{3′}$$

$$\bar{r}_1(a,t) = \delta_1(a)\bar{v}_1(t) = \delta_1(a)\left[\sum_{l=1}^{k}\bar{n}_{lo}(t) + \bar{j}_l(t)\right]. \tag{10}$$

Again the chain reaction of vacancies above grade 1 is observed. The age band for the selection of recruits is determined by the preference distribution $\delta_1(a)$. This hiring decision parameter, $\delta(a)$, will be used as a managerial policy alternative in the chapter. An initial estimate, however, will serve as a basis for these changes.

That is,

$$\hat{\delta}_i(a) = \frac{\Sigma_t\, r_i(a,t)}{\Sigma_t\, r_i(t)}. \tag{11}$$

Since opportunities in higher grades affect all lower ones, the mechanics for deriving the probabilities and staff flows are sequential:

1. Exits from grade k occur and new job vacancies enter, Eq. (3), $i+1 = k$.
2. Promotions from grade $k - 1$ to k are made, Eq. (1).
3. Exits from grade $k - 1$ take place conditional on not being promoted; Eq. (7) if using the residual nonpromoted population and Eq. (8) if using the population at the start of the time interval; new job vacancies also enter grade $k - 1$, Eq. (3).
4. Steps (2) and (3) are repeated iteratively for grades $k - 2$ to Grade 1.
5. Recruits are selected to fill the vacancies at grade 1, Eq. (10) and (11).

PARAMETER ESTIMATES AND SIMULATION DESIGN

Four types of parameter estimates are sufficient to simulate ILM staff flows: managerial selection preferences of seniority levels for promotion, $\hat{\lambda}_{i+1,i}(s)$; managerial hiring preferences by age, $\hat{\delta}_i(a)$; managerial allocation of new jobs per grade, $\hat{\rho}_i$ and worker exit probabilities by age conditional on not being promoted, $\hat{p}_{io}^*(a)$.

I selected the relative organizational grade distribution by examining recent studies of ILM staff movements. The organizational ILMs included a managerial staff of a large British firm (Young and Vassiliou

The probability of a given internal–external mix is given by λ_{io} in Eq. (10′), with the age band for the selection of recruits determined at each grade by the preference distributions $\delta_i(a)$. The chain reaction of vacancies in Eq. (3′) remains, but there is a dampening effect on this chain reaction by all higher level recruitment decisions, as denoted by $\prod_\tau(1 - \lambda_{\tau o})$.

1974), a managerial–professional–technical staff of a United States insurance company (Mahoney and Milkovich 1971), a managerial staff and work force of a United States state police organization (Stewman 1978), a government work force of British physical scientists (Sales 1971), a women's military (naval) organization (Forbes 1971), and a managerial staff of the United States government (current work by the author). Selected profiles, depicted as the percentage of total ILM staff in each grade, are shown below:

Grade	ILM Grade Profiles									
	(1)	(2)	(3)	(4)	(5)	(6)	(7)	(8)	(9)	(10)
G6	—	—	—	—	—	—	—	—	—	.02
G5	.03	.015	.004	—	—	—	—	—	—	.05
G4	.04	.015	.01	.05	—	—	—	—	—	.16
G3	.07	.09	.07	.11	—	—	—	—	.15	.45
G2	.28	.20	.24	.33	.37	.32	.26	.49	.65	.25
G1	.58	.68	.67	.52	.63	.68	.74	.51	.20	.07
Total size	1,102	1,374	112,000	242	333	483	288	122	2,909	3,172

(1)	managerial staff, private firm
(2)	managerial staff, state police
(3)	managerial staff, government
(4)	military hierarchy
(5)–(9)	managerial–professional–technical staff, insurance firm
(10)	scientific staff, government

I was somewhat surprised at the similarity appearing in profiles (1)–(7). Profile (8) stands alone, and no information is provided in the article to aid speculation. However, profiles (9) and (10) also show similarity, with the bulge at the middle perhaps due to the lower grades' serving as a training program. I selected profile (1), a managerial staff of a private firm, buttressed with the somewhat delighted surprise at the overall similarity in the first set of profiles. Furthermore, the ILM size in these simulations was set at 10,000 for convenience.

Second, it was necessary to determine a realistic staff profile by age and seniority within each grade. Fortunately, a large-scale study of the United States government labor force currently under way provided help at this point. The initial distribution per grade was then imposed on the ILM staff selected above. This newly constructed ILM staff profile is shown in Table 10.1, with Figure 10.1 providing the corresponding graphics. A summary by age group and then by seniority is given in Tables 10.4 and 10.8 in the section on results. A concentration in Grades 3, 4,

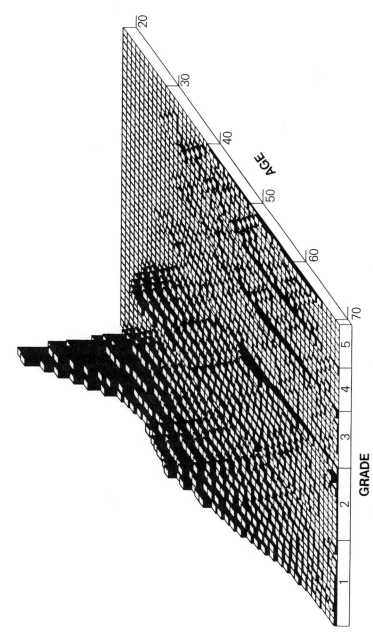

Figure 10.1. Initial age–seniority staff profile by grade.

Table 10.1
Initial Age–Seniority Staff Profile by Grade

Age	Grade 1												Grade 2									
	1	2	3	4	5	6	7	8	9	10	11	12	1	2	3	4	5	6	7	8	9	10
18	0	0	0	0	0	0	0	0	0	0	0	0	0	0	0	0	0	0	0	0	0	0
19	0	0	0	0	0	0	0	0	0	0	0	0	0	0	0	0	0	0	0	0	0	0
20	0	0	0	0	0	0	0	0	0	0	0	0	0	0	0	0	0	0	0	0	0	0
21	1	0	0	0	0	0	0	0	0	0	0	0	0	0	0	0	0	0	0	0	0	0
22	5	1	0	0	0	0	0	0	0	0	0	0	0	0	0	0	0	0	0	0	0	0
23	30	4	0	0	0	0	0	0	0	0	0	0	0	0	0	0	0	0	0	0	0	0
24	64	25	2	0	0	0	0	0	0	0	0	0	0	0	0	0	0	0	0	0	0	0
25	89	54	11	1	0	0	0	0	0	0	0	0	1	0	0	0	0	0	0	0	0	0
26	90	70	25	4	0	0	0	0	0	0	0	0	4	1	0	0	0	0	0	0	0	0
27	79	69	32	11	3	0	0	0	0	0	0	0	12	3	1	0	0	0	0	0	0	0
28	72	61	32	16	6	2	0	0	0	0	0	0	17	10	3	0	0	0	0	0	0	0
29	64	54	31	15	10	3	1	0	0	0	0	0	21	14	7	1	0	0	0	0	0	0
30	57	47	27	16	10	6	2	1	0	0	0	0	23	16	9	4	1	0	0	0	0	0
31	48	44	25	14	10	7	3	1	0	0	0	0	24	18	12	6	3	0	0	0	0	0
32	39	38	25	15	8	6	4	2	0	0	0	0	25	18	14	8	4	2	0	0	0	0
33	37	30	24	16	10	6	4	3	1	0	0	0	23	20	14	10	6	3	2	0	0	0
34	36	30	19	15	10	7	3	3	2	1	0	0	23	19	15	10	7	4	2	1	0	0
35	34	29	19	12	10	8	5	2	2	1	1	0	20	19	15	11	6	6	3	1	1	0
36	33	29	20	13	9	7	5	3	1	1	1	0	20	16	14	11	8	6	4	2	1	0
37	33	27	21	14	9	6	5	3	2	1	1	1	21	16	12	11	8	6	3	3	1	1
38	37	27	19	15	11	7	5	4	2	2	1	1	21	17	13	8	9	7	4	2	2	1
39	35	31	20	14	11	8	5	3	3	1	1	1	19	17	14	11	6	7	5	3	1	2
40	39	29	23	14	12	9	6	4	2	2	1	2	19	15	14	11	9	5	5	4	2	2
41	40	32	22	17	11	9	7	4	2	1	1	2	19	16	13	10	9	7	4	4	3	3
42	41	34	25	17	14	9	6	5	3	2	1	2	17	16	13	11	8	8	6	3	3	4
43	41	35	26	18	14	11	8	5	4	2	1	2	21	14	14	11	9	6	6	4	2	5
44	43	35	26	20	15	11	9	6	4	3	1	2	21	18	12	12	9	7	5	5	3	5
45	45	36	26	20	17	13	9	7	4	3	2	2	19	17	15	10	10	7	6	4	3	6
46	39	38	27	20	16	13	11	7	5	3	2	3	19	16	15	12	8	8	6	4	3	6
47	40	33	30	21	16	13	10	9	6	4	2	3	17	15	14	12	11	7	7	5	3	7
48	34	34	25	24	17	13	11	8	7	4	3	4	17	14	13	12	10	9	6	6	4	8
49	35	29	26	20	20	14	11	8	7	6	3	5	18	14	12	11	9	9	8	5	5	8
50	35	29	23	21	16	17	12	9	6	5	4	6	17	15	13	10	10	8	8	6	4	9
51	29	27	23	19	17	13	13	9	7	5	4	7	15	13	13	10	8	8	7	6	5	11
52	28	22	20	19	16	14	11	11	7	6	4	8	15	12	11	11	9	7	7	6	4	13
53	26	22	16	16	15	12	11	8	8	5	5	8	15	12	10	9	9	8	6	6	4	13
54	25	20	17	12	13	13	10	9	6	7	4	8	13	12	10	9	8	7	7	5	5	12
55	23	20	16	13	10	11	10	7	7	4	6	8	14	11	10	9	7	6	6	4	5	12
56	19	17	15	12	10	8	9	8	5	5	3	8	9	10	8	8	7	6	5	5	4	9
57	17	14	13	11	10	7	6	7	5	3	3	6	6	7	8	6	7	6	5	4	4	7
58	15	13	11	10	8	8	6	4	5	4	2	6	7	5	6	7	5	6	5	3	3	7
59	12	12	10	8	8	6	6	4	3	4	3	5	6	5	3	5	6	4	5	4	3	6
60	9	9	9	8	6	6	4	5	3	2	3	5	5	4	4	2	4	5	4	4	3	6
61	8	7	7	7	6	5	5	3	3	2	2	4	5	4	3	3	2	3	4	2	3	6
62	6	6	5	5	5	5	4	3	2	2	1	3	3	3	3	2	2	1	2	3	2	6
63	6	4	4	4	3	3	4	3	2	1	1	2	2	3	2	2	2	2	1	1	2	4
64	4	4	3	3	3	3	3	3	1	1	1	2	3	2	2	2	1	2	1	1	1	4
65	3	3	3	2	3	2	2	2	2	1	1	1	2	2	1	2	1	1	1	1	1	3
66	3	2	2	3	2	2	2	1	1	1	1	1	2	2	2	1	1	1	1	1	1	2
67	3	3	2	1	2	1	1	1	1	1	1	1	1	1	1	1	1	1	1	1	1	2
68	2	2	2	1	1	1	1	1	1	0	1	1	1	1	1	1	1	0	0	1	1	2
69	2	2	1	2	1	1	1	0	0	0	0	1	1	1	1	1	1	1	0	0	1	1
70	2	2	3	2	2	2	2	1	1	0	2	1	1	1	1	1	1	1	2	1	5	1

Table 10.1 (Continued)

Grade 3								Grade 4						Grade 5					
1	2	3	4	5	6	7	8	1	2	3	4	5	6	1	2	3	4	5	6
0	0	0	0	0	0	0	0	0	0	0	0	0	0	0	0	0	0	0	0
0	0	0	0	0	0	0	0	0	0	0	0	0	0	0	0	0	0	0	0
0	0	0	0	0	0	0	0	0	0	0	0	0	0	0	0	0	0	0	0
0	0	0	0	0	0	0	0	0	0	0	0	0	0	0	0	0	0	0	0
0	0	0	0	0	0	0	0	0	0	0	0	0	0	0	0	0	0	0	0
0	0	0	0	0	0	0	0	0	0	0	0	0	0	0	0	0	0	0	0
0	0	0	0	0	0	0	0	0	0	0	0	0	0	0	0	0	0	0	0
0	0	0	0	0	0	0	0	0	0	0	0	0	0	0	0	0	0	0	0
0	0	0	0	0	0	0	0	0	0	0	0	0	0	0	0	0	0	0	0
0	0	0	0	0	0	0	0	0	0	0	0	0	0	0	0	0	0	0	0
1	0	0	0	0	0	0	0	0	0	0	0	0	0	0	0	0	0	0	0
1	0	0	0	0	0	0	0	0	0	0	0	0	0	1	0	0	0	0	0
1	1	0	0	0	0	0	0	0	0	0	0	0	0	1	1	0	0	0	0
2	1	1	0	0	0	0	0	0	0	0	0	0	0	1	1	1	0	0	0
3	1	0	0	0	0	0	0	1	0	0	0	0	0	1	1	1	1	0	0
3	2	1	0	0	0	0	0	1	1	0	0	0	0	0	1	1	0	0	0
5	2	2	1	0	0	0	0	3	1	1	0	0	0	3	0	0	0	0	0
4	4	2	1	0	0	0	0	2	2	1	0	0	0	4	1	0	0	0	0
4	3	3	2	1	0	0	0	3	1	2	0	0	0	2	3	1	0	0	0
5	4	2	2	1	0	0	0	3	2	1	1	0	0	3	2	3	1	0	0
5	4	3	2	2	1	0	0	2	2	1	1	1	1	3	3	1	3	0	0
5	4	3	2	1	1	1	1	2	1	1	1	0	1	2	2	1	1	2	0
4	4	3	3	2	1	1	1	4	2	1	1	1	1	3	1	1	1	1	1
6	3	4	2	2	1	1	2	3	2	2	1	0	0	2	3	1	0	1	2
5	5	3	3	2	2	1	2	4	3	2	1	1	1	3	1	3	1	0	2
6	4	4	3	2	1	1	3	4	4	1	2	0	2	3	3	1	1	0	1
6	5	4	4	2	2	1	4	5	3	3	1	1	2	4	2	2	0	1	0
5	5	4	3	3	2	1	3	4	3	3	2	1	2	2	3	2	2	0	1
5	5	4	4	2	3	2	4	3	3	3	3	2	3	2	2	2	1	2	1
5	4	4	4	3	2	2	5	4	3	2	2	2	4	5	1	2	2	1	2
5	5	4	3	3	3	2	6	5	2	3	2	2	4	2	3	1	1	1	1
6	4	4	3	3	3	2	6	3	4	2	2	2	5	5	1	3	1	1	2
4	5	4	3	3	2	2	7	4	3	3	1	2	6	3	4	1	3	0	1
4	4	4	3	3	2	2	7	3	3	3	2	1	6	4	2	3	1	3	1
4	3	4	3	3	3	2	7	5	2	3	3	1	6	3	1	1	1	1	3
5	3	3	3	3	2	2	7	3	4	2	3	2	6	2	2	1	1	1	3
4	3	3	2	3	2	2	8	3	3	4	2	3	6	3	2	2	1	1	4
4	3	3	2	2	2	2	8	2	3	3	4	1	6	3	1	2	1	0	3
4	3	3	3	2	1	2	8	3	2	2	2	3	6	4	2	1	1	1	2
2	3	3	2	2	2	1	7	2	1	2	2	2	6	2	2	2	1	1	2
2	1	2	2	2	2	2	6	2	2	1	2	1	6	2	1	2	2	0	3
2	1	1	2	2	1	1	5	1	1	2	1	1	5	0	1	0	2	1	3
2	2	1	1	2	2	1	5	1	0	0	1	1	5	2	0	1	0	2	3
2	2	2	1	1	1	1	4	1	0	0	0	1	5	0	1	0	1	0	3
1	1	1	1	1	1	1	4	0	0	0	0	0	4	2	0	1	0	0	3
1	1	1	1	1	0	0	4	1	0	0	0	0	4	1	1	0	1	0	3
1	1	1	1	1	1	0	3	1	1	0	0	0	3	2	1	0	0	1	3
1	1	0	1	1	1	1	2	1	1	1	0	0	2	0	1	0	0	0	2
1	1	0	0	1	0	1	2	0	0	1	0	0	1	0	0	0	0	0	1
1	0	0	0	0	1	0	1	1	0	0	1	0	0	0	0	0	0	0	0
0	1	0	0	0	0	0	1	0	1	0	0	1	0	0	0	0	0	0	0
0	0	1	0	0	0	0	1	0	0	0	0	0	1	0	0	0	0	0	0
0	0	1	1	1	1	0	2	0	0	0	0	0	1	0	0	0	0	0	0

and 5 of individuals in their forties and fifties is noticeable. Moreover, in Figure 10.1, slight concentrations in the highest seniority levels may be seen in Grades 2–5. These concentrations are centered, for the most part, in the age band 50–59.

Allocation of new jobs to each grade, $\hat{p}_i$, was fixed at the initial relative grade size taken from Young and Vassiliou (1974): G1.58, G2.28, G3.07, G4.04, and G5.03.

Estimates of managerial preference by seniority were taken from Konda and Stewman (1980), with intentional smoothing of the preferences to form an inverse unimodal selection rule. The modified estimates are as follows:

Grade	\multicolumn{12}{c}{Seniority level within grade}
	1	2	3	4	5	6	7	8	9	10	11	12
4	.1482	.4815	.2222	.0741	.0741	—	—	—	—	—	—	—
3	0	.0182	.2909	.1818	.1818	.1455	.1273	.0545	—	—	—	—
2	0	.0411	.1370	.1496	.1781	.1644	.1301	.0753	.0685	.0559	—	—
1	0	.0194	.0543	.0620	.0755	.1744	.1589	.1473	.1163	.1008	.0504	.0388

The reader may note, as Konda and Stewman (1980) have observed, that an individual's best selection chances occur earlier, the higher the grade, suggestive of an acceleration effect, the higher one rises.

Age exit probabilities by grade and recruitment probabilities were chosen using the same data as for the joint age-seniority distribution per grade from the United States government work force. These rates will be modified as desired, but their initial estimation served as a baseline for departure.

The recruitment probabilities by age may be thought of as the probability distribution for filling a vacancy by a person of age a. I will refer to the estimate obtained from the data as the "normal" recruitment rates, but this conveys neither rationality nor optimality. It does connote one realistic ILM hiring practice, however. The $\hat{\delta}(a)$'s, Eq. (11), are:

$\hat{\delta}(a)$:	20–24	25–29	30–39	40–49	50–59	60–64	65–59	70+
	.061	.325	.277	.215	.099	.014	.001	.008

The bulk of the hiring (60%) in this instance occurs in the late twenties and the thirties, with 22% of the hires in the forties and 10% in the fifties. The remaining 8% is at the youngest and oldest age ranges considered—6% in the early twenties and 1% each in the age band 60–64 and 70 or older.

The following age-specific exit rates, $\hat{p}_{io}^{*}(a)$, were assumed to represent Eq. (7):

Grade	Age group							
	20–24	25–29	30–39	40–49	50–59	60–64	65–69	70+
5	0	0	.168	.075	.081	.091	.2	.5
4	0	0	.061	.032	.039	.106	.158	.5
3	0	.052	.050	.035	.064	.124	.156	.5
2	.006	.047	.043	.033	.065	.141	.156	.5
1	.044	.087	.064	.049	.072	.143	.176	.5

A few modifications were made, primarily at the age 70 or older grouping, in which all rates were set to .5.

Having constructed the above initial distributions and behavioral parameters, the remaining simulation design may be described. It involves three hiring alternatives, two exit variations, and four overall ILM changes: constant size, and uniform growth at a constant rate: 2%, 4%, and 6% per year. For only one of the simulations was the modified exit behavior utilized. The alternative hiring practices posed two very divergent policies from the estimated "normal hires" policy. On one hand, all hires were assumed to be in their twenties—ages 20–24: .1 and age 25–29: .9. I will refer to this policy as "young hires." A third variation set hiring policy to be equal at all ages:

$$\delta(a) \; \frac{20\text{–}24}{.1} \; \frac{25\text{–}29}{.1} \; \frac{30\text{–}39}{.2} \; \frac{40\text{–}49}{.2} \; \frac{50\text{–}59}{.2} \; \frac{60\text{–}64}{.1} \; \frac{65\text{–}69}{.03} \; \frac{70+}{.07} \; .$$

This policy will be called "equal hires." In some respects, it does not consider labor availability (or at least the unemployed), especially those first entering the labor force. While this "criticism" may be true on the younger end of the age distribution, it very well may not be so at the highest ages, especially age 65 and older. More important, my intent here is to examine possible futures as well as the present trends, and to do so in an exaggerated way by no means is out of order to reveal certain underlying thrusts of a type of hiring practice. Finally, I note simply that if mid-career change from age 40 on became a common event and persons age 60 or older were "encouraged"—with proper social and economic supports to employer and employee—to choose whether they wished to work, then a much larger available labor pool at higher ages would be expected. Since in the future the United States will have a larger relative pool of potential older workers, this, too, might move hiring practice further in the "equal hires" direction than is now "accepted."

If hiring policies ever behaved in an "equal hires" mode, then exits by age would have to be modified accordingly to include much higher exit rates per ILM at these same ages—40 and older. Thus, I have also changed exit behavior in this circumstance to see both sides of this process. These exits will be referred to as "modified exits." The new parameters are modified only for age 40 upward. Hence, 20–39 age exit behavior at ages 20–39 will not be repeated. The modified exit probabilities are:

Grade	40–49	50–59	60–64	65–69	70+
5	.1	.1	.2	.3	.7
4	.1	.1	.2	.3	.7
3	.15	.15	.25	.25	.6
2	.15	.15	.25	.25	.6
1	.25	.25	.2	.2	.5

The greatest increases were made in their forties and fifties for persons in Grade 1. Why shouldn't they move? However, decreases are made for these age groups at Grades 2 and 3, since much greater expectation of reaching the top seems reasonable. For these grades, individuals in their sixties are expected to have higher exit rates in this highly mobile labor force, since they have not hit the higher grades at this point. Exit rates for individuals age 70 or older was also increased, indicating the lessening of mobility barriers and the choice of some of these workers to actively continue in the labor force. The same logic applies to Grades 4 and 5 for ages 65 and older—moving on to new challenges. For earlier ages, on the other hand, continued reign at the top seemed plausible. The greatest modifications are at the earlier ages in Grade 1 and the later ages in Grades 4 and 5; changes in Grades 2 and 3 are roughly 10% at all ages.

The overall simulation design includes the following four scenarios, each having no growth and uniform growth at 2, 4, and 6%:

Scenario 1: "Normal hires," "normal exits"
Scenario 2: "Young hires," "normal exits"
Scenario 3: "Equal hires," "normal exits"
Scenario 4: "Equal hires," "modified exits"

Attempts to examine cyclic growth or long-term rapid growth followed by no growth produced few additional insights and are not presented in the findings.

RESULTS

The assumption of unstable age and seniority distributions is recognized as a starting place only since relatively fixed growth, exit, hiring, and promotion selection rates are extended over a 20-year period within a fixed grade distribution, thus moving the ILM staff flow process toward an equilibrium. The intended use of the vacancy model here is to pursue the process by which more stable patterns emerge. Of most concern, then, are two factors: (1) insight into the underlying process generating the observed pattern and (2) the managerial and worker decision impacts that may be varied to obtain alternative futures. This second focus suggests that instability is in our favor, if it is ours to control or direct.

The results obtained are by no means a full parametric analysis either of the model or the aging of work organizations, nor are they intended to be. They are, however, an initial start in that pursuit. As noted in the introduction, the results will be organized by five topics:

1. Promotion probabilities by age
2. Age distributions within a grade
3. Grade distributions within an age group
4. Seniority distributions within a grade
5. Joint age-seniority staff profiles

Promotion

Table 10.2 presents the first and twentieth year promotion probabilities by age, grade, and alternative growth rates. Scenarios 1–3 have "normal exits" but vary by hiring policy. Since new hires during Year 1 are not considered for promotion here, these three scenarios have the same initial age groups, growth rate, and exit behavior, and therefore the same promotion probabilities by age. Scenario 4, on the other hand, raises exits and thus promotion chances due to the vacancy pull effect both at the initial grade of entrance and throughout the lower grades. Scenario 1 has "normal hires," Scenario 2 "young hires," and Scenarios 3 and 4 "equal hires." Scenario 3 results are given so that the reader can separate the effects of the hire and exit changes from the first two scenarios. Otherwise, it is unimportant, since a manager cannot hire older employed workers who will not change firms or change ILMs within the same firm.

The first question to be addressed is what age group has the highest promotion chances per grade. The findings generally hold across all scenarios. In Grade 1, it is the thirties; in Grade 2, the thirties and

Table 10.2
Promotion Probabilities by Age, Grade, Scenario, and Time

| | Grade 4 | | | | | | Grade 3 | | | | | |
| | Year 1 | | Year 20 | | | | Year 1 | | Year 20 | | | |
Age 20–24	S1–S3	S4	S1	S2	S3	S4	S1–S3	S4	S1	S2	S3	S4
G = .0	0	0	0	0	0	0	.07	.12	0	0	0	0
.02	0	0	0	0	0	0	.09	.13	0	0	0	0
.04	0	0	0	0	0	0	.11	.15	0	0	0	0
.06	0	0	0	0	0	0	.13	.17	0	0	0	0
25–29												
G = .0	.10	.14	.12	.12	.12	.11	.02	.03	.03	.03	.03	.03
.02	.12	.16	.12	.12	.12	.11	.02	.03	.03	.03	.03	.03
.04	.15	.17	.12	.12	.12	.11	.03	.04	.03	.03	.03	.04
.06	.17	.20	.12	.12	.12	.12	.03	.04	.03	.03	.03	.05
30–39												
G = .0	.10	.13	.16	.16	.17	.15	.05	.09	.08	.08	.10	.10
.02	.12	.15	.16	.16	.17	.15	.07	.10	.09	.08	.10	.12
.04	.14	.16	.17	.17	.17	.16	.09	.12	.09	.08	.11	.14
.06	.15	.17	.17	.17	.17	.17	.10	.14	.09	.09	.11	.16
40–49												
G = .0	.09	.11	.15	.15	.15	.13	.07	.12	.12	.12	.12	.14
.02	.10	.13	.15	.16	.15	.14	.09	.14	.13	.13	.13	.16
.04	.12	.14	.16	.16	.16	.14	.11	.16	.14	.14	.14	.17
.06	.14	.16	.17	.17	.17	.15	.13	.17	.15	.16	.16	.18
50–59												
G = .0	.07	.09	.09	.07	.09	.08	.07	.12	.10	.09	.10	.14
.02	.08	.10	.10	.08	.10	.09	.09	.14	.12	.11	.12	.16
.04	.09	.11	.11	.09	.12	.10	.11	.16	.14	.16	.14	.17
.06	.11	.13	.12	.10	.13	.12	.13	.17	.16	.23	.16	.18
60–64												
G = .0	.03	.04	.07	.05	.07	.06	.07	.11	.09	.07	.10	.12
.02	.04	.05	.08	.06	.09	.07	.09	.13	.12	.10	.12	.13
.04	.04	.05	.09	.07	.10	.09	.11	.15	.14	.15	.14	.14
.06	.05	.06	.11	.08	.11	.11	.13	.17	.17	.23	.16	.16
65–69												
G = .0	.08	.10	.06	.05	.07	.06	.07	.12	.08	.06	.09	.11
.02	.09	.11	.07	.06	.08	.08	.09	.14	.12	.10	.12	.12
.04	.11	.13	.09	.07	.10	.09	.11	.16	.15	.15	.14	.13
.06	.12	.14	.10	.08	.11	.11	.13	.17	.17	.23	.16	.14
70 +												
G = .0	.03	.04	.06	.05	.08	.09	.07	.12	.08	.06	.09	.08
.02	.04	.05	.08	.07	.09	.10	.10	.14	.11	.09	.11	.09
.04	.04	.05	.09	.08	.11	.11	.12	.16	.14	.14	.12	.10
.06	.05	.06	.10	.08	.12	.13	.14	.17	.17	.22	.14	.11
Average												
G = .0	.07	.10	.09	.09	.10	.11	.07	.11	.10	.10	.10	.12
.02	.09	.11	.11	.11	.11	.12	.09	.13	.12	.11	.12	.14
.04	.10	.12	.12	.12	.12	.13	.11	.15	.13	.13	.14	.15
.06	.12	.12	.13	.13	.13	.13	.13	.17	.15	.14	.13	.17
Total number of promotions												
G = .0	29	38	39	37	39	43	48	80	70	68	73	87
.02	35	44	49	62	64	69	62	93	119	115	123	142
.04	41	49	101	100	103	108	76	106	195	190	202	228
.06	47	56	159	157	163	174	89	120	313	304	324	364

Table 10.2 (Continued)

	Grade 2						Grade 1					
Year 1		Year 20				Year 1		Year 20			
S1–S3	S4	S1	S2	S3	S4	S1–S3	S4	S1	S2	S3	S4
.02	.04	.01	.01	.01	.01	0	0	.01	.01	.01	.02
.03	.04	.01	.01	.01	.01	0	0	.01	.01	.02	.03
.03	.05	.01	.01	.01	.01	0	.01	.02	.01	.02	.04
.04	.06	.01	.01	.01	.01	0	.01	.02	.02	.02	.06
.01	.01	.03	.02	.03	.03	.01	.01	.03	.02	.06	.10
.01	.02	.03	.02	.03	.03	.01	.02	.03	.02	.06	.12
.01	.02	.03	.02	.03	.04	.01	.02	.03	.02	.07	.14
.01	.02	.03	.03	.03	.04	.01	.02	.03	.02	.09	.16
.02	.05	.05	.05	.06	.07	.03	.06	.07	.08	.07	.11
.03	.06	.05	.05	.06	.07	.04	.07	.08	.09	.08	.13
.04	.06	.06	.06	.07	.08	.05	.08	.09	.11	.09	.14
.05	.07	.06	.06	.07	.10	.06	.09	.10	.14	.10	.15
.03	.07	.05	.05	.06	.06	.05	.10	.05	.01	.06	.09
.04	.07	.06	.05	.06	.08	.06	.11	.07	.02	.08	.10
.05	.08	.06	.07	.07	.09	.08	.12	.08	.05	.10	.11
.06	.09	.07	.08	.07	.10	.09	.14	.10	1.00	.11	.12
.04	.07	.04	.01	.04	.05	.07	.14	.05	.01	.06	.06
.05	.08	.05	.01	.05	.06	.09	.16	.07	.02	.08	.07
.06	.09	.06	.02	.06	.07	.11	.18	.09	.05	.10	.09
.07	.10	.07	.03	.07	.08	.14	.21	.11	0	.11	.10
.04	.08	.03	.01	.04	.05	.07	.15	.04	.01	.06	.06
.05	.09	.04	.01	.05	.06	.10	.17	.07	.02	.07	.08
.06	.10	.05	.02	.06	.06	.12	.20	.10	.05	.09	.09
.07	.11	.06	.03	.07	.07	.15	.23	.12	0	.10	.11
.04	.07	.03	.01	.04	.04	.07	.15	.04	.01	.07	.11
.05	.08	.04	.01	.05	.05	.10	.17	.07	.02	.09	.14
.06	.09	.05	.02	.06	.05	.12	.20	.13	.05	.11	.16
.07	.10	.06	.03	.07	.06	.15	.23	.17	0	.13	.17
.05	.10	.02	.01	.04	.04	.08	.17	.02	.01	.04	.05
.07	.11	.03	.01	.05	.05	.11	.20	.03	.02	.04	.06
.08	.13	.05	.02	.06	.06	.14	.23	.04	.05	.05	.06
.10	.14	.06	.03	.07	.06	.17	.26	.05	0	.05	.07
.03	.06	.04	.04	.05	.06	.04	.09	.05	.05	.06	.08
.04	.07	.05	.05	.05	.07	.06	.10	.06	.06	.07	.10
.05	.08	.06	.05	.06	.08	.07	.11	.07	.07	.09	.11
.06	.09	.07	.06	.07	.08	.08	.13	.09	.08	.10	.12
89	173	119	108	129	167	240	504	302	262	351	492
116	198	204	186	221	275	321	582	535	471	614	821
143	223	341	315	366	445	402	659	916	822	1039	1345
169	248	555	517	596	713	483	737	1523	1385	1713	2167

forties; in Grade 3, the forties and fifties and in Grade 4, the thirties and forties again.

Scenario 4, depicting much higher exit behavior at age 40 or older and also much higher rates for these "older" workers, generally has the higher promotion rates at all ages. This might appear obvious once we examine the last row of the table, which gives the total number of promotions generated in each scenario per grade. However, it is not true at Grade 4, indicating the intervention of seniority level of the worker and its relative supply at the more preferred levels. In Grades 1–3, the more mobile older worker scenario (Scenario 4) appears more advantageous for increasing any individual worker's promotion chances. With "equal hiring" across ages and a higher overall grade level promotion rate, this larger set of opportunities is divvied up for all to share as their seniority level changes. The second most "promotable" scenario is Scenario 1, a continuation of "normal" hiring policy. The workers most benefited are those over 40. Few differences between Scenarios 1 and 2 are seen for the workers in their twenties or thirties. There is one major exception to the above findings, whereby workers in Scenario 2 have the highest promotion rates of any scenario. In the case of a high growth rate (.06), promotions are accelerated for workers in their forties in Grade 1 (probability 1.0 of promotion) and ages 40 or above in Grade 3 (probabilities of .22 or .23, rather than .16). This particular case is rather interesting and calls for an analysis of promotion rates over time to view the manner in which these large jumps occur. Table 10.3 provides these data, comparing Scenarios 2 and 4 for Grade 1 promotions.

Several features of Table 10.3 are worth noting. First, of course, is the finding that in Scenario 2 any individual aged 40 and older is promoted with probability 1.00 in Year 14. That is, all workers at these ages were promoted. Second, the overall promotion rate from Grade 1 is lower in Scenario 2 than in Scenario 4. Thus, even when the overall chances are worse, some individual's chances may be far better, depending on the volume of opportunities to be filled and the available labor supply at the seniority level of that individual. The volume of opportunities affecting Grade 1 and, consequently, the small number of younger workers reaching high seniority levels, generates a decreasing labor supply in the seniority levels that the older workers hold. With the fixed selection rule and increasing opportunities, the demand for these workers is growing, resulting in their all being promoted. Third, no such differences occur between the various scenarios at the slower growth rates of 2% and 4%. Only at the 6% growth rate was the impact so striking. However, at this level of growth, the internal mechanisms were operating at different levels of relative supply and demand, sweeping the older workers into

TABLE 10.3
Promotion Probabilities from Grade 1 by Age and Year under Different Hiring and Exit Conditions

Year	20–24	25–29	30–39	40–49	50–59	60–64	65–69	70+	Grade average
Grade 1, Scenario 2, G = .06 [Young Hires, Normal Exits]									
1	0	.01	.06	.09	.14	.15	.15	.17	.08
2	0	.01	.08	.11	.16	.17	.17	.17	.08
3	.01	.01	.09	.14	.18	.21	.22	.20	.09
4	.01	.02	.10	.17	.21	.23	.24	.22	.09
5	.02	.02	.10	.21	.26	.25	.28	.26	.09
6	.02	.03	.11	.26	.29	.32	.34	.34	.09
7	.02	.03	.13	.30	.30	.30	.32	.32	.09
8	.02	.03	.14	.30	.30	.30	.30	.30	.09
9	.02	.03	.15	.35	.35	.35	.35	.35	.09
10	.02	.03	.15	.40	.40	.40	.40	.40	.09
11	.02	.03	.06	.41	.41	.41	.41	.41	.09
12	.02	.03	.16	.37	.37	.37	.37	.37	.09
13	.02	.03	.16	.65	.65	.65	.65	.65	.09
14	.02	.03	.16	1.00	1.00	1.00	1.00	1.00	.08
15	.02	.03	.16	0	0	0	0	0	.08
16	.02	.02	.15	0	0	0	0	0	.08
17	.02	.02	.15	0	0	0	0	0	.08
18	.02	.02	.15	1.00	0	0	0	0	.08
19	.02	.02	.15	1.00	0	0	0	0	.08
20	.02	.02	.14	1.00	0	0	0	0	.08
Grade 1, Scenario 4, G = .06 [Equal Hires, Modified Exits]									
1	.01	.02	.09	.14	.21	.23	.23	.26	.13
2	0	.04	.11	.16	.20	.16	.17	.03	.13
3	.01	.09	.15	.16	.16	.11	.11	.03	.13
4	.04	.13	.17	.14	.12	.08	.09	.04	.13
5	.05	.13	.20	.12	.10	.08	.10	.04	.13
6	.06	.13	.18	.12	.10	.09	.13	.05	.12
7	.06	.16	.16	.12	.10	.11	.17	.07	.12
8	.06	.16	.16	.12	.10	.11	.17	.07	.12
9	.06	.16	.16	.12	.10	.11	.17	.07	.12
10	.06	.16	.16	.12	.10	.11	.17	.07	.12
11	.06	.16	.16	.12	.10	.11	.17	.07	.13
12	.06	.16	.16	.12	.10	.11	.17	.07	.13
13	.06	.16	.16	.12	.10	.11	.17	.07	.13
14	.06	.16	.16	.12	.10	.11	.17	.07	.12
15	.06	.16	.16	.12	.10	.11	.17	.07	.12
16	.06	.16	.16	.12	.10	.11	.17	.07	.12
17	.06	.16	.16	.12	.10	.11	.17	.07	.12
18	.06	.16	.16	.12	.10	.11	.17	.07	.12
19	.06	.16	.15	.12	.10	.11	.17	.07	.12
20	.06	.16	.16	.12	.10	.11	.17	.07	.12

Grade 2. In times of high demand, preference structures may reach down and select persons who hitherto had little chance. Hence, individual careers may reveal sudden spiked jumps in promotion chances when demand dramatically alters the underlying supply distributions from which previous selections had been made. Organizationally, such impacts may also suddenly alter the staff mix in a new fashion and thus such potential consequences of present employment policies need to be preexamined and major modifications considered. Below, staff impacts of such policies are considered by looking at age, seniority, and joint age–seniority distributions.

Aging of the ILM Work Force

Two major foci will guide the discussion on the work force aging process within an ILM. The first focus will be age distributions within each grade and for the entire ILM. How age is horizontally distributed, that is, at each grade, is an interesting process to observe and raises the issue of age lumps. The initial distribution portrays an instance known to exist, and it will serve as a baseline for comparison. Aging effects of alternative hiring and exit conditions will be viewed after 20 years and after 40 years or more. The latter data will reveal the long-term age distributions resulting from the hiring policies and exit behavior, independent of the starting distribution. Finally, aging impacts of the high growth, "young hires" policy, which generated the sudden promotion rate changes just noted, will be examined. The second focus, vertical in nature, will view age distributions across grades, addressing how individuals of a certain age are distributed among grades. It is this view that permits comparisons from the individual worker's standpoint, sorting out how aging and hierarchical location are related.

Table 10.4 shows age distributions within each grade and within the total ILM for the staff at the initiation of the simulation and after 20 years. Three 20-year scenarios are shown, each having a zero growth rate. If we use 30% and 40% concentrations in a 10-year age group, as a measure of concentration, then we find the following:

1. The initial population is massed in the 40-year-old and 50-year-old age groups in the three upper grades and has 30% or more in the forties in Grades 1 and 2.
2. Scenario 1, which maintains "normal" hiring and exit patterns, shifts the mass of the two upper grades to the fifties (37%) and sixties (41%); has Grades 2 and 3 populations concentrated in the forties and fifties and has 30% of the staff in Grade 1 in the thirties.

TABLE 10.4
Age Distribution within Grade and for the Total ILM Staff under Different Hiring and Exit Conditions

Grade	Age							
	20–24	25–29	30–39	40–49	50–59	60–64	65–69	70+
			Initial Distribution, t=0					
5	0	.01	.17	.32	.35	.11	.02	0
4	0	0	.10	.34	.43	.08	.04	.01
3	0	0	.14	.37	.35	.08	.03	.01
2	0	.03	.26	.34	.28	.05	.02	.01
1	.02	.16	.23	.30	.23	.04	.01	0
Total	.01	.10	.23	.32	.26	.05	.02	0
			Scenario 1, G=0, t=20 [Normal Hires, Normal Exits]					
5	0	0	.01	.15	.37	.24	.17	.05
4	0	0	.02	.23	.35	.20	.14	.04
3	0	0	.11	.35	.32	.12	.07	.02
2	0	.01	.21	.32	.30	.10	.05	.01
1	.02	.13	.30	.28	.18	.05	.02	.01
Total	.01	.08	.25	.29	.24	.08	.04	.01
			Scenario 2, G=0, t=20 [Young Hires, Normal Exits]					
	0	0	.01	.24	.30	.22	.17	.05
	0	0	.05	.37	.25	.16	.12	.04
	0	0	.23	.52	.12	.07	.05	.01
	0	.02	.44	.32	.12	.05	.03	.01
	.03	.32	.46	.12	.04	.02	.01	0
Total	.02	.18	.41	.22	.08	.04	.03	.01
			Scenario 4, G=0, t=20 [Equal Hires, Modified Exits]					
	0	0	.03	.30	.41	.13	.09	.02
	0	0	.11	.43	.32	.09	.05	.01
	0	.01	.32	.44	.15	.04	.03	.01
	0	.05	.37	.32	.13	.05	.05	.02
	.07	.13	.26	.18	.16	.09	.05	.04
Total	.04	.09	.29	.26	.17	.07	.05	.03

3. Scenario 2, which restricts the hiring to the twenties, has Grade 5 populated largely with persons in their fifties (30%) and sixties (39%) and Grades 3 and 4 with large proportions of persons in their forties (52% in Grade 3); Grade 2 is massed in the 30-year-old and 40-year-old age groups and Grade 1 has almost 50% of its staff in the thirties.

4. Scenario 4, which has hiring at all levels and modifies exit rates of persons over 40, has its Grade 4 and 5 populations centered in

the forties (30%) and fifties (41%), more like the initial population; persons in Grades 2 and 3 are primarily in their thirties and forties and there is diverse staff mixture in Grade 1.

These concentrations per scenario (S) are summarized in Figure 10.2, with differences from the initial distribution (I) being shown by the arrows.

If we pursue more detailed relative changes in the age distribution from the initial or present day staffing, we generally see an aging of the upper grades and a younger staff in the lower grades. The specific shifts per grade are shown in Table 10.5. In Scenario 1, there is a shift at Grades 4 and 5 from the thirties and forties in the initial worker population to the sixties or older. This shift also occurs at Grade 5 in Scenario 2, but at Grade 4 it is the thirties and fifties (instead of forties) being replaced by those over 60. In Scenario 4, the decrease at the thirties in Grade 5 is gained by the fifties and late sixties; large gains in the sixties and seventies are also seen in Grade 1, at the expense of the forties and fifties. Increases in younger staff in Scenario 4 occur in Grade 1 for the early twenties and in Grades 2 and 3 for the thirties. Scenario 2 greatly affects Grade 1 at both the late twenties and thirties and Grade 2 at the thirties. At Grade 3, the fifties become "thirty" and "forty." In Scenario 2, then, the younger effect extends from Grade 1 to Grade 3; at which point aging takes over—perhaps due to decreased competition within these older ages—and Grades 4 and 5 have 32% and 44% in their sixties instead of the original 13% (see Table 10.4).

In brief, whether present hiring policy is continued (Scenario 1) or a radical shift is made to the twenties (Scenario 2) with a continuation of "normal" exit behavior, the upper two grades may be expected to "age" considerably due to the initial age structure's concentration in the forties and fifties. Only with rather "radical" behavioral shocks, permitting large scale mid-career change, are these findings altered.

Looking at the total ILM and returning to Table 10.4, we find around 30% of the initial staff in their forties. Continuing present policies and worker behavior (Scenario 1) maintain the small lump in the forties. Changing hiring policy radically to include only individuals in their twenties (Scenario 2) creates an even larger age lump (40%) which moves to the thirties. A more drastic change, hiring equally at all ages and greatly increasing exits for those over 40 (Scenario 4) results in a more diverse age distribution once again—similar to that in the original distribution and Scenario 1.

The equilibria age distributions for the previous three scenarios are shown in Table 10.6. The greatest departure from the 20-year results is at Scenario 2, where the aging effect of restricting new hires to be in

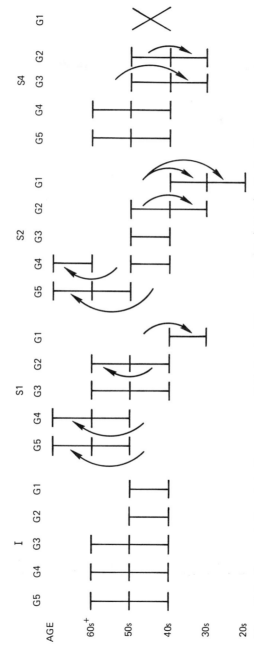

Figure 10.2. Summary of concentrations per scenario(s) showing differences from the initial distribution (I).

TABLE 10.5
Percentage Changes in Age Distributions within Grade from Those of the Initial Staff

Grade	20-24	25-29	30-39	40-49	50-59	60-64	65-69	70+
			Scenario 1, t=20 [Normal Hires, Normal Exits]					
5	–	– 1	–16	–17	+ 2	+13	+15	+5
4	–	–	– 8	–11	– 8	+12	+10	+3
3	–	–	– 3	– 2	– 3	+ 4	+ 4	+1
2	–	– 2	– 5	– 2	+ 2	+ 5	+ 3	0
1	0	– 3	+ 7	– 2	– 5	+ 1	+ 1	+1
Total	0	– 2	+ 2	– 3	– 2	+ 3	+ 2	+1
			Scenario 2, t=20 [Young Hires, Normal Exits]					
5	–	– 1	–16	– 8	– 5	+11	+15	+5
4	–	–	– 5	+ 3	–18	+ 8	+ 8	+3
3	–	–	+ 9	+15	–23	– 1	+ 2	0
2	–	– 1	+18	– 2	–16	0	+ 1	0
1	+1	+16	+23	–18	–19	– 2	0	–
Total	+1	+ 8	+18	–10	–18	– 1	+ 1	+1
			Scenario 4, t=20 [Equal Hires, Modified Exits]					
5	–	– 1	–14	– 2	+ 6	+ 2	+ 7	+2
4	–	–	+ 1	+ 9	–11	+ 1	+ 1	0
3	–	+ 1	+18	+ 7	–20	– 4	0	0
2	–	+ 2	+11	– 2	–15	0	+ 3	+1
1	+5	– 3	0	–12	– 7	+ 5	+ 4	+4
Total	+3	– 1	+ 6	– 6	– 9	+ 2	+ 3	+3

their twenties must run its course. The greatest gains occur in the fifties and these increases are at each grade. In Grades 2 and 3, the main reductions are in the thirties, while in Grades 4 and 5 the decreases are from the sixties and seventies. Permanent and quite large age lumps result in each grade, with the largest being 46% of the staff in Grade 5 in their fifties and 50% of the Grade 3 staff in their forties. Similar increases in the fifties and decreases in the sixties occur at Grades 4 and 5 for Scenarios 1 and 4. Otherwise, the age distributions are largely unchanged from those at 20 years. To reach equilibrium it took Scenario 1 approximately 25 years, Scenario 4 about 50 years (but it was near in 25 years), and Scenario 2 about 90 years, with 40 years to closely approach equilibrium. The equilibria age distributions within grades are quite different for the three scenarios, suggestive of the impacts of alternative hiring practices in particular.

TABLE 10.6
Equilibria Age Distributions within Grade and for the Total ILM Staff under Different Hiring and Exit Conditions

Grade	Age							
	20–24	25–29	30–39	40–49	50–59	60–64	65–69	70+
	Scenario 1, G=0 [Normal Hires, Normal Exits]							
5	0	0	.01	.16	.42	.22	.15	.04
4	0	0	.02	.24	.41	.18	.12	.03
3	0	0	.10	.35	.35	.12	.06	.02
2	0	.01	.20	.32	.30	.10	.05	.01
1	.02	.13	.30	.26	.18	.05	.02	.01
Total	.01	.08	.24	.29	.25	.08	.04	.01
	Scenario 2, G=0 [Young Hires, Normal Exits]							
5	0	0	.01	.28	.46	.15	.08	.02
4	0	0	.03	.37	.37	.13	.07	.02
3	0	0	.17	.50	.22	.06	.03	.01
2	0	.02	.37	.34	.18	.05	.02	.01
1	.03	.30	.44	.14	.07	.02	.01	0
Total	.02	.17	.37	.23	.14	.04	.02	0
	Scenario 4, G=0 [Equal Hires, Modified Exits]							
5	0	0	.03	.34	.44	.13	.06	.01
4	0	0	.10	.43	.34	.09	.03	.01
3	0	.01	.30	.44	.16	.04	.03	.01
2	0	.05	.37	.32	.13	.05	.04	.02
1	.07	.13	.26	.18	.16	.09	.05	.04
Total	.04	.09	.29	.26	.17	.07	.05	.03

Last and most important, I note the proportion of staff aged 60 or older in each scenario (S) at equilibria, compared to the initial (I) distribution. We have

Grade	I	S1	S2	S4
5	.13	.41	.25	.20
4	.13	.33	.22	.13
3	.12	.20	.10	.08
2	.08	.16	.08	.11
1	.05	.08	.03	.18
Total	.07	.13	.06	.15

It is only under the policy of limiting recruits to ages 20–29 (S2) that an increase in the overall proportion of "elderly" is not seen. And, even under these conditions, the internal redistribution is such that about one-fourth of the work force in Grades 4 and 5 is 60 or older, compared to the initial population's one-eighth. If "normal" exit conditions and hiring policy continued (S1), then a rather massive change occurs in Grades 4 and 5, in which one-third and two-fifths of the staff are 60 or older, respectively. Even in Grades 2 and 3 and in the overall staff, the proportion of these older workers is doubled from that of the initial or "present" staff. In the case of "equal hiring" and higher rates of exit at age 40 or above (S4), large gains are seen in Grades 1 and 5 and in the overall proportion of staff, as in Scenario 1.

In summary, from these scenarios large proportional increases may be expected at the age groups 60 or older. Unless major changes occur indicating total withdrawal from the labor force by early retirement or engendering mid-career change, then the above illustrative scenarios indicate rather large-scale redistributions increasing the elderly proportionately "at the top." And, particularly if present hiring practices ("normal hires"; S1) are continued, we may expect increased aging of all grades, with ever greater proportional concentrations, the higher the grade.

The previous analyses have retained a constant size ILM. The sudden spiked promotion rates for all individuals age 40 or older found earlier, occurred only at high growth rate (.06) for Scenario 2—"young hires, normal exits." We now briefly investigate the subsequent age distribution impacts for this case. The results for the process in which growth rate is 6% for the first 15 years and zero for 25 years thereafter are quite similar at Year 40 to the equilibria results of Scenario 2 and thus need no further comment. Table 10.7 indicates the results of a continued high growth rate for Years 20 and 40. Large age lumps may be seen at each grade, especially in Year 40 and extremely large lumps, near 60%, are found in Grades 3 and 4. At Year 40, the proportion of the elderly is very small overall—1%. In this instance, 90% of the staff 60 or older are in the highest seniority level of their grade. There are also large proportions of total staff at these seniority levels and a large labor supply at younger ages in the earlier and more preferred seniority levels. Both of these labor supply circumstances negatively affect the older worker's promotion chances. Recall that all workers age 40 or older were promoted from Grade 1 in Year 14. Thus, our findings here apply only to Grades 2–5. The promotion rates in Year 40 for persons aged 60 or older were as follows: Grade 2 .01; Grade 3 .08 and .09; and Grade 4 .01. The short-term boon enjoyed by older workers in the earlier years of this scenario has passed and the older worker at this point is in a very different internal labor market situation.

TABLE 10.7

Age Distributions within Grade and for the Total ILM Staff under a "Young Hiring" Policy and "Normal Exit" Behavior (Scenario 2)[a]

Grade	Age							
	20–24	25–29	30–39	40–49	50–59	60–64	65–69	70+
				Year 20				
5	0	0	.02	.32	.29	.17	.14	.04
4	0	0	.07	.50	.21	.11	.08	.02
3	0	0	.32	.60	.04	.02	.01	0
2	0	.03	.63	.28	.03	.01	.01	0
1	.05	.48	.46	0	0	0	0	0
Total	.03	.29	.46	.15	.03	.02	.01	0
				Year 40				
5	0	0	.01	.34	.50	.11	.04	0
4	0	0	.05	.48	.35	.08	.02	0
3	0	0	.25	.60	.12	.01	0	0
2	0	.03	.56	.30	.09	.01	0	0
1	.05	.46	.46	.02	0	0	0	0
Total	.03	.28	.45	.17	.06	.01	0	0

[a] Growth rate = .06.

The final view of aging shifts the viewpoint and asks, What is the relative grade distribution given an individual's age group? In other words, What is the probability of a worker age x being in grade y? Since the ILM is not assumed to be in equilibria and many of the parameters of the process are not stationary, there is no fixed relationship between individual aging per se and hierarchical location. Thus, without an intensive analysis of the mixture of cohorts over time, the present framework cannot answer this question adequately. The results of the scenarios after 20 years are presented in Table 10.8 along with the initial distribution, to indicate possible answers and to further support the idea that individual aging per se is not a primary internal mechanism driving the process.

Since too little is known about age distributions within labor market hierarchies, the initial distribution is also of interest in its own right. The major shifts in the probability distributions at Grade 1 occur between the twenties and thirties. At 40 and older, rather small shifts are seen in Grade 1, providing behavioral support for the perceptual importance of the age 40 benchmark noted by Sofer's (1970) managerial staff and Sheehy's (1976) male worker. I wish to stress, however, that this does not indicate that age per se is the factor negating advancement. In the

TABLE 10.8
Grade Distribution within an Age Group under Different Hiring and Exit Conditions

Age	Grade				
	5	4	3	2	1
Initial Distribution					
70+	0	.06	.13	.35	.46
65–69	.03	.08	.12	.29	.48
60–64	.07	.06	.11	.28	.48
50–59	.04	.06	.09	.30	.51
40–49	.03	.04	.08	.30	.54
30–39	.02	.02	.04	.33	.59
25–29	0	0	0	.10	.90
20–24	0	0	0	.01	.99
Scenario 1, G=0 [Normal Hires, Normal Exits]					
70+	.14	.14	.12	.31	.29
65–69	.13	.13	.12	.34	.28
60–64	.09	.10	.11	.34	.36
50–59	.05	.06	.09	.35	.45
40–49	.01	.03	.09	.31	.56
30–39	0	0	.03	.24	.73
25–29	0	0	0	.04	.96
20–24	0	0	0	.01	.99
Scenario 2, G=0 [Young Hires, Normal Exits]					
70+	.19	.18	.12	.32	.19
65–69	.18	.18	.12	.32	.21
60–64	.16	.16	.11	.35	.23
50–59	.11	.12	.10	.41	.26
40–49	.04	.07	.18	.43	.33
30–39	0	0	.04	.30	.66
25–29	0	0	0	.03	.97
20–24	0	0	0	.01	.99
Scenario 4, G=0 [Equal Hires, Modified Exits]					
70+	.01	.01	.03	.19	.75
65–69	.05	.04	.04	.26	.62
60–64	.05	.05	.04	.18	.68
50–59	.08	.08	.06	.22	.57
40–49	.04	.07	.12	.35	.43
30–39	0	.02	.08	.37	.54
25–29	0	0	0	.17	.83
20–24	0	0	0	.02	.98

vacancy model postulated here, it would only be when age and seniority distributions jointly stabilize that such apparent age effects would be seen. To further emphasize the point, recall the sudden promotion probability jump for persons age 40 or older in the high growth, "young hires" scenario.

Seniority Shifts in the ILM

Since seniority within grade was used in these simulations as a surrogate for pertinent job performance attributes, a brief glimpse at the seniority shifts within each grade will be taken. These data are provided in Table 10.9. The initial distribution shows a remarkable similarity in seniority proportions across grades (especially at Seniority Levels 3, 4, and 5) in light of the different number of seniority levels involved. For instance, if we combined all seniority proportions above or equal to Level 6, then the "highest" seniority levels would have the following proportions of staff:

G5	G4	G3	G2	G1
.18	.28	.31	.27	.20

In this respect, there is a slight bulge at Level 6 or above in Grades 2, 3, and 4.

Compared with the outcomes of Scenarios 1 and 2, the initial (I) percentages in the highest seniority levels of Grades 1, 2, 4, and 5 are quite small. In addition, there is less stability in proportionate seniority across grades in all three simulated scenarios than in the initial distribution. In Scenario 4, where there is more upward and outward movement, there are no lumps at the highest seniority levels in Grades 1–3, and the bulge at Grade 4 is similar to that of the initial staff. Of interest is the total absence of workers in Seniority Levels 10, 11, and 12 in Grade 1, again due to the increased mobility effect—upward and outward. The only other instances in which a seniority level is empty are the high growth (.06) scenarios, and once again the impact is the greatest in Scenario 4. Nevertheless, it is this more "radical" hiring policy that most nearly approximates the "current" or initial distribution, in terms of seniority lumps at the highest levels. This comparison is summarized as follows:

Distribution	G5,S6	G4,S6	G3,S8	G2,S10	G1,S12
I	.18	.28	.18	.07	.02
S1	.50	.45	.22	.34	.21
S2	.50	.45	.24	.37	.23
S4	.44	.32	.04	.13	0

The similarity of I and S4 remains, even if we combine all seniority levels at S6 or above. The largest disparity between I and S4 is at Grade 5, where a much higher seniority lump results.

TABLE 10.9
Seniority Distribution within Grade under Different Hiring and Exit Conditions

Grade	Seniority											
	1	2	3	4	5	6	7	8	9	10	11	12
	Initial Distribution, t=0											
5	.29	.20	.14	.10	.08	.18	—	—	—	—	—	—
4	.23	.16	.13	.11	.09	.28	—	—	—	—	—	—
3	.20	.15	.13	.11	.09	.07	.06	.18	—	—	—	—
2	.22	.17	.14	.11	.09	.07	.06	.04	.03	.07	—	—
1	.26	.21	.14	.10	.07	.06	.04	.03	.02	.02	.01	.02
	Scenario 1, G=0, t=20											
5	.13	.11	.10	.08	.07	.50	—	—	—	—	—	—
4	.17	.15	.10	.07	.06	.45	—	—	—	—	—	—
3	.17	.16	.15	.11	.09	.06	.04	.22	—	—	—	—
2	.11	.10	.10	.08	.07	.06	.05	.04	.04	.34	—	—
1	.12	.11	.10	.09	.08	.07	.06	.05	.04	.03	.02	.21
	Scenario 2, G=0, t=20											
5	.12	.11	.10	.08	.07	.50	—	—	—	—	—	—
4	.17	.15	.10	.07	.06	.45	—	—	—	—	—	—
3	.15	.15	.14	.11	.09	.07	.05	.24	—	—	—	—
2	.09	.09	.09	.08	.07	.06	.05	.05	.04	.37	—	—
1	.12	.11	.10	.09	.08	.07	.06	.05	.04	.03	.03	.23
	Scenario 4, G=0, t=20											
5	.14	.13	.11	.10	.08	.44	—	—	—	—	—	—
4	.22	.17	.12	.09	.07	.32	—	—	—	—	—	—
3	.24	.21	.17	.13	.09	.06	.04	.04	—	—	—	—
2	.17	.15	.13	.11	.09	.07	.05	.04	.03	.13	—	—
1	.24	.20	.16	.13	.10	.08	.05	.03	.01	0	0	0

Joint Age–Seniority Staff Profiles

The last aspect of the aging process to be viewed is the joint age–seniority staff profiles at the end of a 20-year period. I think the impacts of the alternative hiring practices and exit behavior are most easily grasped with these profiles. They are shown in Tables 10.10, 10.11, and 10.12 and Figures 10.3, 10.4, and 10.5. Table 10.1 and Figure 10.1 gave the initial staff profile. The basic overall profiles are the same for growth rates 0–6% and thus only one set are presented.[5]

The basic imagery seems to speak quite loudly on overall impact. In particular, the comparisons seem to cast doubt on the advisability of a restricted hiring policy such as is used in Scenario 2, which is perhaps more the rule than the exception in many firms using highly technical staff freshly groomed by our universities. In a complementary vein, much more thought seems needed to providing mechanisms for hiring a mix of staff. In large firms, the transfer of workers between ILMs may be such a device. For movement between firms, however, mid-career change may be necessary and it must have economic and social supports such as transferable pension "rights," retraining pitstops, permitting a time of non-full-time employment; possibly the redefinition of seniority toward more flexibility—sometimes carrying over across ILMs, as used in equal employment opportunity planning; and the use of short-term and long-term leaves to engender more breadth in the worker, thereby potentially increasing productivity and also better accommodating dual careers. Should such leaves be for work in other firms in a different type of ILM, "trade secrets" would be less of a problem. Alternatively, should these leaves be between firms with noncompeting product lines, then no change of ILM type would be necessary. In any event, the above items by no means probe very far into the possibilities for establishing employment mechanisms whereby a mix of staff is available and aging is more fully utilized as an organizational resource to be effectively managed and directed.

SUMMARY

Some of the basic ideas underlying this chapter include the importance of breaking apart the organization's labor force into its internal labor

---

[5] In order to more fully visualize the smaller differences in the higher grades, a data transformation was necessary for the figures; the square root of the number in the corresponding table was utilized.

Table 10.10
Age–Seniority Staff Profile for "Normal Hiring" Policy and "Normal Exit" Behavior (Scenario 1), Growth Rate = .06, Year 20

Age	|				Grade 1									|					Grade 2				
		1	2	3	4	5	6	7	8	9	10	11	12		1	2	3	4	5	6	7	8	9	10
18		0	0	0	0	0	0	0	0	0	0	0	0		0	0	0	0	0	0	0	0	0	0
19		0	0	0	0	0	0	0	0	0	0	0	0		0	0	0	0	0	0	0	0	0	0
20		45	0	0	0	0	0	0	0	0	0	0	0		0	0	0	0	0	0	0	0	0	0
21		45	41	0	0	0	0	0	0	0	0	0	0		0	0	0	0	0	0	0	0	0	0
22		45	41	36	0	0	0	0	0	0	0	0	0		0	0	0	0	0	0	0	0	0	0
23		45	41	36	32	0	0	0	0	0	0	0	0		2	0	0	0	0	0	0	0	0	0
24		45	41	36	32	27	0	0	0	0	0	0	0		3	1	0	0	0	0	0	0	0	0
25		240	41	36	32	27	23	0	0	0	0	0	0		5	3	1	0	0	0	0	0	0	0
26		240	207	35	30	26	22	16	0	0	0	0	0		8	4	2	1	0	0	0	0	0	0
27		240	207	176	29	25	21	16	11	0	0	0	0		13	8	4	2	1	0	0	0	0	0
28		240	207	176	147	24	20	15	10	6	0	0	0		20	12	7	3	2	1	0	0	0	0
29		240	207	176	147	121	19	14	10	6	3	0	0		27	18	11	6	3	1	1	0	0	0
30		102	207	176	147	121	98	14	9	6	3	1	0		35	24	16	9	5	2	1	0	0	0
31		102	90	181	151	124	100	71	9	6	3	1	0		48	31	22	14	7	4	2	1	0	0
32		102	90	79	155	128	103	73	48	6	3	1	0		60	44	28	18	11	6	3	1	1	0
33		102	90	79	68	131	105	74	50	29	3	1	0		69	54	39	24	15	9	4	2	1	1
34		102	90	79	68	57	108	76	51	30	15	1	0		76	63	49	33	20	12	7	3	2	1
35		102	90	79	68	57	47	78	52	31	16	4	0		81	69	56	41	27	16	9	5	3	3
36		102	90	79	68	57	47	34	53	32	16	4	0		75	73	61	47	34	22	12	7	4	4
37		102	90	79	68	57	47	34	23	32	17	5	0		67	68	65	52	39	27	16	9	6	7
38		102	90	79	68	57	47	34	23	14	17	5	0		58	60	60	55	43	31	21	12	7	11
39		102	90	79	68	57	47	34	23	14	7	5	0		52	53	54	51	46	34	24	15	10	15
40		79	90	79	68	57	47	34	23	14	7	2	0		46	47	47	45	42	36	26	18	12	19
41		79	71	80	69	58	48	35	24	14	8	2	0		44	42	42	40	38	34	28	20	14	25
42		79	71	63	70	59	49	35	24	15	8	2	0		44	40	38	36	33	30	26	21	16	32
43		79	71	63	55	60	49	36	24	15	8	2	0		44	40	36	32	30	27	23	19	17	43
44		79	71	63	55	47	50	36	25	15	8	2	0		44	40	36	31	27	24	20	18	16	57
45		79	71	63	55	47	40	37	25	15	8	2	0		44	40	36	31	26	21	18	16	14	62
46		79	71	63	55	47	40	29	26	16	8	2	0		43	40	36	31	26	20	16	14	13	64
47		79	71	63	55	47	40	29	20	16	8	2	0		41	39	36	31	26	21	16	13	11	63
48		79	71	63	55	47	40	29	20	13	8	2	0		40	38	35	31	26	21	16	12	10	59
49		79	71	63	55	47	40	29	20	13	7	2	0		39	37	34	30	26	21	16	13	10	55
50		37	71	63	55	47	40	29	20	13	7	2	0		38	35	33	29	25	21	16	13	10	56
51		37	32	62	54	46	39	28	20	12	6	2	0		37	33	31	27	23	19	15	12	10	54
52		37	32	28	52	45	38	28	19	12	6	2	0		36	33	29	25	22	18	14	11	9	52
53		37	32	28	24	44	37	27	19	12	6	2	0		34	32	29	24	21	17	13	11	9	51
54		37	32	28	24	20	36	26	18	11	6	2	0		32	30	28	24	19	16	13	10	8	49
55		37	32	28	24	20	16	26	18	11	6	2	0		30	28	26	23	19	15	12	9	8	47
56		37	32	28	24	20	16	12	17	11	6	2	0		26	27	25	22	18	15	11	9	7	46
57		37	32	28	24	20	16	12	8	11	6	2	0		23	23	23	20	17	14	11	8	7	44
58		37	32	28	24	20	16	12	8	5	5	2	0		20	20	20	19	16	13	11	8	6	43
59		37	32	28	24	20	16	12	8	5	2	2	0		17	17	18	17	15	13	10	8	6	42
60		10	32	28	24	20	16	12	8	5	2	1	0		16	15	15	14	13	12	10	8	6	42
61		10	8	26	22	18	15	11	7	4	2	1	0		15	13	12	11	11	9	8	7	5	38
62		10	8	7	20	17	14	10	7	4	2	1	0		13	12	10	9	8	8	7	6	5	35
63		10	8	7	5	16	13	9	6	4	2	1	0		12	11	10	8	7	6	5	5	4	32
64		10	8	7	5	4	12	8	6	3	2	0	0		10	10	9	7	6	5	4	4	3	29
65		1	8	7	5	4	3	8	5	3	2	0	0		9	9	8	7	5	4	3	3	3	26
66		1	1	6	5	4	3	2	5	3	1	0	0		7	7	7	6	5	4	3	2	2	23
67		1	1	0	5	4	3	2	1	3	1	0	0		5	6	6	5	4	3	2	2	2	19
68		1	1	0	0	4	3	2	1	1	1	0	0		4	4	4	4	4	3	2	2	1	16
69		1	1	0	0	0	3	2	1	1	0	0	0		3	3	3	3	3	3	2	2	1	14
70		30	15	7	4	2	1	2	2	1	1	0	0		5	4	4	4	4	4	3	3	2	25

Table 10.10 (Continued)

			Grade 3								Grade 4						Grade 5			
1	2	3	4	5	6	7	8	1	2	3	4	5	6	1	2	3	4	5	6
0	0	0	0	0	0	0	0	0	0	0	0	0	0	0	0	0	0	0	0
0	0	0	0	0	0	0	0	0	0	0	0	0	0	0	0	0	0	0	0
0	0	0	0	0	0	0	0	0	0	0	0	0	0	0	0	0	0	0	0
0	0	0	0	0	0	0	0	0	0	0	0	0	0	0	0	0	0	0	0
0	0	0	0	0	0	0	0	0	0	0	0	0	0	0	0	0	0	0	0
0	0	0	0	0	0	0	0	0	0	0	0	0	0	0	0	0	0	0	0
0	0	0	0	0	0	0	0	0	0	0	0	0	0	0	0	0	0	0	0
0	0	0	0	0	0	0	0	0	0	0	0	0	0	0	0	0	0	0	0
0	0	0	0	0	0	0	0	0	0	0	0	0	0	0	0	0	0	0	0
0	0	0	0	0	0	0	0	0	0	0	0	0	0	0	0	0	0	0	0
1	0	0	0	0	0	0	0	0	0	0	0	0	0	0	0	0	0	0	0
1	1	0	0	0	0	0	0	0	0	0	0	0	0	0	0	0	0	0	0
2	1	1	0	0	0	0	0	0	0	0	0	0	0	0	0	0	0	0	0
3	2	1	0	0	0	0	0	0	0	0	0	0	0	0	0	0	0	0	0
5	3	2	1	0	0	0	0	0	0	0	0	0	0	0	0	0	0	0	0
7	4	3	1	0	0	0	0	1	0	0	0	0	0	0	0	0	0	0	0
10	6	4	2	1	0	0	0	1	1	0	0	0	0	0	0	0	0	0	0
13	9	6	3	1	1	0	0	2	1	0	0	0	0	0	0	0	0	0	0
16	11	8	4	2	1	0	0	2	1	1	0	0	0	0	0	0	0	0	0
19	14	10	5	3	1	0	0	3	2	1	0	0	0	1	0	0	0	0	0
23	17	13	7	4	2	1	0	5	3	1	1	0	0	1	1	0	0	0	0
25	20	15	9	5	2	1	0	6	4	2	1	0	0	2	1	1	0	0	0
26	22	18	11	6	3	1	0	8	5	2	1	1	1	2	1	1	0	0	0
26	23	20	13	8	4	2	1	9	6	3	1	1	1	3	2	1	0	0	0
25	23	21	14	9	5	2	1	11	8	4	2	1	1	3	2	1	1	0	0
23	23	21	15	10	6	3	1	14	10	5	3	2	2	5	3	2	1	1	1
22	22	21	16	12	7	4	2	16	13	7	4	3	4	7	5	3	2	1	1
21	20	20	15	12	8	4	3	16	14	8	5	3	5	8	6	4	3	2	2
20	19	18	14	11	7	4	3	16	14	8	5	4	6	8	6	5	3	2	3
19	18	17	13	10	7	4	3	15	13	8	5	4	8	8	6	5	4	3	4
18	17	16	12	9	6	4	3	13	12	7	5	4	9	7	6	5	4	3	6
18	17	15	11	8	5	3	2	12	10	6	4	3	10	6	5	4	4	3	8
18	17	15	11	8	5	3	2	12	10	6	4	3	11	6	5	4	4	3	9
17	16	14	10	8	5	3	2	12	10	6	4	3	12	6	5	4	4	3	10
17	15	14	10	7	5	3	2	11	10	6	4	3	13	6	5	4	4	3	12
16	15	13	9	7	4	2	2	10	9	6	4	3	14	6	5	4	4	3	13
15	14	13	9	7	4	2	2	10	9	5	4	3	16	6	5	4	4	3	14
14	13	12	9	6	4	2	2	10	8	5	4	3	16	5	5	4	3	3	15
13	12	11	8	6	4	2	2	9	8	5	4	3	17	5	5	4	3	3	16
13	12	11	8	6	4	2	2	9	8	5	3	3	18	5	4	4	3	3	17
12	11	10	7	5	4	2	2	8	7	5	3	3	19	5	4	4	3	3	18
12	11	10	7	5	3	2	2	8	7	5	3	3	19	5	4	4	3	3	18
11	10	10	7	5	3	2	2	8	7	5	3	3	19	5	4	4	4	3	19
10	9	9	6	5	3	2	2	8	7	4	3	3	19	5	4	4	4	3	19
8	8	8	6	4	3	2	2	7	6	4	3	2	18	5	4	4	4	3	20
7	7	7	5	4	3	2	1	7	6	4	3	2	18	4	4	4	4	3	20
6	6	6	5	3	2	1	1	6	5	4	3	2	18	4	4	4	4	3	21
5	5	5	4	3	2	1	1	5	5	3	3	2	17	4	4	4	4	3	21
4	4	4	3	2	2	1	1	5	4	3	2	2	15	3	3	3	3	3	18
4	3	3	2	2	1	1	1	4	4	2	2	2	13	3	3	2	2	2	16
3	3	3	2	2	1	1	1	3	3	2	1	1	12	2	2	2	2	2	13
3	3	2	2	1	1	1	1	3	2	2	1	1	10	2	2	2	2	1	11
6	5	5	3	2	2	1	1	6	5	3	2	2	18	6	5	4	4	3	20

Table 10.11
Age–Seniority Staff Profile for "Young Hiring" Policy and "Normal Exit" Behavior (Scenario 2), Growth Rate = .06, Year 20

	Grade 1												Grade 2									
Age	1	2	3	4	5	6	7	8	9	10	11	12	1	2	3	4	5	6	7	8	9	10
18	0	0	0	0	0	0	0	0	0	0	0	0	0	0	0	0	0	0	0	0	0	0
19	0	0	0	0	0	0	0	0	0	0	0	0	0	0	0	0	0	0	0	0	0	0
20	73	0	0	0	0	0	0	0	0	0	0	0	0	0	0	0	0	0	0	0	0	0
21	73	66	0	0	0	0	0	0	0	0	0	0	0	0	0	0	0	0	0	0	0	0
22	73	66	59	0	0	0	0	0	0	0	0	0	1	0	0	0	0	0	0	0	0	0
23	73	66	59	52	0	0	0	0	0	0	0	0	2	1	0	0	0	0	0	0	0	0
24	73	66	59	52	45	0	0	0	0	0	0	0	4	2	1	0	0	0	0	0	0	0
25	656	66	59	52	45	39	0	0	0	0	0	0	7	4	2	0	0	0	0	0	0	0
26	656	567	57	50	43	37	28	0	0	0	0	0	12	6	4	2	0	0	0	0	0	0
27	656	567	486	47	41	35	27	19	0	0	0	0	21	11	6	3	1	0	0	0	0	0
28	656	567	486	408	39	34	26	18	12	0	0	0	37	20	10	5	3	1	0	0	0	0
29	656	567	486	408	339	32	24	18	12	7	0	0	54	34	18	9	4	2	1	0	0	0
30	0	567	486	408	339	276	23	17	11	7	3	0	73	49	31	15	7	3	2	1	0	0
31	0	0	498	418	348	283	205	16	11	7	3	1	110	67	45	27	13	6	3	1	1	0
32	0	0	0	429	356	290	210	145	11	6	3	1	141	101	61	38	22	10	5	2	1	1
33	0	0	0	0	365	297	216	149	94	6	3	1	161	130	92	52	32	18	8	4	2	1
34	0	0	0	0	0	305	221	153	97	56	3	1	173	148	118	79	44	26	14	6	3	2
35	0	0	0	0	0	0	227	157	99	57	25	1	178	159	134	101	66	36	21	11	5	5
36	0	0	0	0	0	0	0	161	102	59	25	9	147	164	144	115	85	54	28	16	9	8
37	0	0	0	0	0	0	0	0	104	60	26	9	113	135	148	124	97	69	42	22	13	15
38	0	0	0	0	0	0	0	0	0	62	27	9	76	102	122	127	104	79	54	33	18	24
39	0	0	0	0	0	0	0	0	0	0	27	9	46	68	90	105	107	85	62	42	27	35
40	0	0	0	0	0	0	0	0	0	0	0	9	20	40	59	77	87	87	66	48	35	49
41	0	0	0	0	0	0	0	0	0	0	0	0	7	16	35	50	64	71	69	52	40	69
42	0	0	0	0	0	0	0	0	0	0	0	0	0	4	13	29	42	52	54	54	44	91
43	0	0	0	0	0	0	0	0	0	0	0	0	0	0	2	10	24	33	39	42	45	117
44	0	0	0	0	0	0	0	0	0	0	0	0	0	0	0	0	8	18	25	30	35	144
45	0	0	0	0	0	0	0	0	0	0	0	0	0	0	0	0	0	5	13	19	25	137
46	0	0	0	0	0	0	0	0	0	0	0	0	0	0	0	0	0	0	2	10	15	121
47	0	0	0	0	0	0	0	0	0	0	0	0	0	0	0	0	0	0	1	1	7	96
48	0	0	0	0	0	0	0	0	0	0	0	0	0	0	0	0	0	0	1	1	1	64
49	0	0	0	0	0	0	0	0	0	0	0	0	0	0	0	0	0	0	1	1	1	32
50	0	0	0	0	0	0	0	0	0	0	0	0	0	0	0	0	0	0	0	1	1	32
51	0	0	0	0	0	0	0	0	0	0	0	0	0	0	0	0	0	0	0	1	0	31
52	0	0	0	0	0	0	0	0	0	0	0	0	0	0	0	0	0	0	0	0	0	30
53	0	0	0	0	0	0	0	0	0	0	0	0	0	0	0	0	0	0	0	0	0	29
54	0	0	0	0	0	0	0	0	0	0	0	0	0	0	0	0	0	0	0	0	0	28
55	0	0	0	0	0	0	0	0	0	0	0	0	0	0	0	0	0	0	0	0	0	27
56	0	0	0	0	0	0	0	0	0	0	0	0	0	0	0	0	0	0	0	0	0	27
57	0	0	0	0	0	0	0	0	0	0	0	0	0	0	0	0	0	0	0	0	0	27
58	0	0	0	0	0	0	0	0	0	0	0	0	0	0	0	0	0	0	0	0	0	27
59	0	0	0	0	0	0	0	0	0	0	0	0	0	0	0	0	0	0	0	0	0	27
60	0	0	0	0	0	0	0	0	0	0	0	0	0	0	0	0	0	0	0	0	0	27
61	0	0	0	0	0	0	0	0	0	0	0	0	0	0	0	0	0	0	0	0	0	26
62	0	0	0	0	0	0	0	0	0	0	0	0	0	0	0	0	0	0	0	0	0	24
63	0	0	0	0	0	0	0	0	0	0	0	0	0	0	0	0	0	0	0	0	0	22
64	0	0	0	0	0	0	0	0	0	0	0	0	0	0	0	0	0	0	0	0	0	21
65	0	0	0	0	0	0	0	0	0	0	0	0	0	0	0	0	0	0	0	0	0	19
66	0	0	0	0	0	0	0	0	0	0	0	0	0	0	0	0	0	0	0	0	0	17
67	0	0	0	0	0	0	0	0	0	0	0	0	0	0	0	0	0	0	0	0	0	15
68	0	0	0	0	0	0	0	0	0	0	0	0	0	0	0	0	0	0	0	0	0	13
69	0	0	0	0	0	0	0	0	0	0	0	0	0	0	0	0	0	0	0	0	0	11
70	0	0	0	0	0	0	0	0	0	0	0	0	0	0	0	0	0	0	0	0	0	21

Table 10.11 (Continued)

Grade 3								Grade 4						Grade 5					
1	2	3	4	5	6	7	8	1	2	3	4	5	6	1	2	3	4	5	6
0	0	0	0	0	0	0	0	0	0	0	0	0	0	0	0	0	0	0	0
0	0	0	0	0	0	0	0	0	0	0	0	0	0	0	0	0	0	0	0
0	0	0	0	0	0	0	0	0	0	0	0	0	0	0	0	0	0	0	0
0	0	0	0	0	0	0	0	0	0	0	0	0	0	0	0	0	0	0	0
0	0	0	0	0	0	0	0	0	0	0	0	0	0	0	0	0	0	0	0
0	0	0	0	0	0	0	0	0	0	0	0	0	0	0	0	0	0	0	0
0	0	0	0	0	0	0	0	0	0	0	0	0	0	0	0	0	0	0	0
0	0	0	0	0	0	0	0	0	0	0	0	0	0	0	0	0	0	0	0
0	0	0	0	0	0	0	0	0	0	0	0	0	0	0	0	0	0	0	0
1	0	0	0	0	0	0	0	0	0	0	0	0	0	0	0	0	0	0	0
1	0	0	0	0	0	0	0	0	0	0	0	0	0	0	0	0	0	0	0
2	1	0	0	0	0	0	0	0	0	0	0	0	0	0	0	0	0	0	0
3	2	1	0	0	0	0	0	0	0	0	0	0	0	0	0	0	0	0	0
6	3	2	1	0	0	0	0	0	0	0	0	0	0	0	0	0	0	0	0
9	5	3	1	0	0	0	0	1	0	0	0	0	0	0	0	0	0	0	0
13	8	5	2	1	0	0	0	1	0	0	0	0	0	0	0	0	0	0	0
20	12	7	3	1	1	0	0	2	1	0	0	0	0	0	0	0	0	0	0
27	18	11	5	2	1	0	0	3	1	1	0	0	0	0	0	0	0	0	0
36	25	16	8	4	2	1	0	5	2	1	0	0	0	1	0	0	0	0	0
44	33	23	12	6	3	1	0	7	4	2	1	0	0	1	1	0	0	0	0
51	40	29	16	9	4	2	1	10	6	2	1	1	0	2	1	1	0	0	0
54	46	36	21	12	6	2	1	14	9	4	2	1	1	3	2	1	0	0	0
54	49	42	26	15	8	3	1	18	11	5	2	1	1	5	2	1	1	0	0
49	50	45	30	19	10	5	2	22	15	7	3	2	1	6	4	2	1	0	0
42	45	45	33	22	13	6	3	26	19	10	5	3	2	8	5	3	2	1	1
33	38	41	33	25	16	8	5	30	23	12	7	4	4	11	8	5	3	2	1
23	30	35	30	25	17	10	7	32	27	16	9	6	7	14	11	8	5	3	2
15	21	26	24	21	16	10	7	29	25	15	10	6	9	14	11	8	5	3	3
8	13	17	17	16	13	8	7	23	22	14	9	6	10	13	11	8	6	4	4
4	7	10	11	11	9	6	6	17	16	11	8	6	11	11	9	7	5	4	5
2	3	5	5	5	4	4	4	10	10	7	5	4	10	7	7	6	4	3	7
1	1	2	2	2	2	1	2	4	4	3	3	2	9	3	3	3	3	2	7
1	1	2	2	2	2	1	2	4	4	3	3	2	10	3	3	3	3	3	9
1	1	2	2	2	2	1	2	3	4	3	2	2	11	3	3	3	3	3	10
1	1	1	1	1	1	1	2	3	3	3	2	2	12	3	3	3	3	3	11
1	1	1	1	1	1	1	2	3	3	3	2	2	13	3	3	3	3	3	13
1	1	1	1	1	1	1	2	3	3	2	2	2	15	3	3	3	3	3	14
1	1	1	1	1	1	1	1	3	3	2	2	2	15	3	3	3	3	3	15
1	1	1	1	1	1	1	1	2	3	2	2	2	16	3	3	3	3	3	15
1	1	1	1	1	1	1	1	2	3	2	2	2	17	3	3	3	3	3	16
1	1	1	1	1	1	1	1	3	3	2	2	2	18	3	3	3	3	3	17
1	1	1	1	1	1	1	2	3	3	2	2	2	18	3	3	3	3	3	18
1	1	1	1	1	1	1	2	3	3	2	2	2	19	3	3	3	3	3	19
1	1	1	1	1	1	1	2	3	3	2	2	2	18	3	3	3	3	3	19
1	1	1	1	1	1	1	1	3	3	2	2	2	18	3	3	3	3	3	20
1	1	1	1	1	1	1	1	2	3	2	2	2	17	3	3	3	3	3	20
1	1	1	1	1	1	1	1	2	3	2	2	2	17	3	3	3	3	3	21
1	1	1	1	1	1	1	1	2	2	2	2	2	16	2	3	3	3	3	21
0	1	1	1	1	1	1	1	2	2	2	2	1	15	2	2	2	3	3	18
0	1	1	1	1	1	1	1	2	2	2	1	1	13	2	2	2	2	2	16
0	0	1	1	1	1	0	1	1	2	1	1	1	11	2	2	2	2	2	13
0	0	1	1	1	0	0	1	1	1	1	1	1	10	2	2	2	2	1	11
1	1	1	1	1	1	1	1	3	3	2	2	2	18	4	4	4	3	3	20

Table 10.12

Age–Seniority Staff Profile for "Equal Hiring" Policy and "Modified Exit" Behavior (Scenario 4), Growth Rate = .06, Year 20.

	Grade 1												Grade 2									
Age	1	2	3	4	5	6	7	8	9	10	11	12	1	2	3	4	5	6	7	8	9	10
18	0	0	0	0	0	0	0	0	0	0	0	0	0	0	0	0	0	0	0	0	0	0
19	0	0	0	0	0	0	0	0	0	0	0	0	0	0	0	0	0	0	0	0	0	0
20	118	0	0	0	0	0	0	0	0	0	0	0	0	0	0	0	0	0	0	0	0	0
21	118	106	0	0	0	0	0	0	0	0	0	0	0	0	0	0	0	0	0	0	0	0
22	118	106	93	0	0	0	0	0	0	0	0	0	3	0	0	0	0	0	0	0	0	0
23	118	106	93	75	0	0	0	0	0	0	0	0	13	3	0	0	0	0	0	0	0	0
24	118	106	93	75	55	0	0	0	0	0	0	0	26	12	3	0	0	0	0	0	0	0
25	118	106	93	75	55	32	0	0	0	0	0	0	44	24	11	2	0	0	0	0	0	0
26	118	102	89	71	53	31	0	0	0	0	0	0	74	40	22	9	2	0	0	0	0	0
27	118	102	85	68	50	29	0	0	0	0	0	0	71	67	35	18	8	1	0	0	0	0
28	118	102	85	65	48	28	0	0	0	0	0	0	68	64	59	30	15	6	1	0	0	0
29	118	102	85	65	46	27	0	0	0	0	0	0	65	61	56	49	24	11	4	1	0	0
30	118	102	85	65	46	26	0	0	0	0	0	0	63	59	54	47	40	18	8	3	0	0
31	118	104	87	67	47	26	0	0	0	0	0	0	62	57	52	45	38	30	13	5	2	0
32	118	104	89	68	48	27	0	0	0	0	0	0	64	56	51	44	37	29	22	9	4	1
33	118	104	89	70	49	28	0	0	0	0	0	0	65	58	50	43	36	28	21	15	6	3
34	118	104	89	70	51	28	0	0	0	0	0	0	67	59	51	42	35	27	20	14	10	6
35	118	104	89	70	51	29	0	0	0	0	0	0	68	60	52	43	34	26	19	13	10	10
36	118	104	89	70	51	29	0	0	0	0	0	0	68	61	53	44	35	26	19	13	9	13
37	118	104	89	70	51	29	0	0	0	0	0	0	68	62	54	45	36	27	18	13	9	15
38	118	104	89	70	51	29	0	0	0	0	0	0	68	62	55	46	37	27	19	12	9	16
39	118	104	89	70	51	29	0	0	0	0	0	0	68	62	55	46	37	28	19	13	8	16
40	118	104	89	70	51	29	0	0	0	0	0	0	68	62	55	46	37	28	20	13	9	16
41	118	84	72	56	41	23	0	0	0	0	0	0	68	55	49	41	33	25	18	12	8	14
42	118	84	57	45	33	19	0	0	0	0	0	0	55	55	43	36	30	22	16	11	7	13
43	118	84	57	36	26	15	0	0	0	0	0	0	44	44	43	32	26	20	14	10	6	12
44	118	84	57	36	21	12	0	0	0	0	0	0	37	36	35	32	23	18	13	8	6	11
45	118	84	57	36	21	10	0	0	0	0	0	0	33	30	28	26	23	16	11	8	5	11
46	118	84	57	36	21	10	0	0	0	0	0	0	30	26	24	21	19	16	10	7	5	10
47	118	84	57	36	21	10	0	0	0	0	0	0	30	25	21	18	15	13	10	6	4	9
48	118	84	57	36	21	10	0	0	0	0	0	0	30	25	19	15	13	10	8	6	4	8
49	118	84	57	36	21	10	0	0	0	0	0	0	30	25	19	14	11	9	6	5	4	7
50	118	84	57	36	21	10	0	0	0	0	0	0	30	25	19	14	10	8	5	4	3	6
51	118	84	57	36	21	10	0	0	0	0	0	0	30	25	19	14	10	7	5	3	2	5
52	118	84	57	36	21	10	0	0	0	0	0	0	30	25	19	14	10	7	4	3	2	5
53	118	84	57	36	21	10	0	0	0	0	0	0	30	25	19	14	10	7	4	3	2	4
54	118	84	57	36	21	10	0	0	0	0	0	0	30	25	19	14	10	7	4	3	2	3
55	118	84	57	36	21	10	0	0	0	0	0	0	30	25	19	14	10	7	4	3	2	3
56	118	84	57	36	21	10	0	0	0	0	0	0	30	25	19	14	10	7	4	3	2	3
57	118	84	57	36	21	10	0	0	0	0	0	0	30	25	19	14	10	7	4	3	2	3
58	118	84	57	36	21	10	0	0	0	0	0	0	30	25	19	14	10	7	4	3	2	2
59	118	84	57	36	21	10	0	0	0	0	0	0	30	25	19	14	10	7	4	3	2	2
60	118	84	57	36	21	10	0	0	0	0	0	0	30	25	19	14	10	7	4	3	2	2
61	118	89	61	38	22	10	0	0	0	0	0	0	30	22	17	13	9	6	4	2	1	2
62	118	89	65	41	24	11	0	0	0	0	0	0	33	22	15	11	8	5	3	2	1	2
63	118	89	65	44	25	12	0	0	0	0	0	0	35	23	15	10	7	5	3	2	1	2
64	118	89	65	44	27	12	0	0	0	0	0	0	36	24	16	10	6	4	3	2	1	1
65	35	89	65	44	27	13	0	0	0	0	0	0	37	26	17	11	6	4	2	1	1	1
66	35	27	65	44	27	13	0	0	0	0	0	0	38	27	18	11	7	4	2	1	1	1
67	35	27	20	44	27	13	0	0	0	0	0	0	36	27	19	12	7	4	2	1	1	1
68	35	27	20	13	27	13	0	0	0	0	0	0	32	26	19	12	8	4	2	1	1	1
69	35	27	20	13	8	13	0	0	0	0	0	0	26	22	18	12	8	4	2	1	1	1
70	413	222	121	64	33	14	0	0	0	0	0	0	74	47	33	23	16	10	5	3	1	2

Table 10.12 (Continued)

Grade 3								Grade 4						Grade 5					
1	2	3	4	5	6	7	8	1	2	3	4	5	6	1	2	3	4	5	6
0	0	0	0	0	0	0	0	0	0	0	0	0	0	0	0	0	0	0	0
0	0	0	0	0	0	0	0	0	0	0	0	0	0	0	0	0	0	0	0
0	0	0	0	0	0	0	0	0	0	0	0	0	0	0	0	0	0	0	0
0	0	0	0	0	0	0	0	0	0	0	0	0	0	0	0	0	0	0	0
0	0	0	0	0	0	0	0	0	0	0	0	0	0	0	0	0	0	0	0
0	0	0	0	0	0	0	0	0	0	0	0	0	0	0	0	0	0	0	0
0	0	0	0	0	0	0	0	0	0	0	0	0	0	0	0	0	0	0	0
0	0	0	0	0	0	0	0	0	0	0	0	0	0	0	0	0	0	0	0
1	0	0	0	0	0	0	0	0	0	0	0	0	0	0	0	0	0	0	0
3	1	0	0	0	0	0	0	0	0	0	0	0	0	0	0	0	0	0	0
7	3	1	0	0	0	0	0	0	0	0	0	0	0	0	0	0	0	0	0
11	6	3	1	0	0	0	0	0	0	0	0	0	0	0	0	0	0	0	0
16	10	5	2	0	0	0	0	1	0	0	0	0	0	0	0	0	0	0	0
21	15	9	3	1	0	0	0	3	1	0	0	0	0	0	0	0	0	0	0
25	19	13	6	2	0	0	0	5	2	1	0	0	0	1	0	0	0	0	0
28	23	17	8	3	1	0	0	7	4	1	0	0	0	1	0	0	0	0	0
30	25	20	11	5	1	0	0	11	6	2	1	0	0	2	1	0	0	0	0
31	27	23	13	6	1	0	0	14	9	4	2	1	0	3	2	1	0	0	0
31	28	24	14	7	2	0	0	16	11	6	3	1	1	5	3	1	1	0	0
32	28	25	15	8	2	0	0	18	13	7	4	2	2	6	4	2	1	0	0
32	28	25	15	9	3	0	0	19	15	8	5	3	3	8	5	3	2	1	1
33	29	25	15	9	3	0	0	20	16	9	6	4	5	9	6	4	2	1	1
33	29	25	15	9	3	0	0	20	16	9	6	4	5	8	6	4	2	1	1
33	26	23	14	8	2	0	0	20	15	9	5	3	5	8	6	4	2	1	1
30	27	21	13	7	2	0	0	18	15	8	5	3	4	8	6	4	3	2	1
27	24	21	11	7	2	0	0	17	14	9	5	4	6	8	7	5	4	2	2
24	22	19	12	6	2	0	0	16	14	9	6	4	8	9	8	6	5	3	4
22	20	17	11	6	2	0	0	16	14	9	6	5	11	9	9	8	6	5	7
19	18	16	10	6	2	0	0	15	13	9	6	5	13	9	9	8	7	5	9
17	16	14	9	5	2	0	0	13	12	8	6	5	14	9	8	7	7	6	12
15	14	12	8	5	1	0	0	12	11	7	5	4	15	8	7	7	6	6	14
13	12	11	7	4	1	0	0	10	9	6	5	4	15	7	7	6	6	5	16
11	10	9	6	4	1	0	0	9	8	6	4	4	15	6	6	6	5	5	17
10	9	8	5	3	1	0	0	8	7	5	4	3	14	5	5	5	5	4	17
10	8	7	4	3	1	0	0	7	6	4	3	3	13	5	4	4	4	4	18
9	8	7	4	2	1	0	0	6	5	4	3	2	13	4	4	4	3	3	17
9	7	6	4	2	1	0	0	5	5	3	2	2	12	3	3	3	3	3	17
9	7	6	3	2	1	0	0	5	4	3	2	2	11	3	3	3	3	3	16
9	7	6	3	2	1	0	0	4	4	2	2	2	10	3	3	2	2	2	15
9	7	6	3	2	0	0	0	4	4	2	2	1	9	2	2	2	2	2	15
9	7	6	3	2	0	0	0	4	3	2	1	1	9	2	2	2	2	2	14
9	7	6	3	2	0	0	0	4	3	2	1	1	8	2	2	2	2	2	13
9	7	6	3	2	0	0	0	4	3	2	1	1	7	2	2	2	2	1	12
9	6	5	3	1	0	0	0	4	3	2	1	1	7	2	2	2	1	1	12
8	6	4	2	1	0	0	0	4	3	2	1	1	7	2	2	1	1	1	11
7	5	4	2	1	0	0	0	3	3	2	1	1	6	2	2	1	1	1	10
6	5	4	2	1	0	0	0	3	2	1	1	1	6	2	1	1	1	1	10
6	4	3	2	1	0	0	0	3	2	1	1	1	5	1	1	1	1	1	9
6	4	3	2	1	0	0	0	2	2	1	1	1	4	1	1	1	1	1	8
6	4	3	2	1	0	0	0	2	2	1	1	0	4	1	1	1	1	1	7
6	4	3	1	1	0	0	0	2	1	1	0	0	3	1	1	1	1	1	7
6	4	3	1	1	0	0	0	2	1	1	0	0	2	1	1	1	1	1	6
18	11	7	3	1	0	0	0	6	3	1	1	0	3	2	1	1	1	1	8

284

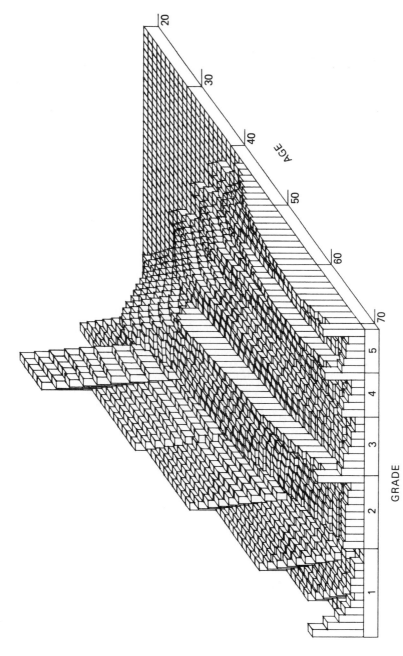

Figure 10.3. Age–seniority staff profile for "normal hiring" policy and "normal exit" behavior (S1). Growth rate = .06, Year 20.

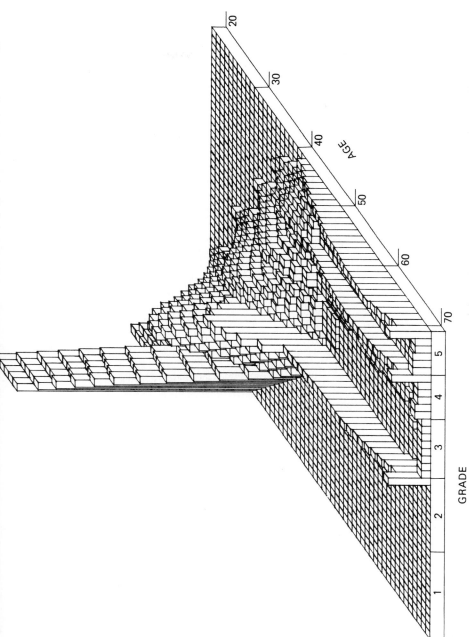

Figure 10.4. Age–seniority profile for "young hiring" policy and "normal exit" behavior (S2). Growth rate = .06, Year 20.

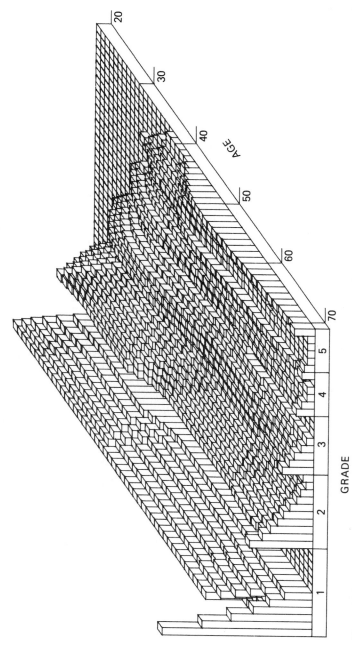

Figure 10.5. Age–seniority staff profile for "equal hiring" policy and "modified exit" behavior (S4). Growth rate = .06, Year 20.

markets (ILMs); the necessity within some of these ILMs to give jobs and job vacancies, which is the demand side of the labor market process, equal weight with that of labor supply; the simultaneous interaction of opportunities and labor supply, with managerial and worker decisions conditional on the demand–supply ratio; that age per se is not a key attribute for promotion, but other factors sometimes associated with aging are important—namely, seniority within grade; that age is a key factor affecting exit behavior; that the promotion process is not stable over time but can be theoretically derived; that aging and age distributions are treated as an outcome of exit behavior and managerial hiring and promotion practices, hence enabling planning and direction for these indirect aging impacts. Five basic types of findings were reported and will be partially summarized here.

1. *Initial Data.* The initial design of the simulation required the construction of a hypothetical but empirically based internal labor market. Thus, in some cases, prior results were recast, while in others they were incorporated as the "best available" guesstimates for our newly built hodgepodge ILM. Of most interest, perhaps, is the preliminary discovery of quite similar relative grade distributions for the ILMs in both public and private firms. If additional data can further confirm this, then a parametric simulation on this dimension would be helpful. Here, I simply selected one such distribution—a private firm managerial ILM. Second, the initial joint age–seniority staff profile of the ILM is instructive of how a firm's staff may be distributed by grade. Third, the earlier finding by Konda and Stewman (1980), which was used in these simulations, suggested an acceleration of promotion rates at earlier seniority levels, the higher an individual is in the firm.

2. *Promotion.* The relation between aging and promotion, though indirect, held generally across the various scenarios investigated. Individuals in their thirties and forties had the highest promotion rates for the most part. But it should be stressed that this is not a zero/one relationship, with other ages thereby being overlooked. Even more important, perhaps, is the finding that under certain internal labor market conditions the highest promotion rates are for older workers. In one scenario, a promotion rate of 1.00 was found for all workers age 40 or older! Also important is that this event was not generated by a corresponding jump for the total grade.

3. *Aging.* In all scenarios, there is a grade redistribution for older workers. Especially noteworthy is the finding of substantially more "elderly" (60 or older) in the top grades and fewer at the lower grades than currently (from the initial distribution). Whether there will be an overall increase in workers 60 or older is dependent on the hiring practice.

Age lumps at 20 years and equilibria were generally found, but their location and size were greatly affected by the managerial hiring practice.

The age-40 barrier to promotion cited in perceptual studies was supported using the lowest grade, but the general findings indicated that age per se is not the important factor here. Further analysis of the dynamics between demand and supply ratios over time is needed.

4. *Seniority.* Alternative employment practices were also found to affect seniority distributions per grade. In general, unless there is a major shift toward an "equal hiring" policy, it appears that we may expect much larger lumps in the highest seniority levels than we now have, using the initial distribution as a baseline. And, if we continue current ("normal hires") employment practice, we may expect much larger age and seniority lumps as the overall proportion of older workers increases.

5. *Joint Age–Seniority Staff Profiles.* The most dramatic impacts of alternative hiring policies were shown in the joint age–seniority staff profiles for the entire ILM. Radically different profiles were found, indicating two things: the importance of examining aging and job performance in much greater detail and the probable necessity of looking for more equitable hiring policies regarding age, with one possibility being much greater mid-career change.

Given these "findings" from asking what-if questions and using empirically informed parameters in the opportunity model, three of the more important policy implications will be reiterated in somewhat more detail. The first is an earlier empirical finding by Konda and Stewman (1980), which I have used in the parameter set of this chapter and on which I will now comment with regard to careers and aging. That is, the managerial selection probabilities indicated that an individual's promotion chances peaked earlier, the higher his or her grade. To the extent that aging and hierarchical level are associated, the career ladder has an accelerator associated with but not caused by age. Thus, one possible direction in an individual's career development is that vertical mobility will accelerate, the higher one climbs, providing an achievement process to look forward to as one ages. If promotion and productivity are related, then one implication is that we may find an increase in productivity with this joint aging–mobility process.

There are other possibilities, of course, including mid-career change (with varying shades of change), thereby changing career streams; a change in firm, possibly changing career ladders; or further development within a hierarchical grade. In any such path, including the accelerated one, developmental training programs may serve to foster these human resources. For example, the concept of proactive (rather than reactive) vacancy training is currently being used by some firms, whereby several persons who are interested in a certain type of job are informed more fully of its requirements and trained accordingly, before the vacancy opens. Such concepts provide more individual choice to career development as one ages.

The second policy issue stems around the findings of rather large-scale redistributions of staff aged 60 or older than we have "currently." Continuation of a hiring policy with hires in the 25–49 age band will result in greater proportions of these older workers at every grade over the next 20 years and permanently thereafter, with possible increases by 150–200% at the higher grades. Reverting to a restricted policy of hiring only in the twenties may result in permanent proportional increases of workers aged 60 or older by 70–100% at the top grades. Only a policy of more equal hires and higher exit behavior shifts these results.

The third and final policy implication to be noted was highlighted in the joint age–seniority staff profiles of Figures 10.3, 10.4, and 10.5. In particular, the concentrated stair-step age bands by grade and the concomitant high concentrations of staff in the highest seniority level of each grade raises strong questions regarding the use of a hiring policy largely restricted to the twenties, as is perhaps the most common employment practice today. As noted earlier, much more thought should be given to the desirability of such effects and the alternative possibilities of providing employment mechanisms for hiring a mix of staff and more fully utilizing aging and experience blends in managing our alternative organizational futures.

REFERENCES

Bartholomew, D. J. (1963) A multi-stage renewal process. *Journal of the Royal Statistical Society* B-25:150–168.

Bartholomew, D. J. (1973) *Stochastic Models for Social Processes*. New York: John Wiley and Sons.

Doeringer, P. B., and Piore, M. J. (1971) *Internal Labor Markets and Manpower Analysis*. Lexington, Mass.: D. C. Heath.

Faunce, W. A. (1972) Self-Investment in the Occupational Role. Paper presented at a meeting of the Southern Sociological Society, New Orleans, La.

Forbes, A. F. (1971) Markov chain models for manpower systems. Pp. 93–113 in D. J. Bartholomew and A. R. Smith, eds., *Manpower and Management Science*. Lexington, Mass.: D. C. Heath.

Keyfitz, N. (1973) Individual mobility in a stationary population. *Population Studies* 27:335–352.

Konda, S., and Stewman, S. (1980) An opportunity labor demand model and Markovian labor supply models: Comparative tests in an organization. *American Sociological Review* 45:276–301.

Mahoney, T. A., and Milkovich, G. T. (1971) The internal labor market as a stochastic process. In D. J. Batholomew and A. R. Smith, eds., *Manpower and Management Science.* Lexington, Mass.: D. C. Heath.

Sales, P. (1971) The validity of the Markov chain model for a class of the Civil Service. *The Statistician* 20:85–110.

Sheehy, G. (1976) *Passages; Predictable Crises of Adult Life.* New York: E. P. Dutton.

Sofer, C. (1970) *Men in Mid-Career; A Study of British Managers and Technical Specialists.* Cambridge, England: Cambridge University.

Stewman, S. (1975) An application of job vacancy chain model to a civil service internal labor market. *Journal of Mathematical Sociology* 4:37–59.

Stewman, S. (1976a) Markov models of occupational mobility: Theoretical development and empirical support. Part 1: Careers. *Journal of Mathematical Sociology* 4:201–245.

Stewman, S. (1976b) Markov models of occupational mobility: Theoretical development and empirical support. Part 2: Continuously operative job systems. *Journal of Mathematical Sociology* 4:247–278.

Stewman, S. (1978) Markov and renewal models for total manpower system. *OMEGA. The International Journal of Management Science.* 6:344–351.

Stewman, S., and Konda, S. (1981a) Careers and Organizational Labor Markets: Demographic Models of Organizational Behavior. *American Journal of Sociology* (in press).

Stewman, S., and Konda, S. (1981b) A Model of Opportunities, Choice and Individual Careers. Unpublished paper. School of Urban and Public Affairs, Carnegie-Mellon University.

White, H. C. (1970) *Chains of Opportunity: System Models of Mobility in Organizations.* Cambridge, Mass.: Harvard University Press.

Young, A., and Vassiliou, P-C. G. (1974) A non-linear model on the promotion of staff. *Journal of the Royal Statistical Society* A137:584–595.

chapter 11

Some Consequences of Organizational Demography: Potential Impacts of an Aging Work Force on Formal Organizations

JEFFREY PFEFFER

Some years ago Stinchcombe *et al.* (1968) noted:

> Organizations, like communities or nations, are made up of people. These people enter the population of the organization, stay awhile, and leave. Organizations grow and decline by a net flow across their boundaries. At any given time the composition of the organization will be determined by the past history of the social composition of net flows into it. In short, all of the variables of demographic theory that apply to communities also apply to organizations [p. 221].

Yet organizational demography and demographic processes in formal organizations remain both theoretically and empirically unexplored. McNeil and Thompson's (1971) speculative paper on regeneration processes in organizations remains an exceptional example of concern with issues of rank and tenure distribution of organizational members and the consequences such demographic distributions may have for issues such as the size of the administrative component, time and attention focused on socialization, and coordination and communication processes within the organization.

This chapter has two purposes. First, an attempt is made to argue that organizational demography, particularly the age, rank, and organi-

AGING
Social Change

zational tenure distribution of members or employees, is an important theoretical variable that has been too long omitted from organizational analysis. Control and governance processes in organizations, adaptation and change, leadership succession, socialization and inculturation, forms and amount of interorganizational linkage, power, politics, and conflict, organizational investments in training, the size of the administrative component, and career processes are only some of the theoretically important issues in organizational analysis that might be enriched by the inclusion of demography as an explanatory variable. Second, in the context of developing some arguments about the relationship of demography to these issues, the potential effects of an aging work force on the operation and structure of formal organizations are considered. An analysis of demographic effects in organizations provides one point of theoretical linkage between the analysis of social change and demography in the population as a whole and the analysis of work organizations more specifically. As Aldrich (1979) has recently argued in advocating the development of an ecological perspective, the analysis of formal organizations has been too long separated and isolated from the analysis of social change and broader sociological concerns. The argument developed here is that demography as well as ecology afford an opportunity to join the analysis of organizational processes to issues of social change and general population trends.

DEFINITION AND MEASUREMENT OF ORGANIZATIONAL DEMOGRAPHY

Demographic variables have been frequently used to describe cities, states, and nations and to explain attitudes (e.g., Glenn 1969), political structures (e.g., Kessel 1962, Schnore and Alford 1963), and the operation of interest group politics (e.g., Cutler 1977) in such settings. Similar demographic descriptions can be applied to formal organizations. Thus, one can assess the sex distribution of organizations, or the sex distribution by general hierarchical level within organizations, the racial or ethnic composition of organizations, the educational level of participants, the income level of members, and the age and tenure distribution characterizing the organization's work force. It is likely that each demographic descriptor might be productively employed to enrich the analysis of numerous variables of interest to organizational researchers. As an example, building on the notion of the token woman and the consequences of such tokenism mentioned by Kanter (1977), Spangler et al.

(1978) examined the effect of the proportion of women in schools of law on women's academic achievement. Also, observed differences between schools of business in terms of their prestige, placement, and career success of their graduates and the schools' ability to obtain resources might be explained, in part, in terms of the income levels characterizing the backgrounds of their student bodies and, perhaps, the faculties as well. Indeed, the development of educational curricula in universities may be a function of the universities' role in the system of social stratification (Collins 1971) and thus related to the demographic composition of their client population and work force.

The opportunities to include demographic variables in the analyses of aspects of formal organizations are numerous and potentially quite productive. However, constraints of time and space limit the present discussion to the effects of one class of demographic variable in particular, the age and organizational tenure of the work force. By age, I mean the chronological age of the organization's work force. Tenure refers to the length of time a given person has been employed in or a member of a particular organization. It is likely that organizational tenure is a more important explanatory variable, at least in terms of the processes to be described in this chapter, than chronological age. The term organizational demography shall be used to refer to the tenure distribution of the organization's work force and, in particular, its managerial work force. The tenure distribution of the organization is probably correlated empirically with the distribution of the work force in terms of chronological age. Although it is conceptually possibly to observe an organization comprised primarily of 40-year-olds who have worked there for 15 years and another organization comprised of 50-year-olds who have worked primarily for the organization for only 5 years, such a result is not likely, especially when it is considered that the organizations themselves have been in existence for some time.

For a variety of reasons, older people are less likely to leave an organization voluntarily, and they are also less likely to be involuntarily separated, except for retirement. Laws protecting older workers from age discrimination help to reduce involuntary separation. Also, to the extent that older workers have longer tenure in the organization, stable working relationships and stable positions will have been established over time so that the individual will be more likely to fit better into the organization. Pension benefits that require some minimum amount of time for vesting and that typically increase with years of service, become more salient and more important with advancing age, decreasing the likelihood of voluntary quitting. Increasing family commitments such as children in school, increasing involvement in community and political

TABLE 11.1
Median Years on Job by Age of Worker[a]

Age	Median years on job
20–24 years	1.2
25–29 years	2.3
30–34 years	3.6
35–39 years	4.7
40–44 years	5.9
45–49 years	7.7
50–54 years	9.6
55–59 years	11.4
60–64 years	12.5

[a] From Bureau of Labor Statistics 1975: A-8.

activities that tends to accompany aging as well as commitments to houses, neighborhoods, and friendship networks make it less likely that older workers will voluntarily leave. Thus, reviews of the literature on voluntary turnover (Porter and Steers 1973) have seldom separated the effects of organizational tenure from the effects of age per se, finding that both age and organizational tenure are negatively associated with intentions to quit and with actual turnover. The failure to make such a distinction may not be empirically significant, given the association between tenure and age that is frequently observed.[1] Table 11.1 presents some illustrative data on the aggregate relationship between age and job tenure.

Although there is an empirical relationship between age and tenure distributions in organizations and in the society as a whole, it is also clear that this relationship is far from perfect. The data in Table 11.1 indicate, for instance, that for each 10 years of age past the age of 20, the average tenure of workers goes up only 2.8 years. Furthermore, although the average tenure of older workers tends to increase with age at a rate slightly faster than that for younger workers, the difference is quite small. In the 10 years from age 40 to age 50, the largest gain in average tenure is achieved, and that is a gain of only 3.7 years (from 5.9 to 9.6 years of service on the job). That compares with an average increase of 2.3 years of job tenure in the age difference between those workers 30 to 40 years old, the smallest average increase in the table.

Thus, although age does have some effect on tenure and through tenure on other aspects of organizational functioning, it is clear that age

[1] Stevens et al. (1978), for example, in a study of 634 supervisors in 71 federal government installations, observed a correlation of .44 ($p < .001$) between the respondent's age and years in the organization.

is only one, and perhaps not even the most important, determinant of the tenure distribution of organizations. In a subsequent section, other determinants of tenure are considered. At the same time, it is the effect of age on average tenure that may be one of the most significant effects of the aging work force on formal organizations.

The Measurement of Organizational Tenure

To measure the effects of organizational demography, a methodology must be employed that enables the researcher to capture variations in tenure distributions across organizations or organizational subunits. It seems clear that the distributional properties, not merely the proportion of workers who have been in an organization a given length of time, may affect organizational properties such as power and influence patterns, control practices, and structure.

One measure of organizational demography, suggested by McNeil and Thompson (1971), is a regeneration index based on the idea of a half-life standard as borrowed from the physical sciences. McNeil and Thompson defined a regeneration index as "the time elapsing before the ratio of new members to old reaches 1:1 [1971, p. 625]." This measure presumably reflects the rate of change in the ratio of new members to old in the organization. As McNeil and Thompson recognized, the operationalization of the index requires one additional decision, whether to use Time 1 as a base (looking forward) or Time 2 as a base (looking backward). The two methods will yield different results. Their suggestion was to use Time 2 as a base because of the emphasis on organizational regeneration rather than degeneration. Particularly for the case of organizations that are adding personnel, the regeneration index will differ depending on the base year used. However, the validity of comparisons will be virtually unimpaired as long as a consistent procedure is followed.

Although at first glance a clever idea, the regeneration index as defined has two problems. First, it is analytically equivalent to finding the median years of service in the organization—for at the median, the ratio of people with less than that number of years of service to those with more years (the ratio of newcomers to old-timers) is 1:1. Thus, the regeneration index is not really a new or unique measurement at all. Second, the index captures only one property of the distribution, the median. In Table 11.2, I present hypothetical data for two organizations with the same median tenure. The magnitude of cohort effects and the requirements and burdens of socialization, however, are likely to be quite different for the organizations.

TABLE 11.2
Hypothetical Data for Two Organizations with Same Median Years of Tenure but Different Distributional Properties

Years of service	Organization A (percentage)	Organization B (percentage)
0–3 years	49	14
4–7 years	0	14
8–10 years	0	14
11–15 years	1	8
16–20 years	0	17
21–25 years	25	17
26–30 years	25	16

A similar but not identical measure is the mean years of service of organizational members. This is computed by taking the number of persons at each level of the years of service distribution multiplied by the number of years served, then dividing this result by the total number of people in the organization. Either median or mean years of service both fail to provide information about the distributional properties of the years of service variable.

There are several ways of incorporating additional distributional information into the analysis of the effects of organizational tenure distributions. One way involves identifying theoretically significant lengths of service and then computing the proportion of organizational personnel with more or less than these tenures. For instance, in academic organizations, the time to tenure is approximately 7 years, and the distinction between having and not having tenure is consequential for inclusion in governance, commitment to the organization, and in status. Thus, in academic organizations, in addition to mean or median years of service for the entire faculty, it might be useful to know what proportion of the faculty have been in the organization less than 7 years. Similarly, socialization and inculturation into the organization may take a somewhat longer period of time to be completely effective. Thus, one might define the proportion of organizational members who have been in the organization longer than 20 years as an indicator of the extent to which the organization is populated by individuals who have spent the bulk of a long working life in the same organization.

All of the measures just described, median years of service (which is equivalent to the regeneration index), mean years of service, or the proportion of persons with more or less than some given number of years of service, fail to fully provide information on other important properties of the demographic distribution, in particular, the extent to which the organization's membership is concentrated in one or a few or spread out evenly over many tenure categories. Two measures of inequality or dispersion in distributions are an index of heterogeneity and the Gini index of concentration. Both measures were used by Blau (1977) in his discussion of inequality and heterogeneity and their consequences in social systems. The index of heterogeneity is defined as $1 - \Sigma_i p_i^2$ where p_i is the fraction of the organization's membership in each tenure or length of service category (Blau 1977, p. 78). If everyone is in one category, then the index takes on a value of zero. When persons are spread evenly over a large number of categories, the index approaches larger and larger values with the value of one as an asymptote. The degree of heterogeneity in a social system, according to this formulation, is a function of the number of groups or categories into which the population is distributed and the relative dispersion of persons over these various categories.

The amount of inequality (in this case, inequality in years of service) in a social system has frequently been measured using the Gini index. This index was operationalized by Blau (1977, p. 67) as:

$$G = \frac{2\Sigma s_i P_i (P_{b_i} - P_{a_i})}{2\Sigma s_i P_i}$$

where s_i is the mean value in a category, p_i is the fraction of the population in that category, and P_{b_i} and P_{a_i} are the fractions of the population with values below and above the category in question. The numerator represents the amount of absolute inequality, computed as the mean distance between statuses. The denominator is twice the mean status. The ratio of the two measures relative inequality in a status distribution.

In Table 11.3, the relationships among the various measures of tenure distributions are illustrated employing data from a sample of 36 academic departments on two University of California campuses. Eight categories were used to measure the length of service, and department heads were asked to report the number of regular faculty in each years-of-service category. The equivalence of the average or mean years of service and the regeneration index can be seen in the very high correlation between the two variables. Although average years of service also correlates highly with the two measures of the proportion of long-tenured and short-tenured persons, average tenure is not highly correlated with either the Gini index of concentration or with the measure of heterogeneity. Furthermore, these measures are only moderately correlated with each other and with the regeneration index. It seems fair to conclude that there is no single measure, inluding those assessing the distributional properties,

TABLE 11.3

Correlations among Measures of Length of Service Distributions of Faculty in Thirty-Six Academic Departments

	2.	3.	4.	5.	6.
1. Average years of service of faculty	.94[b]	.86[b]	−.65[b]	−.27	.36[a]
2. Regeneration index	—	.76[b]	−.70[b]	−.42[a]	.24
3. Proportion of faculty with more than 21 years of service	—	—	−.34[a]	.04	.42[a]
4. Proportion of faculty with less than 7 years of service	—	—	—	.82[b]	.17
5. Gini Index	—	—	—	—	.55[b]
6. Index of heterogeneity	—	—	—	—	—

[a] $p < .05$.
[b] $p < .001$.

that fully captures all the important and relevant information about the distribution of length of service in organizations.

Two other analytical strategies are also available for analyzing length of service distributions. One strategy involves correlating increasingly inclusive tenure categories with the variable or variables of interest to assess at what point a significant break in the relationship is observed. And, if the sample size is large enough, another strategy involves entering the separate categories, as well as the Gini index and the heterogeneity measure, as separate variables in a multiple regression. If the categories are defined in proportional terms, then one category would be omitted because of its linear dependence with the others. In such ways, the effects of demography on organizational outcomes can be examined in an exploratory fashion. Given the present lack of empirical research on this subject, it is difficult to specify a priori if it is 5, 10, or 20 years of service at which different effects on control and behavior are likely to be observed. And, the effects of demography are likely to vary by the type of organization and its context, with demographic effects in academic departments occurring at different times and being different in consequence from, for example, demographic effects in industrial firms. Thus, exploratory analyses using various sets of categories assessing demography are useful.

The principal point emerging from considering demography in this sample of university departments is that no single measure, and certainly not the average years of service or its equivalent, the regeneration index, fully captures the distributional properties characterizing tenure in organizations. The use of a single measure is likely to be misleading because of the lack of information about the rest of the distribution. What is required is the development of a vector measure of distributions that incorporates information about the extremes and the dispersion of the distribution simultaneously.

SOME DETERMINANTS OF ORGANIZATIONAL DEMOGRAPHY

Before considering some of the potential consequences of organizational demography, it is necessary to briefly consider some of the factors that can operate to affect the tenure distribution of formal organizations. This analysis is important because the consequences of demography may be, in part, a function of the causes of the particular length of service distributions. And, these causes of the tenure distribution need to be included in modeling the effects of demography on organizational outcomes. This point can be developed better after some of the causes of organizational demography are reviewed.

Growth

One important factor, if not the most important factor, affecting the demography of organizations is the rate of growth of both the organization itself and the industry in which the organization operates. An organization growing at the rate of 25–30% per year cannot have a long-tenured work force even if everyone hired is young and stays until retirement. Such rates of growth have been experienced by individual firms for some period of time and by industries such as the semiconductor industry for surprisingly long periods of time. The rate of growth in the industry is an important factor affecting the average tenure of any single organization's work force because, in an expanding job market, one of the sources of labor for an expanding firm will be the labor of another firm, as this is probably a less risky way to build a labor force than to bring in outsiders new to the industry. Therefore, even if the specific firm is growing little, if the industry in which it operates is expanding rapidly, there will be forces at work that will tend to make average tenure of its work force shorter. For an organization growing at a rate of 20% per year, the regeneration index is approximately four, which means that half the people in the organization will not have worked there longer than 4 years, and this assumes no voluntary quitting, retirements, or firing. In a survey of professionals at two semiconductor firms, the average job tenure was observed to be only 3.9 years (Pfeffer 1980).

Growth has a profound effect on the potential for individual mobility up a status hierarchy in which there are relatively fewer positions the higher in the hierarchy one progresses. Keyfitz (1973) argued that growth provides additional opportunities for mobility that exist almost independently of any other factors such as skill, luck, or social connections that might affect the promotion process. Using numerical analysis, Keyfitz (1973, p. 339) estimated that growth was three times as important a factor as mortality in the system in affecting the rate of individual mobility up a status hierarchy. Keyfitz's suggestion (1973, p. 343) to choose an expanding industry in terms of additional promotional opportunities is good advice not only because of the direct effect of industry growth on promotion just noted but also because, as previously argued, the expanding industry is also likely to increase the mortality of persons in the organization who are likely to be lured away by other jobs within the industry.

Retirement

Retirement, like growth, is both an organization-specific and contextual variable affecting demography. In the society as a whole, laws proscribing compulsory retirement affect the tenure distributions in individual organizations both directly and through the effect on social values and norms concerning working at various ages. However, within the general laws governing retirement, individual organizations can to some extent manage their demographic distributions through the use of various financial incentives, particularly pensions and buy-outs, to increase the frequency of voluntary retirement at an earlier age. As an effect on individual organizational demography, the data from Table 11.1 suggest that retirement is not an important contributor to length of service distributions in individual organizations—though clearly retirement policies aged 60–64, with a work history of 30–40 years, the median tenure on the job was less than 13 years. Thus, it seems that policies affecting firing and quitting may have more effect on job tenure than do retirement practices in individual firms.
practices in individual firms.

One other comment should be made about retirement. Both social norms and laws as well as company policies affecting retirement are probably quite sensitive, in terms of their effects, to the rate of inflation characterizing the economy or at least the inflationary expectations of individuals contemplating retirement. Virtually all private pension plans are based on the amount of contributions made and the age at retirement. These two factors together, along with some options for the length of a guaranteed pay-out, determine the size of the monthly benefit to be received. The assessment of whether a pension will be adequate will be affected by the expectations for future price increases in items that are important to the individual making the retirement decision. It is quite likely that the rapid inflation experienced in the late 1970s did more to forestall retirement from the labor force than the changes in the retirement laws that occurred at about the same time.

Personnel Policies

Personnel policies refer to policies on hiring, firing, promotion, and compensation that affect the probability of being involuntarily dismissed as well as the likelihood of voluntarily quitting. Some organizations adopt the practice of promoting only from within at a certain level of supervision. In such organizations, there will be a restricted range of tenure at those supervisory levels, and the median tenure will be longer for persons occupying those positions than in organizations in which hiring from the outside is permitted or even encouraged at almost all managerial levels. The military offers an extreme example of this, as promotion through the ranks is the only route to higher rank. Thus, while it is possible to find corporate chief executives with few years in their organization, there are no generals with comparably few years of service.

As already noted, the evidence from the census data is consistent with the position that voluntary turnover is probably one of the greatest determinants of organizational demography. Such voluntary turnover is partly related to the job conditions in the industry as well as in the larger economy. At the same time, programs of company benefits, promotional opportunities, and other personnel practices can either encourage or discourage frequent voluntary quitting. A review of the literature on turnover is well beyond the scope of this chapter and has been done by others (e.g., Porter and Steers 1973). Suffice it to note that these factors affecting turnover also, then, come to affect the demography of the organization.

Technology

The level and rate of change characterizing the technology employed by the organization and by the industry in which the organization operates can also have an effect on organizational demography. Clearly, the level of technology can affect the level of education of the organization's work force. And the rate of change in technology can affect length of service distributions. In organizations with rapidly changing technology, there will be some premium for the hiring of persons recently graduated or for those with the most advanced level of training and expertise. An industry based on proprietary knowledge provides a context in which the purchase of such knowledge by recruiting away personnel with the specialized expertise is likely. One of the important ways in which technology and expertise is diffused in such high-technology industries is by the hiring away of persons with this knowledge. An industry or organization using highly specialized technical expertise is one in which there are few incentives for employing persons with detailed organizational knowledge—rather, it is the technology and knowledge of that technology which is more important. This encourages the movement of personnel among organizations and encourages the organizations to recruit younger, more up-to-date employees and to provide few rewards for staying in the organization beyond the point at which the individual's knowledge is current and important.

Rapidly changing technology is frequently associated with organizational growth, so empirically the two factors are not always independent. Conceptually, however, technology can be seen to have an independent effect on organizational demography tending to produce a tenure distribution with fewer persons with long service in the organization.

Determinants of Demography in Theories
of the Effects of Demography

Any dependent variable to be explored using organizational demography as an independent variable will have already been investigated using other causal explanations. In this endeavor, then, demography is an additional factor to be added in either an additive or, possibly, an interactive fashion. In the arguments that follow, the *ceteris paribus* condition is always assumed. But special concern is necessary for those factors such as growth, technology, retirement policy, and personnel practices that are at once potential determinants of demography as well as possible causes of the effects that have been hypothesized to result from demography. Not only is growth likely to cause a distribution of length of service in the organization biased toward less tenure, but it also can reduce conflict, provide additional promotional opportunities, increase resources including status and prestige, and lead to more positive feelings about the job and the organization. Growth may occur, in turn, because of a newly developing technology, and the technological basis of growth may itself be associated with a more professionalized work force and a more competitive and turbulent environment. Then, to observe an effect of demography may be to overstate its real impact as the effect may have been due to the factors that were associated with the demographic distribution in the first place.

This analytical problem is clearly solvable. It requires simultaneous attention to both the determinants of demography as well as its hypothesized effects. The effects of demography must be examined controlling statistically for those factors that are causally related to the tenure distributions in the first place. And, it is likely that the effects of demography may be an interactive function of the determinants and the particular distribution that has resulted. For example, either rapid growth or rapid voluntary turnover can produce a length of service distribution that is skewed toward relatively brief tenure in the organization, but the consequences of this brief length of tenure are likely to differ depending on whether the distribution was produced by growth or by voluntary turnover. More generally, the consequences of demography may be a function of the causes of the demographic distribution, including the nature of the labor supply and the organizational and industry context.

ORGANIZATIONAL DEMOGRAPHY, CHANGE, AND LEADERSHIP SUCCESSION

One likely effect of demography on the operation of formal organizations involves its effect on change and adaptation in organizations, including the process of administrative succession. The argument relating demography, defined in terms of the tenure distribution, to change and adaptation is reasonably straightforward.

First, there is the frequently observed relationship between tenure and turnover, such that persons with more years of service are more likely to report being satisfied with the organization and are more likely to remain in it. Becker (1960) noted that people develop commitments to organizations the longer they remain, making it more difficult and costly to leave. Indeed, the relationship between tenure and either turnover or intentions to quit is one of the more reliable findings in the organization's literature (Stevens *et al.* 1978, Sheldon 1971, Hrebiniak and Alutto 1972). Thus, it is reasonable to argue that organizations with participants who have longer tenure experience less voluntary turnover.

The second part of the argument relating tenure distributions to change and adaptation concerns the critical role of personnel replacement or turnover in the change process. As persons act in organizational contexts, they become committed to and associated with their actions and decisions. Such commitment is particularly likely to arise when the actions or decisions are taken publicly, when they are explicit, when they are irrevocable, and when choice is involved (Salancik 1977). A statement made with respect to some organizational issue such as strategy, curriculum, hiring, or investment is most frequently public, explicit, and, once made, irrevocable. In such a way, persons become bound by their past behaviors. Staw (1976) has illustrated in an experimental context how failure and personal accountability for the failure can lead to an escalating commitment of resources to the chosen course of action. In addition to the processes by which individuals commit themselves to their actions and decisions, social expectations develop that further constrain them by associating the persons with past actions and policies. The effect of social expectations on behavior has also been examined in a variety of theoretical contexts including the literature on roles (Kahn et al. 1964, Thornton and Nardi 1975) and the literature on expectations effects and the self-fulfilling prophecy (Miller et al. 1975, Dweck, 1975). Thus, organization actors become committed to past decisions and policies. Others associate decisions and decision consequences with those who made such decisions, causing a process of self-justification and rationalization for the past that further commits the individuals involved to these existing practices.

In addition to commitment and expectation effects, organizational members become constrained by the limited information that they see as a consequence of their role and membership. It is generally believed that the familiar effect of selective perception is a consequence of one's organizational position (Dearborn and Simon 1958), in that perceptions are affected by both the organization one is in and one's position in that organization. What is usual, reasonable, and customary depends very much on the person's location in society and in particular social organizations. The phenomenon of joining an organization, initially finding various procedures unusual, and subsequently becoming accustomed and acclimated to the organization's way of doing things is an effect that has been experienced by practically everyone. It is this acculturation, in part produced by a process of informational social influence, that causes individuals within a given organization to come to share a common perspective or organizational paradigm (Brown 1978) and to be cognitively unable to break out of that paradigm to initiate novel or innovative action.

Thus, innovation and adaptation require the importation of new ideas into the organization. This introduction of new perspectives and new concepts is facilitated by the introduction of new people not bound by past commitments within the social structure, not previously subjected to the organization's perspective and information, and not subject to the same set of social expectations and role demands. Academic organizations worry about becoming too highly tenured and about steady-state staff planning for this reason—the need to incorporate innovation through bringing in new personnel. Studies of changes in corporate strategy (Miles and Snow 1978) find that such changes are often accompanied by changes in personnel.

The argument, then, is that tenure is negatively related to turnover, and replacement and turnover of personnel is, in turn, positively related to change and adaptation. Therefore, organizations characterized by a more senior demographic distribution may, other things being equal, be less capable of change, innovation, and adaptation. In Table 11.4 I present some illustrative data on average years of service of personnel in various industries. These data suggest, among other things, that the customary positive preference for low turnover found in the organizational behavior literature may be misguided, a point made also by Staw

TABLE 11.4
Median Years on Job by Industry for Male Workers[a]

Industry	Median years on job
Railroads and railway express	19.6
Agriculture	11.5
Postal service	10.3
Federal public administration	7.6
Automobile manufacturing	7.0
Chemical and allied products manufacturing	6.8
Mining	6.4
Electrical machinery manufacturing	5.7
Communications	5.2
Instrument manufacturing	5.1
Food and kindred products manufacturing	5.1
Finance, insurance, and real estate	4.0
Rubber and plastics manufacturing	4.0
Medical and other health services	2.8
Construction	2.7
Wholesale and retail trade	2.6
Entertainment and recreation services	1.9

[a] From Bureau of Labor Statistics 1975: A-13.

and Oldham (1978). Certainly, there is little association between those industries with long-tenured work forces and effective performances and innovation. Ryder's (1965, p. 851) argument that the age of an industry is correlated with the age of its workers is reasonably consistent with these data, given the previously described association between age and average job tenure.

Inside versus Outside Administrative Succession

One particularly critical position in organizations is that of the chief executive or chief administrator. If nothing else, the replacement of top managers has symbolic value (Gamson and Scotch 1964), signifying to those inside and outside the organization that things are changing. Pfeffer and Salancik (1978, Chapter 9) have argued that one of the ways that organizations become aligned with their social environments is through the effect of environment on internal power and influence distributions and the effect of power on administrative succession. Pfeffer and Salancik (1977) found, in a study of the background and characteristics of administrators in 57 hospitals in Illinois, that the correlations between context and administrator characteristics appropriate for the context were higher in the case of more recently appointed administrators.

Not only is the frequency of administrative succession important, but even more important may be whether the successor is from inside or outside the organization. A series of studies have found that change is more likely when outside succession occurs (Carlson 1967, Helmich and Brown 1972). Such a prediction is completely consistent with the preceding argument concerning the function of replacement and turnover in bringing in new ideas and perspectives. Helmich and Brown (1972) found that there was greater turnover in the executive's immediate subordinates and staff when outside succession occurred, and Helmich (1974) found that organizational performance was negatively associated with a series of inside successions to the chief executive position.

Organizational demography may be expected to affect both succession rate and whether inside or outside succession occurs. A higher proportion of long-tenured persons within the organization provides more inside aspirants to the job, making it politically more difficult to bring in an outsider. Furthermore, an organization in which persons have longer years of service is more likely to employ socialization or inculturation as mechanisms of control rather than explicit, formalized, objective assessments. Ouchi and Johnson (1978) distinguish between two types of organizations on the basis of the type of control used, the primary distinguishing characteristic being whether employment is long-term or short-term. Organizations in which people are employed longer also tend to be characterized by informal methods of evaluation and by nonspecialized careers in which people work in a greater number of business functions. Knowledge of the organization's culture and the ability to fit in are likely to be more important criteria for career advancement and success, and it is highly unlikely that an outsider would be appointed to a high-level position in such an organization. Thus, organizations with a large proportion of long-tenured persons, in which both tenure and average tenure expectations are longer, are more likely to experience inside succession to high-level executive positions. The stability of cultures and cultural control also means that such organizations are likely to experience less frequent turnover.

Consistent with this argument, Harris (1979) reports that railroads are managed by executives who are older than the average corporate executive and who are more likely than average to have come up from the ranks within the organization or certainly within the industry. Harris argues that this pattern of executive development and succession has been partly responsible for management and operating problems within the railroad industry.

The arguments advanced here have been that tenure distributions lead to varying amounts of change and adaptation, in part operating through the frequency and type of executive succession that the organization experiences. It should be recognized, however, that the reverse argument is equally plausible—namely, that an organization that is undergoing change and adaptation is likely to have more executive succession, more outside succession, and is likely to be staffed with persons who have been in the organization a shorter period of time. Thus, just as the tenure distribution affects change and adaptation within organizations so does such change affect the tenure distribution. This instance is only one of many in which organizational variables feed back on each other in a way that reinforces the original effect. An organization characterized by long-tenured persons is less likely to change policies, and this stability in the organization's policies and operations encourages stability in employment within the organization, which in turn helps to ensure a continued stability in organizational practices and so forth. One of the reasons why organizations are so difficult to change may be precisely this feedback process in which organizations that are stable produce processes that facilitate continued stability. By the same token, organizations that are undergoing change are likely to have in place processes which facilitate the continuation of the innovation and change. Analyses of these effects need to account for the reciprocal nature of the relationships.

Organizational Change in the Future

It is interesting to speculate about how the projected increase in the average age of the American population (Cutler and Harootyan 1975) will affect organizational change and adaptation. Unfortunately, we do not have even rudimentary theory or evidence on organizational demography to provide answers that are reasonably grounded in scientific research. It is clear that a simple extrapolation of the argument just developed would imply that: (1) An increasing average age of the work force will lead to reduced interorganizational mobility and increased average organizational tenure; and (2) this increased tenure will, in turn, be associated with less change and adaptation, less-frequent executive succession, and a tendency for organizations to have insiders succeed to high executive positions when such positions become vacant. But such a simple extrapolation may not be warranted.

In the first place, the relationship between age and interorganizational mobility may be a function of organizational recruiting practices as well as personal tastes. The recruitment of younger workers tends to be less expensive in terms of both immediate salary and fringe benefits such as retirement, and such recruitment may be enhanced by the general prejudice against age that is evident in many aspects of current American culture. With increasing average age of the work force, values and attitudes toward age may change, making the older worker a more desirable recruiting target. Also, to the extent that the supply of younger managerial talent is reduced while demand for managerial talent continues, organizations may find it increasingly necessary to recruit at more advanced age levels. Indeed, one can observe that when middle-management talent became scarce, organizational recruitment of middle managers in their forties and fifties intensified. Thus, the link between age and tenure may be reduced in the future.

Another possibility is that the link between tenure and commitment to current policies or practices may be reduced. In this context, it is worthwhile to note that although in their major organizations the Japanese practice lifetime employment and almost no interorganizational mobility at advanced executive levels, these organizations have been able to innovate, change, and adapt to new technologies, new political constraints, new markets, and new products. One hypothesis as to the source of this adaptability is to be found in Staw's (Staw 1976, Staw and Fox 1977) work on the determinants of commitment. Staw found that commitment to a chosen course of action was intensified by the personal accountability of the individual for the results of his or her decisions. The practice of consensual decision making and collective responsibility

(Ouchi and Jaeger 1978) that seems to characterize Japanese organizations reduces this personal association with decisions, perhaps also reducing commitment to the decisions, which makes it difficult to admit mistakes or to change. Thus, as organizations are confronted with requirements for change that are not so readily accomplished by changes in personnel, other mechanisms producing change may evolve. Such mechanisms might include the increased use of group decision making to reduce individual commitment and identification with specific courses of action, increased training and professionalization of the managerial work force, which is likely to encourage innovation (Carlson 1967), and the structural institutionalization of experimentation and innovation in the form of decision experimentation and review (Staw 1977) or the development of additional innovative capacity in the planning or research departments. In any event, it is clear that the future effects of the general population's demography on organizational functioning depends not only on the accuracy of the arguments advanced here on a comparative basis but also on future changes that may occur in response to the issues outlined.

ORGANIZATIONAL CONTROL AND DEMOGRAPHY

In referring to the distinction between American and Japanese firms in their forms of control and coordination in the discussion of change and adaptation, the issue of the relationship between organizational demography and organizational control has already been introduced. Ouchi and Jaeger (1978) distinguish between United States' and Japanese firms on the basis of seven dimensions: (1) length of employment (short-term versus lifetime); (2) specialization of career within the organization or the number of different functions in which a manager is likely to work; (3) speed of evaluation and advancement within the organization; (4) explicitness of the evaluation system on a quantitative to qualitative distinction; (5) whether decision making is individual or consensual; (6) whether responsibility for decisions and results is shared or is individual; and (7) the extent to which the individual's whole life is of concern to the organization. Of the seven elements, average tenure is probably the most important, as nonspecialized career paths, slow evaluation and promotion, implicit evaluation in terms of fitting into the organization, and a collectivist orientation are all facilitated by having the individual in the organization for a longer period of time. Thus, the distinction between the two forms of control—control through socialization and inculturation, or through formal bureaucratic mechanisms such as the hierarchy of authority, rules and procedures, and management information systems—is based importantly on the average tenure of the work force. Bureaucratic, impersonal control is likely to be observed in situations of more turnover and shorter average tenure; cultural control based on socialization and shared norms and beliefs is likely to be found in organizations in which average tenure is relatively longer.

McNeil and Thompson (1971) have argued in a similar vein: "for the newcomer is less familiar with the organization's recent history, its activities in process, its local customs (which we usually recognize as carried in the 'informal' organization) than he is with the 'formal' preparation for joining the organization [p. 628]." Although they argued that this effect should be observed in greater efforts expended on socialization, the argument developed here is that an organization with a large number of new members would rely on more bureaucratic mechanisms of control instead of socialization. The use of bureaucratic control is particularly likely when turnover is the cause of new members. Socialization may still be used in conditions of growth. Thus, in academic departments in which most of the faculty have been in the department (and therefore together) for 20 or more years, implicit, informal understandings and norms emerge that govern the conduct of business within the department and that regulate conflict and dissent. In departments in which many of the faculty are relatively new, written procedures and formal rules are more likely to be employed as these formal procedures must be called upon when the memory of most in the organization is short and when shared values and perspectives have not had time to develop.

Clearly, not only are the forms of control likely to be different, but the roles of persons of various tenures also are likely to be different. If the tenure distribution is skewed toward brief tenure, there will be a greater amount of authority and power possessed by persons with shorter tenure. In organizations that have many people with long tenure, inclusion of the newcomer into the organization's decision making, at least in an influential role, will be accomplished more slowly. This is one of the consequences of socialization as a form of control—little discretion or influence can be permitted until those in the organization are certain that the socialization has taken. As a general proposition, one might argue that there is a contest for control over the organization or subunit and that one distinguishing dimension among the participants is their length of time in the organization. Gusfield (1957) wrote: "Conflicts of power and policy between age-groups are a common feature of many organizational structures [p. 323]." The group that has a relatively greater proportion of the total membership is likely to enjoy somewhat more influence than those who are a smaller part of the whole.

An interesting and theoretically important issue relevant to the preceding discussion is the direction of the causal connection between organizational demography and form of control. Ouchi and Johnson (1978) appear to imply that organizations choose the form of control they wish to employ, and then structure their personnel policies accordingly. We have argued that the existing demography of an organization affects the form and nature of control employed. Both arguments predict an association between demography and the form of control; the difference is in whether control strategy causes demography or whether demography causes the control strategy. Of course, it is possible that both types of effects operate or that they operate in a feedback or mutually reinforcing fashion.

Form of Control and Size of the Administrative Component

One of the possible effects of the form of control employed is on the relative size of the administrative component in the organization. Control accomplished through bureaucratic mechanisms such as rules and procedures, formal evaluations, and a hierarchy of authority and responsibility may require more administrative personnel to operate than control accomplished through a socialization process. Formal evaluation and measurement systems require people to design and operate them; the reduced familiarity with the organization's goals and values necessitates more hierarchical control and probably also results in more questions and issues being referred up the hierarchy for resolution; the fact of more frequent turnover means that communication and coordination patterns are more frequently disrupted, requiring more formal efforts in communication and control. McNeil and Thompson (1971) argued: "If our reasoning is correct, a high rate of regeneration places important burdens on the administrative process. . . . And if the administrative load is increased, then we would expect the ratio of administrative activities to other activities to expand [p. 634]." The argument advanced here is that it is not the rate of regeneration or new accessions to the organization per se that requires a larger administrative component but rather the bureaucratic form of control that would be expected to develop in an organization confronting a higher level of personnel turnover. Control and coordination accomplished through bureaucratic mechanisms requires personnel to design, operate, and update such mechanisms; control accomplished through an inculturation or socialization process requires fewer formal positions with designated responsibility for the control and coordination activities.

In any attempt to relate organizational demography to the size of the administrative component, care must be taken to measure the intervening construct of control type or the forms of coordination or control employed. Furthermore, other determinants of the size of the administrative component, such as whether the organization is growing or declining in size (Freeman and Hannan 1975), the age of the organization, the degree of task interdependence within the organization (Thompson 1967), and the conditions of the organization's task environment (Freeman 1973) must be statistically controlled to observe the effect of demography after these other determinants of administrative component size have been accounted for.

Future Organizational Control Mechanisms

Again, it is possible to speculate on how the increasing age and probably increasing tenure of organizational work forces will affect functioning. In this case, the prediction would be that the increasingly senior distribution of organizational tenure of the work force will lead to less reliance on formal rules, explicit evaluation, and other bureaucratic forms of control and to increased reliance on socialization, shared organizational paradigms, and consensual control and governance. Such a prediction would itself have implications for organizational change and innovation. As Blau (1955) demonstrated, new reporting forms introduced into a bureaucracy lead to relatively rapid changes in behavior. The effect of formal measurement and budgeting systems on behavior have been noted by Ridgway (1956). Cultures and shared systems of belief and meaning, however, are probably changed much more slowly and with greater difficulty.

If such were the case, a reasonable question might be: How do organizations that do use cultural rather than bureaucratic mechanisms of control change and adapt? Interestingly, Ouchi and Johnson (1978) contrast two United States firms that, although ostensibly in the same industry, use the two different control strategies. However, one firm systematically avoids going into highly competitive markets where rapid response, price competition, and close control over costs and operations are necessary, preferring instead to pursue a strategy of developing proprietary, high-technology products that are sold in a less competitive environment. Again, the issue of reciprocal causation is relevant. The question is: Does demography cause the choice of a strategy, or does a particular strategy cause the demography of the organization? Thus it is not clear, based on the limited evidence available, that the cultural form of control can be employed in a highly competitive economic environment. With respect to Japanese organizations, it is important to note that the Ministry of Trade and Industry and the banks and large trading companies are all tightly interconnected with little or none of the kind of antitrust enforcement and separation of economic power that characterizes the United States economy. Thus, again, one might raise the issue of the necessary preconditions for observing the successful implementation of cultural forms of organizational control.

INTERORGANIZATIONAL LINKAGE AND ORGANIZATIONAL DEMOGRAPHY

As previously noted, tenure is negatively associated with the likelihood of interorganizational movement. Such movement not only brings new ideas and perspectives into the organization involved, but personnel movement across organizations is an important mechanism of interorganizational coordination. Baty *et al.* (1971) noted that when individuals move across organizations, they take with them to their new environment knowledge of the old organization's culture, methods of operation, and beliefs about the connections between actions and outcomes. These authors examined the movement of business school faculty among schools and found that there were relatively well-defined clusters of interorganizational recruiting, such that some schools tended to recruit graduate students and more senior faculty only from a limited set of other schools, and such recruiting activity was often mutual. Though not quantitatively tested, the argument is plausibly made that such clusters of faculty movement have consequences for the development of curriculum, points of view on the discipline, research styles, and styles of pedagogy. In other words, the movement of personnel among a limited set of organizations, in this case business schools, will tend to make these organizations more similar to each other as ideas are transmitted through the movement of personnel.

In another context, Pfeffer and Leblebici (1973) argued that the movement of personnel among business firms is one way in which stable structures of coordinated activity emerge to manage interfirm competition. They found that there was more executive recruitment from within the same industry when industrial concentration was intermediate—a condition in which there were too many firms to coordinate behavior implicitly through mutual observation—but when there were not so many separate firms that organization and coordination of the system would be impossible from a limited number of interfirm linkages. Fusfeld (1958) reported interesting sociometric data analyzing clusters of joint ventures among firms in the iron and steel industry; similar analyses might be conducted for interfirm movements of personnel, assessing the consequences of such movements for the development of a common industry or industry segment culture.

Of course, there are other interorganizational coordinating mechanisms beside the movement of personnel. Curricula become standardized through accrediting organizations as well as through the movement of faculty. Industry coordination may be achieved through regulation and the accompanying planning, through industry or trade associations, through government planning and intervention in markets, or through interlocking directorates. Levine (1972) has illustrated, using data from large United States corporations, the central role that banks play in networks of interlocking directors of nonfinancial corporations. The role of banks in coordinating and linking together enterprises in Japan is well known, even if not so graphically demonstrated.

There are three possible results, then, if interorganizational mobility of personnel is negatively related to increasing average tenure: first, the amount of coordination will decline; second, the relative use of some of the alternate forms of coordination will increase; or third, new norms of mobility may emerge, making it both easier and more acceptable to move and diminishing the negative relationship between tenure and interorganizational mobility. Cross-culturally, when the case of Japan is considered, there is some support for the position that other forms of interorganizational coordination emerge when interfirm movement diminishes. This argument is consistent with the position of Pfeffer and Salancik (1978) who argued, for example, that trade associations and more formal mechanisms of interorganizational coordination would become more prominent when the number of firms increased to the point that semiformal mechanisms such as personnel movement were no longer adequate. On the other hand, Harris (1979) argues that in the railroad industry, with an older tenure distribution and less interfirm movement, no alternative forms of coordination such as joint ventures have arisen, leading to some of the problems of facilities duplication and interdependence management confronting that industry. Clearly, an important issue for investigation is the relationship of organizational demography to interorganizational movement and the consequences of such organizational movement for the development of alternative forms of interorganizational coordination or for the level of systemwide coordination and planning achieved. Such analyses might focus on university departments and scientific disciplines as well as on industrial firms. It is interesting to conjecture how the lack of growth in faculty size and the increasingly high tenure distribution will affect not only change and innovation in the discipline but the development of cosmopolitan versus local orientations and the development of shared paradigms across departments that will no longer engage in so much exchange of personnel.

COHORT EFFECTS IN FORMAL ORGANIZATIONS

Cohort effects are another phenomenon associated with the demography of organizations that has been relatively neglected in theorizing and empirical research on formal organizations. Ryder (1965) has argued that social change occurs through the introduction of new cohorts into social systems; and cohort effects have been used to explain differences in voting behavior across age groups (Hyman 1959, Crittenden 1962). Cohorts are defined in terms of groups of individuals who experience the same event at approximately the same time. Thus, for example, people who entered the labor force during the Great Depression would have had a relatively similar and powerful experience at the same time, which may shape their subsequent attitudes and behavior toward risk taking and job and career mobility. The cohort concept as an explanation for behavior is predicated on an imprinting notion—that people are relatively more malleable at some life stages than at others, and experiences at these malleable periods exert a lasting influence on beliefs and actions. The forcefulness of the external event (e.g., the depression, the Vietnam war) affects the extent of the imprinting. One need not accept the premise that personality is fixed early in life and that socialization ceases to expect some cohort effect. Transitions to new occupations or new organizations may engender the type of uncertainty that would lead to the development of new social referents and new patterns of behaving. But clearly, the cohort concept requires some assumption of more or less fixed effects, so that once the new socialization is acquired, this history has continuing impact on the subsequent development of attitudes and actions.

In organizations, there are two types of cohort effects that are of interest. First, there is the general issue of conflict between different cohorts in the organization. Intergenerational conflict is an important theme in discussions of society and social change (Davis 1940). In an insightful analysis of problems of adaptation confronted by the Women's Christian Temperance Union (WCTU), Gusfield (1957) details a generational split within an organization, the consequences for the organization, and some mechanisms that were developed to partially alleviate the negative effect of the conflict. Two groups could be identified in the WCTU: (1) the older group, also the group in control, had entered the movement in the days before prohibition and had viewed abstinence as a solution to problems of poverty and lower-income groups' deviant behavior; (2) the group that entered after the repeal of prohibition entered during a time of increasing social liberalism and were oriented more to treating problems of alcoholism and to education and persuasion, viewing the issue in less narrowly moralistic terms. The two groups favored different tactics and different responses to the crisis of declining membership and prestige faced by the WCTU. Problems of succession and control over the organization illustrated the conflict between the two cohorts comprising the membership.

Universities are another context in which differences in cohorts might be both visible and important. There have been changes over time in the relative income levels of academics, the importance of teaching versus research, and the importance of outside funding and research grants. All of these changes may be reflected in divisions among faculty cohorts entering academia in the different periods. In the 1930s and 1940s, academic work paid relatively little compared to other occupations. The explosion in the research industry following Sputnik in 1957, coupled with the arrival of the postwar baby boom in the 1960s, led to an expansion in university size that was accompanied by an increase in resources, including financial remuneration. With the decline of the college-age population now beginning to be felt, and with the current mood against public expenditures, financial stringency has returned and real income levels of many academics have declined in recent years. Such changes in financial condition affect the attitudes and values of people entering academia in different periods. People beginning work in the late 1940s entered with low financial expectations and at a time when resources were scarce. People starting work in the middle 1960s entered when expansion was rapid, salaries were increasing rapidly, and thus with higher expectations for the level of support. The current relative decline in support for higher education affects the two groups differently, and there is some conflict between those who see the period of affluence as a nice but temporary interlude and those who view such resource munificence as a minimum level of aspiration for the future.

One can observe similar cohort conflicts over the role of research both over time, as research has grown in importance since the late 1950s, and within single institutions as new deans, department heads, or presidents arrive to change the character of the organization and make it more prestigious. Such changes both threaten and are resisted by the cohort accustomed to a less competitive environment. Various strategies for buying off the opposition emerge, including the creation of additional administrative positions, using early retirement policies, and, on occasion, simply driving the old cohort out through brutal power struggles. One can probably tell much about an academic organization by the demography of its faculty and the associated conditions that characterized the period in which these individuals entered their academic careers. Cartwright (1979), in a review of research in social psychology, has persuasively argued that the choice of research topics and theoretical focus in the field has been affected by the demography of the discipline. Early concerns with authoritarianism and democratic styles of leadership were partly a product of the infusion of scholars fleeing Germany at the time of the Nazi rise to power. The field then became interested in attitudes and attitude change as the early 1950s saw increasing concern with racial integration following the Brown versus Board of Education school decision. In the field of organizational behavior, it has been argued that the shift toward more political and, at times, more cynical views of organizations was a result of the emergence in the discipline of students who were in graduate school during the time of the Vietnam war. Clearly, Staw's (1976) work on escalating commitment as well as his earliest research on the attitudinal effects on Reserve Officer Training Corps (ROTC) cadets of the draft lottery (1974) both reflect the impact of a particular period of history.

It is likely that conflicts among cohorts are more severe when the distribution of tenure in the organization is more like Organization A in Table 11.2 than Organization B. Large bursts of new hiring, followed by long periods of few new accessions, produces an organization in which the cleavages among the cohorts are more sharply defined. When hiring is done on a more constant and continuing basis, sharp distinctions among segments of the organization are less pronounced, and the likelihood and severity of conflict among the cohorts is probably reduced. In this regard, it is interesting to speculate how the demography of universities will affect their operations in the future. With little or no future growth and the possibility of future contraction, tenure has become increasingly difficult to obtain, particularly in private institutions. Since there are rules and norms governing the number of years of service before tenure becomes granted, it is quite possible that distributions approaching that of Organization A can emerge in universities with some nontenured persons of fewer than 7 years of service, some persons who have long-tenured service in the organization, and very few in between. The possibilities for young-old conflict in such a situation are clearly increased. One mechanism for the young to employ to obtain some additional power and control over their fate might be unionization, and one prediction would be that the degree of conflict among cohorts, related to organizational demography, is a factor affecting the propensity for faculty to unionize.

Power struggles and political fighting across cohort groups, however, is only one cohort effect that is important. Another important effect is on the development of common bonds among persons in a given cohort or the extent to which cohorts also give rise to the development of peer groups that are structured primarily along cohort lines. Clearly, in some professional organizations such as law firms, accounting firms, and academic departments, there is reason to believe that informal social contacts, friendship patterns, and perhaps even job-related interactions fall primarily within rather than across cohort boundaries. The distinctions between tenure and nontenure in academia and the distinction between partner and associate in law and accounting firms are particularly important lines of demarcation among groups. One research issue is the conditions under which interaction primarily within cohort groups is most likely to arise. It might be expected that the arrival of persons in some number in clusters would increase the tendency for within-group association. Law firms, accounting firms, and universities tend to hire with starting dates at specific times in the year. Some accounting firms send new employees off to training sessions in groups, and law firms and academic departments may have social gatherings so that the new employees get to know one another. The effect of numbers, a common starting date, and common fate may act to increase interaction within the cohort group and diminish contact across cohorts. These organizations also tend to be smaller and have less horizontal and vertical differentiation. And rank in these organizations is highly related to length of service.

Such situations are in contrast to firms in which hiring is more continuous throughout the year, and the new employee is likely to enter alone into a setting in which there are more finely graded status distinctions (hierarchical position rather than the dichotomous partner–associate, tenure–untenured), and in which there is more horizontal differentiation and specialization. Thus, the prediction is that the congruence in entry date and the sharpness of distinctions among cohorts are positively associated with the development of a peer group or groups within the cohort and the consequent restriction of interactions and informal social ties.

A second issue is not what causes the development of psychologically important identification with a cohort but what the consequences of such identification are. One such consequence can be seen in the form of subsequent choice behavior when one member of a cohort is in a position to allocate positions or resources. Because of identification and intense social interaction within the cohort, such selections are more likely to be made from others within that cohort. Thus, lawyers, accountants, or academics begin with a group in an employing organization. Subsequently, some are promoted and others leave for positions in other organizations. The prediction would be that the effect of cohort identification results in the selection of persons from that cohort when there are decisions about subsequent hiring or client referral. The operation of search committees, referral networks, and patterns of resource allocation would be expected to follow cohort lines to the extent that cohort identification was facilitated at the time of entry into the organization or the occupation. Sponsorship mobility, in other words (Turner 1960), may be one of the consequences of cohort development.

Another potential cohort effect can be the imprinting of the organization with the dominant beliefs, patterns of practice, and values from the time the cohort currently in control entered the organization. One consequence of close association within the cohort is that there is probably less contact with other cohorts both more senior and more junior in the organization. Thus, socialization into the organization and the development of a relatively uniform organizational culture is hindered. When the cohort assumes positions of authority within the organization, the organization will come to reflect the beliefs and values that the individuals brought with them at the time of entry. Clearly, such perseverance of initial psychological states is far from complete. Nevertheless, to the extent cohorts are strongly identifiable and engage in extensive informal social interaction, there will be some maintenance of the history of the cohort, which will come to affect the organization's operations when that cohort assumes control. Such effects are particularly likely to be noticed and important when a large number of governing positions turn over at once from one cohort to the next, and when cohort effects are particularly strong. In such a way, organizations become imprinted with the values, attitudes, and standards of activity and practice from the time the governing cohort entered the organization. Although one might suspect that this might produce an organization seriously out of phase with its environment, such is not inevitably the case. To the extent that other organizations in the task environment are governed by persons from the same cohort, each will be in harmony with the other. This leads to the prediction that organizations of different demographies, particularly when cohort effects are stronger, will have more difficulty in interacting and transacting with each other than organizations with similar tenure and age distributions.

As another example of the effect just described, consider the effect of college cohorts on subsequent career and life activity. Not only does one often marry (at least for the first time) within that cohort, but there is some evidence that such friendships and contacts are lasting (Granovetter 1974), providing access to jobs and to transaction networks throughout one's life. Again, such cohort effects can be magnified or reduced by the size of the cohort, the extent of common fate and identification, and maintenance activities taken when the cohort begins to dissolve by taking jobs and moving away.

Cohort effects are another way that age of an organization's work force can affect organizational functioning. Organizational employees born and raised during a certain time come to the organization with training, skills, and points of view that are, in part, a function of their early socialization experiences. A simple example can illustrate the general point. Educational levels have risen during the past decades. This means that not only is there the customary relationship between education and occupational achievement, but also that for any given occupational level, the younger the cohort in that level, the more education they are likely to have obtained. Whereas older executives may have high school, some college, or college degrees, younger executives have a much higher probability of having completed college and obtaining advanced management degrees and training.

To the extent that this additional education has imparted new or different analytical approaches and managerial strategies, then the strategies and analysis in use in an organization will be, in part, a function of the age of its administrative cohort and will reflect the practices and level of training common when they were being educated and socialized.

The point is that it is not the age of the organization's work force, per se, that affects organizational functioning but those elements correlated with age that affect organizations. One such element is the tenure distribution. Another such element is the imprinting in terms of level of skills, type of skills, and practices that are residues of the time in which education and early experience was obtained. Although, as will be discussed in the next section, continuing education can be used in attempts to keep training and perspectives current, the committing effects of a point of view, once adopted, particularly when it is reinforced by others in the cohort, are powerful. In this way, effects from the society that become represented in a cohort get imported into organizations and come to affect organizational functioning.

Clearly, there is tremendous potential for analyzing organizational belief systems and activities employing the concept of cohorts. Also, the concept of cohort can potentially help explain the operation of resource exchanges and stratification systems within organizations. For such cohort effects to occur, the development of peer groups and interaction patterns along cohort lines is essential. Understanding the factors producing such cohort identification can enable the management of cohort effects, if desired, and the diagnosis of cohort effects in social systems.

CAREER GROWTH AND DEVELOPMENT

The concept of cohort explicitly introduces the idea of groups of people moving through time, carrying with them the effects of history modified by subsequent experiences. In most organizations, there is some degree of pyramidal structure with more positions at the bottom than at the top. Thus, only some proportion of assistant professors will be promoted to tenure; only a proportion of associates will become partners in law firms; and only some new managers will advance up the hierarchy, and only a very small proportion will reach top management ranks. Thus, in pyramidal organizations, cohorts tend to decline in size over time. Large cohorts entering at one time will fill up the pyramid, leaving fewer opportunities for subsequent entrants.

This fact of the pyramid interacts with the organization's tenure distribution to cause a number of problems for organizations and their participants. Hall (1976) has described occupational careers in terms of a learning or exploration phase, a career growth phase, and then a phase in which earnings and positional influence plateaus—or a maintenance phase. Such a pattern is illustrated in Figure 11.1. Occupations differ in terms of the time in life at which various phases are encountered. Occupations in which a relatively early plateau is reached pose problems of motivating the individual for effective performance over the long time remaining in the working career. Such problems occur regardless of the absolute level of the plateau achieved.

Similar diagrams could be constructed for formal organizations. Such organizations also differ in terms of the length of the career ladder and time required to traverse it. Problems of career plateauing in organizations are well known and serious. What happens to a cohort when most of the people in it, because of fewer positions in higher levels, come to realize that they have progressed as far as they ever will in their current organization? For persons conditioned by the organization and by the

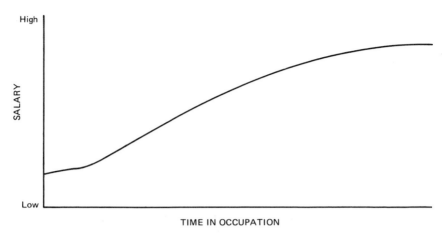

Figure 11.1. Illustration of maintenance phase in pyramidal organization.

larger society to seek achievement, not only achievement but achievement that is measured by the attainment of status, the recognition that there is little likelihood of further advance, coupled with the fact that firing at such levels is rare, can cause serious problems of motivation and performance. Hall (1976) describes numerous strategies that various organizations have employed, including lateral transfers, downward transfers protecting salary, and the development of the managerial role into a training role as well, in efforts to solve the problems of boredom, motivation, and performance.

Career plateauing most frequently occurs at the time in one's life when the issue of mortality becomes salient. The combination of recognition of one's career problems with the recognition of the finiteness of the working and nonworking life can be debilitating. A major radio station in San Francisco recently faced just such a problem with its broadcast employees. At the top of their field in that station, they recognized that they were not going to go on to network television, and thus their careers had plateaued, albeit at a high level. At the same time, they recognized and became more concerned about the fact that this meant they would be doing the same thing for the rest of their working lives. It is one thing to be recently promoted to reading and preparing weather forecasts on a major radio station. It is another thing to contemplate doing the weather for the next 15–20 years. The problems of employee attitudes and morale were becoming evident, and the station cast about madly for some kind of personal growth or personal development seminars to divert the employees' attention from their work situation.

Such mid-career plateauing problems are probably more severe in organizations with longer-tenured work forces. If nothing else, the change in organizations provides the challenge of learning new roles and building new patterns of interaction. Thus, the demography of the organization may predict the extent to which it confronts problems of motivation and morale as a consequence of career plateauing.

The rotation of people into new jobs is one recommended strategy for coping with career plateauing. The cost of such a strategy, however, is the resources required to train the person in the new job and the performance lost while such training is being accomplished. Indeed, if part of the problem is a cohort effect in which new insights and new skills need to be brought into the higher organizational levels, merely rotating the old actors into new roles may not solve the problem. In such situations, new positions, particularly honorific, training, administrative, or planning positions may be created to take people out of their old roles, give them new tasks to perform, and at the same time free the past positions so that younger people or persons from another cohort can be placed in them. Thus, one might hypothesize a relationship between the demography of the organization and the size of the administrative component that is directly opposite to the prediction derived from considerations of control and coordination. Considering control and coordination problems, a long-tenured work force should require fewer administrative positions as control is more internalized. However, considering issues of career plateauing and motivation, long-tenured work forces may be associated with more administrative positions as new jobs and new roles are created to provide variety and to free other management positions for new persons. The argument assumes that, in part, the demand for staff, administration, or similar roles is dictated by the supply of persons willing and ready to fill such positions. Such an assumption is most likely to hold in organizations not subject to rigorous discipline from market competition, so that there is enough slack available to create such excess positions.

Again, we can use the university as an example to illustrate the argument. Many institutions have experienced a proliferation of academic administrators since the late 1960s. Over the period 1967–1974, the University of California at Berkeley experienced virtually no change in the number of students, a 6.9% decrease in faculty, and a 144% increase in the number of senior positions in the chancellor's office while the number of positions in systemwide administration increased 58.9%. There are a number of factors that could account for such an increase, including the increasingly hostile environment, increasing regulations at the federal level, and more complex and differentiated sources of funding. It is also the case that this was a period characterized by the cessation of growth in the university and by a rapidly deteriorating job market in many graduate disciplines. Furthermore, the university was becoming very highly tenured. Thus, the organization faced persons who were reaching career plateaus, students who could not find jobs after years of graduate study, and an environment that made increasingly greater regulatory and informational demands. The factors together made it attractive to expand administrative positions to absorb both faculty and graduate students who cannot find work while at the same time developing more information to cope with the environment. Although parceling out the various factors involved in the growth of the administrative component is complex, there are clear examples of instances in which the demography of the institution had a significant effect on the development of administrative positions to provide additional jobs and mobility within the academic structure.

The Rise of Continuing Education

In the early 1970s, the University of California developed the UC Management Institute, an executive program for administrators solely from within the university system held every summer for 2 weeks. Although, again, many factors were at work, the relationships between continuing education and the factors of organizational demography discussed throughout this chapter are significant. First, if new positions and new position assignments are to be used to help solve motivational problems arising from career plateauing, then education and training must be available to help the new position occupants perform in their new roles. Unemployed Ph.D.s in English and senior physics professors probably have little formal or informal knowledge about budgeting, planning, personnel policies and regulations, and organizational design; senior production executives may know little about executive development or long-range planning. Training for older employees undergoing position changes is an important component of such transitions.

Second, continuing education can provide new insights, new experiences, and variety for those bothered by career plateauing. For some organizations, continuing education can be a reward offered as a consolation prize to those who did not get the promotion but who are still valued by the company. Eight weeks at the Stanford program, 13 weeks at Harvard, or 4 weeks at one of the numerous executive programs of such length breaks up the work routine and provides the manager with new associations, new insight, challenge, and variety that may be lacking on the job.

Third, such new acquaintances and knowledge can help to overcome problems of commitment and stability that may be associated with demography. In the absence of the ability to import new people, new ideas can be obtained by sending the same people off to meet new people, learn new things, and get new insights. Thus, continuing education can provide help for the career-plateauing problems confronted by organizations as well as help solve problems of innovation and adaptation that may arise with a long-tenured work force. And, the associations made at such intensive, residential training sessions may provide important avenues for additional interorganizational linkage.

One might predict, then, that continuing education would grow in importance as the average age of the work force increases. And, one would predict that the use of continuing education would be, in part, a function of the demography of the organization. An organization would be willing to invest in expensive continuing education more if the employee were going to be around for the organization to benefit. At the same time, such an investment is more necessary in long-tenured organizations because of the need to solve career plateau problems and to facilitate change, innovation, and linkage with elements in the organization's environment. One proviso is necessary for the preceding hypothesis: Organizations that are thoroughly committed to current practices may not recognize the need for innovation or change. Thus, the relationship between organizational demography and investment in continuing education and training may be curvilinear, peaking at some moderate-to-high level of tenure but declining after that because of resistance to change and innovation. In that regard, it is interesting to note that most of the attendees at the Berkeley business school's executive education activities come from industries moderate in average tenure, while few come either from the very low- or very high-tenured industries of Table 11.4. Of course, the analysis of the use of continuing education should be undertaken on a much more formal and systematic basis.

CONCLUSION

The arguments developed in this chapter can be briefly summarized at only a very aggregate level: Demography is a variable that can link general social processes with formal organizations and their structures and processes; organizational demography, and particularly the tenure distribution of organizational participants, is an important but virtually unexplored variable that can be employed productively to develop hypotheses about change, adaptation, and leadership succession, the forms and mechanisms of control employed, interorganizational linkage mechanisms, the use of continuing education and training, and the form and amount of conflict and cleavages within the organization. The arguments and the illustrative data presented are speculative, reflecting the lack of attention that organization theorists have given demographic variables and the lack of attention that those interested in aging and demography have paid to organizations and organizational processes and structures.

There clearly does exist a theoretical literature that can be employed to begin to develop hypotheses about organizational demography. Furthermore, there are data on organizational tenure that can be used to at least begin the process of empirically exploring some of the issues raised. If greater understanding of the impact of an aging population and work force on organizations is to be obtained, the first step will be to develop some understanding of the effects of demography on organizations. Only then will we have the theoretical knowledge necessary to understand what the various demographic projections for the population as a whole may mean in terms of the operation and structuring of formal organizations.

ACKNOWLEDGMENTS

The research assistance of J. Richard Harrison and the comments of J. Richard Harrison, Joanne Martin, Valerie Oppenheimer, and Melvin Kohn are gratefully acknowledged.

REFERENCES

Aldrich, H. E. (1979) *Organizations and Environments*. Englewood Cliffs, N.J.: Prentice-Hall.

Baty, G., Evan, W., and Rothermel, T. (1971) Personnel flows as interorganizational relations. *Administrative Science Quarterly* 16:430–443.

Becker, H. S. (1960) Notes on the concept of commitment. *American Journal of Sociology* 66:32–40.

Blau, P. M. (1955) *The Dynamics of Bureaucracy*. Chicago: University of Chicago Press.

Blau, P. M. (1977) *Inequality and Heterogeneity*. New York: The Free Press.

Brown, R. H. (1978) Bureaucracy as praxis: Toward a political phenomenology of formal organizations. *Administrative Science Quarterly* 23:365–382.

Bureau of Labor Statistics (1975) Job Tenure of Workers, January 1973. Special Labor Report 172. Washington, D.C.: U.S. Bureau of Labor Statistics.

Carlson, R. O. (1967) *Adoption of Educational Innovations*. Eugene, Oregon: University of Oregon.

Cartwright, D. (1979) Contemporary Social Psychology in Historical Perspective. *Social Psychology Quarterly* 42:82–93.

Collins, R. (1971) Functional and conflict theories of educational stratification. *American Sociological Review* 36:1002–1019.

Crittenden, J. (1962) Aging and party affiliation. *Public Opinion Quarterly* 26:648–657.

Cutler, N. E. (1977) Demographic, social-psychological, and political factors in the politics of aging: A foundation for research in "political gerontology." *American Political Science Review* 71:1011–1025.

Cutler, N., and Harootyan, R. A. Demography of the aged. Pp. 31–69 in D. S. Woodruff and J. E. Birren, eds., *Aging: Scientific Perspectives and Social Issues.* New York: Van Nostrand Reinhold.

Davis, K. (1940) The sociology of parent-youth conflict. *American Sociological Review* 5:523–535.

Dearborn, D. C., and Simon, H. A. (1958) Selective perception. *Sociometry* 21:140–143.

Dweck, C. S. (1975) The role of expectations and attributions in the alleviation of learned helplessness. *Journal of Personality and Social Psychology* 31:674–685.

Freeman, J. H. (1973) Environment, technology, and the administrative intensity of manufacturing organizations. *American Sociological Review* 38:750–763.

Freeman, J., and Hannan, M. T. (1975) Growth and decline processes in organizations. *American Sociological Review* 40:215–228.

Fusfeld, D. (1958) Joint subsidiaries in the iron and steel industry. *American Economic Review* 48:578–587.

Gamson, W., and Scotch, N. (1964) Scapegoating in baseball. *American Journal of Sociology* 70:6–29.

Glenn, N. D. (1969) Aging, disengagement, and opinionation. *Public Opinion Quarterly* 33:17–33.

Granovetter, M. (1974) *Getting a Job: A Study of Contacts and Careers.* Cambridge, Mass.: Harvard University Press.

Gusfield, J. R. (1957) The problem of generations in an organizational structure. *Social Forces* 35:323–330.

Hall, D. T. (1976) *Careers in Organizations.* Santa Monica, Ca.: Goodyear.

Harris, R. G. (1979) *The Potential Effects of Deregulation Upon Corporate Structure, Merger Behavior and Organizational Relations in the Rail Freight Industry.* Draft Report. Washington, D.C.: Public Interest Economics Center.

Helmich, D. L. (1974) Organizational growth and succession patterns. *Academy of Management Journal* 17:771–775.

Helmich, D., and Brown, W. B. (1972) Successor type and organizational change in the corporate enterprise. *Administrative Science Quarterly* 17:371–381.

Hrebiniak, L. G., and Alutto, J. A. (1972) Personal and role-related factors in the development of organizational commitment. *Administrative Science Quarterly* 17:555–573.

Hyman, H. (1959) *Political Socialization.* Glencoe, Ill.: The Free Press.

Kahn, R. L., Wolfe, D. M., Quinn, R. P., and Snoek, J. D. (1964) *Organizational Stress: Studies in Role Conflict and Ambiguity.* New York: John Wiley and Sons.

Kanter, R. M. (1977) Some effects of proportions on group life: Skewed sex ratios and responses to token women. *American Journal of Sociology* 82:965–990.

Kessel, J. H. (1962) Governmental structure and political environment: A statistical note about American cities. *American Political Science Review* 56:615–620.

Keyfitz, N. (1973) Individual mobility in a stationary population. *Population Studies* 37:335–352.

Levine, J. H. (1972) The sphere of influence. *American Sociological Review* 37:14–27.

McNeil, K., and Thompson, J. D. (1971) The regeneration of social organizations. *American Sociological Review* 36:624–637.

Miles, R. E., and Snow, C. E. (1978) *Organizational Strategy, Structure, and Process.* New York: McGraw-Hill.

Miller, R. L., Brickman, P., and Bolen, D. (1975) Attribution versus persuasion as a means for modifying behavior. *Journal of Personality and Social Psychology* 31:430–441.

Ouchi, W. G., and Jaeger, A. M. (1978) Type Z organization: Stability in the midst of mobility. *Academy of Management Review* 3:305–314.

Ouchi, W. G., and Johnson, J. B. (1978) Types of organizational control and their relationship to emotional well being. *Administrative Science Quarterly* 23:293–317.

Pfeffer, J. (1980) A partial test of the social information processing model of job attitudes. *Human Relations* 33:457–476.

Pfeffer, J., and Leblebici, H. (1973) Executive recruitment and the development of interfirm organizations. *Administrative Science Quarterly* 18:449–461.

Pfeffer, J., and Salancik, G. R. (1977) Organizational context and the characteristics and tenure of hospital administrators. *Academy of Management Journal* 20:74–88.

Pfeffer, J., and Salancik, G. R. (1978) *The External Control of Organizations: A Resource Dependence Perspective.* New York: Harper and Row.

Porter, L. W., and Steers, R. M. (1973) Organizational, work, and personal factors in employee turnover and absenteeism. *Psychological Bulletin* 80:151–176.

Ridgway, V. F. (1956) Dysfunctional consequences of performance measurements. *Administrative Science Quarterly* 1:240–247.

Ryder, N. B. (1965) The cohort as a concept in the study of social change. *American Sociological Review* 30:843–861.

Salancik, G. R. (1977) Commitment and the control of organizational behavior and belief. Pp. 1–54 in B. M. Staw and G. R. Salancik, eds., *New Directions in Organizational Behavior.* Chicago: St. Clair Press.

Schnore, L. F., and Alford, R. A. (1963) Forms of government and socioeconomic characteristics of suburbs. *Administrative Science Quarterly* 8:1–17.

Sheldon, M. E. (1971) Investments and involvements as mechanisms producing commitment to the organization. *Administrative Science Quarterly* 16:143–150.

Spangler, E., Gordon, M. A., and Pipkin, R. A. (1978) Token women: An empirical test of Kanter's hypothesis. *American Journal of Sociology* 85:160–170.

Staw, B. M. (1974) Attitudinal and behavioral consequences of changing a major organizational reward: A natural field experiment. *Journal of Personality and Social Psychology* 29:742–751.

Staw, B. M. (1976) Knee-deep in the big muddy: A study of escalating commitment to a chosen course of action. *Organizational Behavior and Human Performance* 16:27–44.

Staw, B. M. (1977) The experimenting organization: Problems and prospects. Pp. 466–486 in B. M. Staw, ed., *Psychological Foundations of Organizational Behavior.* Santa Monica, Ca.: Goodyear.

Staw, B. M., and Fox, F. V. (1977) Escalation: The determinants of commitment to a chosen course of action. *Human Relations* 30:431–450.

Staw, B. M., and Oldham, G. R. (1978) Reconsidering our dependent variables: A critique and empirical study. *Academy of Management Journal* 21:539–559.

Stevens, J. M., Beyer, J. M., and Trice, H. M. (1978) Assessing personal, role, and organizational predictors of managerial commitment. *Academy of Management Journal* 21:380–396.

Stinchcombe, A. L., McDill, M. S., and Walker, D. R. (1968) Demography of organizations. *American Journal of Sociology* 74:221–229.

Thompson, J. D. (1967) *Organizations in Action.* New York: McGraw-Hill.

Thornton, R., and Nardi, P. M. (1975) The dynamics of role acquisition. *American Journal of Sociology* 80:870–885.

Turner, R. H. (1960) Sponsored and contest mobility and the school system. *American Sociological Review* 25:855–867.

chapter **12**

Reform Movements and Organizations: The Case of Aging

W. RICHARD SCOTT

The fundamental notion that governments should intervene in the social condition of aging persons has been firmly established in industrialized societies
[Binstock and Levin 1976, p. 511].

Although in times past the care of the elderly was mainly a problem for
families or philanthropic institutions, in recent decades it has also come to
be regarded as another of the responsibilities of government [Lakoff 1976,
p. 643].

Sentiments such as these are repeated many times over in the recent
literature on aging. They are consistent with the general trend in modern
nation states both to distinguish among populations of various types and
to bring these differentiated categories clearly under the jurisdiction of
the state. Boli-Bennett and Meyer (1978) have shown how modern societies act to institutionalize the role of children, differentiating them
from adults and managing their protection and socialization. Lakoff asserts that a similar process is under way that differentiates the aged from
other adults and insists on their special needs for assistance and
protection:

The political response to the problems of the elderly is in part a reflection
of a general commitment to social welfare that has become a standard element

AGING
Social Change

in modern government. Older people are classed, for this purpose, with children and the handicapped on the assumption that people in these categories must be regarded as dependents and that society as a whole has a responsibility to assure that all who are dependent are not deprived of some measure of assistance [1976, p. 645].

And Cain (1974, 1976) has documented the increasing extent to which a distinctive legal status has been created for the elderly.

THE RATIONALIZATION OF REFORM

It is possible and it may be useful to view these developments as part of a general rationalizing process that has characterized Western societies during the past few centuries (Weber 1927) and that operates in virtually all societies at the present time. In some countries, rationalization tendencies have been closely linked with the formation of a strong central state; in other societies, such as the United States, rationalizing tendencies have been much more decentralized, associated with voluntaristic efforts and the emergence of many professionalized occupations. However, in recent years, centralization in this country has proceeded rapidly, with more and more activities being controlled or financed at the federal level.

Rationalizing processes operate at several levels—ideological or institutional, organizational, individual—and developments at one level may not coincide with developments at the others, a point to which I return at the conclusion of this chapter. I begin by briefly noting some of the general features of this societal process, illustrated with more specific references to the area of aging.

1. A category of individuals or an area of concern is identified as a candidate for rationalization. Much is made of the current chaotic state of the area identified. Thus, an exposé of nursing homes coauthored by Senator Moss begins with the assertion: "It's hell to be old in this country. This is a simple truth for most of our 21 million elderly [Moss and Halamandaris 1977, p. 3]." Graphic depictions of intolerable conditions become best sellers (Mendelson 1974); congressional committees are formed and hold hearings; and White House conferences are convened. In these and other ways, attention is directed to the current state of affairs, and it is declared to be unsatisfactory.

2. Forces are mobilized calling for reform. Mass-based organizations are developed to mobilize interested citizens and pressure legislators. Existing organizations, such as the National Retired Teachers Association, are activated and joined by newer associations, which often tend to be more radical in character—(e.g., the Gray Panthers or the National Caucus on the Black Aged). (See Pratt 1974, Butler 1975, pp. 321–343.) The aging movement has, of course, been greatly strengthened by demographic changes that are producing a larger proportion of older citizens, which in turn has increased their economic and political power (Riley and Foner 1968).

3. *Among these forces are professional groups having a direct interest in promoting reform.* Moynihan (1965) was among the first to call attention to the extent to which modern reform movements have come to be dominated by those whose job it is to initiate such reforms. Noting that earlier reform efforts in this country were primarily the result of citizens and interest groups imposing pressure on the agencies of government, Moynihan argued:

> By mid-century, however, the process of external pressure and internal encouragement had acquired a degree of institutionalization and expertise that might be described as the professionalization of reform. Increasingly, efforts to change the American social system for the better arose from initiatives undertaken by persons whose profession was to do just that [1970, pp. 22–23].

Piven and Cloward (1972) have challenged Moynihan's thesis by insisting that federal political leaders (and political considerations) dominated the reform process in the case of the war on poverty. But they do not disagree that various types of professionals and experts working both within and outside the government have promoted and helped to shape the content of the reforms. Focusing specifically on reforms in the area of aging, Calhoun (1978) has ascribed a very large role to the "social engineers"—gerontologists, educators, social workers—in promoting and directing this movement.

4. *Reform efforts are viewed as resting on a rational and scientific base that must be extended.* The promise is held out that the area of concern can be reorganized and put on a more scientific basis. Beattie states this premise quite explicitly with respect to reforms in aging:

> It is essential that the fundamental questions as to the goals of services for the aging and the design of delivery systems be predicated upon scientific knowledge and a conceptual and philosophical understanding of aging. . . . Knowledge gained from biological, behavioral, and social research on the processes and conditions of aging, while at times tentative and in beginning stages of development, is essential as a basis for formulating service goals [1976, p. 632].

Calls are made for more research, for more and better trained personnel, and for the more efficient organization of services. In particular, the need for a rational plan is emphasized that can guide the allocation of resources and eliminate waste and duplication. The current dependence on untrained workers and on volunteer and private agencies is viewed as a situation requiring correction.

5. *Needs of clients are defined as being independent of demands for services.* The professional model of service is built on the general proposition that the practitioner, not the client, knows what is in the best interests of the client (Goode 1957). Services created for the elderly often go unused (see Beattie 1976, p. 629, Moen 1978), but such problems are dismissed as being due to ignorance, the absence of mechanisms to ensure access, or a state of apathy and disengagement born of previous neglect. The proposed remedies are to provide better, more professional, services and outreach programs designed to seek out the clients in order to deliver the needed services (see Butler 1975, pp. 170–171).

Those groups specializing in services for the aged recognize that they confront a rather special problem in attempting to ascertain the needs of their clientele. As Boulding (1966) has cogently observed, the professional concept of a client's needs is based on some definition of homeostasis or state maintenance, departures from which require attention. However, the aging process represents not departures from a constant state but changes in the state itself; as Boulding suggests: Aging "might almost be defined as that adverse change in state of the organism which no known input can remedy [p. 206]." This raises very difficult problems for those designing services for the aging, as Kamerman and Kahn have noted: "In the area of community-based services for the aged, there are almost no standards for well-being or service quality. The process of aging may be slowed temporarily but cannot be stopped; there is no 'cure.' What criteria can be utilized to evaluate effectiveness [1976, p. 359]?" We do not propose to resolve these issues in this chapter—only to raise them.

The rationalization of an area of behavior may not entail all of these developments but will involve many of them as well as others. Once an area has been "opened up" by these processes, it becomes much easier to justify and claim support for a large range of professional and scientific activity. The development of new professional specialties, occupational roles, and types of services is greatly facilitated. And older professions begin to explore ways in which they can expand their range of services and involve themselves more heavily in the new area (see Riley *et al.* 1969). In all these ways, rationalizing processes let the light of legitimacy shine in, encouraging new ventures to grow.

THE IMPORTANCE OF CONTEXT

The features just reviewed appear to broadly characterize a large number of reform movements that have occurred during the last century and a half, including the development of child protective and care services, mental health services, antipoverty programs, and services for the educationally and physically handicapped. It is important to identify general features of these movements, but it is no less important to specify ways in which each reform effort assumes distinctive features and moves in specific directions. I would argue that such distinctive features are best explained by noting the particular conditions present at the time of their unfolding. General social processes are shaped by distinctive historical circumstances (see Lipset and Rokkan 1967). More particularly, as Stinchcombe (1965) has argued, organizations founded at a particular point in time tend to share certain characteristics with other organizations established at the same time. These characteristics also tend to be quite stable over time. It is as if organizations in the same cohort are imprinted in some fashion by administrative images, technological imperatives, and environmental constraints prevalent at the time of their founding. It becomes especially important, then, to assess factors present at the time at which social movements give rise to new types of formal organizations.

This is not the place to attempt a detailed analysis of the specific contextual factors affecting the development of organized services for the aged. Rather, I will illustrate the general approach by calling attention to three of the most salient conditions that appear to have shaped the form and direction of current developments.

1. An anti-institutionalization sentiment has been gaining strength since the 1950s. At the time of their founding in the late nineteenth century, institutions designed for the care of many types of client groups differentiated at that time—including criminals, the mentally ill, and orphans—were believed to represent an important step forward in enlightened and humane treatment (Granville 1877, McKelvey 1936). In recent years, however, in most developed societies and for most client groups, prisons, mental hospitals, and orphanages are increasingly regarded as the source of more problems than they solve; a massive move toward deinstitutionalization is under way (see Scull 1977), which represents an important change in both ideology and practice: "Increasingly, this theme has been stressed as a major national policy objective. Concern has been expressed about the need to 'deinstitutionalize' the elderly, to develop 'alternatives to institutions,' and to expand community-based living and care facilities [Kamerman and Kahn 1976, p. 315]."

In the area of aging, the vast majority of persons are not currently institutionalized. Slightly less than 5% of the current population in the United States over age 65 is currently institutionalized; for those over 85, the figure is 18%. Hence, it would appear that the issue for planners in this area is not primarily one of how to dismantle an existing institutionalized system—as is the case in mental health services—but how to develop services for the aged that are based on a noninstitutional model.

A large variety of services to support the elderly in their own homes has been proposed, and some are now available in some communities. Such services include: escort services, homemaker/home-health aides, friendly visiting, portable meals, organized home medical and nursing services, home repair services, transportation services, and telephone lifelines (see Beattie 1976). But, as Kamerman and Kahn conclude: "Home-based help and care, with a full panoply of home health services, is not readily available under current social policy [1976, p. 381]."

2. *Current professional and organizational systems are not congruent with a decentralized model of services.* The relatively small proportion of services now available to clients in their own homes is not just due to the absence of adequate funding—although the lack of federal support for services of this type is a serious constraint. There is also professional and bureaucratic resistance to the development and staffing of truly decentralized service programs. Sussman's observations on these types of constraints facing new programs merit quotation at some length:

> The provision of alternatives to the institutionalization of services and people in complex societies is difficult because of its potential effects upon all societal systems, institutions, and organizations. For example, to move to a client-centered human service system requires radical changes in the current professional–client model regarding the dispensation of services, and this can contaminate the operation of all other formally organized structures. To meet the needs and demands of aged individuals and families for health and social services, for example, may require bringing such activities into the home or utilization of a decentralized organizational model with the provision of services at the client's call. Such proposed "business irregularities" from conventional practices immediately create linkage, relational, and communication problems; resistance from human service staffs; and if not reluctance, at least controlled ambivalence from governmental and community elites. . . .
>
> One logical substitute for the continued proliferation of impersonal institutions and large bureaucratic agencies is the channeling of some of the funds used for service provision directly to the families of the elderly who can provide more personalized general care at perhaps less cost. In some societies with family-centered traditions, this "reversal" of the bureaucratic mode is not overly traumatic. For highly professionalized provider systems, however, the impact is potentially devastating [1976, p. 236].

It would appear, then, that the movement to provide more services to the elderly is not going to result at this time in the creation of a new round of large-scale public hospitals or long-term care facilities. On the other hand, it does not appear that current professional and organizational arrangements will support the creation of truly decentralized, family-centered service programs. Within these constraints, a third set of forces may be seen as creating the new generation of service agencies.

3. The political environment has been of primary importance in shaping the institutions that have developed in recent years to serve the aged. This impact of the political environment can be illustrated by considering the development of two quite different organizational forms: the nursing home and the Area Agencies on Aging.

The development of nursing homes has been greatly influenced by two pieces of federal legislation (Moss and Halamandaris 1977). First, the Social Security Act of 1935, in reaction to the prevailing conditions in public poor houses at that time, barred the payment of Old Age Assistance funds to individuals housed in public institutions, thus encouraging the development of a private, for-profit system of nursing home care. Second, in 1965, the enactment of Medicaid, which provided financing for unlimited extended care to the elderly poor, brought vast amounts of public money into the field. As a consequence, between 1960 and 1976, the number of nursing homes increased from just under 10,000 to over 23,000, and the number of patients increased from just under 300,000 to over 1 million. Moss and Halamandaris note another effect of the sudden availability of funds from Medicaid: "Nursing homes changed from a family enterprise to big business. Major corporations, including several hotel/motel chains, purchased large numbers of facilities and nursing home issues became the hottest item on the stock exchange [1977, p. 6]." Mendelson and Hapgood emphasize the importance of the government's role in creating the nursing home industry: "The nursing home industry, although privately owned, is a government industry much like the Lockheed Aircraft Corporation. By 1971, two-thirds of the million people in nursing homes were supported by the government, and more than three-quarters of the $3.5 billion income of nursing homes was public money [1974, p. 96]."

Numerous analysts have concluded that the industry thus created is more interested in profit margins than in the provision of humane, quality care. This undesirable situation has been attributed to deficiencies in the incentive structures, which tie profits to reduced levels of service and to inadequacies in the state-administered regulatory systems, which appear to be often corrupt or ineffective or both (see Mendelson 1974, Mendelson and Hapgood 1974, Moss and Halanmandaris 1977).

It is clear that the rapid growth of nursing homes during the past decade is out of keeping with the current ideology opposing the institutionalization of dependent groups. Without denying that deplorable conditions may exist in some of these facilities, it is likely that the great amount of hostility and condemnation directed toward these organizations is partially due to the lack of congruence between this institutional type and the idealized models of service organizations prevailing at the time of their development.

Some analysts have begun to acknowledge that decentralized, community-based facilities cannot supplant the need for some institutions of the more conventional type (see Collins *et al.* 1967). As Kamerman and Kahn conclude: "To formulate the problem as 'deinstitutionalization' is to ignore the fact that aging is a degenerative and irreversible process, occurring over time, and that the need is not for 'no care' versus 'intensive' or 'extensive' care but rather for a continuum of care [1976, p. 380]." This note of realism also helps to make more explicable the continued operation of nursing homes that do not meet current standards of care. While corruption and indifference may be a part of the story, it is not the whole of it as even Moss and Halamandaris finally acknowledge:

> Many state health departments take a permissive attitude toward the nursing homes in their state. Vigorous enforcement of standards creates only problems for them. First and foremost is the problem of where to put the patients who would be dispossessed if homes were closed [1977, p. 159].

While the growth of nursing homes represents adherence to earlier institutional models, organizations such as the Area Agencies on Aging are part of the new generation of service institutions. Hence, we will examine this development at greater length.

A NEW MODE OF FEDERAL ACTION

The Area Agencies on Aging were established in 1973 by the Comprehensive Service Amendments to the Older Americans Act of 1965. The original 1965 act authorized funds to encourage individual states to designate a State Unit on Aging whose function was to plan, coordinate, and administer programs for the aged. The 1973 amendments created smaller units within each state to coordinate, encourage, and evaluate services within each of approximately 600 planning areas. The specific administrative location of each area agency was to be determined by individual state plans, but the function of the regional units was defined as to survey the needs in each area; conduct an inventory of resources; develop plans with and for existing agencies, both public and private; coordinate the delivery of existing services; and provide leadership in the development of new services. Federal funds were made available through this legislation only to support planning and some linking functions; support for actual services was to be secured from state or local governments, voluntary agencies, users, or other federal programs (see Special Committee on Aging 1973, Gold 1974).

As Binstock and Levin (1976) have argued, this approach to the problem of aging is consistent with a quite general model of federal action, which first appeared in the 1960s during the Kennedy and Johnson administrations. Lowi (1969) has analyzed these programs under the label of the "New Welfare" programs, and others have referred to them as the "Great Society" programs (e.g., Ginzberg and Solow 1974). Common elements in these programs that deal with a large variety of problem areas—for example, poverty, urban renewal, and health care—include:

1. "A distribution of funds to state and local entities with only the most general rules about what should be done with the distributed resources. . . . The substantive responsibilities of these implementing entities are usually described in the most general of terms: develop services and comprehensive plans; coordinate; undertake advocacy [Binstock and Levin 1976, p. 519]."
2. The distribution of funds not to existing organizations but to "newly designated or newly created implementation entities [Binstock and Levin 1976, p. 520]."
3. Federal requirements stipulation that provision must be made for substantial participation in policy decisions at the state and local levels by members of the client population in the service area.

Several astute analysts have proposed explanations to account for the emergence of one or another of the elements of this pattern. Thus, Binstock and Levin (1976, p. 519) suggest that Congress formulated general programs while avoiding the specific substantive issues of policy implementation in order to cope with the overload of demands for public initiatives. (I note, parenthetically, that at the time of this writing, the demand for new public programs seems to have substantially declined.) Piven and Cloward were among the first to point out an important feature of the new administrative model: "The hallmark of the Great Society programs was the direct relationship between the national government and the ghettoes, a relationship in which both state and local governments were undercut [1972, p. 261]." We observe that in the area agencies—

unlike the community action agencies, which constituted the first generation of the Great Society program—there is more involvement of existing state and local political units. However, a direct linkage between the federal government and local constituencies remains an important element of the model. Krause (1968) has suggested that this linkage is facilitated by the ideology of citizen participation, which helps to legitimate bureaucratic intervention that might otherwise be resisted. However, lest we conclude that it is always the central government that coopts the local interests, we should remember the occasions on which the locals have successfully "mau-maued" or radicalized the bureaucrats (see Moynihan 1970, Wolfe 1970). Indeed, Lowi (1969) is most concerned about this later process, viewed at a more general level. He has stressed the extent to which the new governmental arrangements, such as decentralized administration and citizen participation, legitimate the involvement of special interests in the policymaking process, and asserts that these better organized and more vocal interests drive out those of the general welfare. Finally, the creation of new entities to carry out these programs is consistent with more recent views of organizations, which stress limitations on the capacity of existing organizations to adapt to new circumstances or to accept new assignments (see Hannan and Freeman 1977). It is easier to create new organizations to carry out new functions than it is to modify or transform existing ones.

A NEW MODEL OF ORGANIZATION

While forms of organizations like nursing homes and area agencies are quite different in many ways, they may be viewed as similar in one respect: They are creatures of the institutional environment. The conception of a class of "institutionalized organizations" is currently being developed by Meyer and his colleagues. The model was originally developed to account for some of the special features of educational organizations (Meyer and Rowan 1977, Meyer et al. 1981). The argument, in brief, is as follows: In highly developed societies such as our own, a premium is placed on the rationalization of spheres of activity. In addition to the growth of science and technology, the elaboration of rules and procedures for conducting all manner of activities tends also to occur. Some of these rules are laid down by legal processes, through the actions of legislatures, and the judgments and interpretations of courts and administrative agencies; others are embodied in professional codes and practices. Organizations are likely to develop in both types of arenas:

in technical areas as well as in areas in which institutional rules have been elaborated. However, organizations relate to these two environments in different ways.

The conventional "technical" model of organizational structure argues that formal organizations arise to coordinate technical work flows that prepare outputs that are evaluated in a market. In order to secure stability of work process and to allow standardized procedures to be employed, the "technical core" of the organization is sealed off from the environment. Techniques such as coding, stockpiling, leveling, and rationing help to buffer the technical processes from external disturbances (see Thompson 1967).

By contrast, institutional organizations do not arise as structures to coordinate and regulate technical work processes but come into existence in conformity with and as a reflection of institutionalized rules and codes. Their survival is not based on effectiveness and efficiency of market transactions but rather on conformity with externally defined rules. The actual work performed in these organizations is not tightly regulated by the administrative system: Rather, it tends to be delegated to professionalized or certified workers and infrequently inspected or evaluated. When evaluations do occur, the emphasis is placed on conformity to rules, not on outcomes achieved. As we note in a recent paper: "Thus, the technical organization faces in toward its technical core and turns its back toward the environment; the institutional organization turns its back on its technical core in order to concentrate on conformity to its institutional environment [Meyer *et al.* 1981, p. 153]."

The model of an institutionalized organization appears to fit nursing homes quite well. These organizations survive not by concentrating their energies on the effective and efficient performance of their technical work but on conforming to the requirements of state licensure and regulatory agencies. They seem also to be in the enviable position of being able to collectively help to determine the standards by which they will be evaluated as well as the strictness with which these rules will be enforced (see Moss and Halamandaris 1977, pp. 147–161). Since such regulations are a crucial part of their environment, we should not be surprised at the eagerness with which the nursing home owners involve themselves in these decisions as well as in the political processes that determine the conditions of their existence. All organizations strive to gain control over crucial contingencies in their environments (see Pfeffer and Salancik 1978, pp. 100–101).

The Area Agencies on Aging may also be viewed as examples of institutionalized organizations. Their success is primarily dependent on their conformity with federal laws and regulations. since they are funded to develop a comprehensive service plan for these areas and evaluated on their conformity to this mission, we would expect more of their energies to go into the laying out of plans than into attempts to actually implement them. As Hudson argues, their orientation will be primarily up, toward the sources that fund them rather than down toward the actual delivery of the proposed services: "In the social system model [which Hudson favors as a guide to analysis] the area agencies become organizations established by superordinate actors on whose support they are totally dependent. This being the sole source of their support, they must conform to the demands which these actors make upon them [1974, p. 48]." The new agencies are created and funded in order to plan and coordinate the distribution of services to the aging at the local level. Congress passes on to these agencies a type of symbolic control: They represent our belief in the virtues of planning and the value of an integrated program of action. But the agencies are given no formal authority over the organizations whose services they are to coordinate and few funds to use as incentives to stimulate the cooperation of these existing organizations. To give the new agencies these powers would be highly unsettling for existing organizations, all of whom have their own agendas, constituencies, and funding sources. Congress appears to be aware of the limitations under which such agencies operate and, accordingly, makes adjustments in what they accept as evidence of "successful results." Binstock and Levin suggest the criteria of effectiveness that are employed: "Virtually all that is required is to report on the number of entities and programs that have been established, and the number of dollars that have been widely distributed among constituencies throughout the nation [1976, p. 520]."

I stated at the outset of this chapter that it is possible for rationalization processes to proceed at various levels and for developments at one level to be relatively independent of those at others. The work of the area agencies may exemplify this situation: Here we have an attempt to rationalize a field of action, to plan and coordinate all services to the aged in a specified geographical area, but their integration may occur primarily at the institutional level—at the level of rules and policies—rather than at the operational level. Area plans are produced and revised, but actual services may be unaffected. Indeed, services specified in plans may be nonexistent because of lack of funds, because of conflicts among local units that prevent implementation, or because no one knows how to supply the actual services in question.

In technical organizations, the development of a rational plan is a prelude to the reconstruction and reintegration of a pattern of production activities. In institutionalized organizations, the creation of a rational plan constitutes an alternative to changes in the actual provision of services. For in the latter case, the plans are more likely to be regarded as ends in themselves: as evidence that we are a humane and scientific people who have brought yet another problem area under rational control.

Whether the institutional model of organizations is useful and applicable to the analysis of some of the new organizational forms that have developed in recent years to provide services to the aged is a matter to be decided by future study. I have only suggested the possible utility of this model and illustrated some of its implications; we have precious little in the way of empirical evidence at this time. Even careful descriptive studies are rare. Students of organizations confront a rich and virtually untapped area of study as services to the aged rapidly assume an organizational character.

ACKNOWLEDGMENTS

My thinking about many of the issues addressed in this chapter has been informed and stimulated by numerous discussions with my colleague John W. Meyer. I am happy to acknowledge his contributions.

REFERENCES

Beattie, W. M., Jr. (1976) Aging and the social services. Pp. 619–642 in R. H. Binstock and E. Shanas, eds., *Handbook of Aging and the Social Sciences.* New York: Van Nostrand Reinhold.

Binstock, R. H., and Levin, M. A. (1976) The political dilemmas of intervention policies. Pp. 511–535 in R. H. Binstock and E. Shanas, eds., *Handbook of Aging and the Social Sciences.* New York: Van Nostrand Reinhold.

Boli-Bennett, J., and Meyer, J. W. (1978) Ideology of childhood and the state. *American Sociological Review* 43(December):797–812.

Boulding, K. E. (1966) The concept of need for health services. *Milbank Memorial Fund Quarterly* 44, part 2 (October):202–220.

Butler, R. N. (1975) *Why Survive? Being Old in America.* New York: Harper and Row.

Cain, L. D. (1974) Political factors in the emerging legal age status of the elderly. *Annals of the American Academy of Political and Social Science* 415(September):70–79.

Cain, L. D. (1976) Aging and the law. Pp. 342–368 in R. H. Binstock and E. Shanas, eds., *Handbook of Aging and the Social Sciences.* New York: Van Nostrand Reinhold.

Calhoun, R. (1978) *In Search of the New Old: Redefining Old Age in America: 1945–1970.* New York: Elsevier.

Collins, J. A., Stotsky, B. A., and Dominick, J. R. (1967) Is the nursing home the mental hospital's back ward in the community? *Journal of the American Geriatric Society* 15:75–81.

Ginzberg, E., and Solow, R. M., eds. (1974) The great society: Lessons for the future. *The Public Interest* 34(Winter).

Gold, B. (1974) The role of the federal government in the provision of social services to older persons. *Annals of the American Academy of Political and Social Science* 415:55–69.

Goode, W. J. (1957) Community within a community: The professions. *American Sociological Review* 22(April):194–200.

Granville, J. M. (1877) *The Care and Cure of the Insane.* London: Hardwicke and Bogue.

Hannan, M. T., and Freeman, J. (1977) The population ecology of organizations. *American Journal of Sociology* 82(March):929–964.

Hudson, R. B. (1974) Rational planning and organizational imperatives: Prospects for area planning in aging. *Annals of the American Academy of Political and Social Science* 415(September):41–54.

Kamerman, S. B., and Kahn, A. J. (1976) *Social Services in the United States: Policies and Programs.* Philadelphia: Temple University Press.

Krause, E. A. (1968) Functions of a bureaucratic ideology: "Citizen participation." *Social Problems* 16(Fall):129–143.

Lakoff, S. A. (1976) The future of social intervention. Pp. 643–663 in R. H. Binstock and E. Shanas, eds., *Handbook of Aging and the Social Sciences.* New York: Van Nostrand Reinhold.

Lipset, S. M., and Rokkan, S. (1967) Cleavage structure, party systems, and voter alignments: An introduction. Pp. 1–64 in S. M. Lipset and S. Rokkan, eds., *Party Systems and Voter Alignments.* New York: The Free Press.

Lowi, T. J. (1969) *The End of Liberalism.* New York: W. W. Norton.

McKelvey, B. (1936) *American Prisons: A Study in American Social History Prior to 1915.* Chicago: University of Chicago Press.

Mendelson, M. A. (1974) *Tender Loving Greed.* New York: Alfred Knopf.

Mendelson, M. A., and Hapgood, D. (1974) The political economy of nursing homes. *Annals of the American Academy of Political and Social Science*, 415(September):95–105.

Meyer, J. W., and Rowan, B. (1977) Institutionalized organizations: Formal structure as myth and ceremony. *American Journal of Sociology* 83(September):440–463.

Meyer, J. W., Scott, W. R., and Deal, T. E. (1980) Institutional and technical sources of organizational structure: Explaining the structure of educational organizations. Pp. 151–179 in H. D. Stein, ed., *Organization and the Human Services: Cross-Disciplinary Reflections.* Philadelphia, Pa.: Temple University Press.

Moen, E. (1978) The reluctance of the elderly to accept help. *Social Problems* 25(February):293–303.

Moss, F. E., and Halamandaris, V. J. (1977) *Too Old, Too Sick, Too Bad: Nursing Homes in America.* Germantown, Md.: Aspen Systems.

Moynihan, D. P. (1965) The professionalization of reform. *The Public Interest.* 1(Fall):6–16.

Moynihan, D. P. (1970) *Maximum Feasible Misunderstanding.* New York: The Free Press.

Pfeffer, J., and Salancik, G. R. (1978) *The External Control of Organizations: A Resource Dependence Perspective.* New York: Harper and Row.

Piven, F. F., and Cloward, R. A. (1972) *Regulating the Poor: The Functions of Public Welfare.* New York: Random House.

Pratt, H. J. (1974) Old age associations in national politics. *Annals of the American Academy of Political and Social Science* 415(September):106–119.

Riley, M. W., and Foner, A. (1968) *Aging and Society: Volume One: An Inventory of Research Findings.* New York: Russell Sage Foundation.

Riley, M. W., Riley, J. W., Jr., and Johnson, M. E., eds. (1969) *Aging and Society: Volume Two: Aging and the Professions.* New York: Russell Sage Foundation.

Scull, A. T. (1977) *Decarceration.* Englewood Cliffs, N.J.: Prentice-Hall.

Special Committee on Aging, U.S. Senate (1973) *Older Americans Comprehensive Services Amendments of 1973*. Washington, D.C.: Government Printing Office.

Stinchcombe, A. L. (1965) Social structure and organizations. Pp. 142–193 in J. G. March, ed., *Handbook of Organizations*. Chicago: Rand McNally.

Sussman, M. B. (1976) The family life of old people. Pp. 218–243 in R. H. Binstock and E. Shanas, eds., *Handbook of Aging and the Social Sciences*. New York: Van Nostrand Reinhold.

Thompson, J. D. (1967) *Organizations in Action*. New York: McGraw-Hill.

Weber, M. (1927) *General Economic History*. New York: Greenberg.

Wolfe, T. (1970) *Radical Chic & Mau-Mauing the Flak Catchers*. New York: Farrar, Straus and Giroux.

PART IV

SOCIAL AND
EMOTIONAL RESOURCES

chapter 13

Dilemmas of Social Support: Parallels between Victimization and Aging[1]

CHRISTINE DUNKEL-SCHETTER
CAMILLE B. WORTMAN

They don't know that I am here imprisoned in old age, trying to make contact with the world [Maclay 1977].

There is considerable research suggesting that close supportive relationships can play an important role in preserving mental and physical health. Though many questions about the impact of social support remain unresolved, we believe that this research may have powerful implications for the elderly. As social psychologists, we became interested in the topic of social support while studying how people cope with uncontrollable, aversive life events. Those who have experienced misfortune appear to benefit greatly from the support of family, friends, and professionals. Ironically, however, there is evidence to indicate that sufficient support is often not available. Research suggests that because people feel discomfort in the presence of suffering and distress, they are often unable to provide the help and attention that victims need. Thus, the very nature of victims' unfortunate circumstances prohibits others from extending the help and attention that are required.

This paradox was sufficiently intriguing that we examined it among

[1] Preparation of this chapter was supported by National Science Foundation Grant BNS 78-04743 to the second author.

AGING
Social Change

individuals suffering from a number of different problems including cancer and depression. In this chapter, we explore the possible relevance of our perspective to the elderly. First, our analysis concerning the social support needs and dilemmas of those victimized by life crises is described in some detail. In the second section of the chapter, we consider the applicability of this victimization perspective to the elderly by addressing several specific questions: In what ways might the elderly benefit from social support? What are their specific support needs? Do they receive adequate support? Or like victims of life crises, might the elderly elicit reactions in others that reduce the probability that support will be extended? In the concluding section of the chapter, we explore both research and policy implications of our analysis.

SOCIAL SUPPORT AND COPING WITH VICTIMIZATION

The Adaptiveness of Social Support

An examination of the available research on coping with serious life crises reveals a consistent relationship between the support people receive and their psychological adjustment. Individuals suffering from malignant disease (Bloom and Ross 1977, Carey 1974, Ferlic *et al.* 1979, Jamison *et al.* 1978, Sheldon *et al.* 1970, Vachon 1979, Weidman Gibbs and Achterberg-Lawlis 1978, Weisman 1976), physical disability (Kelman *et al.* 1966, Kemp and Vash 1971, Litman 1962), the death of a family member (Bornstein *et al.* 1973, Clayton *et al.* 1972, Gerber *et al.* 1975, Parkes 1975, Raphael 1977, Vachon 1979), rape (Burgess and Holmstrum 1978), job loss (Cobb and Kasl 1977) and other misfortunes (Davidson *et al.* 1979, Findlayson 1976) appear to adjust more successfully when social support is available to them than when it is not (and see review papers by Cobb 1976, Dean and Lin 1977, DiMatteo and Hays, in press, Heller 1979, House, in press, and Silver and Wortman 1980). Among those coping with stress, there also appears to be a positive relationship between social support and indices of physical health status (Cobb and Kasl 1977, deAraujo *et al.* 1973, Dudley *et al.* 1969, Gerger *et al.* 1975, Gore 1978, Holmes *et al.* 1961, Kimball 1969, Lynch *et al.* 1974, Maddison and Walker 1967, Nuckolls *et al.* 1972, Weisman and Worden 1975). For example, widows who do not receive support from others are more likely to experience symptoms of illness and to have poor health than those who do (Maddison and Walker 1967, Porritt 1979, Raphael 1977).

The mechanisms through which perceived support affects coping and health status have not yet been clearly delineated (see Cobb 1976, 1979, Kahn 1979, and Silver and Wortman 1980, for a more detailed discussion of this issue). Moreover, there are alternative explanations for the findings in many of the individual studies showing a relationship between perceived support and adjustment to life crises. Since most of these studies are correlational, for example, it is not clear whether support facilitates coping or whether one's coping or prognosis determines the amount of support available. However, it is noteworthy that social support has also been found to facilitate adjustment to crises in studies where participants have been assigned to a supportive treatment or a control condition (e.g., Bloom and Ross 1977, Raphael 1977). There is also evidence to suggest that the benefits of social support are not limited to those undergoing a particular life stressor (e.g., Brown et al. 1975, Hinkle 1974, Lynch 1977). For example, Berkman and Syme (1979) conducted a large-scale survey on a population that was very heterogeneous with respect to the types and levels of stressors experienced. They found that people who were lacking in social ties (i.e., marital status, close friends and relatives, participation in groups) were from 3 to 300 times more likely to die within several years of follow-up than those who had such ties. Taken together, the consistent findings regarding the benefits of social support are remarkable given the wide variety of disciplines, methodologies, and populations involved.

Converging evidence regarding the advantages of social support have aroused widespread interest in this construct and have fostered attempts to specify conceptually distinct components or types of support (e.g., Caplan 1974, Caplan 1979, Caplan and Killilea 1976, Cobb 1976, 1979, Heller 1979, House, in press, Kahn 1979, Pinneau 1975). Emotional support—the attempt to communicate positive regard (i.e., love, concern, or respect)—is one frequently mentioned type (Cobb 1976, 1979, House in press, Kahn 1979, Kahn and Antonucci, in this volume). Another is instrumental or tangible support; for example, material aid or help with tasks (Dean and Lin 1977, Caplan 1974, House in press, Kahn 1979, Kahn and Antonucci, in this volume).

A third type, appraisal support, involves providing information to others that they can use to evaluate themselves or their experiences. This includes expressing agreement with or acknowledgment of a person's beliefs or feelings (Caplan 1974, Caplan and Killilea 1976, Dunkel-Schetter and Wortman in press, House in press, Kahn 1979, Kahn and Antonucci, in this volume, Walker et al. 1977, Wortman and Dunkel-Schetter 1979). These components of support are not entirely independent of one another. A given behavior may provide two or more types of support simultaneously (see House in press); for example, gift-giving, which usually conveys affection (i.e., emotional support), can also be a way of helping meet material needs (i.e., instrumental support). Further theoretical and empirical work on the components of social support may highlight the process through which support influences physical and mental well-being.

Ventilation and Validation: Types of Support Especially Valuable for Those Victimized by Life Crises

In our previous work with victims, we became especially interested in emotional and appraisal support. A careful examination of prior research, clinical experience, and our ongoing research with cancer patients, spinal cord injured persons, and rape victims have helped us to identify two specific support needs often experienced by these populations. These are the need to express one's feelings (*ventilation*) and the need to know that one's feelings are normal given the circumstances (*validation*). Actions that encourage ventilation are a specific kind of emotional support, while those providing validation are a form of appraisal support.

In previous papers, we have argued that people who are confronted with undesirable life events usually experience considerable uncertainty and anxiety. Such events may challenge one's assumptions about the world and create feelings of fear and confusion. Many victims of life crises experience an intense need to clarify what is happening and to receive support. For these reasons, they may wish to talk with others about their feelings (Coates *et al.* 1979, Dunkel-Schetter and Wortman in press, Silver and Wortman 1980, Wortman and Dunkel-Schetter 1979). Verbalizing personal concerns during a time of stress can help people to clarify their feelings, to manage them more effectively, and to begin active problem-solving. A person's need to ventilate can best be met by supportive others who encourage open communication and who listen attentively to expressions of feelings, especially negative ones, without judging the person or feeling compelled to provide a solution. Silver and Wortman (1980) review considerable evidence that people appreciate and benefit from the opportunity to express their feelings and that lack of such opportunities can intensify their distress.

The second support need that we have emphasized is validation (Coates and Wortman 1980, Dunkel-Schetter and Wortman in press, Silver and Wortman 1980, Wortman and Dunkel-Schetter 1979). It is common, we have argued, for those who suffer from undesirable life events to worry that their uncertainty, confusion, and anxiety are abnormal. The intensity of these feelings leads many victims to believe that they are coping poorly or are losing their sanity. Learning that their reactions are prevalent among others in similar situations can reduce some of this secondary anxiety. Such knowledge can be gained by acquiring relevant information about others' reactions and then comparing one's own responses to theirs (see Festinger 1954, Schachter 1959). For example, a cancer patient can learn that it is normal to become angry or depressed following diagnosis or to be plagued by fears of recurrence.

In principle, comparison information is available from educational materials (e.g., pamphlets, films), from media accounts and books about others, from professionals who work closely with the specific populations, and from direct contact with others who have had similar experiences. We believe that the last of these—interactions with similar others—is particularly effective in obtaining validation and is beneficial for other reasons as well. Interacting with peers provides a chance to gain direct and vivid comparison information. It also offers excellent opportunities to ventilate and may allow for exchange of valuable practical information and useful suggestions about methods of coping.

The Adequacy of Social Support Available to Those Victimized by Life Crises

While we have argued that the need for ventilation and validation are particularly acute for many victims of undesirable life events, there is also evidence that opportunities to fulfill these needs are frequently unavailable. In a study of cancer patients undergoing radiation therapy, for example, less than half of the sample could identify a person with whom they could discuss emotional difficulties. Moreover, 86% of the respondents indicated that they wished they were able "to discuss the situation more fully" with someone (Mitchell and Glicksman 1977). Similarly, in several studies on bereavement reactions, respondents have reported that they are encouraged to be "strong" and to avoid open expression of their grief (see, e.g., Glick et al. 1974, Helmrath and Steinitz 1978, Schwab et al. 1975). In each of these investigations, respondents reported that such advice from others was not helpful. Those who allowed or encouraged the expression of their feelings were more likely to be regarded as supportive (see also Schoenberg et al. 1975).

The Victimization Perspective: Reactions to Victims and Their Impact

If victims desire support from others and profit when it is forthcoming, why are these needs so infrequently met? In past papers, we have devoted considerable attention to analyzing the interpersonal difficulties that often seem to accompany a victimized status (Coates *et al.* 1979, Coates and Wortman 1980, Dunkel-Schetter and Wortman, in press, Silver and Wortman 1980, Wortman and Dunkel-Schetter 1979). We have argued that while others are usually motivated to help, the victim's plight is a powerful stimulus in its ability to arouse negative feelings in others. One reason why victims may elicit such feelings is that they unwittingly make others feel vulnerable to a similar fate. Second, victims may arouse feelings of helplessness and inadequacy if there is little that one can say or do to alleviate the victim's problems. In short, interactions with people who are suffering are distressing because they may force us to think about things we would rather not contemplate and confront us with problems that we are unable to solve.

In addition, there is evidence that many people hold erroneous assumptions about how victims should respond to the crisis and how they should be treated to facilitate good coping. These assumptions may interfere with the provision of effective support. Past work has indicated that people feel victims should not discuss their negative feelings, and that they should attempt to be optimistic and cheerful (Dunkel-Schetter and Wortman in press, Silver and Wortman 1980, Wortman and Dunkel-Schetter 1979). In reviewing research on widows, for example, Walker, MacBride, and Vachon (1977) concluded that "even intimates do not support the need to mourn the loss beyond the first few days after the death [p. 38]." Similarly, Helmrath and Steinitz (1978) report that although mothers who have lost an infant experience a strong desire to talk about the child, "friends and family steadfastly avoided mentioning the infant or the death [pp. 787–788]." Conversely, victims who do ventilate their negative feelings may be seen as coping poorly. In one study, rape victims who indicated, 6 months after the assault, that they were having some difficulty in getting over the incident were judged as less attractive and more maladjusted than rape victims who did not indicate difficulties (Coates *et al.* 1979).

As a result of prevailing assumptions and negative feelings, people often behave toward victims in a variety of ways that are detrimental to them. Some of these actions are meant to help, while others may be unintentional or unthinking. People frequently avoid victims and may discourage or even prevent open communication. In addition, they typically attempt to be cheerful while concealing their negative feelings. This can result in negative nonverbal behavior and other signs of insincerity that confuse victims and, over time, can undermine their self-esteem.

In examining the needs of victims and the reactions of others to them,

deserve special attention because they may be the most likely to be isolated. As we have mentioned, work with victims suggests that those who are suffering are frequently avoided by others (see Dunkel-Schetter and Wortman in press, Wortman and Dunkel-Schetter 1979). If this holds true for the victimized elderly, they would be a group especially in need of social support services.

Third, although the majority of older people appear to have some intact relationships, changes in one's social support network over time may take their toll (see Bengtson 1973, Kahn 1979). A reality of aging is that as one grows older, there is a high likelihood of being widowed, particularly for women. The elderly must also contend with the gradual diminishing of their former peer group (Butler and Lewis 1977). Rosow (1970) calls this phenomenon a "contracting social world." Consistent with the point, Bultena (1968) found that older retirees had less inter- action with age peers than did younger retirees. He notes that the in- creased likelihood of death of one's spouse and friends can sever the individual from an important source of contact within his or her age group. The loss of relatives and lifelong friends necessarily creates in- stability or gaps in the social network of an older person. Although it may be possible to fill these gaps with other relationships, these shifts in patterns of support may cause stress, while simultaneously reducing the resources the individual has to manage it. Thus, substantial changes in the nature of one's network over time may not be reflected in measures of the sheer number of relationships or frequency of interaction.

Finally, intact social relationships and frequent interaction with others do not ensure that support needs are being met effectively. It is con- ceivable that some social relationships can contribute to rather than solve one's problems (see Caplan 1979, Heller 1979, House in press). For example, some spouses or children are habitual recipients, not sources, of support; they are a burden in both their demands for help and in their failure to reciprocate. Therefore, it is extremely important to examine the content of interactions or the quality of support received by the elderly (see Conner et al. 1979, Henkin 1979, Longino and Lippman 1979, Troll 1971, who also make this point). A recent study by Connor et al. (1979) underscores this problem. In this study, 22 quantitative aspects of social interaction (e.g., frequency of interaction, number of social relationships) were measured among 218 noninstitutionalized re- spondents over 70 years of age, but only four variables were significantly associated with life satisfaction. Moreover, these four measures ac- counted for only a small portion of the variance (3%). The authors conclude that quantity of interaction is not crucial to understanding adaptation to old age and they add: "It is in the quality of interactional experience that a broader understanding of adjustment to the process of aging will ultimately be found [p. 121]."

The few studies that have probed the quality of support available to the elderly raise some doubts about whether they receive the socio-emotional support they need. In one study (Lopata 1978), over 1000 Chicago widows were interviewed about the extent to which families and friends provided 52 types of support organized into four categories (financial, service, social, emotional). With the exception of children, Lopata found that family members provided little support of any kind to respondents. In fact, less than 12% could indicate any relative who would supply each of 13 specific types of emotional support. Although some family members reportedly spent time with their elderly relatives, Lopata states that this "does not translate into real emotional supports. Such relatives are particularly ineffective as comforters, confidants, or suppliers of the self-feelings of usefulness, independence or self-sufficiency [p. 361]."

Two other investigations also raise doubts about the adequacy of support available to the elderly, despite their conclusions to the contrary (Babchuk 1978–1979, Seelbach and Hansen 1980). Seelbach and Hansen (1980) examined satisfaction with family relations among institutionalized and community-dwelling elderly persons. Although they conclude that the elderly are generally satisfied with their families, sizable minorities indicated support problems. For instance, 32% of the respondents wished their families would pay more attention to them, 16% felt their families did not care, and 15% indicated their families tried to boss them. Furthermore, these results may be biased in a favorable direction because of the probable tendency toward socially desirable responses, which the authors point out.

Using a different approach to studying social support from that of Lopata (1978) or Seelbach and Hansen (1980), Babchuk (1978–1979) asked middle-aged and elderly persons to identify relatives and friends with whom they felt very close and then to determine which of these were confidants. The overall pattern of results suggests that few were without close ties of any kind. However, on closer examination, 15% of the sample had no relatives in whom they could confide, and 37% had no friends who were confidants. Many questions are left unanswered by this investigation; for example, how many respondents had neither a relative nor a friend in whom to confide? How many felt a need for more confidants? Is having a confidant a good indication of the receipt of emotional support? Is it better to confide in someone who is unsupportive or who responds negatively than not to confide in anyone at all?

These questions are only a few of those not yet answered by the research on the quality of support available to the elderly.

Reactions to the Elderly That May Interfere with the Provision of Effective Social Support

We suspect that for many reasons, the elderly, like victims, are unlikely to receive as much effective or high-quality support as they need. Some of these reasons are inherent aspects of the elderly person's situation (e.g., the death of friends, discussed above, or impaired hearing or speech); others involve the specific feelings people have toward the elderly and the ways in which they are likely to behave toward them. As previously discussed, a complete understanding of support requires analyzing both the perspective of the elderly individual and that of others in the social environment. Up to this point, we have considered support only from the perspective of the elderly. In the following section, the viewpoint of others toward the elderly will be examined in light of what is known about peoples' reactions to victims of life crises.

As we have discussed, there is a strong and consistent body of research in the field of social psychology suggesting that people often hold negative feelings about those who are suffering, unhappy, or in need of help. Although most of us would agree that the elderly should be treated with compassion and respect, actual encounters with suffering elderly people may be very threatening and upsetting to us, especially if they have serious problems. Like other victimized populations, the elderly may generate negative affect because they threaten our assumptions about the world, shatter our illusions of invulnerability, and engender strong feelings of helplessness. These possibilities are explored further.

Feelings Possibly Elicited by the Elderly

Vulnerability.   One consequence of being confronted with individuals who are suffering, disadvantaged, or treated unfairly is that it can make us feel vulnerable to a similar fate. Such encounters can threaten our perception of our ability to influence and control our future and our assumptions about the world in general. The theorist who has provided the most cogent discussion of this issue is Lerner (1975, Lerner *et al.* 1976), who has argued that we are motivated to believe that the world is a just place in which people are rewarded for their efforts. (See also Walster 1966, for a similar theoretical statement and Wortman 1976, for a comparative analysis of these theoretical perspectives.) The belief in a just world begins with early socialization. People implicitly agree to give up certain immediate gratifications, to work, and to invest their efforts in return for greater fulfillment in the future. Lerner (1975) has maintained that people want to believe that such sacrifices will pay off: "If the person becomes aware that someone else—who lives in and is 'vulnerable' to the same environment—has received undeserved suffering or failed to get what he deserved, the issue must arise as to whether the person himself can trust his environment [p. 8]."

Considering the need to believe in a just world, it is not hard to understand why encounters with the elderly may sometimes be threatening. People believe that this is a time of life when rewards for one's earlier sacrifices should be realized. Encounters with an elderly person whose existence is characterized by loneliness, disability, or inadequate financial resources can make us feel apprehensive about our own future and doubtful about whether our sacrifices and efforts will be rewarded.

Both Lerner and Walster have pointed out a number of ways in which people can reduce the distress that exposure to suffering can cause. People may look for weaknesses in the victim's behavior to explain the incident or outcome. For example, if we learn that an acquaintance has been hurt in an automobile accident, we may sift through the available information in search of some shortcomings on her part. Was she driving too fast? Under bad conditions? In an unsafe car? Under the influence of alcohol? Alternatively, we may attempt to identify weaknesses in the victim's character that would help account for her fate. Lerner and his colleagues have conducted a number of laboratory experiments that provide support for these theories (e.g., Lerner and Matthews 1967).

The implications of the above for attitudes toward the elderly are straightforward (see Perloff 1980). Following the logic of Lerner and Walster, we may often derogate or blame the elderly for their fate. For example, we may attempt to cope with the abject financial condition of an elderly person by attributing it to past laziness, poor planning, or other personal characteristics. Similarly, we may conclude that an elderly person deserves to be lonely because he or she is self-centered, cantankerous, and difficult. By convincing ourselves that we are different, we can feel protected from these predicaments.

Suffering that is specific to the aging process (e.g., the physical changes and growing limitations that occur) may be especially likely to arouse feelings of vulnerability. Interactions with elderly individuals who maintain a good physical appearance and much of their vigor may not be especially troubling. In contrast, a confrontation with a frail elderly person who has trembling hands, wrinkled skin, a stooped back, and failing eyesight or hearing may be very threatening. This makes it difficult to deny that the deterioration and physical decline that accompany aging will happen to us. Because the elderly are like a mirror of our future, they force us to face the potentially fearsome prospects of our own aging and death. For this reason, we believe that many people may find contact with the elderly to be aversive and upsetting.

Helplessness. We believe that the elderly may also be very likely to produce feelings of helplessness among many of the people with whom they interact. There is clearly nothing that can be done to alter the progressive physical deterioration or prevent the death of an elderly person. Moreover, there are often no actions that can be taken to alleviate many of the problems that are typically encountered, including the loss of a spouse, the inability to find meaningful work, or inadequate financial resources. Finally, it is possible to become overwhelmed by the sheer number of problems facing many elderly people. How does one respond to an elderly man, for example, who is depressed by the recent death of his wife or who is unable to find work because he is immobilized by pain from arthritis? Or an elderly divorced woman who is extremely lonely, who is unable to care for herself because her eyesight is failing, and whose resources are not adequate to cope with rising housing and food costs?

There is evidence from the literature that people feel more positive about helping others when they believe that such help leads to concrete improvements in the target person's situation. Conversely, efforts to help that result in no noticeable change are likely to be frustrating and upsetting (see Brickman *et al.* in press for a review). This is most convincingly documented in research on "burnout," a series of attitudinal changes that occur among helping professionals as a result of job stress (see, for example, Cherniss *et al.* 1976, Doherty 1971, Edelwich and Brodsky 1980, Maslach 1976 and 1978, Pines and Aronson 1980, Pines and Maslach 1978, Segel 1970, Wasserman 1971, and see Wills 1978 for a review). Maslach (1976, 1978) has suggested that it occurs because providers feel overwhelmed by the magnitude and complexity of their clients' problems. Over time, burnout can lead to withdrawal either physically (e.g., quitting or avoiding difficult clients) or psychologically (e.g., treating clients in detached or dehumanized ways, or even derogating or blaming them for their problems). Interactions with the elderly and exposure to their difficulties may result in feelings of helplessness and inadequacy among service providers and others similar to burnout (see Hughes *et al.* 1979 for empirical results on negative attitudes toward patients of nursing home personnel of varying tenures).

In summary, contacts with the elderly may generate considerable negative affect for people. In light of this, how do they behave when they encounter an elderly person who is having difficulties? In general, people's feelings of distress may lead them to minimize the frequency of interaction with the elderly and may markedly alter the nature of those interactions that do occur. Thus, the elderly may find that as their health declines and their problems increase, their social relationships become more and more strained. In discussing the interpersonal dynamics of cancer, we have proposed that feelings of discomfort are often displayed in a pattern of negative behavioral reactions. These may include avoidance, reluctance to have open discussions about the suffering person's situation, and verbal as well as nonverbal signs of rejection (Wortman and Dunkel-Schetter 1979). Each of these behaviors will be considered.

Resultant Behaviors

Avoidance. There is considerable evidence that nurses and doctors avoid patients who are dying or who are seriously ill (see Schulz 1978 for a review). When the elderly are institutionalized, hospitalized, or dying, there is good reason to suspect that they are also avoided by staff and family. As we have discussed, interacting with a suffering person forces people to confront their own negative feelings about the situation; indeed it may heighten these feelings since the person's suffering and deterioration are usually more evident in face-to-face interaction. Often the easiest solution is to minimize contact.

To our knowledge, little research has been done on actual behavioral avoidance of the elderly. A few studies on attitudes toward them suggests that the elderly may be avoided by health care professionals (e.g., Campbell 1971, Troll and Schlossberg 1970) and younger people (e.g., Kidwell and Booth 1977, Kogan and Shelton 1962). Anecdotal reports also indicate that avoidance is common among therapists (Kastenbaum 1963, LeShan and LeShan 1961). Although attitudinal findings may suggest behavioral tendencies, it is important to distinguish negative perceptions of the aged from avoidance of them. People may not report negative attitudes toward the elderly as a group yet avoid actual encounters with specific older people. Thus, attitudinal findings taken alone may be misleading. Future research on this topic might combine attitudinal and behavioral measures in order to get a broader picture of reactions to the elderly.

Preventing Open Communication. When interactions occur between suffering individuals and those in their social environment, many empirical studies suggest that open communication is avoided (Jamison *et al.* 1978, Sanders and Kardinal 1977, Vachon *et al.* 1977). In most of these studies, it is unclear whether this reluctance to discuss the person's problems was initiated by the victim or by others. However, the available evidence suggests that it is common for family members, friends, and medical staff to discourage open communication with the seriously ill or dying and that patients see this as a problem (see Bard 1952, Gordon *et al.* 1977, Kastenbaum and Aisenberg 1972, Mitchell and Glicksman 1977, Pearlman *et al.* 1969). For example, Kastenbaum and Aisenberg (1972) asked nurses and orderlies how they responded when elderly geriatric patients attempted to discuss their feelings about death. Approximately 80% of the time, nurses and orderlies reported that they avoided the subject, denied the implications of the patient's remark, or ended the discussion. A comment like "I think I'm going to die soon," for example, was often met with replies such as "That's silly, you'll probably live to be 100."

There is also research that family, friends, and medical personnel try to influence distressed individuals to conceal negative feelings (see Binger *et al.* 1969, Dyk and Sutherland 1956, Glaser and Strauss 1965, Klein 1971, Maddison and Walker 1967, Quint 1965). For example, Glick *et al.* (1974) have reported data suggesting that widows perceive others to be very intolerant of their expressions of grief. Respondents reported that they were continually admonished to focus on the positive, on all they had to live for, and to avoid displays of sadness. Moreover, the widows indicated that such statements from others were not helpful in coming to terms with their loss.

The avoidance of open communication with other distressed populations raises a number of intriguing questions about the elderly. How do others react when older people describe their problems, talk about their past, or attempt to give others advice? Do others exert pressure on the elderly to keep their feelings and opinions to themselves? Lack of open communication may result from false assumptions by others (e.g., assumptions that the older people do not want or need to talk [see Garfinkel 1975], or that they have speech and hearing problems [see Bettinghaus and Bettinghaus 1976, Oyer and Oyer 1976, Oyer *et al.* 1976]). However, avoidance of open communication may also result from lack of interest. Butler and Lewis (1977) have stated that "one of the greatest difficulties for younger persons . . . (including mental health personnel) is to listen thoughtfully to the reminiscence of older people [p. 50]." They go on to say that we believe reminiscence represents living in the past and self-centeredness, that it is "boring, meaningless, and time consuming." If these statements are well founded, it seems probable that the elderly do encounter barriers to open communication that interfere with meeting important social needs.

Negative Nonverbal Behavior. Although others may often attempt to cope with their own distress by avoiding contact with the elderly or their problems, this is not always possible. Many people have some obligation to visit the elderly, see them on a regular basis, and therefore must show some attentiveness to their problems. Among family members, in fact, obligation may be a primary motive for interacting with an elderly relative (cf. Adams 1967, Arling 1976) and it is an obvious factor for service providers. In all likelihood, these individuals may try to hide negative feelings and be as supportive as possible when in the presence of the older person. However, any negative affect experienced during the interaction is likely to be communicated to the elderly person in subtle and insidious ways.

One way in which negative feelings may be communicated is through discrepancies between the person's verbal and nonverbal behaviors. A family member or health care professional may be verbally reassuring but simultaneously show nonverbal signs of distress. Although nonverbal behaviors between the elderly and others have not been carefully studied, research on interactions between able-bodied and handicapped individuals suggests that such discrepancies often occur (see, e.g., Farina *et al.* 1966, Kleck 1968, Kleck *et al.* 1968, Kleck *et al.* 1966). This is another potentially fruitful area of study for enhancing our understanding of social interactions between the elderly and others (see Dunkel-Schetter and Wortman in press, Wortman and Dunkel-Schetter 1979).

Impact of Others' Reactions on the Elderly

The model we have proposed in this chapter suggests that the support needs of the elderly may be met with reactions from others that only magnify their feelings of anxiety, confusion, and isolation. If this reasoning is carried to its logical conclusion, the implications are both paradoxical and distressing. One unfortunate aspect of social encounters between the elderly and others is that the topics that are most beneficial for an elderly person to discuss may be the very topics most likely to threaten and upset others. For example, the elderly may be especially interested in focusing on past conflicts or present distresses in order to view them from a meaningful perspective and resolve them. However, listening to accounts of these problems may heighten others' feelings of vulnerability and helplessness.

A second, equally problematic aspect of the portrait we have been painting is that the more unfortunate an elderly person's situation is, the more negatively others are likely to feel and behave. Most people would probably not find it particularly upsetting to interact with an elderly person who has few serious problems and who is in relatively good health. In fact, such conversations can make one feel optimistic about the later stages of life. In contrast, it may be threatening and upsetting to interact with an elderly person who has many problems and who is coping unsuccessfully with them. As both Lerner and Walster have suggested, the more serious another's problems are, the more threatened we feel and the more likely we are to derogate or blame them. Thus, the elderly who most need support from others may be the least likely to get it, and at the times when they especially need it, they may be particularly likely to alienate others. Some implications of the ideas previously presented for future research and policy on the elderly are explored in the following section.

IMPLICATIONS

Since social support has been demonstrated to be an important mediating variable of physical and mental health across life stages and circumstances, it is incumbent upon us to enhance the opportunities for support available to the elderly of the future. Pursuant to this, research strategies and interventions that may be derived from the foregoing analysis are now discussed.

Research Implications

The gerontological research on social support has some notable gaps. As emphasized earlier, past research has rarely examined the content of the interactions taking place between the elderly and others. When interactions have been studied, the methodologies were usually descriptive and nonempirical (e.g.,Hochschild 1978). In our judgment, rigorous, empirical studies on the actual exchanges between the elderly and others are needed.

In this chapter, we have argued that the elderly may be most likely to receive effective social support from similarly aged peers. We maintained that such peers may be more likely to permit and encourage ventilation and validation of the elderly person's experiences. These ideas could be examined empirically by a systematic study of the interactions between the elderly and various others (e.g., children, siblings, spouse, age peer acquaintances, age peer friends, etc.). How do such interactions differ? Is an elderly person more likely to bring up problems with one type of target person than another? What types of social support are most likely to be offered by particular target individuals? How do the various target persons respond when problems are brought up? To what extent do the elderly and particular targets agree that the interaction went well or that particular behaviors were helpful? In order to conduct this type of research, it would be necessary to conceptualize and quantify many dimensions of the interaction (e.g., types of social support offered, nonverbal signs of rejection). It would also be important to examine the feelings and attitudes of both participants after the interaction had terminated.

These hypotheses could be studied both by monitoring naturally oc-curring conversations (e.g., those that occur between the institutional-ized elderly and their visitors), or by arranging conversations between the elderly and others in which certain factors are manipulated experi-mentally (see, e.g., Coates *et al.* 1979, Coyne 1976, Perloff 1980, Schulz 1976). For example, one could experimentally vary the number, type, or severity of problems discussed by elderly stimulus persons, or their ability to cope with these problems, and examine the feelings and be-haviors of those with whom they interact. Such a design should make it possible to determine whether elderly persons who have many prob-lems, or who are coping poorly, are especially likely to elicit negative feelings in others. In order to determine whether elderly people profit from opportunities to ventilate their feelings, one could experimentally vary the listener's response to the elderly. For example, some listeners could be instructed to permit ventilation, while others could be instructed to try to offer solutions for the elderly person's problems. The elderly person's reaction to the conversation and subsequent feelings could then be behavior assessed.

The reason why we have advocated interactions between the elderly and similarly aged peers is because, generally speaking, such peers are more likely to have similar problems and concerns than other targets. Interactions with such peers not only provide an opportunity for ven-tilation about these problems, but also enable the person to receive validation information. During such an interaction, an elderly person can compare his or her behavioral reactions to those of the peer and judge the appropriateness of these reactions. An elderly widow, for example, can learn that it is normal to have hallucinations about her dead spouse.

The argument we have advanced in this chapter about the benefits of receiving validation information raises a number of issues that could be studied empirically. Similarly aged peers are clearly not a homoge-neous group. While some peers are likely to have similar problems (e.g., financial concerns or having lost a spouse), others are not. Some will be doing better or worse, physically or psychologically, than the elderly person. What is the psychological impact of interacting with a similarly aged peer who has many more problems, and/or who is coping poorly with these problems? Under what conditions is an elderly person likely to feel fortunate in comparison with the other, and under what conditions is he or she likely to feel threatened and vulnerable to the other's fate?

It follows from our analysis that an elderly person with a particular problem should be most likely to receive effective support from a similarly aged peer with similar problems. For example, an elderly widow should be especially likely to benefit from interactions with other elderly widows. But persons with highly similar problems may not always be available. Will an elderly widow receive more effective support from a similarly aged peer who has not lost her husband, or from a younger friend or family member? Is the elderly peer more likely to be emphatic and supportive, since a similar fate may happen to her? Or is the elderly peer more likely to feel vulnerable and threatened, and therefore derogate or blame the widow for her problems? Clearly, these issues are in need of more empirical research.

Policy and Intervention Implications

On the basis of our analysis of the parallels between victimization and aging, we would propose two general types of interventions that may be support-enhancing. First, treatment programs with the objective of improving communication can be designed to alleviate problems that often occur between the elderly and their families. Second, interventions can aim to encourage meaningful interactions among elderly peers.

Since the families of older people seem to be an important source of support, it might be advisable to target some interventions at improving the effectiveness of the support that they are able to offer. We believe that families of older people are very susceptible to feelings of helplessness and vulnerability and are likely to prevent open communication, partly due to lack of understanding of the elderly person's need to talk. When an elderly family member is suffering, families are likely to experience stress (see Egerman 1966), intense negative feelings, and the desire to avoid the person. They may also exhibit negative nonverbal signals that convey rejection to the elderly person. In light of this, interventions are probably often needed by families of older people.

Hausman has recently developed a program for troubled adult children of the aged and has emphasized that communication is one of the primary concerns they mention: "Communication—with parents, other relatives, parents' doctors, nursing home personnel—was another major problem. The need to communicate without complaining, to be assertive, to state needs without accusations, was expressed at nearly every session [1979, p. 105]." Therapeutic interventions that improve communication within the family and that diffuse negative feelings may have important benefits. They can help relatives learn about some of the usual concerns and problems associated with aging. For example, family members may learn that the tendency to review one's life is very common and probably therapeutic among the elderly. The knowledge that merely listening is helpful and that they need not offer a solution may partially alleviate feelings of helplessness. Family members can also learn from discussions with other families that the negative feelings they are experiencing are frequently felt by others who are in similar situations. By providing families with a setting in which to ventilate and validate their feelings and to learn about aging, family interventions can increase the chances that the elderly will receive satisfying emotional support. Thus, it is our contention that making the families of the elderly aware of the complicated social environment in which they exist can improve the quality of support extended to the elderly.

Rosow (1967) has suggested that the best opportunities for socially integrating the elderly are with age peers. Similarly, we previously asserted that contact with others who are facing similar experiences and problems may be helpful to the elderly. We suspect that because elderly persons share common experiences, they are much more capable of meeting one another's support needs than are family or younger friends. A first step in providing peer support is to increase the likelihood that elderly people will meet and get to know others of their own age. To this end, it might be worthwhile to consider various living arrangements that offer proximity to other older people (e.g., communal households, retirement communities, public housing for senior citizens). Another setting in which elderly people congregate are local community centers or senior centers. Contrary to some opinions that the elderly should not be segregated in this way, there may be some important psychological advantages to age-segregated housing and recreational facilities because they provide primary access to age peers.

However, just as quantity of social support need not imply quality, proximity to age peers does not imply meaningful exchanges. Troll, in a paper on kin relationships late in life, agrees: "Residential proximity does not guarantee interaction. Presumably people who live near each other see each other frequently, but they may not be in any kind of intimate or meaningful contact [1971, p. 278]." It is therefore important to determine how different age-segregated environments vary in the extent to which they foster or inhibit interaction and communication among the elderly. Moreover, it is important to develop interventions that aim to facilitate the formation of friendships and communication among older people.

One promising intervention is the peer support group. These groups have multiplied rapidly across the country in recent years and now exist for cancer patients, diabetics, widowed persons, single parents, bereaved parents, and rape victims (for an overview, see Lieberman and Borman 1979, and Levy 1976). They are usually founded on the principle that open and honest communication among people with similar previous experiences (or similar present circumstances) is valuable and therapeutic.

There are a number of outcomes of peer support that could be helpful to the elderly. Foremost among them are the valuable opportunities for ventilation and validation, previously discussed. Similar others are generally more interested in hearing one's concerns, can more easily empathize or share one's perspective, and can provide feedback from firsthand experience that one's concerns are also prevalent in others. Since such groups include a number of individuals with particular problems or concerns, it is usually possible to obtain comparison information that is personally relevant. For example, a widow who cannot sleep or who is afraid to go out at night may compare herself with other widows experiencing these problems. In addition to sharing one's feelings and learning that they are shared by others, peer support groups can provide a source of advice regarding how to cope with common problems (e.g., arthritis, social security benefits, or conflict with one's children). Finally, access to age peers may allow the elderly person to feel less dependent on family members for support, thereby reducing the strain placed on the family.

One example of a peer counseling program for older people has been in operation at the Continuum Center at Oakland University in Michigan (Waters *et al.* 1976). In this program, older people learn communication skills and have small group discussions led by peer paraprofessionals. Informal and formal evaluations conducted on the program suggest that it increases confidence, warmth, and positive feelings among the elderly who participate. Learning to communicate positive and negative feelings enables them to be more direct with their families, to hold fewer resentments, and to improve their interpersonal relationships. In addition to the evident positive effects for participants in the program, peer leaders appear to benefit greatly from their training and involvement.

A similar type of intervention for the institutionalized aged is described in a publication entitled *Old Is Part of the Whole* by Miller *et al.* This program involves a group experience with structured activities that focus discussion and interaction on the participants' feelings about themselves, their lives, and their current condition. One of the authors describes the inferred positive effects of this program: "I have seen many group participants . . . become more positive about themselves and more tolerant of others. . . . I have seen them share losses and comfort each other. In the group, I have watched them mull over out loud what consequences the changes in their lives have brought about, explore a variety of alternatives, describe to each other what works and what no longer works for them, and make choices [1978, p. 3]." Although peer interaction programs like these must be empirically tested to ensure their beneficial effects, we believe that they provide unique opportunities for meeting social support needs.

CONCLUSIONS

In this chapter, several parallels have been examined between the experiences of victims of undesirable life events and those of the elderly. This process yielded several major themes: (1) The elderly can be seen as "victimized" in many different ways; (2) social support is beneficial to the elderly as it is to victims, although more research is needed; (3) the elderly may need more opportunities both to express their feelings (ventilation) and to receive feedback that they are normal given the circumstances (validation); (4) significant segments of the elderly population may experience deficiencies in the quality of support available to them at times when they especially need it; (5) the causes of ineffective support may include feelings of helplessness and vulnerability among others and resultant tendencies to avoid the elderly, prevent open communication with them, and convey nonverbal rejection. We believe that theory and research on victims of life crises offers a unique perspective for understanding the elderly, and are hopeful this analysis will be useful in stimulating further research.

ACKNOWLEDGMENTS

The authors wish to thank Philip Brickman and Joan Robinson for critical comments on this manuscript.

REFERENCES

Adams, B. N. (1967) Occupational position, mobility, and the kin of orientation. *American Sociological Review* 32:364–377.
Arling, G. (1976) The elderly widow and her family, neighbors and friends. *Journal of Marriage and the Family* November: 757–768.

Babchuk, N. (1978–79) Aging and primary relations. *International Journal of Aging and Human Development* 9(2):137–151.

Bard, M. (1952) The sequence of emotional reactions in radical mastectomy patients. *Public Health Reports* 67:1144–1148.

Berkman, L. F., and Syme, S. L. (1979) Social networks, host resistance, and mortality: A nine year follow-up of Alameda County residents. *American Journal of Epidemiology* 109(2):186–204.

Bettinghaus, C. O., and Bettinghaus, E. P. (1976) Communication considerations in the health care of the aging. In H. J. Oyer, and E. J. Oyer, eds., *Aging and Communication*. Baltimore, Md.: University Park Press.

Binger, C. M., Ablin, A. R., Feuerstein, R. C., Kushner, J. H., Zoger, S., and Mikkelson, C. (1969) Childhood leukemia: Emotional impact on patient and family. *The New England Journal of Medicine* 280(8):414–418.

Bloom, J. R., and Ross, R. D. (1977) Comprehensive Psychosocial Support for Initial Breast Cancer: Preliminary Report of Results. Paper presented at the meeting of the American Psychological Association, San Francisco.

Bornstein, P. E., Clayton, P. J., Halikas, J. A., Maurice, W. L., and Robins, E. (1973) The depression of widowhood after 13 months. *British Journal of Psychiatry* 122:561–566.

Brewer, M. B. (1979) Perceptions of the aged: Basic Studies and Institutional Implications. Paper presented at the meeting of the American Psychological Association, New York.

Brickman, P., and Bulman, R. J. (1977) Pleasure and pain in social comparison. In J. M. Suls and R. L. Miller, eds., *Social Comparison Processes*. Washington, D.C.: Hemisphere.

Brickman, P., Rabinowitz, V. C., Karuza, J., Coates, D., Cohn, E., and Kidder, L. Models of Helping and Coping. *American Psychologist*, in press.

Brown, G. W., Bhrolchain, M. N., and Harris, T. (1975) Social class and psychiatric disturbance among women in an urban population. *Sociology* 9:225–254.

Bultena, G. L. (1968) Age grading in the social interaction of an elderly male population. *Journal of Gerontology* 23:539–543.

Burgess, A. W., and Holmstrom, L. L. (1978) Recovery from rape and prior life stress. *Research in Nursing and Health* 1:165–174.

Butler, R. N., and Lewis, M. I. (1977) *Aging and Mental Health: Positive Psychosocial Approaches*, 2nd ed. St. Louis: C. V. Mosby Co.

Campbell, M. E. (1971) Study of the attitudes of nursing personnel toward the geriatric patient. *Nursing Research* 20:147–151.

Caplan, G. (1974) *Support Systems and Community Mental Health*. New York: Behavioral Publications.

Caplan, R. (1979) Social support, person–environment fit and coping. In L. A. Ferman and J. P. Gordus, eds., *Mental Health and the Economy*. Kalamazoo, Mich.: The Upjohn Institute.

Caplan, G., Killilea, M., eds. (1976) *Support Systems and Mutual Help*. New York: Grune and Stratton, Inc.

Carey, R. C. (1974) Emotional adjustment in terminal patients: A quantitative approach. *Journal of Counseling Psychology* 21:433–439.

Cherniss, C., Egnatios, E. S., and Wacker, S. (1976) Job stress and career development in new public professionals. *Professional Psychology* November:428.

Clayton, P. J., Halikas, J. A., and Maurice, W. L. (1972) The depression of widowhood. *British Journal of Psychiatry* 120:71–78.

Coates, D., and Wortman, C. B. (1980) Depression maintenance and interpersonal control. in A. Baum and E. J. Singer, eds., *Advances in Environmental Psychology, Volume 2: Applications of Personal Control*. Hillsdale, N.J.: Lawrence Erlbaum Associates.

Coates, D., Wortman, C. B., and Abbey, A. (1979) Reactions to victims. In I. H. Frieze, D. Bar-Tel, and J. S. Carroll, eds., *New Approaches to Social Problems*. San Francisco: Jossey-Bass.

Cobb, S. (1976) Social support as a moderator of life stress. *Psychosomatic Medicine* 38:300–314.

Cobb, S. (1979) Social support and health through the life course. In *Aging from Birth to Death: Interdisciplinary Perspectives*. Washington, D.C.: American Association for the Advancement of Science.

Cobb, S., and Kasl, S. (1977) *Termination: The Consequences of Job Loss*. Publication #77-224. Washington, D.C.: U.S. Department of Health, Education, and Welfare.

Conner, K. A., Powers, E. A., and Bultena, G. L. (1979) Social interaction and life satisfaction: An empirical assessment of late-life patterns. *Journal of Gerontology* 34(1):116–121.

Coyne, J. C. (1976) Toward an interactional description of depression. *Psychiatry* 39:28–40.

Davidson, T. N., Bowden, L., and Tholen, D. (1979) Social support as a moderator of burn rehabilitation. *Archives of Physical Medicine and Rehabilitation* 60:556.

Dean, A., and Lin, N. (1977) The stress-buffering role of social support. *Journal of Nervous and Mental Disease* 165(6):403–417.

de Araujo, G., van Arsdel, P. R., Holmes, T. H., and Dudley, D. L. (1973) Life change, coping ability, and chronic intrinsic asthma. *Journal of Psychosomatic Research* 17:359–363.

DiMatteo, M. R., and Hays, R. (in press) Social support in the fact of serious illness. In B. H. Gottlieb, ed., *Social Networks and Social Support in Community Mental Health*. Beverly Hills, Calif.: Russell Sage Publications.

Doherty, E. G. (1971) Social attraction and choice among psychiatric patients and staff: A review. *Journal of Health and Social Behavior* 12:279–290.

Dudley, D. L., Verhey, J. W., Masuda, M., Martin, C. J., and Holmes, T. H. (1969) Long term adjustment, prognosis and death in irreversible diffuse obstructive pulmonary syndromes. *Psychosomatic Medicine* 31(4):310–325.

Dunkel-Schetter, C., and Wortman, C. B. (in press) The interpersonal dynamics of cancer: Problems in social relationships and their impact on the patient. In H. S. Friedman and M. R. DiMatteo, eds., *Interpersonal Issues in Health Care*. New York: Academic Press.

Dyk, R. B., and Sutherland, A. M. (1956) Adaptation of the spouse and other family members to the colostomy patient. *Cancer* 9:123–138.

Edelwich, J., and Brodsky, A. (1980) *Burn-out: Stages of Disillusionment in the Helping Professions*. New York: Human Sciences Press.

Egerman, L. E. (1966) Attitudes of adult children toward parents and parents' problems. *Geriatrics* 21:217–222.

Eisdorfer, C., and Altrocchi, J. (1961) A comparison of attitudes toward old age and mental illness. *Journal of Gerontology* 16:340–343.

Farina, A., Holland, C., and Ring, K. (1966) The role of stigma and set in interpersonal attraction. *Journal of Abnormal Psychology* 71(6):421–428.

Federal Council on Aging (1978) *Public Policy and the Frail Elderly*. Office of Human Development Services, Publication No. 79-20959. Washington, D.C.: U.S. Department of Health, Education, and Welfare.

Ferlic, M., Goldman, A., and Kennedy, B. J. (1979) Group counseling in adult patients with advanced cancer. *Cancer* 43:760–766.

Festinger, L. (1954) A theory of social comparison processes. *Human Relations* 7:117–140.

Findlayson, A. (1976) Social networks as coping resources: Lay help and consultation patterns used by women in husbands' post infarction career. *Social Science and Medicine* 10:97–103.

Gaitz, C. M., and Scott, J. (1975) Analysis of letters to "Dear Abby" concerning old age. *The Gerontologist* 15(1):47–50.

Garfinkel, R. (1975) The reluctant therapist 1975. *The Gerontologist* 15(2):136–317.

Gerber, I., Rusalem, R., Hannon, N., Battin, D., and Arkin, A. (1975) Anticipatory grief and aged widows and widowers. *Journal of Gerontology* 30(2):225–229.

Glaser, B. G., and Strauss, A. L. (1965). *Awareness of Dying*. Chicago: Aldine.

Glick, I. W., Weiss, R. S., and Parkes, C. M. (1974) *The First Years of Bereavement*. New York: John Wiley and Sons.

Gore, S. (1978) The effect of social support in moderating the health consequences of unemployment. *Journal of Health and Social Behavior* 19:157–165.

Hausman, C. P. (1979) Short-term counseling groups for people with elderly parents. *The Gerontologist* 19(1):102–107.

Heller, K. (1979) The effects of social support: Prevention and treatment implications. In A. P. Goldstein and F. H. Kanfer, eds., *Maximizing Treatment Gains: Transfer Enhancement in Psychotherapy*. New York: Academic Press.

Helmrath, T. A., and Steinitz, E. M. (1978) Death of an infant: Parental grieving and the failure of social support. *Journal of Family Practice* 6(4):785–790.

Henkin, N. Z. (1979) Self-Disclosure Patterns of Older Adults. Paper presented at the 32nd Annual Meeting of the Gerontological Society, Washington, D.C.

Hinkle, L. E., Jr. (1974) The effect of exposure to cultural change, social change, and changes in interpersonal relationships on health. In B. Dohrenwend and B. Dohrenwend, eds., *Stressful Life Events: Their Nature and Effects*. New York: John Wiley and Sons.

Hochschild, A. (1978) *The Unexpected Community*. Berkeley, Calif.: University of California Press.

Holmes, T. H., Joffe, J. R., Ketcham, J. W., and Sheehy, T. F. (1961) Experimental study of prognosis. *Journal of Psychosomatic Research* 5:235–252.

House, J. (in press) *Work, Stress, and Social Support*. Reading, Mass.: Addison-Wesley.

Hughes, D. C., Peters, G. R., and Steidle, E. (1979) Attitudes Toward the Aged and Aged Ill. Paper presented at the 32nd Annual Meeting of the Gerontological Society, Washington, D.C.

Jamison, K. R., Wellisch, D. K., and Pasnau, R. O. (1978) Psychosocial aspects of mastectomy: I. The woman's perspective. *American Journal of Psychiatry* 134(4):432–436.

Kahn, R. L. (1979) Aging and social support. In *Aging from Birth to Death: Interdisciplinary Perspectives*. Washington, D.C.: American Association for the Advancement of Science.

Kastenbaum, R. (1963) The reluctant therapist. *Geriatrics* 18:296–301.

Kastenbaum, R., and Aisenberg, R. (1972) *The Psychology of Death*. New York: Springer.

Kelman, H. R., Lowenthal, M., and Muller, J. N. (1966) Community status of discharged rehabilitation patients: Results of a longitudinal study. *Archives of Physical Medicine and Rehabilitation* 47:670–675.

Kemp, B. J., and Vash, C. L. (1971) Productivity after injury in a sample of spinal cord injured persons: A pilot study. *Journal of Chronic Disease* 24:259–275.

Kidwell, I. J., and Booth, A. B. (1977) Social distance and intergenerational relations. *The Gerontologist* 17(5):412–420.

Kimball, C. P. (1969) Psychological responses to the experience of open heart surgery. *American Journal of Psychiatry* 126(3):96–107.

Kleck, R. (1968) Physical stigma and nonverbal cues emitted in face-to-face interaction. *Human Relations* 21:19–28.

Kleck, R., Buch, P. L., Goller, W. L., London, R. S., Pfeiffer, J. R., and Vukcevic, D. P. (1968) Effects of stigmatizing conditions on the use of personal space. *Psychological Reports* 23:111–118.

Kleck, R., Ono, H., and Hastorf, A. H. (1966) The effects of physical deviance upon face-to-face interaction. *Human Relations* 19:425–436.

Klein, R. (1971) A crisis to grow on. *Cancer* 28:1660–1665.

Kogan, N., and Shelton, F. C. (1962) Beliefs about "old people": A comparative study of older and younger samples. *Journal of Genetic Psychology* 100:93–111.

Larson, R. (1978) Thirty years of research on subjective well-being of older Americans. *Journal of Gerontology* 33:109–125.

Lerner, M. J. (1975) "Just World" Research and the Attribution Process: Looking Back and Ahead. Unpublished manuscript, University of Waterloo.

Lerner, M. J., and Matthews, G. (1967) Reactions to suffering of others under conditions of direct responsibility. *Journal of Personality and Social Psychology* 5:319–325.

Lerner, M. J., Miller, D. T., and Holmes, J. (1976) Deserving and the emergence of forms of justice. In *Advances in Experimental Social Psychology*. New York: Academic Press.

LeShan, L., and LeShan, E. (1961) Psychotherapy and the patient with a limited life span. *Psychiatry* 24:318–323.

Levy, L. H. (1976) Self-help groups: Types and psychological processes. *Journal of Applied Behavioral Science* 12:310–322.

Lieberman, and Borman, L. D. (1979) *Self-Help Groups for Coping with Crisis*. San Francisco: Jossey-Bass.

Litman, T. J. (1962) The influence of self-conception and life orientation factors in the rehabilitation of the orthopedically disabled. *Journal of Health and Human Behavior* 3:249–256.

Longino, C. F., Jr., and Lipman, A. (1979) Support Network Differentials Between Older Married and Nonmarried Men and Women. Paper presented at the 32nd Annual Meeting of the Gerontological Society, Washington, D.C.

Lopata, M. Z. (1978) Contributions of extended families to the support systems of metropolitan area widows: Limitations of the modified kin network. *Journal of Marriage and the Family* May:355–364.

Lowenthal, M. F., and Haven, C. (1968) Interaction and adaptation: Intimacy as a critical variable. *American Sociological Review* 33:20–31.

Lowenthal, M. F., and Robinson, B. (1976) Social networks and isolation. In R. H. Binstock and E. Shanas, eds., *Handbook of Aging and the Social Sciences*. New York: Van Nostrand Reinhold.

Lutsky, N. S. (1978) Patterns of Personal and Interpersonal Subjective Age Perception. Paper presented at the 31st Annual Meeting of the Gerontological Society, Northfield, Minnesota.

Lynch, J. J. (1977) *The Broken Heart: The Medical Consequences of Loneliness*. New York: Basic Books.

Lynch, J. J., Thomas, S. A., Mills, M. E., Malinow, K., and Katcher, A. H. (1974) The effects of human contact on cardiac arrhythmia in coronary care patients. *Journal of Nervous and Mental Disease* 158(2):88–99.

Maclay, E. (1977) *Green Winter: Celebrations of Old Age*. New York: Thomas Y. Crowell.

Maddison, D., and Walker, W. L. (1967) Factors affecting the outcome of conjugal bereavement. *British Journal of Psychiatry* 113:1057–1067.

Markides, K. S., and Martin, H. W. (1979) A causal model of life satisfaction among the elderly. *Journal of Gerontology* 34(1):86–93.

Maslach, C. (1976) Burnt out. *Human Behavior* 5:16–22.

Maslach, C. (1978) The client role in staff burn-out. *Journal of Social Issues* 34(4):111–124.

McTavish, D. G. (1971) Perceptions of old people: A review of research methodologies and findings. *The Gerontologist* 11:90–101.

Miller, E., Moore, E., and Sadowski, L. (1978) *Old Is Part of the Whole.* Royal Oak, Mich.: Lincoln Park Press.

Mitchell, G. W., and Glicksman, A. S. (1977) Cancer patients: Knowledge and attitudes. *Cancer* 40:61–66.

Nuckolls, K. B., Cassell, J., and Kaplan, B. H. (1972) Psychosocial assets, life crisis and the prognosis of pregnancy. *American Journal of Epidemiology* 95:431–441.

Oyer, H. J., Kapur, Y. P., and Deal, L. V. (1976) Hearing disorders in the aging: Effects upon communication. In H. J. Oyer and E. J. Oyer, eds., *Aging and Communication.* Baltimore, Md.: University Park Press.

Oyer, H. J., and Oyer, E. J. (1976) *Aging and Communication.* Baltimore, Md.: University Park Press.

Parkes, C. M. (1975) The emotional impact of cancer on patients and their families. *Journal of Laryngology and Utology* 89:1271–1279.

Pearlman, J., Stotsky, B. A., and Dominick, J. R. (1969) Attitudes toward death among nursing home personnel. *Journal of Genetic Psychology* 114:63–75.

Perloff, L. S. (1980) Similarity, Empathy, and Young People's Reactions to the Elderly. Paper presented at the meeting of the American Psychological Association, Montreal.

Pines, A., and Aronson, E. (1980) *Burnout: From Tedium to Personal Growth.* San Francisco: The Free Press.

Pines, A., and Maslach, C. (1978) Characteristics of staff burnout in mental health settings. *Hospital & Community Psychiatry* 29(4):233–237.

Pinneau, S. R., Jr. (1975) Effects of Social Support on Psychological and Physiological Strains. Doctoral dissertation, University of Michigan.

Porritt, D. (1979) Social support in crisis: Quantity or quality. *Social Science and Medicine* 13A:715–721.

Quint, J. C. (1965) Institutionalized practice of information control. *Psychiatry* 28:119–132.

Raphael, B. (1977) Preventive intervention with the recently bereaved. *Archives of General Psychiatry* 34:1450–1454.

Richman, J. (1977) The foolishness and wisdom of age: Attitudes toward the elderly as reflected in jokes. *The Gerontologist* 17(3):210–219.

Rosow, I. (1967) *Social Integration of the Aged.* New York: The Free Press.

Rosow, I. (1970) Old people: Their friends and neighbors. *American Behavioral Scientist* 14:59–69.

Sanders, J. B., and Kardinal, C. G. (1977) Adaptive coping mechanism in adult acute leukemia patients in remission. *Journal of American Medical Association* 238(9):952–954.

Sauer, W. (1977) Morale of the urban aged: A regression analysis by race. *Journal of Gerontology* 32:600–608.

Schachter, S. (1959) *The Psychology of Affiliation.* Stanford, Calif.: Stanford University Press.

Schoenberg, B., Gerber, I., Wiener, A., Kutscher, A. H., Peretz, D., and Carr, A., eds. (1975) *Psychosocial Aspects of Bereavement.* New York: Columbia University Press.

Schulz, R. (1976) Effects of control and predictability on the physical and psychological well-being of the institutionalized aged. *Journal of Personality and Social Psychology* 33:563–573.

Schulz, R. (1978) *The Psychology of Death and Dying and Bereavement.* New York: Appleton.

Schwab, J. J., Chalmers, J. M., Conroy, S. J., Farris, P. B., and Markush, R. E. Studies in grief: A preliminary report. In B. Schoenberg, I. Gerber, A. Wiener, A. H. Kutscher, D. Peretz, and A. Carr, eds., *Psychosocial Aspects of Bereavement.* New York: Columbia University Press.

Seelbach, W. C., and Hansen, C. J. (1980) Satisfaction with family relations among the elderly. *Family Relations* 29:91–96.

Shanas, E. (1975) Gerontology and the social and behavioral sciences: Where do we go from here? *The Gerontologist* December:499–502.

Shanas, E. (1979) Social myth as hypothesis: The case of the family relations of old people. *The Gerontologist* 19(1):3–9.

Shanas, E., and Maddox, G. L. (1976) Aging, health, and the organization of health resources. In R. H. Binstock and E. Shanas, eds., *Handbook of Aging and the Social Sciences.* New York: Van Nostrand Reinhold.

Sheldon, A., Ryser, C. P., and Krant, M. (1970) An integrated family oriented cancer care program: The report of a pilot project in the socio-emotional management of chronic diseases. *Journal of Chronic Diseases* 22:743–755.

Segel, A. (1970) Workers' perceptions of mentally disabled clients: Effect on service delivery. *Social Work* 15(3):39–46.

Silver, R. L., and Wortman, C. B. (1980) Coping with undesirable life events. In J. Garber and M. E. P. Seligman, eds., *Human Helplessness.* New York: Academic Press.

Troll, L. E. (1971) The family of later life: A decade review. *Journal of Marriage and the Family* 33(2):263–290.

Troll, L. E., and Schlossberg, N. (1970) A preliminary investigation of "age bias" in helping professions. *The Gerontologist* 10(3):46.

Vachon, M. L. S. (1979) The Importance of Social Support in the Longitudinal Adaptation to Bereavement and Breast Cancer. Paper presented at the meeting of the American Psychological Association, New York.

Vachon, M. L. S., Freedman, K., Formo, A., Rogers, J., Lyall, W. A. L., and Freeman, S. J. J. (1977) The final illness in cancer: The widow's perspective. *Canadian Medical Association Journal* 177:1151–1154.

Walker, K. N., MacBride, A., and Vachon, M. L. S. (1977) Social support networks and the crisis of bereavement. *Social Science and Medicine* 11:35–41.

Walster, E. (1966) Assignment of responsibility for an accident. *Journal of Personality and Social Psychology* 3:73–79.

Wasserman, H. (1971) The professional social worker in a bureaucracy. *Social Work* 16(1):89–95.

Waters, E., Fink, S., and White, B. (1976) Peer group counseling for older people. *Educational Gerontology* 1:157–170.

Weidman Gibbs, H., and Achterberg-Lawlis, J. (1978) Spiritual values and death anxiety: Implications for counseling with terminal cancer patients. *Journal of Counseling Psychology* 25(6):563–569.

Weisman, A. D. (1976) Coping with an untimely death. In F. J. Moss, ed., *Human Adaptation.* Lexington, Mass.: D. C. Heath.

Weisman, A. D., and Worden, J. W. (1975) Psychological analysis of cancer deaths. *Omega* 6(1):61–75.

Wills, T. (1978) Perceptions of clients by professional helpers. *Psychological Bulletin* 85:968–1000.

Wortman, C. B. (1976) Causal attributions of personal control. In J. H. Harvey, W. J. Ickes, and R. F. Kidd, eds., *New Directions in Attribution Research,* Vol. 1. Hillsdale, N.J.: Lawrence Erlbaum Associates.

Wortman, C. B., and Dunkel-Schetter, C. (1979) Interpersonal relationships and cancer: A theoretical analysis. *Journal of Social Issues* 35(1):120–155.

Wortman, C. B., and Dunkel-Schetter, C. (1980) Social Interaction and Depression. Paper presented at the meeting of the American Psychological Association, Montreal.

chapter 14

Convoys of Social Support:
A Life-Course Approach

ROBERT L. KAHN
TONI C. ANTONUCCI

AGING AND THE LIFE COURSE

The central proposition of this chapter is that social support moderates many of the stresses and strains encountered throughout life, including some often ascribed to the process of aging itself. To put this case convincingly, we begin with a brief exposition of the life-course perspective and of the appropriateness of the concept of role in describing the demands and expectations confronted by individuals at any given time. We next discuss the concept of social support, and the convoy as the structure within which support is given and received. The convoy structure is illustrated at different stages in life, and the chapter concludes with some proposals for research and policy.

Research on stress has tended to neglect the dimension of time in general and the phenomenon of aging in particular. Both in the laboratory and in the field, stress research has concentrated on the immediate effects of task content, physical conditions, and social–psychological content. Some field studies have inquired into the correlates of chronic stress, for example, in particular occupations—but few of these studies have included age as a variable and none to our knowledge has treated current

383

ROBERT L. KAHN AND TONI C. ANTONUCCI

stress in the context of the life course. This static or episodic approach is no less characteristic of most intervention strategies for dealing with stress; they have tended to be developed and prescribed as unaffected by age or previous life experience.

What is called the life-course perspective emphasizes the importance of past experiences in explaining current behavior and predicting responses to future situations. The assumption that all people reach age 65 with similar requirements for social support, for example, is too grossly oversimplified to be tenable. Moreover, the differences among people are not merely idiosyncratic; they are likely also to involve cohort effects—economic, political, and technological.

Consider a few of the factors that create differences among individuals and cohorts, and that will influence both the stresses and the supports of the elderly. The lengthening of the life-span makes it increasingly inappropriate to treat the elderly as a single demographic group, and gerontologists have begun to speak of the young-old (50–65), the middle-old (65–80), and the old-old (80 or older). A combination of improved social benefits (medical care, social security, pension plans, etc.) enables people to retire early from work if they choose, at the same time that legislation extends the right of elderly people to continue working if they choose. The decline in family size and the geographical mobility of families contribute to smaller networks of accessible relatives, but gains in longevity are at the same time increasing the number of four-generation families. To the extent that the life-course perspective informs our theories and research, such factors enter as variables rather than as error variance.

To advocate a life-course perspective, however, is by no means sufficient; the notion is too general to guide research. The life course must be disaggregated in order to be researchable. We propose role as one of the key concepts for understanding stress throughout life. An individual's life at any given time can be defined to a considerable extent in terms of the roles that he or she holds and enacts, and the sequential pattern of these roles over the years in large part defines the life course. The nature of those roles and the changes in them and in their compatibility define the expectations and demands that an individual encounters; they are the major sources of external stress in the life of the person.

Some of the resources with which people manage role stress are internal. Others are provided as part of the role; jobs, for example, typically provide access and entitlement to needed resources as well as demands for performance. Social support, however, is a resource of major importance in coping with stress, and it is neither internal nor role-defined. The support that enables a person to cope with stress at work, for example, may come from family and friends away from the job. We propose to think of such support as coming from a personal network of family, friends, and others—a network that is no less structured and tangible than roles and role sets but that often cuts across their boundaries in its interpersonal relationships and interactions. Such networks, seen in the perspective of the life course, we call convoys. We regard the concept of convoy as complementary to that of role, and we propose to use these concepts jointly to understand the way in which patterns of stress and coping change with age, in individual cases and in general.

ROLES AND THE LIFE COURSE

The concept of role is well established in social science—in anthropology, sociology, and psychology. Its adoption in these several disciplines, each of which tends otherwise to be addicted to its own conceptual terminology, is remarkable in itself. That convergence reflects the unique quality of the concept as a link between the social and individual levels. Communities and organizations, groups and extended families are all structures of roles, but the life of the individual can also be conceptualized in terms of the roles that he or she plays.

Role is a behavioral concept, and its defining components are position and expectation (expected activities). Thus, a role is defined as a set of activities that are expected of a person by virtue of his or her occupancy of a particular position in social space. Positions are interdependent, and any given position is defined in terms of its relationship to some set of others. The dominant content of roles is prescriptive and consists of activities that the role occupant is expected to perform. Roles also contain proscriptive aspects, consisting of activities that the role occupant is expected to refrain from engaging in. And there is to many roles a stylistic component; the expectations not only stipulate what is to be done, but also how it shall be done—costume, demeanor, tone of voice, and the like. The voice of command, the ministerial inflection, the quiet acquiescence of the subordinate in a hierarchical organization are all parts of roles.

Research on roles has concentrated on their demand aspect, especially in the context of work and especially under conditions such that the role demands constitute stresses on the individual. The nature and origins of such role stresses—conflict, ambiguity, overload, underutilization, responsibility for others, and the like—have been described elsewhere in some detail (Cobb 1974, Kahn 1974, French 1974, McGrath 1976, Coelho *et al.* 1974, House 1977). The literature on the effects of role stress is also extensive and includes alterations in physiology and performance as well as subjective states.

The constructive aspects of roles have been less well studied, although there is agreement that they sometimes provide opportunities for the acquisition of skills and abilities and for the use of valued skills and abilities that have already been acquired. They also provide the settings in which relationships with others develop, often in ways that supersede the formal requirements of the roles themselves. Research on work illustrates these points. Until they are very old, most people who are employed say that they would prefer to continue working rather than quit, even if they had sufficient resources to do so. They explain that the things they would miss most about relinquishing the work role are the structuring of time and the interaction with others in the work setting.

Many of these role properties have relevance for understanding the movement of individuals through the life course and the phenomenon of aging in the later years. We have said that, as an individual's life at any moment in time can be thought of as the array of roles that he or she enacts, so can that person's life course be conceptualized as the sequence of roles enacted. Throughout a lifetime, each person occupies a variety of roles. Some are explicitly age-related; for example, most people are students (in the formal sense of being enrolled in an educational institution) during their youth, relinquish the student role in early adulthood, and do not resume it in any formal sense. Worker, spouse, and parent are all age-connected roles. Moreover, many roles change in content and style with age, even though they remain nominally unchanged. The role of parent, for example, assumes very different content as children become adults.

Thus, the experience of aging inevitably involves role change and, sooner or later, diminution and loss as well as transition of other kinds. Certain roles, or valued aspects of them, must be relinquished. Jobs are retired from; spouses die. The interaction of parents with adult children, however valued and valuable, is less enveloping and sustained than child-rearing. One moves from player to spectator, from activist to adviser. Indeed, if role demands are not adjusted, the aging individual may experience the stress of prolonged overload. A crucial problem, for both research and social invention, is the coordination of such role changes with individual needs. We have yet to learn how to build into the major life roles enough flexibility so they can be age-responsive in an individual sense rather than imposing on some people the strain of overload and on others that of underutilization.

The potential of role-generated relationships to supersede the roles in which they developed is important throughout life. It seems likely that most close relationships with others begin within the structure of some role. Co-worker becomes friend as interaction in the work setting proceeds; in similar fashion, neighbor becomes confidant. Roles require proximity and interaction, often around some group or organizational outcome. In such circumstances, people of like mind tend to come together, and people who have come together tend to become of like mind. Common goals and interests develop, and matters held in common become matters discussed and shared.

Relationships developed in such role-defined settings, given time and resources, grow beyond the boundaries of roles in several ways. They can endure after the roles are relinquished, as the friendship of co-workers may extend into retirement. They can also cut across the boundaries of roles still active, for example, as marriage partners help each other manage the stresses of their work roles or as co-workers join together in community or leisure activities away from the job.

CONVOYS OF SOCIAL SUPPORT

We have emphasized the demand character of roles, and much of their stressfulness stems from these properties—demand for quantity of performance, quality, style, timing, and the like. Almost all the research on work roles and most research on other roles has concentrated on their demands. But in addition to demanding that we do certain things, roles typically provide the opportunity to do them—access to the places where they are to be done, to the people with whom they are to be done, and to the tools and equipment for doing them. Roles involve opportunities and resources as well as expectations and demands.

When a role is relinquished (as when a worker retires), or even when a role is exchanged for another of the same type (as when a worker changes jobs), the changes necessarily involve all of these role components—opportunities and resources as well as demands. If we are concerned with stress throughout life, therefore, we must look not only to the chronic stresses of continuing enactment of specific roles but also to the more acute stresses of relinquishing them, with or without replacement in kind.

Similarly, when we search for factors that reduce stress or that buffer the effects of stress, we must look both for alleviating factors in chronically stressful situations and for factors that moderate the more acute stresses of loss or transition. Relatively little research has been done on such buffering or moderating factors and still less on the conditions under which different factors are effective in reducing or buffering stress. Social support is an exception in that it has been shown to be widely beneficial in moderating the effects of both chronic and acute stress. The convergence of such findings is less than perfect, but it is persuasive, partly because the findings appear in the work of many investigators whose research includes a considerable range of conceptual definitions and methods.

Social Support in the Work Situation

Early studies in work settings established correlations between supportive supervisory behavior and worker or group performance. Likert (1961, 1967) summarized the results of a number of such studies in terms of three principles, the first of which was that each interaction with the supervisor should be seen by the subordinate as "one which builds and maintains his sense of personal worth and importance [1969, p. 103]." A long series of studies, initiated at Ohio State University and replicated elsewhere, identified consideration (measured in terms of demonstrated concern for members of the group) as one of the main predictors of effective leadership (Stogdill 1974). Measures of supportive behavior were generally predictive of individual satisfaction and, to a lesser extent, of performance.

More recent research in our own program at the Institute for Social Research has concentrated primarily on the moderating effects of social support in the presence of work-related stresses. French (1974) and his colleagues, in a comparative study of scientists, engineers, and administrators at two government scientific centers, found the administrators to be under greater stress and to be showing more symptoms of strain. Their demands were more urgent, their work more often interrupted, and their telephone calls more numerous; they scored higher than their research and engineering colleagues on scales of work load and of role ambiguity. In all three groups, however, the effects of these stresses were altered by the presence of social support on the part of supervisors, colleagues, and subordinates. Among men in the low social support condition (reported poor relationships with these others), work load was positively correlated with such risk factors as blood pressure and serum glucose level; among those reporting good relationships with others, these correlations did not hold. Similarly, a correlation was found between role ambiguity and serum cortisol, an indicator of physiological arousal tentatively linked to coronary heart disease, but this correlation did not exist among those in the high social support condition (reported good relationships with subordinates).

Findings consistent with these are reported by House (1977) from a study of some 2000 hourly workers employed in manufacturing rubber, chemicals, and plastics. His analysis involved seven measures of stress in the work role (work load, role conflict, responsibility, conflict between work and nonwork life, concern over quality of performance, lack of job satisfaction, and lack of occupational self-esteem); five health outcomes (angina pectoris, ulcer, skin rash, persistent cough and phlegm, and neurotic symptoms); and social support as provided from four sources (supervisor, spouse, coworkers, and friends and relatives). Of the 35 relationships between stress and strain (7 × 5), 19 were significantly reduced by one or more of the sources of social support. As House summarizes the findings, "under maximum levels of social support, marked symptoms of self-reported ill health increase only slightly, if at all, as stress increases. In contrast . . . when social support is minimal, marked symptoms of ill health increase dramatically as stress increases [House and Wells 1977, p. 15]."

A study of workers in 23 occupations (Pinneau 1975) showed consistent inverse relationships between social support and measures of psychological strain (33 of 34 significant effects in the predicted direction). Findings within occupational groups were similar; social support was negatively related to symptoms of depression, for example, in 15 of the 16 occupational groups large enough to permit such analysis.

In all these studies of stress at work, much remains to be explained. Not all relationships between stress and strain are reduced by social support; not all symptoms of strain seem equally responsive to support; and not all sources of support seem equally effective. Moreover, the pattern of such findings from study to study is neither completely consistent nor completely explained. The effects are sufficiently large and the replications sufficiently numerous, however, to encourage the search.

Role Transitions and Losses

One possible explanation for irregularities in the relationships among role stresses, strain, and social support involves the concept of change. The need for social support may be heightened when any of a person's major life roles undergoes change, especially unwanted and unpredicted change. Under those circumstances, the buffering effect of social support on the relationship between an acute stress and strain might be heightened.

A recent longitudinal study of the effects of job loss (Cobb and Kasl 1977) was designed around the closing of two manufacturing plants. A sample of 100 blue-collar workers who lost their jobs in these plants was followed over a 2-year period, with physiological and self-reported measurement at five intervals during that time. Data for these workers were compared also with data for control subjects from similar plants that did not shut down. The main effects of job loss were substantial:

> In the mental health sphere changes were noted in sense of deprivation, affective states, and self identity. In the physical health area . . . physiological changes suggesting an increased likelihood of coronary disease took place as did changes in blood sugar, pepsinogen, and uric acid suggesting increased risk of diabetes, peptic ulcer, and gout. There was an increase in arthritis and hypertension . . . [Cobb and Kasl 1977, p. vi].

Social support from a spouse, relatives, and friends reduced many of these relationships between stress and strain. Such buffering effects occurred for all of the deprivation measures and six of the nine measures of affective states (depression, anomie, anxiety–tension, physical symptoms, anger–irritation, and suspicion). Social support also buffered the negative effects of job loss on self-identity, on the maintenance of other activities, and on social interaction. The buffering effect was less with respect to the physiological impact of job loss, although "the effect of social support in protecting against arthritis (swollen joints observed by nurse interviewers) was notable [Cobb and Kasl 1977, p. 179]."

Cobb (1976) pursued the idea that support might have its major effects during periods of acute stress and role change by reviewing research on such episodes at different times throughout life, from infancy to old age. For example, women encountering stressful life changes during pregnancy were more likely to have complications in delivery but not if they were strongly supported by others (Nuckolls et al. 1972). Surgical patients in a double-blind experiment who were given special supportive care by the anesthetist required less medication for postoperative pain and were discharged an average of 2.7 days earlier than patients in the control group (Egbert et al. 1964). Adult asthmatics hospitalized for steroid therapy after significant life changes of various kinds required less steroid dosage to alleviate symptoms if they received high social support than if they did not (de Araujo et al. 1973).

A statewide study of the elderly in Texas (Stephens et al. 1978) found that as informal social support increased, so did planned and zestful engagement, child-centered participation, leisure activity, and activity with friends. Moreover, depression and alienation decreased monotonically as social support increased.

A 10-year study of mortality in Alameda County, California, found that the highest rates of death from all causes occurred among people with fewest social contacts (Berkman 1977). Moreover, this pattern is independent of self-reported health, socioeconomic status, life satisfaction, and preventive health behavior. Lally and colleagues (1979), reporting similar data for older women in single-room-occupant hotels, suggest that small networks are easily exhausted by prolonged or multiple crises and thus do not provide the potential support given by extensive networks.

Other research (Conner *et al.* 1979) suggests that the quality of the supportive interaction is more important than the number of people involved. The well-being of some 218 noninstitutionalized men and women aged 70 or more was not predictable from frequency of interaction or from the number of people with whom interaction occurred but was explainable in terms of quality of interaction.

This interpretation is consistent with the finding that the most crucial quantitative difference in the size of a support network is between zero and one—between those who must face stressful events with no close relationship and those who are supported by at least one such relationship. Lowenthal and Haven (1968), in a widely quoted study of elderly people, found that the reported availability of a confidant, someone to confide in and to share one's troubles with, was the single strongest indicator that an elderly person would not eventually require institutionalization. Among single and divorced men, the likelihood of suicide was nine times higher for those whose mothers had died during the preceding year, but among married men, the death of the mother was not associated with subsequent higher suicide rates (Burch 1972). The health status of women whose husbands had died during the preceding 13 months tended to worsen, but mainly among those who lacked a confidant (Raphael 1977).

Networks and Convoys

The preceding research, with its emphasis on sources and patterns of social support at various points in life, suggests extension of the support concept in three main ways: substantively, so that the defining properties of supportive transactions are stated in explicit and measurable terms; spatially, so that the entire structure of support-relevant relationships for a given person can be represented and analyzed; and temporally, so that the support structure is seen in dynamic terms, changing throughout life.

Our first proposal for extending the concept of network to that of convoy, which calls for an explicit substantive definition of social support, is perhaps more properly regarded as a corrective measure than an addition. Social support is one of those terms that carries considerable colloquial meaning and has therefore been more often used than defined. We propose that it be defined as interpersonal transactions that include one or more of the following key elements: affect, affirmation, and aid.

By affective transactions we mean expressions of liking, admiration, respect, or love. By transactions of affirmation we mean expressions of agreement or acknowledgment of the appropriateness or rightness of some act or statement of another person. Finally, we include as social support those transactions in which direct aid or assistance is given, including things, money, information, time, and entitlements. The operations for measuring support in these terms are available in tentative form, and their adequacy is being assessed in current research. By making our definitions and measures explicit, we hope to contribute to the process of methodological refinement among investigators concerned with social support.

The representation of interpersonal relationships as networks has a considerable history. References to sociometry date from 1934 (Moreno) and continue; more recently, there has been a surge of substantive and methodological interest in social networks and their analysis (Barnes 1972, Fischer *et al.* 1977, Wellman 1979). Some specialists in graph theory, that branch of mathematics concerned with structures consisting of points and the paths between them, also have become interested in the application of their discipline to the analysis of social networks (Harary 1969).

This body of work is highly relevant for specifying the formal properties of such networks. For our purpose, these properties can be regarded as consisting of two subsets: properties of the network as a whole and properties of the separate dyadic links between the focal person and each of the network members.

Major network properties include size, stability, homogeneity, symmetry, and connectedness. These can be defined respectively as number of network members, average duration of membership, proportion of relationships that are both support-giving and support-receiving, and proportion of network members who are acquainted with each other. Properties of dyadic links within networks include interaction frequency, type, magnitude, initiative, range, duration, and capacity. These can be defined as the number of interactions during some stipulated period of time, the substantive category of such interactions (affect, affirmation, aid), the importance of the interactions to the focal person, the proportion of the interactions initiated by the focal person, the number of life domains included in the interactions, the time elapsed since the relationship began, and the maximum potential support under specified hypothetical circumstances. These listings and definitions are partial and both owe much to Barnes's (1972) work on network analysis.

As graph theory develops, especially in application to social structure, we may hope that a logically complete set of network properties will be specified. For the present, any list of such properties must be open-ended, generated in part from formal sources, but in part from intuitive notions about the giving and receiving of social support and the relationships within which such transactions occur.

The life-course perspective, our interest in transitions, and the concept of aging itself call for the extension of the network concept to include changes over time. The methodological implications of such an extension include an emphasis on longitudinal studies, with the comparison of network properties for the same individuals at different points in time— before and after retirement, for example, or at different ages. The conceptual implications are that each network property or variable shall be thought of both in terms of its magnitude at a given time and in terms of its rate of change. Each network property, in other words, would be regarded both as a "state variable" and as a "delta variable." Thus, the property of network size would be treated both as present size (number of people) and as a rate of change in size (net rate at which people are being added to or lost from the network).

It seems useful to designate these dynamic networks of social support with a unique term. We suggest *convoy*[1] as an appropriate term, and propose its use for studying the process of aging and other life-course changes. By choosing this metaphorical label, we imply that each person can be thought of as moving through the life-cycle surrounded by a set of other people to whom he or she is related by the giving or receiving of social support. An individual's convoy at any point in time thus consists of the set of persons on whom he or she relies for support and those who rely on him or her for support. These two subsets may overlap, of course; there are relationships in which one both gives and receives support, although all relationships are not symmetrical in this sense.

---

[1] The use of the term *convoy* in social science came to our attention in the work of David Plath, who in turn credits Loki Madan for his use of the term in an ethnographic study of Kashmir.

The convoy is a structural concept, shaped by the interaction of situational factors and enduring properties of the person and in turn determining in part the person's well-being and ability to perform successfully his or her life roles. It is thus the central concept in an explanatory framework (Figure 14.1) that can be summarized in terms of five general propositions, each of which identifies a category of more specific hypotheses:

1. A person's requirements for support at any given time are determined jointly by enduring properties of the person (age, other demographic characteristics, personality, etc.) and by properties of the situation (expectations and demands of work, family, and other roles): Arrows 1a and 1b, Figure 14.1.
2. The structure of a person's convoy (size, connectedness, stability, etc.) is determined jointly by enduring properties of the person, by the person's requirements for social support, and by properties of the situation: Arrows 2a, 2b, and 2c, Figure 14.1.
3. The adequacy of social support received by a person is determined by the properties of the convoy, and by personal and situational properties: Arrows 3a, 3b, and 3c, Figure 14.1.
4. Life outcomes, including measures of well-being and performance in major roles, are determined jointly by enduring properties of the person, adequacy of social support, and properties of the situation: Arrows 4a, 4b, and 4c, Figure 14.1.
5. The influence of personal and situational factors on criteria of performance and well-being is moderated by the convoy structure and by the adequacy of social support: Arrows 5a, 5b, 5c, and 5d, Figure 14.1.

If we regard the convoy as the core of this model, the remainder of it consists of the hypothesized causes and consequences of convoy structure, including its moderating or interactive effects as well as its direct outcomes.

CONVOYS OVER THE LIFE COURSE

The framework represented in Figure 14.1 is a summary of concepts and hypotheses, each of which requires elaboration and specification. The concept of the *convoy* is central to our propositions about the functions of social support over an individual's lifetime. We turn, therefore, to an elaboration of the center box in Figure 14.1, which represents the

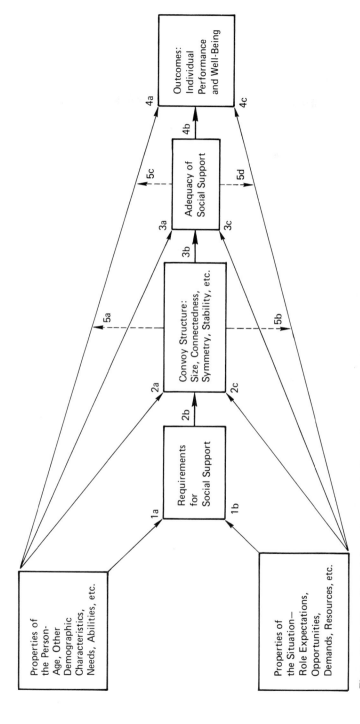

Figure 14.1. Hypothetical determinants and effects of convoy properties.

convoy structure. Specifically, we shall consider the internal structure of a convoy and the manner in which it is likely to develop. In addition, we shall provide an example of the changing convoy of a single individual over 35 years.

To understand the development of convoys, we return to the concept of roles as discussed earlier in this chapter. All individuals enter and leave a variety of roles over their lifetimes (e.g., spouse, parent, worker, supervisor, neighbor, friend). These roles are the bases for contact and interaction with others. Indeed, most role expectations and requirements consist of specifications for interpersonal behavior. In many cases, the actual behavior of individuals in related roles will differ little from these expectations. In other cases, the role behavior may be considerably elaborated in ways that add to the interest and satisfaction of the participants.

Convoy membership develops in this way. Although informal origins of convoy membership are certainly possible, it seems likely that most members of a person's convoy were initially connected to that person through the performance of related roles. The supportive relationships of convoy membership will in some cases continue to be role-constrained; the support of a co-worker may become very important on the job, go far beyond the formal requirements of the work situation, and yet not extend beyond the boundaries of the work situation. In other cases, the relationship grows beyond the role structure in which it originated and comes to be valued for other reasons and active in other contexts.

Figure 14.2 presents an example of a convoy, with indications of the role origins of the various relationships. The smallest circle (P) represents the person in question, the focal person. Membership in a person's convoy is limited to people who are important to him or her in terms of social support and does not include all the people known to P or who merely function in some role in relation to P. Convoy members are shown in the three concentric circles around P. The third (outermost) concentric circle represents people who are least close to P but have nevertheless been identified as sources of support. People in this tertiary convoy circle are very likely to relate to P on the basis of role. Membership is likely to consist of supervisors, co-workers, and neighbors whose relationship to P has achieved some level of importance beyond the formal role requirements. Membership in this third concentric circle is not stable in itself and is extremely vulnerable to concomitant role changes. These are people to whom P feels generally less close and with whom the domain of relationship is likely to be limited. For example, a person in this circle might be a co-worker or supervisor with whom P shares work goals and whose interactions with P are very supportive at work but do not go beyond the work setting.

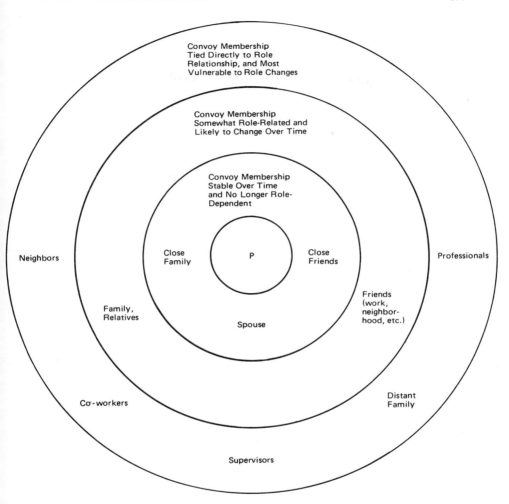

Figure 14.2. Hypothetical example of a convoy.

The second concentric circle consists of people who may be family, friends, or co-workers of the person. Membership in this circle does constitute some special degree of closeness, in that P perceives support from that person above and beyond that implied by the role that he or she fills in the life of P. Times, places, and subjects of interaction are outside the boundaries of the role. However, the relationship is not independent of the role and may not be maintained if either member loses the role. Such relationships are therefore likely to be less stable over adulthood, and substitutions may be readily made as new people fill the roles vacated by others. For example, a supportive relationship with the husband of a close friend may not survive a divorce, but may be replaced after divorce and remarriage by the new husband of the friend. Or a neighbor whom P saw daily and depended upon when they lived in adjacent houses may nevertheless be replaced as friend and convoy member by a new neighbor when P moves into a new house and neighborhood.

The first concentric circle consists of people who are very close to P. They are perceived as important support givers. They are also likely to be close friends or family members, but their location in this first concentric circle is determined by the supportive quality of their relationship to P and not the role or familial relationship. Because it is so highly valued, membership in this inner circle is likely to remain fairly stable through the years, in spite of changes in job or residence. Indeed, geographical proximity or frequency of direct contact may not be a good indicator of membership in this closest of convoy circles. An old friend who now lives several states away and is seen only rarely may nevertheless be the person to whom P turns in a crisis.

People differ in the number of persons with whom they have supportive relationships and in the degree of closeness that characterizes those relationships. We think of the convoy-defining dimensions in absolute rather than relative terms; thus, inclusion anywhere in a person's convoy signifies importance in terms of social support and inclusion in the inner circle signifies a very close relationship, not merely closer than another. Respondents differ, of course, in their frame of reference for assessing closeness and some relativity in response is probably unavoidable. The explanatory power of this approach, however, is greater when the dimension of closeness is absolute, and we are attempting to develop measures that will have this quality.

Thus, in order to qualify for the first concentric circle of a convoy, something like the special relationship of confidant or best friend must be achieved. Such relationships are capable of providing support in a variety of situations. Their support is specific to a person's needs rather than to situational formalities. These are the kinds of relationships that kept Lowenthal and Haven's (1968) older respondents from requiring institutionalization. Individuals differ with respect to such relationships. For some, the inner circle does not exist at all; for others, it includes only one person, and for still others, it may be quite large. We regard both its existence and its size as predictors of well-being and of the ability to cope successfully with stress. Even the loss of support may be better managed by people who have had such relationships. There is some evidence (Bowlby 1969, Lopata 1975) that they are better able to adjust to loss of various kinds and to find substitutes for the lost relationships.

Losses and gains in any circle of the convoy can occur in several ways. Loss in the innermost circle is likely to be the result of death or the kind of break experienced as a major betrayal. Changes in the second and third circle, as we have suggested, may simply reflect changes in role or location. Moreover, the boundaries between these circles are permeable, and flow between them is possible as is flow into and out of the convoy as a whole.

These convoy properties are important with respect to patterns of aging. Recurring role loss is one of the best-documented of age-connected changes; to take the most obvious example, almost all workers relinquish the work role with age. For a person wholly dependent on role membership for convoy support, these role losses will be devastating. For a person with a well-developed inner circle of close relationships, the loss of roles does not imply the loss of these relationships. People whose convoy relationships remain role-linked are thus at greatest risk with increasing age.

To illustrate some changes in convoys over the life course, Figure 14.3 presents convoys of the same individual at two different points in her life. The diagram on the left represents the convoy of a married woman, approximately 35 years of age, with two young children. The diagram on the right presents the convoy of this same woman at 70 years of age as a widow with two adult children. The convoy on the left includes considerably more members than that on the right. Moreover, although membership in the inner circle is hypothesized to be relatively stable, over the 35-year interval there have been several major changes. Parents and spouse have died and remain in some very real sense unreplaced. However, this elderly woman feels particularly close to her daughter, who is now an adult and a major support giver. In addition, P still maintains a close relationship to one of her sisters. Other losses have been compensated for in some degree by a neighbor to whom P feels very close and by an old friend who is now also widowed. The second and third concentric circles have also changed over the years. Convoy membership in these categories has decreased. Relationships with neighbors, friends, and family members remain. Major categorical losses are co-workers, supervisors, and husband's friends and co-workers. These losses are replaced, in part, by a minister and a physician who now play an important part in this woman's life.

These representations of convoy patterns are, of course, illustrative rather than drawn directly from data. They illustrate unavoidably some of the complexities of the convoy concept. We hope that they illustrate

400

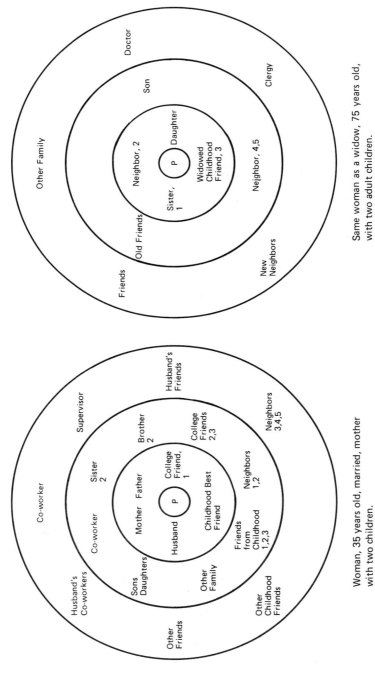

Woman, 35 years old, married, mother
with two children.

Same woman as a widow, 75 years old,
with two adult children.

Figure 14.3. Changing convoy composition over the life course: one woman's convoy at two different points in her life-cycle.

as well some of its potential for the study of social support and the life-course changes in support patterns.

PRIORITIES AND IMPLICATIONS

Three areas of work seem particularly important for the future: (1) methodological development for the measurement of social support; (2) identification of age-related patterns of support, successful and unsuccessful; and (3) development of modes of intervention that supplement and encourage natural support patterns.

Methodological Development

As the convoy of one woman over 35 years (Figure 14.3) suggests, the measurement of support networks is complex. Several modes of network representation have been used and several methods employed to generate network data. These include: the nomination of network members by each respondent in answer to a direct question about "persons you feel closest to"; the keeping of interaction diaries (Fischer *et al*. 1977, Wellman 1979); a spatial representation of the convoy, with the focal person at the center and radial dimensions indicating the closeness of the relationship (Kahn and Quinn 1976, Kahn 1979); and a matrix of support-giving people by role, with a nomination of the people "you feel close to" in each role category (Kahn and Antonucci 1979). All these techniques begin to address the problem of network and convoy membership as well as the quality of the supportive interaction, but many problems still remain.

Most techniques for measuring social support have treated it as if it were unidimensional. We have preferred to consider it multidimensional and have attempted to measure separately social support as affective expression, as affirmation, and as direct aid. Early analyses give empirical support for these distinctions, especially for the dimensions of affect and aid. Further empirical work will be required to determine their explanatory value and to ascertain whether other forms of social support should also be recognized.

Age-Related Patterns of Social Support

The best test of the schema we have proposed for studying convoys over the life-course schema would require a cross-sequential design.

Many research questions can be explored, however, before committing the time and resources necessary for such designs. As Figure 14.3 suggests, patterns of convoy structure are likely to differ both interindividually and intraindividually. One research priority is to explore differences in convoy membership among people of different ages with special attention to distribution of membership in the first, second, and third concentric circles. The relationship between these convoy patterns and criteria of overall well-being could then be analyzed within age groups, a procedure that should permit the tentative delineation of convoys that are most successful, most adaptable, and most able to maintain support throughout life.

Such research should illuminate the relationship between convoy structure and forms of support. For example, it seems likely that the dimension of distance (the radial dimension in Figures 14.2 and 14.3) corresponds to a dimension of generality or specificity in the forms of support provided. A member of the innermost circle of an individual's convoy is likely to give aid, affect, and affirmation, but a member of the tertiary convoy circle may provide only one of these; the relationship is more specified.

As such information is accumulated for representative populations, it becomes possible to describe "normal" social support and also to identify individuals who, because of their convoy compositions, are at maximal or minimal risk. The delineation of a population "at risk" will be useful both for research and application. With specific reference to the aging population, "at risk" convoy composition would earmark people for special attention or intervention, especially at times of major change in their lives (e.g., retirement, widowhood, compelled residential relocation, strenuous medical treatment). Similar applications would be possible for other groups (e.g., pregnant women, unemployed workers, etc.).

The eventual use of a cross-sequential design (which combines the strengths of longitudinal and cross-sectional designs) to study convoys will permit an examination of the development and maintenance of convoys as they affect various criteria of well-being over the life course. Such a design will also provide an assessment of the effectiveness of different convoy patterns for coping with particular life crises and transitions.

Modes of Intervention

Knowledge of convoys and their functions could have several direct applications. In the case of people who do not have convoys that are conducive to successful aging, intervention programs could be devised that specifically address the development of a more supportive convoy pattern. Programs such as Widow-to-Widow and Alcoholics Anonymous suggest that people can be helped through major crises for which they have had no preparation, and that the proper support can be effective despite a history of past failures.

For elderly people who have had successful convoys throughout their lives, knowledge of the composition and functions of convoys may lead to more enlightened behavior, official and familial, and thus prevent the unnecessary disruptions of these convoys by government policies or the decisions of relatives. Among the convoy-disruptive aspects of present policies are: greater government support for the institutionalization of an elderly person than for family members who wish to keep the older person at home; nursing home regulations that separate married couples from each other and enforce other forms of segregation of men and women; regulations that discourage remarriage among elderly women by reducing or eliminating social security benefits upon remarriage; and social security regulations (recently revised) that prevent willing older people from continuing to work, thereby maintaining important supportive relationships.

These examples suggest a history of policy interference with natural support networks. This can be remedied. In addition, supportive services can be invented that will not only provide formal support to the elderly but do so in ways that strengthen the development of natural support networks. Current research (Durlak 1979) indicates that informal and nonprofessional helpers are no less effective than professionals. It is a challenge for research and for application to invent professional modes of support that develop and then give way to the natural networks.

REFERENCES

Barnes, J. A. (1972) *Social Networks*. New York: Addison-Wesley Reprints.

Berkman, L. F. (1977) Social Networks, Host Resistance, and Mortality: A Follow-up Study of Alameda County Residents. Doctoral dissertation, University of California, Berkeley.

Bowlby, J. (1969) *Attachment and Loss, Vol. 1. Attachment*. London: Hogarth, New York: Basic Books.

Burch, J. (1972) Recent bereavement in relation to suicide. *Journal of Psychosomatic Research* 16:361–366.

Cobb, S. (1974) Role responsibility: The differentiation of a concept. In A. McLean, ed, *Occupational Stress*. Springfield, Ill.: Thomas.

Cobb, S. (1976) Social support as a moderator of life stress. *Psychosomatic Medicine* 38(5):300–314.

Cobb, S., and Kasl, S. (1977) *Termination: The consequences of job loss.* (Publication No. 77-224). Washington, D.C.: U.S. Department of Health, Education, and Welfare.

Coelho, G. V., Hamburg, D. A., and Adams, J. E. (1974) *Coping and Adaptation.* New York: Basic Books.

Connor, K. A., Powers, E. A., and Bultena, G. L. (1979) Social interaction and life satisfaction: An empirical assessment of late-life patterns. *Journal of Gerontology* 34(1):116–121.

de Araujo, G., van Arsdel, P. P., Holmes, T. H., and Dudley, D. L. (1973) Life change, coping ability and chronic intensive asthma. *Journal of Psychosomatic Research* 17:359–363.

Durlak, J. A. (1979) Comparative effectiveness of paraprofessional and professional helpers. *Psychological Bulletin* 86(1):80–92.

Egbert, I. D., Battit, G. E., Welch, C. E., and Bartlett, M. K. (1964) Reduction of post-operative pain by encouragement and instruction of patients. *New England Journal of Medicine* 270:825–827.

Fischer, C. S., Jackson, R. M., Stueve, C. A., Gerson, K., and Jones, L. M. (with M. Baldassare). (1977) *Networks and Places: Social Relation in the Urban Setting.* New York: The Free Press.

French, J. R. P., Jr. (1974) Person-role fit. In A. McLean, ed, *Occupational Stress.* Springfield, Ill.: Thomas.

Harary, F. (1969) *Graph Theory.* New York: Addison-Wesley.

House, J. (1977) The three faces of social psychology. *Sociometry* 40(2):161–177.

House, J., and Wells, J. A. (1977) Occupational Stress, Social Support and Health. Paper presented at a conference on reducing occupational stress. Sponsored by Center for Occupational Mental Health, Cornell University and the National Institute of Occupational Safety and Health, White Plains, New York.

Kahn, R. L. (1979) Aging and social support. In M. W. Riley, ed., *Aging From Birth to Death.* Washington, D.C.: American Association for the Advancement of Science.

Kahn, R. L. (1974) Conflict, ambiguity, and overload: Three elements in job stress. Pp. 47–61 in A. McLean, ed, *Occupational Stress.* Springfield, Ill.: Thomas.

Kahn, R. L., and Antonucci, T. (1979) Social Support Networks Among New Teachers. Current study at the Survey Research Center, University of Michigan, Ann Arbor.

Kahn, R. L., and Quinn, R. P. (1976) Mental Health, Social Support, and Metropolitan Problems: A Research Proposal. Ann Arbor, Mich.: Survey Research Center, University of Michigan.

Lally, M., Black, E., Thornock, M., and Hawkins, J. D. (1979) Older women in single room occupant (SRO) hotels: A Seattle profile. *The Gerontologist* 19 (February).

Likert, R. (1961) *New Patterns of Management.* New York: McGraw-Hill.

Likert, R. (1967) *The Human Organization.* New York: McGraw-Hill.

Lopata, H. Z. (1975) Grief work and identity reconstruction. *Journal of Geriatric Psychiatry* 31(November):41–45.

Lowenthal, M. P., and Haven, C. (1968) Interaction and adaptation: Intimacy as a critical variable. *American Sociological Review* 33(1):20–30.

McGrath, J. E. (1976) Stress and behavior in organizations. In M. D. Dunnette, ed., *Handbook of Industrial and Organizational Psychology.* Chicago: Rand McNally.

Moreno, J. L. (1934) *Who Shall Survive?* Washington, D.C.: Nervous and Mental Disease Publishing Co.

Nuckolls, K. B., Cassel, J., and Kaplan, B. H. (1972) Psychosocial assets, life crisis, and the prognosis of pregnancy. *American Journal of Epidemiology* 95:431–441.

Pinneau, S. R. (1975) Effects of Social Support on Psychological and Physiological Strains. Unpublished doctoral dissertation, University of Michigan.

Raphael, B. (1977) Preventive intervention with the recently bereaved. *Archives of General Psychiatry* 34:1450–1454.

Stephens, R. C., Blau, Z. S., Oser, G. T., and Miller, M. D. (1978) Aging, social support systems, and social policy. *Journal of Gerontological Social Work* 1(1)Fall.

Stogdill, R. (1974) *Handbook of Leadership*. New York: The Free Press.

Wellman, B. (1979) The community question: The intimate networks of East Yorkers. *American Journal of Sociology* 84 (February).

chapter 15

The Role of Expectancy in Adaptation to Aging

ROBERT R. SEARS

What do 50-year-old people expect their lives to be like 20 years hence? By and large they do not think much about it (Rosow 1973). They may have a few expectations stemming from extrapolation of their current status or from plans based on financial or housing preparation for retirement. They can predict matters of occupational persistence or sources of income, with an admitted margin of error, but there are many other equally important aspects of life that they cannot predict with the present level of knowledge. Quite aside from the consideration that age 50 is the prime of life and no time to be forecasting—or brooding about— a changed level of activity or enjoyment, there is usually little in a person's current status that offers any obvious hint of the feelings, performance abilities, or environmental circumstances that lie ahead for him or her as an individual. Yet in some degree, a person's adequacy of adaptation to these changes depends on the precision and realistic quality of his or her expectancies about them.

There are various ways in which research could improve the ability to predict events in later life for middle-aged people. Just what effect such an improvement will have is the first question to ask; almost certainly, the answer will be equivocal. Hence, a second type of question is called for: How do the effects of expectancy vary with respect to

AGING
Social Change

different kinds of personal or environmental change in different domains of life experience, such as family life, occupation, and intellectual activity? This approach implies a "tree" of problems, starting with expectancy as the trunk and branching into different types of change as they influence the various domains of motivation and life settings.

The purpose of this chapter is to outline briefly a general theory of expectancy, to provide some illustrative hypotheses with which research in this arena can begin, to describe the methodological requirements for such research, and to suggest some specific ways in which varied degrees of expectancy can influence behavior and feelings in three major domains.

THE MEANING OF EXPECTANCY

Definition

The construct of expectancy is an intervening variable used to account for the directing of action or thought toward specific goals and for providing force or instigation to such action. It plays a role in both cognitive and motivation theory; in everyday usage, it carries meanings appropriate to both. Sometimes it refers to foresight or foreknowledge with the implication that a person has ideas or images of some event that will (or may) occur in the future—for example, "It looks as if it might rain," or "If I do that, I'll be too tired to enjoy myself tonight." Alternatively, it may imply a heightening of motivation—for example, "The prospect of victory drove the team to frenzy." Equally, it can refer to conflictive interference with motivated behavior—for example, "His dread of another failure made him drop out of school." All such examples incorporate both cognitive and motivational elements, of course, and in applying the concept of expectancy to an understanding of behavior we need consider only what functions it serves as an intervening variable in general behavior theory.

Origin

An expectancy is established by some kind of learning experience. Such an experience can be very limited in its extent, both in instigation and action. Pavlov's dogs learned to expect food at the sound of a signal, and the evidence for the existence of expectancy was premonitory salivation. At the other extreme of complexity, in the learning process as well as in the actions required, there are such elaborate cognitive processes as foreseeing the outcome of a series of moves in a chess game, or the more socially interactive processes of planning a political campaign, or the emotion-bound dread of bereavement. Regardless of the degree of complexity involved, we may assume that the exact nature of the expectancy, its strength, the extent to which it is conscious and verbalized, and the kinds of actions attached to it as responses will be determined by the general laws of learning operating in a specific context, both intrapersonal and environmental. This conjunction of the learning process with specific conditions of learning provides for individual differences in expectancies.

Functions

The functions of expectancy belong to both action and learning theory. Once the expectancy has been learned, it serves as an hypothesized cue stimulus to direct thought and action toward the goal represented in the expectation. An ambitious man may seek a competitive task in order to succeed at a public undertaking and thus increase his status. The expectancy in this instance consists of the ideational representation of increased status, and the seeking of a competitive task is the action elicited by that cue stimulus.

A second function is to increase the strength of instigation to the actions initiated either by the expectancy itself or by some other instigative system. This function is that of a facilitative agent. When the ambitious man perceives that his task can be used for status improvement, he works harder or faster or more efficiently.

A third function is derivative from the second. The increased motivational strength provides the necessary condition for increased frustration if the expected goal cannot be achieved. The strength, or severity, of frustration is a direct function of the total strength of instigation to an action that suffers interference. If our ambitious man fails at his competitive task, he will suffer greater distress than he would have if the task had not initially seemed to offer a chance for status improvement.

A fourth function is derived from combining the first three, namely, to reduce or evade potential frustration. At first glance, this appears to be the opposite of the third function itself. How can expectancy both increase and decrease frustration? In fact, different time-and-action frames and different expectancies are involved in the two functions. The third refers to expectancy-cued direct action toward a positive goal. The fourth refers to action directed by an expectation of an aversive outcome; the anticipated frustration of the goal-directed behavior is the cue stimulus that directs the adaptive avoidance or evasive action. The ambitious man, foreseeing competitive failure rather than success, discontinues the first task and seeks another, or (defensively) simply denies to himself that success would have improved his status.

These four functions were recognized long ago by Hull (1930, 1931), Tolman (1932) and Lewin (1935), who incorporated them in their various minitheories of learning and action. In recent years, some have appeared again in other contexts, as in Aronson's (1969) analysis of dissonance theory and in occupational psychology (e.g., Mitchell and Beach 1976, Eran and Jacobson 1976). They are presented here in terms that permit their assimilation into more general behavior theory with the added predictive power provided by that broader systematic setting and its propositions about learning, action, and frustration.

Frustration

As we consider the application of these concepts to aging, frustration stands out as a promising field for investigation. Expectancy, in the sense of foresight or foreknowledge, provides the image of a future event—either positive or aversive—that can be reacted to by thought and planning as well as by evoked feelings of pleasure, displeasure, or anxiety. If the event is likely to be frustrating, the planning can be directed to circumventing the frustration, if that is possible, or to arranging alternative satisfactions, or to rehearsing preparatory rationalizations or other defenses when the frustration is seen as inevitable. To the extent that such anticipatory activity can reduce the strength of motivation toward the goals that will not be achieved, the severity of the frustration will be lessened. Expectancy in this context is the main mechanism for "anticipatory socialization," some recent discussions of which have been well summarized by Hultsch and Plemons (1979, p. 25).

This reduction can be important for a person's adaptation to his or her changing circumstances. In addition to the associated unpleasant feelings, frustration serves as an instigator to a number of maladaptive reactions such as aggression, depression, and anxiety. We do not know to what extent the frustration of different motivational systems is characteristically associated with particular forms of response, although there is good evidence that depression is unusually common when the love-attachment-dependence system suffers interference. The effect of variation in strength or severity of frustration is clear, however. There appears to be a hierarchy of potential responses that are elicited by different strengths. Severe frustration calls forth aggression more frequently than mild frustration does. Effective problem solving, on the other hand, is more frequently a response to mild than to severe frustration. It seems reasonable to suppose, therefore, that anything that can reduce antici-pated frustration will reduce the probability of ineffective, maladaptive feelings and actions and will increase the chances that a person will be able to circumvent potential frustrations or discover means for amelio-rating them in advance.

My hypothesis is that expected aversive events are less frustrating than randomly occurring ones. In consequence, expectancy ordinarily will reduce the probability of aggression, dependency, regression, depres-sion, and denial as products of deleterious changes that accompany aging. Concomitantly, there will be a greater frequency of planful eliminating of the source of the frustration; then, when the latter is inevitable, as with many physical changes, coping by substitution, rationalization, dis-sonance-reduction and other useful defenses will be more frequent.

Some Hypotheses

To exemplify the usefulness of this theoretical approach, I will suggest three researchable hypotheses that rest on the assumption that expec-tancy or foresight will provide better opportunity for adaptive response. Thus, adaptation will be better if:

1. The timing of the event is highly predictable—for example, a stan-dard and non-negotiable retirement age in contrast with a flexible age that is determined unilaterally by the employer. Reasoning: Foresight exists in some degree for both retirement procedures, but it is stronger for the non-negotiable one. Furthermore, when the conditions within which adaptive action must take place are more clearly specified, a person can plan more effectively and does not have to anticipate alternative contingent plans. The "work load" of adaptation is therefore lighter and there is less uncertainty, which is itself ordinarily an instigator of anxiety.
2. The event is occasioned by the person's own choice rather than being imposed by uncontrollable circumstances—for example, moving to smaller living quarters to save housework as contrasted with moving because the property has been condemned for a free-way. Reasoning: A free choice implies a greater probability that alternative sources of satisfaction can be foreseen and that planning

has already begun. The sudden forced move does not provide opportunity for such planning. Note, however, that as with many real-life comparisons, more than one antecedent variable is involved; it must be presumed that anyone who chooses to change homes is less attached to the old one than is someone who has had this choice forced by outside circumstances. Therefore, strength of frustration varies independently of the amount of foresight.

3. The event is far enough away in time to permit planning and rehearsal of adaptive responses to it—for example, elective surgery for cataract as contrasted with emergency surgical repair of an aneurysm. Reasoning: The anticipatory planning period reduces the severity (strength) of frustration and hence also reduces the probability of maladaptive responses.

It is possible to go a little further with these principles and consider the effects of expectancy when the strength of motivation and severity of frustration vary together. If they are high, a given degree of expectancy should provide a greater motivation toward avoiding the frustration, (i.e., circumventing it or adapting to it). Hence, with everything else equal, including time, there should be a greater reduction in maladaptive responses when the frustration does ensue. This hypothesis predicts simply that ultimate persisting maladaptive emotional or other behavior will be less if:

4. The event is central to a strong rather than to an unimportant motivational system—for example, deafness to a performing musician as compared with deafness to a novelist. Reasoning: A person's main career activity usually involves higher motivation, stronger action, and potential for producing more severe frustration than an activity outside his or her career. The stronger the motivation, the more room there is for reduction by expectancy.

One must be cautious, however. Even though these hypotheses may be supportable over the longer term, one immediate reaction to foreknowledge of any change in performance ability or life-style can be anxiety or depression. On the other hand, these emotions themselves are often goads to planful compensation or adaptation. In general it seems reasonable, simply as a hypothesis, to suppose that while there may be wide variability in the effectiveness of precise foreknowledge of future aversive events, the net long-term effect is likely to be positive in most instances. Discovering the conditions that provide exceptions to the principle will be an important task for the next stages of research.

Process Research on Expectancy

The kind of research needed is what I have called elsewhere "process research" (R. Sears 1975, p. 57), that is, investigation directed toward the discovery of presumably universal laws of behavior. For obvious reasons, psychologists ordinarily prefer the experimental method for such study. To illustrate my hypotheses, however, I have chosen deliberately to use examples that cannot fall into the range of experimentable phenomena. While the ultimate refinement of expectancy theory will require experiments, I do not think they are the most fruitful method with which to start. Rather, comparisons of the sort I have suggested, which are taken directly from the real-life experiences and motives and frustrations of aging people, should make it possible to discover some rough principles that can be used for the near-future study of expectancy's role in adaptation to aging.

It is always difficult to convert molecular laboratory operations into comparable defining operations at the naturalistic level. Nowhere is this more difficult than with variables relevant to aging, for there the motives are powerful, the time span for cause-and-effect long, and many of the relevant environmental events unsusceptible to experimental control. Laboratory experiments usually attempt to hold constant the variables implied by "everything else being equal," while in natural situations they can rarely be held constant; in fact, they are often intertwined with the stated independent variables in nonrandom ways. For example, in an experiment, one can examine the influence of subjects' strength of achievement motivation and their expectancy of success at a competitive task on the kinds of reaction they show to failure at the task. This can be done by first selecting subgroups of subjects who display high or low achievement motivation scores on an ambiguous pictures test, then, by appropriate instructions, giving them an expectation of high or low probability of success on a particular task. For the test, all four subgroups can be subjected to experimentally induced failure on the task. We can secure outcome measures by various kinds of observation or test, and we can reach conclusions as to the main effects and interactive effects of strength of motivation and level of expectancy on the occurrence of such reactions as planful coping, self-justification, depression, resentment, and anxiety.

Real life is very different and less orderly. The strength of achievement motivation varies from task to task, and the strength determines whether a person even tries to perform a particular task. Whatever strength does exist has been influenced, in part, by the person's history of success or failure; this conjunction, in turn, influences the kind of expectancies he or she has about the probable outcome of task-directed effort. Hence, there are inescapable built-in correlations among the antecedent variables whose influences we are trying to discover. Worse still, we know that in some age cohorts the strength of achievement motivation varies not only with the kind of task but with the gender of the performer. In sum, the situations faced by real people in the real world include many other variables besides the few that can be controlled in an experiment. These other variables may differ systematically among people according to occupation, intelligence, social-personality attributes, family network status, potential income, housing arrangements, and so on at length (though one hopes not ad infinitum).

From a strategic standpoint, this state of affairs suggests an initial empirical search in whatever longitudinal data may exist for kinds of foreknowledge or expectancy that are associated with satisfying or not satisfying behavioral outcomes. It should be possible to compare subsamples of subjects who have made good versus poor adaptations to such events as bereavement, forced retirement, radically reduced income, changed living arrangements, or incapacitating illness with respect to the amount and kind of preparation they have had for them and the extent of the period during which they have had the expectancy. The distorting effects of systematically correlated independent variables can be somewhat negated by regression analysis. The assumption on which the following sections rest is that expectancy will be shown to have significant effects on the adaptation process. Whether these effects are all positive or not, we need to discover means for providing aging people with more foresight into their future conditions.

METHODS FOR IMPROVING EXPECTANCY

There are two kinds of information that can be useful in making expectations more precise. One is the measure of changes that are universally associated with aging: for example, all people suffer reduced physical strength as they grow older. The other is the parallel set of measures of changes that are associated in some systematic way with individual differences among people: for example, most people also lose some auditory acuity, but there are great individual differences in the age, rate, and tonal levels at which auditory acuity diminishes.

To distinguish between these two kinds of changes is artificial, of course, for certainly there are individual differences in age, rate, and extent of physical strength reduction, and no doubt some reduction in auditory acuity could be demonstrated in all aging people. From a methodological standpoint, however, the two kinds of information are worth distinguishing. Many changes of the first type, those that are universal, can be discovered by comparison of random samples of people of different ages. For changes of the second type, however, longitudinal methods are required in order to establish the antecedent conditions that are predictive of future statuses. After a brief discussion of these two approaches, I will suggest some of the areas in which each can be of particular value.

Normative Cross-Sectional Study

A substantial proportion of the psychological research on aging has been devoted to the single normative question of how older organisms differ from younger (Birren and Schaie 1977). This is a necessary first step if we are to discover the biological determinants of the aging process. There are other and, from a practical standpoint, equally important reasons for such research. Knowledge about the differential growth and decline of abilities is essential for appropriate occupational placement, recreational planning, and the many societal and personal aspects of caretaking for and self-help of the elderly. As these normative data accumulate, it becomes apparent that there are great differences among the various psychological functions in the extent to which they show a general decline in the later years. Some measures of intellectual performance (e.g., language usage) show little or none. Others (e.g., speed tests on reasoning) show at least statistically significant mean declines. More molecular sensory–perceptual processes, such as interference effects of glare (Fozard and Popkin 1978), show radical performance declines with age. Such findings are useful for understanding the aging process itself and may provide help in deciding on certain social policies with respect to elderly persons. Some of the more radical changes associated with aging—loss of physical strength, rate of bladder functioning, the susceptibility to glare—are of a magnitude and a generality that make them relevant to almost everyone. But most of this excellent body of literature has little value for the individual trying to establish realistic expectancies about his or her own personal future as an elderly person.

Under ideal conditions, normative research of this sort is done with large random samples for obvious reasons: There are many variables that influence the measure of any psychological function, and to locate the effects of one single variable, such as aging, all others must be randomized. But of course a random sample is not composed of identical "random" individuals. Hence the variability around the mean of a measured function is often broad, and a person trying to anticipate his or her own future gets little help from the data on a sample of people a decade or two older. There is no way of predicting whether he or she will be at the mean or at some (possibly large) distance above or below it.

To label studies of the effect of aging as normative is not to imply that they have no other value. Obviously, much of this work has not been done with normative purposes in mind but with the far more important purpose of defining changes that are theoretically significant for the reductionistic task of discovering the psychobiological conditions that cause them. The intent of the research is essentially antecedent–consequent—a search for causes.

Individual Differences

There is an alternative strategy for psychological research on aging, however, that can be of value to the individual in attempting to construct realistic expectancies for the future. It is a correlative approach that is sometimes causal. In this case, the consequent (or target, or dependent) variable is not the mean change associated with aging but the size, rate, or age of onset of individual changes. The intent is to discover antecedents of the individual differences among people in the way they respond to aging. For example, a reasonably homogeneous group of intellectually superior men varied widely at age 62 ($SD = 4$ years) in the amount of satisfaction they had gained from their lifetime occupational activity (R. Sears 1977). A regression analysis of a set of predictor variables that had been measured two to four decades earlier showed that expressed feelings about work, health, and ambition were predictive of the later feelings, but that objective or behavioral variables such as actual success, level of occupation, or amount of income were not. On the other hand, the extent to which these men had begun to retire from full-time work was predicted better by these objective events or circumstances than by the earlier expressions of feelings.

Again, analysis of data on family life satisfaction for a comparable group of women showed that married rather than single status was predictive of higher satisfaction, while full-time employment (because of its association with single status) was not (P. Sears and Barbee 1978). But so far as general life satisfaction was concerned (i.e., satisfaction measured over several areas of experience including the occupational), a history of full-time employment was predictive in the positive direction. Knowing these facts, a man or woman of 30–50 years of age would be better able to predict his or her own future feelings and behavior two to four decades hence. More important, such knowledge would enable people to make more enlightened choices of occupational or family activities at early ages to secure the later outcomes desired.

A substantial part of previous research on aging as it affects motivational, personality, and social behavioral variables has followed this strategy (for summaries, see Chown 1977, Neugarten 1977, Neugarten and Hagestad 1976). This correlational approach is not limited to these areas, of course. Intellectual functioning also changes with age, and there are large individual differences with respect to both rate and extent of change. The antecedents of these individual differences can be determined. As an example, in a study of the Terman Gifted Group, we examined the early and late life history variables for predictors and outcomes relating to change in intellectual performance between childhood and middle age (P. Sears and R. Sears 1978). A comparison of those men and women who gained and those who lost in relative position within the total group showed that the gainers were predominantly task-oriented and the losers were more people-oriented. These differences were reflected not only in childhood ratings by parents and teachers but in differences in which areas of life satisfaction, as measured by self-ratings of the subjects themselves in their sixties, had proved most satisfying; the gainers had found relatively greater satisfaction from occupation than family life and the losers vice versa.

This study and others based on our longitudinal research exemplify the strategy for providing information to people in their fifties that will enable them to predict more accurately the feelings, statuses, motives, interests, performance capabilities, and social experiences that will characterize their next two decades. Clearly, the essential element in this research is the use of longitudinal methods. Only by following individuals from one age to another can we determine the experiences and characteristics of the younger person that will eventuate in the outcomes for him or her at an older age.

The difficulties of longitudinal research need no review here. Schaie's authoritative discussion (1977) indicates the various methods that can eliminate the contaminating influence of the time-in-history when measurements are taken. He also describes the designs that can be used to shorten the total research process so that a study can be accomplished within the practical limitations imposed by a research organization's own life-span. The logic of these cross-sequential designs is satisfactory enough, but their practicality remains to be proven. The simultaneous measurement of diverse cohorts at different times creates demands for personnel that may be beyond the financial and administrative resources of any organization. In the meantime, data already exist in several single-cohort longitudinal studies that can provide useful, even if not always definitive, information.

AREAS FOR INVESTIGATION

Between ages 50 and 70, there are several changing aspects of the self and the environment that are worth examining for our purposes. We wish to discover precursor events that can be used to predict an individual's position in some normative group with respect to personal qualities or environmental circumstances for which realistic expectancies will be helpful in adapting to the aging process. Among the domains relating to the self are health and vitality, sensory–motor capacities, intellectual abilities, motivation for work, avocational interests, family relationships, need or desire for income, and levels of desired expenditure or saving. An example illustrates the problem and the possibility: In our 1977 follow-up of the Terman Gifted Group, a list of 33 activities was provided for checking as to how frequently they were now engaged in, whether they had been performed in mid-life but no longer, or had been taken up recently. There was high frequency of both latter responses to competitive sports. Many people had given up golf, and many had begun it! Since any sport is likely to be enhanced by practice in earlier years, it would be useful for people to be able to assess themselves at age 50 and to prepare themselves for what may well become a source of great satisfaction in their postretirement years. A search of the measures that were obtained from these two groups in their earlier years may provide some distinguishing predictors that would make other middle-aged people better able to plan their lives.

In another example, a substantial number of our subjects had taken up gardening as a recreation after retirement and found it very satisfying. Others checked "never." If there is some consistent difference between these two samples, future gardeners would find it wise not to plan for apartment living in their later years.

Intellectual Performance

These examples may seem trivial to a psychologist with a theoretical cast of mind. Without more analysis of relationships among chosen and rejected avocations, the search for differentiating antecedents is but an empirical fishing expedition. Quite the opposite is true of developing changes in intellectual performance. For the scholar, scientist, investor, lawyer, physician or architect, the later years often bring reduced external demands and controls on the person's use of talent. Theoretical analysis of intellectual functioning suggests that different aspects of the processes used in high-level professional work deteriorate at different rates within one person and to different degrees among people (Botwinick 1977). With greater freedom to choose the *kind* of practice they want, elderly professionals should be able to turn their efforts to the kind at which they will be most successful. Some alternatives suggest options: For a scientist, will abstract reasoning deteriorate more rapidly than information processing, so should the writing of a theoretical book or of a textbook be saved for postretirement years? For lawyers and architects, there are often options involving administration, public relations, and detailed design—of briefs or of buildings.

In this area of intellectual functioning, there is probably much to be gained from research on the initial question of what changes come in general with age. The study of the components of intellectual functioning in children and young adults has already produced information about the components that deteriorate differentially in later maturity (Schaie 1979). Cross-sectional studies of cohorts of successive ages can reveal which qualities people in general can expect to hold up relatively well into their seventies and eighties and on which ones they had better not count. When the question of individual differences in the rate and extent of decline arises, however, longitudinal research will be required. Predictors can be discovered only within the own life-cycles of individuals.

Of equal importance, though of less theoretical interest, will be the necessary applied research to discover which of the differentiable intellectual components are most involved in the various real life activities that people want to undertake in their later years. At present, we have little information about the exact relevance of the different Thurstone Primary Mental Abilities or the WAIS subtests to various occupations. For example, intact ability at spatial relations is a necessary but not sufficient condition for architectural work or for some kinds of engineering, and quick memory retrieval is important to seminar teaching. But so far, industrial psychology provides more information about abilities required for occupational success in the early than in the late years of adulthood and in any case does not provide much information about the activities of people outside their occupations.

Family Relations and Networks

The motivational system involving love, attachment, affiliation, dependency, and separation anxiety is of prime importance to aging people. It is a terribly complex one, too, because it has so many significant connections with partially or wholly uncontrollable environmental events. In the first place, people differ widely in the degree to which they develop a dependency on others for expressions of support and affection. Likewise, the significant others who participate in such affectional relations differ greatly. Some aging people draw closer to spouses, some to peers, some to siblings, and some to their children. These others, in turn, have independent lives of their own, lives that may or may not mesh successfully with the needs of the aging person. There are inescapable demographic facts as well that may influence the effectiveness of efforts to obtain or maintain certain kinds of interdependent relationships. Death and the fact that it comes to men and women at different ages, produces uncontrollable changes in the potential population of respondents. Living arrangements are influenced by affiliative needs and in later years by instrumental care-taking needs as well. Over all the variations in initial strength of dependency motivation and in the variety of dyadic partners the motive dictates, hangs the increasing separation anxiety aroused by the approaching death of the self and partners. To the extent that there is identification with a partner, particularly a spouse, a person's own anticipated death can be even more anxiety-arousing than it is in its own right.

These many aspects of love and dependency and the associated fear of loss have been little examined in the elderly. Only bereavement has received much attention. On the other hand, we know a great deal about the origins of love and dependency in early childhood and their manifestations in adolescence and young adulthood (e.g., see Levinson *et al.* 1978). Case materials still constitute our main source of information about them in later years. An example in point is the biographical study of Mark Twain, who had developed an unusually strong dependency motive from his early childhood experiences. Even in his vigorous middle adulthood, he suffered severe separation anxieties; this occurred especially at the times of his wife's pregnancies, which appear to have threatened his dependency relationship to her. Those feelings were expressed mainly in fantasies, but in his older years they became overt in his letter writing (R. Sears *et al.* 1978) and in his social interaction with friends and relatives (Hill 1973). From such biographical materials, it should be possible to define dependent variables describing different styles of response to the threat of loss. Cross-sectional study will be quite adequate for the task of objectifying the measures of these variables, permitting them to be used in longitudinal studies as the outcomes for which antecedents can be determined.

Two major problems are suggested by a dependency-theory approach to this research. First, there is the question as to what earlier life-cycle events are associated with the different reactions to loss. Some hypotheses are as follows:

1. The greater the strength of dependency supplication exhibited in childhood, the greater will be the likelihood of disabling anxiety and depressive reactions to loss or threats of loss in the later years.
2. Effects of losses of dyadic partners will be cumulative, hence a history of divorce, separation, or the death of children will increase the probability of severe anxiety concerning future losses.
3. The greater the number of dyadic partners and the more nearly they are equivalent to one another as sources of dependency gratification, the less probable will be anxious or depressive reactions to any given loss.

A second kind of problem focuses on the role of expectancy. What are the effects of different amounts and kinds of preparation for real losses? Some hypotheses:

1. For any given type of loss, the longer the foreknowledge of its coming, the better will be the adaptation to the final event.
2. There will be an interaction between the person's initial level of dependency and the duration of a clearly posed threat of loss. The higher the initial level, the more rapidly will an enduring threat instigate disabling anxiety.
3. There will be a curvilinear relationship between a person's attribution of probability of a real loss and the severity of his or her anxiety reactions in the first few weeks or months after the threat is presented. The reasoning is that a low probability can be ignored or rationalized, while a near-certainty is more likely to be treated as an actual loss with depressive bereavement and mourning. In between, there will be uncertainty and fear.

The measurement of the variables involved in these propositions will not be simple. The initial strength of dependency or of susceptibility to separation anxiety is not difficult, but the dependent variables in old age will require new indexes of the adequacy of adaptation to loss. A search can be made in biographical data for indexes of anticipatory changes in living accommodations, selection of new dyadic partners, moves toward strengthening or extending family and peer networks, open expression of feelings, and self-ratings of satisfaction concerning the various elements that compose the dependency motivational system. While the construction of these measures will not require longitudinal methods, it will involve interviewing methods of a more open-ended style than have customarily been used in such large data collection enterprises with the elderly as our Stanford study or the researches initiated by the Social Security Administration. Once the variables have been defined operationally, new longitudinal studies will be required to trace the antecedent–consequent relationships suggested by dependency theory.

Occupation, Competition, and Achievement Motivation

Occupational activity reflects the influence of more than one motivational system even within a single person. For many people, perhaps for the majority in a highly industrialized society, work is mainly instrumental. It is what you have to do to keep body and soul together—to secure the medium of exchange that will provide many of the necessary things to bring satisfaction through other motivational systems. Nevertheless, for a substantial part of the adult population, work has its own intrinsic satisfactions or at least provides the conditions under which the satisfactions of other motives are gained simultaneously.

Among the most important of these latter motives are those for competition and achievement. Another is the establishing and maintaining of friendships, a part of the broad spectrum of activities subsumed under the rubric of dependency motivation, as discussed in the previous section. Within the population defined as Classes I and II by the U.S. Bureau of the Census, these probably constitute the major motives involved in occupational activity. There are significant sex differences in the current elderly, however, if we can use our Stanford sample as a criterion group. In their late sixties, men preponderantly reported satisfactions from their work as being related to excellence, higher pay, and competitive success in status seeking, while women more commonly mentioned satisfactions related to personal relationships. These differences are not independent of the kinds of work the employed people performed, however; for both sexes, professional or managerial occupations were associated to a high degree with achievement-motivated satisfactions, while lesser and more routine occupations were associated with dependency satisfaction. There were fewer women at the professional level. The details of these findings will have to be reported elsewhere, but the main sex difference, coupled with the associated differences in occupational level, suggests that the aging process must be examined as a threat to both the achievement motivational system and to that aspect of the dependency system that involves friendships.

The childhood history of competition and achievement has not been so thoroughly studied as that of dependency. Behavioral measures are easily available, of course, and can serve as indexes of early strength even in the absence of solid support for a theory of origin of that strength. For example, in our Stanford longitudinal data on men, there are robust correlations between parents' and teachers' ratings of the 6–12-year-olds on "desire to excel" and "persistence." These, in turn, correlate significantly, though much less robustly, with self-ratings on ambition made by the "children" themselves 40 years later. The consistency over time suggests a modestly stable quality of personality that permits men to make some accurate predictions of the feelings they are likely to have when they reach old age. Likewise, it permits us to use the variable "early strength of achievement motivation" in some hypotheses concerning feelings at later ages.

The dependent variables that seem important in these connections have to do with two aspects of work, feelings of satisfaction–dissatisfaction about changing activity (both level and kind), and behavioral choices to be made with respect to work-persistence either in the same or a different career. A significant research need at present is the careful exploration of the various alternative attitudes toward work at successive stages in the aging process. A set of cross-sectional interview studies of working men and women in a wide sample of occupations, at ages 60–80, would provide a list of options that are open to people as diminishing vitality and/or performance ability forces changes in their work patterns. Even within a seemingly homogeneous occupational class, there are differences in the extent to which alternative work activities are available after retirement. Among university professors, for example, research scientists and creative artists find a continuation of their previous activities relatively easy, often on a reduced time allocation and income basis, while teachers and administrators find such opportunities less easily. Lawyers, physicians, and architects often have the option of reducing their work load if they govern their own employment, but the same kinds of people may have no such option if they have been employed in a large firm. The same holds true for people in managerial occupations.

The same cross-sectional studies can explore and define measures of the feelings that accompany a lessened work load or full retirement. For some, aimlessness and depression—and sometimes rage—often follow the loss of an actively practiced work load that has been either intrinsically pleasurable or has provided accustomed conditions for competition, achievement, and personal relationships. For others, the lessened load may be seen as a relief from external demands, and the affective responses may be more pleasurable than otherwise. If we are to discover antecedents in earlier life that will predict these different outcomes, we will have to have operational measures of the many varieties not only of feelings of satisfaction–dissatisfaction but also of the behavioral adaptations associated with them.

It is in the preparation for the changing work circumstances that expectancy can probably play a useful role. Whatever may be dictated by customs, opportunities, and environmental circumstances, there are also differences among individuals in the extent to which they see their world either as offering new chances or as containing little opportunity for continuing fruitful work. A clear view of what lies ahead may provide the more optimistic with a chance to lay the groundwork for a second career well in advance of the time when it must be adopted. For the more pessimistic or for people who realistically cannot expect any continuation of previous work, a clear understanding of the need for avocations to replace vocations might provide a stimulus to preparatory planning.

These considerations suggest a few more hypotheses that can be tested with longitudinal data. Some refer to the life-experience predictors of later reactions to a change in work activities and some to the possible role of expectancy as an influence on such reactions. Again, we must invoke the cautionary clause, "everything else being equal"—not that it ever is in real life. So, as is the case when one is testing any such abstractly stated propositions, the data analyst will require imagination and ingenuity in selecting subsamples from longitudinal data sets, groups of cases that will control by selection what is uncontrollable in nature.

1. The stronger a person's achievement motivation, the more severely will he or she respond to forced retirement with maladaptive behaviors, at first.
2. Similar propositions hold for: (a) life-cycle duration of the relinquished occupation, (b) limitation to a single occupation, (c) a history of high positive satisfaction from work in the middle years.
3. The more nearly a person has achieved his or her level of aspiration with respect to his or her perception of occupational success, short of actually reaching it, the more: he or she (a) will react maladaptively to mandatory full retirement, or (b) will persist at some form of his or her occupation if retirement is not mandatory, and (c) will seek opportunities to continue in substitute positions similar to the original occupation.
4. This proposition is a corollary to the above: There will be a curvilinear relationship between maladaptive responses and the actual

success achieved at time of forced retirement, both a low degree of success and full success being met with few maladaptive responses.

5. Since new channels for serious occupational competition or achievement are difficult to enter at older ages, those people whose major satisfaction in their work has depended mainly on associated personal relationships will react to retirement more adaptively because it is easier to discover new dyadic partners in avocational or substitute work settings than new ways of satisfying achievement motivation.

6. Realistic foreknowledge of substitute occupational opportunities will be accompanied by relatively low anticipatory anxiety during the immediate preretirement years.

7. The greater the realistic foreknowledge, the shorter will be the interval between retirement and the adoption of effective substitute activities, avocational as well as vocational.

8. The earlier a person shows a recognition of the changes to be expected in working life, the greater will be the probability of a career change prior to the required time of retirement. This proposition is predicated on the supposition that pre-elderly status provides a better opportunity than elderly status to select and prepare for a more lasting occupation or substitute.

These propositions have been presented as hypotheses, but the next stages in research on the outcomes of the relevant motivational systems and the role of foreknowledge or expectancy are not likely to involve much rigorous hypothesis-testing. Few if any existing longitudinal data sets can provide large enough subsamples to permit the necessary "holding constant." Rather, the next steps appear to be construction of operational measures, refinement of the propositions, and elaborating in more precise terms the theories of dependency and achievement motivation, frustration reactions, separation anxiety, and depression in the later years of life.

Discussion

I have considered only a very limited aspect of the expectancy problem here. There are other domains in which it is equally relevant. Expectations as to what the physical, social, political, and economic world will be like 20 years hence play a significant role in a person's planning for that time of life. If the foresight is accurate, the planning will be germane, but if not, the planning may be not only inadequate but even counter-productive, and the arrival of an unexpected kind of environment will be painful and frustrating. From a political and social standpoint, government would be well advised to discover what the maturing public does expect, then try either to meet those expectations or educate the public to more realistic expectations.

The elderly themselves are not the only ones who need realistic fore-knowledge about the effects of aging. As Fozard and Popkin (1978) have emphasized, there are numerous changes of psychological functioning that require special adjustment of the physical environment to suit aging bodies and their abilities. Engineering can progress only as rapidly as knowledge does. In the social realm, a better understanding of motivational and interest changes can provide for better living, recreational, religious, financial, and vocational opportunities and arrangements for the elderly.

All this is commonplace. There is nothing new in the notion that older people need help in ways that younger people do not. Likewise, any politician knows the importance of having a realistically informed electorate. What often seems forgotten in discussing the needs of the elderly is the wish—sometimes, the deep and passionate need—that they have to do things for themselves, to be autonomous, to maintain or even expand the feeling of competence to take care of themselves, and to be as independent as their gradually accumulating frailties permit. My assumption, which obviously must be tested eventually, is that realistic foreknowledge of their own future feelings and performance abilities as they move past the sixties will enable them to plan their lives more effectively and avoid the anxieties, depressions, and aimlessness that come with frustrations caused by unanticipated losses, losses that will occur within themselves as well as in the environment.

The need for autonomy is no more universal than any other need, of course. Just as people vary in the kinds of gratification they gain from their work or the extent to which high dependency places them at risk from bereavement, so they differ in their desires for independence. And, depending on status and circumstances, there are differences in any one person from time to time. This motivational system is as much in need of examination as a part of research on aging as any other system. I have emphasized its existence as a part of the elderly's motivational armamentarium because the temptation is strong among the strong to focus on care-taking of the weak rather than on facilitating the weak to take care of themselves.

Now, if we limit our focus to changes in the self and in those immediate interpersonal aspects of the environment that impinge intimately on the self, what would it be helpful to know in advance? First, and most obvious, the nature of changes in function that can be expected on the average. But since no one can tell in advance whether he or she represents the average, distributional information about the rate, extent, and age of onset of changes will be required also. At the simplest level of psychological functioning, these ranges are sometimes relatively small compared with the mean change, and hence such information can be helpful just as it stands. At the more complex levels, however, at which motivation and cognition are heavily represented, a third kind of information is needed. This is knowledge about the antecedents of individual differences in the kinds of feelings and behavioral changes that accompany the aging process. Here, again, the rate, extent, and age of onset are important, but in addition, we need far more knowledge than we now have of the structural changes in the important motivational systems (e.g., sex, aggression, and autonomy) as well as the achievement and dependency systems that were discussed in the present chapter. In the end, we will be driven to construct life-cycle theories of these motivational systems, extending what we know of their early childhood and adolescent development into the successive stages of adulthood and into the final periods of old age.

Research Priorities

The number of measures of independent and dependent variables that will be required to put such theories to empirical use is awesome to contemplate. So is the complexity of design for the needed research. The construction of theory, the operational defining of variables, and the search for antecedent–consequent relationships in the life-cycle sequence of experiences and behavior will have to go on side by side; so will the two broad types of research, the search for the effects of aging in general and the search for predictable individual differences in the rate, extent, and age of onset of aging changes. Leaving the former type aside (for it needs no special stimulation), we can consider the latter. Given the current state of knowledge, we can anticipate some economy from a priority ordering of steps to be taken.

(1) The defining of dependent or outcome variables will be required before their antecedents can be sought. There are two ways of approaching this task. One is to examine the data already collected in both cross-sectional and longitudinal studies of elderly persons. Both the Stanford and Berkeley longitudinal studies are suitable. Almost any viable

motivational theory will dictate examination of (*a*) feelings of satisfaction–dissatisfaction (whether with attribution to self or to environment), (*b*) forms of overt behavior chosen to satisfy the various motives (e.g., dependency, achievement) in the various domains of activity (e.g., occupation, living arrangements), (*c*) the maladaptive behaviors (e.g., anxiety, depression) that occur in the theoretical context of threat and frustration, and (*d*) the adaptive behaviors that are sequentially adopted at successive stages in the aging process. For this last task, we will also require a developmental definition of discriminable stages.

None of the current data banks will be sufficient for these defining tasks. They can serve as pilot studies, however, to direct the design of new studies, some of which can be cross-sectional without follow-up.

(2) The defining of independent variables that will permit prediction of the dependent variables will be a second step. These independent variables will include (*a*) life-history measures of environmental events occurring from childhood through middle adulthood, (*b*) presumed genetic or constitutional qualities, (*c*) personality, motivational, and cognitive qualities measured in earlier stages of the life history, and (*d*) the concurrent environmental events of old age itself.

Some of these predictive variables will doubtless prove to have causative relations to the outcome variables. Education, occupation, and health are obvious cases in point. Others, particularly those that represent measures of a person's own feelings and behaviors at an earlier period, may have predictive value without a truly causative influence. Feelings about family relationships in the earlier years of marriage and feelings of satisfaction about work or ambition are examples.

Cross-sectional study can have little value in the selection of these independent variables, though it can probably be helpful in the mechanical task of constructing reliable measuring operations. Obviously, the selection of variables will be a companion process to the discovery of what will serve as good predictors. It is here that current longitudinal data banks can be most helpful. Of course, there is no way to avoid the confabulation of social historical events with the individual life-history events of subjects in a single-cohort longitudinal study; for example, all our Stanford subjects experienced the Great Depression in young adulthood. But the effects of such events can be traced, in some degree, and for some aspects of behavior (e.g., sex) may have little importance.

(3) At a later stage we can anticipate the payoff task—the actual discovery of predictors of the outcome variables. For this research, only new longitudinal studies can be effective. The most formidable aspect of this work will be the design of studies—probably cross-sequential— that will permit the discovery of usable principles within the life-spans

of researchers and their organizations. This need for economy in time is dictated not only by the need of researchers to see a terminus, but by the inescapable fact that modern psychological science progresses so rapidly that neither the variables nor the hypotheses that are entered into a research design can remain useful for more than a decade or two at most. I must repeat one more time that this research, in its final form, will all be longitudinal, for that is the only method by which life-cycle antecedent predictors can be found for the great variety of individual differences in the outcome variables to be measured in old age.

(4) Finally, and concurrently with all three task-domains just presented, we must investigate the effects of expectancy itself. I have made the assumption that foreknowledge of the effects of aging will enable people to plan their lives better, reducing anxieties and depressions and permitting the use of problem-solving for making adaptations to the predictable changes. Even if this is generally true, we can be sure that it is not universally so, and one of the tasks for future researchers will be to discover how foreknowledge can help the aging to help themselves.

REFERENCES

Aronson, E. (1969) The theory of cognitive dissonance: A current perspective. Chapter 1 in L. Berkowitz, ed., *Advances in Experimental Social Psychology*. New York: Academic Press.

Birren, J. E., and Schaie, K. W., eds. (1977) *Handbook of the Psychology of Aging*. New York: Van Nostrand Reinhold.

Botwinick, J. (1977) Intellectual abilities. Chapter 24 in J. E. Birren and K. W. Schaie, eds., *Handbook of the Psychology of Aging*. New York: Van Nostrand Reinhold.

Chown, S. M. (1977) Morale, careers and personal potentials. Chapter 28 in J. E. Birren and K. W. Schaie, eds., *Handbook of the Psychology of Aging*. New York: Van Nostrand Reinhold.

Eran, M., and Jacobson, D. (1976) Expectancy theory prediction of the preference to remain employed or to retire. *Journal of Gerontology* 31:605–610.

Fozard, J. L., and Popkin, S. J. (1978) Optimizing adult development. *American Psychologist* 33:975–989.

Hill, H. (1973) *Mark Twain: God's Fool*. New York: Harper and Row.

Hull, C. L. (1930) Knowledge and purpose as habit mechanisms. *Psychological Review* 37:511–525.

Hull, C. L. (1931) Goal attraction and directing ideas conceived as habit phenomena. *Psychological Review* 38:487–506.

Hultsch, D. F., and Plemons, J. R. (1979) Life events and life-span development. Pp. 1–36 in P. B. Baltes and O. G. Brim, Jr., eds., *Life-Span Development and Behavior*, Vol. 2. New York: Academic Press.

Levinson, D. J., Darrow, C. N., Klein, E. B., Levinson, M. H., and McKee, B. (1978) *The Seasons of a Man's Life*. New York: Alfred Knopf.

Lewin, K. (1935) *A Dynamic Theory of Personality*. New York: McGraw–Hill.

Mitchell, T. R., and Beach, L. R. (1976) A review of occupational preference and choice research using expectancy theory and decision theory. *Journal of Occupational Psychology* 49:231–248.

Neugarten, B. L. (1977) Personality and aging. Chapter 26 in J. E. Birren and K. W. Schaie, eds., *Handbook of the Psychology of Aging*. New York: Van Nostrand Reinhold.

Neugarten, B. L., and Hagestad, G. O. (1976) Age and the life course. In R. H. Binstock and E. Shanas, eds., *Handbook of Aging and the Social Sciences*. New York: Van Nostrand Reinhold.

Rosow, I. (1973) The social context of the aging self. *The Gerontologist* 13:82–87.

Schaie, K. W. (1977) Quasi-experimental research designs in the psychology of aging. Chapter 2 in J. E. Birren and K. W. Schaie, eds., *Handbook of the Psychology of Aging*. New York: Van Nostrand Reinhold.

Schaie, K. W. (1979) The primary mental abilities in adulthood: An exploration in the development of psychometric intelligence. Pp. 68–116 in P. B. Baltes and O. G. Brim, eds., *Life-Span Development and Behavior*, Vol. 2. New York: Academic Press.

Sears, P. S., and Barbee, A. H. (1978) Career and life satisfactions among Terman's gifted women. Chapter 3 in J. Stanley, W. George, and C. Solano, eds., *The Gifted and the Creative: A Fifty-Year Perspective*. Baltimore, Md.: The Johns Hopkins University Press.

Sears, P. S., and Sears, R. R. (1978) From Childhood to Middle Age to Later Maturity. Paper presented at the Annual Meeting of the American Psychological Association, Toronto.

Sears, R. R. (1975) *Your Ancients Revisited: A History of Child Development*. Chicago: University of Chicago Press.

Sears, R. R. (1977) Sources of life satisfactions of the Terman gifted men. *American Psychologist* 32:119–128.

Sears, R. R., Lapidus, D., and Cozzens, C. (1978) Content analysis of Mark Twain's novels and letters as a biographical method. *Poetics* 7:155–175.

Tolman, E. C. (1932) *Purposive Behavior in Animals and Men*. New York: Century.

chapter 16

The Self-Concept and Old Age

JOEL COOPER
GEORGE R. GOETHALS

This chapter is a discussion of issues and a call for research. It is a consideration of the way in which self-concept changes as a function of the events that are likely to occur during old age. It is written from the perspective of social psychology, which generally has not paid much attention to issues of aging and life-span development. We would like to consider the literature on the self-concept and functioning of the aged and suggest the utility of a social psychological perspective in understanding success or failure in adapting to old age. We will raise research questions and suggest hypotheses that may deserve particular attention by investigators.

SELF-CONCEPTION AND ADAPTATION IN OLD AGE

Our social psychological perspective will become apparent. We do not believe that any reliable generalizations can be made about the content of the self-concept of the elderly. Some older people have very positive self-concepts and some have negative ones. Some adapt well, some do not. In order to fully understand these individual differences,

431

AGING
Social Change

both personal and situational variables need to be taken into account. We feel that the situational variables deserve particular thought and consideration. It is these that are modifiable at the time of old age—to the benefit or the detriment of those who are affected by them.

Aging and Personality

Before we consider factors relating to the self-concept of the elderly, we should consider some of the findings from research on the personality of aging people. Some of these findings are summarized in Neugarten (1973, 1977), Lowenthal (1977), Baltes and Willis (1977), Birren (1964), and Fozard and Thomas (1975). Fozard and Thomas suggest the following conclusion from their review of the literature. Overall, the mental abilities of most individuals decline after the age of 50. This is especially true of mental abilities for which speed is an important component. However, the personalities of most people are generally stable during old age. Characteristics that were seen in youth and middle age are likely to be found in the aged as well. Nonetheless, there are certain changes. The literature suggests that the elderly are more rigid and introverted and less flexible and energetic. They show less striving for achievement and a lowered degree of sexuality (Fozard and Thomas 1975, p. 139). Consistent with these generalizations is Birren's (1974) conclusion that old age is characterized by a reduction of spontaneous activity and a lack of involvement.

The research that attempts to arrive at generalizations concerning the functioning of the aged cannot be accepted without critical analyses. First, one might question the degree to which measured personality traits reflect actual consistencies in behavior compared with the consistencies in behavior that are due to situational variables. Perhaps any tendency for the elderly to be more introverted is due to the fact that they have fewer social opportunities in which outgoingness might be expressed. Mischel's (1968) analysis implies that personality characteristics have little predictive validity without taking into account the effects of the situations in which persons find themselves. Second, it is not clear that much of the research that has given rise to the foregoing conclusions about personality changes has considered important methodological issues. Take as merely one instance the notion that older adults are intellectually more rigid than younger adults (e.g., Botwinick 1973). Older adults, measured in any particular year, may have had a very different socialization and educational history than younger adults tested during that same year. Since the schooling of the former group took place some

20 to 30 years prior to that of the younger group, the proper explanation for the result is difficult to interpret. Did the cohort of individuals who were educated in the 1920s become more rigid as they aged, or was that cohort trained in a way that would make them more rigid regardless of their chronological age at the time of assessment? Such interpretive issues are important to consider when assessing the meaning of results that purport to show personality differences of old people compared with their younger counterparts.

Aging and Self-Concept

The generalizations that have been made about the changing personalities of aging people are not of primary concern to us. Rather, we focus our attention on their adaptive capabilities and self-concepts. Here it becomes still more difficult to make useful generalizations. Several provocative theories have been suggested, which, at one time, seemed to have some success in accounting for data. For example, Cumming and Henry's (1961) social disengagement theory suggested that adaptation to aging was dependent on willing disengagement from social life and other activities. However, this theory has not been supported by more recent research (see Havighurst *et al.* 1968). Instead, the major implication of the data, as underscored by Neugarten (1977), are that there exist wide ranging differences in the ability of older people to adapt, just as there are large differences in the capacity of younger people to adapt, adjust, and cope.

There have been several attempts to organize the findings about individual differences in success in aging into typologies. For example, Reichard *et al.* (1962) proposed that there are three types of individuals who were able to accept aging and succeed. These include the "mature, philosophical" type, the "rocking chair" type, who looks forward to and enjoys the peace and quiet of old age, and the "armored" type, who keeps compulsively active as a way of coping with his or her new station in life. In addition, Reichard *et al.* proposed that there are aggressive, extrapunitive types and depressed, gloomy, intropunitive types who handled aging badly. Neugarten and her associates (1964) proposed that among both men and women there are integrated types and energetic "defended" types who handled aging well. These typologies are remarkably similar to Reichard *et al.*'s accepting types. In addition, Neugarten found that among men, there were two types who did less well in their later years. These include the introspective, timid type and the dependent type who fears failure. Among older women, Neugarten found one type that is dissatisfied and suffered from feelings of inferiority and another self-doubting and hostile type.

While many of the individual differences in aging undoubtedly reflect differences in personality (see Havighurst 1968) and coping abilities, there are also differences in the situations in which older people find themselves that are important in determining whether they do well or poorly in their later years. Fozard and Thomas suggest that most aging people adapt well to growing old if they remain within the environment they have lived in in the past; they may not cope so well if they face new situations. That is, the environment makes a critical difference to success or failure in aging. This point of view is echoed by Birren (1964), who states that circumstances more than chronological age determine the elderly's attitudes toward themselves and their level of functioning over the age of 60.

Situation and Self-Concept

Though we do not wish to assert that the environment is more important than personality differences developed over many years in determining success or failure in aging, we do think environmental and situational factors are critical and warrant more attention than they have been given thus far. In the discussion to follow, we consider social–psychological processes that are important in the development of self-concepts and examine the various situations and circumstances that might affect these processes during old age. It should be noted that it is our assumption that the basic processes involved in self-conceptualization are the same for the elderly as they are for individuals in other age groups.

THE PROCESSES OF SELF-CONCEPTUALIZATION

By self-concept, we mean the totality of perceptions, beliefs, and evaluations that people have about themselves. Self-concepts include perceptions that people have regarding their beliefs, values, abilities, and characteristics as well as their evaluations of those perceived traits. These evaluations comprise a person's self-esteem. Self-esteem, as Britton and Britton (1972) have shown, can be independent of the particular characteristics that people have and depends instead on the standards that people and significant others in their environment apply to the constellations of characteristics. In discussing self-concept processes, we shall bear in mind both the content of the self-concept and the various factors that lead to positive and negative evaluations.

Recent discussions of the self-concept suggest that it is useful to distinguish several separate processes in the formation of the self-concept (Erikson 1968, Gergen 1971). We shall focus on four: (1) self-attribution, (2) reflected appraisal, (3) social comparision, and (4) identification. Self-attribution is the process of drawing conclusions about the kind of person one is on the basis of observing one's own behavior. Reflected appraisal refers to the process of forming a self-concept on the basis of others' opinions. Social comparison is the process whereby people evaluate their abilities and opinions by comparison with relevant other persons. Finally, identification is the process of attempting to imitate or emulate an admired or powerful person and to become as much like him or her as possible.

In the sections that follow, we discuss each of these processes and consider how the circumstances of the elderly affect the self-concepts they form on the basis of these processes.

Self-Attribution

People use behavior to deduce what they and others are like. When we interact with others, we wish to form judgments and attributions about their characteristics or dispositions. The major information available to us is their overt behavior. When making estimations of our own dispositions, we have available to us a wider array of information. Nonetheless, our own behavior still provides a major proportion of that information. The rules that govern such processes have been discussed in a number of important social psychological theories (Bem 1972, Jones and Davis 1965, Kelley 1967, 1972). Occasionally, the attributions made from behaviors are straightforward and involve the labeling of dominant behavior patterns. For example, a person who sits at home most of the time, avoids social gatherings, and makes few friends may attribute to himself the characteristic of introversion. However, more complex situations require us to view our behavior in terms of the environmental constraints in which the behavior is committed. The combination of the behavior and the constraining forces enables us to deduce whether a behavior is caused by our own dispositions and characteristics, or whether it is committed in response to an environmental stimulus. If the latter is deduced, the behavior is considered to be not revelant to a consideration of what one is like as a person. For example, a man who ceases to work may be considered indolent if he ceases to work of his own accord. However, his same behavior tells him and us nothing about his disposition if his work stoppage is caused by forced retirement. If a behavior is found to be internally produced, then it forms the basis for making an attribution that forms a portion of the self-concept. For example, a man who spends most of his working hours alone may consider himself to be an introvert unless his behavior (i.e., being alone) is a function of what his job as a night watchman requires.

There are a number of factors that make such processes particularly important for understanding the elderly. First, the elderly find themselves in situations that are novel in the totality of their life histories. These situational changes cause behavior changes that, as a typical consequence, cause new attributions to be made about causality. New elements of the self-concept will be formed if people are induced to make internal attributions. Exactly which attributions are made depends on the particular behavior changes that were effected. But the significant point is that events that necessarily occur at this time of life are more than likely to induce the type of attributions that cause changes in the self-concept.

A second important factor is that the most appropriate attribution for a behavior may be difficult to find. For the elderly, situational forces may be ambiguous. Changes of behavior that are in fact caused by situational changes may be erroneously attributed to internal factors. Studies of attribution suggest that people underutilize consensus information (e.g., Nisbett and Borgida 1975). Thus, the elderly might attribute their decisions to personal factors without taking into account the fact that most other old people make similar decisions because of external pressures. Finally, these attributional processes may occur beyond the awareness of the people engaging in them. A social–psychological view of the self-concept of the elderly, then, may take the position that the elderly are engaged in self-attributional processes of which they may be unaware. These processes are provoked by radical changes of behavior which, in turn, may cause significant changes in the self-concept. Unfortunately, many of these changes may not be in an adaptive direction but rather may be consistent with the negative stereotypes of what it is like to be old. And, still more invidiously, these attributions may occur at the same time that other processes, such as the loss of reference groups and clear normative guidelines that shall be discussed in later sections, are causing the elderly to suffer self doubts and make them more vulnerable to changes of self-concepts.

CHANGES OF BEHAVIOR: RETIREMENT

Reaching the age of 65, 68, or 70 brings with it a radical change of circumstance. Most people at these ages cease to do what they have done for nearly 50 years—to work. For many, this retirement is forced as a consequence of company policy, union contract, or law. For others, retirement is self-imposed. Nonetheless, the behavior of people in this category gives rise to the need to make attributions for the causes of the new behavior.

What are the behaviors that replace the daily routine that the elderly had been following for so many years? For some, working is replaced by leisure activities such as increased hobby or sports programs. But for many others, lack of opportunity, lack of finances, or lack of good health force them into a more restricted life-style. Behaviors become more restricted and social contacts may become less frequent (Britton and Britton 1972). Trips to the television set for the latest installment of the noontime soap opera replace trips to the office for productive work. It is by no means clear that the elderly enjoy or can afford this life of leisure. According to Shaver's (1979) analysis of the data collected by the National Council on Aging (1975), it can be estimated that nearly 4 million people over the age of 65 would like to return to work. Yet the elderly must contend with their new life-style.

How are these new behaviors to be attributed? What factors are seen as responsible for the new series of behaviors that the elderly perform? Making an attribution in this circumstance is not simple. Let us take the case of someone whose life-style has become more restricted. Is the new pattern of behavior that is summarized by the word retirement a function of the situation or of the individual? While the answer is bound to be complex and will differ with individual circumstances, there is a major role played by environmental factors. As we have noted, much retirement is forced on an individual by company policy or law. Yet this is often hidden by the carefully elaborated myth of preparing for our own retirement. By convincing ourselves for many years that we are looking forward to retirement and the gold watch that goes with it, the fact that many of us have no choice about retiring is made to vanish.

For the elderly who hold the view that they have diminished capacities and diminished health, can that view have been formed from the attributions made about retirement? Even though retirement is not a matter of complete freedom on the part of an individual, more than 60% of those polled in the National Council on Aging study believed that their retirement was voluntary. The authors of that report suggest ego defense as a reason for viewing retirement as voluntary. Whether this is the case or not, the illusion that one retires by choice implies that the behaviors that one undertakes during retirement have also been freely chosen. If a restricted life-style, restricted social contacts, and less opportunity for creative work are matters of free choice, then internal attributions will be made about causes for the behaviors that comprise that life-style. In effect, the question, "Why am I living this kind of life?" will be answered, "Because that is the kind of person I am. I am less creative, less interested in social contacts, and less energetic than I was when I was younger."

The self-concept of the elderly begins to alter as a function of making an internal attribution for certain behaviors. As we have seen, the reasons for making an internal attribution may be an errant use of the information regarding environmental pressures. If the environment were seen as the cause of the restricted behaviors, then those behaviors would not be expected to have an effect on the elderly's self-concept. But because the cues and pressures are ambiguous, because they most probably have multiple rather than single causes, the appropriate attributions are not often made.

Why would the elderly jeopardize their self-concepts by making internal attributions for the causes of their life-style? Why would the elderly risk the attack on their self-esteem caused by such attributions? Why would they make attributions that do not seem to be in their best interests? Many interlocking interpretations are possible. As we have pointed out, the National Council on Aging study suggested an ego-defensive posture on the part of elderly persons in order to avoid the feeling that society put them out to pasture. Similarly, de Charms (1968) suggests that individuals like to see themselves as "origins" rather than pawns of the environment. Perhaps, too, the belief that "I deserve to retire" blends imperceptibly into the belief, "I chose to retire." The latter belief, which would seem to be the logical outcome of the former belief, would give rise to the internal attributions we have been discussing. Even more likely is the suggestion from research on information processing that people are likely to overattribute causation to the most salient and available stimuli. Tversky and Kahneman (1974) have presented evidence that the logic of causation is altered by what they have called the "availability" and "salience" heuristics. Of the myriad interwoven events that might lead to retirement and then to restrictions in one's life-style, the most available and salient stimulus—even if not the most accurate one—is old age itself. By being the most conspicuous (i.e., salient) explanation, it may also become the most available. The behaviors of the elderly are thus attributed internally to the problem of old age, to ill health, and to a lack of creativity.

QUESTIONS FOR RESEARCH

While this analysis is purely in the form of a hypothesis, it does offer some suggestions for research directions and leads to testable hypotheses. First, a data base on the self-perceptions of the elderly that focuses on attributional phenomena is required. As we have pointed out previously, numerous investigations have considered the self-perceptions of the elderly; however, data are needed that assess the question of attributional styles more directly. What attributions do the elderly make, not only for retirement but also for the subsequent events that occur as a consequence of retirement? Do people who have attributed retirement externally have different views from those who have attributed retirement internally? Are the events that have occurred to the elderly viewed differently by those who have attributed retirement externally? And, as suggested by our hypothesis, are the self-concepts of those who have attributed retirement activity externally less like the stereotype of old age than those who have attributed retirement activities internally?

It should also be possible to alter attributions made by the elderly. This, too, is a researchable question. Do the attributional rules of the elderly follow similar or different lines from those that have been investigated in younger groups? If they are the same, an important question is the degree of resistance to change of those attributions. It should be possible to test this question experimentally by manipulating situational factors in an experimental procedure. Can performance that is internally attributed be changed into an external attribution by revealing the situational pressures that existed but had been subtly disguised? While we usually do not think of using the elderly as subjects in experimental research, their inclusion would allow us to assess the possibility of intervention aimed at altering counterproductive or maladaptive self-attributions.

Finally, it can be hypothesized that one of the aspects of the self-concept that will undergo the greatest shift is the attribution of locus of control. Although the locus of control is considered to be a stable personality characteristic, it would be remarkable if the elderly were not induced to attribute to themselves a sharp reduction in the degree to which they believe that they are in control of their own outcomes. This reduction can also be expected to cause a concomitant reduction in self-esteem. Such attributions would seem entirely plausible, given the changes in behavior and circumstance that accompany retirement. In the financial sphere, for example, prior to age 65 resources are typically flexible, and people manage their finances, take risks with their money, compete for increases in salary, etc. After retirement, social security, pensions, and insurance are more likely to take over. One's financial state shifts into the hands of others. One cannot bargain for an increase in social security; one cannot bargain for protection against the rising cost of living. It is very likely that as control is taken away, a significant shift in one's self-concept occurs. This would be compounded by any infirmities or physical incapacities that might develop at this time. Although the loss of control may be confined to a few—albeit significant— areas, the general feeling of losing control over life may be pervasive. Research is needed to assess this hypothesis, for remedies may exist to protect the elderly's self-concept from the feeling of loss of control.

Reflected Appraisal: Adding the Evaluations of Others to the Self-Concept

Many years ago, Cooley (1902) noted that our opinions of ourselves are very much a function of the appraisal that we receive from others. It is as though we viewed ourselves through a looking glass held by other people. The reflection that we see is dependent on our assessment of the way we believe others view us. Their opinion of us helps to form our own opinion of ourselves.

It is clear that the attitude that others have of the elderly is negatively stereotyped. The National Council on Aging study (1975) showed that young people view old age as a time of trial, a time of loneliness, a time for fear, and a time of ill health. Britton and Britton (1972) intensively interviewed residents of two rural communities in Pennsylvania three times during a period of 9 years. Their data demonstrate a stereotype of the elderly as being uncreative and dependent. Moreover, their data show the elderly's opinions are not valued and they are not thought able to make a contribution to their community.

Cavan (1962) offered an insightful description of the plight of the retired person:

> The man is a lawyer without a case, a bookkeeper without a book. . . . He begins to find a different evaluation of himself in the minds of others from the evaluation he had as an employed person. He no longer sees respect in the eyes of former subordinates, praise in the faces of former superiors, and approval in the manner of former co-workers. The looking glass composed of his former important groups throws back a changed image: He is done for, an old timer, old-fashioned, on the shelf [p. 528].

The elderly cannot be and are not immune from the influence of such evaluations. Although people will differ in the degree to which they will be affected by stereotypes, old age is a time at which people may be more than usually vulnerable. Kuypers and Bengtson (1973) suggested that the dramatic change in friendship patterns and reference groups renders the elderly particularly vulnerable to questioning of their worth and esteem. This vulnerability makes the elderly more readily influenced by the views of people in the environment. And, as we have suggested, these views are antithetical to positive and adaptive self-image.

What makes the elderly even more susceptible to the stereotypes reflected by the evaluation of others? Certainly, there are other stages of development about which negatively toned stereotypes exist. Adolescence is one such stage. Yet, adolescents, unlike the elderly, know that their excursion through their stage of life is brief and changeable. The elderly know that their situation is permanent. Even more pervasive is the vanishing of the reference group that the elderly once used for anchoring their beliefs, attitudes, emotions, and behaviors. As we shall point out shortly, relevant comparison groups are crucial for assessing the value and appropriateness of one's situation. But with whom do the elderly compare themselves? Unlike adolescents and other age groups, the social grouping of the elderly is disappearing, for two reasons. First, the attrition of the group due to death, a very real fact, diminishes the actual number of people who can form a relevant reference group. Second, the elderly do not form a cohesive subgroup within our culture. With the exception of a few groups whose function is social action, the elderly do not have salient reference groups to help them assess those behaviors, values, aspirations, etc. that are appropriate for their age bracket (Rosow 1967). Unfortunately, the most commonly used group for reference and comparison are people who are middle-aged (Bengtson 1973), a comparison that can hardly work to the benefit of the elderly. The vanishing of the reference group, then, robs the elderly of the measuring stick by which their self-worth formerly took its meaning. This provokes a time of crisis characterized by a greater acceptance of society's stereotyped labels. Although this model was initially applied to the role played by the mentally ill, Kuypers and Bengtson (1973) suggest that it could equally well describe the plight of the elderly. In essence, it suggests that the elderly are made to fulfill certain social roles because they are vulnerable to attacks on their self-esteem and because the prevailing view of the worth of the elderly labels them as incompetent and obsolete. The labels are a reification of society's dominant view about the elderly. The labels are accepted by the elderly themselves, and eventually they accept the role that the labels imply: noncreative, nonproductive, lonely, and incompetent.

Thus, the self-concept of the elderly is not only a function of attributions made about the cause of their behavior but also a function of the reflection that the elderly see of themselves when looking in the mirror held by society's stereotypes. The qualities of an individual that may have been dominant in his or her younger years are lost to the

general stereotypes that society has about the group of people known
as elderly.

EXPECTATIONS AND THE SELF-FULFILLING PROPHECY:
A SPECIAL CASE OF REFLECTED APPRAISAL

There is yet another side to the effect that the opinion of others can
have on the elderly. This is a more subtle phenomenon but one whose
effect may be more devastating in causing the deteriorating self-image
that many investigators have documented. We now consider the causative effect that mere expectation can have on the behavior of a group
of people. If we expect the elderly to be incompetent and noncreative,
can those expectations lead directly to the fulfillment of that belief?
Evidence suggests that they can.

Some years ago, Robert Rosenthal and his colleagues began a series
of research efforts to demonstrate the powerful effects of expectation.
In their classic study of classroom behavior of teachers and children,
Rosenthal and Jacobson (1968) found that first- and second-grade teachers
who expected certain of their students to perform well in school actually
produced that effect in their students. Although the children were selected by the investigators on a purely random basis, those children who
were designated as likely to succeed during the school year showed
significant gains in their IQ scores. The expectation apparently held by
the teachers was transmitted to the students, who behaved accordingly.

Are the elderly in the same situation as Rosenthal and Jacobson's
youngsters? Are we, as a society, so convinced of what the elderly are
like that we act in ways to bring about what we expect? The National
Council on Aging study notes, "People in their later years are not that
much different from the way they were in their own youth and the way
the young are now themselves [1975, p. 231]." Yet, as we have noted,
the under-65 age group attributes to the elderly a much greater incidence
of physical disabilities, fear, and loneliness. To the extent that we believe
the commonly held stereotypes, then we establish social structures that
serve to guarantee that those expectations are correct. They are correct
because the social structures actually prompt the behaviors that are
consistent with those expectations. An elderly person may, for a variety
of familial and financial reasons, be placed in a rest home where care
is provided in an antiseptic, medically oriented environment. Even those
who are not ill may come to think of their difficulties in terms of an
illness model. In time, the elderly in this environment may evolve a
series of medical complaints that are, in truth, a function of the medical
environment in which they were placed.

Consider, too, the belief that the elderly are not capable of doing creative and productive work. By enforcing retirement and by restricting opportunities for the fulfillment of creative potential, we may find that the elderly do not act in creative or productive ways—thus fulfilling the expectations about them. What we may not see is the extent to which our rules and limitations of opportunity caused the behavior in question.

Interpersonal behavior also can be tailored to cause the fulfillment of our expectations. If we believe the elderly are not capable of mature thought, we may communicate with them as though they were children. Instances of talking down to elderly persons are not difficult to find in anecdotes and the media. It should not be surprising, then, for the elderly to respond in childish ways that serve to confirm the initial expectation. The extent to which such behavior characterizes a significant portion of our interactions with the elderly is an open question for research. If research were to verify differences in interpersonal communication to the elderly compared with younger persons, a step toward identifying a self-fulfilling prophecy would be taken.

There is a good deal of evidence that people do alter their interpersonal behavior according to their expectations. Although this research does not involve the elderly directly, its implications are clear. The elderly could be victimized by expectations, just as the subjects in these experiments are. One example of self-fulfilling prophecies operating in an interpersonal situation comes from a study by Word et al. (1974). They demonstrated that the expectations of white job interviewers about the performance of blacks could cause black interviewees to behave according to expectation. In the first part of their experiment, interviewers met with either black or white job candidates. Unknown to the interviewers, the candidates were really confederates of the research team who had been trained to act in standardized fashion. However, the interviewers treated the white candidates differently from the black candidates. White candidates were treated with more ''immediacy'' behaviors than black candidates were (Mehrabian 1968)—that is, they received more eye contact, forward body lean, and other behaviors generally associated with positive emotion. In the second portion of the study, white subjects served as applicants. Trained interviewers mimicked the behaviors that the interviewers had used during the first portion of the study. The trained interviewers responded to half of the applicants with precisely the behaviors that had been used with whites during the first phase and to the other half with those behaviors that had been used with blacks. At the conclusion of the second phase, independent raters assessed the performance of the job applicants. They found that the applicants who had been treated as the black applicants had been treated in the first stage (with low immediacy behaviors) performed considerably worse in the second-stage interview. Thus, starting with some assumptions about the way in which blacks would perform on a job interview, the interviewers had acted in a way that was sufficient to produce poor performance in such an interview. Their expectations had formed a self-fulfilling prophecy.

A similar illustration of the self-fulfilling prophecy was offered by Snyder and Swan (1978). They led one member of a dyad to believe that a second (target) member was hostile. The investigators noted that the behavior of the first member changed toward the target and the target actually began to behave in a hostile manner. In fact, the target was a naive subject and the hostile label was not designed to be accurate. Nonetheless, the first dyad member believed it to be correct and behaved in a way to produce hostile behavior from the target. Of still further interest was the fact that when the target member entered into a separate conversation with another individual, he continued to act in a hostile fashion even though the new person had no particular expectation. The hostile behavior, then, that was produced by the expectation of the first dyad member stayed with the target person even after the termination of the interaction with the first member.

There is no reason to believe that the elderly are immune to this process. Our expectations about the elderly may affect our interpersonal interactions with them in a way that cannot be undone without further intervention. Believing that the elderly are in fact like their stereotype, we may act toward them in ways that make them act like their stereotype. And, as we have seen, those actions may persist into other settings with different individuals, only serving to bolster our belief in the correctness of our stereotypes.

Two research directions are clear. If our stereotypes about the elderly affect their behavior, then we must carefully catalogue those stereotypes. Once again, a data base that follows on the 1975 National Council on Aging survey is needed. At that point, experimental studies of the degree to which those stereotypes affect behavior toward the elderly and consequently their behavior are important in identifying the process of the self-fulfilling prophecy about the elderly.

A CAUSAL FEEDBACK LOOP

Thus far in this chapter, we have been suggesting a pattern of causation that forms a causal feedback loop. The elderly, like any other group, form self-attributions on the basis of their behavior. However, the constraints and demands that society places on the elderly are complex and subtle, leading the elderly to attribute to their own internal dispositions behaviors that are to a large extent fostered by societal pressures. Moreover, the expectations of the rest of society about the elderly cause them to behave consistently with those expectations. Their behaviors are also the subject for attribution processes and may, once again, feed into the elderly's erroneous attribution that they are responsible for their restricted and less creative life-styles. At the same time, the behaviors that society's expectations have helped to produce increase the confidence of the rest of society about the dispositions and capacities of the elderly and cause the expectation–attribution cycle to strengthen.

Why do our expectations about the elderly persist? One reason stems from the feedback loop that we have already discussed. Another stems from the value to society of perpetuating the present system. While we as a society may have negative views of the capacities of old people, we also have great sympathy. Their problem comes because they are old. They are not allowed to work because diminished capacity comes with old age. These explanations, fraught with sympathy, nonetheless locate the "problem" within the elderly themselves. As Shaver (1979) has noted, the elderly are perceived as the problem rather than as the victims of the problem. With the locus of the problem residing within the victim, then society does not have to question its institutions and its treatment of the elderly as a group. We can generate social institutions to care for them, social security to feed them, and helping professionals to minister to their needs. If there are elderly individuals who resist society's treatment of them (e.g., they wish to work, remain productive, etc.), then we can treat the deviant cases. We may counsel them on the appropriate ways to spend their golden years or, if necessary, establish ways for them to channel some of their energies. Recognizing the degree to which social institutions may be responsible for the behavior and self-concept of the elderly may require some difficult and fundamental changes in society.

POTENTIAL FOR CHANGE

The potential for bolstering the reflected appraisal of the aged and for altering the attributions that they make for their situation is very much a question in search of an answer. Evidence very much needs to be collected. However, if our hypotheses about attributions and self-fulfilling prophecies are valid, then two avenues would appear to lie open. Both are difficult. First, society must recognize its role in creating the behavior, attitudes, and self-concepts of the elderly. The practice of blaming the victim, which has so long characterized society's relationship with its minority groups, must be transformed into a serious questioning of our institutions, regulations, and personal stereotypes. It is doubtful that society will take such a soul-searching approach unless it is pushed by the elderly themselves.

Therefore, the elderly must alter their totality of self-attributions that we have called the self-concept in order to pressure society to alter its institutions. Here, social scientists and helping professionals can play an important role by investigating and implementing those factors that might cause the elderly to make external rather than internal attributions for their situation after retirement. As we have suggested previously, research may be able to identify the processes by which the attributions of the elderly can be changed. With increasing awareness of the subtle pressure exerted by society, the elderly who find themselves in restricted and less productive positions need not incorporate their situation into their self-concept. And by resisting such attributions, the elderly may be able to pressure society to make the very real changes necessary for a more productive view of themselves.

What changes would the elderly encourage if they were able? The only answer to what will affect the self-concept of the aged in a positive direction must come through research. The theoretical framework that we have discussed thus far would lead one to believe that the elderly must be given more choice and responsibility for positive, productive actions. Kuypers and Bengtson (1973) suggested that institutions for the elderly be revamped to reflect their decision-making responsibilities. They suggested that continuing education programs, old-age homes, and certain governmental committees be run exclusively by the elderly. By vesting decision-making power in the elderly, they will be able to make internal attributions for positive and productive events and may be able to establish expectations on the part of society that they are indeed capable and productive citizens. Although such expectations should lead to positive changes in the self-concept of the elderly, only a massive research effort combining basic and evaluation research can assess the usefulness of these ideas.

Social Comparison Processes and Identification

The processes of social comparison and identification are closely related as they affect the elderly. Social comparison theory was first outlined by Festinger (1950, 1954). Collections of papers on social comparison processes were published by Latané (1966) and Suls and Miller

(1977). These papers have revitalized interest in social comparison and served to reshape the theory. One of the key issues in social comparison theory is with whom people choose to compare. Obviously, the conclusions one draws about one's capacities and competencies on the basis of social comparison will depend on with whom one has compared. The issue of comparison choice is critical in our consideration of self-concept and self-esteem in old age.

Festinger's original formulation of social comparison theory contained two hypotheses that are important for predicting social comparison choice. First, he proposed that when a range of comparison persons is available, people will choose to compare with others who are similar on the ability or opinion being evaluated. Second, Festinger proposed that for abilities there is a "unidirectional drive upwards" such that individuals are concerned with getting better. Although the implications for social comparison choice of the second hypothesis was less than obvious, Wheeler (1966) and others suggested that it implied a tendency to compare with others who are slightly more capable than oneself so that it is possible to see how close one is to a higher ability level and how far one has to go in the future to attain some measure of improvement.

Recent research on social comparison (see Feldman and Ruble in press) has concentrated on the issue of comparison choice. This research together with earlier research (see Suls 1977) suggests that, depending on the circumstances, people will compare in any one of the four ways. First, there is a strong tendency to compare with others who are similar on attributes related to ability. For example, runners often compare with others of the same sex and degree of practice. Comparing with similar others allows people to get a clear idea of their ability by controlling for nonability factors that might affect a comparison. Second, there is a strong tendency to compare with individuals at the ends of the distribution of performances, those who do very well or very poorly. Thus a tennis player might compare both with John McEnroe (or the top-ranked player at the moment) and a novice who is on the courts for the first time. This gives him an idea of where he or she stands in the overall domain of tennis players (Wheeler *et al.* 1969). It should be noted that while people compare with both end points of the distribution, the strongest tendency is to compare with those at the top, the "standard setters" (Zanna *et al.* 1975). A third tendency is the one described by Wheeler (1966). This is a tendency to compare with others who are similar but slightly better. As previously noted, this allows one to set a goal for the immediate future in terms of improving one's ability. Finally, Hakmiller (1966) and Friend and Gilbert (1973) have noted a tendency to compare downward, that is, with people who do or should perform less well than oneself. This tendency is referred to as "defensive comparison." It usually occurs when people are threatened and have reason to expect that they will perform poorly and they wish to comfort themselves by noting that there are indeed others who are worse than they are. They get feelings of having reasonable ability by comparing with those who cannot be expected to do so well as even their own poor performance. Wheeler states of this comparison strategy: "Even a hawk can feel like an eagle among crows [1970]." It should be noted that, though there is evidence that downward comparision tendencies exist, there is more question as to how well they satisfy needs to protect or solidify self-esteem. What is really involved is noting that one is not so bad as the worst, but Sullivan's comments about disparagement as a technique for maintaining security or esteem are relevant here. He notes that "it gradually evolves into 'I am not as bad as the other swine.' To be the best of swine, when it would be nice to be a person, strikes at the very roots of that which is essentially human [1953, p. 242]." What Sullivan suggests is that by comparing with others who are negative references, one has no model to emulate or identify with. This problem can reach serious proportions in old age.

Although social comparison theorists have not considered it, there is another locus of comparison of particular importance to the elderly. This is a comparison with oneself. Such comparisons are usually not considered in traditional treatments of social evaluation (Pettigrew 1967) or equity (Walster *et al.* 1978). Recently, however, Albert (1977) has proposed a "temporal comparison theory" based on a conceptual translation from social comparison theory. Albert's theory suggests the importance of comparison with oneself over time. Similarly, Thibaut and Kelley (1959) refer to self-comparisons in their discussion of how people evaluate their outcomes relative to a comparison level. Thibaut and Kelley note that the comparison level is determined by all the other outcomes of which we are aware, each weighted by its salience. Some of these outcomes are ones that have accrued to us, some are those that have accrued to others. That is, we compare our own fate with how others are doing and how we have done in the past. The distinction between comparing with others and comparing with oneself has not figured prominently in social comparison theory, but it has figured in education. Noncompetitive approaches to education stress getting students to compare with their own earlier performances and to work on improvement relative to their own baseline rather than trying to do better relative to others. Of course, strong tendencies toward interpersonal comparision make this a difficult approach to internalize.

Aging, Social Comparison, and Identification

What do these findings about social comparison tendencies have to tell us about the problems of self-conception among the elderly? First, it is interesting to note how much of social comparison has a future orientation. When people compare with standard setters or those who are slightly ahead of them, there is a concern with improvement in the future. There is an attempt to define goals through comparison with others who are slightly more competent than oneself. These others then serve as models or identification figures. This is the relationship between the self-concept processes of social comparison and identification. Through social comparison we often select persons who serve for us as role models. The standard setters that social comparison theorists discuss are sources of emulation.

To what extent can the elderly engage in this kind of future-oriented, improvement-oriented social comparison? It is probably very difficult. Lowenthal *et al.* (1975) have noted the importance of a future orientation in successful adaptation to growing old, but achieving such an orientation can be difficult. With diminishing capacities, it may be impossible to look forward to improvement. Furthermore, there may be few appropriate role models or similar others to compare with. This stems from not having many similar old people with whom to interact, not having models from whose performances one can set realistic goals, or both. It should be noted that there are old people whose level of competence and achievement is notable, for example, Charles de Gaulle, Ronald Reagan, and Arthur Fiedler. But these standard setters might be as noncomparable for the aged as Paul McCartney is for young musicians. Perhaps they do little more than underline one's inferiority unless there are available for comparison other elderly people who are in an appropriate range of comparability and who can provide examples.

It appears that many older people do not have such role models for comparison purposes. The literature suggests that the most salient reference group for the very old is those who are middle-aged (Bengtson 1973)—that is, older people compare with those who are younger. There can be no hope of matching their performances in the future. In addition, old people make comparisons with themselves at an earlier age. The results can only be damaging to esteem. They can only index one's decline; they cannot provide examples for the future. Ironically, it can be hard to get young people to make comparisons with themselves and note growth and improvement, while older people may engage too much in making comparisons with themselves and note decline.

The implications of these considerations seem fairly straightforward.

If the elderly are to draw positive conclusions about themselves from social comparison, they must have a sufficient number of similar others (i.e., other elderly) with whom to compare so that positive comparisons can result. The alternative is that the elderly will only be able to compare with younger and more vigorous people or earlier images of themselves. A second requirement is that the elderly have access to standard setters or role models who are not so competent that they are noncomparable. The elderly must have others who are doing slightly better and who can provide examples that can be followed. They may be able to devise satisfactory styles of living within their diminished physical and intellectual capacities. There is a great deal of room for research on situations in which older people may find similar others and emulable standard setters and role models for successfully adapting to old age.

REFERENCES

Albert, S. (1977) Temporal comparision theory. *Psychological Review* 84:485–503.
Baltes, P., and Willis, S. (1977) Toward psychological theories of aging and development. In J. Birren and K. Schaie, eds., *Handbook of the Psychology of Aging*. New York: Van Nostrand Reinhold.
Bem, D. (1972) Self-perception theory. In L. Berkowitz, ed., *Advances in Experimental Social Psychology*, Vol. 6. New York: Academic Press.
Bengtson, V. (1973) *The Social Psychology of Aging*. Indianapolis, Ind.: Bobbs-Merrill.
Birren, J. E. (1964) *The Psychology of Aging*. Englewood Cliffs, N.J.: Prentice-Hall.
Birren, J. E. (1974) Psychophysiology and speed of response. *American Psychologist* 29:808–815.
Botwinick, J. (1973) *Aging and Behavior: A Comprehensive Integration of Research Findings*. New York: Sorger.
Britton, J. H., and Britton, J. O. (1972) *Personality Changes in Aging. A Longitudinal Study of Community Residents*. New York: Springer.
Cavan, R. (1962) Self and role in adjustment to old age. In A. M. Rose, ed., *Human Behavior and Social Processes: An Interactionist Approach*. Boston: Houghton Mifflin.
Cooley, C. (1962) *Human Nature and the Social Order*. New York: Scribner's.
Cummings, E., and Henry, W. (1961) *Growing Old: The Process of Disengagement*. New York: Basic Books.
deCharms, R. C. (1968) *Personal Causation: The Internal Affective Determinants of Behavior*. New York: Academic Press.
Erikson, E. (1968) *Identity: Youth and Crisis*. New York: W. W. Norton.
Feldman, N., and Ruble, D. (in press) Social comparison strategies: Dimensions offered and options taken. *Personality and Social Psychology Bulletin*.
Festinger, L. (1950) Informal social communication. *Psychological Review* 57:271–282.
Festinger, L. (1954). A theory of social comparison processes. *Human Relations* 7:117–140.
Fozard, J., and Thomas, J. (1975) Psychology of aging: Basic findings and some psychiatric applications. In J. Howells, ed., *Modern Perspectives in the Psychiatry of Old Age*. New York: Brunner/Mazel.

Friend, R., and Gilbert, J. (1973) Threat and fear of negative evaluation as determinants of locus of social comparison. *Journal of Personality* 41:328–340.

Gergen, K. (1971) *The Concept of Self.* New York: Holt, Rinehart, and Winston.

Hakmiller, K. (1966) Threat as a determinant of downward comparison. *Journal of Experimental Social Psychology*, Supplement 1:32–39.

Havighurst, R. (1968) A social-psychological perspective on aging. *Gerontologist* 8(2):67–71.

Havighurst, R., Neugarten, B., and Tobin, S. (1968) Disengagement and patterns of aging. In B. Neugarten, ed., *Middle Age and Aging.* Chicago: University of Chicago Press.

Jones, E. E., and Davis, K. E. (1965) From acts to dispositions: The attribution process in person perception. In L. Berkowitz, ed., *Advances in Experimental Social Psychology*, Vol. 2. New York: Academic Press.

Kelley, H. H. (1967) Attribution theory in social psychology. In D. Levine, ed., *Nebraska Symposium on Motivation* 15:192–238.

Kelley, H. H. (1972) *Causal Schemata and the Attribution Process.* Morristown, N.J.: General Learning Press.

Kuypers, J. A., and Bengtson, V. L. (1973) Competence and social breakdown: A social psychological view of aging. *Human Development* 16:181–201.

Latané, B., ed. (1966) Studies in social comparison. *Journal of Experimental Social Psychology*, Supplement 1.

Lowenthal, M. (1977) Toward a sociological theory of change in adulthood and old age. In J. Birren and K. Schaie, eds., *Handbook of the Psychology of Aging.* New York: Van Nostrand Reinhold.

Lowenthal, M., Thurnher, M., Chiriboga, D., and associates. (1975) *Four Stages of Life: A Comparative Study of Women and Men Facing Transitions.* San Francisco: Jossey-Bass.

Mehrabian, A. (1968) Relationship of attitudes to seated posture, orientation and distance. *Journal of Personality and Social Psychology* 10:26–30.

Mischel, W. (1968) *Personality & Assessment.* New York: John Wiley and Sons.

National Council on Aging (1975) *The Myth and Reality of Aging in America.* Conducted by Louis Harris & Associates, Inc., Washington, D.C.

Neugarten, B. (1977) Personality and aging. In J. Birren and K. Schaie, eds., *Handbook of the Psychology of Aging.* New York: Van Nostrand Reinhold.

Neugarten, B., and associates. (1964) *Personality in Middle and Late Life.* New York: Atherton.

Neugarten, B. L., and Datan, N. (1973) Sociological perspectives in the life cycle. In P. B. Baltes and K. W. Schaie, eds., *Life-span Developmental Psychology: Personality and Socialization.* New York: Academic Press.

Nisbett, R. E., and Borgida, E. (1975) Attribution and the psychology of prediction. *Journal of Personality and Social Psychology* 32:932–943.

Pettigrew, T. (1967) Social evaluation theory: Convergences and applications. In D. Levine, ed., *Nebraska Symposium on Motivation*, Vol. 15. Lincoln, Neb.: University of Nebraska Press.

Reichard, S., Livson, F., and Peterson, P. (1962) *Aging and Personality: A Study of 87 Older Men.* New York: John Wiley and Sons.

Rosenthal, R. and Jacobson, L. (1968) *Pygmalion in the Classroom: Teacher Expectations and Pupils' Intellectual Development.* New York: Holt, Rinehart, and Winston.

Rosow, I. (1967) *Social Integration of the Aged.* New York: The Free Press.

Shaver, K. G. (1979) Attributional error and attitudes toward aging: A view of the NCOA national attitude survey. *International Journal of Aging and Human Development* 9:101–113.

Snyder, M., and Swann, W. B., Jr. (1978) Behavioral confirmation in social interaction: From social perception to social reality. *Journal of Experimental Social Psychology* 14:148–162.

Sullivan, H. (1953) *The Interpersonal Theory of Psychiatry*. New York: W. W. Norton.

Suls, J. M. (1977) Social comparison theory and research: An overview from 1954. In J. M. Suls and R. L. Miller, eds., *Social Comparison Processes*. Washington, D.C.: Hemisphere.

Suls, J., and Miller, R. (1977) *Social Comparison Processes: Theoretical and Empirical Perspectives*. New York: John Wiley and Sons.

Thibaut, J., and Kelley, H. (1959) *The Social Psychology of Groups*. New York: John Wiley and Sons.

Tversky, A., and Kahneman, D. (1974) Judgment under uncertainty: Heuristics and biases. *Science* 185:1124–1131.

Walster, E., Walster, G., and Berscheid, E. (1978) *Equity: Theory and Research*. Boston: Allyn and Bacon.

Wheeler, L. (1966) Motivation as a determinant of upward comparison. *Journal of Experimental Social Psychology*, Supplement 1:27–31.

Wheeler, L. (1970) *Interpersonal Influence*. Boston: Allyn and Bacon.

Wheeler, L., Shaver, K., Jones, R., Goethals, G., Cooper, J., Robinson, J., Gruder, C., and Butzine, K. (1969) Factors determining the choice of comparison other. *Journal of Experimental Social Psychology* 5:219–232.

Word, C. O., Zanna, M. P., and Cooper, J. (1974) The nonverbal mediation of self-fulfilling prophecies in interracial interaction. *Journal of Experimental Social Psychology* 10:109–120.

Zanna, M., Goethals, G., and Hill, J. (1975) Evaluating a sex related ability: Social comparison with similar others and standard setters. *Journal of Experimental Social Psychology* 11:86–93.

chapter 17

Old Age and Age Differentiation: Anthropological Speculations on Age as a Social Border

JENNIE KEITH

"If you want to do it later, do it now," is the first answer I give to any question about preparation for retirement or old age. For most people, the best predictor of what they will be later is what they are now. On a societal level, the best sources for predictions about old people of the future are old people now. As an anthropologist, accustomed to exploring various people's views of the world and themselves, I have observed how little research on old age has aimed at understanding old people among themselves, in their own eyes or on their own terms. Until recently, most social research about old age has concerned how old people interact with the rest of us—in families or in the realms of public policy. Their position in the equations of social science has typically been the passive one of dependent variable. We have focused on how other factors influence them and on what we should do for or to them in consequence (see Keith 1980b, Holmes 1976, Simmons 1945 for summaries of anthropological research on old age).

More recent ethnographic studies of old people have investigated their ties to each other, and analyses of the consequences of those peer ties promote old people to the position of independent variable. Their age groups may affect family relations, political decisions, and, on the broadest scale, the definitions of old age that will influence all of us as future

453

AGING
Social Change

old people. This chapter explores that link between old people now and in the future in several traditionally anthropological ways. First, ethnographic reports of old people in several industrial societies are described and compared. Second, patterns of living among these old people are held up to the prism of cross-cultural comparisons: What do they have in common with age groups in other cultures and at other points in life? Third, general conditions and consequences of age differentiation are drawn from those comparisons and stated as hypotheses and questions, so that, finally, we can speculate about the presence of those factors in our own future and therefore about the likelihood of significant social boundaries based on old age.

ETHNOGRAPHIC STUDIES OF OLD-AGE COMMUNITIES

"Just because I need help crossing the street doesn't mean I don't know where I'm going." This quotation from an old woman to a young researcher sums up one highly significant aspect of old-age communities. The old people who are creating new lives in those contexts may be able to show us not only where they are going, but where we are going as well. Both old people and gerontologists have invented epithets for the same painful aspects of old age. The terms *roleless, normless, unsocialized* identify the lack of positive cultural direction for continued social participation by the old. The most common feature of communities of old people is that they provide the missing cultural map of shared expectations. My stress on the significance of these maps is not based on the numbers or the representativeness of the old people involved in communal experiments (although estimates of numbers are as high as 10% of the old people in the United States and the diversity of sponsorship of housing for old people produces a corresponding social, economic, and ethnic diversity in its residents). The old people in age-homogeneous communities are influential for the same reasons that they have attracted researchers. They are concentrated and therefore highly visible, and the models they offer for life in retirement are the only ones we have.

The first reports of life in communities of old people show how profoundly they are like the rest of us, and how ingenious they must be at discovering distinctive strategies for staying that way. The likeness appears in the conditions that promote community formation. Comparisons with utopians, squatters, and international organizations show that old people living together develop the structural and affective bases of community in response to exactly the same factors (Keith 1980a, Ross 1977). The differences are between the internal worlds that emerge in the new communities and the wider society outside their borders. Those borders are defined by distinctive norms, rituals, status systems, formal and informal groups, and patterns of socialization. The inside worlds, on the other hand, are remarkably similar to each other, although they develop in different societies and in spatial settings ranging from low-income high-rises to luxury leisure villages.

"We're all old people here," expressed in different words or even different languages, is heard in every community of the elderly. The comment is a kind of border guard's reminder that this is a distinct social universe, with its own rules. Rule number one is that outside statuses may not be smuggled in. "We're all old people here," is, in fact, usually followed by something like "Who does she think she is?" She may have tried to claim higher status on the basis of some past or outside achievement (e.g., former occupation or special attention from some outside group). Resistance to this kind of status smuggling is strong in every old person's community that I know of. A resident who bought two adjoining units in a California condominium (rather than one standard-issue apartment) was voted off the board of directors. Residents in this same community protested the manager's plan to issue a "Who's Who," surely not to prevent people getting the information—in this little community they already knew it—but to avoid emphasis on past distinctions among them. "What matters is who you are now," was their consensus (Hill 1968). Rapid turnovers of resident managers in mobile home parks or of rabbis in a Sephardic home also seem to derive from status contradictions (Fry 1979, Hendel-Sebestyen 1979). Even those who try to use outside connections to benefit their new community may be sanctioned for violation of egalitarian principles: In one California mobile home park, former cooks and salesmen who bought kitchen equipment or bingo prizes for the community at wholesale prices were bitterly accused of profiteering (Johnson 1971).

The acceptable status distinctions among residents of old-age communities are those rooted in their current lives. Elected officers of residents' associations, skilled craftspeople (dollhouse makers, weavers, cabinetmakers), and athletes (shuffleboard, bocce) or exceptionally pleasant and attractive individuals may have more prestige.

Even when some formal status distinction is imported from the outside, its substance is in the internal context. In Les Floralies, the French retirement residence I studied, those who worked had higher status than those who did not. However, the work and leisure roles were all performed inside the residence; in addition, definitions of what was work and what was leisure were part of an arbitrary cultural code shared by the residents (Ross 1977). Those who acquire legitimate prestige still risk quick sanction if they stand out too far from their peers. A ceremonial invitation from the recreation and parks department brought the classic criticism to the president of one California public housing apartment complex: "We're all older people here. The president isn't a day younger than any of us. There's no reason for her to be feeling so special." As a sociologist who studied this community noted, these references to age usually come from those who are not members of the local elite. The "opposition" invokes age as a leveler; the elite are most likely to try to make it irrelevant (Hochschild 1973).

These different uses of age in the microcosm of the age-homogeneous community raise broader questions about the relationship between its significance inside such communities and in the wider social context. The use of age or any other principle of social organization inside a new community might reflect, reverse, or make irrelevant its significance outside. The factors that seem to predict these various patterns are consensus versus dissensus in evaluation of the characteristic by insiders and outsiders, whether the new community is intentionally created or not, and the residents' expectations of temporary or permanent membership in it. As Figure 17.1 suggests, if there is a difference of values, a reversal ("The first shall be last") pattern is most likely in intentional communities, whose members expect to stay permanently. Utopian experiments, formed with the intent of creating community, fit this category, and reversal of some principles of outside social organization is usually one of their explicit goals.

Without the conscious goal-setting of intentional experiments, participants in communities that they see as temporary are likely to develop social patterns reflecting those outside; members of communities that they perceive as permanent are mostly likely to make the outside patterns irrelevant. Communities of old people are typically unintentional: People do not go to them seeking community or with visions of bringing to reality some dream of a better social world. They are looking for security

Value Dissensus		
	Intentional Community	Nonintentional Community
Permanent	REVERSAL	IRRELEVANCE
Temporary		REFLECTION

Figure 17.1. Relationship of social organization inside new community to social organization of wider society.

and independence; they find community. "We're here for the rest of our lives," is a typical statement of the permanent commitment most old people feel to their new communities. We would expect the principles of social organization, about which there is disagreement between these old people and the wider society, to become irrelevant in the new context. This is true of many sources of social status, as we have seen. Status in the past or outside the community is not reversed—it becomes irrelevant. Age itself is a particularly interesting issue, and many expect either reflection (the youngest residents will have higher status) or reversal (the oldest will have most prestige). Our hypothesis predicts that age should be irrelevant, and that is the most common finding. In the French residence, for example, age was simply not correlated with social status. Attempts made by long-time residents to claim privilege were rejected by all but the most naive newcomers, and they learned fast (Ross 1977).

The mixed ethnic populations in some United States public housing are another example of a characteristic highly salient outside an age-homogeneous community, which becomes less so within its borders. Although ethnic subgroups (e.g. black/white or black/Cuban/Anglo) are clearly defined in the communities that have been studied, relationships among individuals of different ethnicities are described as more frequent and smoother than is usual in the outside society. In a national study of public housing for old people, 30% of friendships crossed ethnic lines (Lawton 1979). Several aspects of these communities seem to promote this predominance of common age over ethnic differences: individual culture brokers who link ethnic subgroups; shared participation in desirable, organized activities such as trips or hot meal plans; common opposition to HUD representatives and regulations (Kandel and Heider 1979, Wellin and Boyer 1979). Different types of social ties are also more likely to bridge the ethnic boundaries. In a tri-ethnic housing project in Florida, "health protector" dyads, made up of a stronger individual and one who needs help, are far more likely to cross ethnic lines than "best friend" pairs.

Sex roles are often differently defined inside old-age communities as well. In some cases, such as "Idle Haven" mobile home park in California, men and women become more alike as social actors than previously, as there is less sex segregation in leisure or work domains (Johnson 1971). In other communities, these boundaries are maintained, but the specific markers have changed. Part of the Les Floralies culture was the unofficial identification of the third-floor card tables as a male preserve, while the pottery shop was for women.

The decision to live among age peers could in itself become a distinctive norm for older people. Under what conditions might that occur? The amount of choice that people perceive in making decisions is seen by social psychologists as an important predictor of how they will justify their actions, which in turn is an important factor in norm creation. The justification people give for past actions may become reasons—norms— for similar actions in the future. The element of perceived choice is crucial because if people feel constrained by external forces, they do not need to justify their actions any further than by reference to that constraint, and the process of norm creation is nipped in the bud.

This hypothetical chain of causation, beginning with perceived choice and ending with new norms, might well produce norms about age-homogeneous residence itself. First, as the positive social aspects of old-age communities become better known, they should be used as reasons for decisions to live there. They are a less externally constrained justification than the difficulty of preserving independence and security in "normal" neighborhoods, which is now the most common explanation of these choices. In addition, older people are better off financially than in even the recent past, and future health legislation should protect them and their incomes still more. A decision to live in a retirement community should in that context be perceived as somewhat less constrained, leading to justification in terms of intrinsic rather than enforced reasonableness (see Kiesler, in this volume).

The "health protectors" previously mentioned represent another universal feature of old-age communities. Although the social bonds among these old people encompass the range of human potential—factions, friendships, real and fictional families, sexual ties—the mutual aid represented by roles such as health protector is particularly precious to the elderly. Fears of being injured or falling ill alone haunt many people, but many means of reassurance require a dependence that is viewed with equal dread. Many ingenious schemes for checking up have been invented by residents of old-age communities: "This morning I looked to see if Judson's curtains were open. That's how we do on this floor, when we get up we open our curtains just a bit, so others walking by outside know that everything's all right. And if the curtains aren't drawn by midmorning, we knock to see [Hochschild 1973, p. 53]." Frailer members of every community are helped with housework, walking, eating, mending, and errands. One almost totally blind resident of my French community was guided through her daily life by friends and neighbors. These were, with one exception, people she had known less than a year. This kind of uncommon support offered by new acquaintances is in fact common in communities of old people. It is not, however, extended to all. Deep fears of senility or decrepitude are often projected in hostile attitudes to unknown elderly. The spatial separation of special wings or floors for the ill or senile in many housing complexes is reinforced by the more healthy with epithets and gallows humor. The president and his residents committee once stared stonily at an unfamiliar invalid being helped from an ambulance in front of Les Floralies and coolly suggested that she be taken directly to the basement (where the supposedly secret morgue was located). The need for psychic protection from thoughts of "there but for the grace of God go I" is apparently great. Either of the above strategies could provide it, so the interesting question is why sometimes needs for reassurance lead to help for the frail and the expectation that similar support will be available for oneself, and sometimes to rejection of the less able and denial that one might ever arrive at such a state. The distinction I have observed is commonsensical but also underscores the strength of ties that may develop among age peers in a relatively short time. Those who have already become part of the peer community remain there even if they are bodily removed to a euphemistically labeled "second floor" or "B wing." Friends who probably colluded vigorously to delay the move by masking the failing person's condition continue their support after the change. But individuals who appear in the age-homogeneous context in poor condition and are spatially segregated from their arrival never have the chance to acquire such "health protectors" and become the despised or pitied objects of powerful projected fears.

The sinister significance of "second floor" or "basement" is not, of course, apparent to a stranger, a reminder that members of any community share maps of meaning that they impose on their environment, both spatial and social. The old people who have created communities in age-homogeneous settings do share distinctive norms, like navigational charts for appropriate negotiation of basic human problems in the new context. In the reports about these communities, the two areas of life that appear most normatively different from the society outside are sex and death. To begin with, the fact that we know so much about the attitudes on these topics of old people in age-homogeneous communities is a measure of their significance there. Most younger researchers are diffident enough about these taboo subjects that we would know much less if we had to initiate discussions or ask leading questions. However, norms about sex and death are so central and so distinctive that anyone doing intensive research in an old-age community would have to be a talented ostrich indeed to avoid observing them.

The first feature distinguishing old people's norms about sex and death is the straightforward acknowledgment of their existence, in contrast to our general denial of death and specific denial of sexuality in the old.

In a society in which a gerontologist can still shock a group of nursing-home administrators by suggesting that "petting, kissing or hand-holding would probably go further than a little medication at 10 o'clock [*New York Times,* March 12, 1978, p. 5]," sex is clearly a difficult topic across age lines in our society. Although there is a wide variation in the age combinations considered appropriate for sexual partners in various societies, I do not know of one in which age as a criterion of sexual partnerships is irrelevant. A fair statement of the most general American norm is that approximate age similarity is desirable, with any difference being preferably in the direction of an older man and a younger woman. Just as most Americans probably feel more comfortable talking about sexuality—or enjoying it—with others close to them in age, the elderly are more likely to act and talk like sexual beings among themselves. The most common reason given for decreasing sexual activity is lack of a partner; and (although from a female point of view it would not be fair to call them plentiful) possible partners are more available in an age-homogeneous community. The excitement and tenderness described by lovers in their seventies might be difficult to reveal to many younger people: the risks of embarrassment, patronizing, ridicule, or shame are too great. So, the first distinctive norm about sex in most communities of the old is that it is an appropriate part of life for those who want it. In addition, there are specific norms that differ from those outside. At Les Floralies, there were clear criteria for recognition as a couple (indicated by the titles Mr. and Mrs.), although they did not include legal marriage. There is also acceptance of living together without marriage for commonly understood emotional (What would the children think?) or financial (loss of widow's benefits) reasons. The frivolities of flirtation, risqué jokes, close dancing, or shared fantasies are all much easier to enjoy among peers than with a giggling or disapproving younger generation nearby. Finally, the more technical aspects of sexuality in old age can be discussed among age-mates more comfortably and probably more instructively as well.

In addition to a direct concern with death that is often at first disconcerting to the younger researcher, old people in communities share rituals, myths, and support systems. When the first death since its opening occurred in the French community, its young director hoped to minimize the trauma for residents by minimizing the event altogether. No public announcement was made, the body was quickly removed, no transportation was arranged to take the old people to the funeral. The result was a Pirandello-like scenario of mourners in search of a ritual. Rumors spread that there had been a death; no one was sure whose. People dressed in their best and collected anxiously in the lobby. Some searched for the body; others stood guard at the doors looking for a hearse. When one search squad located the body in the basement, others hurried down to see it. They arrived in time to watch a stick-shift hearse grinding up a steep loading ramp with the coffin sliding out the back. Widespread reaction was "I don't want that to happen to me." As people were quick to explain, "that" did not mean dying, it meant inadequate clumsy recognition of the event. These people needed a ritual; being members of a highly political community, they demanded one and got it.

In many other communities of old people, there are both formal rituals and intensive informal support for the dying, the bereaved, and all those who must expect to be in both of those situations before long. Money is pooled for flowers, funerals are attended, moratoria on other activities leave time for crying, visiting, and preparing food. There is much discussion of the callous attitudes of other age groups, producing a powerful sense that "somebody understands" this painful experience. There are explicit shared values about the best way to go and models of those who were "ready" are close and vivid. Best ways to stay behind are also personified, and the support offered to the bereaved not only reintegrates them into new social roles but also provides a reassuring and instructive model for those who will follow. The importance of age-mates for this kind of support is underlined by the great contrast between the way older people talk about death among themselves and with younger people, in particular their relatives. References to death, especially the older person's own death, are very often squelched with comments such as "Oh Mother, don't talk like that. . . ." If Mother wants to talk about death, she must turn to the peers for whom it has the same immediate reality that it does for her.

Rituals provide something to do when there is in the deepest sense nothing to be done, or they provide a road map for transitions across the no-man's land between two known social situations. Death is not the only area in which old people have demanded or created rituals. The entire transition to old age and retirement is itself one that in industrial societies is marked mainly by exit signs. The classic formula for a rite of passage includes a stage of separation, followed by a marginal or liminal period, and then final reincorporation into society in a new role. Since we offer old people only stage one, it is up to them to provide the rest. Entry into an age-homogeneous community, which gives a spatial dimension to the new social status, is in itself a rite of passage: The screening process and often long waiting period are a liminal stage; and residence in the new setting visibly signals the new role. In addition, within the process of moving to an old-age community, the three stages appear again. Leaving what has often been a home for many years is a separation stage in the sharpest possible sense. The first weeks in the new community are liminal: "Betwixt and between," the new resident is still thinking about family and furniture outside, not yet involved in a new network and often withdrawn, frightened, and tearful. The reincorporation stage representing acceptance of the new identity—by the old person and others outside and inside the community—occurs when the new resident has found a role in the community; it may be signaled in various ways. Finding a role for some may mean having a best friend, for some participation in formal activities, a place at an ongoing card game, a permanent place in the dining hall. The psychic shift is to a focus on life inside the community and self-identification as a member. In many cases, it is expressed as a decision to stay after an initial period defined as probationary. At Les Floralies, as in other communities, real belonging to the new collectivity is often signaled by participation in some important community occasion such as a party, dance, or public meeting; by inclusion of family in community activities, rather than restricting contacts with them to the outside; or by final sale of furniture or a home.

Learning how to participate in these new social worlds has a special significance for the old people involved because these communities are new in two senses. Not only new to their recent recruits, they are also a new form of social life for the societies surrounding them. Since lack of socialization to old age is a source of many of its difficulties, these communities offer a particularly precious learning experience not only to their new participants but also, perhaps, to a wider society.

Inclusion of families in life inside old-age communities is usual, despite the persistent false notion that there is some contradiction between membership in a peer community and satisfactory relationships with children. From one side, it is frequently assumed that children "put" their parents there or that the parents go there only because they have been rejected by their young. From the other side is the idea that the people in retirement housing are childless or not interested in family ties. In fact, about 50% of the residents of the various types of United States retirement housing for which data are available do have children. When distance is controlled, members of age-homogeneous communities have as much contact with their children as other old people (Sherman 1975).

Ties to children are an important part of the cultural patterns created in old people's communities. Like the two friends at a dance who have an agreement that one will "fade" if the other meets an interesting partner, the old people in age-homogeneous communities share understandings about the priorities of relationships with children. Breaking off a conversation when children appear or missing a regular activity because of a visit are not causes for offense. Norms like these as well as time scheduling and spatial separation all prevent friends and kin from being conflicting role partners (Jonas 1979).

Peer ties are often linked to family bonds in a more positive way. Among residents in these communities, those who are the most involved in social networks there are also likely to be most in contact with their kin (Jonas 1979, Ross 1977). The main explanation offered for the non-substitutability of peer and kin ties is that they are qualitatively different (Rosow 1967). There is also evidence that the coexistence of these two types of social bond may improve their quality. Less dependence on children may make both parents and children more relaxed and ready to enjoy less duty-bound encounters (Talmon 1968). A chance to do some occasional griping among peers may also give old people an escape valve that is often only available to younger members of the family (being last in line for the bathroom was a frequent source for joking commiseration when Les Floralies residents returned from visits with their children).

Children are often included in ceremonial occasions in these communities. At Les Floralies, for instance, Christmas was rescheduled so the residents could celebrate one day at their children's home, and the children could celebrate with them at the residence on another.

Children and grandchildren are also a part of everyday life. Many age-homogeneous communities are located near the residents' former homes, so they are not far from at least one child. Drop-in visits several times a week and daily phone calls are not unusual. For those with family farther away, visits are longer and more concentrated; when it is the old person who makes the trip, preparations are often lovingly drawn out and shared with friends (e.g., Hochschild 1973). When the family comes to the residence to visit, restrictions may be imposed on younger members by the community—how long they may be overnight guests, what hours kids may use the pool—but it may be a relief to family relations to have these be community rather than personal restrictions. Children are included in these communities in a less direct way, also. Talking about children and grandchildren, showing pictures, and reporting achievements are appreciated as significant activities and reciprocated. In one sad portrait of old people in Cleveland, an important service rendered by unhappy parents to each other was mutual support of false images of children's prowess and their concern for their aging mothers and fathers (Francis, 1981). This is not a cheerful basis for community but an important interpersonal bond all the same.

Recent research in another notoriously dreary context shows the significance of peer ties for those who wish to avoid rather than cultivate intimacy. Single-room-occupancy hotels, long stigmatized as the very incarnation of urban anomie, under closer scrutiny appear to be an adaptive niche particularly for many elderly, who develop social networks involving hotel staff and other residents. The support provided by these networks allows these loners to maintain independence and freedom from institutional intervention and to avoid involvement in emotional intimacies that many of them have spent a lifetime dodging (Sokolovsky and Cohen 1978, Erickson and Eckert 1977).

Communities of old people, in short, exist. Their members have created informal and formal groups, distinctive norms, autonomous status systems, and networks of mutual aid. The individuals in these communities differ from each other in many respects: income, ethnicity, religion, education, and place of origin; and the contexts in which this social creativity takes place vary in many ways: location, spatial arrangement, services offered, staffing, and ideology. It is remarkable, under these conditions, how similar the communities are. Since what they all have in common is age, we are brought back to the general question of under what conditions age becomes a basis for community and what are the consequences. To answer this requires the comparative perspective of information about age groups in other cultures.

AGE GROUPS IN TRADITIONAL SOCIETIES

A retirement community would probably seem quite reasonable to a Masai; the first goal of this section is to discover why. First, there are separate age villages or sections of villages in several African societies (Nyakyusa in Tanzania; Aboure, Atié of the Ivory Coast), and my preliminary comparisons of a worldwide sample of 60 traditional societies suggest that spatial separation of age groups at some point in life is very common. However, the residential aspect of age grouping in industrial and traditional societies is the most superficial parallel.

Deeper similarities are their egalitarian values, balancing of kin ties, distinctive norms and rituals, mutual aid, opposition to other ages, and peer socialization (Legesse 1979). A closer look at these age organizations may help us understand what old people are doing. This comparison of what are relatively extreme forms of age grouping will also provide the basis for a broader view of age differentiation, the conditions under which it is manifest to various degrees, and the likely significance of old-age borders in our future.

In the anthropological vocabulary for age organization, age grades are categories sliced across the life course; age sets are the individuals in a grade at any one time. Age groups are members of a set in some local area who are in direct contact with each other and at least occasionally act collectively (Turton 1978, p. 103–104). In these terms, old age or retirement is a grade, retired people are members of a set, and residents of a specific age-homogeneous community are an age group. Although there is great variation in the number, clarity, and function of age grades as well as in the number, geographical extent, and duration of age sets or groups, highly developed age organizations have appeared in North and South America, East Asia, Europe, and Africa (Stewart 1977).

Egalitarianism is a widespread characteristic of relations among age-mates, perhaps as a counterbalance to the hierarchy implicit in relations across age-group boundaries. Age-mates are under great social pressure to conform with their peers, especially in terms of external standards (e.g., within warrior grades, exceptional prowess as a warrior is more likely to be acceptable than unusual wealth).

Nuer age-mates in the Sudan "are on terms of entire equality. A man does not stand on ceremony with his age-mates, but jokes, plays and eats with them at his ease. Age-mates associate in work, war, and in all the pursuits of leisure. They are expected to offer one another hospitality and to share their possessions. [Evans-Pritchard 1940, 1968, p. 258]." In some systems (Bartle Bay, New Guinea; Nuba and Masai, East Africa) equality is guarded by shifting out of a set altogether those too markedly strong or weak. In Swiss *Jahrgängervereine* in the nineteenth century, any member who inherited a large estate, made a wealthy marriage, or was otherwise "especially favored by fortune" had to make a special contribution to the age group (Trümpy 1965 cited in Stewart 1977, p. 338). Leadership within age groups is always a delicate matter. Among the Arusha of Tanzania, for example, influential individuals begin to emerge as an age set moves up through the grades, but they must take great precaution not to "become careless of [their] egalitarian obligations to [their] age-mates [or] incline toward authoritarian neglect of their interests or opinions [Gulliver 1963, p. 52]." Anyone too unmindful of egalitarian values is quickly reminded of them as he loses influence and has no choice but to be once again equal to his peers. One influential member of a senior Arusha age grade was very uneasy when, because of his position in the traditional system, he was given the right to vote in the 1958 Tanganyika national elections: He feared being thought "over-ambitious and presumptuous." His solution was to ask for approval of the age set before registering to vote, promising that he would poll his age-mates and vote as they directed (Gulliver 1963, p. 49).

Mutual aid to age-mates is reported around the world. Among the

Hidatsa of North America, for instance, a man's age-mates had the usual brotherly responsibilities to him. They contributed money if he wanted to perform an expensive ritual, restrained him if his participation in ceremonial self-torture was too dangerous, and helped him in times of economic strain, such as theft of his horses (Stewart 1977, p. 277). In many patrilineal African societies, age-mates help an individual obtain the cattle he needs to pay a bride-price. This kind of support appears in modern contexts, also, as among the Atié of the Ivory Coast, who pool resources within an age set to invest in a taxi or lorry, which they operate collectively.

Responses to the death of a member also demonstrate the support given to age-mates. Most often this continues beyond life, as age-mates have specific responsibilities in funerals, often paying some costs and, as among the Hidatsa, giving food and gifts to the bereaved as well (Stewart 1977, p. 277). The Nuer age sets are unusual because their rule is the reverse: Age-mates must not eat meat at each other's funeral feasts and are prohibited from burying each other. The direct reversal of many other rules is, of course, less of an exception than is no rule at all. What is common is some response to death shared by and distinctive to age-mates.

Distinctive norms about sex are also usual in traditional age groups. Age-mates often go courting together, and the hospitality and generosity required among them may extend to wife-sharing. "On some nights all the members (of a Mandan age society) sent for their wives. Then water was poured on the fire, and in the darkness each man seized and hugged someone else's wife [Lowie, 1916, p. 266]." The Arusha prohibit sexual relations with an age-mate's daughter because she is "like your own daughter," but age-mates have the privilege of sexual access to each other's wives as long as it does not occur frequently enough to threaten the couple. In a comparative cross-cultural study, one specialist in African age organization demonstrated the relationship between the presence of formal age grades (in his study this was indicated by named age sets with corporate functions and collective rites of passage through a minimum of two age grades) and permission of premarital promiscuity for men (Legesse 1973a). The explanation for this finding is complex, but for us the significance is the correlation between age-grading and distinctive sexual norms for age-mates. The age-graded systems permitted the younger men promiscuity in various ways—with young married women, older married women, widows, divorcees, or age-mates of the same sex. What is common in all of these examples is that sex is somehow regulated by the age organization and that there are appropriate norms for sexual behavior by and among age-mates.

Rites of passage including genital mutilation, severe hazing, and seclusion for long periods are probably the best-known feature of age-graded societies, as they have been elaborately described by anthropologists. Although some ritual of transition is usual, there is, in fact, wide variation in timing, intensity, and participation. Timing is not always fixed, and conflict among members of adjacent age sets often focuses on demands for advancement from the younger and resistance from the older, who usually determine the date for rituals. The Meru (Kenya) engage in mock battle between novitiates and incumbent warriors and elders; the Kipsigis wage real battle with fists and spears (Holding 1942, p. 59; Peristiany 1939, pp 31–32). In a comparative study of 21 societies with age sets, the only one in which there was no conflict over transitions (Nandi of Kenya) was the one in which their timing was fixed (Foner and Kertzer 1978).

Circumcision or subincision without anesthetics, whipping, scarification, and ridicule are dramatic enough to have created a strong association between the process of age-grade initiation and such painful experiences. However, some transition rituals are much milder, although apparently still effective devices for socialization. The Boran of Ethiopia and Kenya have a complex system of grades based on generation (sons' positions in a grade are determined relative to those of their fathers, regardless of age). Transitions are marked by dances, feasting, ritual songs and poems, and by changes in hair styles, not by torture or trauma. As the anthropologist who studied the Boran points out, the key element of social transitions is a signal to the individuals changing roles and to the others around them that they are now to be treated in a new way and that new behavior is expected of them. The ritual is a signal and, according to Legesse, does not depend for its effectiveness on the psychological trauma of severe hazing (Legesse 1973b, 1979).

The inventory of named sets and grades in some traditional societies may also suggest a false impression of simultaneous movement by all members of a set across the grades. Among the Arusha, as in many other societies, individuals acquire and give up the roles of different grades more gradually and in a less coordinated way. The ritual is more of a recognition that the transition has taken place than a catalyst for its beginning. "What occurs in reality is that there is a gradual, fairly continuous process of changing and becoming. . . . As the system operates in actual practice the ceremonial events . . . mainly give public recognition of an already established change for the majority of men in an age-set; they largely serve to bring formal categories into line with actual roles [Gulliver 1963, p. 39; see also Ruel 1962, p. 22 on the Kuria]."

Older members of society, representatives of more advanced grades, usually have an important role in transition rituals. First, they know the words; they instruct the movers-up in the ritual itself, which often includes teaching them about the "new" attributes they must acquire, which are now legitimized and publicly reinforced. The age-mates who enter Poro secret societies in West Africa are symbolically eaten by the Poro spirit, and then reborn in their new roles. In parts of the reentry ritual, they act like children who cannot walk or talk. They learn a new secret language to be shared only with fellow initiates, and, when they emerge from their seclusion in the bush, they are tied to each other with thread and moss to symbolize the bonds of loyalty they have learned (Little 1965, p. 357). Such rebirth rituals are a kind of symbolic shorthand for the socialization process triggered by or culminated in the ritual signal for new expectations and treatment.

The imagery of fathers and children, which so often appears in transition rituals, raises the question of intergenerational relations in social systems in which age boundaries are highly emphasized. Conflict clearly does occur, as the mock—and real—battles previously referred to demonstrate. However, these conflicts are channeled and constrained in ways that may protect relationships in other spheres, such as kinship. In a comparative study of Masai-type societies in East Africa, Spencer has shown that in each case, conflicts over highly valued and scarce resources, such as women or cattle, are prevented from endangering community harmony by the age organization, which provides means to avoid or manage them.

For the Arusha, the prime scarce resource is land, and intergenerational conflicts over land that take place within patrilineages are kept strictly out of the parish assemblies of the age organization so that they are not allowed to expand village-wide. In the arena of the age organization, competition between adjacent generations is limited. The Samburu's scarce resource is women, and a father's desire for more young wives brings him into direct opposition with sons who want bridewealth for their own marriages. In the Samburu age system, fathers are not the authority figures (fire-stick elders) for their own sons, a fact that prevents family tensions from spilling into the age organization. Finally, among the Masai, whose scarce resource is also women, when a first son becomes a warrior, his mother and her other sons move into a separate warrior village, which increases avoidance between father and sons and formalizes intergenerational relations, so that conflicts arising from possible role ambiguity and competition are less likely (Spencer 1976). The three systems are similar because age and kin relations are in each case complementary: on a more abstract level for the Arusha, for whom the two domains are kept distinct; on a more concrete level for Samburu and Masai, for whom fathers and sons either have less direct relations within the age organization or are kept formally distant from each other according to its rules. Words such as formal or distant should be understood in the structural sense in which they are used: This official estrangement may in fact make personal relations between individual fathers and sons less difficult.

A very common balancing pattern in age organizations is the alliance of alternate generations in the style of the Gray Panthers. In some cases, the balance is extended into a division of the entire organization into two separate "streams." The core feature is the counterweight provided to those in the middle years, who comprise a powerful category in which physical and social resources often coincide. The affective aspect of the tie of alternate generations, similar to our ideal of grandparent–grandchild relations, has been reported in many traditional societies. A comparative study of 75 societies revealed a pattern of affective/authoritative complementarity: When grandparents do not have authority over grandchildren, the ties between them are close, warm, and indulgent (Apple 1956).

The parallels between age organizations in many traditional societies and the definitions of age groups and boundaries by the elderly of many industrial nations are striking. As if they had read the ethnographies, some old people are creating age groups that offer them many supports to a satisfying life that are not provided by their societies. Egalitarianism insulates them from an external status system in which they are losers, often for the first time in their adult lives. Mutual aid among age-mates provides material and psychic security without the price of dependence. Old people in many traditional societies have the roles of norm maintainers or enforcers: They know the rules and may have ritual sanctions to preserve them. In our societies, they have become norm creators as they invent responses to sex, death, and conflict that are distinctive to their new communities. The norms they define and the rites of passage into the new social systems ease the pain of the inhuman situation of social ambiguity in which many old people otherwise exist. In addition—again, considering the traditional age organization—the age-homogeneous communities and the rituals of separation and integration they provide may eventually teach the wider society new roles for old people. Finally, as in the traditional age organizations, old people as a community of age peers seem to perform a better balancing act with their kin, especially their children and grandchildren, as they are less dependent on the family for all social satisfactions, and some intergenerational conflicts are institutionalized away from specific individual relationships.

The first significance of these similarities is the strong suggestion that what old people are doing is perhaps a reasonable and functional adaptation to the situation in which they find themselves. The difficulty of seeing that is, I think, related not only to American attitudes toward old age but also to our unease with explicit emphasis on social differentiation of any kind. Second, to understand what old people are doing now as well as what they may be up to in the future, we need to investigate the conditions of age grouping and age differentiation in general. Having discovered that old people have not invented the age set or even the age village and that the form and function of their age groups has much in common with age organizations in a wide range of cultural contexts, we need to move on to systematic questions about when age is used as the basis of what types of social boundary.

AGE AS A SOCIAL BORDER

Social boundaries based on any characteristic may have one or more dimensions: cognitive, ideological–normative, interactional, and organizational. A characteristic may be the basis of various numbers of borders along any of these dimensions, and each boundary may be higher or lower—that is, defined with varying degrees of sharpness and permeability. Also, by definition, any border has two sides so that perceptions and evaluations of both the border characteristics and its symbolic markers may be different for insiders and outsiders (Ross 1975). The boundary uses of a characteristic such as age can also be charted on more than one level (i.e., social, individual, and situational). A complete map of age differentiation has never been drawn in any cultural context. The goal of this section is to provide a guide for future exploration. We do not yet have enough descriptive data to derive interpretations of dynamic processes, such as sharpening or weakening of age borders. (These dynamics, it should be pointed out, are equally present and mysterious in traditional and modern settings. Age organizations have appeared, altered, disappeared, or intensified in various African and North American societies, for example, in historical times (Levine and Sangree 1962, Stewart 1977, pp. 243–328). Here I will draw on the information we do have about age organization in various settings to propose hypotheses and questions about the conditions and consequences of different types and degrees of age differentiation. The research they require is the first step toward understanding the future significance of age boundaries in our society in general and for old people in particular.

Cognitive Dimension

In a specific social context, the research question on this dimension is about a real-life sorting task. Do people use age in sorting individuals? How many distinctions do they make? What are the indicators that signal age identity?

Individual variation in age categorization has been observed in the United States, where an ethnographer created a sorting experiment to discover the way people used age in real life. The number of age categories reported varied from 2 to 15, and several variables affected the responses: Higher education and higher socioeconomic status are related to more differentiation; women make fewer distinctions than men; married individuals make more distinctions than others; people in the middle years (45–65) make fewer distinctions than those younger or older; and those with children in their late teens name the fewest categories, those whose children are adult, the most. The age heterogeneity of the kin network is the explanatory variable suggested by the author of this research, who argues that at different points in the domestic cycle, age heterogeneity is more or less significant in an individual's kin relations, and that this salience is reflected in categorizations of the life-span (Fry 1976).

It seems likely that there might be less variation in societies in which age is also used as the basis of boundaries around corporate groups and in formal comprehensive categorization of age grades. Or, in a pattern parallel to ethnic stratification, those in the lower ranks of an age hierarchy may make more refined distinctions as they look up the ladder than do those at the top looking down. (Note that, in some societies, the oldest and youngest should therefore be the most sensitive to age stratification as the ranking is not always linear.) Men and women may perceive age categorization differently, also, since in many cultures age organization involves men more intensively than women.

Among the Masai of East Africa ethnographers discovered some consequences of age categorization: variation in evaluation of personality traits, such as disobedience, courage, or laziness, depending on the age category associated with the trait in their experiment (Kirk and Burton 1977). This is reminiscent of Clark and Anderson's finding (1967) that the American traits of independence and aggressiveness that promoted successful living in the middle years were correlated with mental illness in the old. In Nadel's classic controlled comparison of witchcraft in four African societies, the explanation for the difference in intergenerational conflict between the Korongo and the Mesakin (both in Sudan) is that the greater number of age distinctions in Korongo means that these social borders are more congruent to physical capability so that the "old" men are less resentful of the young (Nadel 1960). Nadel's hypothesis could be evaluated on a broader sample and might be examined on the individual as well as the social level. Work such as that of Fry shows that there is variation in age categorization in at least one industrial society, and, for reasons previously discussed, it is plausible that it also occurs in some traditional settings.

Situational ethnicity is a concept introduced by anthropologists who have worked in African cities to describe contextual variation in ethnic categorization. This kind of variation in age differentiation has not been examined, although there are several ways this might be done. The African ethnicity literature suggests that in unfamiliar new settings, ethnicity is a convenient basis of categorization, a means of putting order into a socially undefined situation. The situational label refers to the fact that the ethnic categorization may not be the same in the urban context as in the rural (Southall 1970). Ethnicity is "convenient" both because it is a familiar basis of differentiation and because it is ascriptive and therefore universally available. The same arguments might be made for age.

Ideological Dimension

Individuals who recognize that they share some characteristic (or realize that others perceive them to share it) may in addition develop a sense of collectivity or shared fate, norms about how they should behave, and beliefs about how others should view and treat them.

On the social level, the major factor in discussions of age as an ideological border is change. Rapid social change is argued by many writers to be the cause of age differentiation along an ideological dimension; and the key concept in most of these analyses is generation.

Although it was by no means the first, Mannheim's essay on generations has become the standard reference point for contemporary writers (1952). His concept of historical consciousness exemplifies age boundaries with an ideological dimension: Some members of an age stratum, aware of their shared location in biological and historical time, may become a "generation unit" with shared moral views.

Research on generations has focused narrowly on youth. However, anthropologists studying old age have already made two discoveries that should be integrated into generational theory. First, the communities created by old people show generation units with distinctive norms at another point in the life course. Mannheim argued that the young might develop historical consciousness because their fresh contact with society helped them see it with new, questioning eyes. Certainly the same argument might be made for the young-old today, who, as individuals defined as socially old when they are still physically young, are experiencing a social situation not only new to them as individuals but also unknown to any society past or present (compare Laufer and Bengtson 1974, p. 199). Second, comparative research on alliances of alternate generations demonstrates that the young against everyone else is not the only possible generational alignment.

Rapid social change is identified by Mannheim and many others as a major variable promoting intergenerational conflict (Davis 1940, Foner 1972). The problem is that change as a variable is not seen as variable enough. First, the curvilinearity of the relationship between rate of change and generational conflict pointed out by Mannheim is seldom considered. This is part of a larger problem: Social change as a factor is far too gross to be evaluated without refinement. Although "rapid" so often modifies social change that the words sound comfortably linked, the connection is one of habit, not fact. Mannheim's use of the term *tempo* underlines the need to observe rates of change as a variable if their effects are to be evaluated. The range of societies in which anthropologists work should make this sensitivity to variation both conceptually and practically more likely.

There are also many types of social change as anthropologists have already helped to document. This variation should also affect the relationship between change and age differentiation. Ethnographic studies have already shown, for instance, the ways that different types of change affect the status of old people, refining the widespread idea that change always affects the position of the aged negatively. Old people in a Coast Salish community, for example, have benefited from a revivalistic change pattern that has made them valuable as ritual leaders (Amoss, 1981). The aged among the Asmat of New Guinea, on the other hand, have suffered the more expected loss of status as a result of new economic opportunities for the young, which leave the old men ritual authorities "in a void" (van Arsdale, 1981). The point to be made is that change in relation to age differentiation should be seriously viewed as a variable. Bateson's (1967) "schismogenesis" hypothesis about change and social differentiation in general might be a useful guide to research on age, and data about changing age borders would provide a basis for an empirical evaluation of these propositions. He distinguishes three kinds of contact across social borders: symmetrical, complementary, and reciprocal. Symmetrical relationships exist when both internal and external behaviors and attitudes are similar on either side of the boundary; his example is gangs, which behave similarly toward each other and whose internal behavior patterns are also alike. Complementary relationships occur when both internal and external behaviors of each group are fundamentally different: Outside the border, one is authoritative, one is obedient; within the border, one is hierarchical, one is egalitarian, for example. These two patterns Bateson calls *schismogenic,* because, he argues, unless certain restraining factors are present, they will lead to increasing differentiation and conflict, leading in turn to a break in relations or a new equilibrium. Reciprocity in contacts across a border will, on the other hand, not promote schismogenesis.

According to Bateson, age sets are complementary (1967, p. 193). Clearly, relationships across age borders are usually complementary (e.g., respect in one direction, authority in the other). It is less certain that the internal relationships are also different, which is required for his concept of complementarity. The stress on egalitarianism among Masai warriors or residents of retirement villages suggests that internal behavior in age groups is symmetrical rather than complementary. However, most studies have focused on the internal relations of the age set in one age grade, most often the youthful warriors of traditional societies. As we have already observed, the similarity between that grade and the situation of retired people in our own society is their exclusion from core productive and socially powerful positions. It is that exclusion that seems to explain the emphasis on egalitarianism within the age set. Therefore, it is possible that the internal relations of age sets whose members are in power are different. This would be consistent with hypotheses that age similarity as a social bond is weakened by competition from other loyalties, which are most compelling in most societies in the middle years.

It is also possible that age relations do not fit universally into one of Bateson's categories but are in some societies typically complementary and in others typically symmetrical. His major hypothesis, however, is that either of these patterns, as opposed to reciprocity, should stimulate schismogenesis. Age differentiation should also be accentuated and age boundaries should become foci of conflict when changes occur in the "restraining factors." Schismogenesis should be restrained by: an admixture of symmetrical with complementary relations (an annual ritual rebellion); the development of mutual dependence; the presence of reciprocal elements; or opposition to the outside. His hypothesis needs evaluation in terms of age in both directions. Does the presence of these factors restrain age conflict? Does change away from these factors result in increasing conflict?

Age conflict in general and age polarization in politics in particular have also been discussed in relation to variables other than change.

Spatial segregation of age groups is proposed as a source of conflict by Riley and her associates in their general theory of age stratification (1972, p. 447). The anthropologists who have described age villages or quarters in Africa have made the opposite interpretation, seeing spatial separation as a means of reducing conflict (Wilson 1951, Paulme 1973, pp. 250–252). Also, although there are old people in the United States fighting for their right to live in age-homogeneous communities, there is no evidence that living with age-mates promotes intergenerational conflict. However, systematic comparative research to evaluate Riley's proposition is still to be done. Intervening variables shaping the relationship between age-homogeneous residence and conflict probably include duration, inclusiveness (everyone in the population or certain groups only), extent of separateness, stage of life, and evaluation of age boundary from both sides.

A more direct approach to ideological age borders also proposes age-homogeneous residence as a central factor. Starting from his observation that there is no socialization to an old age role in the United States, Rosow suggests that the emergence of norms among old people should occur in living arrangements for individuals of the same age who also share other major social characteristics (1974). "New norms or used?" is the more subtle question also posed by Rosow: That is, if old people develop a socialization process for themselves, will they define distinctive new norms or maintain youthful norms, but escape invidious judgments of performance through insulation in a peer group? "Viable group" is Rosow's description of the kind of context that would promote new, distinctive norms. The ethnographic descriptions of old-age communities provide examples of groups with high we-feeling and distinctive social organization, including norms, some of them strikingly different from those of the outside world. However, Rosow's specific question has not been investigated, and anthropologists would be especially qualified to do this, both because of their theoretical interest in socialization and norms and because of their methodological expertise in small community research. A broad first hypothesis suggested by Rosow's viable group and also by the community studies is that the higher the level of community, the more likely norms are to be distinctive rather than parallel to those of the younger society. Norms directly concerning age should be reversed, reflected, or irrelevant, according to the factors discussed earlier.

The probability that cross-cutting ties to other social categories will blur age oppositions invokes a basic social principle (e.g., Foner 1972,

Hess 1972). Although this is certainly the core of a testable proposition, it needs to be stated in more precise terms. What types of boundaries do the "competing" ties define (one ideological, one corporate, both corporate, etc.)? Is the priority of one identity over another absolute or varying by context and issue?

A situational variable affecting age polarization in politics is the type of issue central to a conflict. Material issues are less likely than idealistic topics to oppose the generations because, according to Foner, material issues evoke class interests that cross-cut age lines, and the inevitability of aging reduces the salience of economic issues since younger people have hopes of benefiting in the future from advantages given to the old. Material issues are also more easily negotiated to a compromise than idealistic questions. Finally, she argues, ideal issues may lead to feelings that basic political changes are required to resolve the problems; this is the kind of change that older people are most likely to oppose because of their greater "conservative" attachment to the overall structure of their society (Foner 1972, pp. 152–154).

Whether young people believe they will later have access to the rewards they see their elders enjoying is also a predictor of age conflict. In the same direction as Foner, Terray argues that confident anticipation of future benefits is a reason that age does not become a classlike basis of conflict among the Abron of Gyaman (1975). Lack of such belief is suggested by Riley *et al.* as a source of cross-age conflict (1972). Beyond such case studies as that of Terray, there is very little data available to evaluate these propositions, and, for an adequate evaluation, information should include individual perceptions and beliefs about such possibilities. Since even the old in the United States have difficulty identifying themselves as such, do younger people really project themselves into that category? The temporal span of exchanges defined in various cultures as reciprocity is also variable and has important implications for perceptions of support for older people who were once supporters of the young.

Individual differences in receptivity to appeals for age-based political action have been explained for American old people by differences in status inconsistency. The greater the inconsistency among the old person's statuses, the more likely he or she will be to respond to political appeals (Trela 1976). Since the inconsistencies between ascribed and achieved statuses are described as the most stressful, the old people most likely to feel part of an age collectivity with common political interests are those whose achieved statuses are highest, therefore most inconsistent with the low ascriptive position of old age. The resources available to old people with higher class positions may, on the other hand, make it more possible for them to "retain more contact with the larger society than do the poorer and ill-educated and hence acquire less of a distinctive aging sub-culture [Rose 1968, p. 30]."

On the individual level, the first step toward any collective sentiment based on age is self-identification with an age category (compare Bengtson and Cutler 1976, p. 154). In fact, before the age of 75, middle-class individuals in America do seem less likely to identify themselves as old than do members of the working class (Rosow 1967, p. 268). A plausible resolution of the apparent contradiction between Trela and Rose is that for some older people, political attitudes about common problems associated with age may not indicate identification with an age group but rather an attempt to acquire resources that will permit avoidance of that identification (see discussion of "erasure" groups below).

Interactional Dimension

Individuals who share a characteristic such as age may concentrate their social activity inside the social boundary it describes. Calculation of this concentration does not simply require counting hours or individuals. The question is rather what proportion of kinds of social contact people share predominately with others like them. For each type of social tie, such as friendship, an individual may have a more or less homogeneous repertoire of others; and of the entire range of types of social bond (e.g., work-mate, leisure partner, sexual partner, source of emergency help, etc.), a greater or smaller proportion may be predominately homogeneous. A sharp interactional boundary around people who share some characterstic appears to be promoted by reinforcement of that border by other similarities, lack of cross-cutting ties, and inconsistent or ambiguous expectations from outsiders (Ross 1975).

The old people who have created communities in age-homogeneous residences or networks of peer friendships in apartment buildings and neighborhoods with a high proportion of elderly have usually shared many things besides age (e.g., class, ethnicity, and marital status) (Keith 1980a, Rosow 1967, Rosenberg 1970). When populations are more diverse, communal bonds first develop in more homogeneous subgroups, which may be linked to a wider community by cultural brokers or organized activities (Kandel and Heider 1979, Wellin and Boyer 1979). We know very little about the mechanisms through which peer ties develop or the conditions that promote them outside separate residential settings. We know that the proportion of possible age-mates in a residential area makes a difference; and we know that certain individual characteristics (e.g., role loss, working-class status) make it more likely an old person will take advantage of the opportunity to form peer ties. However, the quality of those ties and the details of their creation and functioning are just beginning to be recorded (Fennell, 1981). Under what conditions do encounters with other old people most probably lead to friendships or to mutual support networks? Introduction by younger persons or by age-mates? By kin or friends? In formal or informal situations? Age-homogeneous or not? What influence do earlier patterns of peer contact have on these ties in later life? What factors shape variation in the significance of these peer ties and their integration with other kinds of social relations, such as kin? What parallels are there between the consequence of peer ties for old people in normal neighborhoods and those that live in the more separate worlds of age-homogeneous residences?

We need to go out and do the ethnographies to answer these questions; and in traditional anthropological style, we need to go far and wide to do them. We need to work in different industrial contexts, varying cultures, rural–urban–suburban areas, ethnic groups, and older and newer settlements. Traditional societies must also be included. First, the more informal aspects of age bonds are less well documented than are the formal rules of age organizations; second, social changes, such as migration and participation in urban economies, including pension schemes, raise fascinating questions about possible adaptations of traditional age organization.

Certain life stages apparently stimulate higher age borders on the interactional dimension. The middle years may have more competing roles and memberships and therefore more cross-cutting ties to weaken age bonds (Gulliver 1968, Hess 1972). Among the Akwẽ-Shavante of Brazil, for instance, the bonds of age-set membership are compelling until adulthood, when individuals' ties to their clans and factions take priority (Maybury-Lewis 1967, pp. 147–148). In a Hungarian peasant village, the strong ties among adolescents fade during the middle years but are revived as sources of emotional and social support in late life (Fel and Hofer 1969, cited in Neugarten and Hagestad 1976, p. 42). This view offers a negative reason why adolescence and old age in our own society should be the periods, par excellence, for peer bonds, since they are excluded from either side of social maturity.

There is also a more positive stimulus to peer ties shared by these two stages. Since adolescence and old age are literally on either side of social maturity, they are times of transition into and out of social adulthood. Liminal or threshold states appear to be generally conducive to communal bonds (Turner 1969). In addition, the inconsistent expectations of conflicted roles, such as school superintendents or shop foremen, or the ambiguities of new roles, such as divorced parents, have been described as promoting ties to others in similar positions (Gross *et al.* 1957, Bohannan 1970). Inconsistency and ambiguity of expectations are characteristic of in-between statuses, and both adolescence and the years immediately after retirement could be expected to foster peer bonds on those grounds. Retirement is also, of course, a new social status, and its often-cited "roleless role" should also promote ties among those who share this new and socially undefined old age.

Old people in age-homogeneous communities are offering each other the ritual and personal support through stresses of transition and the communal definition of norms for a new status, which these studies would predict. The higher morale reported in these settings is very likely, at least in part a result of these resolutions of social ambiguity. The research question about age borders on an interactional dimension is to what extent similar peer ties develop, under similar conditions, without residential separation or a planned environment.

The transitional character of age groups in youth was identified by Eisenstadt in his classic *From Generation to Generation* (1956), in which he argued that age groups were likely to appear as an "interlinking sphere" between family and the wider society when the particularistic mode of kin relationships was not adequate preparation for the more universalistic demands of the occupational domain. An extension of this transitional view of age groups to the other end of the life course might suggest that retirement or young-old age is such an intermediate stage between occupation and a return to the predominance of kin in social life. Peer ties might increase in importance among the young-old and decrease again for the oldest.

Situational variation in the age structure of social networks has not been explored, although it is suggested, for example, in descriptions of American society as "age-graded" differently in different institutions (Neugarten and Peterson, 1957). Age has been proposed as a convenient basis of friendship choice in new social aggregates, such as freshman college dormitories (Hess 1972). This could be extended to members of other age categories and to behavior in any unfamiliar group.

Corporate Dimension

Age, like any social characteristic, may also become the basis of recruitment to formal, corporate groups. Although organizations with other manifest purposes may be age-homogeneous, here I am concerned with groups whose explicit definition is in terms of age. Not only are

they formally recruited by age, but also age is central to their corporate
function. This focus on age may take many forms, however, depending
on the orientation of the members to the use of age as a social boundary.

The symmetry or asymmetry of insiders' and outsiders' evaluations
of both the border and its markers are important factors in shaping the
various association goals: confession, erasure, emphasis, or maintenance
of the age border; Table 17.1 summarizes these patterns.

An association that by its existence confesses the presence of a characteristic whose possessors do not value it positively is likely to result
from asymmetry in attitudes of outsiders and insiders about its use to
define a social border. Those with the characteristic do not think it should
be used to mark them off behind a border; outsiders do. An association
that confesses a shared characteristic may make demands on the wider
society or may offer opportunities for friendship, recreation, or power
not available to members in "mixed company." The California Institute
of Social Welfare founded in the 1940s by George McLain is an example

TABLE 17.1
Type of Formal Association and Evaluation of Marker and Border by Insiders and Outsiders[a]

Evaluation[b]				
Marker		Border		Type of
Inside	Outside	Inside	Outside	association
Negative	Negative	Negative	Positive	Confession (request for help)
Negative	Positive	Negative	Positive	Confession (parallel organization)
Positive	Positive	Positive	Negative	Maintenance (defense of border)
Positive	Negative	Positive	Positive	Maintenance (defense of marker)
Positive	Positive	Negative	Positive	Erasure (escape from protection)
Positive	Negative	Negative	Positive	Erasure (escape from rejection)
Positive	Negative	Positive	Negative	Emphasis

[a] Reprinted from Social borders: Definitions of diversity, *Current Anthropology* 16:53–72 by J. K. Ross by permission of The University of Chicago Press. Copyright © 1975 by The University of Chicago Press.

[b] The following configurations of evaluation will not produce formal associations: (1) agreement of insiders and outsiders that a border should not exist; (2) evaluation by insiders of marker as negative and border as positive; (3) agreement of insiders and outsiders on positive evaluation of both marker and border. This last case represents a stable situation which will not produce formal association, but in which already existing formal associations may persist for some time.

of the first type; its main goal was to obtain higher pensions for old people with less bureaucratic humiliation (Pinner *et al.* 1959, Putnam 1970). Many "senior citizens" groups are examples of the second type. Although there is an age restriction on membership, their formal focus is not on age but on various activities to which old people have little access in the wider society.

An association with the goal of erasing a border is likely to appear when individuals who share a characteristic value it positively but do not think it should be a basis for setting them apart, while outsiders think it should. Associations to erase a border are typified by ethnic organizations dedicated to assimilation or integration. Ethel Percy Andrus, founder of the National Retired Teachers Association and the American Association of Retired Persons, often expressed this kind of goal for old people, who she insisted should not be treated like "basket cases." The Gray Panthers now battle against "age-ism." This type of organization usually wages a propaganda campaign to persuade outsiders that the border should be broken down, while at the same time meeting members' needs (e.g., for inexpensive drugs, recreation, or transportation) until the goal is reached.

Creation of an organization and development of self-sufficiency often, of course, have the unintended consequence of making a border more visible to outsiders, more valued to insiders, and consequently more likely to persist than to disappear. For this reason, associations dedicated to erasing a social border are often forerunners of associations with the goal of border emphasis.

An association with the goal of emphasizing a shared characteristic is likely to result from the double asymmetry of a positive evaluation of both border and marker by insiders and negative evaluation of both from the outside. Separatist ethnic organizations are examples of associations that emphasize a border they feel should be maintained. The Townsend organization, which gathered more than 2 million old people in the 1930s, was led by an old man who continually emphasized the distinctiveness of old people as a category in the population, as he demanded respect and appreciation for their contributions to society. Through his revolving pension plan, old people were in addition to be the saviors of the depressed American economy (Holtzmann 1963).

Boundary maintenance is likely to be the goal of an association when insiders evaluate positively both the border and its symbolic markers in contradiction to negative views of either one by outsiders. The Samburu elders, for example, defend their age-based gerontocracy with ritual curses against young men whose disrespectful behavior threatens the senior monopoly on political power and wives (Spencer 1965). Another type of association focused on boundary maintenance may be more centered on the markers than the border characteristic itself. If insiders and outsiders both agree that the boundary should exist but disagree about the value of its marker, insiders may organize a type of antidefamation group to maintain their more positive definition. An old people's group primarily concerned with battling against stereotypes (e.g., through "media watches") would belong in this category.

On the individual level, there are likely to be cognitive, ideological, and interactional correlates of membership in age organizations with varying orientations to the age boundary. For example:

- Members of associations that confess an age border will tend to have negative evaluations both of the existence of an age border and of the characteristics that they see as marking it; they will perceive that others view the existence of the border positively but the marking characteristics negatively.
- Members of associations that want to erase an age border will tend to have a negative evaluation of the existence of an age border but a positive evaluation of the characteristics that they see as marking it; they will perceive that others view the existence of the border positively but the marking characteristics negatively.
- Members of associations that want to emphasize an age border will tend to have a positive evaluation of the existence of an age border and of the characteristics that they see as marking it; they will perceive that others view negatively both the existence of the border and its marking characteristics.
- Age identification will tend to be with the old category for members of associations to emphasize an age border, but not for members of those to confess or erase.
- Old people are most likely to be the reference group for members of associations to emphasize an age border.
- Norms specific to an old-age role are most likely to be shared by members of associations to emphasize an age border; "youthful" or "escapist" norms are most likely to be shared by members of associations to erase an age border.
- Current memberships in other types of association will tend to be most numerous for members of associations to erase; the ratio of previous memberships in other types of associations to current memberships will tend to be highest for members of associations to emphasize.
- Peers will tend to predominate in the informal social networks of members of associations to emphasize an age border, to be less

significant in networks of members of associations to erase and least significant in networks of members of associations to confess.

Situational variation is in one sense less relevant to description of the corporate dimension of age borders since individuals either are or are not members of age groups. It would, however, be possible to examine variation in both strategies and extent of signaling such membership in various social contexts as well as in the priority given to group ideology when not in the company of other members.

CONCLUSION

My conclusions about the future of old age and age differentiation are most relevant to our own future activities as researchers: We have a bulging agenda of work to do in the present before any serious projections of the future are possible. I also predict that comparative study of the conditions and consequences of age differentiation across the life-course and across cultures will be required to provide the data required for those projections. However, I will not resist the forbidden fruit of speculation, first, about the future of age borders and their markers in American society and, second, about the likelihood of conflict across those boundaries.

Corporate groups based on old age will increse in number, and existing groups will increase their memberships, so that a larger proportion of the older population will participate in corporate age associations. My major reason for predicting this is my expectation that more older people will have positive attitudes about their age characteristics as a result of better education, better health, better incomes, and the proliferating media attention to successful agers. I expect old people to be ahead of younger people in attitude change, producing the asymmetry of border evaluation that stimulates formal associations that will be present. There should be more associations with the goals of erasure or emphasis— those to erase with members feeling greater status inconsistency, those to emphasize with members feeling less.

On the interactional dimension, predominance of age peers in older people's social networks should increase, at least in the near future. The very fact that we are speculating about the future of the elderly reveals the kind of social ambiguity that promotes interactional border definition. At first glance, current policy decisions and debates about mandatory retirement might seem to break down age borders at least in the short run; however, they are more likely to produce increased uncertainty about when to retire as well as what to do in retirement. Guidance in all these choices is most likely to come from peers.

The abolition of mandatory retirement would be more likely to produce a redefinition of symbolic markers than an elimination of age borders. Chronological age might be removed as the signal of retirement, but other markers would replace it. In cross-cultural perspective, of course, it is chronological age that is unusual, and redefinition of the indicators of our "retired grade" would make us more like other societies. In the recent Harris study on old age in America, most respondents used a functional rather than a chronological definition of old (National Council on Aging 1975).

On the ideological dimension, I expect the definition of more distinctive norms for old age by the members of age-homogeneous communities, whose visibility will give them a normative influence greater than their numbers might suggest. The conditions promoting community creation among old people living together are present in many cases now, so this process will continue unless those factors change.

If age borders become more explicit on several dimensions, as I predict they will, there will be less individual variation in cognitive mapping of age differentiation and at the same time more situational variation in the salience of age. Age will be less relevant within peer contexts than across age lines, and those situations will be more sharply distinct from each other.

What will be the quality of relationships across these sharper age boundaries? How likely are age borders to become cleavages of conflict? The answers to these questions are peppered with ifs, but at least the ifs will show us where to look for more reliable responses. Abolition of mandatory retirement, for example, would offer the possibility of a better fit between social divisions and physical abilities, which, as the Korongo and Mesakin demonstrate, should reduce the resentment of the old against the young. On the other hand, the comparison of age-set societies revealed that indeterminate timing for transitions led to conflict between age groups because the younger resented the older, who were reluctant to move on. The only solid conclusion to be drawn from these contrasts is that the effect of abolishing mandatory retirement could go either way. Factors that should affect which direction it takes will include with whom the control over retirement decisions lies and, in particular, to what extent decision makers are a relatively age-homogeneous or age-heterogeneous group; the financial attractiveness of retirement; changes in work role patterns so that the most senior do not occupy the most prestigious and well-paid positions; possible changes in career patterns so that seniority is less directly correlated with age. The traditional cases refer to age collectivities, which is a reminder that a particularly influential factor should be the extent to which retirement decisions may be perceived as affecting age-mates similarly. The type of test used to determine capability to continue working could affect this, for instance: Physical strength or response speed might decline quite similarly for people of similar ages. On the other hand, renewable contracts of various lengths would shift attention away from age borders.

If confident anticipation of future benefits lessens age conflict, then the better younger people understand the social security system, the more likely age conflict becomes unless powerful reassurances are offered by the government. Younger people who believe that the social security system is a piggy bank holding their savings until they need them may be shocked into ageism by the understanding that workers pay for nonworkers, combined with the much-publicized increase in the proportion of old people in our population.

If material issues are less likely than ideal ones to provoke intergenrational hostilities, there should be forces pulling in the other direction. This influence seems to me most likely to operate if financial support for old people (e.g., health care) is offered to them as members of families. Policies that enhance the well-documented family support of old people would make most clear the extent to which these are shared benefits.

Schismogenesis of age categories will be constrained by greater reciprocity across them, both actual and perceived. Recent emphasis on life-span studies might promote the longer view of reciprocity that could remove the aura of dependence from support for older people. On the other hand, well-publicized debate about shifting "dependency ratios" and the future of OASDI may heighten perceptions of asymmetrical exchange.

My last prediction is the same as my first: As cross-cultural researchers, we have a lot of work to do on age. I hope to have begun an agenda. My final word is an anthropologist's appeal to tradition: We need to listen to our elders. The best strategy for understanding old age in the future is to pay very close attention to what old people—all over the world—are telling us now.

REFERENCES

Amoss, P. (1981) Religious participation as a route to prestige for the elderly. In C. Fry, ed., *Dimensions: Aging, Culture, and Health.* New York: Praeger.

Apple, D. (1956) The social structure of grandparenthood. *American Anthropologist* 58:656–663.

Bateson, G. (1967) Culture contact and schismogenesis. In P. Bohannan and F. Plog, eds., *Beyond the Frontier*. Garden City, N.Y.: Doubleday.

Bengtson, V., and Cutler, N. (1976) Generations and intergenerational relations: Perspectives on age groups and social change. In R. Binstock and E. Shanas, eds., *Handbook of Aging and the Social Sciences*. New York: Van Nostrand Reinhold.

Bohannan, P. (1970) *Divorce and After*. Garden City, N.Y.: Doubleday.

Clark, M., and Anderson, B. (1967) *Culture and Aging*. Springfield, Ill.: Charles C Thomas.

Davis, K. (1940) The sociology of parent–youth conflict. *American Sociological Review* 5:523–534.

Eisenstadt, S. (1956) *From Generation to Generation: Age Groups and Social Structure*. New York: The Free Press.

Erickson, R., and Eckert, K. (1977) The elderly poor in downtown San Diego hotels. *The Gerontologist* 17:440–446.

Evans-Pritchard, E. E. (1940) *The Nuer*. Oxford: Clarendon Press.

Fel, E., and Hofer, T. (1969) *Proper Peasants: Traditional Life in a Hungarian Village*. Chicago: Aldine.

Fennell, V. (1981) Older women in voluntary organizations. In C. Fry, ed., *Dimensions: Aging, Culture, and Health*. New York: Praeger.

Foner, A. (1972) The polity. In M. Riley, M. Johnson, and A. Foner, eds., *Aging and Society, Vol. 3: A Sociology of Age Stratification*. New York: Russell Sage.

Foner, A., and Kertzer, D. (1978) Transitions over the life-course: Lessons from age-set societies. *American Journal of Sociology* 83:1081–1104.

Francis, D. (1981) Adaptive strategies of the elderly in England and Ohio. In C. Fry, ed., *Dimensions: Aging, Culture, and Health*. New York: Praeger.

Fry, C. (1976) The ages of adulthood: A question of numbers. *Journal of Gerontology* 31:170–177.

Fry, C. (1979) Structural conditions affecting community formation among the aged. *Anthropological Quarterly* 52:7–18. (Special issue on ethnography of old age.)

Gross, N., Mason, W., and McEachern, A. (1957) *Explorations in Role Analysis: Studies of the School Superintendency Role*. New York: John Wiley and Sons.

Gulliver, P. (1963) *Social Control in an African Society*. London: Routledge and Kegan Paul.

Gulliver, P. (1968) Age differentiation. In D. Sills, ed., *International Encyclopedia of the Social Sciences*. New York: Macmillian and The Free Press.

Hendel-Sebestyen, G. (1979) Role diversity: Toward the development of community in a total institutional setting. *Anthropological Quarterly* 52:19–28.

Hess, B. (1972) Friendship. In M. Riley, M. Johnson, and A. Foner, eds., *Aging and Society, Vol. 3: A Sociology of Age Stratification*. New York: Russell Sage.

Hill, J.-K. (Keith) (1968) The Culture of Retirement. Unpublished doctoral dissertation, Northwestern University.

Hochschild, A. R. (1973) *The Unexpected Community*. Englewood Cliffs, N.J.: Prentice-Hall.

Holding, E. (1942) Some preliminary notes on Meru age-grades. *Man* 42:58–65.

Holtzmann, A. (1963) *The Townsend Movement*. New York: Bookman Associates.

Johnson, S. (1971) *Idle Haven: Community Building Among the Working Class Retired*. Berkeley: University of California Press.

Jonas, K. (1979) Factors in development of community among elderly persons in age-segregated housing. *Anthropological Quarterly* 52:29–38. (Special issue on ethnography of old age.)

Kandel, R., and Heider, M. (1979) Friendship and factionalism in a tri-ethnic housing complex for the elderly in North Miami. *Anthropological Quarterly* 52:49–60. (Special issue on ethnography of old age.)

Keith, J. (1980a) Old age and community creation. In C. Fry, ed., *Aging in Culture and Society*. New York: Praeger.

Keith, J. (1980b) The best is yet to be: Toward an anthropology of age. In *Annual Review of Anthropology*, Vol. 9. Palo Alto, Calif.: Annual Reviews, Inc.

Kirk, L., and Burton, M. (1977) Meaning and context: A study of contextual shifts in meaning of Maasai personality descriptors. *American Ethnologist* 4:734–761.

Laufer, R., and Bengtson, V. (1974) Generations, aging, and social stratification: On the development of generational units. *Journal of Social Issues* 30:181–206.

Lawton, M. P. (1979) Comments during Workshop on the Elderly of the Future, Annapolis, Maryland.

Legesse, A. (1973a) The controlled cross-cultural test. *Ethos* I:522–530.

Legesse, A. (1973b) *Gada.* New York: The Free Press.

Legesse, A. (1979) Age sets and retirement communities. *Anthropological Quarterly* 52:61–69. (Special issue on ethnography of old age.)

LeVine, R., and Sangree, W. (1962) The diffusion of age-group organization in East Africa: A controlled comparison. *Africa* 32:97–110.

Little, K. (1965) The political function of the Poro. *Africa* 35:350–365 (part I); *Africa* 36:62–71 (part II).

Lowie, R. (1916) Plains Indian age-societies: Historical and comparative summary. *Anthropological Papers of the American Museum of Natural History* 11:877–984.

Mannheim, K. (1952) The problem of generations. In K. Mannheim *Essays on the Sociology of Knowledge*. London: Routledge and Kegan Paul.

Maybury-Lewis, D. (1967) *Akwē-Shavante Society*. Oxford, England: Clarendon Press.

Nadel, S. F. (1960) Witchcraft in four African societies. In S. Ottenberg and P. Ottenberg, eds., *Cultures and Societies of Africa*. New York: Random House.

National Council on Aging (1975) *Myth and Reality of Aging in America*. Washington, D.C.: National Council on Aging.

Neugarten, B., and Hagestad, G. (1976) Age and the life course. In R. Binstock and E. Shanas, eds., *Handbook of Aging and the Social Sciences*. New York: Van Nostrand Reinhold.

Neugarten, B., and Peterson, W. (1957) A study of the American age-grade system. In *Proceedings of the Fourth Congress of the International Association of Gerontology* 3:497–502.

Paulme, D. (1973) Blood pacts, age classes and castes in Black Africa. In P. Alexandre, ed., *French Perspectives in African Studies*. Oxford, England: Oxford University Press.

Peristiany, J. (1939) *The Social Institutions of the Kipsigis*. London: George Routledge and Sons.

Pinner, F., Jacobs, P., and Selznick, P. (1959) *Old Age and Political Behavior*. Berkeley: University of California Press.

Putnam, J. (1970) *Old-Age Politics in California*. Palo Alto, Calif.: Stanford University Press.

Riley, M., Johnson, M., and Foner, A. (1972) Age strata in society. In M. Riley, M. Johnson, and A. Foner, eds., *Aging and Society, Vol. 3: A Sociology of Age Stratification*. New York: Russell Sage Foundation.

Rose, A. (1968) The subculture of the aging: A topic for sociological research. In B. Neugarten, ed., *Middle Age and Aging*. Chicago: University of Chicago Press.

Rosenberg, G. (1970) *The Worker Grows Old*. San Francisco: Jossey-Bass.

JENNIE KEITH

Rosow, I. (1967) *Social Integration of the Aged*. New York: The Free Press.

Rosow, I. (1974) *Socialization to Old Age*. Berkeley: University of California Press.

Ross, J.-K. (Keith) (1975) Social borders: Definitions of diversity. *Current Anthropology* 16:53–72.

Ross, J.-K. (Keith) (1977) *Old People, New Lives: Community Creation in a Retirement Residence*. Chicago: University of Chicago Press.

Ruel, M. (1962) Kuria generation classes. *Africa* 32:14–37.

Sherman, S. (1975) Patterns of contacts for residents of age-segregated and age-integrated housing. *Journal of Gerontology* 30:103–107.

Simmons, L. (1945) *The Role of the Aged in Primitive Society*. New York: Yale University Press.

Sokolovsky, J., and Cohen, C. (1978) The cultural meaning of personal networks for the inner city elderly. *Urban Anthropology* 7:328–342.

Southall, A. (1970) The illusion of tribe. In P. Gutkind, ed., *The Passing of Tribal Man in Africa*. Leiden: E. J. Brill.

Spencer, P. (1965) *The Samburu*. London: Routledge and Kegan Paul.

Spencer, P. (1976) Opposing streams and the gerontocratic ladder. *Man* 11:153–174.

Stewart, F. H. (1977) *Fundamentals of Age-Group Systems*. New York: Academic Press.

Talmon, Y. (1968) Aging in Israel, a planned society. In B. Neugarten, ed., *Middle Age and Aging*. Chicago: University of Chicago Press.

Terray, E. (1975) Classes and class consciousness in the Abron Kingdom of Gyaman. In M. Bloch, ed., *Marxist Analyses and Social Anthropology*. New York: John Wiley and Sons.

Trela, J. (1976) Status inconsistency and political action. In J. Gubrium, ed., *Time, Roles, and Self in Old Age*. New York: Behavioral Publications.

Trümpy, H. (1965) Jahrgängervereine. In C. Schmitz and R. Wildhaber, eds., *Festschrift Alfred Bühler*. Basel: Pharos-Verlag Hans Rudolf Schwabe.

Turner, V. (1969) *The Ritual Process*. Chicago: Aldine.

Turton, D. (1978) Territorial organisation and age among the Mursi. In P.T.W. Baxter and U. Almagor, eds., *Age, Generation, and Time*. London: C. Hurst.

Van Arsdale, P. (1981) Disintegration of the ritual support network among aged Asmat hunter–gatherers of New Guinea. In C. Fry, ed., *Dimensions: Aging, Culture, and Health*. New York: Praeger.

Wellin, E., and Boyer, E. (1979) Adjustments of black and white elderly to the same adaptive niche. *Anthropological Quarterly* 52:39–48.

Wilson, M. (1951) *Good Company: A Study of Nyakyusa Age Villages*. London: Oxford University Press.

PART V

SOCIAL CONDITIONS AND
SOCIAL PROBLEMS

TABLE 18.1
Percentage Distribution of Living Arrangements among Elderly Men, Fifty-Five Years and over: 1955–1975[a][b]

Living arrangements	1955	1960	1965	1970	1975
In households	96.2%	97.4%	96.8%	96.6%	96.9%
In families	84.4	84.9	84.1	84.3	84.1
Head, spouse present	70.6	73.3	73.3	75.8	77.4
Other male head	4.7	4.2	3.6	3.1	3.0
Other family member	9.1	7.4	7.1	5.3	3.7
Not in families					
Living alone or unrelated household head	8.4	9.6	10.3	10.9	11.5
Living with nonrelatives	3.4	3.2	2.0	1.4	1.3
In institutions or other group quarters[c]	3.8	2.6	3.2	3.4	3.1
Patients/residents[d]	2.3	2.1	2.6	2.6	2.7
Others	1.5	.5	.6	.8	.4
Total	100.0%	100.0%	100.0%	100.0%	100.0%
	(13,602,000)	(14,539,000)	(16,013,000)	(17,073,000)	(18,409,000)

[a] From Bureau of the Census (1955, 1960, 1965, 1970, 1975).

[b] Civilian population only.

[c] Note those institutionalized are not sampled in the Current Population Survey. Estimates of the institionalized population are prepared by forward-surviving the most recent count of those in group quarters.

[d] Estimates of the number of institutionalized persons in 1975 are based on data shown in Table 6-2 of a Current Population Report, "Demographic Aspects of Aging and the Older Population in the United States," Series P-23, No. 59 (May 1976).

their own household, usually alone, balanced by decreases in the proportion of those living with relatives (Mindel 1979). The decline in multigenerational family living also has been offset by slight increases in the proportion of institutionalized elderly. These trends are evident from the data presented in Table 18.1 for older men and in Table 18.2 for older women. Because of the sex differential in mortality, these trends are much more pronounced for women than for men.[8]

Between 1955 and 1975, the older population increased in size. In the 1960s, for example, the population 60 years of age and older increased by nearly 25%, compared with a total population increase of 13%. The

[8] Because of comparability constraints it is possible to assemble data for a 20-year time series only for the population 55 years of age and older.

TABLE 18.2

Percentage Distribution of Living Arrangements among Elderly Women, Fifty-Five Years and over: 1955–1975[a][b]

Living arrangements	1955	1960	1965	1970	1975
In househoulds	96.9%	97.7%	96.8%	96.6%	96.4%
In families	75.8	74.1	70.1	68.0	66.7
Spouse of head	46.6	48.0	47.2	47.5	49.1
Female head	11.2	10.6	10.1	9.7	8.7
Other family member	18.1	15.9	13.6	10.8	8.9
Not in families					
Living alone or unrelated household head	18.2	21.3	24.1	27.3	28.8
Living with non-relative secondary individual	2.8	2.1	1.7	1.2	1.0
In institutions or other group quarters[c]	3.1	2.3	3.2	3.4	3.6
Patients/residents[d]	2.0	1.7	2.8	2.9	3.3
Others	1.1	.6	.4	.5	.3
Total	100.0%	100.0%	100.0%	100.0%	100.0%
	(14,901,000)	(16,656,000)	(18,953,000)	(21,053,000)	(23,496,000)

[a] From Bureau of the Census (1955, 1960, 1965, 1970, 1975).

[b] Civilian population only.

[c] Note those institutionalized are not sampled in the Current Population Survey. Estimates of the institutionalized population are prepared by forward-surviving the most recent Census of those in group quarters.

[d] Estimates of the number of institutionalized persons in 1975 are based on data shown in Table 6-2 of a Current Population Report, "Demographic Aspects of Aging and the Older Population in the United States," Series P-23, No. 59 (May 1976).

proportionate distributions shown in Tables 18.1 and 18.2, while cap-turing the direction of trends in living arrangements among the elderly, mask the very real increase in the number of older persons as a whole and the number of older persons maintaining their own households. In 1960s, the Bureau of the Census enumerated roughly 3 million older persons heading their own nonfamily households; by 1970, this number had doubled.

This increase is particularly noteworthy, since between 1960 and 1970, the older population "aged" as well as increased in size. The aging of the older population might have led a forecaster in the mid-1960s to project a decline in the proportion of elderly living independently, since such arrangements tend to be associated with the younger age groups. Rather, the relative and absolute numbers of individuals living alone or with nonrelatives has continued to increase, but the age structure of these independent types of arrangements also has shifted upward. In 1960, approximately one in every four nonfamily household heads were 75 years of age or older; by 1970, one in three nonfamily household heads were in the older age groups. The data suggest that substantially more older persons are overcoming (or at least confronting) the health and financial problems associated with being very old in order to sustain their preference for independent living.

Accounting for Changes

The dramatic changes in patterns of living arrangements prompted an investigation of the factors for these changes for the periods 1960–1970 and 1970–1975. Our findings are relevant to the overall focus of this chapter—anticipating future trends in living arrangments among the elderly.

In accounting for differences observed from comparing two or more cross-sectional distributions of living arrangements, two distinct hypothesis can be entertained:

1. The distribution of living arrangements changed because the association between determinants of living arrangements (the independent variables) and the outcome variable changed during the time of observation. Changes in the determining process itself could occur as a result of societal changes that altered factors on the supply side, such as the availability of supportive services.
2. Temporal arrangements in patterns of living arrangements reflect changes in the distribution of the independent variables among the population groups under study (i.e., changes in the composition of the older population from one time point to another).

Our research findings with respect to the determinants of aggregate changes in living arrangements are relatively easy to summarize. No matter what variables we examined or in what combination, we found that the factors influencing individual decisions have temporally constant effects. Changes in population composition (i.e., changes in the distribution of these factors among successive cohorts) were identified as the major factor responsible for generating changes in observed patterns of living arrangements.

Changes in the sex-ratio, racial composition, and marital status composition of the older population proved to have relatively minor effects. When only demographic variables were considered, almost all of the observed changes in living arrangements were attributable jointly to changes in the size and age structure of the older population. This conclusion was modified when other factors were considered simultaneously. When attention was restricted to the older ever-married female population and family size was included in the list of explanatory variables, changes in the family size of successive cohorts played the dominant role in accounting for changes in patterns of living arrangements. If living arrangements at the older ages are seen as an outcome of the status achievement process, socioeconomic changes in population composition assume the greatest importance. Increases in the incomes of older women (due to increases in social security benefits and increases in the proportion of older women eligible for their own benefits) accounted in large measure for the substantial increase in the number of older persons heading their own nonfamily households between 1960 and 1975. Our data also suggest that patterns of living arrangements at older ages are much more sensitive to socioeconomic shifts in population composition than they are to demographic changes per se.

COHORT DIFFERENCES

Since our research indicates that changes in population composition, initiated by cohort succession and differentiation, are primarily responsible for changes in living arrangements, projecting the distribution of living arrangements into the near future is largely a matter of projecting the composition of the older population.[9]

The older population of the next 10 or 20 years is currently identifiable in terms of birth cohorts. The cohorts of 1921–1925 and 1926–1930 will be new recruits into the older population by the year 1990; and by the year 2000, the birth cohorts of 1931–1935 and 1936–1940 also will have joined the ranks of the elderly. The effect of cohort flow through the age structure has alternatively been described as permitting temporal change (Ryder 1968), channeling social transformation (Riley et al. 1972), and propelling structural innovation (Taeuber 1964). Regardless of the

---

[9] No two cohorts are born into the same set of circumstances nor do they age in the same way. At each stage in its development, a cohort reciprocates with a unique set and sequence of historical events. The effect of this dialogue with the existing social order endures and accumulates so that each cohort arrives at subsequent stages in its life-cycle with a unique social and demographic configuration. Hence, at any point in time, cohorts are differentiated not only by their age but also by other cohort characteristics such as their sociological composition, pattern of survival up to that point, and behavior.

terminology used, it is clear that the ordering and structuring of cohort flow has innate potential for temporal and social change.

With their fertility, education, and occupational attainment largely completed, the birth cohorts that will fill the ranks of the elderly by 2000 possess a variety of relatively fixed characteristics (Uhlenberg 1977). For purposes of projecting living arrangements based on a compositional change model, it is necessary to anticipate differences in those cohort characteristics that will affect directly or indirectly the demand for different types of living arrangements. In the following list are the kinds of compositional changes that the current structure of mid-life cohorts imply for the older population in the year 2000 or 2020:

- By the turn of the century, the older population is likely to increase in size by about one-third. If current patterns of below-replacement fertility persist, the elderly will account for 18% of our total population in 2020.
- As the older population increases in absolute size, it will age as well. The "implosion of the older population" (Sheppard 1978) will be characterized by a 50% increase in the number of persons 75–84 years of age and a doubling in the number of persons 85 years of age and over between 1978 and 2000.
- If the sex differential in mortality is maintained (and there is no reason to suspect that the gap will narrow), there will be an even greater excess of women as the older population ages.

In addition, it is important to note expected differences in marital status, family size, and socioeconomic status. Because slight improvements in chronic disease mortality are expected to continue, the duration of married life (for those married at the threshold of old age) is likely to increase as well. Current increases in separation and divorce rates also suggest that by the year 2000, proportionately more older persons will have experienced at least one divorce. Glick (1978) estimates that the number of older divorced persons will almost double during the last quarter of the century and increase from 12% in 1975 to 22% in the year 2000. As a result, family ties may become more segmented or diluted. Even for older persons who will have remarried subsequent to a divorce, a disrupted marital history is likely to have had an adverse impact on their asset formation and, consequently, on their economic reserves in old age (Henretta and Campbell 1976).

Women who will be 60–74 years of age in 2000 are the mothers of the baby boom and are likely to have a large family support network available to them in their old cage. The next generation of young-old will be the baby boom cohorts themselves and the parents of the baby bust cohorts. Among the implications of a declining birth rate, we are often told, is a reduction in the size of the family support network potentially available to assist older persons in the future. But completed fertility rates are only half the picture in determining the size of family support networks available to assist the elderly of the future. Equally important is the extent to which children survive until their parents' old age.

Gray (1977), using the Keyfitz techniques (1977) for estimating the probability of living ancestors, compared the survivorship of female children born under the fertility regimes of the 1920s, 1930s, and 1970s and exposed to the mortality schedules of the same year. Not surprisingly, she found that mothers giving birth during the 1920s had more daughters born than did the hypothetical mothers of the 1970s. Because of improvements in mortality, however, these hypothetical mothers would actually have more surviving daughters at the age of 70 than the mothers of the 1920s. For example, a 1920s mother had, on the average, 1.4 female children compared to 1.2 for the mothers giving birth during the 1970s. At age 70, 73.5% of the daughters born to a 1920s mother would still be alive (or an average of .99 surviving daughters). Of the female children born to a mother under the 1970 schedules of fertility and mortality, 90% would be alive by her seventieth birthday (or an average of 1.1 surviving daughters per older mother). This research suggests that fluctuations in the birth rate per se have limited value in predicting kin availability. For purposes of relating kin availability to future patterns of living arrangements, the proximity of the older relatives' homes to those of their adult children is more relevant. The congruency of intergenerational mobility paths, however, is a topic that we, as demographers or gerontologists, have not investigated.

The future elderly, particularly women, also are likely to have quite different socioeconomic backgrounds and resources for coping with age-related changes in health status, and ultimately, in living arrangements. The cohorts of women presently in their young adult and middle-aged years have higher rates of labor force participation than any of their predecessors. Furthermore, these women are not (for the most part) interrupting their work histories either to have or to raise children. Since both the availability of social security worker's benefits and secondary pensions are linked currently to the duration and level of employment, older women in the future, compared with those of today, will have higher mean postretirement incomes. Because of the unknown effects of inflation, however, higher incomes cannot be interpreted as indicating greater purchasing power for tomorrow's elderly.

For cohorts currently middle-aged, it is reasonable to treat as fixed characteristics education, occupational attainment, and family size.

These same cohorts, however, are only now entering the life-cycle stage at which changes in health status are likely to occur most rapidly and to accumulate. Anticipating the morbidity patterns of tomorrow's elderly, however, exceeds the scope of this chapter. The functional health of the various age groups within the older population will improve only if the age-specific rates of the major disabling diseases (such as arthritis and cerebrovascular diseases) decline—either by postponement of the age at onset or by gradual elimination—or the level of functional impairment associated with these disease changes. The age at onset of the major disabling diseases of the elderly may increase slightly as a result of more middle-aged persons embracing the principles of preventive medicine— regular exercise, lower-cholesterol diets, etc. The total net effect of delayed onset for the chronic disabling diseases, however, may be canceled by changes in the age structure of the older population. In addition, analysis of data from the 1970–1974 Health Interview Survey (HIS) indicates that the disabling consequences of the major chronic diseases are relatively constant over at least a 5-year period (Myers and Soldo 1980). For example, arthritis resulted in total mobility restrictions for 11% of its victims in 1970 and 11.8% in 1974. The other major chronic diseases common among the elderly showed similarly stable effects on functional ability. Assuming no major medical breakthrough in chronic disease research and anticipating increasing proportions of the very old, the overall health of tomorrow's elderly is likely to improve slightly, if at all.[10]

If changes in the sociodemographic, economic, and health characteristics of successive cohorts persist as a driving force behind changes in patterns of living arrangements, what do the trends just described imply for future patterns of living arrangements?

ANTICIPATING FUTURE PATTERNS

The only reasonable conclusion to draw from the preceding inventory of the characteristics of today's middle-aged cohorts is that the demand for independent types of living arrangements will increase in the near future. Even if the same age-specific patterns of living arrangements are maintained, by the turn of the century, there will be approximately 8 million older persons (those 65 years of age and over) living alone—a net increase of 3 million since 1970.

Our previous research indicates that the effects of an older age structure are likely to be offset by improvements in the financial status of the

[10] This is not to imply that, in the future, the elderly's capacity to cope with the functional impairments associated with chronic diseases will not improve.

elderly; as generational differences in educational attainment are reduced, more women accumulate their own work histories, and retirement is perhaps postponed. Even older unmarried men may be better equipped to extend independent living into their later years as a result of sharing daily living tasks with their working wives or maintaining their own homes subsequent to divorce. The characteristics of the cohorts that will define the older population in the near future indicate clearly that the demand for independent households will persist, if not increase. The increase in demand will translate into actual increases in the number of persons heading their own households only if the supply and price of housing and supportive services conducive to independent living is sufficient.

For those elderly without financial constraints or physical limitations, the supply of independent living arrangements will be dictated only by the availability of well-sized, well-maintained, and reasonably priced dwelling units. A majority of those who will arrive at old age in good health and with adequate incomes will still be married and will have aged in place. For this group, housing maintenance problems, while not threatening sustained independent living, may compromise their life-style or prompt a move into another housing unit. For the low-income elderly of the future, housing maintenance problems and a scarcity of safe and inexpensive housing units will continue to challenge their ability to live independently (see Struyk, in this volume).

For anticipating future trends in living arrangements, the critical issues involve questions of how long and under what conditions these households of the elderly will continue to function as independent units. The answers we provide to these questions depend much more on the supply of services supportive of independent living than on the demand for independent living arrangements per se. Rather than developing a single forecast of the supply side of the equation, let us consider several alternative scenarios, each corresponding to different assumptions regarding the availability of various service options. Since previous research (Soldo 1977, Newman 1976) indicates that health status is the primary determinant of living arrangements at the older ages, the supply of services compensating for declines in functional capacity are emphasized. Each of the following scenarios also assumes that those without either health or financial problems (most likely the young-old) will satisfy easily their demand for independent living.

Services Are Purchased

The services needed to sustain independent living as functional health declines are those that provide assistance with the daily tasks of living—

cooking, shopping, and personal care. The higher incomes of tomorrow's elderly will enhance the ability of older persons to remain in their own homes only if the necessary services are available for purchase and are well-priced relative to the income of the elderly. Today, the supply of home-health aids and homemaker services is insufficient to meet the demand. The waiting list for such services is often long and, when assistance is provided in the home, it may be limited to only 2–3 hours a day. Older persons who live in rural areas are usually hardest hit by the dearth of service workers. Dunlop (1976a) found that moderately impaired older persons in rural areas often moved to some type of personal care facility for want of in-home services. In the future, the demand may exceed the supply by an even greater amount. The Swedish experience with home-health aids and homemakers indicates that a sufficient number of workers are recruited only when high wages and professional status are accorded these occupations. Neither of these conditions, however, are met in the United States today.

Recruiting an adequate number of service workers will be complicated in the future by changes in the age structure. Workers will be in demand in almost all occupations, and young workers in particular may have the luxury of entering an extremely competitive and flexible job market.

Services Are Provided by Community Groups

Title XX of the Social Security Act and Title III of the Older Americans Act subsidize services provided to older persons by community agencies. Because each state or municipality determines what services are provided, there is considerable variation in the scope and delivery of services. If this pattern continues, independent living will be adequately supported in some areas while in others the absence of needed services may force premature entry into long-term care facilities. In the 1976 Survey of Institutionalized Persons (SIP), the families of 10% of older nursing home residents reported that the availability of home-health aids or delivered meals would have at least postponed the institutionalized placement.

Community services do not account for a large proportion of personal care services consumed by the elderly today. If such services are widely and consistently available in the future, their role may expand. The elderly of today have an abhorrence of anything resembling "welfare." The elderly of tomorrow may be more receptive recipients since they will have aged in a social order where service consumption is more widespread and accepted.

Services Are Provided by the Family

As previously noted, family members are the primary care-givers for today's elderly. Whether the family continues to dominate in service provision depends on the willingness and availability of younger relatives. In terms of sheer numbers, Gray's (1977) research indicates an adequate supply of adult daughters for older parents in the future. If these older parents do not reside near their adult children, however, the potential for care-giving is minimal. It is reassuring to note that, despite the high rates of geographic mobility in the recent past, most older persons have at least one child in the same community (Shanas *et al.* 1968).

Much more difficult to predict than migration are the attitudes and behaviors of adult children toward their parents in the future. There is certainly good reason to suspect that the parent–child bond is relaxing: Children leave their parents' household at an earlier age than previously, move to different cities to attend school or set up their own households, participate in closely knit peer groups, and seek advice and support from professional counselors rather than their parents. As the divorce rate increases and children accumulate a large set of "parents," the strength and quality of the parent–child relationship may be diluted further.

Looking at similar patterns 30 years ago, Pollak wrote: "Dependence on children as the major form of old age adjustment in the family sphere is now seriously endangered by demographic, institutional and attitudinal changes in our society [1948, p. 75]." In forecasting the decline of family supports, we may err, like Pollak previously, by underestimating the strength of family ties and the resiliency, versatility, and adaptiveness of the American family.

Evidence testifying to the family's emotional and service involvement with today's elderly is accumulating. Those in key policymaking positions are becoming increasingly aware of the need to support the family of older persons in their efforts to provide adequate home care (Brody 1978). The service delivery system most likely to extend independent living and postpone (or preclude) institutionalization in the future is one that encourages and supports the family's assumption of the care-giving role. Increases in the number of independent households headed by older persons will continue if day-care and respite-care are not simply isolated demonstration projects but universally available.

Institutionalized Care

Dunlop (1976b) has observed that institutionalized care serves as a "convenient umbrella for the delivery of multiple services." Long-term care facilities provide not only sustained nursing care for those in need but also shelter and personal care for older persons lacking service supports in the community.

Long-term care facilities serve a definite and appropriate need for a select group of older persons, and it is unreasonable to anticipate that some among tomorrow's elderly will not have similar needs (Kane and Kane 1980). But the supply of independent households will increase in the future if long-term care facilities are reserved for those truly requiring skilled nursing care. Providing a continuum of care-giving options and services in the community (through congregate housing and neighborhood centers offering comprehensive service packages, available either regularly or sporadically) will suppress placement rates in institutions if not extend independent living in the strictest sense of the word.

SUMMARY

It is reasonable to anticipate increases in the number of older persons maintaining independent living arrangements in the future. The exact nature of such arrangements is less obvious. There is no single residential environment that is good for all older persons or for the same person at different ages. Efforts must be made to define the types of living arrangements and housing most appropriate for specific levels of functional ability. Are there limits to the feasibility, appropriateness, or costs of programs oriented to maintaining an independent life-style for older persons? At what level of functional disability is an older person better served by transfer to some type of congregate living environment? Is health the only factor that needs to be considered in establishing a threshold for support of independent living?

A wider range of alternatives should be made available to older persons desirous of sustaining independent living as long as possible. With few exceptions, the current choices for those needing assistance are limited to living alone and relying on family or program service delivery, living with a relative, or being institutionalized. Transitional options are seldom available.

The orientation of current service programs targeted at older persons also must be seriously evaluated. Today, subsidized support programs revolve around a medical model. Third-party payment systems absorb the costs of medical expenses such as hip replacement operations, but not of other services supportive of independent living such as the moving expenses of an arthritic woman transferring to a unit without stairs. Service delivery for older persons living alone must emphasize prevention as well as care. For example, regular monitoring and evaluation of older persons, in the home, is a well-established part of the geriatric services in Great Britain.

The family is the primary support system utilized by older persons in need of personal care or assistance. It will continue in this role if efforts are made to shore up the family's ability to be involved in the care of its older members. Tax incentives have been mentioned as one way of accomplishing this objective. Others might include relaxing restrictions for home-health aids under Medicare–Medicaid and increasing the availability of day-care and vacation-care centers for older persons (Comptroller General of the United States 1977b). Cost-sharing moving expenses for older persons wanting to be near but not live with relatives may be another.

Family assistance is the first defense against institutionalization because of the family's commitment and flexibility. A very real challenge for those concerned with program development in the next century will be to orchestrate service delivery to mimic the family's adaptability.

ACKNOWLEDGMENTS

I wish to thank three anonymous reviewers for their constructive comments on an earlier draft of this chapter.

REFERENCES

Barney, J. L. (1977) The prerogative of choice in long-term care. *The Gerontologist* 17:308–314.

Bikson, T. K., and Goodchilds, J. (1978) Old and Alone. Paper presented at a meeting of the American Psychological Association, Toronto.

Bishop, Y. M., Fienberg, S. E., and Holland, P. W. (1975) *Discrete Multivariate Analysis.* Cambridge, Mass.: Massachusetts Institute of Technology Press.

Birren, J., Woodruff, D., and Bergman, S. (1972) Research demonstration and training: Issues and methodology in social gerontology. *The Gerontologist* 12:49–83.

Brody, E. (1978) The aging of the family. *The Annals* 438:13–26.

Brody, S. J., Poulshock, S. W., and Masciocchi, C. F. (1978) The family caring unit: A major consideration in the long-term care support system. *The Gerontologist* 18:556–561.

Bureau of the Census (1955) *Marital Status and Family Status.* Current Population Reports, Series P-20, No. 62. Washington, D.C.: U.S. Department of Commerce.

Bureau of the Census (1960) *Marital Status and Family Status.* Current Population Reports, Series P-20, No. 105. Washington, D.C.: U.S. Department of Commerce.

Bureau of the Census (1965) *Marital Status and Family Status.* Current Population Reports, Series P-20, No. 144. Washington, D.C.: U.S. Department of Commerce.

Bureau of the Census (1970) *Marital Status and Family Status*. Current Population Reports, Series P-20, No. 212. Washington, D.C.: U.S. Department of Commerce.

Bureau of the Census (1972) *Public Use Samples of Basic Records from the 1970 Census: Description and Technical Documentation*. Washington, D.C.: U.S. Department of Commerce.

Bureau of the Census (1975) *Marital Status and Family Status*. Current Population Reports, Series P-20, No. 287. Washington, D.C.: U.S. Department of Commerce.

Bureau of the Census (1976) *Demographic Aspects of Aging and the Older Population in the United States*. Current Population Reports, Series P-23, No. 59. Washington, D.C.: U.S. Department of Commerce.

Cantor, M. H. (1980) The informal support system: Its relevance in the lives of the elderly. In E. F. Borgatta and N. G. McCluskey, eds., *Aging and Society: Current Research and Policy Perspectives*. Beverly Hills, Calif.: Sage Publications.

Comptroller General of the United States (177a) *The Well-Being of Older People in Cleveland, Ohio*. A report to the Congress, April 19, 1977. Washington, D.C.: U.S. General Accounting Office.

Comptroller General of the United States (1977b) *Home Health—The Need for a National Policy to Better Provide for the Elderly*. Washington, D.C.: U.S. General Accounting Office.

Dono, J. E., Falbe, C. M., Kail, B. L., Litwak, E., Sherman, R. H., and Siegel, D. (1979). Primary groups in old age: Structure and function. *Research on Aging* 1:403–433.

Dunlop, B. (1976a) Determinants of Long-Term Care Facility Utilization by the Elderly: An Empirical Analysis. Working Paper No. 963-35. The Urban Institute, Washington, D.C.

Dunlop, B. (1976b) Need for and utilization of long-term care among elderly Americans. *Journal of Chronic Diseases* 29:75–87.

Field, M. (1972) *The Aged, the Family, and the Community*. New York: Columbia University Press.

Glick, P. G. (1978) The Future of the American Family. Statement prepared for Joint Hearings of the House Select Committees on Population and Aging. U.S. House of Representatives, Washington, D.C.

Gray, A. V. (1977) Who Was Really There? An Historical Look at Available Kin. Unpublished paper, University of Southern California.

Hauser, R. M., Koffel, J. N., Travis, H. P., and Kickinson, P. J. (1975) Temporal change in occupational mobility: Evidence for men in the United States. *American Sociological Review* 40:279–297.

Henretta, J. C., and Campbell, R. T. (1976) Status attainment and status maintenance: A study of stratification in old age. *American Sociological Review* 41:981–992.

Kane, R. L., and Kane, R. A. (1980) Alternatives to institutional care: Beyond the dichotomy. *The Gerontologist* 20:249–259.

Keyfitz, N. (1977) The demographic theory of kinship. Pp. 273–302 in *Applied Mathematical Demography*. New York: John Wiley and Sons.

Lopata, H. Z. (1971) *Widowhood in an American City*. Cambridge, Mass.: Sahenkman.

Michael, R. T., Fuchs, V. R., and Scott, S. R. (1980) Changes in the propensity to live alone: 1950–1976. *Demography* 17:39–56.

Mindel, C. H. (1979) Multigenerational family households: Recent trends and implications for the future. *The Gerontologist* 19:456–463.

Mossey, J. M., and Tisdale, W. A. (1979) Measurement of Functional Health Status of the Institutionalized Elderly: Rationale for and Development of an "Index." Working Paper No. 4, Series CPR-MD-79, Center for Population Research, Georgetown University.

Myers, G. C., and Soldo, B. J. (1976) Variations in Living Arrangements Among the Elderly. Final report to the Administration on Aging Grant No. 90-A-313. Center for Demographic Studies, Duke University.

Myers, G. C., and Soldo, B. J. (1980) Changing Household Patterns Among the Elderly. Final report to the Administration on Aging, Grant No. 90-A-1029. Center for Demographic Studies, Duke University.

Newman, S. J. (1976) Housing adjustments of the disabled elderly. *The Gerontologist* 16:312–317.

Pollak, O. (1948) Social Adjustments in Old Age: A Research Planning Report. Bulletin 59. Social Science Research Council, New York.

Riley, M. W., Johnson, M., and Foner, A. (1972) *Aging and Society.* New York: Russell Sage Foundation.

Ryder, N. B. (1968) Cohort analysis. In D. Sills, ed., *International Encyclopedia of the Social Sciences,* Vol. II. New York: Macmillan and The Free Press.

Schaie, J., and Strother, C. (1968) Cross-sequential study of age changes in cognitive behavior. *Psychological Bulletin* 70:671–680.

Shanas, E. (1979) The family as a social support system in old age. *The Gerontologist* 19:169–174.

Shanas, E., Townsend, P., Wedderburn, D., Friis, H., Milhoj, P., and Stehouwer, J. (1968) *Old People in Three Industrial Societies.* New York: Atherton.

Sheppard, H. L. (1978) The economics of population, mortality, and retirement. In *The Economics of Aging: A National Journal Issues Book.* Washington, D.C.: Government Research Corporation.

Soldo, B. J. (1977) The Determinants of Temporal Variations in Living Arrangements Among the Elderly: 1960–1970. Unpublished Ph.D. dissertation, Duke University.

Soldo, B. J., and Myers, G. C. (1976) The Effects of Lifetime Fertility on the Living Arrangements of Older Women. Paper presented at a meeting of the Gerontological Society, New York.

Sternlieb, G., and Hughes, J. W. (1980) Inflationary America: The housing dilemma. *American Demographics* 2(6):21–23.

Taeuber, I. (1964) Population and society. In R. E. L. Faris, ed., *The Handbook of Modern Sociology.* Chicago: Rand McNally.

Townsend, P. (1965) The effects of family structure on the likelihood of admission to an institution in old age: The application of a general theory. In E. Shanas and G. Streib, eds., *Social Structure and the Family Generational Relations.* Englewood Cliffs, N.J.: Prentice-Hall.

Troll, L. E. (1971) The family of later life: A decade review. *Journal of Marriage and the Family* 33:263–290.

Uhlenberg, P. (1977) Changing structure of the older population of the U.S.A. during the twentieth century. *The Gerontologist* 17:197–282.

The Pitkin–Masnick projections were done by age, sex, marital status, and (for women) children ever born. Three distinct sets of projections were made, based on particular assumptions about the future trajectories of marital status and fertility. The basic methodology was to age the different cohorts forward in time and redistribute the survivors among marital status and headship (male versus female) categories. (Women are also distributed among categories of children ever born as well.) The beginning date for the projections is 1976, and the projections were made at 5-year intervals for the 1980–2000 period. The results reported in the following paragraphs are based on the median fertility assumption used, total fertility rate of 1.8 after 1980.

Two alternative housing projection series were used by Pitkin and Masnick to bracket the range of likely trajectories of actual housing consumption patterns. The first is based on the assumption that household preferences for various housing bundles will remain fixed, as observed in 1975. These bundle choices are defined by tenure, structure type, and number of room combinations for 20 specific household types, defined by sex, marital status, and number of children.

The second series reflects the trends in housing consumption patterns actually observed for birth cohorts during the 1960–1975 period. "For each 5-year birth cohort in the projections, the rates of change in housing consumption patterns over each 5-year interval are equal to the average of the rates of change for cohorts who passed through the same age interval between 1960 and 1975 [Pitkin and Masnick 1979]." As an example, the rate of homeownership among those who will be 70–74 in 1980 depends on (1) the rate of homeownership among those who were 65–69 in 1975, and (2) the average rate at which earlier cohorts increased their homeownership rate between 65–69 and 70–74. All of these rates were projected separately for each of the household types within each cohort. Note that the extrapolation projections include the rate at which the elderly have been "uncoupling" from living with children or other arrangements; for this reason, the total count of elderly-headed households increases under this assumption.

Of course, all of these projections rely on the assumption that the distribution of prices per unit of housing services of various housing types will remain fixed over the projection period. This is obviously a strong assumption, but a useful one given the absence of any other strong bases on which to proceed.

The analysis presented here uses only a very small part of the full projections done by Pitkin and Masnick. Table 19.6 displays the 1976 distribution of households headed by a person 65 or older by tenure status and the number of dwelling units in the structure occupied by

TABLE 19.6

Distribution of Households Headed by Person 65 or Older by Tenure and Structure Type, 1976 and 2000, under Alternative Assumptions about Housing Preferences[a]

Tenure and structure type	1976		2000 (constant preference)		2000 (extrapolation preference)	
	Number[b]	Percentage distribution	Number[a,b]	Percentage distribution	Number[a,b]	Percentage distribution
Owner-occupants	8,537	68	11,870	67	14,633	73
Single unit	7,269	58	10,080	57	11,747	59
2–4 units	663	5	930	5	899	4
5 + units	192	2	269	2	418	2
Mobile home	413	3	591	3	1,569	8
Renters	3,987	32	5,811	33	5,371	27
Single unit	1,141	9	1,566	9	1,363	7
2–4 units	1,035	8	1,522	9	1,447	7
5 + units	1,764	14	2,659	15	2,331	12
Mobile home	47	6	74	c	230	1
Total	12,524	100	17,681	100	20,004	100

[a] From Pitkin and Masnick (1979).

[b] In thousands.

[c] Less than one half of 1%.

TABLE 19.7

Distribution of Households Headed by Person 65 or Older by Household Type 1976 and 2000 (in Percentages)[a]

Household type	1976	2000
Married couples	37	31
Males		
Never married	3	3
Other	11	13
Females	4	4
Never married	4	6
Separated, divorced	41	43
Widowed		
Total	100	100

[a] From Pitkin and Masnick (1979).

such households.[6] It also presents two distributions projected to the year 2000—one based on constant housing preferences and one on the extrapolated preferences. There are several important points to be made about the figures in the table:

1. Under the constant preference assumption, there is very little shift in the tenure and structure type distributions; this results from an offsetting combination of the shift in households among household types (see Table 19.7) and the current occupancy patterns displayed by these household types.
2. As expected, there is a substantial increase in the number of elderly households under the extrapolated preferences (13%).
3. Under the extrapolated preferences, there is a major increase in the proportion of elderly households who are homeowners. Because of the recent preferences shown for mobile homes, much of this increase in homeowners is accounted for by a greater share of elderly living in this type of structure.
4. By contrast, the changes in the distribution of renters by structure type in the extrapolated preferences projections are distributed very evenly over the distribution, with only a slight increase in the share accounted for by mobile homes.

[6] The reader may note some divergence from the total household counts and tenure rates shown in this table compared with those from the same year based on the Annual Housing Survey. This divergence has several sources, one being that Pitkin and Masnick (P–M) begin with population counts from the Current Population Survey from July 1976 and then apply AHS headship rates. Second, the ''age'' of the husband–wife households is based on the age of the wife in the P–M computations, while the AHS determines age of household with the husband's age in such cases.

TABLE 19.8
Distribution of Elderly and Middle-Aged Households by Location in 1976[a]

	Inside SMSAs		
	Inside central city	Suburbs	Outside SMSAs
All households, head[b]			
Aged 45–64	26	41	33
Aged 65 +	27	33	39
Owner–occupants, head			
Aged 45–64	23	43	34
Aged 65 +	24	34	42
Renters, head			
Aged 45–64	40	30	30
Aged 65 +	46	29	25

[a] From Bureau of the Census (1978, p.4).
[b] Rows add to 100%.

If we assume that the same patterns of deficiencies and housing expense burden by tenure type that were observed for 1976 in the last section continue to hold into the future, then several tentative conclusions follow. First, the proportion of elderly households living in dwellings with major deficiencies will fall, even without any overall national progress in this area. (The number in deficient units will nevertheless go up because of the very large increase in households.) Second, the proportion of those paying an excessive portion of their income for out-of-pocket housing expenses will also fall. Third, the proportion of elderly who rate their neighborhoods as "good" or "excellent" will increase moderately.

The last section indicated that the satisfaction with neighborhood conditions expressed by elderly-headed households varied significantly by location as well as tenure. To explore the locational aspect somewhat further, the locations of middle-aged households as of 1976 have been contrasted with those of the elderly (Table 19.8). The idea is that the future elderly will reside where middle-aged households are now located. This approach can provide rough guidance on broad locational patterns because of the declining mobility that occurs as households age. Furthermore, examination of data on debt-free homeownership status of households headed by persons 50–64 and 65 and older show remarkably high rates for the former group.[7]

If the patterns shown in Table 19.8 hold up as middle-aged households grow older, then some improvement in neighborhood satisfaction is in

[7] For more on the gross spatial shifts of the elderly see Golant (1972 and 1978).

first things to note is that the various developments are reinforcing in character: the large improvements in dwelling quality anticipated from the continuation of observed trends in housing preferences among the elderly and from government assistance are complemented by the expected increased choice permitted by the widespread existence of cooperatives and condominiums and the early age exemption of capital gains taxes on the sale of owner-occupied units.

Having given the bright side, let me emphasize that there will inevitably be definable groups who do not share in the overall progress. The vast increase in the number of elderly households will make this a major concern. Presumably federal assistance could be focused sharply on such groups to considerable effect. In reality, however, participation requirements for these programs are broadly defined. Thus, as progress is realized by many households, the "target efficiency" of the program—the extent to which it serves those most in need—necessarily declines. It is in the area of efficient use of subsidy resources that the challenge to policy makers is the greatest. Successfully confronting this challenge requires not only conceiving each program efficiently but also properly coordinating the myriad housing and housing-related programs.

ACKNOWLEDGMENTS

I wish to thank Sandra Newman for careful and constructive comments on a draft. The opinions expressed are my own and not necessarily those of either The Urban Institute or the U.S. Department of Housing and Urban Development where I am now employed.

REFERENCES

Ahlbrandt, R. S., Jr. (1978) Home maintenance programs: Are they a necessary ingredient for neighborhood preservation? *Practicing Planner* (September):18–24.
Baer, W. C. (1976) The evaluation of housing indicators and housing standards. *Public Policy* 24:361–393.
Bielby, W. (1978) Measuring Neighborhood Quality in the Annual Housing Survey. Unpublished manuscript, University of California, Santa Barbara.
Bureau of Labor Statistics (1970) *Revised Equivalence Scale for Estimating Incomes or Budget Cast by Family Type.* Washington, D.C.: U.S. Department of Labor.
Bureau of the Census (1972) *Public Use Samples of Basic Records from the 1970 Census.* Washington, D.C.: U.S. Department of Commerce.
Bureau of the Census (1974) *Annual Housing Survey: 1973, United States Regions; Part B, Indicators of Housing and Neighborhood Quality.* Washington, D.C.: U.S. Department of Commerce.

Bureau of the Census (1978) *Annual Housing Survey: 1976; Part A*. Current Housing
    Reports Series H-150-76. Washington, D.C.: U.S. Department of Commerce.
Donahue, W. T., Thompson, M. M., and Curren, D. J. (1977) *Congregate Housing for
    Older People*. Administration on Aging, Publication OHD 77-20284. Washington, D.C.:
    U.S. Department of Health, Education, and Welfare.
Edwards, D. G. (1977) Reverse annuity mortgages. In *Alternative Mortgage Instruments
    Research Study*. Washington, D.C.: Federal Home Loan Bank Board.
Golant, S. M. (1972) *The Residential Location and Spatial Behavior of the Elderly*. De-
    partment of Geography, Research Paper No. 43. Chicago: University of Chicago.
Golant, S. M. (1978) Residential concentrations of the future elderly. *The Gerontologist*
    (February):19–26.
Heintz, K. M. (1976) *Retirement Communities*. New Brunswick: Rutgers University Center
    for Urban Policy Research.
Liebowitz, B. (1978) Implications of community housing for planning and policy. *The
    Gerontologist* 18(April):138–143.
Pitkin, J., and Masnick, G. (1979) *Projection of National Housing Needs—1980–2000*.
    Cambridge, Mass.: Joint Center for Urban Studies, Harvard–MIT.
Rand Corporation (1978) *Fourth Annual Report of the Experimental Housing Allowance
    Program*. Santa Monica, Calif.: Rand Corporation.
Rosenblatt, J. A. (1971) Housing Code Enforcement and Administration. Unpublished
    dissertation, Massachusetts Institute of Technology.
Soldo, B. (1979) Older Neighborhoods and Older Persons. Unpublished manuscript,
    Georgetown University.
Struyk, R., and Devine, D. (1978) Determinants of Dwelling Maintenance Activity by
    Elderly Households. Paper presented at the First Conference on Community Housing
    Options for the Elderly, Philadelphia Geriatric Center.
Struyk, R., and Soldo, B. (1979) *Improving the Elderly's Housing: A Key to Preserving
    the Nation's Housing Stock and Neighborhood*. Cambridge, Mass.: Ballinger Pub-
    lishing Company.
U.S. Department of Housing and Urban Development (1978) *A Summary Report on Current
    Findings from the Experimental Housing Allowance Program*. Washington, D.C.:
    Office of Policy Development and Research.
Welfeld, I., and Struyk, R. (1979) Housing options for the elderly. Vol. 2, pp. 1–134 in
    Occasional Papers in Housing and Community Affairs. Washington, D.C.: U.S. De-
    partment of Housing and Urban Development.

chapter **20**

The Labor Market Behavior
of Older People:
A Framework for Analysis[1]

MARJORIE HONIG
GIORA HANOCH

Several factors distinguish the labor supply decisions of older persons from that of the prime-age labor force: the availability of income maintenance in the form of old-age benefits from the social security program and other public support programs, income from other private and government pension plans and from their own resources accumulated for old age, compulsory retirement provisions, changing preferences for leisure, deteriorating health, and constraints on the demand side regarding the availability of part-time employment in semiretirement.

The standard theoretical and empirical models of the labor market developed for the analysis of prime-age workers must be adapted to these special features relevant to the older population. For example, the social security old-age benefits program entails an earnings test that imposes an implicit tax on earnings (in addition to explicit income taxes). This gives rise to a segmented, noncontinuous individual labor supply curve. The problems of selectivity and endogeneity associated with the individual's choice of budget segment under these conditions require an

[1] This investigation was supported in part by grant number 10-P-90544/2-01 from the Social Security Administration, U.S. Department of Health, Education and Welfare, Washington, D.C.

appropriate econometric methodology. Other provisions of the social security program increase the complexity of the analysis (e.g., past earnings determine current eligibility and current earnings affect future social security benefits). The existence of various other pension plans and work-related sources of income further complicate matters. Market wages, nonwage income, and asset holdings of individuals are correlated in the cross-section with permanent home-productivity and preferences for leisure and therefore with current labor supply behavior. The treatment of these variables as endogenous and the use of some additional simplifying assumptions make it possible to apply the static one-period labor supply model to the analysis of older people, for whom life-cycle and dynamic effects are particularly important.

An additional consideration regarding labor supply that has been pointed out with regard to the decisions of married women (Hanoch 1976a) applies as well to older persons. Individuals are not indifferent to the distribution of a given annual quantity of labor over the year; the treatment of labor supply as merely one-dimensional is, therefore, inappropriate. This effect can best be captured by treating annual weeks and annual hours of work as two endogenous but distinct labor supply variables determined simultaneously. This is especially relevant for women and for semiretired persons, for whom part-time work is common, and has been particularly important for older persons because of special incentives concerning part-year work present in the social security program.[2]

This chapter reviews briefly the research to date on the labor market behavior of older people and proposes a framework for analysis of some of the more important questions concerning this important group.

A longitudinal analysis of a simultaneous model of labor supply, market wage determination, and the asset accumulation behavior of the older population is described, involving estimates of the factors determining labor force participation, annual hours and weeks of work, threshold labor supply quantities, and reservation wages, wage offers and asset holdings. The analysis combines cross-sectional and over-time data, using two merged microdata files (white married males and white female heads of families), including several hundred variables created from three panels (1969, 1971, and 1973) of the Retirement History Study (Irelan 1972) of

---

[2] Until 1978, the earnings test was applied on either a monthly or annual basis, such that benefits were payable for any month in which earnings fell below the monthly maximum, regardless of annual earnings accumulated to date. This resulted in incentives to bunch earnings in as few months as possible. The monthly test was eliminated in the 1977 Amendments to the Social Security Act, which also lowered the upper age limit on the earnings test from 72 to 70.

the Social Security Administration, the largest and most detailed longitudinal survey currently available regarding the older population, merged with social security earnings history records.

The empirical methodology focuses on a longitudinal analysis, which combines cross-sectional and time-series data. The analysis of data of this type has occupied an increasingly central role in a variety of social and economic studies. A focal problem in many of these studies has been the estimation of the separate effects of time period, cohort of birth or vintage, and age. A general solution is offered to the well-known identification problem that arises because current year, year of birth, and age are linearly dependent. The relative weight of the permanent versus the random or transitory variation among individuals in each of the behavioral equations may be estimated as well. Taking account of the longitudinal aspects improves efficiency in the estimation of the model and increases the usefulness and accuracy of the model for detecting current trends as well as for predicting reactions to changing policy parameters.

The estimated model will be applied to analyze current patterns of labor supply and asset accumulation behavior within the older white population in the United States and to predict the effects of various proposed changes in social policy regarding the aged, such as modifications in the benefit structure and earnings test in the social security program, the impact of expanded coverage and benefits under private pension programs, the effect of the recent increase in the compulsory retirement age, and the effect of recent efforts to expand the part-time job market and to reduce the constraints on job mobility for older persons.

A REVIEW OF PREVIOUS STUDIES

Many of the early studies of the labor market behavior of older persons were based on retrospective surveys of retired workers. These tended to attribute falling participating rates to health factors alone (Steiner and Dorfman 1959, Wentworth 1968). Estimates of the importance of health in the labor supply decision must be treated with caution, however. Poor health is undoubtedly the main socially acceptable reason for retirement and therefore the most likely to be offered in retrospective analyses of those already retired, even though other factors may have played the strategic role at the time of retirement. Moreover, health status is one of the more difficult concepts to quantify, in part because of its attitudinal aspects and in part because of the difficulty of distinguishing the investment component. Nevertheless, health factors were viewed as the determining and often the single factor leading to labor force withdrawal of older persons for many years.

With growing interest in the effects of public policy and in particular in the effects of income maintenance programs on labor supply decisions, analyses of the older population began to focus on measures of potential retirement income and the associated implicit tax rates. The effects of the social security program in particular began to receive attention. Social security raises the incomes of older persons and at the same time taxes their benefits for earnings over a given maximum (the earnings or retirement test). On theoretical grounds, a decrease in annual hours of work of the elderly would be predicted from the first of these effects and an increase or decrease in hours from the second, depending on the magnitudes of two offsetting responses.[3]

Some early analyses of the effects of the earnings test found a "bunching" of the annual earnings of social security recipients just under the earnings maximum (Gallaway 1965, Sander 1970, Vroman 1971). The bunching effect is consistent with the predicted effects of the earnings test since the implicit tax on earnings is zero below the earnings maximum and positive above. The earnings maximum (which creates a kink in the budget constraint over a range of wage rates) would be expected to induce a nontrivial proportion of workers to limit their earnings to the maximum.

These studies provided the first suggestive evidence that older persons appeared to respond to the incentives in the social security program. They did not, however, provide any clues to the labor supply effects over the entire wage distribution, nor did they separate the pure income and the tax effects of the program.

In their comprehensive study of labor force participation, Bowen and Finegan (1969) attempted some rough estimates of the effect of the earnings test on the participation rates of the male population aged 65 and over. Their estimates were based on a single-equation model relating total nonlabor income (primarily social security benefits), schooling, age, race, and marital status to participation in the labor force during the census week.

---

[3] The possibility that reductions in the implicit tax rate in social security, undertaken with the view toward increasing the labor supply of older people, may in fact decrease labor supply was developed in a theoretical framework in Hanoch and Honig (1978). A recent empirical analysis of the population 65 years and over confirms this prediction (Pellechio 1978). Similar effects have been found for the Aid to Families with Dependent Children (AFDC) program (Levy 1979), confirming earlier studies indicating response to economic incentives in the AFDC program (Honig 1974, 1976).

They attributed the residual drop in participation between the ages of 64 and 67—that which could not be explained by the above variables—to institutional factors, in particular the earnings test. Their results were no more than suggestive but served to emphasize a point often neglected: Adjustments in labor supply due to the earnings test may take the form of movement in and out of the labor force during the year rather than part-time work on a full-year basis. They also pointed out the intriguing halt in the decline in labor force participation rates for males at age 72 when the earnings test ceases to apply (labor force participation rates adjusted for schooling, other income, marital status, and race were appreciably higher at ages 72 and 73 than at age 71).

Other studies have found significant effects of social security on the retirement decision but have not dealt with the quantities of work supplied by workers (Pechman *et al.* 1968, Barfield and Morgan 1969, Parnes and Nestel 1974, Quinn 1977). Thus they do not treat the implications of the nonlinear budget constraint above the earnings maximum and do not distinguish between income and tax effects. The earnings test alone does not alter incentives to retire from the labor force since it may affect hours of work only in the range of earnings above the maximum exemption in which range the implicit tax (reduction in benefits) is nonzero.[4]

The effects of both social security benefits and the earnings test as well as several other factors were treated in Boskin (1977). This study attempted to distinguish between the effects of the earnings test and the benefits by an ad hoc method that ignored the nonlinearities of the budget constraint and the resulting kinks and discontinuities in the supply function. This was done by measuring the benefits and the tax at a predetermined standard level of hours. Interpretation of the results is difficult in view of the true form of the supply function. In addition, rough approximations of social security benefits were used in the absence of records data on eligibility and on covered earnings, which are likely to be subject to nonnegligible errors.

A later analysis by Boskin and Hurd (1978) estimated probabilities of moving among the states of working, semiretirement, and complete retirement in an effort to capture the effects of the nonlinear budget constraint created by social security. The estimates, however, focused on males aged 62–65 who, because of actuarial increases in benefits for retirement postponed after the age of 62, do not in effect face significant nonlinearities in the budget constraint.[5]

---

[4] This holds true in the absence of restrictions on the demand side that may make it impossible to vary hours of work continuously at a fixed given wage.

[5] If any benefits are withheld from a worker between ages 62 and 65, the benefit check starting at age 65 is raised by .55% of the level of the monthly check that would have been received had benefits started at age 62. Under reasonable assumptions, this amounts in

Two recent analyses have dealt with the implications of the nonlinear budget constraint for the labor supply of the older population both theoretically and empirically (Pellechio 1978, Blinder et al. 1978). The study by Pellechio estimates the probability of retirement as well as the supply of annual hours conditional on working for a sample of males aged 65 and over, drawn from the 1973 CPS-IRS-SSA Exact Match Study (Aziz 1978). The study deals with the effect of the social security program and finds significant effects of social security wealth and the earnings test on the supply of labor.

While the Exact Match Study sample provides social security earnings record data and thereby the possibility of estimating potential social security benefits, it provides only limited information on many of the other variables relevant to labor supply analysis. Moreover, the analysis uses a selective sample and disregards the effects of fixed costs of entry. The methods used for deriving the probabilities of being in each segment of the budget constraint are ad hoc and sometimes unsatisfactory (e.g., probabilities add up to more than one or are negative). The issue is of particular importance since it is possible that the dominant effects of changes in the social security program with respect to the earnings test or the size of benefits will appear in changes in the probabilities of location in various segments rather than in marginal changes within the segments. Finally, while this study recognized the importance of life-cycle effects, the fact that the Exact Match Study file is not a panel survey precluded a full longitudinal analysis.

The latter comment applies to the Blinder et al. study as well. Although three panels of the Retirement History Study were available for this study, each was treated as a separate sample. In the wage equation, observations from these panels were pooled, including as an additional panel information given in 1969 about previous jobs, with high variance in the dates of these jobs and low reliability of the wage data. The labor supply equation used only the 1973 panel and the asset equation used only the 1971 panel. Social security record data for calculating potential and future benefits were not available at the time of the study. Benefits were calculated from lifetime earnings estimated from the partial labor history information available in the surveys and are very rough approximations. Information on current, last, and first jobs used for interpolating the earnings history covers less than half the total labor force experience (time from entry to first job to present), while wage information on early

---

present value terms to 1 month's benefit check. Combined with the practice of concentrating withholding of benefits in any year into as few months as possible, this creates for this age group a budget constraint that is roughly a straight line. See Blinder et al. (1978) for development of this point.

jobs is unreliable. (Although the 1971 survey includes information about the longest job held, it was not used by Blinder *et al.* in the construction of the earnings profiles; by our calculations, experience in current, previous, longest, and first jobs—after netting out the overlaps—accounts for about 70% of total labor force experience.) In addition, large selection biases may exist in the sample used, since many cases with partially missing data were dropped from the sample. This resulted in a reduction of sample size from 28,000 to 13,000 observations in the wage equation and in a sample of only 1972 cases (of 7000) in the asset equation.

The specification of the utility function used by Blinder *et al.* (1978) for estimating the supply equation (by maximum likelihood) seems unnecessarily complex and dictated a very restrictive specification of additional covariates.

These studies have clarified many issues and have added significantly to the stock of current knowledge about the labor market behavior of the older population. None, however, has used the panel-aspect information embedded in the Retirement History Survey and other micropanel surveys.[6] Recent studies have either used cross-sectional data, single cross-sections from panel data, or have pooled the panels to treat them as independent observations. The additional panel information, which identifies the same individual appearing in different years, can be used for increasing the efficiency of the estimates (by allowing the elimination of the permanent cross-sectional variation between years) and for testing the stability of the behavioral functions (by testing for changes in parameters over time and over a variable range of the explanatory variables). In other words, panel data may be used to distinguish between cohort and age effects in the deterministic part of the equations and between permanent and transitory components in the stochastic part.

A FRAMEWORK FOR ANALYSIS

The model that is discussed briefly in this section is based on a theoretical analysis of the individual labor supply curve under conditions of an income maintenance program such as social security (Hanoch and Honig 1978). The simultaneous model consists of the following equations: the probability of participation, annual hours of work, annual weeks,

[6] The Michigan Income Dynamics Panel Study and the National Longitudinal Survey both involve smaller samples on the relevant age groups. In addition, neither can be matched with social security record data, which provide reliable estimates of current potential and future social security benefits.

market wage, reservation wage, and asset holdings in each of the three years, allowing for variations in parameters over time. The variance–covariance matrix of residuals is partitioned into the permanent components, which account for constant differences among individuals in preferences and in productivity, and the transitory components, which are regarded as random. The methodology used for the estimation is chosen with the aim of obtaining consistent but inexpensive estimates, sacrificing some efficiency relative to infeasible or very expensive maximum likelihood methods. However, the simpler estimation methods may be more robust when the models are imperfectly specified. These simpler methods allow more intensive specification search at a lower cost in order to choose the best proxies for given conceptual variables from sets of alternative variables and better exclusion restrictions and functional forms. This specification search may yield higher returns than high-powered and costly estimation methods applied to restrictive, predetermined specifications of the equations and definitions of the variables. A by-product will be added insight about the unique data set that has been developed for this study, which may be useful in a wide variety of analyses concerning the older population. Recommendations for improvements in future microsurveys may also be derived.

This large microdata file includes several hundred variables created from three panels of the Social Security Administration Retirement History Study (1969/1971/1973) (Irelan 1972). It contains several alternative measures for each of many important variables such as wages, labor supply, labor force experience (including job tenure and general market experience), types of assets and incomes, health, retirement status, pension and social security eligibility status, household and family characteristics, and individual background characteristics as well as measures of changes over time in these variables. The data were carefully screened for reporting and recording errors causing extreme outlying observations, and considerable effort was devoted to avoiding exclusions from the sample based on missing information. All variables have been transformed from coded to quantitative form (including many dummy variables). The processed data are stored separately in two merged files— white married males and white female heads of families (aged 58–63 in 1969)—consisting of 3683 and 1514 observations, respectively.

The survey data have been merged with social security record data on annual earnings and quarters of coverage of respondents and spouses for the years 1951–1974. These data provide information on the work histories of respondents from age 40, including movements in and out of the labor force (specifically, employment covered by social security) as well as checks for accuracy in the survey data on earnings and employment. In addition, it is possible to estimate with a high degree of accuracy the potential current and future retirement benefits available to respondents and spouses from social security.

The theoretical development in Hanoch and Honig (1978) proposes a simple model with one individual, one period, two goods (leisure and other consumption), and exogenous wage rate, nonwage income, and benefits. Extensions of the model account for the two-tiered tax system in the social security program, which was in effect in the years covered by the first three RHS panels, as well as for other complexities in social security provisions, such as the effects of current earnings and benefits on future benefits, the endogeneity of wage rates and nonwage incomes, and intrafamily substitution effects. These effects are incorporated into the methodology developed for the empirical application of the model.

A brief description of the main findings of the model follows.[7] The supply function of hours $H^*(\bar{W}, \bar{Y})$ is uniquely associated with the utility function $U(X, L)$, where L is leisure ($L \leq T$) and X is goods, $\bar{W}$ is a fixed hourly wage, and $\bar{Y}$ a given nonwage income.

Given a benefit B, an earnings maximum M, and an implicit tax rate t on benefits ($0 \leq t \leq 1$) for earnings above M, the supply curve can take two alternative forms:

(a) If $t \geq t_0$, where t_0 is an endogenous threshold critical tax rate, the supply curve is of the general form shown in Figure 20.1.
   The critical wages W_1, W_2, and W_4 are also endogenously determined.
(b) If $t < t_0$, the supply curve is as shown in Figure 20.2.

The backward-bending segment $H = M/W$ corresponds to the wage range where the optimal solution for the individual is at the corner; he or she works just enough to earn the maximum exempt amount $M = HW$.

The discontinuity (at W_4 or W_5) occurs where he or she is indifferent between receiving benefits or working and earning more and thereby opting out of the benefits system.

The horizontal distance between $H^*(W, Y)$ and this supply curve represents the total effect of the program, where the difference $H^*(W, Y) - H^*(W, Y+B)$ is the pure benefit effect, and the remaining difference (which may be negative) is the effect of the earnings test and the implicit tax. Changes in t above t_0 do not have any effect, while changes below

---

[7] For proofs and details, see Hanoch and Honig (1978) and for an illustration related to the Israeli social security system, see Hanoch and Honig (1976).

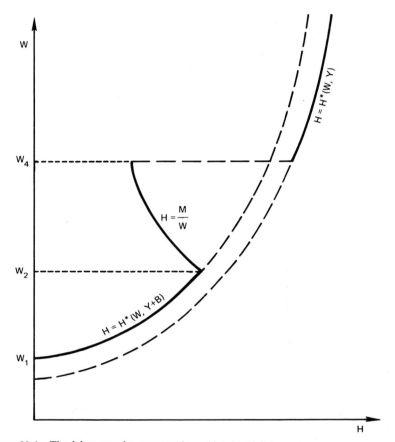

Figure 20.1   The labor supply curve under a high implicit tax rate.

t_0 may increase or decrease work, depending on the individual's location on the wage axis (relative to the supply curve, determined jointly by the individual's preferences and the program parameters).

If fixed money costs C are involved in entering the labor market, the supply curve will have a discontinuity at the point of entry, and the lowest positive segment of the supply curve will be:

$$H = H^*(W, Y - C + B) \geq H_0 \qquad \text{(for } W > W_1^* > W_1)$$

where the minimum supply H_0 equates the utility $U(Y + B, T)$ when retired, with $U(Y - C + B + W_1^* H_0, T - H_0)$, when working H_0 hours, receiving a wage equal to the reservation wage W_1^*.

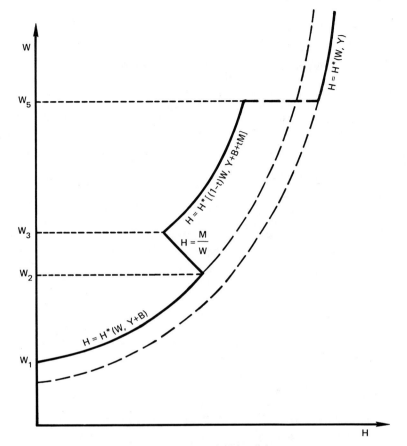

Figure 20.2 The labor supply curve under a low implicit tax rate.

In the empirical application, individual variation in preferences is captured by introducing the effects of various measured variables Z into the basic supply function H^*, and by an additive stochastic component ε; that is,

$$H^* = \bar{H}^*(W, Y; Z) + \varepsilon.$$

Z and ε introduce variation among individuals both in the location and the form of each segment of the supply curve as well as in the critical wage rates that determine its relevant boundaries. Specification of H^* as additive in log W, Y, Z, and ε facilitates the estimation of the function in all the segments jointly, provided the choice of the relevant segment is accounted for as an endogenous choice.

The estimation by maximum likelihood of the complete simultaneous model, including the probabilities of location on each segment and of retirement or nonparticipation, the hours (and perhaps weeks) equation, and the reservation wage as well as the wage equation, is clearly infeasible. Approximate two-stage limited information estimations may be carried out, but they are also costly and complex.

The considerably cheaper, albeit consistent, route to be taken in this study for estimating the model may be sketched as follows:

1. Estimate the probability of participation by maximum likelihood probit analysis, disregarding at this stage the location of workers on other segments of the supply function and the quantity of labor.

2. Estimate conditional probabilities among workers for locating on different segments of the supply function by a multinomial probit (or logit) estimation or by a series of dichotomous probit estimates (if this yields reasonable results such that probabilities are positive fractions adding to one for almost all individuals).

3. Use the inverse Mill's ratios obtained from the probit estimates as additional explanatory variables in each behavioral equation as used in labor supply estimates by Heckman (1976) and Hanoch (1976b). Introducing these estimated variables into the equations corrects for selectivity biases implied by the endogenous choice of segment and their coefficients give estimates for some parameters of the residual variance–covariance matrix.

4. The function $\bar{H}^*$ can be estimated by pooling all the noncorner solution cases together, provided the appropriate wage and income variables are used as arguments (e.g., for individuals whose benefits are reduced via the earnings test at the $t = .5$ segment, the relevant wage is $.5W$, and the relevant income is $[Y + B + .5M]$) and provided the relevant bias-correcting factors (for truncation at both ends of an interior segment) are added to the list of right-side variables.

5. These linearized equations, corrected for the relevant selection biases, may now be estimated by the usual methods applicable to a linear simultaneous model, consisting in this case of the market wage equation, the hours supply equation, and possibly also the asset-holding and the annual weeks supply equations. Allowing for correlations between residuals among these equations, the method of three-stage least squares can be applied to the model (as in Hanoch 1976b, 1980). The coefficients of the reservation wage

equation are estimated in a separate regression later, using the participation (probit) index and the supply-determining variables as the explanatory variables and the predicted wage, imputed from the market wage equation, as the dependent variable.[8]

This procedure uses all the information available and uses asymptotically efficient estimation methods relative to the information used in each stage but sacrifices some efficiency by separating the stages, so that at each stage only part of the information is utilized (e.g., in the probit step, information on hours and weeks of work is ignored).

Thus far, the above description of the methods applies to one given cross-section. Accounting for the panel time-series aspects may be done simply by using levels as well as between-year differences of variables. A brief explanation of the method for two panels indicates the approach to be taken (which is equivalent in efficiency at the limit to full maximum likelihood estimates in a linear model). Let the hours equation in Years 1 and 2 be:

$$H_1 = X_1\alpha_1 + Z\beta_1 + \varepsilon + u_1$$
$$H_2 = X_2\alpha_2 + Z\beta_2 + \varepsilon + u_2$$

where X are variables that change over time (e.g., incomes, wages, experience, children) and Z are fixed variables (race, past education, father's occupation and education, children ever born to older females, etc.). Transitory residuals are u_1 and u_2, while ε is a permanent individual residual component. The coefficients α and β are allowed, in the general case, to change between years but are the same for all individuals in each cross-section.

Writing $X_2 = X_1 + \Delta X$ for the matrix X, allowing for a form of nonlinearity by substituting $(\alpha_{21}X_1 + \alpha_{22}\Delta X)$ for $\alpha_2 X_2$, and taking the difference between the two equations gives:

$$\Delta H = (\alpha_{21} - \alpha_1) X_1 + \alpha_{22}\Delta X + (\beta_2 - \beta_1) Z + \Delta u.$$

Thus, testing for $\alpha_{21} - \alpha_1 = 0$ and $\beta_2 - \beta_1 = 0$ may determine the stability of the equations over time (for a given range of variables $\{X_1, Z\}$), while testing $\alpha_{22} = \alpha_{21}$ detects possible changes in parameters due to nonlinearities associated with changing the range of X from X_1 to X_2. These tests are performed in a simultaneous estimation (by 3SLS) of the first-year level equation and the above difference equation. This provides asymptotically efficient estimates, while allowing for a fixed covariance (equal to $-\sigma_{u_1}^2$) between the corresponding residuals ($\varepsilon + u_1$) and $\Delta u = (u_2 - u_1)$.

[8] See Hanoch (1976b, pp. 35–37).

If any of the tested coefficients are virtually equal, new estimates can be obtained by substituting these equalities into the equations. The covariance structure is also estimated consistently, thus enabling the identification of the permanent versus the transitory components of variance. Extensions to 3 years is straightforward [e.g., using two difference $(H_2 - H_1, H_3 - H_2)$ and one (H_1) level equations]. This can be extended to a simultaneous model with three or four equations for each year in an analogous way.

The identification of the actual segment on which each individual is located is determined by the available data, for example, whether he or she is retired, working and receiving full benefits, or earning above M and receiving partial benefits [where the effective wage is $W(1 - t)$ and the effective nonwage income is $(Y + B + tM)$, or earning still more and receiving no benefits (with $\bar{W} = W$ and $\bar{Y} = Y$)]. As a control group, persons who are not eligible for the benefits (e.g., who were not covered by social security in early jobs) are also included, with their expected supply curve being $H^*(W, Y, Z)$ throughout. The two-tiered tax system with $t_1 = .5$ and $t_2 = 1$ is treated in an analogous fashion.

Effects of current earnings on future benefits (particularly important for ages 62–64 subject to provision for early retirement) can also be incorporated, affecting both the permanent nonwage wealth or income and the relevant current net wage.

The discontinuity of supply at the point of entry is taken into account as in Hanoch (1976b, 1980) by specifying the reservation wage equation $W_1^*(\bar{Y}; Z)$ separately from the basic supply function $H^*(\bar{W}, \bar{Y}; Z)$; the supply function applies conditionally for $W > W_1^*$ only (or $H^* > H_0$). Although W_1^* is not observed, it is estimated using information on participation and on Z for the total sample and on wages of workers as previously explained.

The labor supply in terms of annual weeks worked (which is a major form of variation when weekly hours are constrained by employers) can be specified similarly to H^*, but an additional modification is required (see Hanoch 1980) for the large proportion of individuals who work a full year (52 weeks) and who are subject to a corner-solution effect at that point.

Given the estimated model, if any important and economically meaningful changes in parameters over time are detected, they may be incorporated into the model itself (e.g., by introducing additional interactions with age or time-trends in the coefficients).

A somewhat different approach for separating the effects of age and of changes over time (both long-run and cyclical) is based on a recent study (Hanoch 1979) that provides a strategy for estimating the separate effects of age, year of birth (vintage or cohort effects), and current year on any of the dependent variables. The main idea here is to separate the linear components of the three effects from the nonlinear deviations orthogonal to these linear trends. While the nonlinear components are fully identified as effects of individual year, year of birth, or year of age (using a complete set of individual-year dummy variables in a regression model), only two of the linear trends can vary independently. Thus, one requires either outside information regarding one of the linear trends or the omission of one of these trends (e.g., if the linear cohort trend is omitted, the estimated age trend represents the combined age and cohort cross-sectional linear effect, and the time linear trend estimates the excess of the time trend over the cross-sectional age trend).

The adjusted age profile (purged of cohort and period effects), time profile (adjusted for age and cohort), or cohort differences (net of age and period), may then be related to other explanatory variables as described in the previous discussion.

An alternative strategy for combining the two approaches is simply to incorporate the age, period, and cohort dummy variables into each of the individual-observation equations of the simultaneous model described previously, while imposing the required restrictions on their coefficients in order to provide for identification of the separate effects as implied in the age–period–cohort analysis based on the means of the year-by-cohort cells.

Once a satisfactory version of the model is estimated, it is possible to derive from it the underlying preferences-structure in this population and to use it to predict the labor market behavior of any given individual (for example, the "representative" individual whose residuals equal zero and whose other exogenous variables are equal to the population means) under various hypothetical conditions, such as reformed social security benefits structure or additional pension coverage.

Taking the estimates of the stochastic components into account, predictions with respect to aggregates (in the sample populations) may also be derived analytically for alternative simulated conditions or suggested policy reforms. For example, although in the existing data only two implicit tax rates on social security benefits applied (50% and 100%), the estimated equations and probabilities can be used to predict the aggregate effects on labor supply of changes in these tax rates or of their elimination (such as in the current system where only a 50% tax applies). In addition, predictions about the labor supply behavior of future cohorts of the older population (which were not covered in the RHS data) may also be obtained, if extrapolation of the observed trends in the exogenous variables and in the behavioral coefficients can be expected to remain valid.

ACKNOWLEDGMENTS

The authors are indebted to Lola Irelan, Anthony Pellechio, William Rabin, and Karen Schwab for useful discussions and to Walter Bourne for helpful programming assistance.

REFERENCES

Aziz, F., Kilss, B., and Scheuren, F. (1978) *1973 Current Population Survey—Administrative Record Exact Match File Codebook, Part 1*. Social Security Administration, Report No. 8. Washington, D.C.: U.S. Department of Health, Education and Welfare.

Barfield, R., and Morgan, J. (1969) *Early Retirement: The Decision and the Experience*. University of Michigan: Survey Research Center.

Blinder, A. S., Gordon, R. H., and Wise, D. (1978) An Empirical Study of the Effects of Pensions and the Saving and Labor Supply Decisions of Older Men. Report submitted to U.S. Department of Labor under contract no. J-9-P-6-0173.

Boskin, M. J. (1977) Social security and retirement decisions. *Economic Inquiry* 15(1).

Boskin, M. J., and Hurd, M. (1978) The effect on social security on early retirement. *Journal of Public Economics* 10(4).

Bowen, W. G., and Finegan, T. A. (1969) *The Economics of Labor Force Participation*. Princeton, N.J.: Princeton University Press.

Gallaway, L. E. (1965) The Retirement Decision: An Exploratory Essay. Research Report No. 1. Office of Research and Statistics, Social Security Administration.

Hanoch, G. (1976a) Hours and Weeks in the Theory of Labor Supply. Rand Corporation, R-1787-HEW.

Hanoch, G. (1976b) A Multivariate Model of Labor Supply: Methodology for Estimation. Rand Corporation, R-1869-HEW.

Hanoch, G. (1979) A General Solution for Estimating Period, Cohort, and Age Effects. Discussion paper. Center for the Social Sciences, Columbia University.

Hanoch, G. (1980) A multivariate model of labor supply: Methodology and estimation. Chap. 6 in J. P. Smith, ed., *Female Labor Supply*. Princeton, N.J.: Princeton University Press (forthcoming).

Hanoch, G., and Honig, M. (1976) The Effect of Social Security of Labor Supply. Working paper 88. Department of Economics, The Hebrew University, Jerusalem.

Hanoch, G., and Honig, M. (1978) The labor supply curve under income maintenance programs. *Journal of Public Economics* 9(1).

Heckman, J. (1976) Sample Selection Bias as a Specification Error. Rand Corporation, R-1984-HEW.

Honig, M. (1974) AFDC payments, recipient rates, and family dissolution. *Journal of Human Resources* 9(3).

Honig, M. (1976) AFDC payments, recipient rates, and family dissolution: A reply. *Journal of Human Resources* 11(2).

Irelan, L. M. (1972) Retirement history study: Introduction. *Social Security Bulletin* (February).

Levy, F. (1979) The labor supply of female household heads, or AFDC incentives don't work too well. *Journal of Human Resources* 14(1).

Parnes, H., and Nestel, G. (1974) Early retirement. In H. S. Parnes *et al.*, *The Pre-Retirement Years: Five Years in the Worklives of Middle-Age Men*. Ohio State University: Center for Human Research.

Pechman, J. A., Aaron, H. J., and Taussig, M. K. (1968) *Social Security: Perspective for Reform*. Washington, D.C.: The Brookings Institution.

Pellechio, A. (1978) Social Security and Retirement Behavior. Unpublished Ph.D. dissertation, Harvard University.

Quinn, J. F. (1977) Microeconomic determinants of early retirement: A cross-sectional view of white married men. *Journal of Human Resources* 12(3).

Sander, K. G. (1970) The Effects of the 1966 Retirement Test on the Earnings of Workers Aged 65–72. Research and Statistics Note No. 1. Office of Research and Statistics, Social Security Administration.

Steiner, P., and Dorfman, R. (1959) *The Economic Status of the Aged*. Berkeley, Calif.: University of California Press.

Vroman, W. (1971) Older Worker Earnings and the 1965 Social Security Amendments. Research Report No. 39. Office of Research and Statistics, Social Security Administration.

Wentworth, E. (1968) Employment After Retirement. Research Report No. 21. Office of Research and Statistics, Social Security Administration.

chapter 21

Women's Employment and Its Implications for the Status of the Elderly of the Future[1]

JUDITH TREAS

The trouble with our times is that the future is not what it used to be.
—Paul Valery

Should a social historian of the twenty-first century chronicle our time, he or she might well conclude that ours is the era of working women. Of all the interwoven developments of the postwar period—the burgeoning of a welfare state, the transformation to a service economy, the flowering of social movements for equality—perhaps none has colored the fabric of public and private life as has the rise in women's labor force participation. In the workplace, the working woman has staked a claim for economic opportunity while precipitating a subtle revolution of etiquette and social custom. On the home front, working women have affected both the family's balance of power and its balance of payments. So wide-reaching have been these work force changes that the growth of women's labor force participation has been charged with everything from the rise in fast foods to the fall in fertility.

[1] Support for the preparation of this chapter derives in part from Administration on Aging Grant No. 90-A-1015 and from National Science Foundation Grant No. SOC-7813769. The conclusions, however, are those of the author and not necessarily those of the agencies.

561

Many of the women who pioneered the postwar rise in labor force participation are now old, and each successive cohort promises more and more women who will enter old age with a wealth of labor force experience. Since rising work force involvement of women has touched so many of our social and economic institutions, its implications for the status of the elderly of the future warrant our attention. This chapter traces the trends in women's work force participation, considers its impact on the fiscal and philosophical foundations of social security, and speculates on the ways in which longer working lives may alter the late-life finances of women and their families. The focus on families is deliberate. To be sure, many older persons, especially women, are single, and the unmarried have more modest means than do older couples. Most of these aged singles have been married, nonetheless, and their status in old age reflects a legacy of family income-getting, income-pooling, and income-spending. This family locus is recognized by public programs of old age support, and it is married women with families who are largely responsible for the postwar rise in women's work force involvement.

FEMALE LABOR FORCE PARTICIPATION: WHAT'S IN STORE?

Present-day preoccupation with women's employment may be traced to the dramatic increase in female labor force participation during the postwar period. Historically, some women had always worked outside the home—black women, immigrant women, and young, unmarried women. World War II saw the work force involvement of mature married women as well. This wartime mobilization, however, only hinted at the changes to come in women's social and economic roles. Attracted by the growth of occupations stereotypically held by women, such as teaching and clerical work, middle-aged married women went to work in unprecedented numbers (Gordon 1963) and were welcomed by employers facing an inadequate labor pool of well-educated, young single women (Oppenheimer 1970). Not only were women with grown children seen to enter the labor force, but also those with school-age children. By 1970, it was apparent that the growth in female labor force participation had affected even young mothers, for one-third of women with preschool children were working. The labor force participation of women had soared from 25.4% in 1940 to 48% in 1977. No longer content to work only until marriage, women, it seemed, would be spending a good part of their lives on the job.

The quickening tempo of women's employment was all the more remarkable because it came at a time when work rates for men were plummeting. Of course, prolonged schooling raised the age of labor force entry for young men, and the emerging institution of retirement decreased the work involvement of older men (Kreps and Clark 1975). Although the trend to early retirement emerged in the late 1950s, in more recent decades, labor force participation slipped even among men under age 55. Table 21.1 illustrates the changes that occurred between 1967 and 1977 in the labor force participation rates of men and women aged 25–64. For each 10-year age group, men's participation dropped between the 2 years, with older men registering the sharpest declines. This trend toward "early retirement" has been associated on one hand with unemployment, poor health, and unfavorable working conditions, and on the other hand with the growing availability of disability and retirement income (Katona 1965, Barfield and Morgan 1970, Boskin 1977, Quinn 1977, Rones 1978, Burkhauser 1979). As a matter of policy concern, early retirement has been linked to rising fiscal demands on the social security system. Women have served to offset men's declines in employment, expanding social security's payroll tax base while posing few new demands for the already overburdened system (Pitts 1978).

In contrast to the rates for men, the age-specific labor force participation rates rose for women aged 25–54. Most marked were the increases at the younger ages; although women aged 45–54 showed the highest labor force participation in 1967, the work rates of the middle-aged were exceeded by those of younger women in 1977. For women aged 55–64, 1967 and 1977 rates were almost identical. With each successive cohort evidencing greater work force commitment, the upward trend in women's labor force participation seems sure to continue.

The most recent civilian labor force projections by the Bureau of Labor Statistics (Flaim and Fullerton 1978) estimate female labor force

TABLE 21.1
Labor Force Participation Rates of Men and Women Ages 25–64, March 1967 and 1977[a]

	Men		Women	
	1967	1977	1967	1977
25–34	97.3	95.2	41.4	59.3
35–44	97.4	95.6	47.8	59.6
45–54	95.4	90.9	50.9	56.1
55–64	83.6	74.4	41.7	41.1

[a] From Michelotti (1977).

participation rates for 1990 under assumptions of high, intermediate, and low growth. Rates for women aged 16 and older are expected to rise from 48.4 in 1977 to 53.8, 57.1, or 60.4, depending on growth assumptions. These assumptions are based in large measure on economic growth scenarios, since young women's labor force participation is less and less responsive to trends in marriage and motherhood. More problematic will be the labor force participation of mature women. Continuing declines are foreseen for women above age 65, and women 55–64 are projected to experience declining labor force involvement under assumptions of intermediate or low labor force growth. It remains to be seen whether the participation of these women 55–64 will actually fall from its 1977 level of 41% to 39.8% (or even 36.6%), because it is projected to inch up to 41.8% under high growth assumptions. At issue is whether the rising participation of successive cohorts of mature women will be sufficient to counter a recent and subtle shift toward early retirement by these women workers—a trend emerging only in the 1970s (McEaddy 1975). That women do drop out in later years is seen in Table 21.1 for the cohort of women who were 45–54 in 1967 and 55–64 in 1977. Although at the latter ages their work rates were little different from those of women aged 55–64 a decade earlier, the rate for this cohort has dropped from 50.9 to 41.1. Proportionately, this decline in participation was almost as great as that of men.

As among men, the shift toward early retirement holds mixed blessings for aged women. On the one hand, it reflects the growth in retirement income, which cushions the displacement of older workers and offers affluent leisure for some. On the other hand, it is associated with income below earnings and with permanently reduced social security benefits. Between December 1967 and December 1977, for example, reduced benefits climbed from 64% to 74% of all Old Age and Survivors retirement benefits awarded women workers (Social Security Administration 1978). Comparable figures for men were 49% and 62%.

Since empirical studies of the early retirement phenomenon have focused largely on men, the trends and differentials in labor force participation by mature women merit scrutiny. Both age-specific and education-specific data on labor force participation provide telling, if tentative, evidence of early retirement patterned by personal preference and personnel policies. Consider, for example, changes in age-specific proportions of women aged 55–64 reporting some work experience during the year. The proportion of women aged 55–59 declined only modestly during the 1970s; in 1976, the proportion reporting work experience was 96.2% of that in 1970 (Bureau of Labor Statistics 1971, 1977). Among women aged 60–61, however, it fell to 85.2% of that in 1970. Among women aged 62–64, the dropoff was to 87% of the 1970 figure. In other words, the largest declines were for those ages of eligibility for social security benefits as a retired worker or the spouse of a retired worker. If eligibility for a retirement pension prompts retirement after 60, it is also possible that this tantalizing prospect of qualifying for a pension encourages continued employment of women aged 55–59 who have an eye to eligibility and benefit formulas.

The patterning of work force declines by educational attainment is also of interest. Figure 21.1 charts 1959–1977 labor force participation rates of women, aged 55–64, grouped by years of schooling. As a whole, this age group saw work rates climb steadily until 1971 and then begin to edge down. Among women who finished college—those with 16 or more years of education—the trend was more pronounced. While these well-educated women maintained higher labor force participation rates throughout the period, their participation rose more sharply, peaked earlier (in 1965), and then plummeted. This participation profile is intelligible in terms of the occupational make-up of this college-educated

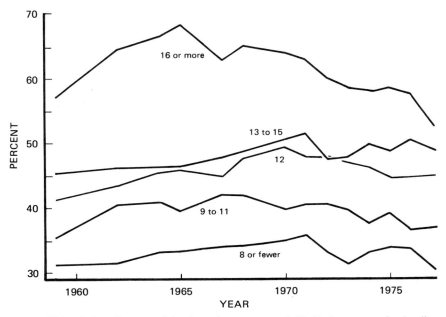

Figure 21.1. Labor force participation of women, aged 55–64, by years of schooling, 1959–1977. (From U.S. Bureau of Labor Statistics, "Educational Attainment of Workers." Selected *Special Labor Force Reports*. Washington, D.C.: U.S. Government Printing Office.)

group. In 1970, half of working women, aged 55–64, with a college degree taught kindergarten, elementary, or secondary school (Bureau of the Census 1973). As largely public employees, these women were probably atypical in their high rates of coverage by retirement plans promising relatively generous retirement incomes—a variable linked to the early retirement decision among men. As teachers, they belonged to a profession in which retirement is so approved and institutionalized as to support the .5 million-member National Retired Teacher's Association. Interestingly, the downturn in participation rates coincided with the high school graduation of children born at the onset of the baby boom. We may speculate that labor force withdrawal by well-educated older women has reflected a decline in demand for their services in the classroom, for there has been no new tide of school-children to offset the loss of baby boom students who have outgrown grades K through 12.

What this data is meant to suggest is that the 1970s trend toward early labor force withdrawal by older women has probably been predicated on many of the same factors as the declining work force participation of older men, particularly on the availability of retirement income. Of course, men's trend toward earlier retirement has reflected in part the 1961 change in social security, which gave men the option of retirement with reduced benefits at age 62—an option that women already enjoyed. Other public and private pension plans have probably played a part, too. The spread of private retirement plans, the associated growth of mandatory retirement rules, and the development of early retirement provisions are among the factors linked with declining labor force participation at the older ages. While these factors predate the recent trend to early retirement by women, it may well be that women are becoming more responsive to these developments due to their longer and more continuous work lives.

Although there is little research to date on the subject, there is reason to suspect that working wives have altered late-life economic behavior and planning by married couples. For example, has the work force involvement of wives led to greater pension eligibility and asset accumulation and, hence, to earlier withdrawal from the labor force? Does the continuing earnings of one spouse enable the other to retire earlier than otherwise? Does earlier retirement free one spouse to assume household tasks while freeing the other partner for paid work? Do couples retire jointly—the better to enjoy shared leisure time?

Any coordination of retirement decisions is complicated by the fact that partners of different ages may not become eligible for social security benefits at the same time. Among married men aged 63–69 in the Social Security Administration's Retirement History Study, nearly half had wives 4 or more years younger than themselves, while less than a quarter had wives born within a year of their own birthdate (Fox 1979). Workers become eligible for reduced OASDI retirement benefits at age 62 and full benefits at age 65, while wives may retire with husbands to claim dependent spouse benefits at age 60. If the partners are covered by other public or private retirement plans, each may face additional age-related eligibility requirements for the receipt of pension benefits.

One empirical analysis indicates that husbands and wives do affect one another's labor supply decisions. Using data from the Retirement History Study, Anderson, Clark, and Johnson (1978) find the labor force participation of wives to influence significantly and positively that of husbands and vice versa—a relationship that held under ordinary least squares, two-stage least squares, logit, and simultaneous logit formulations. In other words, one is more likely to be working if one's spouse is working, net of a host of factors. The labor force participation of both spouses dropped if the wife were 62 or older, and the wife's work force participation fell if the husband were covered by a pension. In short, these findings indicate late-life labor force participation to be sensitive to the spouse's eligibility for retirement benefits as well as to his or her continued involvement in the labor force.

It remains to be seen whether work rates of older men and women in the 1980s will reflect a straight-line extension of early retirement trends of the 1950s, 1960s, and 1970s. Economic growth assumptions, of course, underlie all forecasts of labor supply and demand, and the relative attractions of work and retirement may well depend on the tempo at which jobs are created. Attracting much popular attention has been recent legislation affecting the age of mandatory retirement. To date, there is no firm evidence on how many and what kinds of workers can be expected to stay on the job, and there is no indication whether the option of deferred retirement will be attractive enough to counter the trend toward early retirement. Given the new legislation, one force for postponed retirement may well be the economic insecurity of persistent inflation, eroding retirement savings, and private pensions (if not social security, so long as it is indexed to the cost of living). Perhaps more profound could be possible normative shifts defining 70, rather than 65, as the good and proper age of retirement and making continued work evidence of continued competence. Although the long-run impact of changes in mandatory retirement laws is a matter of speculation, it is clear that more and more women will be moving into old age with a long and continuous work life, and this fact may be expected to influence the labor force response of both men and women to changes in conditions of employment.

SOCIAL SECURITY: FAMILY EQUITY
OR FAMILY ADEQUACY

Although the steady climb in women's work force participation has been a prime age phenomenon, its implications for late life have been far-reaching. Nowhere is this more apparent than in the major social institution for the support of the aged. Founded in an era when relatively few women worked, social security has been influenced on two counts by the changes in women's economic roles. First, basic inconsistencies in the ideological underpinnings of the system have been pointed up by behavioral and normative changes accompanying these labor force trends. Second, the balance sheet of payroll taxes and benefit payments has registered the impact of rising numbers of women in covered employment.

As originally conceived in the Social Security Act of 1935, old age insurance was designed to protect workers against the time when they were too old to work. The pensioner was to be the beneficiary of his or her own lifetime labors. Funded by compulsory contributions, the system was planned to be actuarially fair so that (on average) a worker might expect to get out in old age what he or she put in during working years. As in any annuity or insurance scheme, those who contributed more money or who lived to collect longer might benefit at the expense of others. As a self-contained system, however, social security was to be equitable to the typical worker. It made no pretension of remedying earnings inequities or payout disparities that might arise from individual choice, personal misfortune, or market forces.

Even before the first benefits were issued, the 1939 Amendments to the Social Security Act introduced new considerations emphasizing income adequacy rather than equity. The amendments meant that the distributional forces of the marketplace would figure less prominently in the distribution of benefits. Provisions for a minimum benefit and for a progressive benefit structure illustrate income maintenance concerns diverging from the original social insurance principles.

If the worker's history of income-getting became less important to the determination of benefits, his or her obligations in income-pooling were to be recognized. In providing benefits to the aged wives, widows, dependent children and parents of retired workers, the 1939 amendments recognized that workers share income with other family members, and over the course of the next 40 years, subsequent amendments extended benefits to certain categories of divorced wives, dependent husbands and widowers, and disabled dependents. From a social welfare perspective, it was most appropriate to base benefits on the family consuming unit and its needs rather than on only the individual worker and his or her earnings. Since workers differed in terms of family composition at retirement, insuring the family instead of the worker introduced individual inequities sidestepped by the actuarially fair system, and single workers wound up subsidizing the benefits received by other workers' families. Small families supported larger ones.

This arrangement continues to this day. Bennett (1979) illustrates this point with a simulation designed to predict (under alternative assumptions of family type) benefits and contributions that could be expected by families of workers entering the social security system in 1978. Integrating actuarial data, economic statistics, and social security regulations, the simulation indicates that relatively few families can expect to get out more than they pay in. Among those with average earnings levels, however, married couples with children and with limited labor force participation by the wife turn a profit on their contributions. Comparable single workers, even those with children, do not even break even. Given average earnings, the female family head with two children can ultimately expect benefits totaling 88% of contributions; for the married couple with two children and 5 years of labor force participation by the wife, the family may expect to receive benefits exceeding contributions by 4%. Single males without children can expect only 41%.

Whether or not benefits for dependents reflect an equitable definition of family adequacy also depends on one's viewpoint. Since family benefits are scaled to what the worker has paid into the system, two families with similar composition can receive different benefit amounts for dependents. If one believes that adequacy should be judged relative to the preretirement living standard, that is an acceptable approach. If one believes that adequacy should reflect some absolute standard of welfare, then various families receive more than or less than this minimum standard.[2]

Social security's dual mission—ensuring to families an "adequate" income and providing a safe, equitable social insurance vehicle for the worker's retirement savings—are directly at odds. These two interpretations of social security's purpose have coexisted, nonetheless, as politically expedient fictions reconciling two competing philosophies—one emphasizing the state's responsibility for social welfare and the other stressing the individual's responsibility to provide for himself or herself.

---

[2] Recent research by Holden (1979) illustrates this situation in the context of a discussion of the supplemental spouse benefit—the amount dependent wives receive above and beyond the entitlement on their own work record. Given the association between husband's earnings and wife's supplemental spouse benefit, it is not surprising that these benefits prove to be a poor mechanism for transferring income to aged couples below the poverty line standard of adequacy. Unlike survivor's benefits which go to the neediest of aged women—widows—spouse benefits accrue to couples in all income categories.

In the early years of social security, many recognized that dual goals might be unfair to the individual worker, especially the single worker without a family. Over the years, more and more married women entered the labor force, and the distinction between worker and dependent blurred. A system that seemed in 1940 to favor families over individuals has come increasingly under fire for fostering inequities between famililes with working wives and those without.

These charges arise because social security was not structured to treat income-getting as a family affair. While acknowledging family income-pooling, social security did not anticipate the innovative strategies that families might employ to get income. Informed by the "new home economics," we today are sensitive to the fact that the decision to work is contingent on the way in which other family members allocate time to market work, housework, schooling, or leisure. We appreciate that these decisions are responsive to changes within the family and outside it. Social security was not well suited to women's growing work force involvement because it recognized family interdependency when benefits were paid out but not when contributions were paid in. A legacy of dual goals, this arrangement suited most Americans in an era of stable families looking to a male breadwinner for support. When husband–wife families with working wives came to outnumber those in which only the husband worked, seeming disparities between what families got out and what their working members paid in drew criticism. The shotgun marriage of individual equity and family adequacy was seen as "unfair" to a broad segment of Americans.

A few examples can serve to illustrate such complaints. Some wives who contribute to social security enjoy no greater retirement benefits than had they never worked. In this group are those women who worked too few quarters in covered employment to be eligible in their own right. Also included are wives who worked enough to qualify but who are eligible for less money as a retired worker than as the wife or survivor of a retired worker.[3] In 1975, this situation applied to 18% of women who were married to entitled husbands and who were eligible for their own worker benefits (Social Security Administration 1977, p. 125). To be sure, most eligible wives fare better collecting on their own account than on their husband's. Under the present system by which women collect the larger of the two benefits, however, some portion of own coverage merely duplicates spousal benefits.[4]

---

[3] Benefits to dependent wives and divorcees amount to 50% of the retired worker's benefit. Widows receive 100%.

[4] Few would deny that there are advantages to own entitlement even for those who do not draw on their earnings record. A woman's covered employment insures dependent

To cast the argument somewhat differently, the spouse benefit means that one-earner couples can receive higher benefits than two-earner couples who achieve the same total family earnings. Consider two couples in which both spouses turn age 62 in 1980. Suppose that both couples averaged $12,000 in inflation-indexed earnings for the period over which their benefits are calculated. In Couple A, the husband was the only earner, whereas in Couple B, the husband averaged $8000 while the wife averaged $4000 in earnings. Couple A would receive $7776 in retired worker and spousal benefits. Couple B with two retired workers would receive only $6528.

This overlap in wives' benefits as spouses and workers is a major target of criticism. That more women are qualifying for social security in their own right has prompted proposals to phase out spouse benefits altogether, perhaps with Supplemental Security Income assisting the needy (Campbell 1977, Munnell 1977). On the other hand are proposals to put spouse's benefits on sounder footing through credits for home-making, earnings credits shared between spouses, or the omission of child care years from benefit calculations. Implicit in all these plans is the notion that homemaking is valuable activity, that it facilitates husbands' employment, but that there are tradeoffs in terms of wives' reduced earning power. Rising divorce rates have created a greater perceived need to secure the housewife's stake in social security against marriage breakups and to offset the financial drawbacks of spousal dependency.[5]

While issues about working wives and homemakers do not exhaust the controversy surrounding the social security program, they illustrate the problems arising from the loose link between individual contributions and family benefits. While recognizing the family as the consuming unit in need of income, the system failed to allow for the coordinated efforts of family members in income-getting. In the case of the housewife's support services, the system has been faulted for not adequately protecting the homemaker's community property claim to husband's earned benefits, especially against a rising tide of marital disruption. In the case of the working wife's earnings, the system has been criticized for discounting the second earner's essential role in family finances.

Questions of equity raised by these issues are a far cry from equity issues raised in the early pursuit of an actuarially fair system. In part, this reflects the fact that new issues focus on fairness to families and

---

children against her death or disability, and it qualifies her for the more generous disability standards applied to workers than to widows (Franklin 1975).

[5] Responding to these concerns was the recent reduction from 20 to 10 years in the length of marriage entitling the divorced to benefits on the former spouse's account.

not to individual workers. Perhaps more important, these contemporary issues seem to call social security to account for "inequities" rooted outside the system itself. Whether as homemakers or as working wives, women usually benefit financially from sharing husband's earnings because women usually earn less than men. This disparity in earnings seems to derive from some mix of sex discrimination, occupational choice, and discontinuous job experience. Whatever its determinants, the earnings gap evolves within the social institutions of school, family, and economy and not within social security per se.

Despite a benefit formula that works to the advantage of the low earner, the Primary Benefit Amount (PIA) accorded retired women is less than that of men. In 1975, for example, the average PIA for women was $144.34 and that for men was $190.06 (U.S. Congress 1975, p. 83). Homemaker credits and child care drop out years address one source of these lower benefits—low and zero earnings years, which presently enter into the calculation of benefits. As long as personal pay-outs depend on what is paid in, and as long as women's wage rates are lower than men's, the individual equity considerations built into the social security system will translate into lower average own benefits. Were all adults to work the same amount for the same pay, social security would be in a better position to reconcile its dual missions of individual equity and family adequacy. As things now stand, however, women's changing work lives have served to point up the conflict of goals.

PRIVATE PENSIONS: AN ASIDE

In a leading volume on private pensions, McGill espouses a management perspective:

> The underlying purpose of a pension plan is to enable the employer to remove his superannuated employees from the payroll in a manner that is morally and socially acceptable. In practical terms, this means that a life income in some amount must be made available to an employee who has reached the end of his economically productive life [1975, p. 88].

In keeping with this philosophy, one may anticipate McGill's argument that "death benefits are incidental to the principal purpose of a pension plan [1975, p. 140]." Before the Employee Retirement Income Security Act of 1974, plans were not required to provide death benefits, and plans with no survivor provisions encompassed 20% of workers covered by the common "defined-benefit" plans (Schulz 1978).

Social security concerns with family dependency are paralleled in some private plans with various provisions for the survivors of current and retired employees. The 1974 ERISA legislation set minimal standards for such provisions. Plans were to offer the worker the opportunity to opt for joint and survivor coverage in preretirement years, albeit with a possible reduction in regular retirement benefits. At retirement, the plan was to provide automatically such joint and survivor coverage (again with a possible benefit reduction) unless the worker opted to forego this provision. In case of the employee's death prior to retirement, his or her contributions were to be returned.

Since these awards may be funded by the worker's contributions or reduced benefits, ERISA did not mandate survivor benefits funded by the employer. Nonetheless, some employers do pay for death benefits. In the nonrandom sample of large employers surveyed by the Bureau of Labor Statistics, 35% of employers pay for postretirement death benefits and 62% fund preretirement death benefits (Schulz 1978).

To be sure, these benefits include small lump sum payments and monthly payments of short duration. Nonetheless, they constitute fringe benefits that may not benefit all employees. Although some plans permit the worker to designate a beneficiary, other plans pay death benefits only to spouses or other specified kin. The worker without these family relations loses out on these fringe benefits.

If one views pension benefits as a form of deferred wages, issues of individual equity are raised by employer attempts to provide for the needs of surviving family members. Federal law in no way requires employer-funded death benefits, but several factors suggest that worker's dependents will receive more attention. First is the ERISA mandate to offer at least joint and survivor options to workers. Second is a 1980 Supreme Court decision that permits private pension benefits to be treated as community property in divorce settlements, with pension funds required to pay a share of benefits directly to the worker's former spouse. Third is the growing interest in the "integration" of private pensions and social security—benefit coordination that brings private plans in concert with a public system in which family adequacy concerns are weighed.

SHOULDERING THE LOAD OF OLD-AGE DEPENDENCY

Although the increase in women's labor force participation has highlighted the basic inconsistencies in the philosophy and structure of social security, this change has had implications for old-age support that extend well beyond contemporary political debate over what constitutes equitable treatment for various OASDI constituencies. The postwar shift of women into the paid work force has affected societal capacity to maintain the old-age support programs launched during the depression.

The impact that women workers have had on the balance between economic "dependents" and economic "producers" warrants attention, if only because of growing concern regarding the fiscal solvency of the OASDI trust funds. This well-publicized social security "crisis" has certainly prompted a closer look at the provisions of the program, and the new interest in the adequacy-equity issues raised by the treatment of second earners reflects these fiscal as well as moral issues. Despite the ideological preference that workers finance their own retirement, this "crisis" also has pointed out that the system is basically pay-as-you-go, with one generation of workers supporting a previous generation now retired. The reality of this financing scheme has made the system sensitive to shifts in the relative numbers of covered workers and beneficiaries. Similar considerations attend to other unfunded pension liabilities in the public sector and to all programs funded by tax revenues.

To be sure, women have been among the growing numbers of social security beneficiaries. As recently as 1960, only 58% of women 62 and older were receiving social security. Fourteen years later, fully 86% drew benefits as wives, widows, or former workers. Still more were eligible, but they or their husbands had not yet retired to draw benefits. In both periods, one-third of all women qualified for benefits only as the dependents of husbands who were eligible, but the proportion qualifying on the basis of their own earnings record grew from one-quarter to more than half (U.S. Congress 1975, p. 16). In short, while the number of older women receiving social security had increased, so had the number who, during their work life, had made significant contributions toward their old-age support. Future cohorts may also anticipate high rates of earned own eligibility: In 1970, 68% of women 40–49 had already worked enough quarters to qualify for their own OASDI benefits at age 65 (Reno 1973).

Although women's employment may continue to occasion a shift from dependent to own eligibility, overall eligibility rates are already so high as to preclude the spectacular growth in eligibility witnessed by previous decades. Since the original Social Security Act of 1935, congressional amendments have extended coverage to new categories of workers and dependents (Munnell 1977, pp. 158–161). While the differential effects of the expansion of worker coverage for men and women are not known, some working women, such as domestic laborers, were added by legislative mandate, and today 9 out of 10 jobs in paid or self-employment fall under the program. (Many of those not covered work in government jobs that have their own retirement programs.) As for worker's dependents, few new program participants would be added by the extension of eligibility to, say, economically dependent maiden aunts (Grad 1975). In sum, almost everyone who now turns 65 is entitled to some cash benefit from social security, and neither congressional mandate nor women's lengthening work lives will do much to increase the number of aged on social security rolls.

If rising labor force participation of women is of only modest consequence for the numbers of persons drawing OASDI benefits, it is nonetheless important for the societal carrying capacity of old-age support and, specifically, for social security's balance of payments. Although OASDI financing has received careful study from both within and without the Social Security Administration, Table 21.2 provides a rough appreciation of working women's contributions to the public support of older Americans.

Within families, retired husbands and wives have come to support fewer dependents on their own social security accounts. As the first column of Table 21.2 demonstrates, husbands and wives qualifying only on a spouse's record have declined relative to the numbers of husbands and wives who qualify as retired workers. Between 1955 and 1975, the ratio of dependent spouses to eligible spouses plummeted from .26 to .14. If we include dependent children receiving benefits along with dependent spouses as in Column 2, the family dependency ratio declines from .28 to .17 over the 20 years. Dollar-for-dollar, few families are likely to enjoy any immediate advantage in having the wife's benefits based in whole or part on her own earnings record rather than on that of her spouse. From the societal perspective, however, this declining dependency within families buoys the system providing retirement income.

A popular, if crude, index of the societal "burden" of old-age support is the old-age dependency ratio of persons 65 and older to those 18–64. The third column of Table 21.2 illustrates the rise in the dependency ratio occasioned by shifts in the age structure of the American population. Between 1945 and 1975, this ratio rose from .12 to .18, as an older population with lengthening life-spans confronted a relatively small prime-age population born of the depression birth dearth. This measure, of course, provides only a rough idea of the ratio of older "dependents" to younger "producers." A more refined indicator considers labor force participation, rather than merely age, in determining relative numbers. Column 4 compares persons 65 and older who are not in the labor force with all persons who are in the labor force. This measure, too, demonstrates an increasing dependency load as it rises from .11 to .21 over the 30-year period.

TABLE 21.2
Alternative Dependency Ratios for Selected Years, 1945–1975[a]

Years			Ratios			
	Dependent spouses to retired workers	Dependent spouses and children to retired workers[b]	Persons 65+ to persons 18–64	Persons 65+ not in labor force to persons in labor force	Persons 65+ to total labor force 16–64[c]	Persons 65+ to male labor force 16–64[c]
1945	—	—	.12	.11	.17	.22
1950	—	—	.13	.14	.20	.27
1955	.26	.28	.15	.16	.22	.30
1960	.26	.29	.17	.19	.24	.34
1965	.21	.25	.17	.20	.25	.36
1970	.17	.21	.17	.20	.24	.37
1975	.14	.17	.18	.21	.24	.40

[a] From Bureau of the Census (1975, pp.10, 131, 387) and Social Security Administration (1977).
[b] Retired workers exclude dually entitled husbands and wives who receive a spousal supplement. Figures are for fiscal year.
[c] In 1945, 14–16.

Since this measure is affected by change in older Americans' work and retirement patterns as well as by changes in their numbers relative to younger workers, it is useful to set all persons 65 or older in ratio to younger persons in the labor force. As Column 5 illustrates, this ratio rises from .17 in 1945 to .24 in 1975. During this period, however, the ranks of the labor force were swelled by the entry of women workers. How has the upward trend in their labor force participation affected societal carrying capacity for old-age support? Column 6 compares persons 65 and older to the younger male labor force and demonstrates that the effect of working women has been to offset the growth of the older population by broadening the economically productive base of support for older Americans. If, over the course of three decades, no women had worked, the dependency ratio would have risen from .22 to .40—or 82%. Because women participated in the work force in ever increasing numbers, however, the actual dependency ratio in Column 5 rose only 41%.

These measures provide only a general sense of societal carrying capacity for old-age support programs. They indicate that women's growing participation in paid work constitutes a valuable economic offset against the growing numbers of elderly who do not work. They do not translate readily into a cash-flow analysis of social security, of course. They do not establish how many persons of all ages receive benefits nor how much they receive. They do not indicate how many Americans work at jobs covered by social security nor how much they consequently pay into the system. More importantly, they do not indicate that women's employment might affect family (as opposed to public) support systems— cutting into the time middle-aged women have to run errands for aging kin or discouraging young women from bearing children who might support them in old age (Treas 1977).

To sum up, social security eligibility as worker or dependent is now so universal that further growth in women's labor force participation will have little effect on the number of beneficiaries on social security rolls. Rising participation should continue to pump money into programs of old-age support, nonetheless. With respect to public income transfers between generations, it is clear that women's employment has lightened the old-age dependency "burden" on the middle generation.

WOMEN'S LONGER WORKLIVES AND RETIREMENT INCOME

As we have indicated, tomorrow's aged may predicate household retirement planning on women's employment in a way that previous generations have not. It remains to be seen to what extent future cohorts of elderly will enjoy greater economic well-being by virtue of their cohort's higher levels of female labor force participation. In foretelling the impact of women's paid work on the status of the future elderly, it is tempting to dwell on safe ground, where projections of women's employment patterns intersect with existing pension schedules of eligibility and benefits. Unfortunately, neither social security nor other retirement plans have proved immutable, and it is likely that the elderly of the future will confront pension requirements and provisions that differ from those of today. As we have stressed, women's labor force participation itself is a force for change in social security, both because it has called attention to ideological inconsistencies and because it has had implications for the financing of old-age support in our society.

Despite the likelihood that our observations may be invalidated by future changes, it is informative to consider the way in which women's labor force participation pays off in later life. It has become almost a gerontological cliché to argue that the future elderly will be advantaged because they will be different from their predecessors—better educated, more often native-born and English-speaking, and more comfortable with accepting old-age benefits from public sources (Cain 1967, Moen 1978). In this vein, it is reasonable to argue that, relative to older women today, women who will turn 65 in the years to come will be advantaged by virtue of their longer worklives. To the extent that employment outside the home promotes independence, efficacy, and the acquisition of assorted life skills, future cohorts may well invalidate the stereotype of aged women as ill-prepared to balance checkbooks, negotiate with bureaucracies, drive to the doctor, or fend off swindlers. On a less positive note, women may encounter more health risks as they clock more time in the workplace. Whether we consider the potential stresses of a career, the auto safety hazards of commuting, or the exposure to industrial carcinogens, it seems reasonable that women's work might lead to chronic conditions in later life and that the health status of the older population might be affected accordingly.

Although these by-products of women's worklives may influence the status of the future aged for better or for worse, the most tangible effects of women's paid work are apt to involve their contributions to retirement income and late-life economic resources. The old-age impact of any contributions by working women may be judged relative to some absolute standard of living, relative to the economic circumstances of younger persons or relative to the economic well-being of other older Americans.

There can be no doubt that working women boost absolute family income during their working years. In 1976, for example, husband–wife families in which both spouses worked reported median pretax incomes of $19,327. In families in which only the husband was in the labor force, the median was only $16,267. If we compare the incomes of men whose wives had income with those whose wives did not, we find median figures of $11,609 and $13,751, respectively (Bureau of the Census 1978, Tables 23 and 28A). In other words, working wives tend to raise family income from below the middle to above it.

In the past, the labor force participation of married women has afforded families considerable economic flexibility. Wives have been available for paid work to meet special expenditures or emergencies. In middle years, their employment has meshed both with decreasing household responsibilities and with increasing costs of adolescent children and college students. While younger mothers were preoccupied with the care of small children, the jobs of middle-aged women (in concert with their husbands' high mid-life earnings) permitted their families to pull ahead financially. Looking to retirement, many feathered the empty nest by working.

As suggested by the earlier discussion of work force trends, the labor force participation of women is becoming less discretionary than it once was. A tolerance of working women, it seems, is giving way to the expectation that women will work throughout their lives. That more and more women of childbearing years are in the labor force implies that mid-life work can represent less and less of a relative advantage. As families come to peg their long-run consumption to expectations of the wife's continuous earnings, the wife's employment becomes essential to day-to-day expenditures; it no longer constitutes a resource that can be tapped to provide an interim advantage at the threshold of retirement.[6] We can extend this argument to single women who, in the absence of husband's income, have been more likely to work. With more wives supplementing family incomes, single women may be at more of a disadvantage.

Even if emerging patterns of women's employment leave less room for financial jockeying in the second half of life, this is not to argue that the elderly of the future may not be the better for women's longer and more continuous worklives. With respect to retirement income, economic betterment may come in the area of private pensions rather than social security. As we have indicated, the advantage of the working wife/widow under present social security arrangements is limited by the fact that her

[6] As indication that wives' incomes are now a permanent component of family economic planning, consider the new willingness of banks to approve home loans based on two incomes.

benefit as a retired worker may duplicate in part the entitlement as the wife–widow of a retired worker. Private pension plans, on the other hand, provide for the worker but not for dependents. Thus, the household in which both the husband and wife qualify for private pensions may enjoy a greater advantage than the household in which both spouses qualify for only OASDI retired worker benefits.

From its inception, social security was never intended to provide fully for the income needs of older Americans. It was assumed, for example, that the aged also would draw upon savings and assets to achieve a comfortable living standard in retirement. Increasingly, it is another pension that augments social security benefits or fills in the gaps in social security coverage. Only 55% of all pension benefits in 1973 derived from social security; 45% of aggregate expenditures came from private pension programs, government employee plans, veteran's benefits, and railroad retirement (Schulz 1977). After earnings and asset income, the second pension is the most frequent supplement to social security retirement benefits (Fox 1976).

As eligibility for some type of social security has become almost universal, it is the second pension that has come to differentiate the affluent aged from their poorer counterparts. Among couples receiving social security in 1967 with the husband and/or wife over age 65, 21% received a private pension and 9% received a second public pension from a program for employees of federal, state, or local government, the military, or the railroad (Bixby and Reno 1976). Couples with second pensions enjoyed median earnings 50% higher than those of other married beneficiaries. Although nonmarried beneficiaries were less likely to draw a second pension, those who did so had median incomes almost twice that of single beneficiaries without a supplementary pension benefit.

Estimates of private pension coverage by sex are available from several sources, and they show that women are less likely to be covered by a second pension, public or private (Kolodrubetz 1976, Landay and Kolodrubetz 1973, Hendricks and Peters 1978, Thompson 1978).[7] For example, the April 1972 Current Population Survey contained a special supplement on retirement coverage for the entire population 16 years or older. Among workers in private, full-time, wage and salary jobs, 52% of men and 36% of women reported coverage by a private retirement plan (Landay and Kolodrubetz 1973). Futhermore, 34% of men and 26% of women said they already had a vested or nonforfeitable right to a pension from their present plan. When women draw a second pension, they receive lower benefits than do men (Kolodrubetz 1976).

[7] Coverage refers to eligibility to participate in a plan. To be covered by a contributory plan, worker must elect to participate.

As in the case of OASDI, women's lower private pension benefits reflect lower earnings and fewer years of work. In the Social Security Administration's 1968–1970 Survey of Newly Entitled Beneficiaries, 40% of women with less than 10 years of private-sector service on the longest job were receiving or expected to receive a private pension—as compared with 70% of women with 10 to 15 years on the job (Kolodrubetz 1976). The average working life for women is estimated to have risen from 12.1 years in 1940 to 22.9 in 1970 (Fullerton and Byrne 1976), and longer work lives may well translate into higher rates of eligibility for private pensions as well as higher benefit awards. Furthermore, the Employee Retirement Income Security Act of 1974 limited the service requirements before benefits vest—that is, before rights to accrued benefits are protected from breaks in service (McGill 1975).[8] Even prior to the enactment of ERISA, a gradual liberalization of corporate pension plans meant a waning of long service requirements (Bankers Trust Company 1975).[9] The liberalization of service requirements in conjunction with the earlier growth of private retirement plans has meant that older men and women with more recent participation on the longest job are more likely to be covered than their predecessors who worked as long but left employment in an earlier era (Thompson 1978).

If more and more women qualify for higher and higher second pensions, we may anticipate an increase in the average income of the older population. This increase in overall well-being, however, may well come at the cost of greater income disparities within the older population. First, private pensions, unlike social security, do not favor the low-income worker in benefit calculations. Second, the women who will qualify for second pensions will tend to be skilled employees of a stable, highly capitalized, industrial sector that provides its workers with good pay, job security, career ladders, and fringe benefits. If married, their husbands also are apt to be employed in this privileged sector, albeit in different occupations. In contrast are husbands and wives who (by virtue of low skills, poor education, and residence in depressed areas) are relegated to a peripheral sector of the economy made up of small, highly competitive, low capital enterprises vulnerable to the vagaries of the marketplace. Such enterprises are less likely to offer private pension plans, and the expensive reporting and fiduciary standards required by ERISA deter the expansion of non-OASDI pensions in this sector. Given

[8] Benefits may vest completely at 10 years of service, progressively between 5 and 15 years of service, or progressively based on an age and service schedule.

[9] This may be contrasted with social security where the maturation of the system has lengthened the period over which eligibility is established and benefits are computed (Mallan 1975).

that like marries like, it is not unreasonable to contemplate a future in which more households look to two or more second pensions while others make do on only social security. Third, although women's longer worklives may mean more and higher pensions, it does not follow automatically that sex disparities in retirement income will disappear. The persistence of occupation segregation and sex differentials in earnings suggests that women will continue to average lower pension benefits than men in years to come. In particular, older women without husbands will continue to be overrepresented in poverty.

CONCLUSION

What is most important about women's labor force participation today is its persistence and seeming inevitability. Both the behavior of individuals and the organization of institutions has accomodated to women's employment. The high rates of labor force participation by young women, even those with preschool children, indicate that a good many women will be spending most of their lives in paid employment. The recent trend toward early retirement among older women suggests that already growing numbers of women have worked enough to expect comfortable retirement incomes. These facts argue that household economic planning will be predicated more and more on the continuous earnings of the wife. We would expect retirement decisions, for instance, to entail greater coordination between husband and wife in the future. The growing importance of women's work to later life is apt to stem not from any short-run advantage of labor force reentry, but rather from the accumulation of work experience and retirement rights over a lengthening worklife.

To be sure, the rise in female labor force participation has registered an impact on social security. On one hand, the rise in working women has acted to offset the growing population of older retirees. On the other hand, it has called attention to basic inconsistencies in a system that seeks to square what is paid in by individual workers with what is paid out to families. That both housewives and working women are said to be treated "unfairly" underscores the complexity of the equity-adequacy dilemma. As it is currently structured, a number of features of social security—its lengthening computation period, its near universal eligibility, its overlap between women's coverage as spouses and as workers—suggest that the ultimate impact of women's employment trends on OASDI benefits is unlikely to influence dramatically the economic status of the elderly of the future. Eligibility for private pensions, however, is apt to be more sensitive to women's longer worklives, and it is not unreasonable to expect that a higher proportion of households will enjoy a second or third pension by virtue of women's job tenure. This scenario raises the prospect of a widening gap between households with multiple pensions and less advantaged older persons dependent on social security alone. Renewed interest in the integration of public and private benefits might well result.

REFERENCES

Anderson, K., Clark, R., and Johnson, T. (1978) Retirement in Dual Career Families. Unpublished manuscript, North Carolina State University.

Bankers Trust Company (1975) *Study of Corporate Pension Plans*. New York: Bankers Trust Company.

Barfield, R. E., and Morgan, J. N. (1970) *Early Retirement: The Decision and the Experience*. Ann Arbor, Mich.: Institute for Social Research, University of Michigan.

Bennett, C. T. F. (1979) The social security benefit structure: Equity considerations of the family as its basis. *The American Economic Review* 69(May):227–231.

Bixby, L. E., and Reno, V. (1976) Incidence of second pension rights. Pp. 145–149 in *Reaching Retirement Age*. Social Security Administration Research Report No. 47. Washington, D.C.: U.S. Department of Health, Education, and Welfare.

Boskin, M. J. (1977) Social security and retirement decisions. *Economic Inquiry* 15:1–25.

Bureau of Labor Statistics (1971) *Work Experience of the population, 1970*. Special Labor Force Report No. 141. Washington, D.C.: U.S. Department of Labor.

Bureau of Labor Statistics (1977) *Work Experience of the Population, 1976*. Special Labor Force Report No. 201. Washington, D.C.: U.S. Department of Labor.

Bureau of Labor Statistics (1978) *Educational Attainment of Workers*. Special Labor Force Reports. Washington, D.C.: U.S. Department of Labor.

Bureau of the Census (1973) *Census of Population: 1970*. Subject Reports. Final Report PC(2)-7A, Occupational Characteristics. Washington, D.C.: U.S. Department of Commerce.

Bureau of the Census (1975) *Historical Statistics of the United States, Part 1*. Washington, D.C.: U.S. Department of Commerce.

Bureau of the Census (1978) *Perspectives on American Husbands and Wives*. Current Population Reports Special Studies P-23, No. 77. Washington, D.C.: U.S. Department of Commerce.

Burkhauser, R. V. (1979) The pension acceptance decision of older men. *Journal of Human Resources* 14(Winter):63–75.

Cain, L. D. (1967) Age status and generational phenomena: The new old people in contemporary America. *The Gerontologist* 7:83–92.

Campbell, R. R. (1977) The problems of fairness. In M. J. Boskin, ed., *The Crisis in Social Security: Problems and Prospects*. San Francisco: Institute for Contemporary Studies.

Flaim, P. O., and Fullerton, H. N. (1978) Labor force projections to 1990: Three possible paths. *Monthly Labor Review* 101(December):25–35.

Fox, A. (1976) Income of new beneficiaries by age at entitlement to benefits. In *Reaching Retirement Age*. Social Security Administration Research Report No. 47. Washington, D.C.: U.S. Department of Health, Education, and Welfare.

Fox, A. (1979) Earnings replacement rates of retired couples: Findings from the retirement history study. *Social Security Bulletin* 42(January):17–39.

Franklin, P. A. (1975) The disabled widow. *Social Security Bulletin* 38(January):20–27.

Fullerton, H. N., Jr., and Byrne, J. J. (1976) *Length of Working Life for Men and Women, 1970.* Special Labor Force Report #187. Washington, D.C.: U.S. Bureau of Labor.

Gordon, M. S. (1963) Projecting employment opportunities for middle-aged and older workers. In H. L. Orbach and C. Tibbetts, eds., *Aging and the Economy.* Ann Arbor, Mich.: University of Michigan Press.

Grad, S. (1975) Economically dependent persons without pension coverage in old age. *Social Security Bulletin* 38(October):13–17.

Hendricks, G., and Peters, E. (1978) The Social Security Coverage of Government Workers. Paper presented at the National Bureau of Economic Research workshop on Policy Analysis with Social Security Research Files. March 15–17, Williamsburg, Virginia.

Holden, K. C. (1979) The inequitable distribution of OASDI benefits among homemakers. *The Gerontologist* 19(June):250–256.

Katona, G. (1965) *Private Pensions and Individual Saving.* Ann Arbor, Mich.: Institute for Social Research, University of Michigan.

Kolodrubetz, W. W. (1976) Earnings replacement from private pensions. In *Researching Retirement Age.* Social Security Administration Research Report No. 47. Washington, D.C.: U.S. Department of Health, Education, and Welfare.

Kreps, J., and Clark, R. (1975) *Sex, Age and Work: The Changing Composition of the Labor Force.* Baltimore, Md.: Johns Hopkins University Press.

Landay, D. M., and Kolodrubetz, W. W. (1973) *Coverage and Vesting of Full-Time Employees Under Private Retirement Plans: Findings from the April 1972 Survey.* Bureau of Labor Statistics Report No. 423. Washington, D.C.: U.S. Department of Labor.

Mallan, L. (1975) Young widows and their children: A comparative report. *Social Security Bulletin* 38:3–21.

McEaddy, B. J. (1975) Women in the labor force: The later years. *Monthly Labor Review* 98(November):17–24.

McGill, D. M. (1975) *Fundamentals of Private Pensions.* Homewood, Ill.: Richard D. Irwin, Inc.

Michelotti, K. (1977) Educational attainment of workers, March 1977. *Monthly Labor Review* 100(December):56.

Moen, E. (1978) The reluctance of the elderly to accept help. *Social Problems* 25(February):293–303.

Munnell, A. H. (1977) *The Future of Social Security.* Washington, D.C.: The Brookings Institution.

Oppenheimer, V. K. (1970) *The Female Labor Force in the United States: Demographic and Economic Factors Governing its Growth and Changing Composition.* Berkeley, Calif.: Institute of International Studies.

Pitts, A. M. (1978) Social security benefits and aging populations. In T. J. Espenshade and W. J. Serow, eds., *The Economic Consequences of Slowing Population Growth.* New York: Academic Press.

Quinn, J. F. (1977) Microeconomic determinants of early retirement: A cross-sectional view of white married men. *Journal of Human Resources* 12(Summer): 329–346.

Reno, V. (1973) Women newly entitled to social security benefits. In *Preliminary Findings from the Survey of New Beneficiaries.* U.S. Social Security Administration Report No. 4. Washington, D.C.: U.S. Department of Health, Education and Welfare.

Rones, P. L. (1978) Older men—the choice between work and retirement. *Monthly Labor Review* 101(November):3–10.

Schulz, J. H. (1977) Public policy and future roles of public and private pensions. In G. S. Tolley and R. V. Burkhuaser, eds., *Income Support for the Aged.* Cambridge, Mass.: Ballinger.

Schulz, J. H. (1978) Private pensions and women. In *Women in Midlife: Security and Fulfillment.* House Select Committee on Aging. Washington, D.C.: U.S. Government Printing Office.

Social Security Administration (1977) *Social Security Bulletin Annual Statistical Supplement, 1975.* Washington, D.C.: U.S. Department of Health, Education, and Welfare.

Social Security Administration (1978) Quarterly statistics. *Social Security Bulletin* 41(December):Table Q-4.

Thompson, G. B. (1978) Pension coverage and benefits, 1972: Findings from the Retirement History Study. *Social Security Bulletin* 41(February):3–17.

Treas, J. (1977) Family support systems for the aged: Some social and demographic considerations. *The Gerontologist* 17(April):466–491.

U.S. Congress (1975) Women and Social Security: Adapting to a New Era. Senate Special Committee on Aging. Working paper presented by the Task Force on Women and Social Security.

chapter *22*

Behavioral and Social Science Research and the Future Elderly

JAMES N. MORGAN

Dramatic changes are taking place, and others are likely, that increase both the need for research and for opportunities to learn more about the human behavior and condition. Changes produce natural "experiments," as people, institutions, and systems respond to them. Some needed changes in institutions and laws require public policy decisions, and the complex ways in which those changes might affect the whole system need forecasting. Many of the most dramatic past and future changes affect the elderly.

Massive changes have already taken place in birth, death, marriage, and divorce rates, with implications for the future. The age distribution of the population, family organization, help patterns, and even people's economic status will be affected. Equally dramatic changes have taken place in unemployment, prices, and in the way the economic system functions. Wild, unpredicted, and disparate changes in prices have gone along with rising unemployment, some of it in occupations traditionally regarded as secure. People react to these events in different ways, and the events plus the reactions help determine the future. One might develop a research agenda by asking what kinds of natural experiments or other opportunities the most dramatic and predictable societal changes will produce. Or one could ask which of the intellectually exciting issues

AGING
Social Change

in the social sciences will be most promising to investigate in the next 20 years. Assuming that a principal criterion of a good social order is the well-being of its citizens, what policy issues will be raised by the large future changes that will affect the quality of life (and of people's satisfactions with it), and what research will allow those policy decisions to be made wisely?

I propose to concentrate on the kinds of research that might facilitate the public policy decisions that deal with the new and changing world and people's responses to it. The focus will be research on the condition and behavior of people more than on the ultimate quality of life that results. I leave to psychologists the study of those last linkages between people's situations—health, wealth, and environment—on one hand, and their sense of well-being or happiness on the other. Not only is happiness more than individual health and wealth added up; it may well be greater for everyone at the same time if empathy overwhelms envy. And we might well have a better understanding of people's behavioral responses if we knew more about what makes them happy!

Many policy decisions could be made more wisely if we were able to see how the future might look under alternative policies. Planning ahead for future problems and choices might allow research to be more useful while freeing it from having to address each new legislative proposal as it appears. Policy analysts and politicians should be able to help us spot the main options and issues worth investigating far enough in advance to allow good research. In the meantime, we need to attempt the task ourselves. One guide is in the substantial set of changes that have already occurred in laws relating to work and retirement, income maintenance programs, medical care, philanthropy and bequests, and retirement. The multiple problems created by uneven inflation, unemployment, gyrating asset values, and the energy crisis can also serve as guides.

RESEARCH STRUCTURE AND THE DIVISION OF LABOR

A common reaction of researchers everywhere, including the behavioral scientists, is to decompose problems into manageable pieces, to translate them into questions that can be tackled with existing tools, and to rely on the known advantages of specialization and the division of labor, even in research. The implications of likely changes and of the policies that may be adopted can be researched piecemeal by partial equilibrium analysis that holds other things constant, but economic, political, and social systems are both dynamic and interdependent. So the implications of the bits and pieces are not clear without some overall analysis of the whole complex system. Economists pioneered in the development both of national accounting and of systems of structural equations to deal with dynamic economic systems at the national level.

It was the econometricians who first showed the biases in estimates that did not take account of the full set of interrelationships in a system of equations (feedback). Much recent analysis in both economics and sociology works with submodels and procedures like path analysis, which assume no feedback loops. This vastly simplifies the analysis of behavior—properly so—but full analysis of our socioeconomic system requires that the pieces be assembled in a full model with feedback or simultaneous interactions. And when questions have to do with explicit details or subpopulations, either these models must be substantially disaggregated, or we must move to such other ways of dealing with dynamic interactions as simulation of whole socioeconomic systems in the computer (Orcutt 1965). Even the largest economic models at their present (several hundred equations) level of disaggregation are in desperate need of more behavioral relations than can be approximated from statistical analysis of time-series data, which infer relationships from changes over the past of whole subgroups of people or firms.

Using the future elderly as an example of these interrelationships, it is rather easy to predict the rising number of families that will be approaching retirement age over the next decade or two. We can even predict, though not well, the numbers that will have a history of two earners, a valuable house paid for, and multiple pension coverage. One could simulate the impacts of this on labor force participation and retirement ages, and on the flows of funds into and out of social security.[1] But these alternative futures will also affect aggregate unemployment, interest rates, and the rest of the economic system.

Alternative changes in housing and living arrangements upon retirement need to be predicted and their implications, in turn, spelled out. Affluence may allow retired couples to remain in their very expensive, excessively large houses, but they might also decide to sell and move to nicer climes, particularly with new laws that largely eliminate their capital gains taxes. With each of two spouses eligible for an individual

---

[1] Actually we have startlingly little data on people's retirement plans and expectations and even less on the likely pension rights and coverage of the age groups approaching retirement.

pension, they might be more able to live separately, but the insecurity and uncertainty of the world might well make companionship and staying together more appealing than in the past.

At any rate, if substantial numbers give up their large houses in urban areas and move to new communities or scatter to rural areas when they retire, the housing shortage may ease in the older cities, but a shortage of community facilities and public service capabilities may well appear in the growing areas of retirement communities. It takes time to expand sewer services, city governments, and public utilities. The whole geographic pattern of construction, taxes, demand for government services, and related secondary businesses can be affected by whether people stick to the old pattern of living where they retire, or in increasing numbers move away from the dangerous cities or the cold North or the dull small towns. Spelling out the interlaced implications requires simulation on a computer of representative sets of households, areas, firms, and so forth. The more realistic the individual behavioral responses that are built into such models, the more manageable and accurate their forecasts and estimates of the effects of alternatives can become. It is the failure to build behavioral responses into analytical models that leads to the most extreme and mistaken forecasts, particularly over longer periods in which compound interest without response adjustments produces dramatic growth or decline. A system with reasonably rapid adaptive responses to introduced change can absorb many shocks with little overall alteration. Economists may well put too much faith in possible rational adaptive responses, whereas engineers may exaggerate dangers by implicitly assuming none at all, as the two groups are now doing in discussing the future shortage of energy or minerals.

With such full analysis of the whole system, it may be possible to forecast a little better whether changes in environment, technology, policies, or laws and in behavior (some of which result from the other changes) will have substantial and far-reaching effects on the whole system or will be absorbed and adjusted to with little impact.

THE NEED FOR COOPERATION

Some division of labor is natural between those who construct and manipulate models of the system or of major subsystems and those who provide the estimates of the human responses that become the input assumptions of the models. While behavioral researchers may focus on behavioral responses, particularly since they, in turn, affect the system, it is ultimately the affective responses that matter—what happens to people's feelings of well-being.

Economics and the other "social sciences" are both behavioral and social, if the latter means analysis of not only interactions among people but also system-functioning and its analysis. Close and continued cooperation is required between the two groups. Otherwise, the analysts modeling dynamic systems and attempting to forecast or predict the effects of changes are likely to estimate behavioral relations by deducing what rational people should or would do. Or they may use past relations among aggregate time-series data. These relationships are often of dubious behavioral clarity or stability. There is a tendency of behavioral researchers to frame their questions and hypotheses in terms of the narrow theorems of single disciplines, testing a few variables at a time rather than estimating the relative importance of various influences in the dynamic form most useful for building into the analytical studies. Behavioral research uses models, too, of course, but they are usually subsystem models with little or no feedback (path models). Other researchers can and do estimate the coefficients of dynamic models from past time-series data and then use the models to forecast the future, combining behavioral and social science functions. A heuristic distinction between estimating behavioral responses on one hand and using dynamic models to understand the interrelations in a system or to forecast on the other hand remains useful.

The dynamic models should be responsive to the likely policy issues and national problems and useful for speaking to the implications of alternative policies for the future condition of the aged. Behavioral research, in turn, should be responsive to the needs of the system analysts, by focusing on the study of particular behavioral responses for which better understanding, specification, and prediction are required if forecasts of the models are to be precise enough to be useful. The all-too-common focus on the latest interesting explanatory variable is then replaced by a broader focus on behavioral or attitudinal dependent variables, with a multidisciplinary variety of explanatory variables. The system analysts can use their models to locate the particular behavioral response parameters most in need of better estimation because the system's response is more sensitive to them. With structural equation models, such sensitivity analysis can sometimes be done by manipulating the equations, but, more commonly (particularly with the simulation models) by simulating the system's dynamic paths under alternative assumptions.

The symbiotic relationship between system analysis, forecasting, and policy analysis on one hand and behavioral or psychological research at the individual level on the other is clearest when the models are quite detailed and of short-run change, building in interrelations and constraints and simulating the dynamic processes on the computer. (This is probably the best way to go from what we know about individual behavioral responses to an analysis of how the whole system functions [see Orcutt 1965].)

HOW THE PARTS AFFECT EACH OTHER

The expected behavioral responses of many types of individuals and families can be built directly into the simulation model and explorations made of the effects of changes in laws, policies, environment, and population or of initial changes in behavior. One might also want to build in institutions since they change, too. Such work puts new and specific demands on behavioral researchers for better explanations, understanding, and prediction of individual or group behavior. At the same time, the behavioral researchers may well call for altering the specifications of the models, suggesting that they omit relationships that appear to be absent or weak but add factors and relationships that do matter in behavior.

For example, prior research has already shown that economic factors and constraints swamp any other forces we can measure in explaining when people retire when they do. They retire when their health or job gives out, or when they can afford it—two pensions, house paid for, and no major obligations to children. But in a changing world in which more people can afford to retire earlier, and in which better health, easier work, and new laws make it possible for more people to work past 65, other motives and considerations may come to the fore, such as the relative attractiveness of the job and its alternatives, uncertainty about the future and the effects of inflation, a feeling of obsolescence of work skills, or acquired recreational skills. Most of our research in this area, as in others, like sexual or racial or age discrimination, has inferred process from outcome and motive or cause from process. More attention to the process may reveal missing variables, some of them measurable, which are necessary in order to choose among competing explanations. It is difficult with just economic and behavioral data to distinguish the effects of wage rates in altering people's willingness to substitute leisure for money, from the effects of the higher income from higher wages along with inflation, in affecting general living standards, and then income goals and hence work.

Higher wages make not working more costly in foregone wages—the substitution effect, but higher income from the first 40 hours a week makes one better able to buy back one's own time for more enjoyable pursuits—the income effect. So, in theory, the two effects work in opposite directions, though the income effect seems to dominate behavior. Our recent panel analysis indicates that income goals, which are changeable like any other aspiration level, are more influential than any substitution effects deduced from the rational behavior theory of economics, but more understanding of people's attitudes, expectations, goals, and explanations would help (see Morgan 1979). This is not merely a plea for panel studies, since it is not at all clear that the timing or sequencing of events or changes can really untangle the directions of causal influences.

So far, simulation studies have developed slowly, less because of computer limitations than because of the shortage of good behavioral data in the proper form—relations between initial states and subsequent changes. Those interested in building and testing models have had to devote a good deal of time to searching for data, reanalyzing much of it, or inserting estimates of behavioral relations based on inadequate data or rational deduction. What is needed is data relating initial conditions and perhaps some past events changing during a rather short period, to minimize the amount of structural interaction within each period. The model itself, in the computer, deals with the (limited) interactions, additivities, and constraints within each time period and predicts the changes and hence ending states, which then became the initial states for the next iteration. Models are currently in use for the whole population, for modeling individual cities, and for international relations. Even if we settle for partial or less comprehensive models for much of the analysis, the very notion of a possible complete model gives us a consistent set of long-term objectives, a structure into which the partial models hopefully fit, and a guide to how research on individuals can be built into a larger whole.

A FINAL LINK

If a major societal goal is human satisfaction, there is a final link from the more easily measurable physical conditions like income, assets, health, and environment to the affective senses of well-being that result.

Indeed, we can think of a massive scheme of social measurement and analysis, (I hesitate to use the term *accounting*), starting with the inputs of human time and effort (resources) to produce outputs of goods and services and environmental states, like clean streets, which in turn have some effect on the quality of life and people's happiness. Analysis, then, focuses on two kinds of linkages or relations: There are the linear linkages between inputs of resources and outputs of products—called production functions in economics. And there are linkages between inputs to individuals of goods and services and environment and the resulting human satisfaction—consumption functions to economists but better treated by psychologists.

There are interactions at each of the three levels. Economists deal with technical interactions at the input and at the consumption level, calling them *externalities*, or private versus social costs and benefits. Sociologists and psychologists have paid more attention to interactions among human satisfactions, using terms like *envy, empathy, guilt, altruism,* and *philanthropy.* Again, all these pieces need ultimately to be fit into some overall pattern.

It is in the behavioral area in which, it seems to me, we are most deficient both in the amount of research and in its integration with any kind of system model. And we are probably most deficient in research on economic behavior. Economists have preferred to deduce and test for expected behavior of a rational person maximizing something or to argue that natural selection would allow survival only of firms and individuals that at least approximately followed rational rules. But some of those rules are complex, requiring the capacity to use insights, select facts, process them, and make decisions. Many of the decisions the future elderly must make in the ordinary course or in response to dramatic changes in prices, laws, and so on, require complex problem solving but may be made without it (Bikson and Goodchilds 1978). How well people understand the economic insights involved in their decisions makes a difference. The level of economic education in the general population in this country is very low, particularly in comparison with the complexity of the choices open to people. Their economic future may depend on their capacity to learn and/or on the quality of programs designed to teach them.

Noneconomists often rebel at the notion that economic logic is useful, or used, arguing that most of us successfully avoid it and survive; that "optimal" may be hard to define. What is meant by "good" economic decision making is decisions that the individual would not regret upon acquiring some information or insight that is available. A brief indication of what is involved may help here.

AN OVERVIEW OF ECONOMIC INSIGHTS FOR
INDIVIDUAL BEHAVIOR

Economists treat economic behavior as choice among alternatives by comparing the benefits and costs of the two most attractive alternatives, one of which may be to do nothing or to continue on a present course. Most economic insight involves ways of quantifying benefits and costs and converting them so that they can be compared. A summary statement is that each cost or benefit has a value, which is its:

PRESENT, EXPECTED, REAL, AFTER TAX,
DOLLAR VALUE

Each of the five adjectives involves translation methods or tricks:

Future amounts are "discounted" to present values using interest rates to adjust for inflation and interest. If someone else earns the interest and you lose by inflation, the value to you now of $X to be received in n years is $X/(1 + i)^n$ where i is the market interest rate.

Expected values of uncertain events convert them into "certainty equivalents" by multiplying them by the probability that they will really happen. In a more complex example, the value of a lifetime annuity is the discounted value of each future benefit multiplied by the probability that I will live that long. If there are alternative outcomes from a single alternative, their expected values can be added. Recent research indicates persistent and nonsymmetric biases that make these norms a poor description of actual behavior in choices involving risk (Kahneman and Tversky 1979).

Price levels change, so money amounts must be deflated for inflation.

Federal income taxes take a bite out of some things, not others. Social security benefits are not taxed nor are the benefits of doing one's own repairs nor is time given to tax and philanthropy. Earnings are taxed, and charitable contributions are not excluded unless you itemize deductions, which means probably an income over $17,000 or many expenses. Comparisons thus need to be made in after-tax dollars.

Finally, many costs or benefits do not involve money receipts or payments but can be converted into dollar equivalents, a process called imputation by economists. For example, the money tied up in your house has a cost, which is what you could earn by investing it for financial return. And the depreciation in market value of a house or car is a real cost, even if it only shows up when you must replace it.

Many decisions facing the elderly involve the present value of alternative streams of earnings and/or pension payments over an expected lifetime, requiring either tables or a middle-priced pocket computer to estimate.

Of course, insight is only part of a longer, more complex process in human decisions. Studies of acceptance of innovation in family planning or agriculture use the paradigm of knowledge, attitudes, and practice to describe the process. We suggest that the process starts with the realization that there is a decision to be made, which may itself require some economic insight, then proceeds through a process in which the individual assembles the information that knowledge and insight indicate is relevant; this leads to some expectations and attitudes and intentions and may result in some action or decision. The end result is some level of satisfaction with the outcome. It seems likely that economic choices especially require some understanding of the range of alternative outcomes if a person is to be motivated to do the work of getting information and processing it. The low level of use of available information may result, in part, from the failure of economic understanding. How else is one to select the relevant information from the plethora of irrelevant fact? As Simon writes: "In a world where attention is a major scarce resource, information may be an expensive luxury for it may divert our attention from what is important to what is unimportant [1978, p. 13]." A focus on the many types of retirement plans or insurance and their prices may distract attention from the basic choices about what kind of plan is called for and in what amounts and even distract the individual from a proper cost comparison of appropriately selected alternatives. Decisions may be made on noneconomic criteria simply because of unwillingness or incapacity to grapple with the economic analysis.

RESEARCH ON LEARNING ECONOMIC INSIGHTS

It is possible to do research on people's capacity to handle economic insights and to understand the public economic policies affecting them. It is not just the effects of public policies on behavior that depend on people's understanding or capacity to acquire understanding. It is also often the very acceptability of a public program. The acceptability of social security hinges on whether it is seen as basically equitable and useful. So people need to understand why with changing age distributions pay-as-you-go is unnecessary and meaningless, and why adjusting benefits upward with inflation is not a gift from the currently working to the currently retired but a justified implicit market interest return on prior contributions. Present emotional arguments based on faulty economic logic or attention to largely irrelevant fiscal implications may exacerbate intergenerational tensions and even lead to unwise political changes in the system.

Similarly, the proposed new option allowing people to trade a promise to bequeath their house at death (to a government corporation) in return for a lifetime cash annuity starting now is a complex notion with emotional aspects that may make it difficult for people to focus on its economics. Indeed, if there were such a choice, people would need to be educated enough to insist on an inflation-adjusted annuity.

Any of the substantive areas of research on the future elderly may have aspects of this basic issue of their level of economic understanding and their capacity to learn and achieve more economic insight. Turning now to those substantive areas, we can organize an outline for a program of research by looking at the likely main elements of systematic forecasting models and then at the behavioral research that they will probably call for.

Since much of the research that will have to be done is on the separate parts and pieces, it is useful to itemize the major societal changes and policy issues that are with us now or soon will be, then move on to some guesses as to the main pieces of behavioral research that will be required. An added reason for focusing on the behavioral research is that it takes longer, costs more, and may even help avoid the creation of unrealistic analytic models. The ultimate criterion (dependent variable), however, is human happiness—it is the link to that which we finally need.

MASSIVE CHANGES THAT SHOULD AFFECT THE FUTURE ELDERLY

Inflation, past and expected, is a new and unexpected problem, one that hits the elderly with greatest force. Just when various annuity and retirement programs seemed in control of the risk of outliving one's savings by living too long, the risk of erosion by inflation hit, particularly inflation of costs important to the elderly such as medical care, utilities, food, and personal services. Worse still, uncertainty as to the value of individual savings invested in stocks, etc. compounds the uncertainty about the future course of inflation. Skyrocketing prices of houses provide capital gains more for the elderly than anyone else, but it is difficult to cover the rising cost of utilities, property taxes, repairs, and other expenses with unrealized capital gains.

Past changes in the birth rate—the baby boom and subsequent bust—mean a bulge of workers piled on top of the entry of more and more women and some immigrants into the labor force. This will be followed by a substantial increase in the number and proportion of those who are retired. These changes in the overall ratio of producers to consumers will be tempered by a decrease in the number of dependent young people unless the birth rate rises again. There are implications for unemployment, total output, national investment policy, the flows into and out of the social security system, and even for the political understanding of social security—an understanding that was less necessary when the system was growing and the working population was growing more rapidly than the total population.

Changes in laws affect the elderly more than most, particularly changes in social security, in private pension law, in welfare, in the law related to gifts and inheritances (estate tax), and to the treatment of capital gains and philanthropic contributions.

Somewhat less dramatic but nonetheless important because the aging tend to stay where they lived when they retired, are substantial changes in the geographic distribution of the population and in residential patterns around urban areas. The needed services for recreation, medical care, and so forth of the elderly involve capital investments that have to be located geographically.

There have also been massive recent changes in laws and institutions and policies affecting the elderly—changes in the social security law, estate and gift tax laws, private pensions (company or individual), and the tax treatment of philanthropy and of capital gains. People may see their life savings eroded by inflation, offset by an unexpected capital gain on their house and by a suddenly more important inflation-adjusted social security.

A great deal of systematic and systemic analysis of the implications of these changes and other likely changes can be done with very little behavioral input. But before the results can be precise enough for sound forecasts or policy implications, the distribution of initial impacts and the adjustments people make to these changing situations will have to be built in, which means that we need estimates of behavioral parameters which will require research on possible behavioral responses. It is not really markets or prices that "behave," but human beings. They make choices sometimes as voters or business operators or as elected representatives, but mostly, and most important, as individuals. As individuals, they decide how much to work for money or other rewards, when to retire, how many children to have, with whom to live and share, and what contributions to make to others outside the household—relatives, other people, or organized philanthropies. And they may well influence each other.

In practice, simulation models incorporating these known or easily predicted changes can be used to make initial forecasts of their implications. More important, the sensitivity of the forecasts to changes in the behavioral response coefficients of the models should indicate where the resources for behavioral research should go. But we can make some guesses at the main areas of behavioral research that are needed. And such guesses are needed because behavioral research takes more time and involves more money than work with analytical models, structural equations, or simulation.

We have already indicated the importance of research on possible improvement in the teaching of economic insights to adults at times when they have major decisions to make. Policies about government protection and regulation are based on assumptions about individual capacity to learn how to deal with economic decisions, and the potential acceptance of and support for other policies depends on popular acceptance, which must ultimately be based on understanding of the economic issues involved. We turn now to other substantive research that is needed.

BEHAVIORAL RESEARCH AND THE FUTURE ELDERLY

Some structure is useful in describing the vast range of possible and potentially useful behavioral research. The research that concerns us here has economic implications, that is, it involves the use of economic resources in the form of money or time with results that affect economic well-being. (However, we shall not discuss the final link to happiness here.) Economic choices can be discrete, irregular, but with lasting consequences, such as buying a home or other capital transactions, retiring or changing jobs, making other commitments about time use, moving one's residence, or changing one's family composition (divorce, doubling up). Other choices involve regular flows—using time and/or money for productive or consumption purposes.

Most important of all, we can be concerned either with the cumulative effects of past behavior, combined with experience, as it is revealed or results in current states of health, wealth, and income. Or we can be concerned with the present, with decisions involving either discrete capital transactions or new commitments or with continuous uses of time or money. Or we can be concerned with predicting people's future changes or decisions. The last of these may be our most important policy concern, aside from some evaluative descriptions of the present level and distribution of well-being, but all the other research can contribute to our capacity to forecast future changes and can make us more comfortable with forecasts based on people's own desires, expectations, plans, and commitments. We shall discuss each in turn.

Not all behavior is relevant to policy decisions or a prime target for potentially productive research. The important behavior is that which is likely to change or to need to change, and we have already alluded to some of the massive and known changes in environment and population distributions that will point to the areas of behavioral response we most need to know about. Future decisions about retirement, for example, seem inevitably affected by changes in social security, in private pensions, in inflation and unemployment, and in the rapidly increasing proportion of families with a period of two earners before retirement.

CUMULATIVE RESULTS OF PAST BEHAVIOR AND EXPERIENCE

Particularly among the older age groups, studies of the level and distribution of well-being, of health, wealth, and current income, are implicitly or explicitly studies of the cumulative results of past decisions and behavior, combined with events and experiences that differ among individuals. In addition, such studies of the present state of people, particularly older people in whom change is least likely, can point to inequities and raise policy questions. Where are the main gaps in our knowledge of the present states of people's well-being?

We know a good deal about health and morbidity, a modest amount about income, but little or nothing about the distribution of wealth. The gaps are particularly great in areas of wealth involving rights, equities, or even expectations. The importance of such components of wealth is increasing with the growth of vested private pensions, the improvements in social security coverages and benefits, and the probable increase in the number of family fortunes that will be inherited by someone. Not only have there been no studies of wealth of households in this country for over a decade, but even those did not attempt to estimate a complete family net worth concept. Worse still, the erratic fluctuations in asset values, with skyrocketing house values and plunging stock values, and the cumulative impact of inflation and unemployment may well have changed the distribution of wealth substantially. Since wealth in its broadest sense is the basis of economic security for older people, knowing about its distribution within each age group is essential for forecasting the future condition of the elderly. The closer they are to retirement, the more the adequacy of economic status in retirement can be estimated on the basis of wealth and other rights already accumulated.

Since the full combination of rights and obligations is crucial, it seems essential to start with families, that is, with probability sample surveys. It might be useful to secure access to some official records to get estimates of specific assets, but people's perceptions of their wealth and rights are almost as important as the "facts."

A family has combinations of assets in various members' names plus a set of potential rights and obligations from and to other family members living elsewhere, employers, and the government. It is quite possible that the variety of overlapping the independent rights and obligations result in substantial inequities, with some families having a favorable combination of rights and others with few or none. When we extend the wealth concept to include the probabilistic aspects of insurance coverages, the disparities may well be even greater. Some people can collect from many different coverages; others are sparsely covered—if at all.

Changes in family stability can have substantial effects. The old stereotype of women ending up with the wealth their husbands accumulated because women outlive men may not fit a high-divorce world in which women also work and even marry younger men.

Other results of past behavior, decisions, and experience about which we know little are the accumulated skills and equipment for both vocational and recreational use. The potential earnings of older people may depend on their accumulated skills, seniority, and so forth, and their potential recreational patterns and needs may well depend on the recreational skills, interests, and equipment they have accumulated. The number of older skiers, swimmers, or joggers will surely depend on the numbers in the various age cohorts who are already involved in these activities, while the future needs for public facilities may be affected by extrapolations of the age distributions of the participants in various recreational activities and their geographic location.

CURRENT BEHAVIOR, DISCRETE CHOICES, AND CONTINUOUS PATTERNS

The Present

Some changes in behavior with aging are relatively gradual alterations in flows and in the spending of time and–or money and can probably best be studied by looking at current age differences in a series of cross-sections to see whether the cohorts, as they age, change in the way differences among age groups at one point in time would imply. There is, of course, always the lurking third possibility that current "year of history" effects are also operating to affect behavior, so that if age differences change in a series of cross-sectional studies, we may find it difficult to decide whether that reflects the differences in the historic experience of the different generations (cohort effects) or differences in the current situation, such as prices, extra job availability, or current expectations of the future seen now (period effects).

The most crucial behavioral flows are, of course, total hours of paid work, of productive work around the house, and of unpaid volunteer work. But we need also repeated small surveys to monitor the time spent in recreational activities and in getting from one place to another. The money flows of most policy concern are expenditures on medical care, energy (heat and light, gasoline), and transfers to others (support of parents or children or philanthropic contributions). Our national accounts and other official data are particularly deficient in covering transfers. Official income distribution data are collected subsequent to some official transfers but before many other transfers and taxes. Future demands on public transfer systems will, of course, depend on what happens to private transfers, inside and outside the family living together.

Some of the most crucial behaviors, however, are discrete and irregularly made and consequently more difficult to study. The most obvious is the decision to retire, but people also change jobs, move, change their family composition by divorce, marriage, or other doubling or undoubling (see Duncan and Morgan 1980). They buy or replace cars and other "durables," and they invest in skills, vocational or recreational, with lasting consequences for the benefit-cost situation facing future activity choices. Not only are such decisions irregularly made, but they may well be interlaced or joint. Changing jobs or retiring may lead to, result from, or be decided jointly with a change in residence. With more and more two-earner families approaching retirement age and with separable equities, there may be fewer economic barriers to splitting up if one spouse wants to travel or move south or retire earlier than the other. Research on such decisions must be based on sample surveys that include those who decided not to make changes as well as those who did and must investigate the perceived alternatives and choices—because doing nothing may imply a negative decision or alternatively no conscious decision at all. We need to know more about these decisions involving retirement, alternative jobs in the case of mandatory retirement or job obsolescence, selling the home, moving, and so forth. Many of these choices are so important, crucial, and probably salient that it seems likely that we can start by collecting retrospective (memory) data on past changes, alternatives, constraints, and explanations for the outcomes. Hypotheses from such studies may then require and justify more expensive, slower, longitudinal studies. The before-after nature of panel studies allows better information on perceived alternatives (at the time), desires, expectations and situations of both spouses and more precise information on current conditions. The results may be a long time in coming and even then may require combination with current expectations and information about expected environmental changes, if they are to forecast the future.

Hence, detailed studies of the current situation of each age group plus some recalled information about recent changes would provide an inexpensive and essential base for more complex studies and could be used in combination with data from the same studies on desires, plans, and expectations about the future. We need to broaden the scope of what we consider the current economic condition and behavior of families to include ties with relatives—children and parents and others—that may express themselves not in current dollar flows or current time given but in lending or borrowing or stand-by commitments to help, if and when help is needed. Expectations about inheritances and bequests are difficult to elicit from potential recipients but should be obtainable from the current elderly—the potential donors.

Indeed, survey research on what affects people's sense of security is also needed. It may well reveal that savings and job security are only a part and that the major sources of insecurity today are possible future inflation, uncertainty about health care and its financing, a sense of danger in the streets, or insecure family relations and obligations. The links between people's economic–physical condition and environment, on one hand, and their happiness and mental health, on the other, lead to another but related program of research on quality of life.

There are, of course, some very specific data needs, such as the equity people have in houses, in case a program became possible allowing them to bequeath that equity at death in return for a lifetime annuity commencing immediately. But a broader investigation of responses to fresh insights about the costs of owning a home and of the alternatives might reveal that it was not nostalgia that keeps older people overhoused in inappropriate locations but the lack of alternative protections against inflation and against outliving their money.

Comparisons of older but not retired people with those already retired can usefully indicate biases in expectations, as when the former say they expect to do more volunteer work when they retire, while the latter report that they are not doing any more volunteer work than before they retired.

Panel study data can usefully show the patterns of events and decisions around the retirement ages. We already know that increased unemployment and illness preceded retirement, particularly early retirement. But much more detailed studies of sequencing and studies that include the experience of both spouses and the interrelations of their decisions (since the wife is usually several years younger) might well reveal new patterns and problems arising that will affect the future situation and call for new policy initiatives.

Second only to decisions about retirement are decisions about various contractual saving arrangements such as Independent Retirement Accounts. Monitoring behavior of people in setting up such accounts, studies to show whether they really understand the benefits and costs of the alternative options, and parallel studies of the management of these accounts by the various trustees and institutions that arrange them are clearly needed. The lure of avoiding (or at least postponing) income taxes may well blind people to other problems. The record of institutional management of other people's money in recent years has not been very good (e.g., investment trusts and mutual funds).

Given the growth of second-home ownership and the skyrocketing values of homes (which makes it expensive to own them, economists claim), moving to the second home as a retirement option may well be more attractive. Such decisions can certainly be inquired about as they are gradually made in the years before retirement, as well as after. The future demand for condominiums and for other space in retirement communities is not just a marketing problem for promoters but also a major problem for state and local governments and the public utilities that must provide the community services and facilities. Is there a combination of desire and ability to pay that foretells an increased migration at retirement to nicer climates, better local environments, or lower cost of living?

Research Bearing on Future Behavior

In a rapidly changing world, past and present behavior by itself may be a poor indicator of the future. As we pointed out earlier, the various models that attempt to simulate the future dynamics of the economic system must not only build into them the standard relationships and the known basic changes in population age distribution (ratio of earners to eaters in the population, etc.) but also must deal with potential behavioral responses to changes that people face. Hence, we would like to know not only what people currently hope, expect, and plan to do in the future, but also how they might change those plans or some other behavior if their environment changes in ways they did not expect. Extrapolating from past behavior patterns may give wrong answers.

Anything we can learn about people's basic desires, aspirations, and values should help us to predict their future behavior. In addition, since many of the crucial decisions of individuals involve economic insights plus information, we need to know how they deal with complex economic decisions—how likely they are to see the problem of choice and figure out what information is needed and how to make use of it. Research on problems people have in such economic decision making may even help us improve adult education. The present preretirement counseling programs are developing slowly and with only a partial focus on the hard and complex economic choices.

It is usually dangerous to ask people questions beginning with "if," since our capacity to imagine what we would do in situations we have not encountered or even thought about is limited. However, there are a number of contingencies people are likely to have thought about and for which they might at least be able to indicate the alternative responses they might make. For example, unemployment or serious illness after age 62 raises questions about early retirement or change of job. And a decision to change jobs raises questions about possible moves to other parts of the country. People may have planned what they will do when the mortgage is paid off—where monthly funds so freed will go. They may well have plans to accumulate a fresh set of durables before they retire, "while they have money." They are likely to have ideas about future obligations for actual gifts or loans to children, parents, or other relatives. In particular, we need to study people's notions about their parents and themselves, in case either parent or child becomes disabled or requires a great deal of extra care. There is very little information now about the extent of memory loss unaccompanied by any other physical disability but requiring extensive time and/or costs to protect the affected person. We know even less about the web of family obligations such traumas might engage.

For the group of aging individuals of unknown size who have accumulated substantial assets, more than they are likely to need for themselves for the rest of their lives, we can improve our predictions of their management and ultimate disposition of these assets by asking them about their purposes, sources of information, expected changes in portfolio, reactions to some possible future changes such as an end to inflation, and commitments, plans, or possibilities about what will happen to the assets eventually. Some will have decided on a bequest pattern, others may intend to leave it to fate, and still others may have contingency plans. We might understand better some of the huge flows into and out of the country and into and out of the stock market if we knew what the individual owners were thinking about. There is evidence that such people do not delegate investment decisions to others, so their choices could be investigated directly along with their sources of advice and/or information.

People's plans, expectations, and aspirations about the future range from legal commitments through investments in equipment, skills, and information to vague thoughts and dreams. The extent to which their actual future activities will differ from their present expectations is likely to depend on how firmly the latter are based on planning, information, commitment, and provision. Many people will talk about retiring early and traveling a lot. Some have calculated the economic implications of alternative retirement ages, have itineraries for trips, and will have read about places to visit, whereas others will have done none of these.

Finally, it is important to know what worries people and makes them fearful of the future. It seems likely that inflation, combined with the possibility of extensive unemployment or illness that would wipe out some of their accumulated assets, is the main concern. If inflation is crucial, then the absence of any safe way to protect savings against erosion may be the crucial policy issue of the future. An owned home has been one traditional defense, which may well explain the hostility against rising property taxes, but it is only a partial defense—one cannot use unrealized capital gains for food or medical bills. Should the government offer to sell an inflation-adjusted lifetime annuity calculated at 3% real return and justified as paying a market return, the difference reflecting inflation? Would people understand this and plan to convert their savings upon retirement? Do they appreciate that inflation and erosion of the value of savings is a worse problem than the threat of medical catastrophes, since insurance is available for the latter?

This is a long list of behavioral research topics, but it is not just a random shopping list. It sprang from a consideration of massive past and likely changes in the environment and the economy and some guesses as to which behavioral responses were most likely to be critical in the way the whole socioeconomic system will be affected by those changes. Better behavioral research should improve our capacity to model the whole system and analyze it, whether by systems of time-series equations or iterative simulation of a system of representative households and firms in the computer. When all this leads to policy implications, something more is required.

SOME NEEDED ECONOMIC ANALYSIS OF PUBLIC POLICY

Much legislation intended to protect the individual as consumer, saver, investor, or annuitant has been passed in the heat of political debate and compromise with inadequate input from economists. The result has been a serious omission of good economic analysis of the alternatives. We need sophisticated economic impact statements. Indeed, we need more than that; we need analysis of the longer-term implications. Let us focus here on two examples most relevant for the future elderly: the social security system and the Employees Income and Retirement Security Act of 1974. I have spelled out elsewhere the way in which lack of sophisticated interpretation and analysis of the social security system leaves us without guidance for its modification and with rampant, unchallenged nonsense about intergenerational conflict and imminent bankruptcy of the system (see Conference on the Economic Outlook 1978). It is possible to interpret and analyze the system as though it were intended to be intergenerationally equitable—each generation as a whole paying for that generation's benefits—and calculate the modifications necessary to ensure that goal. Within each generation, it is also possible to analyze the redistributions—insurance and risk-based or welfare and needs-based— to see whether they are politically acceptable or should be left to other programs. Once this is done, it is possible to estimate the likely fiscal and monetary impact of the system—its effect on total saving and spending, and hence, on the employment–inflation mix. Finally, there are implications for a system that does not maintain its own fully funded reserve, the government implicitly borrowing from the social security system, for optimal levels of national real investment, public and private. It is in this order that the research topics should be tackled, however, since starting with impacts of a system that needs (probably minor) alterations can lead to attempts to change the system for reasons other than its own purposes and to the detriment of its equity as a system. And the original theory that with population and real output per capita growing at the same constant rate (and no inflation), the contributions would equal the benefits without any interest on a reserve fund, is increasingly irrelevant and misleading. "Pay-as-you-go" sounds nice but obscures the reality.

The much-heralded Employees Income and Retirement Security Act provides a more specific example. In the interest of fairness, it allows only two kinds of company pension plans. One, called a guaranteed contribution plan, requires the employer to contribute the same fraction of each salary to the pension account; the individual's pension is based on what those contributions plus interest will buy. Since women in particular earn most of their lifetime earnings in the last few years of their working life, this provides a relatively inadequate saving and pension program for them. And if there is a company pension plan, they cannot fill the gap by setting up one of the tax-deferred private Independent Retirement Accounts allowed by the act for those without any company pension. The second type, called a guaranteed benefit plan, can base pensions on formulas that weight the last years' earnings somewhat more heavily (not more than one-third more), but not enough to really equalize "replacement ratios" or allow the kind of saving program many women need. Worse, the pension cost to the employer of a pay raise is different for employees of different ages under such a plan. An across-the-board wage increase might cost the employer 5–10% additional in pension costs for young employees, but 30–60% additional for employees close to retirement.

Perhaps if we were all economically sophisticated, unions would agree that wage increases could be inclusive of pension costs, and older workers could get smaller increases in take-home pay because of the larger increases in contributions to their pensions. What might be more likely would be increased reluctance to hire or promote older workers. So attempting to legislate equity may result in inequity for women and older workers and confusion and costly actuarial complexity. Of course, the main purposes of the act—to insure solvency of pension funds, vesting of rights, and better information—have probably been achieved and are clearly worthy.

Much other consumer protection legislation affects all ages, though it may affect young and old in different ways. But many of the same issues arise and require analysis: Does the legislation really deal with the problem? Would education and publicity about abuses solve the problem better? For example, the Truth in Lending Law tends to legitimize as well as reveal the interest rate and does not require revelation when part of the interest stated in the contract is really a hidden component of the price. That would be revealed if the borrower had to be informed when the lender sold the installment contract for more than the remaining principal due, even if the difference was pooled into a "dealer reserve" as though it were a reserve for bad debts. Sheer publicity of these "kickbacks" might eliminate them and would certainly reduce consumer confusion about what constitutes the price of the product and what constitutes interest charges.

The history of state licensing laws in restricting entry and competition and of ceilings on interest rates that have resulted in illegal lending at exorbitant rates or avoidance through FHA mortgage "points" needs study before we engage in a wave of protective legislation for older people. Are increasingly severe regulations on nursing homes keeping out legitimate competition so that it is difficult to enforce the regulations on those with the scarce permits now (monopolies)? Would encouraging entry and competition do more good? These are potentially researchable questions that require a mixture of behavioral and analytical research.

COOPERATION BETWEEN, BUT COMPETITION WITHIN, RESEARCH COMPONENTS

We have argued for complementary and mutually helpful research components, particularly between behavioral research and system modeling. But within each area, particularly in behavioral research, there is need for some competition. Given the variety of methods, approaches, theories, and variables, there is no agreed-upon best approach. A variety of research teams tackling the same problem will improve methods if they disagree and increase the credibility of findings if they agree. One research administrator reports his own favorable experience with such variability in replication:

> The significance of these projects is sustained through the diversification and variability of scope and approach. Consistent findings on the design, context, and implementation . . . emerge despite this variability and are thereby strengthened by it.
>
> The commonality of findings is a critical concern here, for it is based on the realistic and methodologically supportable position that no particular study or approach is free from both random error and systematic bias. In social research where conditions and circumstances are always changing, where theories have relatively weak explanatory power, and where measurement is approximate (at best), it is fruitless (and for some, immobilizing) to seek the perfect study [Lebowitz, 1979, p. 156].

Careful comparison of the results of research focused on the same problems requires funding, perhaps best by including such comparisons as part of each funded research project. The simple policy of funding more than one project on a single problem would go a long way toward ensuring adequate quality control.

SUMMARY

We have looked forward, not back, outlining a panoply of topics requiring fresh research, mostly on human behavior, understanding, and attitudes. Much of the research can be done relatively inexpensively on small national samples, perhaps oversampled among the older age groups. The focus has not been on precise numerical estimates of states but on relationships, expressed reasons, expectations, and plans.

Much of the research is in areas in which our theories are sufficiently numerous and competing and our methods sufficiently new, so that there is no one best way to do the research. Wherever possible, this speaks for a kind of replication and testing by funding two or three research projects on each topic requiring each of them to compare results with the others. Agreement on general findings would make them quite convincing, and the explanation for disagreements would help science progress and provide evaluations of the quality differences. Competitive analysis of the data by others may also be possible, with similar advantages.

There also needs to be the coordination referred to earlier between behavioral studies and the analytical modeling and simulation. The former can improve the specifications of variables and relations in models, and the models can reveal where we need better behavioral data if we are to be able to spell out the implications of alternative future policies, events, laws, or social changes.

There needs to be coordination also with the quality of life research that relates the physical changes of the future to affective senses of well-being.

We have argued that the behavioral research is in particular need of an early start since it takes longer than the simulation modeling, and its results are more likely to alter the details of the models than the findings of the models are to alter the focus or content of the behavioral research. We already know what many of the behavioral questions are: Who is going to retire when, with what kinds of assets and rights, and with what plans and provisions for future activities? What patterns of time use after retirement can be expected on the basis of investments in recreational skills and equipment and present plans? How many have what kind of protection against various catastrophes? What is happening to extended family obligations? What of future living arrangements?

Finally, a basic criterion for the allocation of research funds on the future of the elderly should be not only the quality of the proposal and the importance, excitement, or promise of its individual topic but also the extent to which it fits into a coherent program of research. Coherence means that attention is paid to the need for interactive complementary relationships among microresearch on individual behavior, modeling and simulation of dynamic implications for a whole economic system, and the relationship of all the physical outcomes to people's sense of well-being. Within such a framework, there should be plenty of room for exciting individual projects competing with those studying the same problem and complementing those studying related problems.

REFERENCES

Bikson, T. K., and Goodchilds, J. D. (1978) *Product Decision Processes Among Older Adults*. Santa Monica, Calif.: Rand Corporation.

Conference on the Economic Outlook (1978) *The Future of Social Security*. Ann Arbor, Mich.: University of Michigan.

Duncan, G., and Morgan, J. (1980) Incidence and some consequences of major life events. Chapter 6 in *Five Thousand American Families: Patterns of Economic Progress*, Vol. VIII. Ann Arbor, Mich.: Institute for Social Research, University of Michigan.

Kahneman, D., and Tversky, A. (1979) Prospect theory: An analysis of decision under risk. *Econometrica* 47(March):263–291.

Lebowitz, B. D. (1979) The management of research on aging: A case study in science policy. *The Gerontologist* 19(April):151–157.

Morgan, J. N. (1979) The work hours of family heads, constraints, marginal choices, and income goals. Chapter 2 in G. Duncan and J. Morgan, eds., *Five Thousand American Families: Patterns of Economic Progress*, Vol. VII. Ann Arbor, Mich.: Institute for Social Research, University of Michigan.

Orcutt, G. (1965) *Microanalysis of Socioeconomic Systems*. New York: Harper and Row.

Simon, H. (1978) Rationality as process and as product of thought. *American Economic Review* 60(May):1–16.

appendix A

The Elderly of the Future
May 3–5, 1979
Annapolis, Maryland

WORKSHOP PARTICIPANTS

Toni Antonucci, University of Michigan
Shirley P. Bagley, National Institute on Aging
Robert N. Butler, National Institute on Aging
Sidney Cobb, Brown University
Yehudi A. Cohen, Rutgers State University
Joel Cooper, Princeton University
Neal E. Cutler, University of Southern California
James R. Dumpson, New York Community Trust Foundation
Christine Dunkel-Schetter, Northwestern University
Richard G. Fox, Duke University
Alan Freiden, Social Security Administration
Victor Fuchs, National Bureau of Economic Research
George R. Goethals, Williams College
D. Richard Greene, University of Pennsylvania
Giora Hanoch, The Hebrew University of Jerusalem
Marjorie Honig, Columbia University
Robert L. Kahn, University of Michigan
Stanislav V. Kasl, Yale University
Jennie Keith, Swarthmore College

Sara B. Kiesler, Carnegie-Mellon University
M. Powell Lawton, Philadelphia Geriatric Center
Richard S. Lazarus, University of California, Berkeley
James G. March, Stanford University
James N. Morgan, University of Michigan
Valerie Kincade Oppenheimer, University of California, Los Angeles
Anthony Pellechio, National Bureau of Economic Research
Irving Rosow, University of California, San Francisco
Michael Ross, University of Waterloo
Joseph A. Schlesinger, Michigan State University
Mildred Schlesinger, Michigan State University
David O. Sears, University of California, Los Angeles
Robert R. Sears, Stanford University
Ethel Shanas, University of Illinois, Chicago
Harold Sheppard, American Institutes for Research
Jacob Siegel, Bureau of the Census
Daniel S. Smith, The Newberry Library, Chicago
Beth J. Soldo, Georgetown University
Shelby Stewman, Carnegie-Mellon University
Myra Strober, Stanford University
Raymond J. Struyk, Department of Housing and Urban Development
Judith Treas, University of Southern California
Wilbur Watson, National Center on Black Aged
Camille B. Wortman, Northwestern University

appendix B

Reviewers

Howard E. Aldrich, Cornell University
Monica D. Blumenthal, Western Psychiatric Institute and Clinic, Pittsburgh
Elizabeth F. Colson, University of California, Berkeley
John Ferejohn, California Institute of Technology
Leon Festinger, New School for Social Research
Susan Green, George Washington University
Heidi I. Hartmann, National Research Council
Elaine Hatfield, University of Wisconsin
James S. Jackson, University of Michigan
Edward E. Jones, Princeton University
Nathan Keyfitz, Harvard University
Charles Kiesler, Carnegie-Mellon University
Francis E. Kobrin, Brown University
John T. Lanzetta, Dartmouth College
M. Powell Lawton, Philadelphia Geriatric Center
Laurence E. Lynn, Harvard University
Karen Matthews, Western Psychiatric Institute and Clinic, Pittsburgh
Sandra J. Newman, Department of Housing and Urban Development
Harold Orbach, Kansas State University
Adrian Ostfeld, Yale University
David W. Plath, University of Illinois, Urbana
Robert D. Putnam, Harvard University

Harvey S. Rosen, Princeton University
Howard Schuman, University of Michigan
Ethel Shanas, University of Illinois, Chicago Circle
Mervyn W. Susser, Columbia University
James Trussel, Princeton University
Linda Waite, University of Illinois, Champaign
Roy L. Walford, University of California, Los Angeles
Harrison C. White, Harvard University
Julian Wolpert, Princeton University
Mark P. Zanna, University of Waterloo
Franklin Zimring, University of Chicago.

Author Index

Numbers in italics indicate the pages on which the complete references can be found.

Q

Quattrone, G., 59, *73*
Quinn, J., 547, *559*, 563, *584*
Quinn, R., 401, *404*
Quint, J., 367, *379*

R

Range, P., 95, *126*
Raphael, B., 350, 351, 358, *379*, 391, *405*
Reichard, S., 433, *451*
Reiter, R., 163, *182*
Reno, V., 574, 580, *584*
Richman, J., 356, *379*
Ridgway, V., 312, *328*
Riker, W., 220, *238*
Riley, M., 141, 151, 152, *157*, 208, 229, *238*, 333, 334, *344*, 475, *487*, 502, *512*
Ripley, R., 209, 221, *238*
Rix, S., 206, *238*
Robinson, B., 357, *378*
Rodin, J., 47, *74*
Rohde, D., 222, 229, *238*
Rokeach, M., 185, *204*
Rokkan, S., 335, *344*
Rones, P., 563, *585*
Rosch, E., 62, *73*
Rose, A., *182*, 477, *487*
Rose, T., 59, *73*
Rosenberg, G., 477, *487*
Rosenblatt, J., 516, *542*
Rosenthal, R., 442, *451*
Rosow, I., 359–361, 372, *379*, 407, *430*, 441, *451*, 463, 475, 477, *488*
Ross, J., 455–457, 463, 470, 477, 480, *488*
Ross, L., 43, 50, 66, 67, *73*
Ross, M., 51, *73*
Ross, R., 350, 351, *375*
Rowan, B., 340, *344*
Rothman, D., 221, *238*
Ruble, D., 447, *450*
Ruel, M., 467, *488*
Ryder, N., 56, *73*, 306, 315, *328*, 502, *512*

S

Sabato, L., 217, 218, *238*
Sahlins, M., 161, *182*

Salancik, G., 304, 306, 314, *328*, 341, *344*
Sales, P., *290*
Samuelson, R., 205, *238*
Sander, K., 546, *559*
Sanders, J., 366, *379*
Sanderson, W., 16, 36, 37, *39*
Sangree, W., 470, *487*
Sauer, W., 357, *379*
Schachter, S., 353, *379*
Schaie, J., 495, *512*
Schaie, K., 141, *157*, 415, 417, 419, *430*
Schenkler, B., 51, *73*
Schlesinger, J., 209, 211–213, 215, 224, *238*
Schlossberg, N., 366, *380*
Schoenberg, B., 353, *379*
Schonfeld, E., 43, *72*
Schneider, W., 12, 62, *73*, 201
Schnore, L., 292, *328*
Schultz, J., 572, 573, 580, *585*
Schulz, R., 356, 370, *380*
Schuman, H., 200, *204*
Schwab, J., 353, *380*
Scott, J., 358, *377*
Scull, A., 335, *344*
Sears, D., 53, 183, 186, 187–189, 194–198, 200, 201, *204*
Sears, P., 413, 416, 417, 420, *430*
Sears, R., 416, 417, *430*
Seelbach, W., 362, *380*
Segel, A., 365, *380*
Seligman, L., 225, *238*
Service, E., 161, *182*
Seward, E., 80, *90*
Shanas, E., 176, 355, 360, *380*, 491, 495, 508, *512*
Shaver, K., 436, 445, *451*
Sheehy, G., 247, 273, *290*
Sheldon, A., 350, *380*
Sheldon, M., 303, *328*
Shelton, F., 366, *378*
Sheppard, H., 137, *157*, 206, *238*, 503, *512*
Sherif, M., 184, *204*
Sherman, S., 462, *488*
Shiffrin, R., 62, *73*
Shin, K., 214, *238*
Sicoly, F., 45, 67, *73*
Siegel, J., 136, 137, *157*, 205, 230, 231, *238*

Subject Index